The

RIVERSIDE READER

NINTH EDITION

Joseph F. Trimmer
Ball State University

Maxine Hairston
Late of University of Texas at Austin

Houghton Mifflin Company   Boston New York

Editor-in-Chief: Carrie Brandon
Senior Sponsoring Editor: Lisa Kimball
Senior Marketing Manager: Tom Ziolkowski
Marketing Assistant: Bettina Chiu
Assistant Editor: John McHugh
Editorial Assistant: Katilyn Crowley
Senior Project Editor: Jane Lee
Editorial Assistant: Carrie Parker
Senior Art and Design Coordinator: Jill Haber
Cover Design Manager: Anne S. Katzeff
Senior Photo Editor: Jennifer Meyer Dare
Composition Buyer: Chuck Dutton
New Title Project Manager: Susan Brooks-Peltier

Cover Image: *Row of Green Trees Reflected in Water.* Copyright © Pete Turner/ Getty Images.

Printed in the U.S.A.

Library of Congress Control Number: 2006936824

Instructor's exam copy:
ISBN 13: 978-0-618-83298-9
ISBN 10: 0-618-83298-X

For orders, use student text ISBNs:
ISBN 13: 978-0-618-81125-0
ISBN 10: 0-618-81125-7

3 4 5 6 7 8 9-EB-11 10 09 08 07

CONTENTS

Thematic Table of Contents   xv
Preface   xxi

INTRODUCTION   1

Guidelines for Reading an Essay   6
Sample Analysis of an Essay: ANNA QUINDLEN   *How Reading Changed My Life*   8
Guidelines for Writing an Essay   12
Student Essay: KRISTIE FERGUSON   *The Scenic Route*   14

NARRATION AND DESCRIPTION   19

MAXINE HONG KINGSTON   *A Song for a Barbarian Reed Pipe* (professional paragraph)   24

LAUREN BRINER   *Deloris* (student paragraph)   25

MARJANE SATRAPI   *The Veil* (visual text)   27

ANDRE DUBUS   *Digging*   28

   A noted essayist who became a paraplegic tells the story of a grueling summer as a seventeen-year-old in Louisiana when he developed muscle, stamina, and courage as he worked alongside seasoned ditch diggers and earned their friendship and respect.

ALICE WALKER   *Beauty: When the Other Dancer Is the Self*   39

An African-American novelist who has won many prizes for her novels tells of the long, slow process of regaining her self-esteem after a childhood accident severely injured one of her eyes.

JUDITH ORTIZ COFER   *The Myth of the Latin Woman: I Just Met a Girl Named María*   49

An acclaimed and widely read Latina author tells of humiliating incidents that she and other Hispanic women frequently experience because of misleading stereotypes about them that are perpetuated by television and movies.

SISTER HELEN PREJEAN   *Memories of a Dead Man Walking*   58

The Catholic nun who wrote of her own experience in *Dead Man Walking* tells how she summoned the courage to accompany a condemned man to the death chamber and stay with him through the execution.

GEORGE ORWELL   *Shooting an Elephant*   65

The English political writer and social critic tells how he was relentlessly drawn into a senseless killing to keep himself and the British Empire from looking foolish.

ALICE ADAMS   *Truth or Consequences* (story)   75

The narrator in this story thinks about the cruel class system in her junior high school and wonders if one of her thoughtless actions changed the life of a boy who rebelled against being ostracized.

PROCESS ANALYSIS   92

SCOTT RUSSELL SANDERS   *Digging Limestone* (professional paragraph)   97

SARA TEMPLE   *Making Stained Glass* (student paragraph)   98

JAMES STEVENSON   *How Many It Takes* (visual text)   100

ANN ZWINGER   *Drawing on Experience*   101

A naturalist and an artist explains how the process of drawing detailed sketches of flowers and plants reveals to her the secrets and wonders of the natural world.

P. J. O'ROURKE   *Third World Driving Hints and Tips*   109

Drawing on the adventures he recounts in his book *Holidays in Hell,* the author offers advice that will make driving exciting for anyone rash enough to get behind the wheel of a car in a Third World country.

NIKKI GIOVANNI   *Campus Racism 101*   115

A prize-winning poet and frequent spokesperson for African-American causes gives some straightforward answers and pragmatic advice to young black college students on how to do well when they attend a predominately white college.

JULIA ALVAREZ   *Grounds for Fiction*   121

A novelist and poet explains how she accumulates clippings about the miniature dramas of people's lives and turns them into stories and books, sometimes successfully, sometimes not.

SERENA NANDA   *Arranging a Marriage in India*   136

An American woman who has lived in India explains the complex and delicate process by which families in that country arrange their children's marriages, a negotiation they believe is too important to leave in the inexperienced hands of young people.

ELIZABETH WINTHROP   *The Golden Darters* (story)   149

Initiated unwillingly into the rituals of tying flies by her fly-fishing father, the girl in the story escapes the designed task by turning the flies she creates to her own uses.

COMPARISON AND CONTRAST   160

DAVID McCULLOUGH   *FDR and Truman* (professional paragraph)   164

NATHAN M. HARMS   *Howard and Rush* (student paragraph)   165

DON HONG-OAI   *At Play, Tianzi Mountains* (visual text)   167

MARK TWAIN   *Two Views of the River*   168

A famous American writer who was once a river pilot contrasts an artist's romantic view of the river with a riverman's pragmatic view of the same stretch of the Mississippi River.

SARAH VOWELL   *Cowboys v. Mounties*   172

This American writer who says she feels like a Canadian most of the time contrasts the impetuous, individualistic, gun-toting style of the American cowboy with the restrained, team-player calm of the Royal Canadian Mounted Police officer.

DAVA SOBEL   *Imaginary Lines*   180

In this opening chapter of her book *Longitude,* Sobel compares latitude and longitude, the imaginary lines travelers use to navigate the world, and explains why calculating longitude remained a formidable challenge for thousands of years.

ANNE ROIPHE   *A Tale of Two Divorces*   188

In comparing a divorce that didn't happen—her parents'—with one that did—her own—this writer concludes that in contemporary America our romantic fantasies so complicate our lives that arranged marriages might mean fewer divorces.

LAURA BOHANNAN   *Shakespeare in the Bush*   199

When she tries to establish common cultural ground with the elders of an African tribe by telling them the story of *Hamlet,* this would-be literary ambassador finds that the elders' views about human nature provide a totally new meaning for the famous play.

WITI IHIMAERA   *His First Ball* (story)   213

An invitation to a splendid government ball threatens to wreak havoc with the life of a young Maori man, but once he arrives at the ball, he turns his chagrin into success when he meets and dances with a young woman who is as much an outsider as he is.

DIVISION AND CLASSIFICATION   229

WENDELL BERRY   *Conservation Is Good Work*
(professional paragraph)   234

GARETH TUCKER   *Gentleman! Start Your Engines*
(student paragraph)   234

ROZ CHAST   *Cloud Chart* (visual text)   236

JAMES H. AUSTIN   *Four Kinds of Chance*   237

This scientist and author, who has an interest in scientific discovery, classifies four kinds of luck and shows their relationship to creativity.

JUDITH VIORST   *The Truth About Lying*   244

A prominent essayist writes about a subject that has intrigued and challenged her for years—the difference between different types of lying.

MARY MEBANE   *Shades of Black*   252

A black essayist tells stories from her youth to illustrate how the culturally conditioned biases of many of the adults led them to classify their fellow African-Americans by the shades of their skin.

PHILLIP LOPATE   *Modern Friendships*   260

An essayist reflects that, as he has matured, he has moved away from expecting to have one Best Friend toward cherishing the differences he finds in a broad range of friends with widely varying personalities and talents.

GARRY WILLS   *The Dramaturgy of Death*   274

This respected writer and scholar begins his essay by describing in gory detail fourteen historical models of capital punishment; he concludes by invoking expert testimony to show that the death penalty is an irrational and ineffective form of punishment.

FLANNERY O'CONNOR   *Revelation* (story)   290

In this short story by a famous southern writer, a sanctimonious woman has a revelation that undermines her obsessive system of categorizing people.

DEFINITION   316

JOYCE CAROL OATES   *When Tristram Met Isolde* (professional paragraph)   320

JASON UTESCH   *Personality* (student paragraph)   321

SHANNON MENDES   *Adbusters* (visual text)   323

JOHN BERENDT   *The Hoax*   324

In this essay, a connoisseur of hoaxes describes a variety of clever deceptions ranging from elaborate practical jokes to ingenious get-rich schemes.

DIANE ACKERMAN   *Pain*   329

Giving a wide range of diverse examples to illustrate her claim, the author asserts that people's responses to and attitudes toward pain vary enormously across cultures.

JAMES GLEICK   *Attention! Multitaskers*   335

In this excerpt from his book *Faster: The Acceleration of Just About Everything,* James Gleick explains how contemporary culture has become adept at packing more and more activities into smaller and smaller amounts of time.

ANTHONY GIDDENS   *Globalisation*   342

England's most prominent sociologist defines a "complex set of processes" that is transforming "our very life circumstances."

STEPHEN HARRIGAN   *The Tiger Is God*   353

Through a dispassionate analysis of the behavior and temperament of a Siberian tiger, the author concludes that, in killing one of its keepers, the tiger "was just being a tiger."

TONI CADE BAMBARA   *The Lesson* (story)   364

In this story, Miss Moore tries to teach several slum children that they are part of the underclass in a society where the definition of "cost" varies greatly, where some people pay more for a toy than others would spend to feed a large family for a year.

CAUSE AND EFFECT   376

JONATHAN WEINER   *Elephant Evolution* (professional paragraph)   379

EMILY LINDERMAN   *Barrier-Free Design* (student paragraph)   380

FRANK HURLEY   *The Endurance* (visual text)   382

KATHA POLLITT   *Why Boys Don't Play with Dolls*   383

This poet and essayist speculates that nurture is more powerful than nature, and that adult attitudes cause their children to perpetuate stereotypical behavior.

DANIEL GOLEMAN   *Peak Performance: Why Records Fall*   388

This science writer reports on research showing that the record-breaking performers in any field, whether sports, music, or chess, are those who start early and practice intensively over long periods of time.

JONATHAN KOZOL   *The Human Cost of an Illiterate Society*   396

A famous commentator on education and poverty analyzes the effects of illiteracy on the daily lives of one-third of our culture.

MALCOLM GLADWELL   *Examined Life*   407

In this profile of Stanley Kaplan, the energetic entrepreneur who created the Kaplan program to coach students for their College Boards, Gladwell shows how Kaplan's success has undermined the standing of the Educational Testing Service and raised serious questions about college admissions practices.

ERIC SCHLOSSER   *Why McDonald's Fries Taste So Good*   422

In this excerpt from his book *Fast Food Nation,* Eric Schlosser takes his readers on a tour of the flavor industry in the United States and reveals how skillful chemists and biotechnicians create the compounds that give fast foods their appealing taste and texture.

ARTHUR C. CLARKE   *The Star* (story)   437

The distressed narrator of this science fiction tale is a Catholic priest and astrophysicist who, on the basis of evidence he cannot deny, finds that he has to accept the connection between a cause and an effect that shakes the foundation of his faith.

PERSUASION AND ARGUMENT   448

NICHOLAS LEMANN   *The Promised Land* (professional paragraph)   454

JIM F. SALOMAN   *Genetic Engineering* (student paragraph)   455

Physicians Against Land Mines (visual text)   457

A Debate About Racism

MARTIN LUTHER KING, JR.   *I Have A Dream*   458

In this landmark speech rich with metaphor and allusion, the most famous civil rights leader of the 1960s urges his listeners to share his vision of freedom and equality.

ERIC LIU   *A Chinaman's Chance: Reflections on the American
Dream*   465

An Ivy League graduate whose parents were poor Chinese immigrants defines the American Dream not as achieving material wealth
but as offering freedom, opportunity, and responsibility.

A Debate About Stem Cell Research

RICHARD DOERFLINGER   *First Principles and the
"Frist Principles"*   478

A passionate spokesman for the pro-life movement argues against
allowing human embryos to be used for stem cell research.

PEGGY PRICHARD ROSS   *Stem Cell Research: It's About Life and
Death, Not Politics*   482

A woman who is dying of a mysterious brain disease argues that scientists must be allowed to pursue stem cell research to develop treatments for illnesses like hers, as well as for common ones like diabetes
and Alzheimer's.

A Debate About Family

BARBARA KINGSOLVER   *Stone Soup*   485

A novelist who writes frequently about the complex issues of family
life argues that there is not necessarily one best model for a successful family, that a single parent who is part of a strong community can
do an excellent job of raising a child.

BARBARA DAFOE WHITEHEAD   *Women and the Future of
Fatherhood*   496

Saying that even the best mothers cannot be good fathers, the
author argues that children's need for a father is so important that
men and women need to negotiate new kinds of marriage contracts
to meet children's needs.

A Debate About Harry Potter

JOAN ACOCELLA   *Under the Spell*   505

A well-known dance and theater critic traces the rich traditions
of myth and legend that form the foundation of the enormously

popular Harry Potter books, and concludes that the strength of their appeal lies partly in the author's willingness to raise universal moral questions but give no easy answers.

HAROLD BLOOM *Can 35 Million Book Buyers Be Wrong? Yes.* 516

A distinguished professor of literature at Yale argues that the Harry Potter books are unimaginative and clichéd, inferior to children's classics of an earlier time.

KURT VONNEGUT, JR. *Harrison Bergeron* (story) 522

In a fantasy about the future, Vonnegut creates a disturbing picture of a world in which the government uses extraordinary measures to ensure that everyone is equal.

RESOURCES FOR WRITING
Energy: A Casebook 533

STEPHEN DOHENY-FARINA *The Grid and the Village* (Narration and Description) 538

A teacher of technical writing describes how a major ice storm destroys his community's electrical power but enables it to create powerful new social connections.

TOM AND RAY MAGLIOZZI *Guide to Better Fuel Economy* (Process Analysis) 548

The brothers who host the widely popular National Public Radio show *Car Talk* provide extensive—and humorous—advice about how drivers can get better miles per gallon.

The Sources of Energy: A Visual Essay

GREENPEACE INTERNATIONAL *Sellafield = Springfield?* (Comparison and Contrast) 557

The international environmental advocacy organization presents a sardonic comparison between a real nuclear accident in England and the attitudes of the people who operate the fictitious nuclear plant on the television cartoon show *The Simpsons*.

SUSAN NEVILLE *Utilities* (Division and Classification) 562

A prize-winning fiction writer explores the mysterious buildings that produce energy, and then reflects on the sources that are used to run other kinds of machines.

JOSEPH J. ROMM   *The Holy Grails of Energy Technology*
(Definition)   573

> A prominent energy consultant defines fuel cells and the possibility
> of a hydrogen economy, suggesting why that economy may never
> become a reality.

EDWARD CODY   *China's Symbol, and Source, of Power*
(Cause and Effect)   582

> A reporter for the foreign desk of the *Washington Post* analyzes the rea-
> sons why the Chinese built the largest hydroelectric dam in the world
> and speculates on the effect it will have on people and the environment.

A Debate About Windmills

ROBERT F. KENNEDY, JR.   *An Ill Wind Off Cape Cod*
(Persuasion and Argument)   587

> An environmental lawyer from a famous American family associated
> with Cape Cod argues that installing windmills in Nantucket Sound
> will create environmental and economic dangers.

FRANCIS BROADHURST   *Cape Wind Is Sound for the Sound*
(Persuasion and Argument)   592

> A longtime resident of Cape Cod and a frequent contributor to the
> *Cape Cod Times* argues that the windmills will create no environ-
> mental dangers and will produce valuable economic benefits.

THOMAS PYNCHON   *Entropy* (story)   596

> By interweaving two plots—one chaotic, the other ordered—
> Pynchon explores the social and cultural interconnections of his
> favorite slippery, scientific word.

USING AND DOCUMENTING SOURCES   615

Student Research Paper: ERIN McMULLEN *The Possibilities and
Limitations of Online Learning*   638

Acknowledgements   651
Index   657

THEMATIC TABLE OF CONTENTS

The Environment

WENDELL BERRY   *Conservation Is Good Work*
(professional paragraph)   234

EMILY LINDERMAN   *Barrier-Free Design*
(student paragraph)   380

THOMAS PYNCHON   *Entropy*
(story)   596

FRANCIS BROADHURST   *Cape Wind Is Sound for
the Sound*   592

EDWARD CODY   *China's Symbol, and Source, of Power*   582

STEPHEN DOHENY-FARINA   *The Grid and the Village*   538

STEPHEN HARRIGAN   *The Tiger Is God*   353

ROBERT F. KENNEDY, JR.   *An Ill Wind Off Cape Cod*   587

DAVA SOBEL   *Imaginary Lines*   180

MARK TWAIN   *Two Views of the River*   168

The Family

MAXINE HONG KINGSTON   *A Song for a Barbarian Reed Pipe*
(professional paragraph)   24

LAUREN BRINER   *Deloris*
(student paragraph)   25

ELIZABETH WINTHROP   *The Golden Darters*
(story)   149

BARBARA KINGSOLVER   *Stone Soup*   485

PHILLIP LOPATE   *Modern Friendships*   260

SERENA NANDA   *Arranging a Marriage in
India*   136

KATHA POLLITT   *Why Boys Don't Play with
Dolls*   383

ANNE ROIPHE   *A Tale of Two Divorces*   188

ALICE WALKER   *Beauty: When the Other Dancer Is
the Self*   39

BARBARA DAFOE WHITEHEAD   *Women and the
Future of Fatherhood*   496

The Other

NICHOLAS LEMANN   *The Promised Land*
(professional paragraph)   454

LAUREN BRINER   *Deloris*
(student paragraph)   25

WITI IHIMAERA   *His First Ball*
(story)   213

LAURA BOHANNAN   *Shakespeare in the
Bush*   199

JUDITH ORTIZ COFER   *The Myth of the Latin Woman:
I Just Met a Girl Named María*   49

ANTHONY GIDDENS   *Globalisation*   342

NIKKI GIOVANNI   *Campus Racism 101*   115

ERIC LIU   *A Chinaman's Chance: Reflections on the
American Dream*   465

MARY MEBANE   *Shades of Black*   252

GEORGE ORWELL   *Shooting an Elephant*   65

Women

JOYCE CAROL OATES   *When Tristram Met Isolde*
(professional paragraph)   320

NATHAN M. HARMS   *Howard and Rush*
(student paragraph)   165

ALICE ADAMS   *Truth or Consequences*
(story)   75

JUDITH ORTIZ COFER   *The Myth of the Latin Woman: I Just Met a Girl Named María*   49

BARBARA KINGSOLVER   *Stone Soup*   485

SERENA NANDA   *Arranging a Marriage in India*   136

KATHA POLLITT   *Why Boys Don't Play with Dolls*   383

ANNE ROIPHE   *A Tale of Two Divorces*   188

ALICE WALKER   *Beauty: When the Other Dancer Is the Self*   39

BARBARA DAFOE WHITEHEAD   *Women and the Future of Fatherhood*   496

Heroes

DAVID McCULLOUGH   *FDR and Truman*
(professional paragraph)   164

JASON UTESCH   *Personality*
(student paragraph)   321

KURT VONNEGUT, JR.   *Harrison Bergeron*
(story)   522

JOAN ACOCELLA   *Under the Spell*   505

HAROLD BLOOM   *Can 35 Million Book Buyers Be Wrong? Yes.*   516

ANDRE DUBUS   *Digging*   28

DANIEL GOLEMAN   *Peak Performance: Why Records Fall*   388

MARTIN LUTHER KING, JR.   *I Have a Dream*   458

GEORGE ORWELL   *Shooting an Elephant*   65

SARAH VOWELL   *Cowboys v. Mounties*   172

Work

SCOTT RUSSELL SANDERS   *Digging Limestone*
(professional paragraph)   97

SARA TEMPLE   *Making Stained Glass*
(student paragraph)   98

FLANNERY O'CONNOR   *Revelation*
(story)   290

ANDRE DUBUS   *Digging*   28

JAMES GLEICK   *Attention! Multitaskers*   335

DANIEL GOLEMAN   *Peak Performance: Why Records
Fall*   388

GREENPEACE INTERNATIONAL   *Sellafield = Springfield?*   557

JONATHAN KOZOL   *The Human Cost of an Illiterate
Society*   396

SUSAN NEVILLE   *Utilities*   562

MARK TWAIN   *Two Views of the River*   168

Teaching and Learning

MAXINE HONG KINGSTON   *A Song for a Barbarian
Reed Pipe* (professional paragraph)   24

LAUREN BRINER   *Deloris*
(student paragraph)   25

TONI CADE BAMBARA   *The Lesson*
(story)   364

LAURA BOHANNAN   *Shakespeare in the Bush*   199

KRISTI FERGUSON   *The Scenic Route*   14

NIKKI GIOVANNI   *Campus Racism 101*   115

MALCOLM GLADWELL   *Examined Life*   407

TOM AND RAY MAGLIOZZI   *Guide to Better Fuel Economy*   548

P. J. O'ROURKE   *Third World Driving Hints and Tips*   109

ANNA QUINDLEN   *How Reading Changed My Life*   8

Arts and Leisure

JOYCE CAROL OATES   *When Tristram Met Isolde* (professional paragraph)   320

GARETH TUCKER   *Gentlemen! Start Your Engines* (student paragraph)   234

KURT VONNEGUT, JR.   *Harrison Bergeron* (story)   522

JOAN ACOCELLA   *Under the Spell*   505

JULIA ALVAREZ   *Grounds for Fiction*   121

JOHN BERENDT   *The Hoax*   324

HAROLD BLOOM   *Can 35 Million Book Buyers Be Wrong? Yes.*   516

LAURA BOHANNAN   *Shakespeare in the Bush*   199

ANNA QUINDLEN   *How Reading Changed My Life*   8

ANN ZWINGER   *Drawing on Experience*   101

Science and Technology

JONATHAN WEINER   *Elephant Evolution* (professional paragraph)   379

JIM F. SALOMAN   *Genetic Engineering* (student paragraph)   455

ARTHUR C. CLARKE   *The Star* (story)   437

DIANE ACKERMAN   *Pain*   329

JAMES H. AUSTIN   *Four Kinds of Chance*   237

RICHARD DOERFLINGER   *First Principles and the*
"Frist Principles"   478

JAMES GLEICK   *Attention! Multitaskers*   335

JOSEPH J. ROMM   *The Holy Grails of Energy
Technology*   573

PEGGY PRICHARD ROSS   *Stem Cell Research: It's About
Life and Death, Not Politics*   482

ERIC SCHLOSSER   *Why McDonald's Fries Taste
So Good*   422

Ethical Issues

MAXINE HONG KINGSTON   *A Song for a Barbarian Reed Pipe*
(professional paragraph)   24

JIM F. SALOMAN   *Genetic Engineering*
(student paragraph)   455

ARTHUR C. CLARKE   *The Star*
(story)   437

RICHARD DOERFLINGER   *First Principles and the*
"Frist Principles"   478

JONATHAN KOZOL   *The Human Cost of an Illiterate
Society*   396

GEORGE ORWELL   *Shooting an Elephant*   65

SISTER HELEN PREJEAN   *Memories of a Dead Man
Walking*   58

PEGGY PRICHARD ROSS   *Stem Cell Research: It's About Life
and Death, Not Politics*   482

JUDITH VIORST   *The Truth About Lying*   244

GARRY WILLS   *The Dramaturgy of Death*   274

PREFACE

For almost three decades, *The Riverside Reader* has set the standard for rhetorical readers. Its explanations of purpose, audience, and strategies have enabled a generation of students to read prose models effectively and to write their own essays successfully. Indeed, its thorough coverage and thoughtful advice about the many issues and problems embedded in the reading and writing processes have established this book as one of the core texts in the college composition curriculum.

The ninth edition of *The Riverside Reader,* like its predecessors, presents essays by acknowledged masters of prose style, including George Orwell, Flannery O'Connor, and Alice Walker, along with many new voices such as Joan Acocella, Malcolm Gladwell, and Susan Neville. Almost one-half of the selections are new to this edition. As always, introductions, readings, study questions, and writing assignments are clear, creative, and cogent.

THE *RIVERSIDE* TRADITION

The first seven sections in this reader are arranged in a sequence familiar to most writing teachers. Beginning with narration and description, moving through the five expository patterns, and ending with persuasion and argument, these sections group readings according to traditional writing strategies.

The readings within each section have been chosen to illustrate what the section introductions say they illustrate: there are no strange hybrids or confusing models. Within each section, the selections are arranged in an ascending order of length and complexity. The ultimate purpose of *The Riverside Reader* is to produce good writing. For that reason, the writing assignments in this book are presented as the culminating activity of each section. Six assignments at the end of each section ask students to write essays that cover a range of writing tasks from personal response to analysis and argument.

REVISIONS TO THE ENDURING FEATURES

At the core of *The Riverside Reader* is our desire to assist students in their reading and writing by helping them see the interaction between the two processes:

- The **connection between the reading and writing process** is highlighted in the general introduction. The familiar terminology of *response, purpose, audience,* and *strategies* provides a framework for the introduction and for subsequent study questions and writing assignments.
- **Guidelines for Reading an Essay** is paired with **Guidelines for Writing an Essay** to enhance and advance the students' understanding of the reading/writing connection.
- A **new annotated essay** on the subject of reading appears in the general introduction: "How Reading Changed My Life" by Anna Quindlen. The annotations illustrate how a reader responds to reading by writing.
- A **student essay** on the subject of writing—Kristie Ferguson's "The Scenic Route"—discusses the beginning experiences of one student writer. The essay is followed by commentary on what the student discovered about her writing and by writing assignments that encourage similar discoveries.

- To demonstrate the increasing importance of visual literacy in our culture, each rhetorical section features a **visual text**—such as a cartoon, an icon, an advertisement. Each of these texts is followed by an assignment that encourages students to look more closely at the image, discuss its significance to the chapter's rhetorical strategy, and write about what they have discovered.

- In each section introduction, an **annotated paragraph by a professional writer**, such as an excerpt from Maxine Hong Kingston's "A Song for a Barbarian Reed Pipe," concisely demonstrates reading and writing at work.

- In each section introduction, a **paragraph by a student writer**, such as Lauren Briner's "Deloris," is followed by questions about writing strategy.

- A **Points to Remember** list concludes each section introduction and provides a convenient summary of the essential tasks and techniques of each strategy.

- This ninth edition of *The Riverside Reader* contains **twenty-two new selections,** among them Alice Walker's "Beauty: When the Other Dancer Is the Self," James Gleick's "Attention! Multitaskers," and Susan Neville's "Utilities." The complete collection, which includes popular essays from previous editions, provides a variety of readings to engage the interest of all students on subjects as wide ranging as the taste of fast food, the impact of ethnic stereotypes, and the problems of energy independence.

- **A new case study, Energy,** presents variations on the theme of energy independence—personal, social, environmental, and scientific. The eight essays and one short story, which are arranged to repeat the patterns presented in the seven rhetorical chapters, illustrate how such strategies enable a writer to investigate a theme from a variety of perspectives. The writing assignments following each reading encourage students to use what they already know or can discover to *respond, analyze,* and *argue* about the texts.

- An eight-page **color photographic essay,** "The Sources of Energy," emphasizes the power of images to evoke ideas and insights. The images present both the possibilities and problems of energy independence, and are followed by assignments that encourage students to connect what they see with what they read and plan to write.

- A **Thematic Table of Contents** is provided for teachers who wish to organize their course by themes or issues.
- Selections in the **Persuasion and Argument** section are paired to present different perspectives on the issues such as race, stem cell research, and the popular Harry Potter books. This feature reflects our continuing emphasis on analytical and interpretive reading and writing.
- A **short story** concludes each section to provide an interesting perspective on a particular writing strategy and to give students opportunities to broaden their reading skills. New to this edition are Toni Cade Bambara's "The Lesson," and Thomas Pynchon's "Entropy."
- **Study questions and writing assignments** throughout the text have been extensively revised.
- The chapter on **using and documenting sources** provides expanded instruction on using and documenting sources in the format of the latest Modern Language Association (MLA) style. Special attention is given to the problem of plagiarism and the citation of electronic sources. The chapter concludes with an annotated student paper, Erin McMullen's "The Possibilities and Limitations of Online Learning," that uses both print and electronic sources.

SUPPLEMENTS FOR THE RIVERSIDE READER

Website

The dynamic, redesigned website encourages further exploration by students into the themes and topics of the book and supplies considerable support to student's writing. Features include suggested rhetorical- and thematic-based assignments or exercises, sample student essays, a writing guidelines checklist, and reading quizzes for each selection.

The website for instructors supplies the comprehensive Instructor's Resource Manual.

For both sites, go to **http://college.hmco.com/english.**

Instructor's Resource Manual

Now available in a downloadable PDF on-line, the *Instructor's Resource Manual,* by Elizabeth Shostak, includes advice on teaching reading and writing strategies and on classroom challenges new writing instructors may encounter. For each selection in the reader, the *Instructor's Resource Manual* provides an extensive rhetorical analysis, reading quiz, and vocabulary list.

ACKNOWLEDGMENTS

We are grateful to the following writing instructors who have provided extensive commentary of *The Riverside Reader* for this edition:

> Barbara Barrett, Washington County Community
>   College
> David Bells, Rutgers University Camden Division
> Amy E. Kalvig, Heidelberg College
> Cate Marvin, College of Staten Island, CUNY
> Patricia Montalbano, College of St. Catherine

We are also grateful to our students for allowing us to reprint their work in this edition: Kristie Ferguson, Lauren Briner, Sara Temple, Nathan Harms, Gareth Tucker, Jason Utesch, Emily Linderman, Jim Saloman, and Erin McMullen.

A special thanks goes to two new friends, our development editor, John McHugh, and our art editor, Ann Schrueder, and two old friends, our production editor, Jane Lee, and our energy researcher, Sarah Helyar Chester. And, of course, our debt to all of our students is ongoing.

J. F. T.
M. H.

The
RIVERSIDE
READER

INTRODUCTION

People who do well in college are nearly always good readers and good writers. They have to read well to absorb and evaluate the wealth of information they encounter on line and in books and articles, and they have to write well to show that they're learning and thinking. In this book we try to help you connect your reading and writing and become skillful at both crafts. For they are complementary skills, and you can master both of them through practice.

BECOMING A GOOD READER

- Step One. When you're reading a piece of writing you need to master, go over it quickly at first to get the main ideas and the flavor of the piece. Just enjoy it for what you're learning. Unless you get lost or confused, don't go back to reread or stop to analyze the writer's argument.

- Step Two. Now slow down. If you're reading from a book or magazine you don't own, photocopy the essay. If you're reading off the Internet, print out the piece. Now go back over it, this time underlining or highlighting key points and jotting notes in the margins—summaries of the main points in the left margin, questions or objections in the right one.
- Step Three. On a separate piece of paper or in a separate file, jot down your response to the reading. What about the writer's ideas appeals to you? What puzzles you? What elements in the piece remind you of some of your own experiences? Remember that there's not necessarily one "right" reaction to what you're reading. Each reader brings different experiences to reading a piece of writing—sees it through his or her unique lens, so to speak. So every response will be individual, and each reader will have a slightly different perspective. The notes you take will help you if you go on to write about the piece or discuss it in class.

The annotated sample essay, "How Reading Changed My Life," which you will find further along in this introduction, shows how one reader responded to an essay by columnist and novelist Anna Quindlen. In that essay, the writer explains how reading influenced her attitude toward and questions about life.

READING TO BECOME A BETTER WRITER

Many people have learned to improve their performance in a sport or activity by watching a professional at work and then patterning their activity on that of the professional. In the same way, student writers can sharpen their skills by paying attention to how professional writers practice their craft. This book is organized around that assumption. Thus you will find tips about what to look for as you read these authors and questions that give you insight into their writing process. Here are three things to look for:

- What is the writer's **purpose**? What does he or she want to accomplish? How does the writer communicate that purpose? For instance, in "The Scenic Route," the sample student essay that comes right after Guidelines for Writing an Essay, the writer's purpose is to explain how she developed her own writing process.

- Who is the writer's **audience**? Why has he or she chosen that audience? In "The Scenic Route" the author, Kristie Ferguson, is writing for other novice writers, who might empathize with her struggles to develop as a writer.
- What are the writer's **strategies**? What can you tell from the way the writer starts out? Does he or she tell stories, argue, give examples, cite personal experience, or empathize with a person or group? In "The Scenic Route" Kristie Ferguson draws on personal experience and narratives to make her point.

When you get in the habit of asking these questions when you read, you'll begin to understand how writers work and also begin to master some elements of the craft for your own writing.

READING TO LEARN ABOUT WRITING STRATEGIES

In *The Riverside Reader* you will find essays and short stories that comment on events and circumstances that affect all our lives. Here are just a few of the topics you may read about:

- The environment
- Racial discrimination and problems
- Capital punishment
- Ethnic conflicts
- Family patterns and values
- Academic testing
- Popular entertainment
- Scientific problems

The essays connect to other strands in your college education and are as pertinent to courses in women's studies, architecture, geology, history, or education as they are in a college writing course. In the short stories you can see how fiction writers explore human problems through narratives.

Common Writing Strategies

The essays in *The Riverside Reader* are arranged according to common patterns of development that we encounter every day.

- Narration and description
- Process analysis
- Comparison and contrast
- Division and classification
- Definition
- Cause and effect
- Persuasion and argument

As you read and get a sense of how professional writers develop their ideas by using one or more of these patterns, you'll probably see how you can adapt these strategies to your writing.

The essays in this reader provide strong examples of each strategy in action, but you don't have to limit yourself to a single pattern for an entire piece of writing. Certainly professional writers don't. But frequently they do structure an essay around one dominant strategy, using other strategies to supplement it. For example, Malcolm Gladwell concentrates on cause and effect in "Examined Life," but he also uses narration to tell the story of Stanley Kaplan.

Strategies for Your Writing

You can also use these traditional strategies as tools of discovery to generate material for your first draft. Suppose you want to write about wind farms as an alternate energy source. Here are some strategies for getting started.

> **Narration and description:** Describe a wind farm.
> **Comparison and contrast:** Contrast wind power with hydroelectric power.

Process analysis: Analyze how wind farms work.

Cause and effect: Show wind power as a clean energy source. Show why it is needed.

Persuasion and argument: Argue for the special benefits of wind power compared to nuclear or coal-generated power.

You can see that, when you begin to think of writing with these patterns in mind, you'll have an easier time getting started.

USING *THE RIVERSIDE READER*

Before you begin to read essays from a section of *The Riverside Reader,* look over the introduction to that section to get a feel for what to expect. The introduction will suggest how you might incorporate the pattern into your own writing and will also illustrate how a professional writer used the pattern and how a student writer incorporated it into a paragraph. Each introduction concludes with a highlighted list of Points to Remember.

Before each essay or story you'll find a headnote about the author's background and work. Following each essay is a set of questions to help you analyze key elements of the piece; after each story, a "comment" discusses some of its high points. After each section, you'll find writing assignments that connect with the section's essay pattern.

On pages 6 to 7 we give Guidelines for Reading an Essay, and after those guidelines you will find a sample analysis of Anna Quindlen's "How Reading Changed My Life." This introduction to *The Riverside Reader* closes with Guidelines for Writing an Essay, followed by student Kristie Ferguson's essay.

Guidelines for Reading an Essay

I. READ THE ESSAY THROUGH CAREFULLY

a. Consider the title and what expectations it raises.

b. Note when the essay was written and where it was first published.

c. Look at the author information in the headnote, and consider what important leads that information gives you about what to expect from the essay.

d. Now go back over the essay, underlining or highlighting key ideas and jotting down any questions you have.

II. THINK ABOUT YOUR RESPONSE TO THE ESSAY

a. Note what you liked and/or disliked about it, and analyze why you had that reaction.

b. Decide what questions you have after reading the essay.

c. Think about the issues the essay raises for you.

III. WRITE A BRIEF STATEMENT OF WHAT SEEMS TO BE THE AUTHOR'S PURPOSE

a. Consider how the information about the author's life and experience may account for that purpose.

b. Decide to what extent you think the author achieved his or her purpose.

IV. AS FAR AS YOU CAN, IDENTIFY THE AUTHOR'S ORIGINAL AUDIENCE

a. Make a guess about what those readers' interests are.

b. Compare your interests and experiences to those of the readers the author had in mind when writing the essay, and decide how similar or different they are.

V. LOOK AT THE STRATEGIES THE WRITER USES TO ENGAGE AND HOLD THE READER'S INTEREST

a. Look at the lead the author uses to engage the reader.

b. Identify the main pattern the writer uses in the essay, and consider how that pattern helps to develop his or her main idea.

c. Pick out the descriptions, events, or anecdotes that make a particular impression, and consider why they're effective.

d. Identify passages or images that you find especially powerful.

VI. REFLECT ON THE ESSAY, AND TRY TO STATE ITS CONTENT AND MAIN ARGUMENT IN TWO OR THREE SENTENCES

Sample Analysis of an Essay

ANNA QUINDLEN

Anna Quindlen was born in 1953 in Philadelphia, Pennsylvania, and was educated at Barnard College. She began her career as a reporter for the New York Post *and then as a reporter and columnist for the* New York Times. *Her columns are collected in* Living Out Loud *(1988) and* Thinking Out Loud: On the Personal, the Political, the Public and the Private *(1994). Quindlen continues to contribute columns to* Newsweek, *but she devotes much of her time to writing the kinds of novels she talks about in* How Reading Changed My Life *(1998). Those best-selling novels include* Object Lessons *(1991),* One True Thing *(1995),* Black and Blue *(1998), and* Blessings *(2002).* One True Thing *was adapted to the screen and starred Renée Zellweger and Meryl Streep. In "How Reading Changed My Life," excerpted from the book of that title, Quindlen explains how her passion for reading shaped her values and work.*

How Reading Changed My Life

Her topic   Perhaps only a truly discontented child can become as seduced by books as I was. <u>Perhaps restlessness is a necessary corollary of devoted literacy.</u> There was a club chair in our house, a big one, with curled arms and a square ottoman; it sat in one corner of the living room, catty-corner to the fireplace, with a barrel table next to

Are only discontented children avid readers?

it. In my mind I am always sprawled in it, reading with my skinny, scabby legs slung over one of its arms. "It's a beautiful day," my mother is saying; she said that always, often, autumn, spring, even when there was a fresh snowfall. "All your friends are outside." It was true; they always were. Sometimes I went out with them, coaxed into the street, out into the fields, down by the creek, by the lure of what I knew intuitively was normal childhood, by the promise of being what I knew instinctively was a normal child, one who lived, raucous, in the world.

Strong image to evoke setting [margin note]

What does she mean by "normal"? [margin note]

I have clear memories of that sort of life, of lifting the rocks in the creek that trickled through Naylor's Run to search for crayfish, of laying pennies on the tracks of the trolley and running to fetch them, flattened, when the trolley had passed. But at base it was never any good. The best part of me was always at home, within some book that had been laid flat on the table to mark my place, its imaginary people waiting for me to return and bring them to life. That was where the real people were, the trees that moved in the wind, the still, dark waters. I won a bookmark in a spelling bee during that time with these words of Montaigne upon it in gold: "When I am reading a book, whether wise or silly, it seems to me to be alive and talking to me." I found that bookmark not long ago, at the bottom of a box, when my father was moving.

Comparisons between outdoor self and reading self [margin note]

What does she mean by the "best part" of her? [margin note]

Good quote [margin note]

In the years since those days in that club chair I have learned that I was not alone in this, although at the time I surely was, the only child I knew, or my parents knew, or my friends knew, who preferred reading to playing kick-the-can or ice-skating or just sitting on the curb breaking sticks and scuffing up dirt with a sneaker in summer. In books I have traveled, not only to other

Other people have had similar experiences with reading [margin note]

What she learned from reading

worlds, but into my own. I learned who I was and who I wanted to be, what I might aspire to, and what I might dare to dream about my world and myself. More powerfully and persuasively than from the "shalt nots" of the Ten Commandments, I learned the difference between good and evil, right and wrong. One of my favorite childhood books, *A Wrinkle in Time,* described that evil, that wrong, existing in a different dimension from our own. But I felt that I, too, existed much of the time in a different dimension from everyone else I knew. There was waking, and there was sleeping. And then there were books, a kind of parallel universe in which anything might happen and frequently did, a universe in which I might be a newcomer but was never really a stranger. My real, true world. My perfect island.

What is this book about?

Reading as a parallel universe

Comment In the left column, the reader underlines what seems to be the key sentence in this text and uses annotations to identify the main points that Quindlen seems to be making. In the right margin, she asks questions that occur to her—questions she might like to ask the author or questions that might lead to other ideas. By interacting with the text in this way, the reader becomes an "active" reader, engaging with the text and digging around for material that might provide good topics for her own writing.

In the first paragraph, the reader identifies the topic— "restlessness is a necessary corollary of devoted literacy." But that topic could go anywhere. What is "restlessness"? What is "devoted literacy"? The reader questions Quindlen's assertion that only "discontented" children become avid readers. She then notes how Quindlen narrows her topic by describing the club chair where she did most of her childhood reading and introducing her mother's comments about "playing outside." Her suggestion that playing outside is "normal childhood" behavior prompts the reader to ask for a definition of "normal."

In the second paragraph, Quindlen expands her comparison between playing in *the* world and living in the world of books. The reader notes this comparison but wonders what Quindlen means by the "best" part of her, sensing what she might mean as she acknowledges Quindlen's effective selection of a quote from Montaigne to illustrate the power of the reading experience.

Finally, the reader notes Quindlen's recognition that she is not alone—that other people have had similar experiences with reading. She then marks the specific things Quindlen says she has learned by reading. Although she is unfamiliar with *A Wrinkle in Time*—and would probably like to ask Quindlen some questions about the book—she recognizes how Quindlen is using it as an example to establish the concept of a parallel universe where Quindlen might be a "newcomer" but never a "stranger."

Guidelines for Writing an Essay

Before you begin a college writing assignment, you need a plan. Here are some suggestions that will get you started and help you work through to a piece of finished writing.

I. ANALYZE YOUR WRITING SITUATION

Any writing task has three components: (1) a topic, (2) a purpose, and (3) an audience. Before you start, analyze these basics and write out the results:

- Decide on your topic and the basic points you want to make. Put your ideas in writing.
- Decide on your purpose, what you want to achieve.
- Identify your audience and their interest in your topic.
- Plan how you will appeal to that audience.

II. SELECT AND NARROW YOUR TOPIC

- If you can choose your own topic, look for one that interests you and on which you already have some knowledge.
- Brainstorm with your classmates about the topic, and talk to friends to get ideas for developing it.
- Check the on-line catalog in your library for leads, and look on the Web for other resources.
- Write a tentative thesis sentence to get you started; it can always be modified later.

III. FINE-TUNE YOUR PURPOSE

- Decide what outcome you want to have.
- Consider what conclusion you want your readers to come to.

IV. ANALYZE YOUR AUDIENCE

- If your readers are going to be your instructor and classmates, consider what will help you appeal to them.
- Also identify a publication where your essay might be published, and analyze the readers of that publication.
- Write out the questions your readers are likely to have.

V. DECIDE ON A PLAN OF ORGANIZATION

- Make a rough outline to put your ideas in order.
- Choose a tentative writing pattern to get you started. Depending on your purpose, you might try narration, comparison and contrast, or cause and effect.
- Consider what kinds of supporting evidence you need.

VI. WRITE A DRAFT, GET FEEDBACK ON IT, REVISE, EDIT, AND PROOFREAD

Student Essay

KRISTIE FERGUSON
The Scenic Route

As a writer, I always seem to take the scenic
route. I don't plan it that way. My teachers provide me with detailed maps pointing me down
the most direct road, but somehow I miss a turn
or make a wrong turn, and there I am—standing
at some unmarked crossroads, head pounding,
stomach churning, hopelessly lost. On such occasions, I used to curse my teachers, my maps,
and myself. But recently, I have come to expect,
even to enjoy, in a perverse way, the confusion
and panic of being lost. Left to my own devices,
I have learned to discover my own way to my
destination. And afterwards, I have a tale to tell.

I did not learn this all at once. In the beginning, I was confused about where I was going.
One day in the second grade, Mrs. Scott told us
that if we wrote a brief theme, we could go to a
movie. I grabbed my #2 pencil and listened for
directions. "You may not use erasers or dictionaries. I may ask for do-overs." Lost! I was the
worst speller in the class. My first draft was "Too
sloppy. Misspelled words." My second, "Misspelled word. Do it over." Now I was really lost.
One misspelled word. They all looked right—
and then they all looked wrong. Blind luck led
me to one of those "ie" words. I rubbed out the
letters, reprinted them, and put the dot between
them. "Kristie, you erased," she hissed. "No
ma'am." She eyed my paper and then me again,
and with a sigh waved me to the auditorium.
Collapsing next to my best friend, Karla, I
arrived in time to watch a film about dental
hygiene. Teeth? All that for teeth!

My next problem was trying to figure out where I was going. Mrs. Pageant, my fifth-grade teacher, was the source of my confusion. Seemingly unaware of my errors, she wrote enthusiastic notes on all my papers, suggesting on one, "Kristie, you're so creative. Why don't you write a book?" Why indeed should the second-grade dummy begin on such a perilous journey? "You should, Kristie. You really should. You could even write a fantasy book like the one we read today." Luckily, fantasy was my forté. I used to make up stories about the family of squirrels in my backyard. And so I wrote *Squirrel Family Starts a Grocery Store* in which, after the hoopla on page one, the squirrels run out of food on page three and close their store on page five.

As she read my book to the class, Mrs. Pageant could hardly contain herself. "What a delightful story, Kristie. You must write another one immediately." My head pounded. My stomach churned. I had stumbled into one story, but why keep going? Because Mrs. Pageant "just loved" those dumb squirrels. So there was the *Squirrel Family Starts a Bank,* in which the dumb squirrels run out of money, and *Squirrel Family Starts a Newspaper* in which they ran out of stories. I couldn't think of another squirrel story, and Karla told me that if she had to listen to one more, she would throw up.

When I got to the eleventh grade, I knew for the first time where I was going and why. The poster on Mr. Logan's bulletin board announced a writing contest: "Threats to the Free Enterprise System." Sponsored by the Blair County Board of Realtors. First prize $200. Now my problem was how to get there. Mr. Logan took us to the school library where he mapped out the first half of his strategy. Look up sources in the data base.

Take notes. Organize notes into an outline for the first draft. It seemed like a sensible plan, but, as usual, I got lost at the first turn. I logged on to Google, but it was pointless. The screen displayed hundreds of sources on free enterprise, but I couldn't find out who was threatening it.

As the deadline for the first draft approached, I was so desperate I asked my parents for directions. "Ask some local business people what they think." Not bad for parents. I borrowed my father's tape recorder and made the rounds—the grocery store, the pizza parlor, the newspaper. Most of the people seemed a lot like me—lost. They talked a lot, but they didn't focus on the question.

Maybe I was asking the wrong question. I listened to the tape a couple of times and picked out some common themes. Then I rewrote my question: "How do taxes, government regulation, or foreign competition threaten your business?" The next time around, people seemed to know what they were talking about. I organized their answers under my three categories, wrote out my draft, and made the deadline.

In class, Mr. Logan announced the second half of his strategy. Read draft. Listen to student and teacher responses. Write another draft. Mail essay. Karla went first. She quoted every book in the school library. Looking down at my paper, I saw myself stranded again. After a few more papers, I felt better. All of them sounded alike. I knew my quotes would be different—the guy at the pizza parlor, the newspaper editor. "You didn't do any research," Karla complained. "I bet you didn't read one article." A chorus of "yeses" came from the guys in the back row. Mr. Logan didn't say anything for a while. Then, smiling, he looked at Karla. "What is research?" Now Karla looked lost. The guys looked at their notebooks.

Silence. Finally, the bell. What's the answer? What am I supposed to do? Mr. Logan never said. I thought about what I had done, considered my options, and, with a sigh, mailed my essay.

A few weeks later I was standing not at some unmarked crossroads, but in the center of town— behind a lectern in front of a room full of people. A man from Blair County Board of Realtors handed me a trophy and an envelope and asked me to tell how I wrote the paper. I started to panic, and then I smiled. "Well . . ." I caught Mr. Logan's eye. "I asked a lot of people what they thought. At first they didn't know what I was talking about. Neither did I. Then I fixed up my question and they helped me figure out what to say." I looked at Mr. Logan one more time. "I guess I did research."

Comment This engaging essay by Kristie Ferguson also tells of one writer's beginnings. It takes readers on a tour of her development as a writer and highlights three memorable experiences along the way. Although the narrative focuses on her personal experiences, they conjure up memories for many fledgling writers. First, the Nazi teacher from the second grade who demands perfection and loves to punish mistakes. Then the sweetie-pie teacher from the fifth grade who gushes and lavishes praise on stuff the writer knows is junk. Finally, the practical and organized eleventh-grade teacher who outlines a writing process and guides the students through it.

But Kristie finds out that one size doesn't fit all. She has to try various approaches and adapt the process to her own style. When she does and trusts her intuition to take her in a direction that feels right to her, she succeeds and writes a winning essay that comes from listening to people talk about their own concerns. She enlivens her account with anecdotes and personal stories, creating a persona that amuses her readers and engages their sympathy. She skillfully works out her metaphor of the road and the crossroads and closes with a nice vignette of her triumph.

Possible Writing Topics

1. Compose a draft that responds to an assignment asking you to write about "How Reading Changed Your Life." You might write about some other activity that changed your life, such as taking dance lessons, playing chess, competing on a baseball team, or speaking as a youth minister for your church.

2. Compose a draft that responds to an assignment asking you to write about "The Scenic Route." You might write about a teacher or coach who influenced you early in your development, or you might write about how you respond to the feeling of being lost.

NARRATION
AND
DESCRIPTION

The writer who *narrates* tells a story to make a point. The writer who *describes* evokes the senses to create a picture. Although you can use either strategy by itself, you will probably discover that they work best in combination if you want to write a detailed account of some memorable experience—your first trip alone, a last-minute political victory, a picnic in some special place. When you want to explain what happened, you will need to tell the story in some kind of chronological order, putting the most important events—I took the wrong turn, she made the right speech, we picked the perfect spot—in the most prominent position. When you want to give the texture of the experience, you will need to select words and images that help your readers see, hear, and feel what happened—the road snaked to a dead end, the crowd thundered into applause, the sunshine softened our scowls. When you show and tell in this way, you can help your readers see the meaning of the experience you want to convey.

PURPOSE

You can use narration and description for three purposes. Most simply, you can use them to introduce or illustrate a complicated subject. You might begin an analysis of the energy crisis, for example, by telling a personal anecdote that dramatizes wastefulness. Or you might conclude an argument for gun control by giving a graphic description of a shooting incident. In each case, you are using a few sentences or a detailed description to support some other strategy, such as causal analysis or argument.

Writers use narration and description most often not as isolated examples but as their primary method when they are analyzing an issue or theme. For example, you might spend a whole essay telling how you came to a new awareness of patriotism because of your experience in a foreign country. Even though your personal experience would be the center of the essay, your narrative purpose (what happened) and your descriptive purpose (what it felt like) might be linked to other purposes. You might want to *explain* what caused your new awareness (why it happened) or to *argue* that everyone needs such awareness (why everyone should reach the same conclusion you did).

The writers who use narration and description most often are those who write autobiography, history, and fiction. If you choose to write in any of these forms, your purpose will be not so much to introduce an example or tell about an experience as to throw light on your subject. You may explain why events happened as they did or argue that such events should never happen again, but you may choose to suggest your ideas subtly through telling a story or giving a description rather than stating them as direct assertions. Your primary purpose is to report the actions and describe the feelings of people entangled in the complex web of circumstance.

AUDIENCE

As you think about writing an essay using narration and description, consider how much you will need to tell your readers and how much you will need to show them. If you are writing from personal experience, few readers will know the story before you tell it. They may know similar stories or have had similar experiences, but they do not know your story. Because you can tell your story in so many different ways—adding or deleting material to fit the occasion—you need to decide how much information your readers will need. Do they need to know every detail of your story, only brief summaries of certain parts, or some mixture of detail and summary?

In order to decide what details you should provide, you need to think about how much your readers know and what they are going to expect. If your subject is unusual (a trip to see an erupting volcano), your readers will need a lot of information, much of it technical, to understand the novel experience you are going to describe. They will expect an efficient, matter-of-fact description of volcanoes but also want you to give them some sense of how it feels to see one erupting. If your subject is familiar to most people (your experience with lawn sprinklers), your readers will need few technical details to understand your subject. But they will expect you to give them new images and insights that create a fresh vision of your subject—for example, portraying lawn sprinklers as the languid pulse of summer.

STRATEGIES

The writers in this section demonstrate that you need to use certain strategies to write a successful narrative and descriptive essay. For openers, you must recognize that an experience and an essay about that experience are not the same thing. When you have any experience, no matter how long it lasts, your memory of that experience is going to be disorganized and poorly defined, but the essay you write about that experience must have a purpose and be sharply focused. When you want to transform your experience into an essay, start by locating the central **conflict.** It may be (1) between the writer and himself or herself, as when George Orwell finds himself in a quandary about whether to shoot the elephant; (2) between the writer and others, as when Alice Walker describes her reaction to family members and school friends; or (3) between the writer and the environment, as when Judith Ortiz Cofer tries to explain the difference between *individuals* and *social stereotypes.*

Once you have identified the conflict, arrange the action so that your readers know how the conflict started, how it developed, and how it was resolved. This coherent sequence of events is called a **plot.** Sometimes you may want to create a plot that sticks to a simple chronological pattern. In "Memories of a Dead Man Walking," Sister Helen Prejean begins her account of the original events at the beginning and describes them as they occur. At other times you may want to start your essay in the middle or even near the end of the events you are describing. In "Digging," Andre Dubus concludes his narrative by speculating about a different "middle." The authors choose a pattern according to their purpose: Sister Helen Prejean wants to describe the evolution of the events leading up to the execution; Dubus wants to describe why coming home for lunch would have changed the whole story.

When you figure out what the beginning, middle, and end of your plot should be, you can establish how each event in those sections should be paced. **Pace** is the speed at which the writer recounts events. Sometimes you can narrate events quickly by omitting details, compressing time, and summarizing experience. For example, Cofer summarizes several episodes that reveal her contact with a stereotype. At other times you may want to pace events more slowly and carefully because they are vital to your purpose. You will need to include every detail, expand on time, and present the situation as a fully realized scene rather than in summary form. Dubus creates such a scene when he describes his first morning of "digging."

You can make your scenes and summaries effective by your careful **selection of details.** Just adding more details doesn't satisfy this requirement. You must select those special details that satisfy the needs of your readers and further your purpose in the essay. For example, sometimes you will need to give *objective* or *technical* details to help your readers understand your subject. Cofer provides this kind of detail when she describes the cultural customs of Puerto Rico. At other times you will want to give *subjective* or *impressionistic* details to appeal to your readers' senses. Orwell provides much of this sort of detail as he tries to re-create his physical and psychological response to shooting the elephant. Finally, you may want to present your details so they form a *figurative image* or create a *dominant impression*. Dubus uses both of these strategies: the first when he describes his father's conversation, and the second when he describes his lunch hour.

In order to identify the conflict, organize the plot, vary the pace, and select details for your essay, you need to determine your **point of view:** the person and position of the narrator (*point*) and the attitude toward the experience being presented (*view*). You choose your *person* by deciding whether you want to tell your story as "I" saw it (as Sister Helen Prejean does in her story about her experiences with death row inmates) or as "he" saw it (as Dubus does when he describes his father's life).

You choose your *position* by deciding how close you want to be to the action in time and space. You may be involved in the action or view it from the position of an observer, or you may tell about the events as they are happening or many years after they have taken place. For example, George Orwell, the young police officer, is the chief actor in his narrative, but George Orwell, the author, still wonders, years after the event, why he shot the elephant. You create your attitude—

how you view the events you intend to present and interpret—by the person and position you choose for writing your essay. The attitudes of the narrators in the following essays might be characterized as reticent (Dubus), nostalgic (Walker), perplexed (Cofer), tormented (Prejean), and ambivalent (Orwell).

USING NARRATION AND DESCRIPTION IN PARAGRAPHS

Here are two narration and description paragraphs. The first is written by a professional writer and is followed by an analysis. The second is written by a student writer and is followed by questions.

MAXINE HONG KINGSTON
A Song for a Barbarian Reed Pipe

Not all of the children who were silent at American school found a voice at Chinese school. One new teacher said each of us had to get up and recite in front of the class, who was to listen. My sister and I had memorized the lesson perfectly. We said it to each other at home, one chanting, one listening. The teacher called on my sister to recite first. It was the first time a teacher had called on the second-born to go first. My sister was scared. She glanced at me and looked away; I looked down at my desk. I hoped that she could do it because if she couldn't, then I would have to. She opened her mouth and a voice came out that wasn't a whisper, but it wasn't a proper voice either. I hoped that she would not cry, fear breaking up her voice like twigs underfoot. She sounded as if she were trying to sing though weeping and strangling. She did not pause or stop to end the embarrassment. She kept going until she said the last word, and then she sat

Sets up conflict

Conflict slows pace; heightens suspense

Appeals to sense

down. When it was my turn, the same voice came out, a <u>crippled animal running on broken legs.</u> You could hear splinters in my voice, bones rubbing jagged against one another. I was loud, though. I was glad I didn't whisper.

Creates new image

Confirms point of view

Comment This paragraph, taken from the final section of *The Woman Warrior,* recounts an embarrassing scene involving two Chinese sisters. Kingston describes how she and her sister prepare for the expected recitation. The conflict occurs when the teacher calls on the second-born sister first—a breach of Chinese etiquette. By describing how she looks down at her desk, Kingston slows the pace and heightens the anxiety of the situation. She then selects details and images to evoke the sound of her sister's and then her own voice as they complete the lesson.

LAUREN BRINER
Deloris

"All right, how do you say 'dollars' in Spanish?" Mrs. Tyrrel was setting the rules for Spanish II, but we wanted the old rules. Last year Mr. Kreuger, who taught Spanish I, loved to throw parties. I guess he thought fiestas would make us want to learn Spanish. What we really wanted was more fiestas. But now, according to Mrs. Tyrrel, the party was over. She peered at us over the top of her glasses looking for a snitch. We avoided her eyes by thumbing the sides of our new books. "Lauren? How about you?" I looked for help. No luck! My party friends were faking it, staring at the unintelligible sentences in *Spanish II.* I was on my own. I looked up at Mrs. Tyrrel. "Lauren?" I was desperate, caught in her gaze. I panicked. In a really hokey accent, I suggested a possible answer, "Dellores?" "Deloris? Who's Deloris? Is she a friend of yours?"

Mrs. Tyrrel was laughing. The whole class began laughing, "Deloris! Deloris! Deloris!" The blood rushed to my face and tears welled in my eyes. So much for old rules and old friends.

1. How does Briner's description of the two teachers establish the conflict in this episode?
2. How do the responses of the teacher and the class to Lauren's answer reveal the writer's point of view?

NARRATION AND DESCRIPTION

Points to Remember

1. Focus your narrative on the "story" in your story—that is, focus on the conflict that defines the plot.
2. Vary the pace of your narrative so that you can summarize some events quickly and render others as fully realized scenes.
3. Supply evocative details to help your readers experience the dramatic development of your narrative.
4. Establish a consistent point of view so that your readers know how you have positioned yourself in your story.
5. Represent the events in your narrative so that your story makes its point.

In this excerpt from her graphic novel Persepolis: The Story of a Childhood *(2003), Marjane Satrapi recounts the reaction of young schoolgirls to the law requiring them to wear "the veil." Some argue that the veil debases and even erases female identity. Others argue that it provides women with safety and secret power. How do the characters in Satrapi's narrative feel about this regulation? Write a narrative describing your own reactions to some obligatory dress code.*

ANDRE DUBUS

Andre Dubus (1936–1999) was born in Lake Charles, Louisiana, and educated at McNeese State College and the University of Iowa. He taught writing at universities such as the University of Alabama and Boston University. His work includes novels such as *The Lieutenant* (1967), *Voices from the Moon* (1984), and several collections of short stories, including *Finding a Girl in America* (1980) and *Dancing After Hours* (1996). In 1986, he barely survived a devastating traffic accident that cost him his leg. He writes about confronting his disability in a series of essays, *Meditations from a Movable Chair* (1998). In "Digging," reprinted from that collection, Dubus remembers the lessons he learned from physical labor.

Digging

THAT HOT JUNE in Lafayette, Louisiana, I was sixteen, I would be seventeen in August, I weighed 105 pounds, and my ruddy, broad-chested father wanted me to have a summer job. I only wanted the dollar allowance he gave me each week, and the dollar and a quarter I earned caddying for him on weekend and Wednesday afternoons. With a quarter I could go to a movie, or buy a bottle of beer, or a pack of cigarettes to smoke secretly. I did not have a girlfriend, so I did not have to buy drinks or food or movie tickets for anyone else. I did not want to work. I wanted to drive around with my friends, or walk with them downtown, to stand in front of the department store, comb our duck-tails, talk, look at girls.

My father was a civil engineer, and the district manager for the Gulf States Utilities Company. He had been working for them since he left college, beginning as a surveyor, wearing boots and khakis and, in a holster on his belt, a twenty-two caliber pistol for cottonmouths. At home he was quiet; in the evenings he sat in his easy chair, and smoked, and read: *Time, The Saturday Evening Post, Collier's, The Reader's Digest,* detective novels, books about golf, and Book-of-the-Month Club novels. He loved to talk, and he did this at parties I listened to from my bedroom, and with his friends on the golf course, and drinking in the clubhouse after playing eighteen holes. I listened to more of my father's conversations about

---

It is time to thank my father for wanting me to work and telling me I had to work . . . and buying me lunch and a pith helmet instead of taking me home to my mother and sister.

---

politics and golf and his life and the world than I ever engaged in, during the nearly twenty-two years I lived with him. I was afraid of angering him, seeing his blue eyes, and reddening face, hearing the words he would use to rebuke me; but what I feared most was his voice, suddenly and harshly rising. He never yelled for long, only a few sentences, but they emptied me, as if his voice had pulled my soul from my body. His voice seemed to empty the house, too, and, when he stopped yelling, the house filled with silence. He did not yell often. That sound was not part of our family life. The fear of it was part of my love for him.

I was shy with him. Since my forties I have believed that he 3
was shy with me too, and I hope it was not as painful for him as it was for me. I think my shyness had very little to do with my fear. Other boys had fathers who yelled longer and more often, fathers who spanked them or, when they were in their teens, slapped or punched them. My father spanked me only

three times, probably because he did not know of most of my transgressions. My friends with harsher fathers were neither afraid nor shy; they quarreled with their fathers, provoked them. My father sired a sensitive boy, easily hurt or frightened, and he worried about me; I knew he did when I was a boy, and he told me this on his deathbed, when I was a Marine captain.

My imagination gave me a dual life: I lived in my body, and at the same time lived a life no one could see. All my life I have told myself stories, and have talked in my mind to friends. Imagine my father sitting at supper with my mother and two older sisters and me: I am ten and small and appear distracted. Every year at school there is a bully, sometimes a new one, sometimes the one from the year before. I draw bullies to me, not because I am small, but because they know I will neither fight nor inform on them. I will take their pushes or pinches or punches, and try not to cry, and I will pretend I am not hurt. My father does not know this. He only sees me at supper, and I am not there. I am riding a horse and shooting bad men. My father eats, glances at me. I know he is trying to see who I am, who I will be.

Before my teens, he took me to professional wrestling matches because I wanted to go; he told me they were fake, and I did not believe him. We listened to championship boxing matches on the radio. When I was not old enough to fire a shotgun he took me dove hunting with his friends: we crouched in a ditch facing a field, and I watched the doves fly toward us and my father rising to shoot, then I ran to fetch the warm, dead and delicious birds. In summer he took me fishing with his friends; we walked in woods to creeks and bayous and fished with bamboo poles. When I was ten he learned to play golf and stopped hunting and fishing, and on weekends I was his caddy. I did not want to be, I wanted to play with my friends, but when I became a man and left home, I was grateful that I had spent those afternoons watching him, listening to him. A minor league baseball team made our town its home, and my father took me to games, usually with my mother. When I was twelve or so, he taught me to play golf, and sometimes I played nine holes with him; more often and more comfortably, I played with other boys.

If my father and I were not watching or listening to some-   6
thing and responding to it, or were not doing something, but were simply alone together, I could not talk, and he did not, and I felt that I should, and I was ashamed. That June of my seventeenth year, I could not tell him that I did not want a job. He talked to a friend of his, a building contractor, who hired me as a carpenter's helper; my pay was seventy-five cents an hour.

On a Monday morning my father drove me to work. I   7
would ride the bus home and, next day, would start riding the bus to work. Probably my father drove me that morning because it was my first day; when I was twelve he had taken me to a store to buy my first pair of long pants; we boys wore shorts and, in fall and winter, knickers and long socks till we were twelve; and he had taken me to a barber for my first haircut. In the car I sat frightened, sadly resigned, and feeling absolutely incompetent. I had the lunch my mother had put in a brown paper bag, along with a mason jar with sugar and squeezed lemons in it, so I could make lemonade with water from the cooler. We drove to a street with houses and small stores and parked at a corner where, on a flat piece of land, men were busy. They were building a liquor store, and I assumed I would spend my summer handing things to a carpenter. I hoped he would be patient and kind.

As a boy in Louisiana's benevolent winters and hot summers   8
I had played outdoors with friends: we built a clubhouse, chased each other on bicycles, shot air rifles at birds, tin cans, bottles, trees; in fall and winter, wearing shoulder pads and helmets, we played football on someone's very large side lawn; and in summer we played baseball in a field that a father mowed for us; he also built us a backstop of wood and chicken wire. None of us played well enough to be on a varsity team; but I wanted that gift, not knowing that it was a gift, and I felt ashamed that I did not have it. Now we drove cars, smoked, drank in nightclubs. This was French Catholic country; we could always buy drinks. Sometimes we went on dates with girls, but more often

looked at them and talked about them; or visited them, when several girls were gathered at the home of a girl whose parents were out for the evening. I had never done physical work except caddying, pushing a lawn mower, and raking leaves, and I was walking from the car with my father toward working men. My father wore his straw hat and seersucker suit. He introduced me to the foreman and said: "Make a man of him."

Then he left. The foreman wore a straw hat and looked old; everyone looked old; the foreman was probably thirty-five. I stood mutely, waiting for him to assign me to some good-hearted Cajun carpenter. He assigned me a pickaxe and a shovel and told me to get into the trench and go to work. In all four sides of the trench were files of black men, swinging picks, and shoveling. The trench was about three feet deep and it would be the building's foundation; I went to where the foreman pointed, and laid my tools on the ground; two black men made a space for me, and I jumped between them. They smiled and we greeted each other. I would learn days later that they earned a dollar an hour. They were men with families and I knew this was unjust, as everything else was for black people. But on that first morning I did not know what they were being paid, I did not know their names, only that one was working behind me and one in front, and they were good to me and stronger than I could ever be. All I really knew in those first hours under the hot sun was raising the pickaxe and swinging it down, raising it and swinging, again and again till the earth was loose; then putting the pick on the ground beside me and taking the shovel and plunging it into dirt that I lifted and tossed beside the trench.

I did not have the strength for this: not in my back, my legs, my arms, my shoulders. Certainly not in my soul. I only wanted it to end. The air was very humid, and sweat dripped on my face and arms, soaked my shirts and jeans. My hands gripping the pick or shovel were sore, my palms burned, the muscles in my arms ached, and my breath was quick. Sometimes I saw tiny black spots before my eyes. Weakly I raised the pick, straightening my back, then swung it down,

9

10

bending my body with it, and it felt heavier than I was, more durable, this thing of wood and steel. that was melting me. I laid it on the ground and picked up the shovel and pushed it into the dirt, lifted it, grunted, and emptied it beside the trench. The sun, always my friend till now, burned me, and my mouth and throat were dry, and often I climbed out of the trench and went to the large tin water cooler with a block of ice in it and water from a hose. At the cooler were paper cups and salt tablets, and I swallowed salt and drank and drank, and poured water onto my head and face; then I went back to the trench, the shovel, the pick.

Nausea came in the third or fourth hour. I kept swinging   11
the pick, pushing and lifting the shovel. I became my sick and hot and tired and hurting flesh. Or it became me; so, for an hour or more, I tasted a very small piece of despair. At noon in Lafayette a loud whistle blew, and in the cathedral the bell rang. I could not hear the bell where we worked, but I heard the whistle, and lowered the shovel and looked around. I was dizzy and sick. All the men had stopped working and were walking toward shade. One of the men with me said it was time to eat, and I climbed out of the trench and walked with black men to the shade of the tool shed. The white men went to another shaded place; I do not remember what work they had been doing that morning, but it was not with picks and shovels in the trench. Everyone looked hot but comfortable. The black men sat talking and began to eat and drink. My bag of lunch and jar with lemons and sugar were on the ground in the shade. Still I stood, gripped by nausea. I looked at the black men and at my lunch bag. Then my stomach tightened and everything in it rose, and I went around the corner of the shed where no one could see me and, bending over, I vomited and moaned and heaved until it ended. I went to the water cooler and rinsed my mouth and spat, and then I took another paper cup and drank. I walked back to the shade and lay on my back, tasting vomit. One of the black men said: "You got to eat."

"I threw up," I said, and closed my eyes and slept for the   12
rest of the hour that everyone—students and workers—had

for the noon meal. At home my nineteen-year-old sister and my mother and father were eating dinner, meat and rice and gravy, vegetables and salad and iced tea with a loaf of mint; and an oscillating fan cooled them. My twenty-two-year-old sister was married. At one o'clock the whistle blew, and I woke up and stood and one of the black men said: "Are you all right?"

I nodded. If I had spoken, I may have wept. When I was a 13 boy I could not tell a man what I felt, if I believed what I felt was unmanly. We went back to the trench, down into it, and I picked up the shovel I had left there at noon, and shoveled out all the loose earth between me and the man in front of me, then put the shovel beside the trench, lifted the pick, raised it over my shoulder, and swung it down into the dirt. I was dizzy and weak and hot; I worked for forty minutes or so; then, above me, I heard my father's voice, speaking my name. I looked up at him; he was here to take me home, to forgive my failure, and in my great relief I could not know that I would not be able to forgive it. I was going home. But he said: "Let's go buy you a hat."

Every man there wore a hat, most of them straw, the oth- 14 ers baseball caps. I said nothing. I climbed out of the trench, and went with my father. In the car, in a voice softened with pride, he said: "The foreman called me. He said the Nigras told him you threw up, and didn't eat, and you didn't tell him."

"That's right," I said, and shamefully watched the road, 15 and cars with people who seemed free of all torment, and let my father believe I was brave, because I was afraid to tell him that I was afraid to tell the foreman. Quietly we drove to town and he parked and took me first to a drugstore with air-conditioning and a lunch counter, and bought me a 7-Up for my stomach, and told me to order a sandwich. Sweet-smelling women at the counter were smoking. The men in the trench had smoked while they worked, but my body's only desire had been to stop shoveling and swinging the pick, to be with no transition at all in the shower at home, then to lie on my bed, feeling the soft breath of the fan on my damp skin. I would not have smoked at work anyway, with men. Now I wanted a cigarette. My father smoked, and I ate a bacon and lettuce and tomato sandwich.

Then we walked outside, into humidity and the heat and glare of the sun. We crossed the street to the department store where, in the work clothes section, my father chose a pith helmet. I did not want to wear a pith helmet. I would happily wear one in Africa, hunting lions and rhinoceroses. But I did not want to wear such a thing in Lafayette. I said nothing; there was no hat I wanted to wear. I carried the helmet in its bag out of the store and, in the car, laid it beside me. At that place where sweating men worked, I put it on; a thin leather strap looped around the back of my head. I went to my two comrades in the trench. One of them said: "That's a good hat."   16

I jumped in.   17

The man behind me said: "You going to be all right now."   18

I was; and I still do not know why. A sandwich and a soft drink had not given me any more strength than the breakfast I had vomited. An hour's respite in the car and the cool drugstore and buying the helmet that now was keeping my wet head cool certainly helped. But I had the same soft arms and legs, the same back and shoulders I had demanded so little of in my nearly seventeen years of stewardship. Yet all I remember of that afternoon is the absence of nausea.   19

At five o'clock the whistle blew downtown and we climbed out of the trench and washed our tools with the hose, then put them in the shed. Dirt was on my arms and hands, my face and neck and clothes. I could have wrung sweat from my shirt and jeans. I got my lunch from the shade. My two comrades said, See you tomorrow. I said I would see them. I went to the bus stop at the corner and sat on the bench. My wet clothes cooled my skin. I looked down at my dirty tennis shoes; my socks and feet were wet. I watched people in passing cars. In one were teenaged boys, and they laughed and shouted something about my helmet. I watched the car till it   20 was blocks away, then took off the helmet and held it on my lap. I carried it aboard the bus; yet all summer I wore it at work, maybe because my father bought it for me and I did not want to hurt him, maybe because it was a wonderful helmet for hard work outdoors in Louisiana.

My father got home before I did and told my mother and sister the story, the only one he knew, or the only one I assumed he knew. The women proudly greeted me when I walked into the house. They were also worried. They wanted to know how I felt. They wore dresses, they smelled of perfume or cologne, they were drinking bourbon and water, and my sister and father were smoking cigarettes. Standing in the living room, holding my lunch and helmet, I said I was fine. I could not tell the truth to these women who loved me, even if my father were not there. I could not say that I was not strong enough and that I could not bear going back to work tomorrow, and all summer, anymore than I could tell them I did not believe I was as good at being a boy as other boys were: not at sports, or with girls; and now not with a man's work. I was home, where vases held flowers, and things were clean, and our manners were good.   21

Next morning, carrying my helmet and lunch, I rode the bus to work and joined the two black men in the trench. I felt that we were friends. Soon I felt this about all the black men at work. We were digging the foundation; we were the men and the boy with picks and shovels in the trench. One day the foundation was done. I use the passive voice, because this was a square or rectangular trench, men were working at each of its sides. I had been working with my comrades on the same side for weeks, moving not forward but down. Then it was done. Someone told us. Maybe the contractor was there, with the foreman. Who dug out that last bit of dirt? I only knew that I had worked as hard as I could, I was part of the trench, it was part of me, and it was finished; it was there in the earth to receive concrete and probably never to be seen again. Someone should have blown a bugle, we should have climbed exultant from the trench, gathered to wipe sweat from our brows, drink water, shake hands, then   22

walk together to each of the four sides and marvel at what we
had made.

On that second morning of work I was not sick, and at   23
noon I ate lunch with the blacks in the shade, then we all
slept on the grass till one o'clock. We worked till five, said
goodbye to each other, and they went to the colored section of town, and I rode the bus home. When I walked into
the living room, into cocktail hour, and my family asked me
about my day, I said it was fine. I may have learned something if I had told them the truth: the work was too hard,
but after the first morning I could bear it. And all summer
it would be hard; after we finished the foundation, I would
be transferred to another crew. We would build a mess hall
at a Boy Scout camp and, with a black man, I would dig a
septic tank in clay so hard that the foreman kept hosing
water into it as we dug; black men and I would push wheel-
barrows of mixed cement; on my shoulder I would carry
eighty-pound bags of dry cement, twenty-five pounds less
than my own weight; and at the summer's end my body
would be twenty pounds heavier. If I had told these three
people who loved me that I did not understand my weak
body's stamina, they may have taught me why something
terrible had so quickly changed to something arduous.

It is time to thank my father for wanting me to work and   24
telling me I had to work and getting the job for me and buying me lunch and a pith helmet instead of taking me home to
my mother and sister. He may have wanted to take me home.
But he knew he must not, and he came tenderly to me. My
mother would have been at home that afternoon; if he had
taken me to her she would have given me iced tea and, after
my shower, a hot dinner. When my sister came home from
work, she would have understood, and told me not to despise myself because I could not work with a pickaxe and a
shovel. And I would have spent the summer at home, nestled
in the love of the two women, peering at my father's face,
and yearning to be someone I respected, a varsity second
baseman, a halfback, someone cheerleaders and drum major-
ettes and pretty scholars loved; yearning to be a man among

men, and that is where my father sent me with a helmet on
my head.

For Study and Discussion

QUESTIONS FOR RESPONSE

1. Have you ever had a summer job that required hard physical
   labor? How did your body respond to the demands of this work?
2. In what ways did your parents teach you about work?

QUESTIONS ABOUT PURPOSE

1. How do Dubus's father's instructions to the foreman—"Make a
   man of him"—reveal the narrator's purpose?
2. How is the narrator's admission that he lived a "dual life" revealed in his story?

QUESTIONS ABOUT AUDIENCE

1. How does Dubus's characterization of himself as sensitive and
   shy help him establish a connection with his audience?
2. How does his friendship with black workmen help him teach his
   audience something about justice?

QUESTIONS ABOUT STRATEGIES

1. How does Dubus pace his first day at work to reveal the intensity
   of his efforts?
2. How do Dubus's speculations about what would have happened
   if he had gone home to lunch help clarify the purpose of the
   narrative?

QUESTIONS FOR DISCUSSION

1. Why is it difficult—according to Dubus—to tell the truth to
   friends and family?
2. What does his father's decision to take him to lunch and buy him
   a pith helmet reveal about the nature of many father-son
   relationships?

ALICE WALKER

Alice Walker was born in 1944 in Eatonton, Georgia, attended Spelman College in Atlanta, and graduated from Sarah Lawrence College. She then became active in the civil rights movement, helping to register voters in Georgia, teaching in the Head Start program in Mississippi, and working on the staff of the New York City welfare department. In subsequent years, she began her own writing career while teaching at Wellesley College, the University of California at Berkeley, and Brandeis University. Her writing reveals her interest in the themes of sexism and racism, themes she embodies in her widely acclaimed novels: *The Third Life of Grange Copeland* (1970), *Meridian* (1976), *The Color Purple* (1982), *Possessing the Secret of Joy* (1992), and *Now Is the Time to Open Your Heart* (2004). Her stories, collected in *In Love and Trouble: Stories of Black Women* (1973) and *You Can't Keep a Good Woman Down* (1981), and essays, found in *Living by the Word* (1988) and *The Same River Twice* (1996), examine the complex experiences of black women. In "Beauty: When the Other Dancer Is the Self," reprinted from *In Search of Our Mothers' Gardens* (1983), Walker recalls how a childhood accident affected her self-perception.

Beauty: When the Other Dancer Is the Self

IT IS A bright summer day in 1947. My father, a fat, funny 1
man with beautiful eyes and a subversive wit, is trying to decide which of his eight children he will take with him to the

county fair. My mother, of course, will not go. She is knocked
out from getting most of us ready: I hold my neck stiff
against the pressure of her knuckles as she hastily completes
the braiding and then beribboning of my hair.

   My father is the driver for the rich old white lady up the   2
road. Her name is Miss Mey. She owns all the land for miles
around, as well as the house in which we live. All I remember
about her is that she once offered to pay my mother thirty-
five cents for cleaning her house, raking up piles of her
magnolia leaves, and washing her family's clothes, and that
my mother—she of no money, eight children, and a chronic

---

*I realize I have dashed about the world
madly, looking at this, looking at that,
storing up images against the fading of
the light.*

---

earache—refused it. But I do not think of this in 1947. I am
two and a half years old. I want to go everywhere my daddy
goes. I am excited at the prospect of riding in a car. Someone
has told me fairs are fun. That there is room in the car for
only three of us doesn't faze me at all. Whirling happily in my
starchy frock, showing off my biscuit-polished patent-leather
shoes and lavender socks, tossing my head in a way that
makes my ribbons bounce, I stand, hands on hips, before my
father. "Take me, Daddy," I say with assurance; "I'm the
prettiest!"

   Later, it does not surprise me to find myself in Miss Mey's   3
shiny black car, sharing the back seat with the other lucky
ones. Does not surprise me that I thoroughly enjoy the fair.
At home that night I tell the unlucky ones all I can remember about the merry-go-round, the man who eats live chickens, and the teddy bears, until they say: that's enough, baby
Alice. Shut up now, and go to sleep.

It is Easter Sunday, 1950. I am dressed in a green, flocked, 4
scalloped-hem dress (handmade by my adoring sister, Ruth)
that has its own smooth satin petticoat and tiny hot-pink
roses tucked into each scallop. My shoes, new T-strap patent
leather, again highly biscuit-polished. I am six years old and
have learned one of the longest Easter speeches to be heard
that day, totally unlike the speech I said when I was two:
"Easter lilies / pure and white / blossom in / the morning
light." When I rise to give my speech I do so on a great wave
of love and pride and expectation. People in the church stop
rustling their new crinolines. They seem to hold their breath.
I can tell they admire my dress, but it is my spirit, bordering
on sassiness (womanishness), they secretly applaud.

"That girl's a little *mess*," they whisper to each other, 5
pleased.

Naturally I say my speech without stammer or pause, un- 6
like those who stutter, stammer, or, worst of all, forget. This
is before the word "beautiful" exists in people's vocabulary,
but "Oh, isn't she the *cutest* thing!" frequently floats my way.
"And got so much sense!" they gratefully add . . . for which
thoughtful addition I thank them to this day.

It was great fun being cute. But then, one day, it ended. 7

I am eight years old and a tomboy. I have a cowboy hat, cow- 8
boy boots, checkered shirt and pants, all red. My playmates are
my brothers, two and four years older than I. Their colors are
black and green, the only difference in the way we are dressed.
On Saturday nights we all go to the picture show, even my
mother; Westerns are her favorite kind of movie. Back home,
"on the ranch," we pretend we are Tom Mix, Hopalong
Cassidy, Lash LaRue (we've even named one of our dogs Lash
LaRue); we chase each other for hours rustling cattle, being
outlaws, delivering damsels from distress. Then my parents decide to buy my brothers guns. These are not "real" guns. They
shoot "BBs," copper pellets my brothers say will kill birds. Because I am a girl, I do not get a gun. Instantly I am relegated
to the position of Indian. Now there appears a great distance

between us. They shoot and shoot at everything with their new guns. I try to keep up with my bow and arrows.

One day while I am standing on top of our makeshift "garage"—pieces of tin nailed across some poles—holding my bow and arrow and looking out toward the fields, I feel an incredible blow in my right eye. I look down just in time to see my brother lower his gun.   9

Both brothers rush to my side. My eye stings, and I cover it with my hand. "If you tell," they say, "we will get a whipping. You don't want that to happen, do you?" I do not. "Here is a piece of wire," says the older brother, picking it up from the roof; "say you stepped on one end of it and the other flew up and hit you." The pain is beginning to start. "Yes," I say. "Yes, I will say that is what happened." If I do not say this is what happened, I know my brothers will find ways to make me wish I had. But now I will say anything that gets me to my mother.   10

Confronted by our parents we stick to the lie agreed upon. They place me on a bench on the porch and I close my left eye while they examine the right. There is a tree growing from underneath the porch that climbs past the railing to the roof. It is the last thing my right eye sees. I watch as its trunk, its branches, and then its leaves are blotted out by the rising blood.   11

I am in shock. First there is intense fever, which my father tries to break using lily leaves bound around my head. Then there are chills: my mother tries to get me to eat soup. Eventually, I do not know how, my parents learn what has happened. A week after the "accident" they take me to see a doctor. "Why did you wait so long to come?" he asks, looking into my eye and shaking his head. "Eyes are sympathetic," he says. "If one is blind, the other will likely become blind too."   12

This comment of the doctor's terrifies me. But it is really how I look that bothers me most. Where the BB pellet struck there is a glob of whitish scar tissue, a hideous cataract, on my eye. Now when I stare at people—a favorite pastime, up to now—they will stare back. Not at the "cute" little girl, but at her scar. For six years I do not stare at anyone, because I do not raise my head.   13

Years later, in the throes of a mid-life crisis, I ask my mother   14
and sister whether I changed after the "accident." "No,"
they say, puzzled. "What do you mean?"

What do I mean?   15

I am eight, and, for the first time, doing poorly in school,   16
where I have been something of a whiz since I was four. We
have just moved to the place where the "accident" occurred.
We do not know any of the people around us because this is
a different county. The only time I see the friends I knew is
when we go back to our old church. The new school is the
former state penitentiary. It is a large stone building, cold
and drafty, crammed to overflowing with boisterous, ill-
disciplined children. On the third floor there is a huge circular imprint of some partition that has been torn out.

"What used to be here?" I ask a sullen girl next to me on   17
our way past it to lunch.

"The electric chair," says she.   18

At night I have nightmares about the electric chair, and   19
about all the people reputedly "fried" in it. I am afraid of the
school, where all the students seem to be budding criminals.

"What's the matter with your eye?" they ask, critically.   20

When I don't answer (I cannot decide whether it was an   21
"accident" or not), they shove me, insist on a fight.

My brother, the one who created the story about the wire,   22
comes to my rescue. But then brags so much about "protecting" me, I become sick.

After months of torture at the school, my parents decide   23
to send me back to our old community, to my old school. I
live with my grandparents and the teacher they board. But
there is no room for Phoebe, my cat. By the time my grandparents decide there *is* room, and I ask for my cat, she cannot
be found. Miss Yarborough, the boarding teacher, takes me
under her wing, and begins to teach me to play the piano.
But soon she marries an African—a "prince," she says—and is
whisked away to his continent.

At my old school there is at least one teacher who loves me.   24
She is the teacher who "knew me before I was born" and

bought my first baby clothes. It is she who makes life bearable. It is her presence that finally helps me turn on the one child at the school who continually calls me "one-eyed bitch." One day I simply grab him by his coat and beat him until I am satisfied. It is my teacher who tells me my mother is ill.

My mother is lying in bed in the middle of the day, something   25
I have never seen. She is in too much pain to speak. She has an abscess in her ear. I stand looking down on her, knowing that if she dies, I cannot live. She is being treated with warm oils and hot bricks held against her cheek. Finally a doctor comes. But I must go back to my grandparents' house. The weeks pass but I am hardly aware of it. All I know is that my mother might die, my father is not so jolly, my brothers still have their guns, and I am the one sent away from home.

   "You did not change," they say.   26

   Did I imagine the anguish of never looking up?   27

I am twelve. When relatives come to visit I hide in my room. My   28
cousin Brenda, just my age, whose father works in the post office and whose mother is a nurse, comes to find me. "Hello," she says. And then she asks, looking at my recent school picture, which I did not want taken, and on which the "glob," as I think of it, is clearly visible, "You still can't see out of that eye?"

   "No," I say, and flop back on the bed over my book.   29

   That night, as I do almost every night, I abuse my eye. I   30
rant and rave at it, in front of the mirror. I plead with it to clear up before morning. I tell it I hate and despise it. I do not pray for sight. I pray for beauty.

   "You did not change," they say.   31

I am fourteen and baby-sitting for my brother Bill, who lives   32
in Boston. He is my favorite brother and there is a strong bond between us. Understanding my feelings of shame and ugliness he and his wife take me to a local hospital, where the "glob" is removed by a doctor named O. Henry. There is still a small bluish crater where the scar tissue was, but the ugly white stuff is gone. Almost immediately I become a different person from the girl who does not raise her head. Or so I

think. Now that I've raised my head I win the boyfriend of my dreams. Now that I've raised my head I have plenty of friends. Now that I've raised my head class-work comes from my lips as faultlessly as Easter speeches did, and I leave high school as valedictorian, most popular student, and *queen,* hardly believing my luck. Ironically, the girl who was voted most beautiful in our class (and was) was later shot twice through the chest by a male companion, using a "real" gun, while she was pregnant. But that's another story in itself. Or is it?

"You did not change," they say.   33

It is now thirty years since the "accident." A beautiful journalist comes to visit and to interview me. She is going to write a cover story for her magazine that focuses on my latest book. "Decide how you want to look on the cover," she says. "Glamorous, or whatever."   34

Never mind "glamorous," it is the "whatever" that I hear. Suddenly all I can think of is whether I will get enough sleep the night before the photography session: if I don't, my eye will be tired and wander, as blind eyes will.   35

At night in bed with my lover I think up reasons why I should not appear on the cover of a magazine. "My meanest critics will say I've sold out," I say. "My family will now realize I write scandalous books."   36

"But what's the real reason you don't want to do this?" he asks.   37

"Because in all probability," I say in a rush, "my eye won't be straight."   38

"It will be straight enough," he says. Then, "Besides, I thought you'd made your peace with that."   39

And I suddenly remember that I have.   40

I remember: 41

I am talking to my brother Jimmy, asking if he remembers anything unusual about the day I was shot. He does not know I consider that day the last time my father, with his sweet home remedy of cool lily leaves, chose me, and that I suffered and raged inside because of this. "Well," he says, "all I remember is standing by the side of the highway with Daddy, trying to flag down a car. A white man stopped, but   42

when Daddy said he needed somebody to take his little girl
to the doctor, he drove off."

I remember: 43

I am in the desert for the first time. I fall totally in love   44
with it. I am so overwhelmed by its beauty, I confront for
the first time, consciously, the meaning of the doctor's
words years ago: "Eyes are sympathetic. If one is blind, the
other will likely become blind too." I realize I have dashed
about the world madly, looking at this, looking at that, storing up images against the fading of the light. *But I might
have missed seeing the desert!* The shock of that possibility—
and gratitude for over twenty-five years of sight—sends me
literally to my knees. Poem after poem comes—which is perhaps how poets pray.

ON SIGHT

I am so thankful I have seen
The Desert
And the creatures in the desert
And the desert Itself.

The desert has its own moon
Which I have seen
With my own eye.

There is no flag on it.

Trees of the desert have arms
All of which are always up
That is because the moon is up
The sun is up
Also the sky
The stars
Clouds
None with flags.

If there *were* flags, I doubt
the trees would point.
Would you?

But mostly, I remember this: 45

I am twenty-seven, and my baby daughter is almost three.   46
Since her birth I have worried about her discovery that her
mother's eyes are different from other people's. Will she be
embarrassed? I think. What will she say? Every day she
watches a television program called "Big Blue Marble." It begins with a picture of the earth as it appears from the moon.
It is bluish, a little battered-looking, but full of light, with
whitish clouds swirling around it. Every time I see it I weep
with love, as if it is a picture of Grandma's house. One day
when I am putting Rebecca down for her nap, she suddenly
focuses on my eye. Something inside me cringes, gets ready
to try to protect myself. All children are cruel about physical
differences, I know from experience, and that they don't
always mean to be is another matter. I assume Rebecca will be
the same.

But no-o-o-o. She studies my face intently as we stand, her   47
inside and me outside her crib. She even holds my face mater-
nally between her dimpled little hands. Then, looking every
bit as serious and lawyerlike as her father, she says, as if it may
just possibly have slipped my attention: "Mommy, there's a
world in your eye." (As in, "Don't be alarmed, or do anything crazy.") And then, gently, but with great interest:
"Mommy, where did you *get* that world in your eye?"

For the most part, the pain left then. (So what, if my broth-   48
ers grew up to buy even more powerful pellet guns for their
sons and to carry real guns themselves. So what, if a young
"Morehouse man" once nearly fell off the steps of Trevor
Arnett Library because he thought my eyes were blue.) Crying
and laughing I ran to the bathroom, while Rebecca mumbled
and sang herself off to sleep. Yes indeed, I realized, looking
into the mirror. There *was* a world in my eye. And I saw that it
was possible to love it: that in fact, for all it had taught me of
shame and anger and inner vision, I *did* love it. Even to see it
drifting out of orbit in boredom, or rolling up out of fatigue,
not to mention floating back at attention in excitement (bearing witness, a friend has called it), deeply suitable to my personality, and even characteristic of me.

That night I dream I am dancing to Stevie Wonder's song 49
"Always" (the name of the song is really "As," but I hear it as
"Always"). As I dance, whirling and joyous, happier than I've
ever been in my life, another bright-faced dancer joins me. We
dance and kiss each other and hold each other through the
night. The other dancer has obviously come through all right, as
I have done. She is beautiful, whole and free. And she is also me.

For Study and Discussion

QUESTIONS FOR RESPONSE

1. What sort of accidents happened to you when you were a child?
2. What kinds of lies did you and your brothers and sisters agree to
   tell your parents?

QUESTIONS ABOUT PURPOSE

1. What does Walker demonstrate about the cause and effect of
   self-perception?
2. How does she use her daughter's observation that "there's a
   world in your eye" to resolve her problem with self-perception?

QUESTIONS ABOUT AUDIENCE

1. What childhood experiences does Walker assume she shares with
   her readers?
2. How might her male readers respond differently to this text than
   her female readers?

QUESTIONS ABOUT STRATEGIES

1. How does Walker link the brief episodes in this text into a coherent narrative?
2. How does she use the doctor's comment about eyes being sympathetic to establish the conflict in the essay?

QUESTIONS FOR DISCUSSION

1. How do people respond to words such as "cute," "beautiful,"
   "handsome," and "ugly"?
2. How does Walker connect *sight* and *insight*?

JUDITH ORTIZ COFER

Judith Ortiz Cofer was born in Hormigueros, Puerto Rico, in 1952. She emigrated to the United States in 1956 and was educated at Augusta College, Florida Atlantic University, and Oxford University. She has taught in the public schools of Palm Beach County, Florida, as well as at several universities such as Miami University and the University of Georgia. Her poetry is collected in *Reading for the Mainland* (1987) and *Terms of Survival* (1987), and her first novel, *The Line of the Sun* (1989), was nominated for the Pulitzer Prize. Her recent books include *The Latin Deli: Prose and Poetry* (1993), *An Island Like You: Stories of the Barrio* (1995), and *Women in Front of the Sun: On Becoming a Writer* (2000). In "The Myth of the Latin Woman: I Just Met a Girl Named María," reprinted from *The Latin Deli,* Cofer describes several experiences that taught her about the pervasive stereotypes of Latin women.

The Myth of the Latin Woman: I Just Met a Girl Named María

O N A BUS trip to London from Oxford University where I was earning some graduate credits one summer, a young man, obviously fresh from a pub, spotted me and as if struck by inspiration went down on his knees in the aisle. With both hands over his heart he broke into an Irish tenor's rendition of "María" from *West Side Story.* My politely amused fellow passengers gave his lovely voice the round of gentle applause it deserved. Though I was not quite

1

as amused, I managed my version of an English smile: no show of teeth, no extreme contortions of the facial muscles— I was at this time of my life practicing reserve and cool. Oh, that British control, how I coveted it. But María had followed me to London, reminding me of a prime fact of my life: you can leave the Island, master the English language, and travel as far as you can, but if you are a Latina, especially one like me who so obviously belongs to Rita Moreno's gene pool, the Island travels with you.

This is sometimes a very good thing—it may win you   2
that extra minute of someone's attention. But with some

When a Puerto Rican girl dressed in her idea of what is attractive meets a man from the mainstream culture who has been trained to react to certain types of clothing, a clash is likely to take place.

---

people, the same things can make *you* an island—not so much a tropical paradise as an Alcatraz, a place nobody wants to visit. As a Puerto Rican girl growing up in the United States and wanting like most children to "belong," I resented the stereotype that my Hispanic appearance called forth from many people I met.

Our family lived in a large urban center in New Jersey   3
during the sixties, where life was designed as a microcosm of my parents' casas on the island. We spoke in Spanish, we ate Puerto Rican food bought at the bodega, and we practiced strict Catholicism complete with Saturday confession and Sunday mass at a church where our parents were accommodated into a one-hour Spanish mass slot, performed by a Chinese priest trained as a missionary for Latin America.

As a girl I was kept under strict surveillance, since virtue   4
and modesty were, by cultural equation, the same as family
honor. As a teenager I was instructed on how to behave as a
proper señorita. But it was a conflicting message girls got,
since the Puerto Rican mothers also encouraged their daughters to look and act like women and to dress in clothes our
Anglo friends and their mothers found too "mature" for our
age. It was, and is, cultural, yet I often felt humiliated when I
appeared at an American friend's party wearing a dress more
suitable to a semiformal than to a playroom birthday celebration. At Puerto Rican festivities, neither the music nor the
colors we wore could be too loud. I still experience a vague
sense of letdown when I'm invited to a "party" and it turns
out to be a marathon conversation in hushed tones rather
than a fiesta with salsa, laughter, and dancing—the kind of
celebration I remember from my childhood.

I remember Career Day in our high school, when teachers   5
told us to come dressed as if for a job interview. It quickly
became obvious that to the barrio girls, "dressing up" sometimes meant wearing ornate jewelry and clothing that would
be more appropriate (by mainstream standards) for the company Christmas party than as daily office attire. That morning
I had agonized in front of my closet, trying to figure out
what a "career girl" would wear because, essentially, except
for Marlo Thomas on TV, I had no models on which to base
my decision. I knew how to dress for school: at the Catholic
school I attended we all wore uniforms; I knew how to dress
for Sunday mass, and I knew what dresses to wear for parties
at my relatives' homes. Though I do not recall the precise details of my Career Day outfit, it must have been a composite
of the above choices. But I remember a comment my friend
(an Italian-American) made in later years that coalesced my
impressions of that day. She said that at the business school
she was attending the Puerto Rican girls always stood out for
wearing "everything at once." She meant, of course, too
much jewelry, too many accessories. On that day at school,
we were simply made the negative models by the nuns who

were themselves not credible fashion experts to any of us. But it was painfully obvious to me that to the others, in their tailored skirts and silk blouses, we must have seemed "hopeless" and "vulgar." Though I now know that most adolescents feel out of step much of the time, I also know that for the Puerto Rican girls of my generation that sense was intensified. The way our teachers and classmates looked at us that day in school was just a taste of the culture clash that awaited us in the real world, where prospective employers and men on the street would often misinterpret our tight skirts and jingling bracelets as a come-on.

Mixed cultural signals have perpetuated certain stereo-   6
types—for example, that of the Hispanic woman as the "Hot Tamale" or sexual firebrand. It is a one-dimensional view that the media have found easy to promote. In their special vocabulary, advertisers have designated "sizzling" and "smoldering" as the adjectives of choice for describing not only the foods but also the women of Latin America. From conversations in my house I recall hearing about the harassment that Puerto Rican women endured in factories where the "boss men" talked to them as if sexual innuendo was all they understood and, worse, often gave them the choice of submitting to advances or being fired.

It is custom, however, not chromosomes, that leads us to   7
choose scarlet over pale pink. As young girls, we were influenced in our decisions about clothes and colors by the women—older sisters and mothers who had grown up on a tropical island where the natural environment was a riot of primary colors, where showing your skin was one way to keep cool as well as to look sexy. Most important of all, on the island, women perhaps felt freer to dress and move more provocatively, since, in most cases, they were protected by the traditions, mores, and laws of a Spanish/Catholic system of morality and machismo whose main rule was: *You may look at my sister, but if you touch her I will kill you.* The extended family and church structure could provide a young woman with a circle of safety in her small pueblo on the island; if a man "wronged" a girl, everyone would close in to save her family honor.

This is what I have gleaned from my discussions as an adult   8
with older Puerto Rican women. They have told me about
dressing in their best party clothes on Saturday nights and
going to the town's plaza to promenade with their girlfriends
in front of the boys they liked. The males were thus given an
opportunity to admire the women and to express their admiration in the form of *piropos:* erotically charged street poems
they composed on the spot. I have been subjected to a few
piropos while visiting the Island, and they can be outrageous,
although custom dictates that they must never cross into ob-
scenity. This ritual, as I understand it, also entails a show of
studied indifference on the woman's part; if she is "decent,"
she must not acknowledge the man's impassioned words. So
I do understand how things can be lost in translation. When
a Puerto Rican girl dressed in her idea of what is attractive
meets a man from the mainstream culture who has been
trained to react to certain types of clothing as a sexual signal,
a clash is likely to take place. The line I first heard based on
this aspect of the myth happened when the boy who took me
to my first formal dance leaned over to plant a sloppy overea-
ger kiss painfully on my mouth, and when I didn't respond
with sufficient passion said in a resentful tone: "I thought
you Latin girls were supposed to mature early"—my first instance of being thought of as a fruit or vegetable—I was supposed to *ripen,* not just grow into womanhood like other
girls.

It is surprising to some of my professional friends that   9
some people, including those who should know better, still
put others "in their place." Though rarer, these incidents are
still commonplace in my life. It happened to me most recently during a stay at a very classy metropolitan hotel favored by young professional couples for their weddings. Late
one evening after the theater, as I walked toward my room
with my new colleague (a woman with whom I was coordi-
nating an arts program), a middle-aged man in a tuxedo, a
young girl in satin and lace on his arm, stepped directly into
our path. With his champagne glass extended toward me, he
exclaimed, "Evita!"

Our way blocked, my companion and I listened as the man 10 half-recited, half-bellowed "Don't Cry for Me, Argentina." When he finished, the young girl said: "How about a round of applause for my daddy?" We complied, hoping this would bring the silly spectacle to a close. I was becoming aware that our little group was attracting the attention of the other guests. "Daddy" must have perceived this too, and he once more barred the way as we tried to walk past him. He began to shout-sing a ditty to the tune of "La Bamba"—except the lyrics were about a girl named María whose exploits all rhymed with her name and gonorrhea. The girl kept saying "Oh, Daddy" and looking at me with pleading eyes. She wanted me to laugh along with the others. My companion and I stood silently waiting for the man to end his offensive song. When he finished, I looked not at him but at his daughter. I advised her calmly never to ask her father what he had done in the army. Then I walked between them and to my room. My friend complimented me on my cool handling of the situation. I confessed to her that I really had wanted to push the jerk into the swimming pool. I knew that this same man—probably a corporate executive, well educated, even worldly by most standards—would not have been likely to regale a white woman with a dirty song in public. He would perhaps have checked his impulse by assuming that she could be somebody's wife or mother, or at least *somebody* who might take offense. But to him, I was just an Evita or a María: merely a character in his cartoon-populated universe.

Because of my education and my proficiency with the 11 English language, I have acquired many mechanisms for dealing with the anger I experience. This was not true for my parents, nor is it true for the many Latin women working at menial jobs who must put up with stereotypes about our ethnic group such as: "They make good domestics." This is another facet of the myth of the Latin woman in the United States. Its origin is simple to deduce. Work as domestics, waitressing, and factory jobs are all that's available to women with little English and few skills. The myth of the Hispanic menial has been sustained by the same media phenomenon that made "Mammy" from *Gone with the Wind* America's idea of the black woman for generations; María, the housemaid or counter girl, is now indelibly etched into the national psyche. The big and the little screens have presented us with the picture of the funny Hispanic maid, mispronouncing words and cooking up a spicy storm in a shiny California kitchen.

This media-engendered image of the Latina in the United   12
States has been documented by feminist Hispanic scholars, who claim that such portrayals are partially responsible for the denial of opportunities for upward mobility among Latinas in the professions. I have a Chicana friend working on a Ph.D. in philosophy at a major university. She says her doctor still shakes his head in puzzled amazement at all the "big words" she uses. Since I do not wear my diplomas around my neck for all to see, I too have on occasion been sent to that "kitchen," where some think I obviously belong.

One such incident that has stayed with me, though I rec-   13
ognize it as a minor offense, happened on the day of my first public poetry reading. It took place in Miami in a boat-restaurant where we were having lunch before the event. I was nervous and excited as I walked in with my notebook in my hand. An older woman motioned me to her table. Thinking (foolish me) that she wanted me to autograph a copy of my brand new slender volume of verse, I went over. She ordered a cup of coffee from me, assuming that I was the waitress. Easy enough to mistake my poems for menus, I suppose. I know that it wasn't an intentional act of cruelty, yet of all the good things that happened that day, I remember that scene most clearly, because it reminded me of what I had to overcome before anyone would take me seriously. In retrospect I understand that my anger gave my reading fire, that I have almost always taken doubts in my abilities as a challenge—and that the result is, most times, a feeling of satisfaction at having won a convert when I see the cold, appraising eyes warm to my words, the body language change, the smile that indicates that I have opened some avenue for communication. That

day I read to that woman and her lowered eyes told me that she was embarrassed at her little faux pas, and when I willed her to look up at me, it was my victory, and she graciously allowed me to punish her with my full attention. We shook hands at the end of the reading, and I never saw her again. She has probably forgotten the whole thing but maybe not.

Yet I am one of the lucky ones. My parents made it pos- 14 sible for me to acquire a stronger footing in the mainstream culture by giving me the chance at an education. And books and art have saved me from the harsher forms of ethnic and racial prejudice that many of my Hispanic *compañeras* have had to endure. I travel a lot around the United States, reading from my books of poetry and my novel, and the reception I most often receive is one of positive interest by people who want to know more about my culture. There are, however, thousands of Latinas without the privilege of an education or the entrée into society that I have. For them life is a struggle against the misconceptions perpetuated by the myth of the Latina as whore, domestic or criminal. We cannot change this by legislating the way people look at us. The transformation, as I see it, has to occur at a much more individual level. My personal goal in my public life is to try to replace the old pervasive stereotypes and myths about Latinas with a much more interesting set of realities. Every time I give a reading, I hope the stories I tell, the dreams and fears I examine in my work, can achieve some universal truth which will get my audience past the particulars of my skin color, my accent, or my clothes.

I once wrote a poem in which I called us Latinas "God's 15 brown daughters." This poem is really a prayer of sorts, offered upward, but also, through the human-to-human channel of art, outward. It is a prayer for communication, and for respect. In it, Latin women pray "in Spanish to an Anglo God/with a Jewish heritage," and they are "fervently hoping/that if not omnipotent,/at least He be bilingual."

For Study and Discussion

QUESTIONS FOR RESPONSE

1. In what ways have people misread your behavior—by focusing on your clothes, your language, or your looks?
2. What strategies do you use to control your anger and resentment when you are misread?

QUESTIONS ABOUT PURPOSE

1. Why does Cofer introduce the conflict between *custom* and *chromosomes*? How does this conflict help explain the concept of *stereotype*?
2. How does this narrative help accomplish Cofer's "personal goal in her public life"?

QUESTIONS ABOUT AUDIENCE

1. In what ways does Cofer use the references to *María* and *Evita* to identify her audience?
2. How does she use the example of the *piropos* to educate her audience?

QUESTIONS ABOUT STRATEGIES

1. How does Cofer use the details of Career Day to explain how a cultural stereotype is perpetuated?
2. How does she manipulate point of view at her "first public poetry reading" to illustrate how she intends to change that stereotype?

QUESTIONS FOR DISCUSSION

1. How does Cofer use *Gone with the Wind* to illustrate how the media create stereotypes?
2. Why does she put so much emphasis on education? What can it do *for* you? What might it do *to* you?

SISTER HELEN PREJEAN

Helen Prejean was born in 1939 in Baton Rouge, Louisiana. At the age of eighteen, she entered the Order of the Sisters of St. Joseph of Medaille and taught English in various Catholic schools until she moved into a New Orleans housing project and co-founded a community service agency. When a friend suggested that she write to Patrick Sonnier, an inmate on death row, Prejean began a correspondence that prompted her to visit him in prison and eventually become his spiritual adviser. These experiences became the subject of her best-selling book, *Dead Man Walking: An Eyewitness Account of the Death Penalty in the United States* (1993). The book was adapted to the screen, and the film version earned Susan Sarandon an Oscar for Best Performance by an Actress in 1996. In "Memories of a Dead Man Walking," Sister Helen watches the making of the movie and is "sucked back into the original scene."

Memories of a Dead Man Walking

T HERE SHE WAS during the filming of *Dead Man Walking*,   1
Susan Sarandon being me, going into the women's room in the death house, putting her head against the tile wall, grabbing the crucifix around her neck, praying, "Please God, don't let him fall apart." It's something to watch a film of yourself happening in front of your eyes, kind of funny to hear somebody saying that she's you, but I don't stay long with this mirror stuff. What happens is that I'm sucked back into the original scene, the white-hot fire of what actually happened.

There in the Louisiana death house on April 4, 1984, I was   2
scared out of my mind. I had never watched anybody be killed.

I was supposed to be the condemned man's spiritual advisor. I was in over my head. All I had agreed to in the beginning was to be a pen pal to Patrick Sonnier. Sure, I said, I could write letters. But the man was all alone. He had no one to visit him, and it was like a current in a river: I got sucked in, and the next thing I was saying was, Okay, sure, I'll come to visit you, and when I filled out the prison application form to be approved

---

The torture happens when conscious human beings are condemned to death and begin to anticipate that death and die a thousand times before they die.

---

as his visitor, he suggested spiritual advisor, and I said, Sure. He was Catholic, and I'm a Catholic nun, and it seemed right, but I didn't know that at the end, on the evening of the execution, everybody has to leave the death house at 5:45 p.m. Everybody but the spiritual advisor. The spiritual advisor stays to the end. The spiritual advisor witnesses the execution.

People ask me all the time, What's a nun doing getting involved with these murderers? You know how people have these stereotypical images of nuns—nuns teach, nuns nurse the sick. I tell people: Look at who Jesus hung out with—lepers, prostitutes, thieves, the throwaways of his day. People don't get it. There's a lot of "biblical quarterbacking" in death penalty debates, with people tossing in quotes from the Bible to back up what they've already decided on, people wanting to practice vengeance and have God agree with them. The same thing happened in this country in the slavery debates and in the debates over women's suffrage. Quote that Bible. God said torture. God said get revenge. Religion is tricky business. 3

But here's the real reason I got involved with death row inmates: I got involved with poor people. And everybody who lives on this planet and has at least one eye open knows 4 that only poor people get selected for death row. On June 1, 1981, I drove a little brown truck into St. Thomas, a black, inner-city housing project in New Orleans, and began to live there with four other sisters (with my scared Catholic Mama kneeling on crushed glass and saying her rosary, praying that her daughter wouldn't be shot). ("Kneeling on crushed glass" is just an expression. Read *fervently*.)

5   Growing up a Southern white girl in Baton Rouge, right on the cusp of the upper class, I had only known black people as my servants. I went to an all-white high school—this was in the fifties—and black people had to sit in the back of the bus and up in the balcony of the Paramount and Hart theaters.

6   I got a whole other kind of education in the St. Thomas Projects. I still go there every Monday to keep close to friends I made there and to keep close to the struggle. Living there, it didn't take long to see that there was a greased track to prison and death row. As one Mama put it: "Our boys leave here in a police car or a hearse."

7   When I began visiting Pat Sonnier in 1982, I couldn't have been more naïve about prisons. The only other experience with prisoners I'd had was in the '60s when Sister Cletus and I—decked in full head-to-toe habits—went to Orleans Parish Prison one time to play our guitars and sing with the prisoners. This was the era of singing nuns, the "Dominica-nica-nica" era, and the guards brought us all into this big room with over one hundred prisoners and I said, "Let's do 'If I Had a Hammer,'" and the song took off like a shot. The men really got into it and started making up their own verses: "*If I had a switchblade . . .*" laughing and singing loud, and the guards were rolling their eyes. Sister Cletus and I weren't invited back to sing there again. And the movie got this scene right, at least the telling of it. Sister Helen/Susan tells this story to the chaplain who has asked her if she's had any experience in prisons. He's not amused.

8   I wrote Patrick Sonnier about life in St. Thomas, and he wrote me about life in a six-by-eight-foot cell. He and forty other men were confined twenty-three out of twenty-four hours a day in cells of this size, and he'd say how glad he was when

summer was over because there was no fresh air in their unventilated cells, and he'd sometimes wet the sheet from his bunk and put it on the cement floor to try to cool off, or he'd clean out his toilet bowl and stand in it and use a small plastic container to get water from his lavatory and pour it over his body. Patrick was on death row four years before they killed him.

I made a bad mistake. When I found out about Patrick   9
Sonnier's crime—he and his brother were convicted of killing two teenage kids—I didn't go to see the victims' families. I stayed away because I wasn't sure how to deal with such raw pain. The movie's got this part down pat. It really takes you over to the victims' families and helps you see their pain and my awful tension with them. In real life I was a coward. I stayed away and only met the victims' families at Patrick's pardon board hearing. They were there to demand the execution. I was there to ask the board to show mercy. It was not a good time to meet.

Here were two sets of parents whose children had been   10
ripped from them, condemned in their pain and loss to a kind of death row of their own. I felt terrible. I was powerless to assuage their grief. It would take me a long time to learn how to help victims' families, a long time before I would sit at their support group meetings and hear their unspeakable stories of loss and grief and rage and guilt. I would learn that the divorce rate for couples who lose a child is over seventy percent—a new twist to "until death do us part." I would learn that often after a murder, friends stay away because they don't know how to respond to the pain. I would learn that black families or Hispanic families or poor families who have a loved one murdered not only don't expect the district attorney's office to pursue the death penalty but are surprised when the case is prosecuted at all. In Louisiana, murder victims' families are allowed to sit on the front row in the execution chamber to watch the murderer die. Some families. Not all. But black families almost never witness the execution of someone who has killed their loved one, because in Louisiana, the hangman's noose, then the electric chair, and now the lethal injection gurney, are almost exclusively reserved for those who killed whites. Ask Virginia Smith's African-American family. She was fourteen when three white youths took her into

the woods, raped, and stabbed her to death. None of them got the death penalty. They had all-white juries.

Patrick tried to protect me from watching him die. He told me he'd be okay, I didn't have to come with him into the execution chamber. "Electric chair's not a pretty sight, it could scare you," he told me, trying to be brave. I said, "No, no, Pat, if they kill you, I'll be there," and I said to him, "You look at me, look at my face, and I will be the face of Christ for you, the face of love." I couldn't bear it that he would die alone. I said, "God will help me." And there in the women's room, just a few hours before the execution, my only place of privacy in that place of death, God and I met, and the strength was there, and it was like a circle of light, and it was just in the present moment. If I tried to think ahead to what would happen at midnight, I started coming unraveled, but there in the present I could hold together, and Patrick was strong and kept asking me, "Sister Helen, are you all right?" 11

Being in the death house was one of the most bizarre, confusing experiences I have ever had because it wasn't like visiting somebody dying in a hospital, where you can see the person getting weaker and fading. Patrick was so fully alive, talking and responding to me and writing letters to people and eating, and I'd look around at the polished tile floors—everything so neat—all the officials following a protocol, the secretary typing up forms for the witnesses to sign, the coffee pot percolating, and I kept feeling that I was in a hospital, and the final act would be to save this man's life. It felt strange and terrifying because everyone was so polite. They kept asking Patrick if he needed anything. The chef came by to ask him if he liked his last meal—the steak (medium rare), the potato salad, the apple pie for dessert. 12

When the warden with the strap-down team came for Patrick at midnight, I walked behind him. In a hoarse, child-like voice he asked the warden, "Can Sister Helen touch my arm?" I put my hand on his shoulder and read to him from Isaiah, Chapter 43; "I have called you by your name . . . if you walk through fire I will be with you." God heard his prayer, "Please, God, hold up my legs." It was the last piece 13 of dignity he could muster. He wanted to walk. I saw this dignity in him, and I have seen it in the other two men I have accompanied to their deaths. I wonder how I would hold up if I were walking across a floor to a room where people were waiting to kill me. The essential torture of the death penalty is not finally the physical method: a bullet or rope or gas or electrical current or injected drugs. The torture happens when conscious human beings are condemned to death and begin to anticipate that death and die a thousand times before they die.

I'm not saying that Patrick Sonnier or any of the condemned killers I've accompanied were heroes. I do not glorify them. I do not condone their terrible crimes. But each of these men was a human being, and each had a transcendence, a dignity, which should assure them of two very basic human rights that the United Nations Universal Declaration of Human Rights calls for: the right not to be tortured, the right not to be killed. To have a firm moral bedrock for our societies we must establish that no one is permitted to kill— and that includes governments.

At the end I was amazed at how ordinary Patrick Sonnier's last moments were. He walked to the dark oak chair and sat in it. As guards were strapping his legs and arms and trunk, he found my face and his voice and his last words of life were words of love to me and I took them in like a lightning rod and I have been telling his story ever since.

When they filmed the execution scene of *Dead Man Walking* on a set in New York City, I was there for the whole last week, watching Sean Penn, as the death row inmate Matthew Poncelet, get executed by lethal injection. It was tense, it was slow, it was hard. They shot each scene ten or more times. It took forever. Sean dying, Susan accompanying him, me remembering. Once, during a break, Sean stayed strapped to the gurney and Susan went to visit with him for a while. He's strapped at his neck, trunk, legs, arms, ankles. The cameras are over him. There's a hushed buzz from other actors and technicians. Susan's standing close and talking softly to him. I notice she's holding his hand. It's just a movie. He's not really dying, but there she is holding his hand. Even playing at dying and killing can be real, real hard on you.

For Study and Discussion

QUESTIONS FOR RESPONSE

1. How has your attitude toward capital punishment been shaped by the movies?
2. How has your attitude toward nuns been shaped by the movies?

QUESTIONS ABOUT PURPOSE

1. How does Prejean's narrative support the United Nations Universal Declaration of Human Rights?
2. What does Prejean's description of the filming of the execution scene contribute to the purpose of her narrative?

QUESTIONS ABOUT AUDIENCE

1. How does Prejean's reference to "biblical quarterbacking" anticipate the reactions of some of her readers?
2. How does her experience in poor neighborhoods help explain to her readers how she got involved with her "pen pal," Patrick Sonnier?

QUESTIONS ABOUT STRATEGIES

1. How does Prejean's explanation of the role of the "spiritual advisor" establish the conflict in her narrative?
2. How does Prejean use the shooting of the film to develop her narrative about the real events?

QUESTIONS FOR DISCUSSION

1. How does Prejean provide a "new twist to 'until death do us part'"?
2. In what ways does Prejean's narrative affect your attitude toward the death penalty?

GEORGE ORWELL

George Orwell, the pen name of Eric Blair (1903–1950), was born in Motihari, Bengal, where his father was employed with the Bengal civil service. He was brought to England at an early age for schooling (Eton), but rather than completing his education at the university, he served with the Indian imperial police in Burma (1922–1927). He wrote about these experiences in his first novel, *Burmese Days.* Later he returned to Europe and worked at various jobs (described in *Down and Out in Paris and London,* 1933) before fighting on the Republican side in the Spanish civil war (see *Homage to Catalonia,* 1938). Orwell's attitudes toward war and government are reflected in his most famous books: *Animal Farm* (1945), *1984* (1949), and *Shooting an Elephant and Other Essays* (1950). In the title essay from the last volume, Orwell reports a "tiny incident" that gave him deeper insight into his own fears and "the real motives for which despotic governments act."

Shooting an Elephant

I N MOULMEIN, IN lower Burma, I was hated by large num-   1
bers of people—the only time in my life that I have been important enough for this to happen to me. I was subdivisional police officer of the town, and in an aimless, petty kind of way anti-European feeling was very bitter. No one had the guts to raise a riot, but if a European woman went through the bazaars alone somebody would probably spit betel juice over her dress. As a police officer I was an obvious target and was baited whenever it seemed safe to do so. When

a nimble Burman tripped me up on the football field and the referee (another Burman) looked the other way, the crowd yelled with hideous laughter. This happened more than once. In the end the sneering yellow faces of young men that met me everywhere, the insults hooted after me when I was at a safe distance, got badly on my nerves. The young Buddhist priests were the worst of all. There were several thousands of them in the town and none of them seemed to have anything to do except stand on street corners and jeer at Europeans.

All this was perplexing and upsetting. For at that time I   2 had already made up my mind that imperialism was an evil thing and the sooner I chucked up my job and got out of it

---

*As soon as I saw the elephant I knew
with perfect certainty that I ought not to
shoot him.*

---

the better. Theoretically—and secretly, of course—I was all for the Burmese and all against their oppressors, the British. As for the job I was doing, I hated it more bitterly than I can perhaps make clear. In a job like that you see the dirty work of Empire at close quarters. The wretched prisoners huddling in the stinking cages of the lock-ups, the gray, cowed faces of the long-term convicts, the scarred buttocks of the men who had been flogged with bamboos—all these oppressed me with an intolerable sense of guilt. But I could get nothing into perspective. I was young and ill educated and I had had to think out my problems in the utter silence that is imposed on every Englishman in the East. I did not even know that the British Empire is dying, still less did I know that it is a great deal better than the younger empires that are going to supplant it. All I knew was that I was stuck between my hatred of the empire I served and my rage against the evil-spirited little beasts who tried to make my job impossible.

With one part of my mind I thought of the British Raj as an unbreakable tyranny, as something clamped down, in *saecula saeculorum,* upon the will of prostrate peoples; with another part I thought that the greatest joy in the world would be to drive a bayonet into a Buddhist priest's guts. Feelings like these are the normal by-products of imperialism; ask any Anglo-Indian official, if you can catch him off duty.

One day something happened which in a roundabout way   3 was enlightening. It was a tiny incident in itself; but it gave me a better glimpse than I had had before of the real nature of imperialism—the real motives for which despotic governments act. Early one morning the sub-inspector at a police station the other end of town rang me up on the 'phone and said that an elephant was ravaging the bazaar. Would I please come and do something about it? I did not know what I could do, but I wanted to see what was happening and I got on to a pony and started out. I took my rifle, an old .44 Winchester and much too small to kill an elephant, but I thought the noise might be useful *in terrorem.* Various Burmans stopped me on the way and told me about the elephant's doings. It was not, of course, a wild elephant, but a tame one which had gone "must." It had been chained up, as tame elephants always are when their attack of "must" is due, but on the previous night it had broken its chain and escaped. Its mahout, the only person who could manage it when it was in that state, had set out in pursuit, but had taken the wrong direction and was now twelve hours' journey away, and in the morning the elephant had suddenly reappeared in the town. The Burmese population had no weapons and were quite helpless against it. It had already destroyed somebody's bamboo hut, killed a cow and raided some fruit-stalls and devoured the stock; also it had met the municipal rubbish van and, when the driver jumped out and took to his heels, had turned the van over and inflicted violences upon it.

The Burmese sub-inspector and some Indian constables   4 were waiting for me in the quarter where the elephant had been seen. It was a very poor quarter, a labyrinth of squalid bamboo huts, thatched with palm-leaf, winding all over a steep hillside. I remember that it was a cloudy, stuffy morning at the beginning of the rains. We began questioning the people as to where the elephant had gone and, as usual, failed to get any definite information. That is invariably the case in the East; a story always sounds clear enough at a distance, but the nearer you get to the scene of events the vaguer it becomes. Some of the people said that the elephant had gone in one direction, some said that he had gone in another, some professed not even to have heard of any elephant. I had almost made up my mind that the whole story was a pack of lies, when we heard yells a little distance away. There was a loud, scandalized cry of "Go away, child! Go away this instant!" and an old woman with a switch in her hand came round the corner of a hut, violently shooing away a crowd of naked children. Some more women followed, clicking their tongues and exclaiming; evidently there was something that the children ought not to have seen. I rounded the hut and saw a man's dead body sprawling in the mud. He was an Indian, a black Dravidian coolie, almost naked, and he could not have been dead many minutes. The people said that the elephant had come suddenly upon him round the corner of the hut, caught him with its trunk, put its foot on his back and ground him into the earth. This was the rainy season and the ground was soft, and his face had scored a trench a foot deep and a couple of yards long. He was lying on his belly with arms crucified and head sharply twisted to one side. His face was coated with mud, the eyes wide open, the teeth bared and grinning with an expression of unendurable agony. (Never tell me, by the way, that the dead look peaceful. Most of the corpses I have seen looked devilish.) The friction of the great beast's foot had stripped the skin from his back as neatly as one skins a rabbit. As soon as I saw the dead man I sent an orderly to a friend's house nearby to borrow an elephant rifle. I had already sent back the pony, not wanting it to go mad with fright and throw me if it smelt the elephant.

The orderly came back in a few minutes with a rifle 5 and five cartridges, and meanwhile some Burmans had arrived and told us that the elephant was in the paddy fields below, only a few hundred yards away. As I started forward practically the whole population of the quarter flocked out of the houses and followed me. They had seen the rifle and were all shouting excitedly that I was going to shoot the elephant. They had not shown much interest in the elephant when he was merely ravaging their homes, but it was different now that he was going to be shot. It was a bit of fun to them, and it would be to an English crowd; besides they wanted the meat. It made me vaguely uneasy. I had no intention of shooting the elephant—I had merely sent for the rifle to defend myself if necessary—and it is always unnerving to have a crowd following you. I marched down the hill, looking and feeling a fool, with the rifle over my shoulder and an ever-growing army of people jostling at my heels. At the bottom, when you got away from the huts, there was a metalled road and beyond that a miry waste of paddy fields a thousand yards across, not yet ploughed but soggy from the first rains and dotted with coarse grass. The elephant was standing eight yards from the road, his left side toward us. He took not the slightest notice of the crowd's approach. He was tearing up bunches of grass, beating them against his knees to clean them, and stuffing them into his mouth.

I had halted on the road. As soon as I saw the elephant I knew with perfect certainty that I ought not to shoot him. It is a serious matter to shoot a working elephant—it is comparable to destroying a huge and costly piece of machinery—and obviously one ought not to do it if it can possibly be avoided. And at that distance, peacefully eating, the elephant looked no more dangerous than a cow. I thought then and I think now that his attack of "must" was already passing off; in which case he would merely wander harmlessly about until the mahout came back and caught him. Moreover, I did not in the least want to shoot him. I decided that I would watch him for a little while to make sure that he did not turn savage again, and then go home. 6

But at that moment I glanced round at the crowd that had followed me. It was an immense crowd, two thousand at the least and growing every minute. It blocked the road for a long distance on either side. I looked at the sea of yellow 7

faces above the garish clothes—faces all happy and excited
over this bit of fun, all certain that the elephant was going to
be shot. They were watching me as they would watch a con-
jurer about to perform a trick. They did not like me, but with
the magical rifle in my hands I was momentarily worth
watching. And suddenly I realized that I should have to
shoot the elephant after all. The people expected it of me and
I had got to do it; I could feel their two thousand wills pressing me forward, irresistibly. And it was at this moment, as I
stood there with the rifle in my hands, that I first grasped the
hollowness, the futility of the white man's dominion in the
East. Here was I, the white man with his gun, standing in
front of the unarmed native crowd—seemingly the leading
actor of the piece; but in reality I was only an absurd puppet
pushed to and fro by the will of those yellow faces behind. I
perceived in this moment that when the white man turns
tyrant it is his own freedom that he destroys. He becomes a
sort of hollow, posing dummy, the conventionalized figure of
a sahib. For it is the condition of his rule that he shall spend
his life in trying to impress the "natives," and so in every crisis he has got to do what the "natives" expect of him. He
wears a mask, and his face grows to fit it. I had got to shoot
the elephant. I had committed myself to doing it when I sent
for the rifle. A sahib has got to act like a sahib; he has got to
appear resolute, to know his own mind and do definite
things. To come all that way, rifle in hand, with two thousand
people marching at my heels, and then to trail feebly away,
having done nothing—no, that was impossible. The crowd
would laugh at me. And my whole life, every white man's life
in the East, was one long struggle not to be laughed at.

But I did not want to shoot the elephant. I watched him   8
beating his bunch of grass against his knees with that preoccupied grandmotherly air that elephants have. It seemed to
me that it would be murder to shoot him. At that age I was
not squeamish about killing animals, but I had never shot an
elephant and never wanted to. (Somehow it always seems
worse to kill a *large* animal.) Besides, there was the beast's
owner to be considered. Alive, the elephant was worth at

least a hundred pounds; dead, he would only be worth the value of his tusks, five pounds, possibly. But I had got to act quickly. I turned to some experienced-looking Burmans who had been there when we arrived, and asked them how the elephant had been behaving. They all said the same thing: he took no notice of you if you left him alone, but he might charge if you went too close to him.

It was perfectly clear to me what I ought to do. I ought to walk up to within, say, twenty-five yards of the elephant and test his behavior. If he charged, I could shoot; if he took no notice of me, it would be safe to leave him until the mahout came back. But also I knew that I was going to do no such thing. I was a poor shot with a rifle and the ground was soft mud into which one would sink at every step. If the elephant charged and I missed him, I should have about as much chance as a toad under a steam-roller. But even then I was not thinking particularly of my own skin, only of the watchful yellow faces behind. For at that moment, with the crowd watching me, I was not afraid in the ordinary sense, as I would have been if I had been alone. A white man mustn't be frightened in front of "natives"; and so, in general, he isn't frightened. The sole thought in my mind was that if anything went wrong those two thousand Burmans would see me pursued, caught, trampled on, and reduced to a grinning corpse like that Indian up the hill. And if that happened it was quite probable that some of them would laugh. That would never do. There was only one alternative. I shoved the cartridges into the magazine and lay down on the road to get a better aim.

The crowd grew very still, and a deep, low, happy sigh, as of people who see the theater curtain go up at last, breathed from innumerable throats. They were going to have their bit of fun after all. The rifle was a beautiful German thing with cross-hair sights. I did not then know that in shooting an elephant one would shoot to cut an imaginary bar running from ear-hole to ear-hole. I ought, therefore, as the elephant was sideways on, to have aimed straight at his ear-hole; actually I aimed several inches in front of this, thinking the brain would be further forward.

When I pulled the trigger I did not hear the bang or feel the   11
kick—one never does when a shot goes home—but I heard the
devilish roar of glee that went up from the crowd. In that instant, in too short a time, one would have thought, even for
the bullet to get there, a mysterious, terrible change had come
over the elephant. He neither stirred, nor fell, but every line of
his body had altered. He looked suddenly stricken, shrunken,
immensely old, as though the frightful impact of the bullet had
paralyzed him without knocking him down. At last, after what
seemed a long time—it might have been five seconds, I dare
say—he sagged flabbily to his knees. His mouth slobbered. An
enormous senility seemed to have settled upon him. One
could have imagined him thousands of years old. I fired again
into the same spot. At the second shot he did not collapse but
climbed with desperate slowness to his feet and stood weakly
upright, with legs sagging and head drooping. I fired a third
time. That was the shot that did for him. You could see the
agony of it jolt his whole body and knock the last remnant of
strength from his legs. But in falling he seemed for a moment
to rise, for as his hind legs collapsed beneath him he seemed to
tower upward like a huge rock toppling, his trunk reaching
skyward like a tree. He trumpeted, for the first and only time.
And then down he came, his belly toward me, with a crash that
seemed to shake the ground even where I lay.

I got up. The Burmans were already racing past me across   12
the mud. It was obvious that the elephant would never rise
again, but he was not dead. He was breathing very rhythmi-
cally with long rattling gasps, his great mound of a side
painfully rising and falling. His mouth was wide open—I
could see far down into caverns of pale pink throat. I waited
a long time for him to die, but his breathing did not weaken.
Finally I fired my two remaining shots into the spot where I
thought his heart must be. The thick blood welled out of him
like red velvet, but still he did not die. His body did not even
jerk when the shots hit him, the tortured breathing continued without a pause. He was dying, very slowly and in great
agony, but in some world remote from me where not even a

bullet could damage him further. I felt that I had got to put an end to that dreadful noise. It seemed dreadful to see the great beast lying there, powerless to move and yet powerless to die, and not even to be able to finish him. I sent back for my small rifle and poured shot after shot into his heart and down his throat. They seemed to make no impression. The tortured gasps continued as steadily as the ticking of a clock.

In the end I could not stand it any longer and went away. 13 I heard later that it took him half an hour to die. Burmans were bringing dahs and baskets even before I left, and I was told they had stripped his body almost to the bones by the afternoon.

Afterward, of course, there were endless discussions 14 about the shooting of the elephant. The owner was furious, but he was only an Indian and could do nothing. Besides, legally I had done the right thing, for a mad elephant has to be killed, like a mad dog, if its owner fails to control it. Among the Europeans opinion was divided. The older men said I was right, the younger men said it was a damn shame to shoot an elephant for killing a coolie, because an elephant was worth more than any damn Coringhee coolie. And afterward I was very glad that the coolie had been killed; it put me legally in the right and it gave me a sufficient pretext for shooting the elephant. I often wondered whether any of the others grasped that I had done it solely to avoid looking a fool.

For Study and Discussion

QUESTIONS FOR RESPONSE

1. How do you feel when you are laughed at? What do you do in order to avoid looking like a fool?
2. How did you react to Orwell's long introduction (paragraphs 1 and 2) to the incident? Were you attentive, bored, or confused? Now that you have finished the essay, reread these two paragraphs. How does your second reading compare with your first?

QUESTIONS ABOUT PURPOSE

1. What thesis about "the real nature of imperialism" does Orwell prove by narrating this "tiny incident"?
2. List the reasons Orwell considers when he tries to decide what to do. According to his conclusion, what was his main purpose in shooting the elephant?

QUESTIONS ABOUT AUDIENCE

1. How does Orwell wish to present himself to his readers in paragraphs 6 through 9? Do you follow the logic of his argument?
2. Which of the three positions stated in the final paragraph does Orwell expect his readers to agree with? Why is he "glad that the coolie had been killed"?

QUESTIONS ABOUT STRATEGIES

1. Although Orwell begins narrating the incident in paragraph 3, we do not see the elephant until the end of paragraph 5. What details do we see? How do they intensify the dramatic conflict?
2. How does Orwell pace the shooting of the elephant in paragraphs 11 and 12? How does the elephant's slow death affect Orwell's point of view toward what he has done?

QUESTIONS FOR DISCUSSION

1. Orwell was young, frightened, and tormented by strangers in a strange land. What parallels do you see between Orwell's plight and the plight of young American soldiers who have served in Afghanistan and Iraq?
2. Much of Orwell's essay assumes a knowledge of the words *imperialism* and *despotism*. What do these words mean? How do they apply to the essay? What current events can you identify in which these words might also apply?

ALICE ADAMS

Alice Adams (1926–1999) was born in Fredericks-
burg, Virginia, and educated at Radcliffe College.
After twelve years of marriage, she began working
at various office jobs, including secretary, clerk,
and bookkeeper, while she mastered the skills of a
writer. Adams published her first book of fiction,
Careless Love (1966), at the age of forty. Later she
published five widely acclaimed novels, *Families
and Survivors* (1975), *Listening to Billie* (1978)—
the title refers to the legendary blues singer Billie
Holiday—*Rich Rewards* (1980), *Superior Women*
(1984), and *Caroline's Daughter* (1991), as well
as three collections of short stories, *Beautiful Girl*
(1979), *To See You Again* (1982), and *Return
Trips* (1985). She contributed numerous short
stories to magazines such as *The New Yorker, The
Atlantic,* and *Paris Review.* Her most recent
novel, entitled *After the War* (2000), was published posthumously. The narrator of "Truth or
Consequences," reprinted from *To See You Again,*
tries to understand the "consequences" that resulted from her truthful answer in a childhood
game.

Truth or Consequences

THIS MORNING, WHEN I read in a gossip column that a   1
man named Carstairs Jones had married a famous
former movie star, I was startled, thunderstruck, for I knew
that he must certainly be the person whom I knew as a child,
one extraordinary spring, as "Car Jones." He was a dangerous and disreputable boy, one of what were then called the
"truck children," with whom I had a most curious, brief and

frightening connection. Still, I noted that in a way I was pleased at such good fortune; I was "happy for him," so to speak, perhaps as a result of sheer distance, so many years. And before I could imagine Car as he might be now, Carstairs Jones, in Hollywood clothes, I suddenly saw, with the most terrific accuracy and bright sharpness of detail, the schoolyard of all those years ago, hard and bare, neglected. And I relived the fatal day, on the middle level of that schoolyard, when we were playing truth or consequences, and I said that I would rather kiss Car Jones than be eaten alive by ants.

Our school building then was three stories high, a formidable brick square. In front a lawn had been attempted, some years back; graveled walks led up to the broad, forbidding entranceway, and behind the school were the playing fields, the playground. This area was on three levels: on the upper level, nearest the school, were the huge polished steel frames for the creaking swings, the big green splintery wooden seesaws, the rickety slides—all for the youngest children. On the middle level older girls played hopscotch, various games, or jumped rope—or just talked and giggled. And out on the lowest level, the field, the boys practiced football, or baseball, in the spring. 2

To one side of the school was a parking space, usually filled with the bulging yellow trucks that brought children from out in the country in to town: truck children, country children. Sometimes they would go back to the trucks at lunchtime to eat their sandwiches, whatever; almost always there were several overgrown children, spilling out from the trucks. Or Car Jones, expelled from some class, for some new acts of rebelliousness. That area was always littered with trash, wrappings from sandwiches, orange peel, Coke bottles. 3

Beyond the parking space was an empty lot, overgrown with weeds, in the midst of which stood an abandoned trellis, perhaps once the support of wisteria; now wild honeysuckle almost covered it over. 4

The town was called Hilton, the seat of a distinguished university, in the middle South. My widowed mother, Charlotte Ames, had moved there the previous fall (with me, Emily, her 5 only child). I am still not sure why she chose Hilton; she never much liked it there, nor did she really like the brother-in-law, a professor, into whose proximity the move had placed us.

An interesting thing about Hilton, at that time, was that there were three, and only three, distinct social classes. (Negroes could possibly make four, but they were so separate, even from the poorest whites, as not to seem part of the social system at all; they were in effect invisible.) At the scale's top were professors and their families. Next were the townspeople, storekeepers, bankers, doctors and dentists, none of whom had the prestige nor the money they were later to acquire. Country people were the bottom group, families living out on the farms that surrounded the town, people who sent their children in to school on the yellow trucks. ⁶

The professors' children of course had a terrific advantage, academically, coming from houses full of books, from parental respect for learning; many of those kids read precociously and had large vocabularies. It was not so hard on most of the town children; many of their families shared qualities with the faculty people; they too had a lot of books around. But the truck children had a hard and very unfair time of it. Not only were many of their parents near-illiterates, but often the children were kept at home to help with chores, and sometimes, particularly during the coldest, wettest months of winter, weather prevented the trucks' passage over the slithery red clay roads of that countryside, that era. A child could miss out on a whole new skill, like long division, and fail tests, and be kept back. Consequently many of the truck children were overage, oversized for the grades they were in. ⁷

In the seventh grade, when I was eleven, a year ahead of myself, having been tested for and skipped the sixth (attesting to the superiority of Northern schools, my mother thought, and probably she was right), dangerous Car Jones, in the same class, was fourteen, and taller than anyone. ⁸

There was some overlapping, or crossing, among those three social groups; there were hybrids, as it were. In fact, I was such a crossbreed myself: literally my mother and I were town people—my dead father had been a banker, but since ⁹

his brother was a professor we too were considered faculty people. Also my mother had a lot of money, making us further élite. To me, being known as rich was just embarrassing, more freakish than advantageous, and I made my mother stop ordering my clothes from Best's; I wanted dresses from the local stores, like everyone else's.

Car Jones too was a hybrid child, although his case was less 10 visible than mine: his country family were distant cousins of the prominent and prosperous dean of the medical school, Dean Willoughby Jones. (They seem to have gone in for fancy names, in all the branches of that family.) I don't think his cousins spoke to him.

In any case, being richer and younger than the others in 11 my class made me socially very insecure, and I always approached the playground with a sort of excited dread: would I be asked to join in a game, and if it were dodge ball (the game I most hated) would I be the first person hit with the ball, and thus eliminated? Or, if the girls were just standing around and talking, would I get all the jokes, and know which boys they were talking about?

Then, one pale-blue balmy April day, some of the older girls 12 asked me if I wanted to play truth or consequences with them. I wasn't sure how the game went, but anything was better than dodge ball, and, as always, I was pleased at being asked.

"It's easy," said Jean, a popular leader, with curly red hair; 13 her father was a dean of the law school. "You just answer the questions we ask you, or you take the consequences."

I wasn't at all sure what consequences were, but I didn't 14 like to ask.

They began with simple questions. How old are you? 15 What's your middle name?

This led to more complicated (and crueler) ones. 16

"How much money does your mother have?" 17

"I don't know." I didn't, of course, and I doubt that she 18 did either, that poor vague lady, too young to be a widow, too old for motherhood. "I think maybe a thousand dollars," I hazarded.

At this they all frowned, that group of older, wiser girls, whether in disbelief or disappointment, I couldn't tell. They moved a little away from me and whispered together. 19

It was close to the end of recess. Down on the playing field below us one of the boys threw the baseball and someone batted it out in a long arc, out to the farthest grassy edges of the field, and several other boys ran to retrieve it. On the level above us, a rutted terrace up, the little children stood in line for turns on the slide, or pumped with furious small legs on the giant swings. 20

The girls came back to me. "Okay, Emily," said Jean. "Just tell the truth. Would you rather be covered with honey and eaten alive by ants, in the hot Sahara Desert—or kiss Car Jones?" 21

Then, as now, I had a somewhat literal mind: I thought of honey, and ants, and hot sand, and quite simply I said I'd rather kiss Car Jones. 22

Well. Pandemonium: Did you hear what she said? Emily would kiss Car Jones! *Car Jones.* The truth—Emily would like to kiss Car Jones! Oh, Emily if your mother only knew! Emily and Car! Emily is going to kiss Car Jones! Emily said she would! Oh, Emily! 23

The boys, just then coming up from the baseball field, cast bored and pitying looks at the sources of so much noise; they had always known girls were silly. But Harry McGinnis, a glowing, golden boy, looked over at us and laughed aloud. I had been watching Harry timidly for months; that day I thought his laugh was friendly. 24

Recess being over, we all went back into the schoolroom, and continued with the civics lesson. I caught a few ambiguous smiles in my direction, which left me both embarrassed and confused. 25

That afternoon, as I walked home from school, two of the girls who passed me on their bikes called back to me, "Car Jones!" and in an automatic but for me new way I squealed out, "Oh no!" They laughed, and repeated, from their distance, "Car Jones!" 26

The next day I continued to be teased. Somehow the boys had   27
got wind of what I had said, and they joined in with remarks
about Yankee girls being fast, how you couldn't tell about
quiet girls, that sort of wit. Some of the teasing sounded mean;
I felt that Jean, for example, was really out to discomfit me, but
most of it was high-spirited friendliness. I was suddenly discovered, as though hitherto I had been invisible. And I continued
to respond with that exaggerated, phony squeal of embarrassment that seemed to go over so well. Harry McGinnis
addressed me as Emily Jones, and the others took that up.
(I wonder if Harry had ever seen me before.)

Curiously, in all this new excitement, the person I thought   28
of least was the source of it all: Car Jones. Or, rather, when I
saw the actual Car, hulking over the water fountain or lounging near the steps of a truck, I did not consciously connect
him with what felt like social success, new popularity. (I didn't
know about consequences.)

Therefore, when the first note from Car appeared on my   29
desk, it felt like blackmail, although the message was innocent, was even kind. "You mustn't mind that they tease you.
You are the prettiest one of the girls. C. Jones." I easily recognized his handwriting, those recklessly forward-slanting
strokes, from the day when he had had to write on the black-
board, "I will not disturb the other children during Music."
Twenty-five times. The note was real, all right.

Helplessly I turned around to stare at the back of the   30
room, where the tallest boys sprawled in their too small
desks. Truck children, all of them, bored and uncomfortable.
There was Car, the tallest of all, the most bored, the least
contained. Our eyes met, and even at that distance I saw that
his were not black, as I had thought, but a dark slate blue;
stormy eyes, even when, as he rarely did, Car smiled. I turned
away quickly, and I managed to forget him for a while.

Having never witnessed a Southern spring before, I was   31
astounded by its bursting opulence, that soft fullness of petal
and bloom, everywhere the profusion of flowering shrubs
and trees, the riotous flower beds. Walking home from
school, I was enchanted with the yards of the stately houses

(homes of professors) that I passed, the lush lawns, the rows of brilliant iris, the flowering quince and dogwood trees, crepe myrtle, wisteria vines. I would squint my eyes to see the tiniest pale-green leaves against the sky.

My mother didn't like the spring. It gave her hay fever, and she spent most of her time languidly indoors, behind heavily lined, drawn draperies. "I'm simply too old for such exuberance," she said.   32

"Happy" is perhaps not the word to describe my own state of mind, but I was tremendously excited, continuously. The season seemed to me so extraordinary in itself, the colors, the enchanting smells, and it coincided with my own altered awareness of myself: I could command attention, I was pretty (Car Jones was the first person ever to say that I was, after my mother's long-ago murmurings to a late-arriving baby).   33

Now everyone knew my name, and called it out as I walked onto the playground. Last fall, as an envious, un-known new girl, I had heard other names, other greetings and teasing-insulting nicknames, "Hey, Red," Harry McGinnis used to shout, in the direction of popular Jean.   34

The new note from Car Jones said, "I'll bet you hate it down here. This is a cruddy town, but don't let it bother you. Your hair is beautiful. I hope you never cut it. C. Jones."   35

This scared me a little: the night before I had been arguing with my mother on just that point, my hair, which was long and straight. Why couldn't I cut it and curl it, like the other girls? How had Car Jones known what I wanted to do? I forced myself not to look at him; I pretended that there was no Car Jones; it was just a name that certain people had made up.   36

I felt—I was sure—that Car Jones was an "abnormal" per-son. (I'm afraid "different" would have been the word I used, back then.) He represented forces that were dark and strange, whereas I myself had just come out into the light. I had joined the world of the normal. (My "normality" later included three marriages to increasingly "rich and promi-nent" men; my current husband is a surgeon. Three children, and as many abortions. I hate the symmetry, but there you   37 are. I haven't counted lovers. It comes to a normal life, for a woman of my age.) For years, at the time of our coming to Hilton, I had felt a little strange, isolated by my father's death, my older-than-most-parents mother, by money. By being younger than other children, and new in town. I could clearly afford nothing to do with Car, and at the same time my literal mind acknowledged a certain obligation.

Therefore, when a note came from Car telling me to meet him on a Saturday morning in the vacant lot next to the school, it didn't occur to me that I didn't have to go. I made excuses to my mother, and to some of the girls who were getting together for Cokes at someone's house. I'd be a little late, I told the girls. I had to do an errand for my mother.   38

It was one of the palest, softest, loveliest days of that spring. In the vacant lot weeds bloomed like the rarest of flowers; as I walked toward the abandoned trellis I felt myself to be a sort of princess, on her way to grant an audience to a courtier.   39

Car, lounging just inside the trellis, immediately brought me up short. "You're several minutes late," he said, and I noticed that his teeth were stained (from tobacco?) and his hands were dirty: couldn't he have washed his hands, to come and meet me? He asked, "Just who do you think you are, the Queen of Sheba?"   40

I am not sure what I had imagined would happen between us, but this was wrong; I was not prepared for surliness, this scolding. Weakly I said that I was sorry I was late.   41

Car did not acknowledge my apology; he just stared at me, stormily, with what looked like infinite scorn.   42

Why had he insisted that I come to meet him? And now that I was here, was I less than pretty, seen close up?   43

A difficult minute passed, and then I moved a little away. I managed to say that I had to go; I had to meet some girls, I said.   44

At that Car reached and grasped my arm. "No, first we have to do it."   45

Do it? I was scared.   46

"You know what you said, as good as I do. You said kiss Car Jones, now didn't you?"   47

I began to cry.   48

Car reached for my hair and pulled me toward him; he 49
bent down to my face and for an instant our mouths were
mashed together. (Christ, my first kiss!) Then, so suddenly
that I almost fell backward, Car let go of me. With a last look
of pure rage he was out of the trellis and striding across the
field, toward town, away from the school.

For a few minutes I stayed there in the trellis; I was no 50
longer crying (that had been for Car's benefit, I now think)
but melodramatically I wondered if Car might come back
and do something else to me—beat me up, maybe. Then a
stronger fear took over: someone might find out, might have
seen us, even. At that I got out of the trellis fast, out of the
vacant lot. (I was learning conformity fast, practicing up for
the rest of my life.)

I think, really, that my most serious problem was my utter 51
puzzlement: what did it mean, that kiss? Car was mad, no
doubt about that, but did he really hate me? In that case, why
a kiss? (Much later in life I once was raped, by someone to
whom I was married, but I still think that counts; in any case,
I didn't know what he meant either.)

Not sure what else to do, and still in the grip of a monu- 52
mental confusion, I went over to the school building, which
was open on Saturdays for something called Story Hours,
for little children. I went into the front entrance and up to
the library where, to the surprise of the librarian, who may
have thought me retarded, I listened for several hours of
tales of the Dutch Twins, and Peter and Polly in Scotland.
Actually it was very soothing, that long pasteurized drone,
hard even to think about Car while listening to pap like that.

When I got home I found my mother for some reason in a 53
livelier, more talkative mood than usual. She told me that a
boy had called while I was out, three times. Even before my
heart had time to drop—to think that it might be Car, she
babbled on, "Terribly polite. Really, these *bien élevé* Southern
boys." (No, not Car.) "Harry something. He said he'd call
again. But, darling, where were you, all this time?"

I was beginning to murmur about the library, homework, 54
when the phone rang. I answered, and it was Harry McGinnis,

asking me to go to the movies with him the following Saturday afternoon. I said of course, I'd love to, and I giggled in a
silly new way. But my giggle was one of relief; I was saved, I
was normal, after all. I belonged in the world of light, of
lightheartedness. Car Jones had not really touched me.

I spent the next day, Sunday, in alternating states of agita-   55
tion and anticipation.

On Monday, on my way to school, I felt afraid of seeing   56
Car, at the same time that I was both excited and shy at the
prospect of Harry McGinnis—a combination of emotions
that was almost too much for me, that dazzling, golden first
of May, and that I have not dealt with too successfully in later
life.

Harry paid even less attention to me than he had before; it   57
was a while before I realized that he was conspicuously not
looking in my direction, not teasing me, and that that in itself
was a form of attention, as well as being soothing to my shyness.

I realized too, after a furtive scanning of the back row, that   58
Car Jones was *not at school* that day. Relief flooded through
my blood like oxygen, like spring air.

Absences among the truck children were so unremarkable,   59
and due to so many possible causes, that any explanation at
all for his was plausible. Of course it occurred to me, among
other imaginings, that he had stayed home out of shame for
what he did to me. Maybe he had run away to sea, had joined
the Navy or the Marines? Coldheartedly, I hoped so. In any
case, there was no way for me to ask.

Later that week the truth about Car Jones did come out—   60
at first as a drifting rumor, then confirmed, and much more
remarkable than joining the Navy: Car Jones had gone to the
principal's office, a week or so back, and had demanded to be
tested for entrance (immediate) into high school, a request
so unprecedented (usually only pushy academic parents
would ask for such a change) and so dumbfounding that
it was acceded to. Car took the test and was put into the
sophomore high-school class, on the other side of town,
where he by age and size—and intellect, as things turned out;
he tested high—most rightfully belonged.

I went to a lot of Saturday movies with Harry McGinnis,   61
where we clammily held hands, and for the rest of that
spring, and into summer, I was teased about Harry. No one
seemed to remember having teased me about Car Jones.

Considering the size of Hilton at that time, it seems   62
surprising that I almost never saw Car again, but I did not,
except for a couple of tiny glimpses, during the summer that
I was still going to the movies with Harry. On both those occasions, seen from across the street, or on the other side of a
dim movie house, Car was with an older girl, a high-school
girl, with curled hair, and lipstick, all that. I was sure that his
hands and teeth were clean.

By the time I had entered high school, along with all those   63
others who were by now my familiar friends, Car was a freshman in the local university, and his family had moved into
town. Then his name again was bruited about among us, but
this time was an underground rumor: Car Jones was reputed
to have "gone all the way"—to have "done it" with a pretty
and most popular senior in our high school. (It must be remembered that this was more unusual among the young then
than now.) The general (whispered) theory was that Car's
status as a college boy had won the girl; traditionally, in
Hilton, the senior high-school girls began to date the freshmen in the university, as many and as often as possible. But
this was not necessarily true; maybe the girl was simply drawn
to Car, his height and his shoulders, his stormy eyes. Or
maybe they didn't do it after all.

The next thing I heard about Car, who was by then an   64
authentic town person, a graduate student in the university,
was that he had written a play which was to be produced by
the campus dramatic society. (Maybe that is how he finally
met his movie star, as a playwright? The column didn't say.) I
think I read this item in the local paper, probably in a clipping
forwarded to me by my mother; her letters were always thick
with clippings, thin with messages of a personal nature.

My next news of Car came from my uncle, the French   65
professor, a violent, enthusiastic partisan in university affairs,

especially in their more traditional aspects. In scandalized tones, one family Thanksgiving, he recounted to me and my mother, that a certain young man, a graduate student in English, named Carstairs Jones, had been offered a special sort of membership in D.K.E., his own beloved fraternity, and "Jones had *turned it down.*" My mother and I laughed later and privately over this; we were united in thinking my uncle a fool, and I am sure that I added, Well, good for him. But I did not, at that time, reconsider the whole story of Car Jones, that most unregenerate and wicked of the truck children.

But now, with this fresh news of Carstairs Jones, and his wife   66
the movie star, it occurs to me that we two, who at a certain time and place were truly misfits, although quite differently— we both have made it: what could be more American dream-y, more normal, than marriage to a lovely movie star? Or, in my case, marriage to the successful surgeon?

And now maybe I can reconstruct a little of that time; spe-   67
cifically, can try to see how it really was for Car, back then. Maybe I can even understand that kiss.

Let us suppose that he lived in a somewhat better than   68
usual farmhouse; later events make this plausible—his fam-ily's move to town, his years at the university. Also, I wish him well. I will give him a dignified white house with a broad front porch, set back among pines and oaks, in the red clay countryside. The stability and size of his house, then, would have set Car apart from his neighbors, the other farm families, other truck children. Perhaps his parents too were somewhat "different," but my imagination fails at them; I can easily imagine and clearly see the house, but not its population. Brothers? sisters? Probably, but I don't know.

Car would go to school, coming out of his house at the   69
honk of the stained and bulging, ugly yellow bus, which was crowded with his supposed peers, toward whom he felt both contempt and an irritation close to rage. Arrived at school, as one of the truck children, he would be greeted with a total lack of interest; he might as well have been invisible, or been black, *unless* he misbehaved in an outright, conspicuous way.

And so he did: Car yawned noisily during history class, he hummed during study hall and after recess he dawdled around the playground and came in late. And for these and other assaults on the school's decorum he was punished in one way or another, and then, when all else failed to curb his ways, he would be *held back,* forced to repeat an already insufferably boring year of school.

One fall there was a minor novelty in school: a new girl (me), a Yankee, who didn't look much like the other girls, with long straight hair, instead of curled, and Yankee clothes, wool skirts and sweaters, instead of flowery cotton dresses worn all year round. A funny accent, a Yankee name: Emily Ames. I imagine that Car registered those facts about me, and possibly the additional information that I was almost as invisible as he, but without much interest.

Until the day of truth or consequences. I don't think Car was around on the playground while the game was going on; one of the girls would have seen him, and squealed out, "Oooh, there's Car, there *he is!*" I rather believe that some skinny little kid, an unnoticed truck child, overheard it all, and then ran over to where Car was lounging in one of the school buses, maybe peeling an orange and throwing the peel, in spirals, out the window. "Say, Car, that little Yankee girl, she says she'd like to kiss you."

"Aw, go on."

He is still not very interested; the little Yankee girl is as dumb as the others are.

And then he hears me being teased, everywhere, and teased with his name. "Emily would kiss Car Jones—Emily Jones!" Did he feel the slightest pleasure at such notoriety? I think he must have; a man who would marry a movie star must have at least a small taste for publicity. Well, at that point he began to write me those notes: "You are the prettiest one of the girls" (which I was not). I think he was casting us both in ill-fitting roles, me as the prettiest, defenseless girl, and himself as my defender.

He must have soon seen that it wasn't working out that way. I didn't need a defender, I didn't need him. I was having a wonderful time, at his expense, if you think about it, and I am pretty sure Car did think about it.

Interestingly, at the same time he had his perception of my triviality, Car must have got his remarkable inspiration in regard to his own life: there was a way out of those miserably boring classes, the insufferable children who surrounded him. He would demand a test, he would leave this place for the high school. 76

Our trellis meeting must have occurred after Car had taken the test, and had known that he did well. When he kissed me he was doing his last "bad" thing in that school, was kissing it off, so to speak. He was also insuring that I, at least, would remember him; he counted on its being my first kiss. And he may have thought that I was even sillier than I was, and that I would tell, so that what had happened would get around the school, waves of scandal in his wake. 77

For some reason, I would also imagine that Car is one of those persons who never look back; once kissed, I was readily dismissed from his mind, and probably for good. He could concentrate on high school, new status, new friends. Just as, now married to his movie star, he does not ever think of having been a truck child, one of the deprived, the disappointed. In his mind there are no ugly groaning trucks, no hopeless littered playground, no squat menacing school building. 78

But of course I could be quite wrong about Car Jones. He could be another sort of person altogether; he could be as haunted as I am by everything that ever happened in his life. 79

COMMENT ON "TRUTH OR CONSEQUENCES"

"Truth or Consequences" is an excellent illustration of how narration and description are used in short fiction. The catalyst for the story is the narrator's reading in a gossip column about Car Jones's marriage to a famous former movie star. His name sparks a memory, and the narrator (Emily) tries to reconstruct the events that occurred during her

school years. The story is paced at two speeds: the opening is
slow, as Emily describes the various social divisions on the
playground; the action speeds up once Emily says she would
rather kiss Car Jones than be eaten by ants. The plot reaches
its climax when Car Jones calls Emily's bluff and asks her to
meet him by the trellis near the school. The story concludes
as Emily (older and wiser?) continues to wonder about the
"truth" and "consequences" of this brief encounter.

Narration and Description as a Writing Strategy

1. Recount the details of an accident or disaster in which you were a witness or a victim. You may wish to retell the events as a reporter would for a front-page story in the local newspaper, or you may recount the events from a more personal point of view, as Sisten Helen Prejean does in her account of her experiences on death row. If you were a witness, consider the points of view of the other people involved so that you can give your readers an objective perspective on the event. If you were a victim, slow the pace of the major conflict, which probably occurred quickly, so you can show your readers its emotional impact.

2. Report an experience in which you had to commit an extremely difficult or distasteful deed. You may wish to begin, as George Orwell does, by telling your readers about the conditions you encountered before you confronted the problem of whether to commit the questionable act. Be sure to list all the options you considered before you acted, and conclude by reflecting on your attitude toward your choice. And, of course, make sure to plot your essay so that the *act* is given the central and most dramatic position.

3. In "Beauty: When the Other Dancer Is the Self," Alice Walker presents a series of brief narratives that picture the way she thinks people see her and the way she sees herself at various ages. These narratives form a kind of photograph album. Study photographs of yourself at different ages. Then write a narrative that establishes a thematic connection among these photographs.

4. Describe a significant event in your life when you were unfairly stereotyped. You may want to point out certain features of your dress or behavior that sent—unknown to you—mixed signals. Like Cofer, you may want to speculate on how these signals were the result of custom or caricature.

5. Describe how people who are different are treated within your community. Like Andre Dubus, you may want to document how the shy and sensitive feel shame and attract bullies. Or you may want to describe how you discovered an injustice in your community's way of acknowledging those who are different.

6. Demonstrate the effects of perception on values (how "seeing is believing"). All the writers in this section deal with this subject. Dubus recounts how his summer of physical labor changed his body and his thinking. Walker remembers how her childhood accident affected her self-perception. Cofer reveals how people from mainstream culture believe that they should be applauded for their ability to perpetuate stereotypes. Sister Helen Prejean relives her own experiences on death row when watching an actress (Susan Sarandon) play her in the making of a movie. Orwell shows how seeing the crowd's mocking faces convinces him to shoot the elephant. And Emily Ames, the narrator in Alice Adams's short story, tells how her concern for social acceptance made her misread the actions of someone who was different.

PROCESS ANALYSIS

A **process** is an operation that moves through a series of steps to bring about a desired result. You can call almost any procedure a process, whether it is getting out of bed in the morning or completing a transaction on the stock exchange. A useful way to identify a particular kind of process is by its principal function. A process can be *natural* (the birth of a baby), *mechanical* (starting a car engine), *physical* (dancing), or *mental* (reading).

Analysis is an operation that divides something into its parts in order to understand the whole more clearly. For example, poetry readers analyze the lines of a poem to find meaning. Doctors analyze a patient's symptoms to prescribe treatment. Politicians analyze the opinions of individual voters and groups of voters to plan campaigns.

If you want to write a process-analysis essay, you need to go through three steps: (1) divide the process you are going to explain into its individual steps; (2) show the movement of the process, step by step, from beginning to end; and (3) explain how each step works, how it ties into other steps in the sequence, and how it brings about the desired result.

PURPOSE

Usually you will write a process analysis to accomplish two purposes: *to give directions* and *to provide information*. Sometimes you might find it difficult to separate the two purposes. After all, when you give directions about how to do something (hit a baseball), you also have to provide information on how the whole process works (rules of the game—strike zone, walks, hits, base running, outs, scoring). But usually you can separate the two because you're trying to accomplish different goals. When you give directions, you want to help your readers do something (change a tire). When you give information, you want to satisfy your readers' curiosity about some process they'd like to know about but are unlikely to perform (pilot a space shuttle).

You might also write a process analysis to demonstrate that (1) a task that looks difficult is really easy or (2) a task that looks easy is really quite complex. For instance, you might want to show that selecting a specific tool can simplify a complex process (using a microwave oven to cook a six-course dinner). You might also want to show why it's important to have a prearranged plan to make a process seem simple (explaining the preparations for an informal television interview).

AUDIENCE

When you write a process-analysis essay, you must think carefully about who your audience will be. First, you need to decide whether you're writing *to* an audience (giving directions) or writing *for* an audience (providing information).

If you are writing *to* an audience, you can address directly readers who are already interested in your subject: "If you want to plant a successful garden, you must follow these seven steps." If you are writing *for* an audience, you can write from a more detached point of view, but you have to find a way to catch the interest of more casual readers: "Although many Americans say they are concerned about nuclear power, few understand how a nuclear power plant works."

Second, you have to determine how wide the knowledge gap is between you and your readers. Writing about a process suggests you are something of an expert in that area. If you can be sure your readers are also experts, you can make certain assumptions as you write your analysis. For instance, if you're outlining courtroom procedure to a group of fellow law students, you can assume you don't have to define the special meaning of the word *brief.*

On the other hand, if you feel sure your intended audience knows almost nothing about a process (or has only general knowledge), you can take nothing for granted. If you are explaining how to operate a VCR to readers who have never used one, you will have to define special terms and explain all procedures. If you assume your readers are experts when they are not, you will confuse or annoy them. If you assume they need to be told everything when they don't, you will bore or antagonize them. And, finally, remember that to analyze a process effectively, you must either research it carefully or have firsthand knowledge of its operation. It's risky to try to explain something you don't really understand.

STRATEGIES

The best way to write a process analysis is to organize your essay according to five parts:

> Overview
> Special terms
> Sequence of steps

Examples
Results

The first two parts help your readers understand the process, the next two show the process in action, and the last one evaluates the worth of the completed process.

Begin your analysis with an *overview* of the whole process. To make such an overview, you take these four steps:

1. Define the objective of the process
2. Identify (and number) the steps in the sequence
3. Group some small steps into larger units
4. Call attention to the most important steps or units

For example, Julia Alvarez begins her analysis of how she writes a story by breaking down this process into short steps. Nikki Giovanni makes her recommendations for black students in sequence and then goes on to illustrate some of the common problems that occur with each recommendation.

Each process has its own *special terms* to describe tools, tasks, and methods, and you will have to define those terms for your readers. You can define them at the beginning so your readers will understand the terms when you use them, but often you do better to define them as you use them. Your readers may have trouble remembering specialized language out of context, so it's often practical to define your terms throughout the course of the essay, pausing to explain their special meaning or use the first time you introduce them. Ann Zwinger follows this strategy by describing the various drawing tools she keeps in her purse.

When you write a process-analysis essay, you must present the *sequence of steps* clearly and carefully. As you do so, give the reason for each step and, where appropriate, provide these reminders:

1. *Do not omit any steps.* A sequence is a sequence because all steps depend on one another. Nikki Giovanni explains the importance of going to class to establish "a consistent presence in the classroom."

2. *Do not reverse steps.* A sequence is a sequence because each step must be performed according to a necessary and logical pattern. Ann Zwinger describes how the sequence of drawing a picture can lead to a learning experience.

3. *Suspend certain steps.* Occasionally, a whole series of steps must be suspended and another process completed before the sequence can resume. P. J. O'Rourke suggests that a whole sequence of steps can be avoided if you suspend the sequence and give everybody "big wads of American money."

4. *Do not overlook steps within steps.* Each sequence is likely to have a series of smaller steps buried within each step. Julia Alvarez reminds her readers that collecting curious information is not the same as researching it.

5. *Avoid certain steps.* It is often tempting to insert steps that are not recommended but that appear "logical." Serena Nanda discovers that her American logic does not work in an Indian context.

You may want to use several kinds of examples to explain the steps in a sequence.

1. *Pictures.* You can use graphs, charts, and diagrams to illustrate the operation of the process. Although none of the writers in this section uses pictures, Ann Zwinger's purpose is to demonstrate what you can learn by drawing them.

2. *Anecdotes.* Because you're claiming some level of expertise by writing a process analysis, you can clarify your explanation by using examples from your own experience. O'Rourke uses this method—for comic effect—when he describes roadblocks and animals in the right of way.

3. *Variants.* You can mention alternative steps to show that the process may not be as rigid or simplistic as it often appears. Giovanni uses sample questions and answers to illustrate different ways to participate in class.

4. *Comparisons.* You can use comparisons to help your readers see that a complex process is similar to a process they already know. Nanda uses this strategy when she compares

the complexities of arranging an Indian marriage to the "love matches" made in America.

Although you focus on the movement of the process when you write a process-analysis essay, finally you should also try to evaluate the *results* of that process. You can move to this last part by asking two questions: How do you know it's done? How do you know it's good? Sometimes the answer is simple: the car starts; the trunk opens. At other times, the answer is not so clear: the student may need further instruction; the jury may have difficulty reaching a decision.

USING PROCESS ANALYSIS IN PARAGRAPHS

Here are two process-analysis paragraphs. The first is written by a professional writer and is followed by an analysis. The second is written by a student writer and is followed by questions.

SCOTT RUSSELL SANDERS
from "Digging Limestone"

Dealing with the stone itself involves a whole new set of machines. Great mobile engines called channelers, powered by electricity, chug on rails from one side of the bed to the other, chiseling ten-foot-deep slots. Hammering and puffing along, they look and sound and smell like small locomotives. By shifting rails, the quarriers eventually slice the bed into a grid of blocks. The first of these to be removed is called the key-block, and it always provokes a higher than usual proportion of curses. There is no way to get to the base of this first block to cut it loose, so it must be wedged , hacked, splintered and worried at, until something like a clean hole has been

[margin notes:] Topic sentence predicts content

Names special tools

Identifies first step

Describes subsequent steps

Makes
comparison
(earth's
crust to
cement job)

excavated. <u>Men can then</u> climb down and, by drilling holes and driving wedges, <u>split the neighboring block</u> free at its base, <u>undoing in an hour a three-hundred-million-year-old cement job.</u>

Comment This paragraph, excerpted from "Digging Limestone," analyzes the complicated process of removing large slabs of limestone from the earth. The opening sentences name the special machines required to begin the work. Sanders makes sure his readers understand the importance of removing the keyblock. Only after this slice of stone is removed can the workers proceed with the rest of the process, "undoing in an hour a three-hundred-million-year-old cement job."

SARA TEMPLE
Making Stained Glass

Before you begin making stained glass, you will need to purchase the right tools—most of which you can find at your local hardware store. First, select a glass cutter. It looks like a steel fork with a wheel at one end. The wheel is the blade that allows you to cut out the shape of each piece of glass. Second, you will need another tool to "break" the glass along the line you have scored with your cutter. I've always called this object "the tool." Tell the hardware clerk what you want and she'll show you what you need. Third, pick out a glass grinder to polish each piece of glass to the right size. Finally, buy a soldering iron to fuse the various pieces of glass into your design. These last two tools can be "pricey," so you may want to find a partner to share the cost. In the process, you may discover that your stained glass will become more creative when you design it with a friend.

1. How does Temple list and describe the special tools needed in the process?
2. What advice does Temple provide about how to purchase and use the "pricey" tools?

PROCESS ANALYSIS

Points to Remember

1. Arrange the steps in your process in an orderly sequence.
2. Identify and explain the purpose of each of the steps in the process.
3. Describe the special tools, terms, and tasks needed to complete the process.
4. Provide warnings, where appropriate, about the consequences of omitting, reversing, or overlooking certain steps.
5. Supply illustrations and personal anecdotes to help clarify aspects of the process.

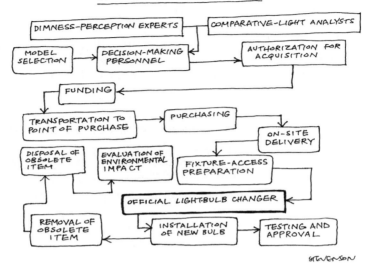

HOW MANY IT TAKES

In this comic drawing, James Stevenson offers yet another variation on the old joke "How many [fill in the blank] does it take to change a light bulb?" Trace the various steps in this overwrought flow chart. Has Stevenson missed a step or placed steps out of sequence? Construct your own flow chart for a simple process such as making an ATM transaction or hitting a golf ball. Then write an analysis of your chart demonstrating why this simple process contains hidden steps or must be explained in a larger context.

ANN ZWINGER

Ann Zwinger was born in Muncie, Indiana, in 1925, and was educated at Wellesley College and Indiana University. She has taught art at Smith College and the University of Arizona, and served as naturalist-in-residence at Carleton College. She is best known for books she has written and illustrated about the environment, such as *Beyond the Aspen Grove* (1970); *Run, River Run: A Naturalist's Journey Down One of the Great Rivers of the West* (1975); *The Mysterious Lands: The Four Deserts of the United States* (1989); and *Shaped by Wind and Water: Reflections of a Naturalist* (2000). Her artwork has been exhibited throughout the country and in her hometown, Colorado Springs, and she has published (with her daughter) a book of writings and photographs, *Women in the Wilderness* (1995). In "Drawing on Experience," reprinted from a collection of essays on nature and culture from *Orion* magazine, *Finding Home* (1992), Zwinger explains the "simple act of pencil rotating softly on paper."

Drawing on Experience

IT REALLY DOESN'T matter whether you can draw or not— just the time taken to examine in detail, to turn a flower or a shell over in your fingers, opens doors and windows. The time spent observing pays, and you can better observe with a hand lens than without one. A hand lens is a joy and a delight, an entrée to another world just below your normal vision. Alice in Wonderland never had it so good—no mysterious potions are needed, just a ten- or fifteen-power hand lens hung around your neck. There's a kind of magic in

seeing stellate hairs on a mustard stem, in seeing the
retrorsely barbed margin of a nettle spine—there all the time
but never visible without enhancement.

But to take the next step—to draw these in the margin of   2
your notebook, on the back of an envelope, in a sketch pad,
or even in the sand—establishes a connection between hand
and eye that reinforces the connection between eye and
memory. Drawing fastens the plant in memory.

I speak of plants because they are what I enjoy drawing. I   3
find small plants easier to translate to paper than a minute
ant's antennae or a full-blown, horizon-to-horizon landscape.
Landscapes are beautiful for what you leave out; the
most magnificent landscapes I know are those Rembrandt did

---

*I think of drawing not as an end in itself
but as a learning process, of doing research
with a hand lens and pencil instead of a
book and note cards.*

---

with a wash from a couple of brush strokes enlivened with a
crisp pen. But that took years of practice and a large dose
of genius, which are not the point here—I speak of the enjoyment of learning from precise observation.

With a plant, I start with a small detail and build up because   4
it's easier to extend outward into the infinite space of the page
than to be caught in the finite space of an outline. If you begin
with the big outline and fill in, and if you have any of the proportion problems I do, you often draw yourself into a corner.
I begin with the stigma and stamens, or perhaps a petal, or
perhaps the part that's closest, and work outward, relating
each part to what's been put down before rather than block-
ing in a general outer shape and working down to detail.

When I begin in the center, as it were, and move outward,   5
I build up a reality in which each detail relates to the one

before. I wonder if this is also a way of apprehending a world, of composing it from many observations, a detail here, a detail there, creating an infinitely expandable universe. I always thought I worked this way because I was myopic, but maybe it's deeper than that and has to do with judgments, perceived realities, and whether there are five or six stamens.

Small things, large enough to see easily, but small enough 6 to hold in the hand or put on the table in front of you, small enough to translate more or less one-to-one, seem to me the easiest subjects for the neophyte illustrator. Why deal with complex proportions if you don't have to? Forget the tea rose and the peony. Forgo the darlings of the garden that have been bred into complex, complicated flowers with multiple petals and fancy shapes. Try instead an interesting leaf, noting how the veining webs, or the edges curl or notch. Or try a simple flower—a phlox or lily-of-the-valley or an open, five-petaled wild rose.

Pale-colored plants are easier to draw: dark or brilliant 7 colors often obscure the shape and character of the flower. Seedheads, summer's skeletons, are often felicitous subjects. So are cow parsnip's umbrella ribs or pennycress's orbicular pods, shepherd's purse or lily pods, which likewise give a sense of seasons past and springs to come.

Plants are nice because they stay still. I draw insects but 8 only deceased ones, collected, pinned, and dried. Trying to portray a moving bug is a ridiculous task ending only in frustration.

Quick sketches of larger moving animals are difficult but 9 greatly rewarding. If you are a birdwatcher and have the patience, drawing is a good way to learn how birds move, orient and tilt their bodies, and to pick up a lot on animal behavior because the observation is focused. (I happen to find birds hard to draw but suspect it's because I don't practice.) An afternoon sketching at the zoo with pencil and pad will astound anyone who's never tried it before. Pick out the movement, never mind the details, and by the end of the afternoon the improvement, both in drawing and observation, is measurable.

Shells, beach debris, offer endless possibilities. Think of   10
what you are doing as doodling, not immortalizing a shell for
posterity. Play with different points of view and different
scales. Find out how a snail builds its shell by the Fibonacci
numbers, how the inside of an oyster shell reveals in color
and pattern where the oyster was attached and how it lived.

Or go to your local natural history museum and draw   11
stuffed animals, although a weasel in the bush is worth two in
the display. I remember wanting to draw a pocket gopher,
and the sole specimen easily available was in a natural history
museum. Only the front part was visible, the rest of the specimen having presumably been blown to bits on capture. It
was not a successful drawing, and I never used it.

Drawing is like practicing the piano: you have to do it on   12
a fairly regular basis to keep your hand in.

I have no patience with the "Oh,-if-I-could-only-draw!"   13
school. Drawing is a state of mind—how much you want to
do it, how much time you're willing to practice. It is, after all,
simply a neural connection between eye and mind and hand,
and the more that connection is reinforced, the more satisfying the result is going to be. I knew an art teacher who required students in his class to draw their own hand, once a
week. His theory was that the subject was always on the
premises, had infinite possibilities of outline and pose and
was not very easy to draw. The difference between the first
hand drawn and the last was remarkable, a real confidence
builder.

I'm also impatient with those who say "It doesn't *look* like   14
what I wanted it to look like!" So what? Don't demand of
yourself what you're not able to do at the time. Enjoy the feel
of pencil on paper without imposing goals you can't meet.

I don't know why this setting of impossible goals happens   15
more with drawing than with other creative endeavors. People who accept that they can't sit down and write a symphony
in a week expect to produce a skilled drawing the first time
out. Potters spend hours learning how to center on the
wheel; violinists practice scales all their lives. Drawing is in
the same category: it takes time to develop the basic skills.

And patience. When you hit a wrong note on the piano it fades off into the air before you play the correct one. If you make a wrong line, you can erase it. Or start over.

There are some wonderful books on drawing—Frederick 16 Franck's *The Zen of Drawing* and, best of all, *Drawing on the Right Side of the Brain* by Betty Edwards. The exercises she suggests, along with her practical how-tos, open a whole new way of looking and seeing.

A drawing class can also be useful, but it's not necessary. 17 What *is* necessary is to toss out some preconceived notions, and to accept and appreciate your fallibility and then forget it. Masterpieces of self-expression are not devoutly to be wished. Drawing is an experience of the facts and figures of a visual world that you can learn about in no other way.

Fancy tools aren't necessary either. Although I used to 18 carry a full complement of pencils, I now carry a single automatic one with a .5 mm lead that I buy at the supermarket. I prefer a spiral sketch pad because the papers remain anchored better, and I like one with little "tooth," as smooth as will comfortably take pencil. And if there's space in your pack or purse, carry a can of workable spray fixative. It's dismaying in the extreme to see a labored-over drawing reduced to a smear, and know that it can't be restored.

Colored pencils are a delight to use, but there's a great 19 deal to be said for learning with black pencil on white paper. The analogy of black-and-white and color photography comes to mind: color is lively, but color obfuscates. I don't learn as much about a plant when I draw with color. The structure and the detail are clearer in black and white.

When I am drawing I am usually very content in the pleasures of focusing outward. I think of drawing not as an end in itself but as a learning process, of doing research with a hand lens and pencil instead of a book and note cards. I think of it as seeing what I did not see before, of discovering, of walking around in the stamens and the pistil, of pacing off the petals, of touching the plant and knowing who it is.

In touch, you are given knowledge in an immediate and 21 practical way. You find out quickly that a cholla spine stings, that a blue spruce stabs, that a juniper prickles, that a mullein leaf is soft. There is also a communication established, an intimacy between mind and plant.

I remember a morning an April ago. I had been out in the   22 desert for three days and had an ice chest full of plants. No matter how hard I worked in the evening, I couldn't catch up with all there was to draw, so I took that morning just to draw. And I'm not sure but what it isn't a good time for drawing—your mind is yet uncluttered, energy is high, the capacity for concentration undiluted. The light tends to be bright and cool and better for drawing than the artificial light needed at night.

Two days prior a kindly hostess had said, "Let me get you   23 a glass to put the lily in so you don't have to hold it in your hand." I had replied without thinking, "No thank you—I need to see what's on the other side." I thought of that that morning as I drew the lily, which had been carefully cossetted in the ice chest since.

When I had acquired the lily, it had five buds. That   24 morning only one remained closed, two were open, and two were spent. It was a delicate, difficult flower, spreading its sepals and petals into a six-pointed star, stretching out goldpowdered sepals that would attract no pollinator, extending a white, three-partite stigma beyond where it could catch its own pollen, a stigma that now, in the end, would catch none. But even as I had plucked the stalk (there was no time to draw it on site) I knew the bulb would endure, to produce another stalk of flowers next year, nourished by the ruffled leaves that spread across the dry, hard ground.

I propped the lily up in the folds of the bedspread,   25 arranged it so that the two open flowers gave different aspects of the same reality, arranged it so it said not only *Hemerocallis* but *undulata* and Sonoran Desert at ten o'clock on an April morning. A light breeze came in the window at my right shoulder and the perfect light, bright but soft, illuminated the ruffled edges of the petals, revealing a trace of where they had overlapped in the bud.

The quintessential lily, based on a trinity of shapes: I drew   26
three lines, enough to put a turned-back sepal on paper, lay-
ered pencil lines to limn the greenish stripe down the middle,
checked the proportions, width against length, ruffle against
sweep of edge. And picked it up. Unconsciously. Turned it
over, looked it round, set it back, realized that knowing what
was on the other side mattered a great deal. How do you know
where you're going if you don't know where you've been?

The appearance of the lily on the page is the future, but   27
I've already seen it in my mind's eye, turned it in my hand,
seen all lilies in this lily, known dryness in my roots, spreading in my leaves, sunshine polishing my stalk. Because of this
lily, which I never saw until a few days ago, I know all about
waiting for enough warmth, all about cool dawns and wilting
noons. Because of this lily I know about desert heat and winter sleep and what the desert demands.

This lily is fixed in my mind's memory, on the page and   28
blowing in a desert spring. No matter what the season, this
lily blooms as part of experience, part of understanding, a
deep part of knowledge beyond words. Words, visual images,
straight memory—none bring that lily to flower in the
mind like the notation of its curve and the line of its flare, a
memory of the eye and the hand inscribed in the simple act
of pencil rotating softly on paper.

For Study and Discussion

QUESTIONS FOR RESPONSE

1. When was the last time you tried to draw a picture? Why does
   the prospect of drawing produce anxiety?
2. How do you respond to the "mistakes" you see in your drawing?

QUESTIONS ABOUT PURPOSE

1. According to Zwinger, what is the purpose of drawing?
2. Why does she encourage her readers to enjoy "the feel of pencil
   on paper without imposing goals you can't meet"?

QUESTIONS ABOUT AUDIENCE

1. How does Zwinger address her readers who belong to the "Oh,-if-I-could-only-draw!" school?
2. How does she respond to those readers who say "It doesn't *look* like what I wanted it to look like"?

QUESTIONS ABOUT STRATEGY

1. Why does Zwinger recommend drawing small things? Why does she begin at the center?
2. What sort of tools and techniques does Zwinger recommend? Why is black and white more effective than color?

QUESTIONS FOR DISCUSSION

1. How does Zwinger use the example of the lily to illustrate how "drawing is an experience of the facts and figures of a visual world that you can learn about in no other way"?
2. In what way is "drawing a state of mind"? How does it depend on practice?

P. J. O'ROURKE

Patrick Jake O'Rourke was born in 1947 in Toledo, Ohio, and was educated at Miami University and Johns Hopkins University. He began his writing career working for underground newspapers such as *Harry* in Baltimore before landing jobs as a feature editor and freelance writer for the *New York Herald,* executive editor for *National Lampoon,* and correspondent for *Rolling Stone* and *Atlantic Monthly.* His humorous style is showcased in *The 1964 High School Yearbook Parody* (1974), *Modern Manners: An Etiquette Book for Rude People* (1983), *The Bachelor's Home Companion: A Practical Guide to Keeping House Like a Pig* (1987), and *Holidays in Hell* (1988). O'Rourke's humor always has a political edge, evident in books such as *Republican Party Reptile: Essays and Outrages* (1987), *Give War a Chance: Eyewitness Accounts of Mankind's Struggle Against Tyranny, Injustice and Alcohol-Free Beer* (1992), and *The CEO of the Sofa* (2001). In "Third World Driving Hints and Tips," reprinted from *Holidays in Hell,* O'Rourke analyzes the rules of the road for driving in a different country.

Third World Driving Hints and Tips

D URING THE PAST couple of years I've had to do my   1
share of driving in the Third World—in Mexico, Lebanon, the Philippines, Cyprus, El Salvador, Africa and Italy. (Italy is not technically part of the Third World, but no one has told the Italians.) I don't pretend to be an expert, but I have been making notes. Maybe these notes will be

useful to readers who are planning to do something really stupid with their Hertz #1 Club cards.

ROAD HAZARDS

What would be a road hazard anywhere else, in the Third   2
World is probably the road. There are two techniques for coping with this. One is to drive very fast so your wheels "get on top" of the ruts and your car sails over the ditches and gullies. Predictably, this will result in disaster. The other technique is to drive very slowly. This will also result in disaster. No matter how slowly you drive into a ten-foot hole, you're

---

Never look where you're going—
you'll only scare yourself.

---

still going to get hurt. You'll find the locals themselves can't make up their minds. Either they drive at 2 m.p.h.—which they do every time there's absolutely no way to get around them. Or else they drive at 100 m.p.h.—which they do coming right at you when you finally get a chance to pass the guy going 2 m.p.h.

BASIC INFORMATION

It's important to have your facts straight before you begin   3
piloting a car around an underdeveloped country. For instance, which side of the road do they drive on? This is easy. They drive on your side. That is, you can depend on it, any oncoming traffic will be on your side of the road. Also, how do you translate kilometres into miles? Most people don't know this, but one kilometre = ten miles, exactly. True, a kilometre is only 62 per cent of a mile, but if something is one hundred kilometres away, read that as one thousand

miles because the roads are 620 percent worse than anything you've ever seen. And when you see a 50-k.p.h. speed limit, you might as well figure that means 500 *m.p.h.* because nobody cares. The Third World does not have Broderick Crawford and the Highway Patrol. Outside the cities, it doesn't have many police at all. Law enforcement is in the hands of the army. And soldiers, if they feel like it, will shoot you no matter what speed you're going.

TRAFFIC SIGNS AND SIGNALS

Most developing nations use international traffic symbols. 4 Americans may find themselves perplexed by road signs that look like Boy Scout merit badges and by such things as an iguana silhouette with a red diagonal bar across it. Don't worry, the natives don't know what they mean, either. The natives do, however, have an elaborate set of signals used to convey information to the traffic around them. For example, if you're trying to pass someone and he blinks his left turn signal, it means go ahead. Either that or it means a large truck is coming around the bend, and you'll get killed if you try. You'll find out in a moment.

Signalling is further complicated by festive decorations 5 found on many vehicles. It can be hard to tell a hazard flasher from a string of Christmas-tree lights wrapped around the bumper, and brake lights can easily be confused with the dozen red Jesus statuettes and the ten stuffed animals with blinking eyes on the package shelf.

DANGEROUS CURVES

Dangerous curves are marked, at least in Christian lands, by 6 white wooden crosses positioned to make the curves even more dangerous. These crosses are memorials to people who've died in traffic accidents, and they give a rough statistical indication of how much trouble you're likely to have at that spot in the road. Thus, when you come through a curve in a full-power slide and are suddenly confronted with a veritable forest of crucifixes, you know you're dead.

LEARNING TO DRIVE LIKE A NATIVE

It's important to understand that in the Third World most   7
driving is done with the horn, or "Egyptian Brake Pedal," as
it is known. There is a precise and complicated etiquette of
horn use. Honk your horn only under the following circumstances:

1. When anything blocks the road.
2. When anything doesn't.
3. When anything might.
4. At red lights.
5. At green lights.
6. At all other times.

ROAD-BLOCKS

One thing you can count on in Third World countries is   8
trouble. There's always some uprising, coup or Marxist insurrection going on, and this means military road-blocks. There
are two kinds of military road-block, the kind where you slow
down so they can look you over, and the kind where you
come to a full stop so they can steal your luggage. The important thing is that you must *never* stop at the slow-down
kind of road-block. If you stop, they'll think you're a terrorist about to attack them, and they'll shoot you. And you must
always stop at the full-stop kind of road-block. If you just
slow down, they'll think you're a terrorist about to attack
them, and they'll shoot you. How do you tell the difference
between the two kinds of road-block? Here's the fun part:
you can't!

(The terrorists, of course, have road-blocks of their own.   9
They always make you stop. Sometimes with land mines.)

ANIMALS IN THE RIGHT OF WAY

As a rule of thumb, you should slow down for donkeys, speed   10
up for goats and stop for cows. Donkeys will get out of your
way eventually, and so will pedestrians. But never actually

stop for either of them or they'll take advantage, especially the pedestrians. If you stop in the middle of a crowd of Third World pedestrians, you'll be there buying Chiclets and bogus antiquities for days.

Drive like hell through the goats. It's almost impossible to hit a goat. On the other hand, it's almost impossible *not* to hit a cow. Cows are immune to horn-honking, shouting, swats with sticks and taps on the hind quarters with the bumper. The only thing you can do to make a cow move is swerve to avoid it, which will make the cow move in front of you with lightning speed. 11

Actually, the most dangerous animals are the chickens. In the United States, when you see a ball roll into the street, you hit your brakes because you know the next thing you'll see is a kid chasing it. In the Third World, it's not balls the kids are chasing, but chickens. Are they practising punt returns with a leghorn? Dribbling it? Playing stick-hen? I don't know. But Third Worlders are remarkably fond of their chickens and, also, their children (population problems not withstanding). If you hit one or both, they may survive. But you will not. 12

ACCIDENTS

Never look where you're going—you'll only scare yourself. Nonetheless, try to avoid collisions. There are bound to be more people in that bus, truck or even on that moped than there are in your car. At best you'll be screamed deaf. And if the police do happen to be around, standard procedure is to throw everyone in jail regardless of fault. This is done to forestall blood feuds, which are a popular hobby in many of these places. Remember the American consul is very busy fretting about that Marxist insurrection, and it may be months before he comes to visit. 13

If you do have an accident, the only thing to do is go on the offensive. Throw big wads of American money at everyone, and hope for the best. 14

SAFETY TIPS

One nice thing about the Third World, you don't have to   15
fasten your safety belt. (Or stop smoking. Or cut down on
saturated fats.) It takes a lot off your mind when average life
expectancy is forty-five minutes.

For Study and Discussion

QUESTIONS FOR RESPONSE

1. How were you taught to drive? What procedures—for example,
   parallel parking—gave you the most trouble?
2. What difficulties have you encountered driving in a strange car
   or in an unfamiliar place?

QUESTIONS ABOUT PURPOSE

1. How do O'Rourke's travels establish his credentials to provide
   advice to drivers?
2. At what point in the essay do you realize that his purpose is to
   entertain rather than inform?

QUESTIONS ABOUT AUDIENCE

1. How does O'Rourke identify his readers when he refers to
   "Hertz #1 Club cards" and "big wads of American money"?
2. How might the "natives" referred to in this essay respond to
   O'Rourke's characterization of their driving habits?

QUESTIONS ABOUT STRATEGIES

1. How does O'Rourke's analysis of the "Egyptian Brake Pedal" and
   the road-blocks reveal that his hints are not really meant to help?
2. How does his discussion of "animals in the right of way" and
   children complicate his analysis?

QUESTIONS FOR DISCUSSION

1. To what extent does O'Rourke's use of the words *Third World* and
   underdeveloped suggest an attitude of smug, cultural superiority?
2. How might some of his analysis apply to the driving habits you
   have encountered in your hometown?

NIKKI GIOVANNI

Nikki Giovanni was born in 1943 in Knoxville, Tennessee, and was educated at Fisk University, the University of Pennsylvania, and Columbia University. She has taught creative writing at Rutgers University and Virginia Tech and worked for the Ohio Humanities Council and the Appalachian Community Fund. Her poems have appeared in the collections *My House* (1972), *The Women and the Men* (1975), *Those Who Ride the Night Winds* (1983), and *Girls in the Circle* (2004). Her nonfiction work appears in books such as *Gemini: An Extended Autobiographical Statement on My First Twenty-Five Years Being a Black Poet* (1971), *Sacred Cows . . . and Other Edibles* (1988), and *Racism 101* (1994). In "Campus Racism 101," Giovanni tells black students how to succeed at predominantly white colleges.

Campus Racism 101

THERE IS A bumper sticker that reads: TOO BAD IGNO- 1
RANCE ISN'T PAINFUL. I like that. But ignorance is. We just seldom attribute the pain to it or even recognize it when we see it. Like the postcard on my corkboard. It shows a young man in a very hip jacket smoking a cigarette. In the background is a high school with the American flag waving. The caption says: "Too cool for school. Yet too stupid for the real world." Out of the mouth of the young man is a bubble enclosing the words "Maybe I'll start a band." There could be a postcard showing a jock in a uniform saying, "I don't need school. I'm going to the NFL or NBA." Or one showing a young man or woman studying and a group of young

115

people saying, "So you want to be white." Or something equally demeaning. We need to quit it.

I am a professor of English at Virginia Tech. I've been here   2
for four years, though for only two years with academic rank. I am tenured, which means I have a teaching position for life, a rarity on a predominantly white campus. Whether from malice or ignorance, people who think I should be at a predominantly Black institution will ask, "Why are you at Tech?" Because it's here. And so are Black students. But even if Black students weren't here, it's painfully obvious that this nation and this world cannot allow white students to go through higher education without interacting with Blacks in authoritative positions. It is equally clear that predominantly Black

---

Your job is not to educate white people; it is to obtain an education.

---

colleges cannot accommodate the numbers of Black students who want and need an education.

Is it difficult to attend a predominantly white college?   3
Compared with what? Being passed over for promotion because you lack credentials? Being turned down for jobs because you are not college-educated? Joining the armed forces or going to jail because you cannot find an alternative to the streets? Let's have a little perspective here. Where can you go and what can you do that frees you from interacting with the white American mentality? You're going to interact; the only question is, will you be in some control of yourself and your actions, or will you be controlled by others? I'm going to recommend self-control.

What's the difference between prison and college? They   4
both prescribe your behavior for a given period of time. They both allow you to read books and develop your writing. They both give you time alone to think and time with your

peers to talk about issues. But four years of prison doesn't give you a passport to greater opportunities. Most likely that time only gives you greater knowledge of how to get back in. Four years of college gives you an opportunity not only to lift yourself but to serve your people effectively. What's the difference when you are called nigger in college from when you are called nigger in prison? In college you can, though I admit with effort, follow procedures to have those students who called you nigger kicked out or suspended. You can bring issues to public attention without risking your life. But mostly, college is and always has been the future. We, neither less nor more than other people, need knowledge. There are discomforts attached to attending predominantly white colleges, though no more so than living in a racist world. Here are some rules to follow that may help:

Go to class. No matter how you feel. No matter how you think the professor feels about you. It's important to have a consistent presence in the classroom. If nothing else, the professor will know you care enough and are serious enough to be there.   5

Meet your professors. Extend your hand (give a firm handshake) and tell them your name. Ask them what you need to do to make an A. You may never make an A, but you have put them on notice that you are serious about getting good grades.   6

Do assignments on time. Typed or computer-generated. You have the syllabus. Follow it, and turn those papers in. If for some reason you can't complete an assignment on time, let your professor know before it is due and work out a new due date—then meet it.   7

Go back to see your professor. Tell him or her your name again. If an assignment received less than an A, ask why, and find out what you need to do to improve the next assignment.   8

Yes, your professor is busy. So are you. So are your parents who are working to pay or help with your tuition. Ask early what you need to do if you feel you are starting to get into academic trouble. Do not wait until you are failing.   9

Understand that there will be professors who do not like you; 10
there may even be professors who are racist or sexist or both.
You must discriminate among your professors to see who will
give you the help you need. You may not simply say, "They
are all against me." They aren't. They mostly don't care.
Since you are the one who wants to be educated, find the
people who want to help.

Don't defeat yourself. Cultivate your friends. Know your en- 11
emies. You cannot undo hundreds of years of prejudicial thinking. Think for yourself and speak up. Raise your hand in class.
Say what you believe no matter how awkward you may think it
sounds. You will improve in your articulation and confidence.

Participate in some campus activity. Join the newspaper 12
staff. Run for office. Join a dorm council. Do something that
involves you on campus. You are going to be there for four
years, so let your presence be known, if not felt.

You will inevitably run into some white classmates who are 13
troubling because they often say stupid things, ask stupid
questions—and expect an answer. Here are some comebacks
to some of the most common inquiries and comments:

Q: What's it like to grow up in a ghetto? 14
A: I don't know. 15

Q: (from the teacher): Can you give us the Black perspective 16
on Toni Morrison, Huck Finn, slavery, Martin Luther King,
Jr., and others?
A: I can give you *my* perspective. (Do not take the burden of 17
22 million people on your shoulders. Remind everyone that
you are an individual, and don't speak for the race or any
other individual within it.)

Q: Why do all the Black people sit together in the dining hall? 18
A: Why do all the white students sit together? 19

Q: Why should there be an African-American studies course? 20
A: Because white Americans have not adequately studied 21
the contributions of Africans and African-Americans. Both

Black and white students need to know our total common history.

Q: Why are there so many scholarships for "minority" students?   22
A: Because they wouldn't give my great-grandparents their forty acres and the mule.   23

Q: How can whites understand Black history, culture, literature, and so forth?   24
A: The same way we understand white history, culture, literature, and so forth. That is why we're in school: to learn.   25

Q: Should whites take African-American studies courses?   26
A: Of course. We take white-studies courses, though the universities don't call them that.   27

Comment: When I see groups of Black people on campus, it's really intimidating.   28
Comeback: I understand what you mean. I'm frightened when I see white students congregating.   29

Comment: It's not fair. It's easier for you guys to get into college than for other people.   30
Comeback: If it's so easy, why aren't there more of us?   31

Comment: It's not our fault that America is the way it is.   32
Comeback: It's not our fault, either, but both of us have a responsibility to make changes.   33

It's really very simple. Educational progress is a national concern; education is a private one. Your job is not to educate white people; it is to obtain an education. If you take the racial world on your shoulders, you will not get the job done. Deal with yourself as an individual worthy of respect, and make everyone else deal with you the same way. College is a little like playing grown-up. Practice what you want to be. You have been telling your parents you are grown. Now is your chance to act like it.   34

For Study and Discussion

QUESTIONS FOR RESPONSE

1. How have you responded to situations in which you were convinced that your teacher did not like you?
2. How have you felt when a teacher or fellow student placed you in a group (characterized by stereotypes) and then asked you to speak *for* that group?

QUESTIONS ABOUT PURPOSE

1. How does Giovanni explain her reasons for teaching at a predominantly white school?
2. In what ways does the issue of control, particularly self-control, explain the purpose of her advice?

QUESTIONS ABOUT AUDIENCE

1. How do the examples in the first paragraph and the advice in the last paragraph identify Giovanni's primary audience?
2. How does Giovanni's status as professor at a predominantly white college establish her authority to address her audience on "Racism 101"?

QUESTIONS ABOUT STRATEGIES

1. How does Giovanni arrange her advice? Why is her first suggestion—"Go to class"—her *first* suggestion? Why is her last suggestion—"Participate in some campus activity"—her *last* suggestion?
2. How does she use sample questions and answers to illustrate the experience of learning on a white campus?

QUESTIONS FOR DISCUSSION

1. What does Giovanni's attitude toward *individual* as opposed to *group* perspective suggest about the nature of "racism"?
2. How might white students learn as much as black students from following her advice?

JULIA ALVAREZ

Julia Alvarez was born in New York City in 1950 but was raised in the Dominican Republic until her family was forced to flee the country because her father's involvement in the plot to overthrow dictator Rafael Trujillo was uncovered. She was educated at Middlebury College, Syracuse University, and Bread Loaf School of English and worked as a Poet-in-the-Schools in several states. She then began teaching writing at George Washington University, the University of Illinois, and Middlebury College. Her major works of fiction include *How the Garcia Girls Lost Their Accents* (1991), *In the Time of Butterflies* (1994), *¡YO!* (1996), and *In the Name of Salomé: A Novel* (2000). Her poems appear in *Homecoming* (1984), *The Other Side/El Otro Lado* (1995), and *The Woman I Kept to Myself* (2004). In "Grounds for Fiction," reprinted from *Something to Declare* (1998), Alvarez analyzes the sources and strategies of her writing process.

Grounds for Fiction

EVERY ONCE IN a while after a reading, someone in the audience will come up to me. *Have I got a story for you!* They will go on to tell me the story of an aunt or sister or next-door neighbor, some moment of mystery, some serendipitous occurrence, some truly incredible story. "You should write it down," I always tell them. They look at me as if they've just offered me their family crown jewels and I've refused them. "I'm no writer," they tell me. "You're the writer." 1

"Oh, you never know," I reply, so as to encourage them.   2
What I should tell them is that writing ideas can't really be
traded in an open market. If they could be, writers would be
multimillionaires. Who knows what mystery (or madness) it
is that drives us to our computers for two, three, four years,
in pursuit of some sparkling possibility that looks like dull
fact to everyone else's eyes. One way to define a writer is she
who is able to make what obsesses her into everyone's
obsession. I am thinking of Goethe, whose *Sorrows of
Young Werther,* published in 1774, caused a spate of suicides
in imitation of its young hero. Young Werther's blue frock
coat and yellow waistcoat became the fad. We have all been
the victims of someone's too-long slide show of their white-

*I told the young man that if he didn't want
to spend hours and hours finding out if the
kernel of an idea, the glimmer of an
inspiration, the flash of a possibility would
make a good story, he should give up the idea
of wanting to be a writer.*

water rafting trip or their recounting of a convoluted, boring
dream. But a Mark Twain can turn that slide show into the
lively backdrop of a novel, or a Jorge Luis Borges can take the
twist and turn of a dream and wring the meaning of the universe from it.

But aside from talent—and granted, that is a big aside, one   3
that comes and goes and shifts and grows and diminishes, so
it is also somewhat unpredictable—how can we tell when
we've got it: that seed of experience, of memory, that voice of
a character or fleeting image that might just be grounds for
fiction? The answer is that we can never tell. And so another
way to define a writer is someone who is willing to find out.
As James Dickey once explained to an audience, "I work on

the process of refining low-grade ore. I get maybe a couple of nuggets of gold out of fifty tons of dirt. It is tough for me. No, I am not inspired."

"Are you all here because you want to muck around in fifty tons of dirt?" I ask my workshop of young writers the first day. Not one hand goes up unless I've told them the Dickey story first.

In fact, my students want to know ahead of time if some idea they have will make a good story. "I mean, before I spend hours and hours on it," one young man explained. I told my students what Mallarmé told his friend the painter Degas, when Degas complained that he couldn't seem to write well although he was "full of ideas." Mallarmé's famous answer was, "My dear Degas, poems are not made out of ideas. Poems are made out of words." I told my student that if a young writer had come up to me and told me that he was going to write a story about a man who wakes up one morning and finds out that he has been turned into a cockroach, I would have told him to forget it. That story would never work. "And I would have stopped Kafka from writing his 'Metamorphosis,'" I concluded, smiling at my student, as if he might be a future Kafka.

"Well, it's just two pages," he grumbled. "And I have this other idea that might be better. About a street person who is getting Alzheimer's."

"Write both stories, and I'll read them and tell you what I think of them," I said. He looked alarmed. So I leveled with him. I told him that if he didn't want to spend hours and hours finding out if the kernel of an idea, the glimmer of an inspiration, the flash of a possibility would make a good story, he should give up the *idea* of wanting to be a writer.

As much as I can break down the process of writing stories, I would say that this is how it begins. I find a detail or image or character or incident or cluster of events. A certain luminosity surrounds them. I find myself attracted. I come forward. I pick it up, turn it around, begin to ask questions, and spend hours and weeks and months and years trying to answer them.

I keep a folder, a yellow folder with pockets. For a long time   9
it had no label because I didn't know what to label it:
WHATCHAMACALLITS, filed under *W,* or also under *W,*
STORY-POEM-WANNABES. Finally, I called the folder
CURIOSIDADES, in Spanish so I wouldn't have to commit
myself to what I was going to do in English with these random little things. I tell my students this, too, that writing begins before you ever put pen to paper or your fingers down
on the keyboard. It is a way of being alive in the world.
Henry James's advice to the young writer was to be someone
on whom nothing is lost. And so this is my folder of the little
things that have not been lost on me; news clippings, headlines, inventory lists, bits of gossip that I've already sensed
have an aura about them, the beginnings of a poem or a short
story, the seed of a plot that might turn into a novel or a
query that might needle an essay out of me.

Periodically, when I'm between writing projects and   10
sometimes when I'm in the middle of one and needing a
break, I go through my yellow folder. Sometimes I discard a
clipping or note that no longer holds my attention. But most
of my curiosidades have been in my folder for years, though
some have migrated to new folders, the folders of stories and
poems they have inspired or found a home in.

Here's one of these curiosidades that is now in a folder   11
that holds drafts of a story that turned into a chapter of my
novel *¡YO!* This chapter is in the point of view of Marie
Beaudry, a landlady who, along with other narrators, gets to
tell a story on Yolanda García, the writer. The little curiosity
that inspired Marie's voice was a note I found in the trash of
an apartment I moved into. It has nothing at all to do with
what happens in my story.

> *Re and Mal: Here's the two keys to your father's apt.*
> *Need I say more excepting that's such a rotten thing*
> *you pulled on him. My doing favors is over as of this*
> *morning. Good luck to you two hard-hearted*
> *hannahs. I got more feeling in my little finger than*
> *the two of you got in your whole body.*
>
> *Jinny*

I admit that when I read this note, I wanted to move out   12
of that apartment. I felt the place was haunted by the ghost
of the last tenant against whom some violation had been perpetrated by these two hard-hearted hannahs, Re and Mal.
Over the years that handwritten note stayed in my yellow
folder and eventually gave me the voice of my character
Marie Beaudry.

Here's another scrap from deep inside one of the pockets.   13
It's the title of an article in one of my husband's ophthal-
mological journals: "Treatment of Chronic Postfiltration
Hypotony by Intrableb Injection of Autologous Blood." I
think I saved that choice bit of medical babble because of the
delight I took in the jabberwocky phenomenon of that title.

> *'Twas brillig and the slithy toves*
> *Did gyre and postfiltrate the wabe;*
> *All hypotonious was the blood,*
> *And autologous the intrableb.*

I have not yet used it in a story or poem, but who knows,
maybe someday you will look over the shoulder of one of my
characters and see that he is reading this article or writing it.
I can tell you that this delight in words and how we use and
misuse them is a preoccupation of mine.

Maybe because I began my writing life as a poet, the   14
naming of things has always interested me:

> *Mother, unroll the bolts and name*
> *the fabrics from which our clothing came,*
> *dress the world in vocabulary:*
> *broadcloth, corduroy, denim, terry.*

Actually, that poem, "Naming the Fabrics," besides being inspired, of course, by the names of fabrics, was also triggered
by something I picked up while reading *The 1961 Better
Homes and Garden Sewing Book,* page 45: "During a question and answer period at a sewing clinic, a woman in the audience asked this question: 'I can sew beautifully; my fitting
is excellent; the finished dress looks as good as that of any

professional—but how do I get up enough courage to cut the fabric?'" I typed out this passage and put it away. A few months later, this fear found its way from my yellow folder to my poem, "Naming the Fabrics":

> *I pay a tailor to cut his suits*
> *from seersucker, duck, tweed, cheviot,*
> *those names make my cutting hand skittish—*
> *either they sound like sex or British.*

Since I myself have no sewing skills to speak of, I didn't know about this fear that seamstresses experience before cutting fabric. Certainly, the year 1961, when this sewing book was published, brings other fears to mind: the Berlin Wall going up; invaders going down to the Bay of Pigs; Trujillo, our dictator of thirty-one years, being assassinated in the Dominican Republic. But this housewife in Indiana had her own metaphysical fears to work out on cloth. "How do I get up enough courage to cut the fabric?" Her preoccupation astonished me and touched me for all kinds of reasons I had to work out on paper.

You might wonder what a "serious writer" was doing   15
reading *The 1961 Better Homes and Garden Sewing Book*. Wouldn't my time have been better spent perusing Milton or Emily Dickinson or even the *New York Review of Books* or *The Nation*? All I can say in my defense is that I believe in Henry James's advice: be someone on whom nothing is lost. Or what Deborah Kerr said in *Night of the Iguana*, "Nothing human disgusts me." I once heard a writer on *Fresh Air* tell Terry Gross that one of the most important things he had ever learned in his life was that you could learn a lot from people who were dumber than you. You can also learn a lot from publications that are below your literary standards: housekeeping books, cookbooks, manuals, cereal boxes, and the local newspapers of your small town.

These last are the best. Even if some of this "news" is re-   16
ally glorified gossip—so what? Most of our classics are

glorified gossip. Think of the Wife of Bath's inventory of husbands or the debutante's hair-rape in "The Rape of the Lock." How about Madame Bovary's seamy affair? Is what happened to Abelard over his Héloïse or to Jason for pissing off Medea any less infamous than the John and Lorena Bobbit story of several years ago? The wonderful Canadian writer Alice Munro admits that she likes reading *People* magazine, and "not just at the checkout stand. I sometimes buy it." She goes on to say that gossip is "a central part of my life. I'm interested in small-town gossip. Gossip has that feeling in it, that one wants to know about life."

I've gotten wonderful stories from the *Addison Independent,* the *Valley Voice,* even the *Burlington Free Press* that would never be reported in the *Wall Street Journal* or the *New York Times:*   17

11-YEAR-OLD GIRLS TAKE CAR
ON TWO-STATE JOYRIDE

Two 11-year-old girls determined to see a newborn niece secretly borrowed their grandfather's car, piled clothes on the front seat so they could see over the steering wheel and drove more than 10 hours.

Neither one of them had ever driven a car before, said Michael Ray, Mercer County's juvenile case worker. The youngsters packed the Dodge Aries with soda, snacks, and an atlas for their trek from West Virginia to the central Kentucky town of Harrodsburg. "They were determined to see that baby," said caseworker Ray.

You could write a whole novel about that. In fact, in Mona   18
Simpson's latest novel, *A Regular Guy,* eleven-year-old Jane di Natali is taught by her mother to drive their pickup with wood blocks strapped to the pedals so her short legs can reach them. Little Jane takes off on her own to see her estranged father hundreds of miles away. I wonder if Mona Simpson got her idea for Jane's odyssey from reading about these two eleven-year-olds.

Here's another article I've saved in my yellow folder: 19

MISDIAGNOSED PATIENT FREED AFTER 2 YEARS

A Mexican migrant worker misdiagnosed and kept sedated in an Oregon mental hospital for two years because doctors couldn't understand his Indian dialect is going home.

Adolfo Gonzales, a frail 5-foot-4-inch grape picker who doesn't speak English or Spanish, had been trying to communicate in his native Indian dialect of Trique.

Gonzales, believed to be in his 20s, was born in a village in Oaxaca, Mexico. He was committed in June 1990 after being arrested for indecent exposure at a laundromat. Charges later were dropped.

I couldn't get this story out of my head. First, I was—and am—intensely interested in the whole Scheherazade issue of how important it is to be able to tell our stories to those who have power over us. Second, and more mundanely, I was intensely curious about those charges that were later dropped: indecent exposure at a laundromat. What was Adolfo Gonzales doing taking his clothes off in a laundromat? Why was he in town after a hard day of grape picking? I had to find answers to these questions, and so I started writing a poem. "It's a myth that writers write what they know," the writer Marcie Hershman has written. "We write what it is that we need to know."

> *The next payday you went to town*
> *to buy your girl and to wash your one*
> *set of working clothes.*
> *In the laundromat, you took them off*
> *to wring out the earth you wanted*
> *to leave behind you.*
>
> *from "Two Years Too Late"*

Of course, you don't even have to go to your local paper.   20
Just take a walk downtown, especially if you live in a small

town, as I do. All I have to do is have a cup of coffee at Steve's Diner or at Jimmy's Weybridge Garage and listen to my neighbors talking. Flannery O'Connor claimed that most beginners' stories don't work because "they don't go very far inside a character, don't reveal very much of the character. And this problem is in large part due to the fact that these characters have no distinctive speech to reveal themselves with." Here are some examples of my fellow Vermonters talking their very distinctive and revealing speech.

> He's so lazy he married a pregnant woman.
> I'm so hungry I could eat the north end out of a southbound skunk.
> The snow's butt-high to a tall cow.
> More nervous than a long-tailed cat in a room full of rocking chairs.
> I'm so sick that I'd have to get well to die.

Of course if, like Whitman, you do nothing but listen, you will also hear all kinds of bogus voices these days, speaking the new doublespeak. In our litigious, politically overcorrected, dizzily spin-doctored age, politicians and public figures have to use language so that it doesn't say anything that might upset anyone. Here's a list of nonterms and what they really stand for:

Sufferer of fictitious disorder syndrome:	Liar
Suboptimal:	Failed
Temporarily displaced inventory:	Stolen
Negative gain in test scores:	Lower test scores
Substantive negative outcome:	Death

We're back to "Treatment of Chronic Postfiltration Hypotony by Intrableb Injection of Autologous Blood," what Ken Macrorie in his wonderful book about expository writing, *Telling Writing,* calls "Engfish"—homogenized, doctored-up, approximate language that can't be traced to a human being.

I tend to agree with what Dickinson once said about   21
poetry, "There are no approximate words in a poem." Auden
even went so far as to say that he could pick out a potential
poet by a student's answer to the question, "Why do you
want to write poetry?" If the student answered, "I have
important things to say," then he was not a poet. If he
answered, "I like hanging around words listening to what
they say," then maybe he was going to be a poet.

I got enmeshed in one such string of words when I visited   22
the United Nations to hear my mother give a speech on violation of human rights. At the door an aide handed me the
list of voting member countries and the names caught my
eye: Dem Kampuchea, Dem Yemen, Denmark, Djibouti,
Dominica, Dominican Republic, Ecuador, Egypt. . . . When I
got home, I started writing a poem, ostensibly about hearing
my mother give that speech, but really because I wanted to
use the names of those countries:

> *I scan the room for reactions,*
> *picking out those countries*
> *guilty of her sad facts.*
> *Kampuchea is absent,*
> *absent, too, the South African delegate.*
> *I cannot find the United States.*
> *Nervous countries predominate,*
> *Nicaragua and Haiti,*
> *Iraq, Israel, Egypt.*
> > *from "Between Dominica and Ecuador"*

But of course, it's not just words that intrigue writers, but the
stories, the possibilities of human character that cluster
around a bit of history, trivia, gossip.

For instance, Anne Macdonald's book, *Feminine Ingenu-*   23
ity, inspired a character trait of the mother in *How the García*
Girls Lost Their Accents. According to Macdonald, at the
beginning of the twentieth century, 5,535 American women
were granted patents for inventions, including a straw-weaving
device, an open-eye needle for sewing hot-air balloons,

and special planking designed to discourage barnacles from attaching themselves to warships. These intriguing facts gave me a side of the mother's character I would never have thought up on my own. Inspired by the gadgetry of her new country, Laura García sets out to make her mark: soap sprayed from the nozzle head of a shower when you turn the knob a certain way; instant coffee with creamer already mixed in; time-released water capsules for your potted plants when you were away; a key chain with a timer that would go off when your parking meter was about to expire. (And the ticking would help you find your keys easily if you mislaid them.)

Sometimes the inspiration is history. History . . . that subject 24 I hated in school because it was so dry and all about dead people. I wish now my teachers had made me read novels to make the past spring alive in my imagination. For years, I wanted to write about the Mirabal sisters, but I admit I was put off by these grand historical abstractions. It wasn't until I began to accumulate several yellow folders' worth of vivid little details about them that these godlike women became accessible to me. One of my first entries came from my father, who had just returned from a trip to the Dominican Republic: "I met the man who sold the girls pocketbooks at El Gallo before they set off over the mountain. He told me he warned them not to go. He said he took them out back to the stockroom supposedly to show them inventory and explained they were going to be killed. But they did not believe him." I still get goosebumps reading my father's letter dated June 5, 1985. It went in my yellow folder. That pocketbook-buying scene is at the end of the novel I published nine years later.

So what are you to conclude from this tour of my yellow 25 folder? That this essay is just an excuse to take you through my folder and share my little treasures with you? Well, one thing I don't want you to conclude is that this preliminary woolgathering is a substitute for the real research that starts once you have a poem or story going. In "Naming the Fabrics," for instance, though I was inspired by the plaintive question asked at a sewing clinic, I still had to go down to the fabric store and spend an afternoon with a very kind and

patient saleslady who taught me all about gingham and calico, crepe and gauze. I spent days reading fabric books, and
weeks working on the poem, and years going back to it, revising it, tinkering with it. For my story, "The Tent," I had to
call up the National Guard base near Champaign, Illinois,
and get permission from the base commander to go observe
his men setting up a tent. ("What exactly do you need this
for?" he asked at least half a dozen times.) Sometimes I think
the best reason for a writer to have a reputable job like being
a professor at a university or a vice president of Hartford Insurance Company is so you can call up those base command-
ers or bother those salesladies in fabric stores as if you do
have a real job. Otherwise, they might think you are crazy
and lock you up like poor Adolfo Gonzales.

   On the whole, I have found people to be kind and gener-   26
ous with their time, especially when you ask them to talk
about something they know and care about. Many people
have actually gone beyond kindness in helping me out. I remember calling up the local Catholic priest, bless his heart,
who really deserves, I don't know, a plenary indulgence for
tolerance in the face of surprise. Imagine getting an early-
morning call (my writing day starts at 6:30, but I really don't
do this kind of phone calling till about 7:30 since I do want
my sources to be lucid). Anyhow, imagine an early-morning
call at your rectory from a woman you don't know who asks
you what is the name of that long rod priests have with a hole
on one end to sprinkle people with holy water? I'd be lying if
I tried to make drama out of the phone call and say there was
a long pause. Nope. Father John spoke right up, "Ah yes, my
aspergill."

   One thing I should add—the bad news part of all this fun,   27
but something writers do have to think about in this litigious
age—what is grounds for fiction can also be, alas, grounds for
suing. All three of my novels have been read by my publisher's lawyer for what might be libelous. Thank goodness
Algonquin's lawyer is also a reader who refuses to vacuum all
the value out of a book in order to play it safe. Still, I have
had to take drinks out of characters' hands and make abused

ladies disabused and make so many changes in hair coloring and hairstyle that I could start a literary beauty parlor.

But even if your fictional ground is cleared of litigious material, there might still be grounds for heartache. Your family and friends might feel wounded when they can detect—even if no one else can—the shape of the real behind the form of your fiction. And who would want to hurt those very people you write for, those very people who share with you the world you are struggling to understand in your fiction for their sake as well as your own? ₂₈

I don't know how to get around this and I certainly haven't figured out what the parameters of my responsibility are to the real people in my life. One of my theories, which might sound defensive and self-serving, is that there is no such thing as straight-up fiction. There are just levels of distance from our own life experience, the thing that drives us to write in the first place. In spite of our caution and precaution, bits of our lives will get into what we write. I have a friend whose mother finds herself in all his novels, even historical novels set in nineteenth-century Russia or islands in the Caribbean where his mother has never been. A novelist writing about Napoleon might convey his greedy character by describing him spooning gruel into his mouth, only to realize that her image of how a greedy man eats comes from watching her fat Tío Jorge stuff his face with sweet habichuelas. ₂₉

I think that if you start censoring yourself as a novelist— *this is out of bounds, that is sacrosanct*—you will never write anything. My advice is to write it out, and then decide, by whatever process seems fair to you—three-o'clock-in-the-morning insomniac angst sessions with your soul, or a phone call with your best friend, or a long talk with your sister— what you are going to do about it. More often than not, an upset reaction has more to do with people's wounded vanity or their own unresolved issues with *you* rather than what you've written. I'm not speaking now of meanness or revenge thinly masquerading as fiction, but of a writer's serious attempts to render justice to the world she lives in, which includes, whether she wants it to or not, the people she loves or ₃₀

has tried to love, the people who have been a part of the memories, details, life experiences that form the whole cloth of her reality—out of which, with fear and a trembling hand, she must perforce cut her fiction.

But truly, this is a worry to put out of your head while you   31 are writing. You'll need your energy for the hard work ahead: tons and tons of good *ideas* to process in order to get those nuggets of pure prose. What Yeats once said in his poem, "Dialogue of Self and Soul," could well be the writer's pledge of allegiance:

> *I am content to follow to its source,*
> *every event in action or in thought.*

And remember, no one is probably going to pay you a whole lot of money to do this. You also probably won't save anyone's life with anything you write. But so much does depend on seeing a world in a grain of sand and a heaven in a wildflower. Maybe we are here only to say: house, bridge, aspergill, gingham, calico, gauze. "But to say them," as Rilke said, "remember oh, to say them in a way that the things themselves never dreamed of existing so intensely."

But this is too much of an orchestral close for the lowly   32 little ditty that starts with a newspaper clipping or the feel of a bolt of gingham or a cup of coffee at the Weybridge Garage. The best advice I can give writers is something so dull and simple you'd never save it in your yellow folder. But go ahead and engrave it in your writer's heart. If you want to be a writer, anything in this world is grounds for fiction.

For Study and Discussion

QUESTIONS FOR RESPONSE

1. Have you ever read a news story or overheard some gossip that you think would make a good story? Explain the features that made it "good."

2. Have you ever tried to write about a personal experience that meant a great deal to you? Why were you satisfied or disappointed with the results?

QUESTIONS ABOUT PURPOSE

1. How does Alvarez use Henry James's advice—to be someone on whom nothing is lost—to explain the purpose of the process she is trying to analyze?
2. How does she use "the Scheherazade issue" to explain the purpose of writing?

QUESTIONS ABOUT AUDIENCE

1. In what ways do the people who attend Alvarez's poetry readings serve as the imaginary audience for her essay?
2. How does she use Auden's question to student writers (page 130) to expand her audience?

QUESTIONS ABOUT STRATEGIES

1. Identify the steps in the little paragraph Alvarez uses to "break down the process of writing fiction." What steps are hidden within this sequence?
2. How does Alvarez's "tour" of her CURIOSIDADES help her illustrate the way she *finds* stories?

QUESTIONS FOR DISCUSSION

1. How does Alvarez suggest you solve the problem of the conflict between grounds for fiction and grounds for suing?
2. How does Alvarez support her argument that there is no such thing as "straight-up fiction"?

SERENA NANDA

Serena Nanda was educated at New York University and taught cultural anthropology at John Jay College of Criminal Justice at City University of New York. Her books include *Cultural Anthropology* (1998), *American Cultural Pluralism and Law* (1996), *Neither Man nor Woman: The Hijras of India* (1999), and *Gender Diversity: Cross-Cultured Variations* (2000). Nanda's current research focuses on non-European representations of Europeans in art and performance. In "Arranging a Marriage in India," reprinted from *The Naked Anthropologist: Tales from Around the World* (1992), Nanda contrasts the Indian and American processes of getting married.

Arranging a Marriage in India

Sister and doctor brother-in-law invite correspondence from North Indian professionals only, for a beautiful, talented, sophisticated, intelligent sister, 5' 3 ", slim, M.A. in textile design, father a senior civil officer. Would prefer immigrant doctors, between 26–29 years. Reply with full details and returnable photo.

A well-settled uncle invites matrimonial correspondence from slim, fair, educated South Indian girl, for his nephew, 25 years, smart, M.B.A., green card holder, 5' 6 ". Full particulars with returnable photo appreciated.
—*Matrimonial Advertisements,* India Abroad

I N INDIA, ALMOST all marriages are arranged. Even among   1
the educated middle classes in modern, urban India, marriage is as much a concern of the families as it is of the individuals. So customary is the practice of arranged marriage

that there is a special name for a marriage which is not arranged: It is called a "love match."

On my first field trip to India, I met many young men and women whose parents were in the process of "getting them married." In many cases, the bride and groom would not meet each other before the marriage. At most they might meet for a brief conversation, and this meeting would take

---

I found it difficult to accept the docile manner in which this well-educated young woman awaited the outcome of a process that would result in her spending the rest of her life with a man she hardly knew, a virtual stranger, picked out by her parents.

---

place only after their parents had decided that the match was suitable. Parents do not compel their children to marry a person who either marriage partner finds objectionable. But only after one match is refused will another be sought.

As a young American woman in India for the first time, I found this custom of arranged marriage oppressive. How could any intelligent young person agree to such a marriage without great reluctance? It was contrary to everything I believed about the importance of romantic love as the only basis of a happy marriage. It also clashed with my strongly held notions that the choice of such an intimate and permanent relationship could be made only by the individuals involved. Had anyone tried to arrange my marriage, I would have been defiant and rebellious!

At the first opportunity, I began, with more curiosity than tact, to question the young people I met on how they felt about this practice. Sita, one of my young informants, was a college graduate with a degree in political science. She had been waiting for over a year while her parents were arranging a match for her. I found it difficult to accept the docile manner in which this well-educated young woman awaited the outcome of a process that would result in her spending the rest of her life with a man she hardly knew, a virtual stranger, picked out by her parents.

"How can you go along with this?" I asked her, in frustration and distress. "Don't you care who you marry?"   5

"Of course I care," she answered. "This is why I must let   6
my parents choose a boy for me. My marriage is too important to be arranged by such an inexperienced person as myself. In such matters, it is better to have my parents' guidance."

I had learned that young men and women in India do not   7
date and have very little social life involving members of the opposite sex. Although I could not disagree with Sita's reasoning, I continued to pursue the subject.

"But how can you marry the first man you have ever met?   8
Not only have you missed the fun of meeting a lot of different people, but you have not given yourself the chance to know who is the right man for you."

"Meeting with a lot of different people doesn't sound like   9
any fun at all," Sita answered. "One hears that in America the girls are spending all their time worrying about whether they will meet a man and get married. Here we have the chance to enjoy our life and let our parents do this work and worrying for us."

She had me there. The high anxiety of the competition to   10
"be popular" with the opposite sex certainly was the most prominent feature of life as an American teenager in the late fifties. The endless worrying about the rules that governed our behavior and about our popularity ratings sapped both our self-esteem and our enjoyment of adolescence. I reflected that absence of this competition in India most certainly may have contributed to the self-confidence and natural charm of so many of the young women I met.

And yet, the idea of marrying a perfect stranger, whom   11
one did not know and did not "love," so offended my American ideas of individualism and romanticism, that I persisted with my objections.

"I still can't imagine it," I said. "How can you agree to   12
marry a man you hardly know?"

"But of course he will be known. My parents would never   13
arrange a marriage for me without knowing all about the
boy's family background. Naturally we will not rely only on
what the family tells us. We will check the particulars out ourselves. No one will want their daughter to marry into a family
that is not good. All these things we will know beforehand."

Impatiently, I responded, "Sita, I don't mean know the   14
family, I mean, know the man. How can you marry someone
you don't know personally and don't love? How can you think
of spending your life with someone you may not even like?"

"If he is a good man, why should I not like him?" she said.   15
"With you people, you know the boy so well before you
marry, where will be the fun to get married? There will be no
mystery and no romance. Here we have the whole of our
married life to get to know and love our husband. This way is
better, is it not?"

Her response made further sense, and I began to have sec-   16
ond thoughts on the matter. Indeed, during months of meeting many intelligent young Indian people, both male and
female, who had the same ideas as Sita, I saw arranged marriages in a different light. I also saw the importance of the
family in Indian life and realized that a couple who took their
marriage into their own hands was taking a big risk, particularly if their families were irreconcilably opposed to the
match. In a country where every important resource in life—
a job, a house, a social circle—is gained through family connections, it seemed foolhardy to cut oneself off from a supportive social network and depend solely on one person for
happiness and success.

Six years later I returned to India to again do fieldwork, this   17
time among the middle class in Bombay, a modern, sophisticated city. From the experience of my earlier visit, I decided
to include a study of arranged marriages in my project. By
this time I had met many Indian couples whose marriages
had been arranged and who seemed very happy. Particularly

in contrast to the fate of many of my married friends in the United States who were already in the process of divorce, the positive aspects of arranged marriages appeared to me to outweigh the negatives. In fact, I thought I might even participate in arranging a marriage myself. I had been fairly successful in the United States in "fixing up" many of my friends, and I was confident that my matchmaking skills could be easily applied to this new situation, once I learned the basic rules. "After all," I thought, "how complicated can it be? People want pretty much the same things in a marriage whether it is in India or America."

An opportunity presented itself almost immediately. A 18
friend from my previous Indian trip was in the process of arranging for the marriage of her eldest son. In India there is a perceived shortage of "good boys," and since my friend's family was eminently respectable and the boy himself personable, well educated, and nice looking, I was sure that by the end of my year's fieldwork, we would have found a match.

The basic rule seems to be that a family's reputation is 19
most important. It is understood that matches would be arranged only within the same caste and general social class, although some crossing of subcastes is permissible if the class positions of the bride's and groom's families are similar. Although dowry is now prohibited by law in India, extensive gift exchanges took place with every marriage. Even when the boy's family do not "make demands," every girl's family nevertheless feels the obligation to give the traditional gifts, to the girl, to the boy, and to the boy's family. Particularly when the couple would be living in the joint family—that is, with the boy's parents and his married brothers and their families, as well as with unmarried siblings—which is still very common even among the urban, upper-middle class in India, the girl's parents are anxious to establish smooth relations between their family and that of the boy. Offering the proper gifts, even when not called "dowry," is often an important factor in influencing the relationship between the bride's and groom's families and perhaps, also, the treatment of the bride in her new home.

In a society where divorce is still a scandal and where, in   20
fact, the divorce rate is exceedingly low, an arranged marriage
is the beginning of a lifetime relationship not just between
the bride and groom but between their families as well. Thus,
while a girl's looks are important, her character is even more
so, for she is being judged as a prospective daughter-in-law as
much as a prospective bride. Where she would be living in a
joint family, as was the case with my friend, the girl's ability
to get along harmoniously in a family is perhaps the single
most important quality in assessing her suitability.

My friend is a highly esteemed wife, mother, and daughter-   21
in-law. She is religious, soft-spoken, modest, and deferential.
She rarely gossips and never quarrels, two qualities highly de-
sirable in a woman. A family that has the reputation for gossip and conflict among its womenfolk will not find it easy to
get good wives for their sons. Parents will not want to send
their daughter to a house in which there is conflict.

My friend's family were originally from North India. They   22
had lived in Bombay, where her husband owned a business,
for forty years. The family had delayed in seeking a match for
their eldest son because he had been an Air Force pilot for
several years, stationed in such remote places that it had
seemed fruitless to try to find a girl who would be willing to
accompany him. In their social class, a military career, despite
its economic security, has little prestige and is considered
a drawback in finding a suitable bride. Many families
would not allow their daughters to marry a man in an occu-
pation so potentially dangerous and which requires so much
moving around.

The son had recently left the military and joined his fa-   23
ther's business. Since he was a college graduate, modern, and
well traveled, from such a good family, and, I thought, quite
handsome, it seemed to me that he, or rather his family, was
in a position to pick and choose. I said as much to my friend.

While she agreed that there were many advantages on   24
their side, she also said, "We must keep in mind that my son
is both short and dark; these are drawbacks in finding
the right match." While the boy's height had not escaped my

notice, "dark" seemed to me inaccurate; I would have called him "wheat" colored perhaps, and in any case, I did not realize that color would be a consideration. I discovered, however, that while a boy's skin color is a less important consideration than a girl's, it is still a factor.

An important source of contacts in trying to arrange her 25 son's marriage was my friend's social club in Bombay. Many of the women had daughters of the right age, and some had already expressed an interest in my friend's son. I was most enthusiastic about the possibilities of one particular family who had five daughters, all of whom were pretty, demure, and well educated. Their mother had told my friend, "You can have your pick for your son, whichever one of my daughters appeals to you most."

I saw a match in sight. "Surely," I said to my friend, "we 26 will find one there. Let's go visit and make our choice." But my friend held back; she did not seem to share my enthusiasm, for reasons I could not then fathom.

When I kept pressing for an explanation of her reluctance, 27 she admitted, "See, Serena, here is the problem. The family has so many daughters, how will they be able to provide nicely for any of them? We are not making any demands, but still, with so many daughters to marry off, one wonders whether she will even be able to make a proper wedding. Since this is our eldest son, it's best if we marry him to a girl who is the only daughter, then the wedding will truly be a gala affair." I argued that surely the quality of the girls themselves made up for any deficiency in the elaborateness of the wedding. My friend admitted this point but still seemed reluctant to proceed.

"Is there something else," I asked her, "some factor I have 28 missed?" "Well," she finally said, "there is one other thing. They have one daughter already married and living in Bombay. The mother is always complaining to me that the girl's in-laws don't let her visit her own family often enough. So it makes me wonder, will she be that kind of mother who always wants her daughter at her own home? This will prevent the girl from adjusting to our house. It is not a good thing." And so, this family of five daughters was dropped as a possibility.

Somewhat disappointed, I nevertheless respected my   29
friend's reasoning and geared up for the next prospect. This
was also the daughter of a woman in my friend's social club.
There was clear interest in this family and I could see why.
The family's reputation was excellent; in fact, they came from
a subcaste slightly higher than my friend's own. The girl, who
was an only daughter, was pretty and well educated and had
a brother studying in the United States. Yet, after expressing
an interest to me in this family, all talk of them suddenly died
down and the search began elsewhere.

"What happened to that girl as a prospect?" I asked one   30
day. "You never mention her any more. She is so pretty and
so educated, what did you find wrong?"

"She is too educated. We've decided against it. My hus-   31
band's father saw the girl on the bus the other day and
thought her forward. A girl who 'roams about' the city by
herself is not the girl for our family." My disappointment this
time was even greater, as I thought the son would have liked
the girl very much. But then I thought, my friend is right, a
girl who is going to live in a joint family cannot be too independent or she will make life miserable for everyone. I also
learned that if the family of the girl has even a slightly higher
social status than the family of the boy, the bride may think
herself too good for them, and this too will cause problems.
Later my friend admitted to me that this had been an important factor in her decision not to pursue the match.

The next candidate was the daughter of a client of my   32
friend's husband. When the client learned that the family was
looking for a match for their son, he said, "Look no further,
we have a daughter." This man then invited my friends to
dinner to see the girl. He had already seen their son at the office and decided that "he liked the boy." We all went together
for tea, rather than dinner—it was less of a commitment—
and while we were there, the girl's mother showed us around
the house. The girl was studying for her exams and was
briefly introduced to us.

After we left, I was anxious to hear my friend's opinion.   33
While her husband liked the family very much and was

impressed with his client's business accomplishments and reputation, the wife didn't like the girl's looks. "She is short, no doubt, which is an important plus point, but she is also fat and wears glasses." My friend obviously thought she could do better for her son and asked her husband to make his excuses to his client by saying that they had decided to postpone the boy's marriage indefinitely.

By this time almost six months had passed and I was becoming impatient. What I had thought would be an easy matter to arrange was turning out to be quite complicated. I began to believe that between my friend's desire for a girl who was modest enough to fit into her joint family, yet attractive and educated enough to be an acceptable partner for her son, she would not find anyone suitable. My friend laughed at my impatience: "Don't be so much in a hurry," she said. "You Americans want everything done so quickly. You get married quickly and then just as quickly get divorced. Here we take marriage more seriously. We must take all the factors into account. It is not enough for us to learn by our mistakes. This is too serious a business. If a mistake is made we have not only ruined the life of our son or daughter, but we have spoiled the reputation of our family as well. And that will make it much harder for their brothers and sisters to get married. So we must be very careful."

What she said was true and I promised myself to be more patient, though it was not easy. I had really hoped and expected that the match would be made before my year in India was up. But it was not to be. When I left India my friend seemed no further along in finding a suitable match for her son than when I had arrived.

Two years later, I returned to India and still my friend had not found a girl for her son. By this time, he was close to thirty, and I think she was a little worried. Since she knew I had friends all over India, and I was going to be there for a year, she asked me to "help her in this work" and keep an eye out for someone suitable. I was flattered that my judgment was respected, but knowing now how complicated the process was, I had lost my earlier confidence as a matchmaker. Nevertheless, I promised that I would try.

It was almost at the end of my year's stay in India that I met   37
a family with a marriageable daughter whom I felt might be a
good possibility for my friend's son. The girl's father was related to a good friend of mine and by coincidence came from
the same village as my friend's husband. This new family had
a successful business in a medium-sized city in central India
and were from the same subcaste as my friend. The daughter
was pretty and chic; in fact, she had studied fashion design in
college. Her parents would not allow her to go off by herself
to any of the major cities in India where she could make a
career, but they had compromised with her wish to work by
allowing her to run a small dressmaking boutique from their
home. In spite of her desire to have a career, the daughter was
both modest and home-loving and had had a traditional,
sheltered upbringing. She had only one other sister, already
married, and a brother who was in his father's business.

I mentioned the possibility of a match with my friend's   38
son. The girl's parents were most interested. Although their
daughter was not eager to marry just yet, the idea of living in
Bombay—a sophisticated, extremely fashion-conscious city
where she could continue her education in clothing design—
was a great inducement. I gave the girl's father my friend's
address and suggested that when they went to Bombay on
some business or whatever, they look up the boy's family.

Returning to Bombay on my way to New York, I told my   39
friend of this newly discovered possibility. She seemed to feel
there was potential but, in spite of my urging, would not
make any moves herself. She rather preferred to wait for the
girl's family to call upon them. I hoped something would
come of this introduction, though by now I had learned to
rein in my optimism.

A year later I received a letter from my friend. The family   40
had indeed come to visit Bombay, and their daughter and my
friend's daughter, who were near in age, had become very
good friends. During that year, the two girls had frequently
visited each other. I thought things looked promising.

Last week I received an invitation to a wedding: My   41
friend's son and the girl were getting married. Since I had

found the match, my presence was particularly requested at the wedding. I was thrilled. Success at last! As I prepared to leave for India, I began thinking, "Now, my friend's younger son, who do I know who has a nice girl for him . . . ?"

FURTHER REFLECTIONS ON ARRANGED MARRIAGE

The previous essay was written from the point of view of a family seeking a daughter-in-law. Arranged marriage looks somewhat different from the point of view of the bride and her family. Arranged marriage continues to be preferred, even among the more educated, Westernized sections of the Indian population. Many young women from these families still go along, more or less willingly, with the practice, and also with the specific choices of their families. Young women do get excited about the prospects of their marriage, but there is also ambivalence and increasing uncertainty, as the bride contemplates leaving the comfort and familiarity of her own home, where as a "temporary guest" she has often been indulged, to live among strangers. Even in the best situation, she will now come under the close scrutiny of her husband's family. How she dresses, how she behaves, how she gets along with others, where she goes, how she spends her time, her domestic abilities—all of this and much more—will be observed and commented on by a whole new set of relations. Her interaction with her family of birth will be monitored and curtailed considerably. Not only will she leave their home, but with increasing geographic mobility, she may also live very far from them, perhaps even on another continent. Too much expression of her fondness for her own family, or her desire to visit them, may be interpreted as an inability to adjust to her new family, and may become a source of conflict. In an arranged marriage, the burden of adjustment is clearly heavier for a woman than for a man. And that is in the best of situations.

In less happy circumstances, the bride may be a target of resentment and hostility from her husband's family, particularly her mother-in-law or her husband's unmarried sisters, for whom she is now a source of competition for the affection, loyalty, and economic resources of a son or brother. If she is psychologically or even physically abused, her options are limited, as returning to her parents' home or getting a divorce is still very stigmatized. For most Indians, marriage and motherhood are still considered the only suitable roles for a woman, even for those who have careers, and few women can comfortably contemplate remaining unmarried. Most families still consider "marrying off" their daughters as a compelling religious duty and social necessity. This increases a bride's sense of obligation to make the marriage a success, at whatever cost to her own personal happiness.

The vulnerability of a new bride may also be intensified by the issue of dowry that, although illegal, has become a more pressing issue in the consumer-conscious society of contemporary urban India. In many cases, where a groom's family is not satisfied with the amount of dowry a bride brings to her marriage, the young bride will be harassed constantly to get her parents to give more. In extreme cases, the bride may even be murdered and the murder disguised as an accident or a suicide. This also offers the husband's family an opportunity to arrange another match for him, thus bringing in another dowry. This phenomenon, called "dowry death," calls attention not just to the "evils of dowry" but also to larger issues of the powerlessness of women as well.

For Study and Discussion

QUESTIONS FOR RESPONSE

1. Have you ever been fixed up on a blind date? How did you feel about spending an evening with someone you didn't know? How did it work out?
2. Have you ever tried to fix people up? Why were you so sure that they would make a good match? How did it work out?

QUESTIONS ABOUT PURPOSE

1. How does Nanda's conversation with Sita help illustrate her thesis that in India marriage is a family, not an individual, decision?
2. How does Sita's criticism of American marriages help Nanda clarify her purpose?

QUESTIONS ABOUT AUDIENCE

1. In what ways does Nanda address her essay to American rather than Indian readers?
2. How does Nanda serve as a substitute for her readers? For example, how does she, and thus her readers, learn about the criteria for a good marriage?

QUESTIONS ABOUT STRATEGIES

1. How does Nanda use the example of the family with five daughters to illustrate the importance of social caste and financial status in Indian marriages?
2. How does Nanda use the example of the well-educated girl to illustrate the importance of finding a good daughter-in-law—as opposed to finding a good wife?

QUESTIONS FOR DISCUSSION

1. What arguments would you use to defend "love matches" as opposed to "arranged marriages"? Compare Anne Roiphe's observation on these issues (pages 196–197).
2. How do issues such as "dowry death" enable Nanda to present the arranged marriage from the point of view of the bride and her family?

ELIZABETH WINTHROP

Elizabeth Winthrop was born in 1948 in Washington, D.C., and educated at Sarah Lawrence College. She worked for Harper and Row editing Harper Junior Books before she began her own career as author of books for children. She has written more than thirty such books, including *Bunk Beds* (1972), *Potbellied Possums* (1977), *In My Mother's House* (1988), *The Battle for the Castle* (1993), and *As the Crow Flies* (1998). Winthrop has twice won the PEN Syndicated Fiction Contest, once in 1985 with her story "Bad News" and again in 1990 with "The Golden Darters." In the latter story, reprinted from *American Short Fiction,* a young girl betrays her father by using their creation for the wrong purpose.

The Golden Darters

I WAS TWELVE years old when my father started tying flies. It was an odd habit for a man who had just undergone a serious operation on his upper back, but, as he remarked to my mother one night, at least it gave him a world over which he had some control.

The family grew used to seeing him hunched down close to his tying vise, hackle pliers in one hand, thread bobbin in the other. We began to bandy about strange phrases—foxy quills, bodkins, peacock hurl. Father's corner of the living room was off limits to the maid with the voracious and destructive vacuum cleaner. Who knew what precious bit of calf's tail or rabbit fur would be sucked away never to be seen again?

Because of my father's illness, we had gone up to our summer cottage on the lake in New Hampshire a month early.

None of my gang of friends ever came till the end of July, so in the beginning of that summer I hung around home watching my father as he fussed with the flies. I was the only child he allowed to stand near him while he worked. "Your brothers bounce," he muttered one day as he clamped the vise onto the curve of a model-perfect hook. "You can stay and watch if you don't bounce."

So I took great care not to bounce or lean or even breathe   4
too noisily on him while he performed his delicate maneuvers, holding back hackle with one hand as he pulled off the final flourish of a whip finish with the other. I had never been so close to my father for so long before, and while he studied his tiny creations, I studied him. I stared at the large pores of his skin, the sleek black hair brushed straight back from the soft dip of his temples, the jaw muscles tightening and slackening. Something in my father seemed always to be ticking. He did not take well to sickness and enforced confinement.

When he leaned over his work, his shirt collar slipped   5
down to reveal the recent scar, a jagged trail of disrupted tissue. The tender pink skin gradually paled and then toughened during those weeks when he took his prescribed afternoon nap, lying on his stomach on our little patch of front lawn. Our house was one of the closest to the lake and it seemed to embarrass my mother to have him stretch himself out on the grass for all the swimmers and boaters to see.

"At least sleep on the porch," she would say. "That's why   6
we set the hammock up there."

"Why shouldn't a man sleep on his own front lawn if he so   7
chooses?" he would reply. "I have to mow the bloody thing. I might as well put it to some use."

And my mother would shrug and give up.   8

At the table when he was absorbed, he lost all sense of any-   9
thing but the magnified insect under the light. Often when he pushed his chair back and announced the completion of his latest project to the family, there would be a bit of down or a tuft of dubbing stuck to the edge of his lip. I did not tell him about it but stared, fascinated, wondering how long it would take to blow away. Sometimes it never did, and I

imagine he discovered the fluff in the bathroom mirror when he went upstairs to bed. Or maybe my mother plucked it off with one of those proprietary gestures of hers that irritated my brothers so much.

In the beginning, Father wasn't very good at the fly-tying. 10
He was a large, thick-boned man with sweeping gestures, a robust laugh, and a sudden terrifying temper. If he had not loved fishing so much, I doubt he would have persevered with the fussy business of the flies. After all, the job required tools normally associated with woman's work. Thread and bobbins, soft slippery feathers, a magnifying glass, and an instruction manual that read like a cookbook. It said things like, "Cut off a bunch of yellowtail. Hold the tip end with the left hand and stroke out the short hairs."

But Father must have had a goal in mind. You tie flies be- 11
cause one day, in the not-too-distant future, you will attach them to a tippet, wade into a stream, and lure a rainbow trout out of his quiet pool.

There was something endearing, almost childish, about his 12
stubborn nightly ritual at the corner table. His head bent under the standing lamp, his fingers trembling slightly, he would whisper encouragement to himself, talk his way through some particularly delicate operation. Once or twice I caught my mother gazing silently across my brothers' heads at him. When our eyes met, she would turn away and busy herself in the kitchen.

Finally, one night, after weeks of allowing me to watch, he 13
told me to take his seat. "Why, Father?"

"Because it's time for you to try one." 14

"That's all right. I like to watch." 15

"Nonsense, Emily. You'll do just fine." 16

He had stood up. The chair was waiting. Across the room, 17
my mother put down her knitting. Even the boys, embroiled in a noisy game of double solitaire, stopped their wrangling for a moment. They were all waiting to see what I would do. It was my fear of failing him that made me hesitate. I knew that my father put his trust in results, not in the learning process.

"Sit down, Emily." 18

I obeyed, my heart pounding. I was a cautious, secretive   19
child, and I could not bear to have people watch me doing
things. My piano lesson was the hardest hour in the week.
The teacher would sit with a resigned look on her face while
my fingers groped across the keys, muddling through a
sonata that I had played perfectly just an hour before. The
difference was that then nobody had been watching.

"—so we'll start you off with a big hook." He had been   20
talking for some time. How much had I missed already?

"Ready?" he asked.   21

I nodded.   22

"All right then, clamp this hook into the vise. You'll be   23
making the golden darter, a streamer. A big flashy fly, the
kind that imitates a small fish as it moves underwater."

Across the room, my brothers had returned to their game,   24
but their voices were subdued. I imagined they wanted to hear
what was happening to me. My mother had left the room.

"Tilt the magnifying glass so you have a good view of the   25
hook. Right. Now tie on with the bobbin thread."

It took me three tries to line the thread up properly on the   26
hook, each silken line nesting next to its neighbor. "We're
going to do it right, Emily, no matter how long it takes."

"It's hard," I said quietly.   27

Slowly I grew used to the tiny tools, to the oddly enlarged   28
view of my fingers through the magnifying glass. They
looked as if they didn't belong to me anymore. The feeling in
their tips was too small for their large, clumsy movements.
Despite my father's repeated warnings, I nicked the floss
once against the barbed hook. Luckily it did not give way.

"It's Emily's bedtime," my mother called from the kitchen.   29

"Hush, she's tying in the throat. Don't bother us now."   30

I could feel his breath on my neck. The mallard barbules   31
were stubborn, curling into the hook in the wrong direction.
Behind me, I sensed my father's fingers twisting in imitation
of my own.

"You've almost got it," he whispered, his lips barely mov-   32
ing. "That's right. Keep the thread slack until you're all the
way around."

I must have tightened it too quickly. I lost control of the   33
feathers in my left hand, the clumsier one. First the gold
mylar came unwound and then the yellow floss.

"Damn it all, now look what you've done," he roared, and   34
for a second I wondered whether he was talking to me. He
sounded as if he were talking to a grown-up. He sounded the
way he had just the night before when an antique teacup had
slipped through my mother's soapy fingers and shattered
against the hard surface of the sink. I sat back slowly, resting
my aching spine against the chair for the first time since
we'd begun.

"Leave it for now, Gerald," my mother said tentatively   35
from the kitchen. Out of the corner of my eye, I could see her
sponging the kitchen counter with small, defiant sweeps of
her hand. "She can try again tomorrow."

"What happened?" called a brother. They both started across   36
the room toward us but stopped at a look from my father.

"We'll start again," he said, his voice once more under   37
control. "Best way to learn. Get back on the horse."

With a flick of his hand, he loosened the vise, removed my   38
hook, and threw it into the wastepaper basket.

"From the beginning?" I whispered.   39

"Of course," he replied. "There's no way to rescue a mess   40
like that."

My mess had taken almost an hour to create.   41

"Gerald," my mother said again. "Don't you think—"   42

"How can we possibly work with all these interruptions?"   43
he thundered. I flinched as if he had hit me. "Go on upstairs,
all of you. Emily and I will be up when we're done. Go on,
for God's sake. Stop staring at us."

At a signal from my mother, the boys backed slowly away   44
and crept up to their room. She followed them. I felt all
alone, as trapped under my father's piercing gaze as the hook
in the grip of its vise.

We started again. This time my fingers were trembling so   45
much that I ruined three badger hackle feathers, stripping off
the useless webbing at the tip. My father did not lose his
temper again. His voice dropped to an even, controlled

monotone that scared me more than his shouting. After an
hour of painstaking labor, we reached the same point with
the stubborn mallard feathers curling into the hook. Once,
twice, I repinched them under the throat, but each time they
slipped away from me. Without a word, my father stood up
and leaned over me. With his cheek pressed against my hair,
he reached both hands around and took my fingers in his. I
longed to surrender the tools to him and slide away off the
chair, but we were so close to the end. He captured the curling stem with the thread and trapped it in place with three
quick wraps.

"Take your hands away carefully," he said. "I'll do the   46
whip finish. We don't want to risk losing it now."

I did as I was told, sat motionless with his arms around   47
me, my head tilted slightly to the side so he could have the
clear view through the magnifying glass. He cemented the
head, wiped the excess glue from the eye with a waste feather,
and hung my golden darter on the tackle box handle to dry.
When at last he pulled away, I breathlessly slid my body back
against the chair. I was still conscious of the havoc my clumsy
hands or an unexpected sneeze could wreak on the table,
which was cluttered with feathers and bits of fur.

"Now, that's the fly you tied, Emily. Isn't it beautiful?"   48
I nodded. "Yes, Father."   49
"Tomorrow, we'll do another one. An olive grouse.   50
Smaller hook but much less complicated body. Look. I'll
show you in the book."

As I waited to be released from the chair, I didn't think he   51
meant it. He was just trying to apologize for having lost his
temper, I told myself, just trying to pretend that our time together had been wonderful. But the next morning when I
came down, late for breakfast, he was waiting for me with the
materials for the olive grouse already assembled. He was
ready to start in again, to take charge of my clumsy fingers
with his voice and talk them through the steps.

That first time was the worst, but I never felt comfortable   52
at the fly-tying table with Father's breath tickling the hair on
my neck. I completed the olive grouse, another golden darter

to match the first, two muddler minnows, and some others. I don't remember all the names anymore.

Once I hid upstairs, pretending to be immersed in my summer reading books, but he came looking for me. 53

"Emily," he called. "Come on down. Today we'll start the lead-winged coachman. I've got everything set up for you." 54

I lay very still and did not answer. 55

"Gerald," I heard my mother say. "Leave the child alone. You're driving her crazy with those flies." 56

"Nonsense," he said, and started up the dark, wooden stairs, one heavy step at a time. 57

I put my book down and rolled slowly off the bed so that by the time he reached the door of my room, I was on my feet, ready to be led back downstairs to the table. 58

Although we never spoke about it, my mother became oddly insistent that I join her on trips to the library or the general store. 59

"Are you going out again, Emily?" my father would call after me. "I was hoping we'd get some work done on this minnow." 60

"I'll be back soon, Father," I'd say. "I promise." 61

"Be sure you do," he said. 62

And for a while I did. 63

Then at the end of July, my old crowd of friends from across the lake began to gather and I slipped away to join them early in the morning before my father got up. 64

The girls were a gang. When we were all younger, we'd held bicycle relay races on the ring road and played down at the lakeside together under the watchful eyes of our mothers. Every July, we threw ourselves joyfully back into each other's lives. That summer we talked about boys and smoked illicit cigarettes in Randy Kidd's basement and held leg-shaving parties in her bedroom behind a safely locked door. Randy was the ringleader. She was the one who suggested we pierce our ears. 65

"My parents would die," I said. "They told me I'm not allowed to pierce my ears until I'm seventeen." 66

"Your hair's so long, they won't even notice," Randy said. "My sister will do it for us. She pierces all her friends' ears at college." 67

In the end, only one girl pulled out. The rest of us sat in a   68
row with the obligatory ice cubes held to our ears, waiting
for the painful stab of the sterilized needle.

Randy was right. At first my parents didn't notice. Even   69
when my ears became infected, I didn't tell them. All alone in
my room, I went through the painful procedure of twisting
the gold studs and swabbing the recent wounds with alcohol.
Then on the night of the club dance, when I had changed my
clothes three times and played with my hair in front of the
mirror for hours, I came across the small plastic box with di-
viders in my top bureau drawer. My father had given it to me
so that I could keep my flies in separate compartments, un-
tangled from one another. I poked my finger in and slid one
of the golden darters up along its plastic wall. When I held it
up, the mylar thread sparkled in the light like a jewel. I took
out the other darter, hammered down the barbs of the two
hooks, and slipped them into the raw holes in my earlobes.

Someone's mother drove us all to the dance, and Randy   70
and I pushed through the side door into the ladies' room. I
put my hair up in a ponytail so the feathered flies could twist
and dangle above my shoulders. I liked the way they made
me look—free and different and dangerous, even. And they
made Randy notice.

"I've never seen earrings like that," Randy said. "Where   71
did you get them?"

"I made them with my father. They're flies. You know, for   72
fishing."

"They're great. Can you make me some?"   73

I hesitated. "I have some others at home I can give you,"   74
I said at last. "They're in a box in my bureau."

"Can you give them to me tomorrow?" she asked.   75

"Sure," I said with a smile. Randy had never noticed any-   76
thing I'd worn before. I went out to the dance floor, swinging my ponytail in time to the music.

My mother noticed the earrings as soon as I got home.   77

"What has gotten into you, Emily? You know you were   78
forbidden to pierce your ears until you were in college. This
is appalling."

I didn't answer. My father was sitting in his chair behind 79
the fly-tying table. His back was better by that time, but he
still spent most of his waking hours in that chair. It was as if
he didn't like to be too far away from his flies, as if something
might blow away if he weren't keeping watch.

I saw him look up when my mother started in with me. 80
His hands drifted ever so slowly down to the surface of the
table as I came across the room toward him. I leaned over so
that he could see my earrings better in the light.

"Everybody loved them, Father. Randy says she wants a 81
pair, too. I'm going to give her the muddler minnows."

"I can't believe you did this, Emily," my mother said in a 82
loud, nervous voice. "It makes you look so cheap."

"They don't make me look cheap, do they, Father?" I 83
swung my head so he could see how they bounced, and my
hip accidentally brushed the table. A bit of rabbit fur floated
up from its pile and hung in the air for a moment before it
settled down on top of the foxy quills.

"For God's sake, Gerald, speak to her," my mother said 84
from her corner.

He stared at me for a long moment as if he didn't know 85
who I was anymore, as if I were a trusted associate who had
committed some treacherous and unspeakable act. "That is
not the purpose for which the flies were intended," he said.

"Oh, I know that," I said quickly. "But they look good 86
this way, don't they?"

He stood up and considered me in silence for a long time 87
across the top of the table lamp.

"No, they don't," he finally said. "They're hanging upside 88
down."

Then he turned off the light and I couldn't see his face 89
anymore.

COMMENT ON "THE GOLDEN DARTERS"

"The Golden Darters" questions the purpose of learning a
particular process. Emily's father decides to tie fishing flies to
help him recuperate from back surgery. Although he is

clumsy at first, he masters the tools, the procedure, and the artistry of tying. He has a goal in mind—to "attach [the flies] to a tippet, wade into a stream, and lure a rainbow trout out of his quiet pool." Emily's father decides to teach her what he has learned, even though his presence makes her nervous and her mistakes complicate the work process. Emily eventually escapes his obsession and joins her girlfriends to learn other procedures—smoking, leg-shaving, ear-piercing. The last procedure enables Emily to experiment—to wear two yellow darters as earrings to the club dance. Although she dazzles her friends, she disappoints her father, who sees her experiment as a betrayal.

Process Analysis as a Writing Strategy

1. Write an essay for readers of a popular magazine in which you give directions on how to complete a mechanical or artistic project. Like Julia Alvarez, anticipate the resistance of those readers who are certain before they start that they can't do it.

2. Provide information for the members of your writing class on the steps you followed to complete an educational project, such as writing a research paper. Like Nikki Giovanni, you may want to explain these steps to a particular group of students.

3. Analyze the process for using your favorite tool. There are, of course, standard methods for using every tool, but because this tool is your favorite you should—like Ann Zwinger—supply "insider's" instructions that have made the tool work effectively for you.

4. Analyze the various steps in a political process (casting a vote), an economic process (purchasing stock), or a social process (getting married). Assume that your audience watches a lot of television. Explain how the process you are analyzing (such as finding a spouse) differs from the process they see represented on the tube.

5. Analyze a process that tests the ability to reach consensus and capture others. Like P. J. O'Rourke, you may want to describe the common courtesy required if drivers are going to avoid accidents. Or you may want to analyze the process illustrated in children's play, athletic contests, or human mating games.

6. Analyze a process that confuses or intimidates people, particularly when other people are watching. Elizabeth Winthrop's short story "The Golden Darters" is obviously a good source for this assignment. Your job is to describe the intricate steps of the physical tasks and to speculate on why the presence of the observer (a teacher, a relative, a friend) makes the task so difficult.

COMPARISON AND CONTRAST

Technically speaking, when you **compare** two or more things, you're looking for similarities; when you **contrast** them, you're looking for differences. In practice, of course, the operations are opposite sides of the same coin, and one implies the other. When you look for what's similar, you will also notice what is different. You can compare things at all levels, from the trivial (plaid shoelaces and plain ones) to the really serious (the differences between a career in medicine and one in advertising). Often when you compare things at a serious level, you do so to make a choice. That's why it's helpful to know how to organize your thinking so that you can analyze similarities and differences in a systematic, useful way that brings out significant differences. It's particularly helpful to have such a system when you are going to write a comparison-and-contrast essay.

PURPOSE

You can take two approaches to writing comparison-and-contrast essays; each has a different purpose. You can make a *strict* comparison, exploring the relationship between things in the same class, or you can do a *fanciful* comparison, looking at the relationship among things from different classes.

When you write a *strict* comparison, you compare only things that are truly alike—actors with actors, musicians with musicians, but *not* actors with musicians. You're trying to find similar information about both your subjects. For instance, what are the characteristics of actors, whether they are movie or stage actors? How are jazz musicians and classical musicians alike, even if their music is quite different? In a strict comparison, you probably also want to show how two things in the same class are different in important ways. Often when you focus your comparison on differences, you do so in order to make a judgment and, finally, a choice. That's one of the main reasons people make comparisons, whether they're shopping or writing.

When you write a *fanciful* comparison, you try to set up an imaginative, illuminating comparison between two things that don't seem at all alike, and you do it for a definite reason: to help explain and clarify a complex idea. For instance, the human heart is often compared to a pump—a fanciful and useful comparison that enables one to envision the heart at work. You can use similar fanciful comparisons to help your readers see new dimensions to events. For instance, you can compare the astronauts landing on the moon to Columbus discovering the New World, or you can compare the increased drug use among young people to an epidemic spreading through part of our culture.

You may find it difficult to construct an entire essay around a fanciful comparison—such attempts tax the most creative energy and can quickly break down. Probably you can use this method of comparison most effectively as a device for enlivening your writing and highlighting dramatic similarities. When you're drawing fanciful comparisons, you're not very likely to be comparing to make judgments or recommend choices. Instead, your purpose in writing a fanciful comparison is to catch your readers' attention and show new connections between unlike things.

AUDIENCE

As you plan a comparison-and-contrast essay, think ahead about what your readers already know and what they're going to expect. First, ask yourself what they know about the items or ideas you're going to compare. Do they know a good deal about both—for instance, two popular television programs? Do they know very little about either item—for instance, Buddhism and Shintoism? Or do they know quite a bit about one but little about the other—for instance, football and rugby?

If you're confident that your readers know a lot about both items (the television programs), you can spend a little time pointing out similarities and concentrate on your reasons for making the comparison. When readers know little about either (Eastern religions), you'll have to define each, using concepts they are familiar with, before you can point out important contrasts. If readers know only one item in a pair (football and rugby), then use the known to explain the unknown. Emphasize what is familiar to them about football, and explain how rugby is like it but also how it is different.

As you think about what your readers need, remember that they want your essay to be fairly balanced, not 90 percent about Buddhism and 10 percent about Shintoism, or two paragraphs about football and nine or ten about rugby. When your focus seems so unevenly divided, you appear to be using one element in the comparison only as a springboard to talk about the other. Such an imbalance can disappoint your readers, who expect to learn about both.

STRATEGIES

You can use two basic strategies for organizing a comparison-and-contrast essay. The first is the *divided* or *subject-by-subject* pattern. The second is the *alternating* or *point-by-point* pattern.

When you use the *divided* pattern, you present all your information on one topic before you bring in information on the other topic. Mark Twain uses this method in "Two Views of the River." First he gives an apprentice's poetic view, emphasizing the beauty of the river; then he gives the pilot's practical view, emphasizing the technical problems the river poses.

When you use the *alternating* pattern, you work your way through the comparison point by point, giving information first on one aspect of the topic, then on the other. If Mark Twain had used an alternating pattern, he would have given the apprentice's poetic view of a particular feature of the river, then the pilot's pragmatic view of that same feature. He would have followed that pattern throughout, commenting on each feature—the wind, the surface of the river, the sunset, the color of the water—by alternating between the apprentice's and the pilot's points of view.

Although both methods are useful, you'll find that each has benefits and drawbacks. The divided pattern lets you present each part of your essay as a satisfying whole. It works especially well in short essays, such as Twain's, where you're presenting only two facets of a topic and your reader can easily keep track of the points you want to make. Its drawback is that sometimes you slip into writing what seems like two separate essays. When you're writing a long comparison essay about a complex topic, you may have trouble organizing your material clearly enough to keep your readers on track.

The alternating pattern works well when you want to show the two subjects you're comparing side by side, emphasizing the points you're comparing. You'll find it particularly good for longer essays, such as Laura Bohannan's "Shakespeare in the Bush," when you want to show many complex points of comparison and need to help your readers see how those points match up. The drawback of the alternating pattern is that you may reduce your analysis to an exercise. If you use it for making only a few points of comparison in a short essay on a simple topic, your essay sounds choppy and disconnected, like a simple list.

Often you can make the best of both worlds by *combining strategies*. For example, you can start out using a divided pattern to give an overall, unified view of the topics you're going to compare. Then you can shift to an alternating pattern to show how many points of comparison you've found between your subjects. Dava Sobel uses a version of this strategy in "Imaginary Lines." She begins by establishing the difference between latitude and longitude; then she demonstrates the complex process by which longitude was established.

When you want to write a good comparison-and-contrast analysis, keep three guidelines in mind: (1) *balance parts,* (2) *include reminders,* and (3) *supply reasons.* Look, for example, at how Sarah Vowell balances the American and Canadian approaches to frontier law.

Laura Bohannan uses similar strategies when she contrasts her version of *Hamlet* with the African elders' reinterpretation of the play.

USING COMPARISON AND CONTRAST IN PARAGRAPHS

Here are two comparison-and-contrast paragraphs. The first is written by a professional writer and is followed by an analysis. The second is written by a student writer and is followed by questions.

DAVID McCULLOUGH
FDR and Truman

Uses alternating pattern | Both [FDR and Truman] were men of exceptional determination, with great reserves of personal courage and cheerfulness. They were alike too in their enjoyment of people. (The human race, Truman once told a reporter, was an "excellent outfit.") Each had an active sense of | Establishes point of comparison humor and was inclined to be dubious of those who did not. <u>But Roosevelt, who loved stories, loved also to laugh at his own, while Truman was more of a listener and laughed best when somebody else told "a good one."</u> Roosevelt enjoyed flattery, Truman was made uneasy by it. Roosevelt loved the subtleties of human relations. <u>He was a master of the circuitous solution to problems, of</u> the pleasing if ambiguous answer to difficult questions. He was sensitive to nuances in a way <u>Harry Truman never was and never would be.</u> Truman, with his rural Missouri background, and partly, too, because of the limits of his education, was inclined to see things in far simpler terms, as right or wrong, wise or foolish. He dealt little in abstractions. His answers to questions, even complicated questions, were nearly always direct and assured, plainly said, and followed often by a conclusive "And that's all there is to it," an old Missouri expression, when in truth there may have been a great deal more "to it."

Sets up points of contrast

Expands on significant difference between two men (circuitous versus direct)

Comment This paragraph illustrates how the alternating pattern can be used to point out many levels of comparison between two subjects. McCullough acknowledges that President Roosevelt and President Truman shared many common virtues—determination, courage, and cheerfulness. But he also contrasts (point by point) how the two men's personal styles—love of complex subtleties (FDR) versus preference for direct simplicity (Truman)—contributed to their uniqueness.

NATHAN M. HARMS
Howard and Rush

Howard [Stern] and Rush [Limbaugh] seem like the ying and yang of talk radio. Howard is thin and shaggy and loves to bash entrenched, stodgy Republicans. Rush is fat and dapper and loves to bash traditional liberal Democrats. Howard, the defender of individual freedom, wants to sleep with every woman in America. Rush, the defender of family values, wants every American woman to stay home and take care of the kids. Although they may think the world works in different ways, Howard and Rush work in the world in the same way. They focus their shows on controversy, belittle those who disagree with them, package their "philosophies" in best-selling books, and thrive on their ability to create publicity and fame for themselves.

1. What specific points of difference does Harms see between Howard Stern and Rush Limbaugh?
2. What major personality trait does Harms suspect they share?

COMPARISON AND CONTRAST

Points to Remember

1. Decide whether you want the pattern of your comparison to focus on complete units (*divided*) or specific features (*alternating*).
2. Consider the possibility of combining the two patterns.
3. Determine which subject should be placed in the first position and why.
4. Arrange the points of your comparison in a logical, balanced, and dramatic sequence.
5. Make sure you introduce and clarify the reasons for making your comparison.

In this photograph, Don Hong-Oai recreates the look of a classical Chinese landscape scroll. The Chinese characters in the upper right provide the title "At Play, Tianzi Mountains." In what ways do the line strokes in these words resemble the lines pictured in the limbs of the trees and the gibbon monkeys "at play"? Select a particularly evocative photograph, and then explain why your picture is worth *a thousand words, or why it* takes *a thousand words (to explain).*

Mark Twain (the pen name of Samuel Clemens, 1835–1910) was born in Florida, Missouri, and grew up in the river town of Hannibal, Missouri, where he watched the comings and goings of the steamboats he would eventually pilot. Twain spent his young adult life working as a printer, a pilot on the Mississippi, and a frontier journalist. After the Civil War, he began a career as a humorist and storyteller, writing such classics as *The Adventures of Tom Sawyer* (1876), *Life on the Mississippi* (1883), *The Adventures of Huckleberry Finn* (1885), and *A Connecticut Yankee in King Arthur's Court* (1889). His place in American writing was best characterized by editor William Dean Howells, who called Twain the "Lincoln of our literature." In "Two Views of the River," taken from *Life on the Mississippi,* Twain compares the way he saw the river as an innocent apprentice to the way he saw it as an experienced pilot.

Two Views of the River

N OW WHEN I had mastered the language of this water, and had come to know every trifling feature that bordered the great river as familiarly as I knew the letters of the alphabet, I had made a valuable acquisition. But I had lost something, too. I had lost something which could never be restored to me while I lived. All the grace, the beauty, the poetry, had gone out of the majestic river! I still keep in mind a certain wonderful sunset which I witnessed when steamboating was new to me. A broad expanse of the river was turned to blood; in the middle distance the red hue brightened into gold, through which a solitary log came floating

1

black and conspicuous; in one place a long, slanting mark lay
sparkling upon the water; in another the surface was broken
by boiling, tumbling rings that were as many tinted as an
opal; where the ruddy flush was faintest, was a smooth spot
that was covered with graceful circles and radiating lines, ever
so delicately traced; the shore on our left was densely
wooded, and the somber shadow that fell from this forest was
broken in one place by a long, ruffled trail that shone like silver; and high above the forest wall a clean-stemmed dead tree
waved a single leafy bough that glowed like a flame in the

When I mastered the language of this
water . . . I had made a valuable acquisition.
But I had lost something too.

---

unobstructed splendor that was flowing from the sun. There
were graceful curves, reflected images, woody heights, soft
distances; and over the whole scene, far and near, the dissolving lights drifted steadily, enriching it every passing moment
with new marvels of coloring.

I stood like one bewitched. I drank it in, in a speechless 2
rapture. The world was new to me, and I had never seen anything like this at home. But as I have said, a day came when I
began to cease from noting the glories and the charms which
the moon and the sun and the twilight wrought upon the
river's face; another day came when I ceased altogether to
note them. Then, if that sunset scene had been repeated, I
should have looked upon it without rapture, and should have
commented upon it, inwardly, after this fashion: "This sun
means that we are going to have wind to-morrow; that floating log means that the river is rising, small thanks to it; that
slanting mark on the water refers to a bluff reef which is
going to kill somebody's steamboat one of these nights, if it
keeps on stretching out like that; those tumbling 'boils' show

a dissolving bar and a changing channel there; the lines and circles in the slick water over yonder are a warning that that troublesome place is shoaling up dangerously; that silver streak in the shadow of the forest is the 'break' from a new snag, and he has located himself in the very best place he could have found to fish for steamboats; that tall dead tree, with a single living branch, is not going to last long, and then how is a body ever going to get through this blind place at night without the friendly old landmark?"

No, the romance and beauty were all gone from the river.   3 All the value any feature of it had for me now was the amount of usefulness it could furnish toward compassing the safe piloting of a steamboat. Since those days, I have pitied doctors from my heart. What does the lovely flush in a beauty's cheek mean to a doctor but a "break" that ripples above some deadly disease? Are not all her visible charms sown thick with what are to him the signs and symbols of hidden decay? Does he ever see her beauty at all, or doesn't he simply view her professionally, and comment upon her unwholesome condition all to himself? And doesn't he sometimes wonder whether he has gained most or lost most by learning his trade?

For Study and Discussion

QUESTIONS FOR RESPONSE

1. Mark Twain is one of America's most famous historical personalities. Which of his books or stories have you read? What ideas and images from this selection do you associate with his other works?
2. Do you agree with Twain when he argues that an appreciation of beauty depends on ignorance of danger? Explain your answer.

QUESTIONS ABOUT PURPOSE

1. What does Twain think he has gained and lost by learning the river?
2. What does Twain accomplish by *dividing* the two views of the river rather than *alternating* them beneath several headings?

QUESTIONS ABOUT AUDIENCE

1. Which attitude—poetic or pragmatic—does Twain anticipate his readers have toward the river? Explain your answer.
2. How does he expect his readers to answer the questions he raises in paragraph 3?

QUESTIONS ABOUT STRATEGIES

1. What sequence does Twain use to arrange the points of his comparison?
2. Where does Twain use transitional phrases and sentences to match up the parts of his comparison?

QUESTIONS FOR DISCUSSION

1. Besides the pilot and the doctor, can you identify other professionals who lose as much as they gain by learning their trade?
2. How would people whose job is to create beauty—writers, painters, musicians, architects, gardeners—respond to Twain's assertion that knowledge of their craft destroys their ability to appreciate beauty?

SARAH VOWELL

Sarah Vowell was born in 1969, raised in rural Oklahoma, and educated at Montana State University and School of the Art Institute in Chicago. She started contributing her witty essays to the radio program *This American Life* (Public Radio International) and the Internet magazine *Salon.com*. Her experience with radio is documented in *Radio On: A Listener's Diary* (1997). Her other essays are collected in *Take the Cannoli: Stories from the New World* (2000), *The Partly Cloudy Patriot* (2002), and *Assassination Vacation* (2005). In "Cowboys v. Mounties," reprinted from *The Partly Cloudy Patriot,* Vowell compares the American and Canadian frontier experience.

Cowboys v. Mounties

C ANADA HAUNTS ME. The United States's neighbor to   1
the north first caught my fancy a few years back when I started listening to the CBC. I came for the long-form radio documentaries; I stayed for the dispatches from the Maritimes and Guelph. On the CBC, all these nice people, seemingly normal but for the hockey obsession, had a likable knack for loving their country in public without resorting to swagger or hate.

A person keen on all things French is called a Francophile.   2
One who has a thing for England is called an Anglophile. An admirer of Germany in the 1930s and '40s is called Pat Buchanan. But no word has been coined to describe Americans obsessed with Canada, not that dictionary publishers have been swamped with requests. The comedian Jon Stewart used to do a bit in which a Canadian woman asked him to come clean with what Americans *really* think of Canada. "We don't," he said.

Keeping track of Canadians is like watching a horror ₃
movie. It's *Invasion of the Body Snatchers* in slow-mo. They
look like us, but there's something slightly, eerily off. Why is
that? The question has nagged me for years. Asking why they
are the way they are begs the follow-up query about how we
ended up this way too.

There's a sad sack quality to the Canadian chronology I find ₄
entirely endearing. I once asked the CBC radio host Ian Brown
how on earth one could teach Canadian school-children their

---

*Everyone knows what the individualistic
American cowboy fetish gets us: shot.*

---

history in a way that could be remotely inspiring, and he answered, "It isn't inspiring."

Achieving its independence from Britain gradually and ₅
cordially, through polite meetings taking place in nice rooms,
Canada took a path to sovereignty that is one of the most hi-
lariously boring stories in the world. One Canadian history
textbook I have describes it thus, "British North Americans
moved through the 1850s and early sixties towards a modestly spectacular resolution of their various ambitions and
problems." Modestly spectacular. Isn't that adorable?

One day, while nonchalantly perusing the annals of ₆
Canadian history, I came across mention of the founding of
the Mounties. The Royal Canadian Mounted Police, called
the North-West Mounted Police at its inception, was created,
I read, to establish law and order on the Canadian frontier in
anticipation of settlement and the Canadian Pacific Railroad.
In 1873, Canada's first prime minister, John Macdonald, saw
what was happening in the American Wild West and organized a police force to make sure Canada steered clear of
America's bloodbath.

That's it. Or, as they might say in Quebec, voilà! That ex-   7
plains how the Canadians are different from Americans. No
cowboys for Canada. Canada got Mounties instead—Dudley
Do-Right, not John Wayne. It's a mind-set of "Here I come
to save the day" versus "Yippee-ki-yay, motherfucker." Or
maybe it's chicken and egg: The very idea that the Canadian
head of state would come to the conclusion that establishing
law and order *before* large numbers of people migrated west,
to have rules and procedures and authorities waiting for
them, is anathema to the American way.

Not only did the Mounties aim to avoid the problems we   8
had faced on our western frontier, especially the violent,
costly Indian wars, they had to clean up after our spillover
mess. In a nineteenth-century version of that drug-war movie
Traffic, evil American whiskey traders were gouging and poisoning Canadian Indian populations. Based in Fort Benton,
Montana, they sneaked across the border to peddle their
rotgut liquor, establishing illegal trading posts, including the
infamous Fort Whoop-up, in what is now Alberta. You can't
throw a dart at a map of the American West without hitting
some mass grave or battleground—Sand Creek, Little Bighorn,
Wounded Knee—but it's fitting that the most famous such
Canadian travesty, the Cypress Hills Massacre, happened
because American whiskey and fur traders were exacting
revenge on a few Indians believed to have stolen their
horses. The Americans slaughtered between one and two
hundred Assiniboine men, women, and children. Never
mind that the horse thieves had been Cree. That was 1873.
The Mounties were under formation, but they hadn't yet
marched west.

The most remarkable thing about the Mounties was their   9
mandate: one law. One law for everyone, Indian or white.
The United States makes a big to-do about all men being created equal, but we're still working out the kinks of turning
that idea into actual policy. Reporting to the force's commissioner in 1877, one Mountie wrote of Americans in his jurisdiction, "These men always look upon the Indians as their
natural enemies, and it is their rule to shoot at them if they

approach after being warned off. I was actually asked the other day by an American who has settled here, if we had the same law here as on the other side, and if he was justified in shooting any Indian who approached his camp after being warned not to in advance."

Word of the Canadians' fairness got around. Some north- 10 western tribes referred to the border between the United States and Canada as the "medicine line." Robert Higheagle, a Lakota Sioux from Sitting Bull's band, recalled, "They told us this line was considered holy. They called that a holy trail. They believe things are different when you cross from one side to another. You are altogether different. On one side you are perfectly free to do as you please. On the other you are in danger."

To Canada's dismay, the northern side of the medicine line 11 became an attractive destination for American Indians, including the most famous, most difficult one of all, Sitting Bull. On the run after Little Bighorn, Sitting Bull and entourage settled near Canada's Fort Walsh, under the command of Major James Walsh. Walsh and, as he called him, Bull became such great friends that the Canadian government had Walsh transferred to another post to separate him from Sitting Bull. Sitting Bull was an American problem and the Canadian government wanted to boot him south. Walsh even defied orders and went to Chicago to lobby on Sitting Bull's behalf, but to no avail, ensuring that Sitting Bull would die south of the medicine line.

All the Sitting Bull complications make Walsh my favorite 12 Mountie. But he's a very American choice—he bucked the system, he played favorites for a friend, he defied policy, he stuck out. (Apparently, even having a favorite Mountie is an American trait. When I asked the twentieth commissioner of Mounties, Giuliano "Zach" Zaccardelli, who was his favorite RCMP commissioner in history, he answered Canadianly, "Every one of them has contributed tremendously to the legacy of the RCMP, and I hope that during my tenure I will be able to add some value to the legacy that those nineteen who came before me left for this organization.") When Walsh heard that Sitting Bull had been fatally shot in Minnesota, he wrote, "Bull's ambition is I am afraid too great to let him settle down and be content with an uninteresting life." This strikes me as almost treasonously individualistic, with American shades of "pursuit of happiness" and "liberty or death."

Everyone knows what the individualistic American cowboy fetish gets us: shot. It all comes down to guns. The population of the United States is ten times that of Canada, but we have about thirty times more firearms. Two-thirds of our homicides are committed with firearms, compared with one-third of theirs. (Which begs the question, just what are Canadian killers using, hair dryers tossed into bathtubs?)   13

The famous (well, in Canada) historian Pierre Berton, in his surprisingly out-of-print book *Why We Act Like Canadians,* informs an American friend that it has to do with weather. Having been to Edmonton in January, I cede his point. He wrote,   14

> *Hot weather and passion, gunfights and race riots go together. Your mythic encounters seem to have taken place at high noon, the sun beating down on a dusty Arizona street. I find it difficult to contemplate a similar gunfight in Moose Jaw, in the winter, the bitter rivals struggling vainly to shed two pairs of mitts and reach under several layers of parka for weapons so cold that the slightest touch of flesh on steel would take the skin off their thumbs.*

Most of the time, I feel Canadian. I live a quiet life. I own no firearms (though, as a gunsmith's daughter, I stand to inherit a freaking arsenal). I revere the Bill of Rights, but at the same time I believe that anyone who's using three or more of them at a time is hogging them too much. I'm a newspaper-reading, French-speaking, radio-documentary-loving square. A lot of my favorite comedians, such as Martin Short, Eugene Levy, the Kids in the Hall, are Canadian. I like that self-deprecating Charlie Brown sense of humor. As Canadian-born *Saturday Night Live* producer Lorne Michaels once put it in   15 a panel discussion devoted to the question of why Canadians are so funny at the Ninety-second Street Y, a Canadian would never have made a film called *It's a Wonderful Life* because "that would be bragging." The Canadian version, he said, would have been titled "It's an All Right Life."

So I mostly walk the Canadian walk, but the thing about a 16 lot of Canadian talk is that it sounds bad. When I went to Ottawa, the "Washington of the North," to see the RCMP's Musical Ride, which is sort of like synchronized swimming on horseback, I was telling a constable in the Mounties about a new U.S. Army recruiting ad. The slogan was "an army of one." It aimed to reassure American kids that they wouldn't be nameless, faceless nobodies, that they could join the army and still do their own thing.

The Mountie was horrified. He said, "I think we have to 17 try and work as a team and work together. If you start to be an individualist, then everybody's going their own way. One person might be doing something and the other person might be doing something else and everybody wants to put their word in and thinks, I'm better than him or My idea's better than his. You need conformity. You need everybody to stick together and work as a team."

It hurt my ears when he said "you need conformity." I 18 know he's probably right, and what organization more than a military one requires lockstep uniformity so that fewer people get killed? But still. No true American would ever talk up the virtue of conformity. Intellectually, I roll my eyes at the cowboy outlaw ethic, but in my heart I know I buy into it a little, that it's a deep part of my identity. Once, when I was living in Holland, I went to the movies, and when a Marlboro Man ad came on the screen, I started bawling with homesickness. I may be the only person who cried all the way through *Don't Tell Mom the Babysitter's Dead.*

The Mounties on the Musical Ride dress in the old- 19 fashioned red serge suits and Stetson hats, like Dudley Do-Right. Seeing them on their black horses, riding in time to music, was entirely lovable, yet lacking any sort of, for lack of a better word, edge. I tried to ask some of them about it.

I say, "In the States, the Mountie is a squeaky-clean icon.   20
Does that ever bother you that the Mountie is not 'cool'?"

He stares back blankly. I ask him, "You know what I mean?"   21

"No, I don't."   22

"There's no dark side," I tell him. "The Mounties have no   23
dark side."

He laughs. "That might be one of the things that upset   24
the Americans, because we're just that much better." Then
he feels so bad about this little put-down that he repents,
backtracking about how "there's good and bad in everybody," that Americans and Canadians "just have different
views," and that "Canadians are no better than anyone else."

Another constable, overhearing, says, "Our country is far   25
younger than the United States, but at the same time, the
United States is a young country when you compare it to the
countries of Europe."

"Yeah," I answer, "but you're a very well-behaved young   26
country."

"Well"—he smiles—"that's just the way my mum raised   27
me."

For Study and Discussion

QUESTIONS FOR RESPONSE

1. How have the movies shaped your perception of "cowboys" and
"Mounties"?
2. How much do you know about the history and culture of Canada?
For example, can you name its provinces and their capitals?

QUESTIONS ABOUT PURPOSE

1. In what ways does Vowell's characterization of Canadian history
help her reinterpret American history?
2. How does Vowell reverse her friend's assertion that Canadian
history "isn't inspiring"?

QUESTIONS ABOUT AUDIENCE

1. How does Vowell anticipate her readers when she quotes an American as saying he doesn't think about Canada?
2. What does Vowell mean when she says she feels Canadian? Is she trying to connect with her Canadian readers or help her American readers understand the appeal of Canadian values?

QUESTIONS ABOUT STRATEGIES

1. How does Vowell use the "medicine line" to distinguish between American and Canadian culture?
2. How does Pierre Berton use weather to explain the difference between Americans and Canadians?

QUESTIONS FOR DISCUSSION

1. What cultural values are embedded in the U.S. Army recruiting ad? Why does the Mountie object to the ad?
2. What is the difference—according to Vowell—between being "cool" and "well-behaved"?

DAVA SOBEL

Dava Sobel was born in 1947 in New York City and was educated at the State University of New York at Binghamton. She has worked as a science reporter for the *New York Times* and the Discovery Channel On-line. She has contributed articles to magazines such as *Audubon, Discover,* the *New Yorker,* and *Vogue.* Her books include *Is Anyone Out There? The Scientific Search for Extraterrestrial Intelligence* (1992), *Longitude: The True Story of a Lone Genius Who Solved the Greatest Scientific Problem of His Time* (1995), *Galileo's Daughter: A Historical Memoir of Science* (1999), and *The Planets* (2005). In "Imaginary Lines," reprinted from *Longitude,* Sobel compares and contrasts the imaginary lines that travelers have used to navigate the world.

Imaginary Lines

When I'm playful I use the meridians of longitude and parallels of latitude for a seine, and drag the Atlantic Ocean for whales.
—MARK TWAIN, *Life on the Mississippi*

O NCE ON A Wednesday excursion when I was a little girl, my father bought me a beaded wire ball that I loved. At a touch, I could collapse the toy into a flat coil between my palms, or pop it open to make a hollow sphere. Rounded out, it resembled a tiny Earth, because its hinged wires traced the same pattern of intersecting circles that I had seen on the globe in my schoolroom—the thin black lines of latitude and longitude. The few colored beads slid along the wire paths haphazardly, like ships on the high seas. 1

My father strode up Fifth Avenue to Rockefeller Center with me on his shoulders, and we stopped to stare at the statue of Atlas, carrying Heaven and Earth on his. 2

The bronze orb that Atlas held aloft, like the wire toy in   3
my hands, was a see-through world, defined by imaginary
lines. The Equator. The Ecliptic. The Tropic of Cancer. The
Tropic of Capricorn. The Arctic Circle. The prime meridian.
Even then I could recognize, in the graph-paper grid imposed on the globe, a powerful symbol of all the real lands
and waters on the planet.

Today, the latitude and longitude lines govern with more   4
authority than I could have imagined forty-odd years ago, for
they stay fixed as the world changes its configuration under-

---

*The zero-degree parallel of latitude is fixed
by the laws of nature, while the zero-degree
meridian of longitude shifts like the
sands of time.*

---

neath them—with continents adrift across a widening sea, and
national boundaries repeatedly redrawn by war or peace.

As a child, I learned the trick for remembering the differ-   5
ence between latitude and longitude. The latitude lines, the
parallels, really do stay parallel to each other as they girdle the
globe from the Equator to the poles in a series of shrinking
concentric rings. The meridians of longitude go the other
way. They loop from the North Pole to the South and back
again in great circles of the same size, so they all converge at
the ends of the Earth.

Lines of latitude and longitude began crisscrossing our   6
worldview in ancient times, at least three centuries before the
birth of Christ. By A.D. 150, the cartographer and astronomer
Ptolemy had plotted them on the twenty-seven maps of his
first world atlas. Also for this landmark volume, Ptolemy listed
all the place names in an index, in alphabetical order, with the
latitude and longitude of each—as well as he could gauge them
from travelers' reports. Ptolemy himself had only an armchair

appreciation of the wider world. A common misconception of his day held that anyone living below the Equator would melt into deformity from the horrible heat.

The Equator marked the zero-degree parallel of latitude   7
for Ptolemy. He did not choose it arbitrarily but took it on higher authority from his predecessors, who had derived it from nature while observing the motions of the heavenly bodies. The sun, moon, and planets pass almost directly overhead at the Equator. Likewise the Tropic of Cancer and the Tropic of Capricorn, two other famous parallels, assume their positions at the sun's command. They mark the northern and southern boundaries of the sun's apparent motion over the course of the year.

Ptolemy was free, however, to lay his prime meridian, the   8
zero-degree longitude line, wherever he liked. He chose to run it through the Fortunate Islands (now called the Canary & Madeira Islands) off the northwest coast of Africa. Later mapmakers moved the prime meridian to the Azores and to the Cape Verde Islands, as well as to Rome, Copenhagen, Jerusalem, St. Petersburg, Pisa, Paris, and Philadelphia, among other places, before it settled down at last in London. As the world turns, any line drawn from pole to pole may serve as well as any other for a starting line of reference. The placement of the prime meridian is a purely political decision.

Here lies the real, hard-core difference between latitude   9
and longitude—beyond the superficial difference in line direction that any child can see: The zero-degree parallel of latitude is fixed by the laws of nature, while the zero-degree meridian of longitude shifts like the sands of time. This difference makes finding latitude child's play, and turns the determination of longitude, especially at sea, into an adult dilemma—one that stumped the wisest minds of the world for the better part of human history.

Any sailor worth his salt can gauge his latitude well   10
enough by the length of the day, or by the height of the sun or known guide stars above the horizon. Christopher Columbus followed a straight path across the Atlantic when he "sailed the parallel" on his 1492 journey, and the technique

would doubtless have carried him to the Indies had not the Americas intervened.

The measurement of longitude meridians, in comparison, is tempered by time. To learn one's longitude at sea, one needs to know what time it is aboard ship and also the time at the home port or another place of known longitude—at that very same moment. The two clock times enable the navigator to convert the hour difference into a geographical separation. Since the Earth takes twenty-four hours to complete one full revolution of three hundred sixty degrees, one hour marks one twenty-fourth of a spin, or fifteen degrees. And so each hour's time difference between the ship and the starting point marks a progress of fifteen degrees of longitude to the east or west. Every day at sea, when the navigator resets his ship's clock to local noon when the sun reaches its highest point in the sky, and then consults the home-port clock, every hour's discrepancy between them translates into another fifteen degrees of longitude.

Those same fifteen degrees of longitude also correspond to a distance traveled. At the Equator, where the girth of the Earth is greatest, fifteen degrees stretch fully one thousand miles. North or south of that line, however, the mileage value of each degree decreases. One degree of longitude equals four minutes of time the world over, but in terms of distance, one degree shrinks from sixty-eight miles at the Equator to virtually nothing at the poles.

Precise knowledge of the hour in two different places at once—a longitude prerequisite so easily accessible today from any pair of cheap wristwatches—was utterly unattainable up to and including the era of pendulum clocks. On the deck of a rolling ship, such clocks would slow down, or speed up, or stop running altogether. Normal changes in temperature encountered en route from a cold country of origin to a tropical trade zone thinned or thickened a clock's lubricating oil and made its metal parts expand or contract with equally disastrous results. A rise or fall in barometric pressure, or the subtle variations in the Earth's gravity from one latitude to another, could also cause a clock to gain or lose time.

For lack of a practical method of determining longitude,   14
every great captain in the Age of Exploration became lost at
sea despite the best available charts and compasses. From
Vasco da Gama to Vasco Núñez de Balboa, from Ferdinand
Magellan to Sir Francis Drake—they all got where they were
going willy-nilly, by forces attributed to good luck or the
grace of God.

As more and more sailing vessels set out to conquer or ex-   15
plore new territories, to wage war, or to ferry gold and com-
modities between foreign lands, the wealth of nations
floated upon the oceans. And still no ship owned a reliable
means for establishing her whereabouts. In consequence,
untold numbers of sailors died when their destinations suddenly loomed out of the sea and took them by surprise. In a
single such accident, on October 22, 1707, at the Scilly Isles
near the southwestern tip of England, four home-bound
British warships ran aground and nearly two thousand men
lost their lives.

The active quest for a solution to the problem of longitude   16
persisted over four centuries and across the whole continent
of Europe. Most crowned heads of state eventually played a
part in the longitude story, notably King George III of England and King Louis XIV of France. Seafaring men such as
Captain William Bligh of the *Bounty* and the great circum-
navigator Captain James Cook, who made three long voy-
ages of exploration and experimentation before his violent
death in Hawaii, took the more promising methods to sea to
test their accuracy and practicability.

Renowned astronomers approached the longitude chal-   17
lenge by appealing to the clockwork universe: Galileo Galilei,
Jean Dominique Cassini, Christiaan Huygens, Sir Isaac Newton, and Edmond Halley, of comet fame, all entreated the
moon and stars for help. Palatial observatories were founded
at Paris, London, and Berlin for the express purpose of determining longitude by the heavens. Meanwhile, lesser minds
devised schemes that depended on the yelps of wounded
dogs, or the cannon blasts of signal ships strategically anchored—somehow—on the open ocean.

In the course of their struggle to find longitude, scientists   18
struck upon other discoveries that changed their view of the
universe. These include the first accurate determinations of
the weight of the Earth, the distance to the stars, and the
speed of light.

As time passed and no method proved successful, the   19
search for a solution to the longitude problem assumed legendary proportions, on a par with discovering the Fountain
of Youth, the secret of perpetual motion, or the formula for
transforming lead into gold. The governments of the great
maritime nations—including Spain, the Netherlands, and
certain city-states of Italy—periodically roiled the fervor by
offering jackpot purses for a workable method. The British
Parliament, in its famed Longitude Act of 1714, set the highest bounty of all, naming a prize equal to a king's ransom
(several million dollars in today's currency) for a "Practicable
and Useful" means of determining longitude.

English clockmaker John Harrison, a mechanical genius   20
who pioneered the science of portable precision timekeeping,
devoted his life to this quest. He accomplished what Newton
had feared was impossible: He invented a clock that would
carry the true time from the home port, like an eternal flame,
to any remote corner of the world.

Harrison, a man of simple birth and high intelligence,   21
crossed swords with the leading lights of his day. He made a
special enemy of the Reverend Nevil Maskelyne, the fifth astronomer royal, who contested his claim to the coveted prize
money, and whose tactics at certain junctures can only be described as foul play.

With no formal education or apprenticeship to any watch-   22
maker, Harrison nevertheless constructed a series of virtually
friction-free clocks that required no lubrication and no cleaning, that were made from materials impervious to rust, and
that kept their moving parts perfectly balanced in relation to
one another, regardless of how the world pitched or tossed
about them. He did away with the pendulum, and he combined different metals inside his works in such a way that
when one component expanded or contracted with changes

in temperature, the other counteracted the change and kept the clock's rate constant.

His every success, however, was parried by members of the 23 scientific elite, who distrusted Harrison's magic box. The commissioners charged with awarding the longitude prize—Nevil Maskelyne among them—changed the contest rules whenever they saw fit, so as to favor the chances of astronomers over the likes of Harrison and his fellow "mechanics." But the utility and accuracy of Harrison's approach triumphed in the end. His followers shepherded Harrison's intricate, exquisite invention through the design modifications that enabled it to be mass produced and enjoy wide use.

An aged, exhausted Harrison, taken under the wing of 24 King George III, ultimately claimed his rightful monetary reward in 1773—after forty struggling years of political intrigue, international warfare, academic backbiting, scientific revolution, and economic upheaval.

All these threads, and more, entwine in the lines of longitude. To unravel them now—to retrace their story in an age 25 when a network of orbiting satellites can nail down a ship's position within a few feet in just a moment or two—is to see the globe anew.

For Study and Discussion

QUESTIONS FOR RESPONSE

1. How did you first learn about latitude and longitude?
2. What did you learn about other imaginary lines, such as the Equator, Tropic of Cancer, and Tropic of Capricorn?

QUESTIONS ABOUT PURPOSE

1. According to Sobel, what is the "hard-core" difference between latitude and longitude?
2. What is the relationship between time and longitude?

QUESTIONS ABOUT AUDIENCE

1. What assumptions does Sobel make about the historical knowledge of her readers?
2. How does she use the example of the orbiting satellite to help her readers see how much our perception of the world has changed?

QUESTIONS ABOUT STRATEGIES

1. How does Sobel use a childhood toy to introduce her comparison?
2. How does she explain the solution to the "longitude challenge"?

QUESTIONS FOR DISCUSSION

1. What are the mathematical strategies necessary to calculate longitude?
2. Why was the problem of establishing longitude considered a political as well as a scientific problem?

ANNE ROIPHE

Anne Roiphe was born in New York City in 1935 and educated at Sarah Lawrence College. Perhaps best known for the novel *Up the Sandbox!* (1970), her works explore a woman's search for identity in the wake of marriage and divorce. In some of her fiction, *The Pursuit of Happiness* (1991), and non-fiction, *Generation Without Memory: A Jewish Journey in Christian America* (1981), *A Season of Healing: Reflections on the Holocaust* (1988), *1185 Park Avenue: A Memoir* (1999), and *An Imperfect Lens* (2006), Roiphe explores the special issues confronted by Jewish women. In "A Tale of Two Divorces," reprinted from *Women on Divorce* (1995), Roiphe compares two marriages, one that should have ended in divorce and one that did.

A Tale of Two Divorces

E VERY DIVORCE IS a story, and while they can begin to   1
sound the same—sad and cautionary—each one is as
unique as a human face. My divorce is the tale of two divorces, one that never was and one that was. The first is the story of my parents' marriage.

My mother was the late fifth child, raised in a large house   2
on Riverside Drive in New York City. Her father, who came
to America as a boy from a town outside of Suvalki, Poland,
had piled shirts on a pushcart and wandered the streets of the
Lower East Side in the 1880s. His pushcart turned into a loft
with twenty women sewing shirts for him and before he was
twenty-five he owned a small company called Van Heusen
Shirts. He was one of the founding members of Beth Israel
Hospital and I have a photo of him, shovel in hand, black hat
on his head, as the foundation stone is placed in the ground.

My mother grew up, small, plump, nervous, fearful of   3
horses, dogs, cats, cars, water, balls that were hit over nets,
tunnels, and bridges. She was expected to marry brilliantly
into the world of manufacturers of coats, shoes, gowns, store
owners, prosperous bankers whose sons attended the dozens
of teas and charity events where she—always afraid her hair
was wrong, her conversation dull, her dress wrinkled—tried

In twentieth-century America we place so
much emphasis on romance that we barely
notice the other essentials of marriage that
include economics and child rearing.

---

to obey the instructions of her older sister and sparkle. A girl
after all had to sparkle. She was under five feet. She was near-
sighted. Without her thick glasses she stumbled, recognized
no one, groped the wall for comfort. Her lipstick tended to
smear. She chain-smoked. She lost things. She daydreamed.
Her father died of a sudden heart attack when she was just
thirteen. Her older sisters married millionaires, her brothers
inherited the business. She was herself considered an heiress,
a dangerous state for a tremulous girl, whose soul was perpet-
ually fogged in uncertainty.

At a Z.B.T. Columbia University fraternity party she met   4
my father. He was the Hungarian-born son of a drug salesman who bet the horses and believed that he had missed his
grander destiny. My paternal grandfather was never able to
move his family out from the railroad flat under the Third
Avenue El. His wife, my grandmother, was a statuesque
woman, taller than her husband but overwhelmed by noise,
the turmoil of her American days. She never learned English.
She stayed home in her nightgown and slippers, sleeping
long hours. My father was in law school. He was tall and
handsome with black hair slicked down like Valentino and

cold eyes set perfectly in an even face. He was an athlete who had earned his college expenses by working summers as a lifeguard in the Catskills. His shoes were perfectly polished. His white shirt gleamed. He loathed poverty. He claimed to speak no other language than English though he had arrived in America at age nine. He told my mother he loved her. Despite the warnings of her siblings, she believed him. If she was not his dream girl, she was his American dream. They went on their honeymoon to Europe and purchased fine china and linen at every stop.

My father became a lawyer for the family shirt company. He   5
was edgy, prone to yell at others; he ground his teeth. He suffered from migraines. He could tolerate nothing out of place, nothing that wasn't spotless. He joined a club where men played squash, steamed in the sauna, and drank at the bar. He stayed long hours at his club. He told his wife she was unbeautiful. She believed him although the pictures of her at the time tell a different story. They show a young woman with soft amused eyes and a long neck, with a shy smile and a brave tilt of the head. My father explained to my mother that he could never admire a short woman, that long legs were the essence of glamour.

My father began to have other ladies. He would meet   6
them under the clock at the Biltmore, at motels in Westchester. He had ice in his heart, but he looked good in his undershirt. He looked good in his monogrammed shirts. He lost his nonfamily clients. They didn't like his temper, his impatience. It didn't matter. He took up golf and was gone all day Saturday and Sunday in the good weather. He made investments in the stock market. He had a genius for bad bets. My mother made up the heavy losses. She had two children and she lived just as she was expected to do, with servants to take care of the details, to wake with the babies, to prepare the food, to mop the floors. She spent her days playing cards and shopping. She went to the hairdresser two, sometimes three times a week. A lady came to the house to wax her legs and do her long red nails. She had ulcers, anxiety attacks,

panic attacks. In the evening at about five o'clock she would begin to wait for my father to come home. She could do the crossword puzzle in five minutes. She was a genius at canasta, Oklahoma, bridge, backgammon. She joined a book club. She loved the theater and invested cleverly in Broadway shows. She took lessons in French and flower arranging.

At the dinner table, as the food was being served, my fa- 7 ther would comment that he didn't like the way my mother wore the barrette in her hair. She would say bitterly that he never liked anything she wore. He would say that she was stupid. She would say that she was not. Their voices would carry. In the kitchen the maid would clutch the side of the sink until her fingernails were white. My mother would weep. My father would storm out of the house, slamming doors, knocking over lamps. She would shout after him, "You don't love me." He would scream at her, "Who could love you?" She would lie in bed with ice cubes on her swollen eyes, chain-smoking Camel cigarettes. She would call her sister for comfort. Her sister would say, "Don't give him an argument." She would say, "I'll try to do better, I really will."

When I was seven years old, she lay in the bathtub soaking 8 and I was sitting on the rim keeping her company. "I could divorce him," she said. "I could do it." Her eyes were puffed. I felt a surge of electricity run through me, adrenaline flowed. "Leave him?" I asked. "Yes," she said. "Should I?" she asked me. "Should I leave him? Would you mind?" I was her friend, her confidante. I did not yet know enough of the world to answer the question. I thought of my home split apart. I thought my father would never see me again. I wondered what I would tell my friends. No one I knew had parents who were divorced. I was afraid. "Who will take care of us?" I asked. My mother let the ashes of her cigarette fall into the tub. "God!" she said. "Help me," she said. But she'd asked the wrong person.

Then she did a brave thing. She went to a psychiatrist. I 9 would wait for her downstairs in the lobby. She would emerge from the elevator after her appointment with her mascara smeared over her cheeks. "When I'm stronger," she said, "I'll leave him." But the years went on. He said she was demanding. He said, "I spend enough time with you. Go to Florida with your sister. Go to Maine with your brother. Stop asking me to talk to you. I've already said everything I want to say." She said, "I need you to admire me. I need you to say you love me." "I do," he said, but then they had a party and I found him in the coat closet with a lady and lipstick all over his face.

He talked about politics. He read history books. He hit on the chin a man who disagreed with him. He yelled at my mother that she had no right to an opinion on anything. He said, "Women with opinions smell like skunks." She said, "He's so smart. He knows so much." She said, "If I leave him no other man will marry me." She said, "I can't leave him." 10

Week after week, she would say something that irritated him. He would make her cry and then he would scream at her for crying. His screams were howls. If you listened to the sound you would think an animal was trapped and in pain. Dinner after dinner my brother and I would silently try to eat our food as the same old fight began again, built and reached its crescendo. 11

Finally I was old enough. "Leave him," I said. "I don't know," she said, "maybe." But she couldn't and she wouldn't and the dance between them had turned into a marathon. She quit first. She died at age fifty-two, still married, still thinking, if only I had been taller, different, better. He inherited her money and immediately wed a tall woman, with whom he had been having an affair for many years, whose hands shook when she spoke to him. He called her: "That stupid dame." "That dumb broad," he would say. He went off to his club. He went for long walks. He had migraines. 12

This was a story of a divorce that should have been. 13

When I was twenty-seven I found myself checking into a fleabag hotel in Juárez. My three-year-old daughter was trying to pull the corncob out of the parrot cage and the parrot was trying to bite her fingers. I was there, my room squeezed 14 between those of the local drunks and prostitutes, to get a divorce. This was a divorce that should have been and was. I had married a man whom I thought was just the opposite of my father. He was a playwright, a philosopher. He was from an old southern family. He talked to me all the time and let me read and type his manuscripts. I worked as a receptionist to support him. Our friends were poets and painters, beatniks and their groupies. I had escaped my mother's home or so I thought. What I didn't notice was that my husband was handsome and thought me plain, that my husband was poor and thought me a meal ticket, that my husband—like my father—was dwarfed of spirit and couldn't imagine another soul beside himself. What I didn't know was that I—like my mother—had no faith, no confidence, no sense that I could fly too. I could even write.

My husband had other women and I thought it was an 15 artist's privilege. My husband said, "If Elizabeth Taylor is a woman, then you must be a hamster." I laughed. My husband went on binges and used up all our money. I thought it was poetic although I was always frightened; bill collectors called. I was always apologizing. We didn't fight so I thought I had achieved matrimonial heaven, a place where of course certain compromises were necessary.

Then after I had a child I thought of love as oxygen and I 16 felt faint. In the middle of the night when I was nursing the baby and my husband was out at the local bar I discovered that loneliness was the name of my condition. I noticed that my husband could not hold his child because he was either too drunk, out of the house, closed into his head, or consumed with nervousness about the applause the outside world was giving or withholding from him. I discovered that I had married a man more like my father than not and that, more like my mother than not, I had become a creature to be pitied. Like moth to flame I was drawn to repeat. My divorce was related to her undivorce, so the generations unfold back to back handing on their burdens—by contamination, memory, experience, identification, one's failure becomes the other's. The courage it takes to really make things better, to change, is rare and won only at great cost. Yes, we are responsible for ourselves, but nevertheless our family stories course and curse through our veins: our memories are not free.

If my mother had been brave enough to go it alone I 17
might have seen myself differently. I might have been brave enough to let myself be loved the first time around. At least I didn't wait for my entire life to pass before leaping up and away. So this is why I listen with tongue in cheek to all the terrible tales of what divorce has done to the American family. I know that if my mother had left my father not only her life but mine too might have been set on more solid ground. I know that if I had stayed in my marriage my child would have lived forever in the shadow of my perpetual grief and thought of herself as I had, unworthy of the ordinary moments of affection and connection.

In twentieth-century America we place so much emphasis on 18
romance that we barely notice the other essentials of marriage that include economics and child rearing. My mother was undone by the economic equation in her marriage. Money, which we know to be a part of the bitterness of divorce, is in there from the beginning, a thread in the cloak of love, whether we like it or not.

History clunking through our private lives certainly af- 19
fected my mother's marriage and my bad marriage. Woman's proper role, woman's masochistic stance, immigration, push to rise in social status, the confusion of money damned my mother to a lifetime of tears and almost caught me there too. But history is always present without our always being able to name its nasty work.

The women's movement, which came too late for my 20
mother, sent some women off adventure bound, free of suburb, unwilling to be sole caretakers to find, at the end of their rainbow isolation, disappointment, bitterness. The sexual revolution, which soon after burned like a laser through our towns and sent wives running in circles in search of multiple pleasures, freedom from convention, and distance from the burdens of domesticity, was a balloon that popped long

before the arrival of AIDS. We found we were not, after all, in need of the perfect orgasm. We were in need of a body to spoon with in bed, a story we could tell together as well as sexual equality.

But there is more. Divorce is also the terrible knife that rends family asunder, and for the children it can be the tilting, defining moment that marks them ever after, walking wounded, angry, sad souls akimbo, always prone to being lost in a forest of despair. They can be tough, too tough. They can be helpless, too helpless. They can never trust. They can be too trusting. They can accept a stepparent for a while and then revoke their acceptance. They can protest the stepparent for a while and then change their mind, but either way their own parents' divorce hangs over them, threat, reminder, betrayal always possible. My stepdaughter, now a married woman and a mother herself, speaks of her own parents' breakup, which came when she was only seven, as the most terrible moment in her life. As she says this I have only to listen to the tightness in her voice, watch the slight tremble in her hand to know that the divorce seemed to her like an earthquake. The divorce caused a before and after and everything after is tarnished, diminished by what went before. 21

I wish this were not so. I wish that we could marry a new 22 mate, repair, go on to undo the worst of our mistakes without leaving ugly deep scars across our children's psyches, but we can't. And furthermore the children will never completely forgive us, never understand how our backs were against the wall: They may try to understand our broken vows but they don't. Of course there are other things our children don't forgive us for. If we die, if we withdraw, if we let ourselves drown in misery, addictions, if we fail at work or lose our courage in the face of economic or other adversity, that too will eat at their hearts and spoil their chances for the gold ring on life's carousel. There are, in other words, many ways to damage children, and divorce is only the most effective and perhaps most common of them.

For a while, in the seventies, divorce was everywhere, a 23 panacea for the heart burdened. We were too excited by the prospects of freedom to see the damage that was done. The wounds are very severe for both partners and children. It may be worth it as it would have been for my mother. It may be necessary, but divorce is never nice. I felt as if the skin had been stripped from my body the first months after my divorce, and I was only twenty-seven years old. I felt as if I had to learn anew how to walk in the streets, how to set my face, how to plot a direction, how to love. I had to admit to failure, take back my proud words, let others help me. It was a relief, but it was a disaster. I had lost confidence in my decisions. It took a long while to gain back what I had lost. I understand why my mother did not have the strength to do it, although she should have.

24   I cannot imagine a world in which divorce would not sometimes occur. Men and women will always fail each other, miss each others' gestures, change in fatally different ways. There are men who cannot love, who abuse their wives or themselves or some substance. There are women who do the same. There are some disasters that wreck a marriage, a sick or damaged child, an economic calamity, a professional failure. There are marriages that are simply asphyxiated by daily life.

25   But I can imagine a world in which divorce would be rare, in which the madness, meanness, mess of everyday life were absorbed and managed without social cataclysm. It is perhaps our American obsession with the romantic that leads to so much trouble. If we were able to see marriage as largely an economic, child-rearing institution, as a social encounter involving ambition, class, money, we might be better off. Never mind our very up-to-date goals of personal fitness and fulfillment; we are still characters, all of us, in a nineteenth-century novel.

26   At the moment, now that my children are of marriageable age I have become a believer in the arranged betrothal. Such marriages could not possibly cause more mischief than those that were created by our free will rushing about in heavy traffic with its eyes closed. Perhaps we should consider love as a product of marriage instead of the other way around. Of course those societies that arrange marriages have other tragic stories of bride burning, lifelong miserable submission

experienced by women, sexual nightmares, poor young girls and dirty old men. We are the only animal species that cannot seem to figure out how to pair off and raise children without maiming ourselves in the process.

We can bemoan the social disorder caused by divorce until the moon turns to cream cheese, but we are such fragile souls, so easily cast adrift, wounded, set upon by devils of our own making, that no matter how we twist or turn, no system will protect us from the worst. There is cruelty in divorce. There is cruelty in forced or unfortunate marriage. We will continue to cry at weddings because we know how bitter-sweet, how fragile is the troth. We will always need legal divorce just as an emergency escape hatch is crucial in every submarine. No sense, however, in denying that after every divorce someone will be running like a cat, tin cans tied to its tail: spooked and slowed down.

27

For Study and Discussion

QUESTIONS FOR RESPONSE

1. How have your friends or members of your family reacted to a divorce?
2. How do you characterize divorce—as a failure or liberation? Can you tell a story about a couple that might fit into each category?

QUESTIONS ABOUT PURPOSE

1. In what ways does Roiphe's sentence—"my divorce is the tale of two divorces, one that never was and one that was"—state the purpose of her essay?
2. How do her stories demonstrate her thesis that marriage requires more than romance?

QUESTIONS ABOUT AUDIENCE

1. How does Roiphe's assertion that all divorce stories sound the same, and yet each is as "unique as a human face," help her identify her audience?
2. These two contemporary tales focus on women. How does Roiphe anticipate the responses of her male readers?

QUESTIONS ABOUT STRATEGIES

1. How does Roiphe balance her two stories to demonstrate that although they seem different, her husband was like her father and she was like her mother?
2. How does Roiphe use her stepdaughter's experience to make a transition to the final part of her essay?

QUESTIONS FOR DISCUSSION

1. What effects does Roiphe think the women's movement has had on divorce?
2. How does she justify her assertion that we will always need divorce as "an emergency escape hatch"?

LAURA BOHANNAN

Laura Bohannan was born in New York City in 1922 and educated at Smith College, the University of Arizona, and Oxford University. She has taught anthropology at Northwestern University, the University of Chicago, and the University of Illinois, Chicago Circle. She has held several fellowships to conduct research in East Africa that have resulted in books such as *The Tiv of Central Nigeria* (1953) and *A Sourcebook on Tiv Religion* (1972). In "Shakespeare in the Bush," reprinted from *Natural History* magazine, Bohannan compares her version of *Hamlet* with the interpretation of the elders of an African tribe.

Shakespeare in the Bush
An American Anthropologist Set Out to Study the Tiv of West Africa and Was Taught the True Meaning of Hamlet

J UST BEFORE I left Oxford for the Tiv in West Africa, conversation turned to the season at Stratford. "You Americans," said a friend, "often have difficulty with Shakespeare. He was, after all, a very English poet, and one can easily misinterpret the universal by misunderstanding the particular." 1

I protested that human nature is pretty much the same the whole world over; at least the general plot and motivation of the greater tragedies would always be clear—everywhere—although some details of custom might have to be explained and difficulties of translation might produce other slight changes. To end an argument we could not conclude, my friend gave me a copy of *Hamlet* to study in the African 2

bush: it would, he hoped, lift my mind above its primitive surroundings, and possibly I might, by prolonged meditation,
achieve the grace of correct interpretation.

It was my second field trip to that African tribe, and I thought   3
myself ready to live in one of its remote sections—an area difficult to cross even on foot. I eventually settled on the hillock of
a very knowledgeable old man, the head of a homestead
of some hundred and forty people, all of whom were either
his close relatives or their wives and children. Like the other

---

*Before the end of the second month, grace
descended on me. I was quite sure that
Hamlet had only one possible interpretation,
and that one universally obvious.*

---

elders of the vicinity, the old man spent most of his time performing ceremonies seldom seen these days in the more
accessible parts of the tribe. I was delighted. Soon there
would be three months of enforced isolation and leisure,
between the harvest that takes place just before the rising of
the swamps and the clearing of new farms when the water
goes down. Then, I thought, they would have even more
time to perform ceremonies and explain them to me.

I was quite mistaken. Most of the ceremonies demanded   4
the presence of elders from several homesteads. As the swamps
rose, the old men found it too difficult to walk from one
homestead to the next, and the ceremonies gradually ceased.
As the swamps rose even higher, all activities from one came to
an end. The women brewed beer from maize and millet. Men,
women, and children sat on their hillocks and drank it.

People began to drink at dawn. By midmorning the whole   5
homestead was singing, dancing, and drumming. When it
rained, people had to sit inside their huts: there they drank
and sang or they drank and told stories. In any case, by noon

or before, I either had to join the party or retire to my own hut and my books. "One does not discuss serious matters when there is beer. Come, drink with us." Since I lacked their capacity for the thick native beer, I spent more and more time with *Hamlet*. Before the end of the second month, grace descended on me. I was quite sure that *Hamlet* had only one possible interpretation, and that one universally obvious.

Early every morning, in the hope of having some serious 6
talk before the beer party, I used to call on the old man at his reception hut—a circle of posts supporting a thatched roof above a low mud wall to keep out wind and rain. One day I crawled through the low doorway and found most of the men of the homestead sitting huddled in their ragged cloths on stools, low plank beds, and reclining chairs, warming themselves against the chill of the rain around a smoky fire. In the center were three pots of beer. The party had started.

The old man greeted me cordially. "Sit down and drink." 7
I accepted a large calabash full of beer, poured some into a small drinking gourd, and tossed it down. Then I poured some more into the same gourd for the man second in seniority to my host before I handed my calabash over to a young man for further distribution. Important people shouldn't ladle beer themselves.

"It is better like this," the old man said, looking at me approvingly and plucking at the thatch that had caught in my 8
hair. "You should sit and drink with us more often. Your servants tell me that when you are not with us, you sit inside your hut looking at a paper."

The old man was acquainted with four kinds of "papers": 9
tax receipts, bride price receipts, court fee receipts, and letters. The messenger who brought him letters from the chief used them mainly as a badge of office, for he always knew what was in them and told the old man. Personal letters for the few who had relatives in the government or mission stations were kept until someone went to a large market where there was a letter writer and reader. Since my arrival, letters were brought to me to be read. A few men also brought me bride price receipts, privately, with requests to change the

figures to a higher sum. I found moral arguments were of no avail, since in-laws are fair game, and the technical hazards of forgery difficult to explain to an illiterate people. I did not wish them to think me silly enough to look at any such papers for days on end, and I hastily explained that my "paper" was one of the "things of long ago" of my country.

"Ah," said the old man. "Tell us."   10

I protested that I was not a storyteller. Storytelling is a   11
skilled art among them; their standards are high, and the audiences critical—and vocal in their criticism. I protested in
vain. This morning they wanted to hear a story while they
drank. They threatened to tell me no more stories until I told
them one of mine. Finally, the old man promised that no one
would criticize my style "for we know you are struggling with
our language." "But," put in one of the elders, "you must
explain what we do not understand, as we do when we tell
you our stories." Realizing that here was my chance to prove
Hamlet universally intelligible, I agreed.

The old man handed me some more beer to help me on   12
with my storytelling. Men filled their long wooden pipes and
knocked coals from the fire to place in the pipe bowls; then,
puffing contentedly, they sat back to listen. I began in the
proper style, "Not yesterday, not yesterday, but long ago, a
thing occurred. One night three men were keeping watch
outside the homestead of the great chief, when suddenly they
saw the former chief approach them."

"Why was he no longer their chief?"   13

"He was dead," I explained. "That is why they were trou-   14
bled and afraid when they saw him."

"Impossible," began one of the elders, handing his pipe   15
on to his neighbor, who interrupted, "Of course it wasn't the
dead chief. It was an omen sent by a witch. Go on."

Slightly shaken, I continued. "One of these three was a   16
man who knew things"—the closest translation for scholar,
but unfortunately it also meant witch. The second elder
looked triumphantly at the first. "So he spoke to the dead
chief saying, 'Tell us what we must do so you may rest in your
grave,' but the dead chief did not answer. He vanished, and

they could see him no more. Then the man who knew things—his name was Horatio—said this event was the affair of the dead chief's son, Hamlet."

There was a general shaking of heads round the circle. "Had the dead chief no living brothers? Or was this son the chief?" 17

"No," I replied. "That is, he had one living brother who became the chief when the elder brother died." 18

The old men muttered: such omens were matters for chiefs and elders, not for youngsters; no good could come of going behind a chief's back; clearly Horatio was not a man who knew things. 19

"Yes, he was," I insisted, shooing a chicken away from my beer. "In our country the son is next to the father. The dead chief's younger brother had become the great chief. He had also married his elder brother's widow only about a month after the funeral." 20

"He did well," the old man beamed and announced to the others, "I told you that if we knew more about Europeans, we would find they really were very like us. In our country also," he added to me, "the younger brother marries the elder brother's widow and becomes the father of his children. Now, if your uncle, who married your widowed mother, is your father's full brother, then he will be a real father to you. Did Hamlet's father and uncle have one mother?" 21

His question barely penetrated my mind; I was too upset and thrown too far off balance by having one of the most important elements of *Hamlet* knocked straight out of the picture. Rather uncertainly I said that I thought they had the same mother, but I wasn't sure—the story didn't say. The old man told me severely that these genealogical details made all the difference and that when I got home I must ask the elders about it. He shouted out the door to one of his younger wives to bring his goatskin bag. 22

Determined to save what I could of the mother motif, I took a deep breath and began again. "The son Hamlet was very sad because his mother had married again so quickly. 23

There was no need for her to do so, and it is our custom for a widow not to go to her next husband until she has mourned for two years."

"Two years is too long," objected the wife, who had ap- 24 peared with the old man's battered goatskin bag. "Who will hoe your farms for you while you have no husband?"

"Hamlet," I retorted without thinking, "was old enough 25 to hoe his mother's farms himself. There was no need for her to remarry." No one looked convinced. I gave up. "His mother and the great chief told Hamlet not to be sad, for the great chief himself would be a father to Hamlet. Furthermore, Hamlet would be the next chief: therefore he must stay to learn the things of a chief. Hamlet agreed to remain, and all the rest went off to drink beer."

While I paused, perplexed at how to render Hamlet's dis- 26 gusted soliloquy to an audience convinced that Claudius and Gertrude had behaved in the best possible manner, one of the younger men asked me who had married the other wives of the dead chief.

"He had no other wives," I told him. 27

"But a chief must have many wives! How else can he brew 28 beer and prepare food for all his guests?"

I said firmly that in our country even chiefs had only one 29 wife, that they had servants to do their work, and that they paid them from tax money.

It was better, they returned, for a chief to have many wives 30 and sons who would help him hoe his farms and feed his people; then everyone loved the chief who gave much and took nothing—taxes were a bad thing.

I agreed with the last comment, but for the rest fell back 31 on their favorite way of fobbing off my questions: "That is the way it is done, so that is how we do it."

I decided to skip the soliloquy. Even if Claudius was here 32 thought quite right to marry his brother's widow, there remained the poison motif, and I knew they would disapprove of fratricide. More hopefully I resumed, "That night Hamlet kept watch with the three who had seen his dead father. The dead chief again appeared, and although the others were afraid, Hamlet followed his dead father off to one side. When they were alone, Hamlet's dead father spoke."

"Omens can't talk!" The old man was emphatic.   33

"Hamlet's dead father wasn't an omen. Seeing him might   34
have been an omen, but he was not." My audience looked as
confused as I sounded. "It *was* Hamlet's dead father. It was a
thing we call a 'ghost.'" I had to use the English word, for
unlike many of the neighboring tribes, these people didn't
believe in the survival after death of any individuating part of
the personality.

"What is a 'ghost'? An omen?"   35

"No, a 'ghost' is someone who is dead but who walks   36
around and can talk, and people can hear him and see him
but not touch him."

They objected. "One can touch zombies."   37

"No, no! It was not a dead body the witches had animated   38
to sacrifice and eat. No one else made Hamlet's dead father
walk. He did it himself."

"Dead men can't walk," protested my audience as one man.   39

I was quite willing to compromise. "A 'ghost' is the dead   40
man's shadow."

But again they objected. "Dead men cast no shadows."   41

"They do in my country," I snapped.   42

The old man quelled the babble of disbelief that arose im-   43
mediately and told me with that insincere, but courteous,
agreement one extends to the fancies of the young, ignorant,
and superstitious, "No doubt in your country the dead can
also walk without being zombies." From the depths of his
bag he produced a withered fragment of kola nut, bit off one
end to show it wasn't poisoned, and handed me the rest as a
peace offering.

"Anyhow," I resumed, "Hamlet's dead father said that his   44
own brother, the one who became chief, had poisoned him.
He wanted Hamlet to avenge him. Hamlet believed this in
his heart, for he did not like his father's brother." I took another swallow of beer. "In the country of the great chief, living in the same homestead, for it was a very large one, was an
important elder who was often with the chief to advise and

help him. His name was Polonius. Hamlet was courting his daughter, but her father and her brother . . . [I cast hastily about for some tribal analogy] warned her not to let Hamlet visit her when she was alone on her farm, for he would be a great chief and so could not marry her."

"Why not?" asked the wife, who had settled down on the edge of the old man's chair. He frowned at her for asking stupid questions and growled, "They lived in the same homestead." 45

"That was not the reason," I informed them. "Polonius was a stranger who lived in the homestead because he helped the chief, not because he was a relative." 46

"Then why couldn't Hamlet marry her?" 47

"He could have," I explained, "but Polonius didn't think he would. After all, Hamlet was a man of great importance who ought to marry a chief's daughter, for in his country a man could have only one wife. Polonius was afraid that if Hamlet made love to his daughter, then no one else would give a high price for her." 48

"That might be true," remarked one of the shrewder elders, "but a chief's son would give his mistress's father enough presents and patronage to more than make up the difference. Polonius sounds like a fool to me." 49

"Many people think he was," I agreed. "Meanwhile Polonius sent his son Laertes off to Paris to learn the things of that country, for it was the homestead of a very great chief indeed. Because he was afraid that Laertes might waste a lot of money on beer and women and gambling, or get into trouble by fighting, he sent one of his servants to Paris secretly, to spy out what Laertes was doing. One day Hamlet came upon Polonius's daughter Ophelia. He behaved so oddly he frightened her. Indeed"—I was fumbling for words to express the dubious quality of Hamlet's madness—"the chief and many others had also noticed that when Hamlet talked one could understand the words but not what they meant. Many people thought that he had become mad." My audience suddenly became much more attentive. "The great chief wanted to know what was wrong with Hamlet, so he sent for two of Hamlet's age mates [school friends would 50 have taken long explanation] to talk to Hamlet and find out what troubled his heart. Hamlet, seeing that they had been bribed by the chief to betray him, told them nothing. Polonius, however, insisted that Hamlet was mad because he had been forbidden to see Ophelia, whom he loved."

"Why," inquired a bewildered voice, "should anyone be- 51
witch Hamlet on that account?"

"Bewitch him?" 52

"Yes, only witchcraft can make anyone mad, unless, of 53
course, one sees the beings that lurk in the forest."

I stopped being a storyteller, took out my notebook and de- 54
manded to be told more about these two causes of madness. Even while they spoke and I jotted notes, I tried to calculate the effect of this new factor on the plot. Hamlet had not been exposed to the beings that lurk in the forests. Only his rela-tives in the male line could bewitch him. Barring relatives not mentioned by Shakespeare, it had to be Claudius who was at-tempting to harm him. And, of course, it was.

For the moment I staved off questions by saying that the 55
great chief also refused to believe that Hamlet was mad for the love of Ophelia and nothing else. "He was sure that some-thing much more important was troubling Hamlet's heart."

"Now Hamlet's age mates," I continued, "had brought 56
with them a famous storyteller. Hamlet decided to have this man tell the chief and all his homestead a story about a man who had poisoned his brother because he desired his brother's wife and wished to be chief himself. Hamlet was sure the great chief could not hear the story without making a sign if he was indeed guilty, and then he would discover whether his dead father had told him the truth."

The old man interrupted, with deep cunning, "Why 57
should a father lie to his son?" he asked.

I hedged: "Hamlet wasn't sure that it really was his dead 58
father." It was impossible to say anything, in that language, about devil-inspired visions.

"You mean," he said, "it actually was an omen, and he 59
knew witches sometimes send false ones. Hamlet was a fool

not to go to one skilled in reading omens and divining the truth in the first place. A man-who-sees-the-truth could have told him how his father died, if he really had been poisoned, and if there was witchcraft in it; then Hamlet could have called the elders to settle the matter."

The shrewd elder ventured to disagree. "Because his fa-   60
ther's brother was a great chief, one-who-sees-the-truth might therefore have been afraid to tell it. I think it was for that reason that a friend of Hamlet's father—a witch and an elder—sent an omen so his friend's son would know. Was the omen true?"

"Yes," I said, abandoning ghosts and the devil; a witch-   61
sent omen it would have to be. "It was true, for when the storyteller was telling his tale before all the homestead, the great chief rose in fear. Afraid that Hamlet knew his secret he planned to have him killed."

The stage set of the next bit presented some difficulties of   62
translation. I began cautiously. "The great chief told Hamlet's mother to find out from her son what he knew. But because a woman's children are always first in her heart, he had the important elder Polonius hide behind a cloth that hung against the wall of Hamlet's mother's sleeping hut. Hamlet started to scold his mother for what she had done."

There was a shocked murmur from everyone. A man   63
should never scold his mother.

"She called out in fear, and Polonius moved behind the   64
cloth. Shouting, 'A rat!' Hamlet took his machete and slashed through the cloth." I paused for dramatic effect. "He had killed Polonius!"

The old men looked at each other in supreme disgust.   65
"That Polonius truly was a fool and a man who knew noth-ing! What child would not know enough to shout, 'It's me!'" With a pang, I remembered that these people are ardent hunters, always armed with bow, arrow, and machete; at the first rustle in the grass an arrow is aimed and ready, and the hunter shouts "Game!" If no human voice answers immedi-ately, the arrow speeds on its way. Like a good hunter Hamlet had shouted, "A rat!"

I rushed in to save Polonius's reputation. "Polonius did 66
speak. Hamlet heard him. But he thought it was the chief and
wished to kill him to avenge his father. He had meant to kill
him earlier that evening. . . ." I broke down, unable to describe to these pagans, who had no belief in individual after-
life, the difference between dying at one's prayers and dying
"unhousell'd, disappointed, unaneled."

This time I had shocked my audience seriously. "For a man 67
to raise his hand against his father's brother and the one who
has become his father—that is a terrible thing. The elders
ought to let such a man be bewitched."

I nibbled at my kola nut in some perplexity, then pointed 68
out that after all the man had killed Hamlet's father.

"No," pronounced the old man, speaking less to me than 69
to the young men sitting behind the elders. "If your father's
brother has killed your father, you must appeal to your father's age mates; *they* may avenge him. No man may use violence against his senior relatives." Another thought struck
him. "But if his father's brother had indeed been wicked
enough to bewitch Hamlet and make him mad that would be
a good story indeed, for it would be his fault that Hamlet,
being mad, no longer had any sense and thus was ready to kill
his father's brother."

There was a murmur of applause. *Hamlet* was again a good 70
story to them, but it no longer seemed quite the same story
to me. As I thought over the coming complications of plot
and motive, I lost courage and decided to skim over dangerous ground quickly.

"The great chief," I went on, "was not sorry that Hamlet 71
had killed Polonius. It gave him a reason to send Hamlet
away, with his two treacherous age mates, with letters to a
chief of a far country, saying that Hamlet should be killed.
But Hamlet changed the writing on their papers, so that the
chief killed his age mates instead." I encountered a reproachful glare from one of the men whom I had told undetectable
forgery was not merely immoral but beyond human skill. I
looked the other way.

"Before Hamlet could return, Laertes came back for his   72
father's funeral. The great chief told him Hamlet had killed
Polonius. Laertes swore to kill Hamlet because of this, and
because his sister Ophelia, hearing her father had been killed
by the man she loved, went mad and drowned in the river."

"Have you already forgotten what we told you?" The old   73
man was reproachful. "One cannot take vengeance on a mad-
man; Hamlet killed Polonius in his madness. As for the girl,
she not only went mad, she was drowned. Only witches can
make people drown. Water itself can't hurt anything. It is
merely something one drinks and bathes in."

I began to get cross. "If you don't like the story, I'll stop."   74

The old man made soothing noises and himself poured me   75
some more beer. "You tell the story well, and we are listening.
But it is clear that the elders of your country have never told
you what the story really means. No, don't interrupt! We believe you when you say your marriage customs are different,
or your clothes and weapons. But people are the same everywhere; therefore, there are always witches and it is we, the elders, who know how witches work. We told you it was the great
chief who wished to kill Hamlet, and now your own words
have proved us right. Who were Ophelia's male relatives?"

"There were only her father and her brother." Hamlet was   76
clearly out of my hands.

"There must have been many more; this also you must ask   77
of your elders when you get back to your country. From what
you tell us, since Polonius was dead, it must have been Laertes
who killed Ophelia, although I do not see the reason for it."

We had emptied one pot of beer, and the old men argued the   78
point with slightly tipsy interest. Finally one of them demanded
of me, "What did the servant of Polonius say on his return?"

With difficulty I recollected Reynaldo and his mission. "I   79
don't think he did return before Polonius was killed."

"Listen," said the elder, "and I will tell you how it was and   80
how your story will go, then you may tell me if I am right.
Polonius knew his son would get into trouble, and so he did.
He had many fines to pay for fighting, and debts from gam-
bling. But he had only two ways of getting money quickly.
One was to marry off his sister at once, but it is difficult to

find a man who will marry a woman desired by the son of a chief. For if the chief's heir commits adultery with your wife, what can you do? Only a fool calls a case against a man who will someday be his judge. Therefore Laertes had to take the second way: he killed his sister by witchcraft, drowning her so he could secretly sell her body to the witches."

I raised an objection. "They found her body and buried it. Indeed Laertes jumped into the grave to see his sister once more—so, you see, the body was truly there. Hamlet, who had just come back, jumped in after him." 81

"What did I tell you?" The elder appealed to the others. "Laertes was up to no good with his sister's body. Hamlet prevented him, because the chief's heir, like a chief, does not wish any other man to grow rich and powerful. Laertes would be angry, because he would have killed his sister without benefit to himself. In our country he would try to kill Hamlet for that reason. Is this not what happened?" 82

"More or less," I admitted. "When the great chief found Hamlet was still alive, he encouraged Laertes to try to kill Hamlet and arranged a fight with machetes between them. In the fight both the young men were wounded to death. Hamlet's mother drank the poisoned beer that the chief meant for Hamlet in case he won the fight. When he saw his mother die of poison, Hamlet, dying, managed to kill his father's brother with his machete." 83

"You see, I was right!" exclaimed the elder. 84

"That was a very good story," added the old man, "and you told it with very few mistakes. There was just one more error, at the very end. The poison Hamlet's mother drank was obviously meant for the survivor of the fight, whichever it was. If Laertes had won, the great chief would have poisoned him, for no one would know that he arranged Hamlet's death. Then, too, he need not fear Laertes' witchcraft; it takes a strong heart to kill one's only sister by witchcraft. 85

"Sometime," concluded the old man, gathering his ragged toga about him, "you must tell us some more stories of your country. We, who are elders, will instruct you in their true 86 meaning, so that when you return to your own land your elders will see that you have not been sitting in the bush, but among those who know things and who have taught you wisdom."

For Study and Discussion

QUESTIONS FOR RESPONSE

1. What has been your experience reading *Hamlet?* What aspects of the play confuse you?
2. Have you ever tried to tell a story to a group of people who interrupted and misunderstood you? How did you react to the situation?

QUESTIONS ABOUT PURPOSE

1. What belief convinces Bohannan that *Hamlet* is universally intelligible?
2. How does her attempt to tell Hamlet's story prove that her friend was right: "one can easily misinterpret the universal by misunderstanding the particular"?

QUESTIONS ABOUT AUDIENCE

1. How does Bohannan translate concepts—*chief* for *king, farm* for *castle*—to help her African audience understand her story?
2. How does she reveal her frustration and anger in trying to tell her audience what she thought was a simple story?

QUESTIONS ABOUT STRATEGIES

1. How does Bohannan's discussion of Hamlet's *madness* reveal differences in the English and African culture?
2. Ironically, what feature of her version of Hamlet's story convinces her African audience that "people are the same everywhere"?

QUESTIONS FOR DISCUSSION

1. How does Bohannan's audience interpret Hamlet's story? What convinces them that Bohannan's elders have not told her the true story?
2. How do the elders suggest that Hamlet should have resolved his conflict with Claudius? What does this solution suggest about the presumed superiority of the English culture?

WITI IHIMAERA

Witi Ihimaera was born in 1944 in Gisborne, New Zealand, and educated at the University of Auckland. After working as a newspaper reporter, he accepted a position as a diplomatic officer in New Zealand's Ministry of Foreign Affairs. He began writing to document the two landscapes of New Zealand, the Maori (the indigenous people) and the Pakeha (the Europeans). In particular, he wanted to ensure that "my Maori people were taken into account." His short stories have been collected in *Pounamu, Pounamu* (1972) and *The New Net Goes Fishing* (1976). His books include *Tangi* (1973), *Whanau* (1974), *The Whale Rider* (1992), *The Dream Swimmer* (1997), and *Sky Dancer* (2003). He has also edited a collection of Maori writing, *Into the World of Light* (1978). "His First Ball," reprinted from *Dear Miss Mansfield* (1989), recalls a similar story by a Pakeha New Zealander who spent most of her life in England, Katherine Mansfield.

His First Ball

J UST WHY IT was that he, Tuta Wharepapa, should receive the invitation was a mystery to him. Indeed, when it came, in an envelope bearing a very imposing crest, his mother mistook it for something entirely different—notice of a traffic misdemeanour, a summons perhaps, or even worse, an overdue account. She fingered it gingerly, holding it as far away from her body as possible—just in case a pair of hands came out to grab her fortnightly cheque—and said, "Here, Tuta. It must be a bill." She thrust it quickly at her son before he could get away and, wriggling her fingers to get rid of the taint, waited for him to open it.

1

213

"Hey—" Tuta said as he stared down at the card. His face dropped such a long way that his mother—her name was Coral—became alarmed. Visions of pleading in court on his behalf flashed through her mind. "Oh, Tuta, how bad is it?" she said as she prepared to defend her son against all-comers. But Tuta remained speechless and Coral had to grab the card from his hands. "What's this?" she asked. The card was edged with gold:

The Aide-de-Camp in Waiting
Is Desired By Their Excellencies

"Oh, Tuta, what have you done?" Coral said. But Tuta was still in a state of shock. Then, "Read on, Mum," he said.

To Invite Mr Tuta Wharepapa
To A Dance At Government House

Coral's voice drifted away into speechlessness like her son's. Then she compressed her lips and jabbed Tuta with an elbow. "I'm tired of your jokes," she said. "It's not my joke, Mum," Tuta responded. "I know you, Tuta," Coral continued. "True, Mum, honest. One of the boys must be having me on." Coral looked at Tuta, unconvinced. "Who'd want to have *you* at their flash party?" she asked. "Just wait till I get the joker who sent this," Tuta swore to himself. Then Coral began to laugh. "You? Go to Government House? You don't even know how to bow!" And she laughed and laughed so much at the idea that Tuta couldn't take it. "Where are you going, Your Highness?" Coral asked. "To find out who sent this," Tuta replied, waving the offending invitation in her face. "By the time I finish with him—or her—" because he suddenly realised Coral herself might have sent it—"they'll be laughing on the other side of their face." With that, he strode out of the kitchen. "Oh, Tuta?" he heard Coral call, all la-di-da, "If you ore gooing pahst Government Howse please convay may regahrds to—" and she burst out laughing again.

Tuta leapt on to his motorbike and, over the rest of the   3
day, roared around the city calling on his mates from the factory. "It wasn't me, Tuta," Crazy-Joe said as he sank a red
ball in the billiard saloon, "but I tell you, man, you'll look
great in a suit." Nor was it Blackjack over at the garage, who
said, "But listen, mate, when you go grab some of those
Diplo number plates for me, ay?" And neither was it Des,
who moonlighted as Desirée Dawn at the strip club, or
Sheree, who worked part time at the pinball parlour. "You
couldn't take a partner, could you?" Desirée Dawn breathed
hopefully. "Nah, you wouldn't be able to fit on my bike,"
Tuta said—apart from which he didn't think a six-foot trans-
vestite with a passion for pink boas and slit satin dresses
would enjoy it all that much. By the end of the day Tuta was
no wiser, and when he arrived at Bigfoot's house and found
his mate waiting for him in a tiara, he knew that word was
getting around. Then it came to him that perhaps the invitation was real after all. Gloria Simmons would know—she was
the boss's secretary and knew some lords.

"Oh," Mrs. Simmons whispered reverently as Tuta handed   4
her the crested envelope. She led Tuta into the sitting-
room. "It looks real," she said as she held it to the light.
Then she opened the envelope and, incredulous, asked, " *You*
received this?" Tuta nodded. "You didn't just pick it up on
the street," Mrs. Simmons continued, "and put your name
on it?" Offended, Tuta shook his head, saying "You don't
think I want to go, do you?" Mrs. Simmons pursed her lips
and said, "Perhaps there's another Tuta Wharepapa, and you
got his invitation in error." And Mrs. Simmons's teeth smiled
and said, "In that case, let me ring Government House and
let them know." With that, Mrs. Simmons went into another
room, where Tuta heard her dialling. Then *her* voice went all
la-di-da too as she trilled, "Ooo, Gahverment Howse? May
ay speak to the Aide-de-Camp? Ooo, har do yoo do. So sorry
to trouble you but ay am ringing to advayse you—" Tuta
rolled his eyes—how come everybody he told about the invitation got infected by some kind of disease! Then he became
acutely aware that Mrs. Simmons had stopped talking. He

heard her gasp. He heard her say in her own lingo, "You mean to tell me that this is for real? That you people actually sent an invite to a—a—boy who packs batteries in a factory?" She put down the telephone and returned to the sitting-room. She was pale but calm as she said, "Tuta dear, difficult though this may be, can you remember the woman who came to look at the factory about two months ago?" Tuta knitted his eyebrows. "Yeah, I think so. That must have been when we opened the new extension." Mrs. Simmons closed her eyes. "The woman, Tuta. The woman." Tuta thought again. "Oh yeah, there *was* a lady, come to think of it, a horsey-looking lady who—" Mrs. Simmons interrupted him. "Tuta, dear, that lady was the wife of the Governor-General."

Dazed, Tuta said, "But she didn't say who she was." And   5
he listened as Mrs. Simmons explained that Mrs. Governor-General had been very impressed by the workers at the factory and that Tuta was being invited to represent them. "Of course you will have to go," Mrs. Simmons said. "One does not say 'No' to the Crown." Then Mrs. Simmons got up and telephoned Tuta's mother. "Coral? Gloria here. Listen, about Tuta, you and I should talk about what is required. What for? Why, when he goes to the ball of course! Now—" *Me? Go to a ball?* Tuta thought. *With all those flash people, all those flash ladies with their crowns and diamonds and emeralds? Not bloody likely—Bigfoot can go, he's already got a tiara, yeah. Not me. They'll have to drag me there. I'm not going. Not me. No fear. No WAY.* But he knew, when he saw the neighbours waiting for him at home that, of course, his mother had already flapped her mouth to everybody. "Oh yes," she was telling the neighbours when Tuta walked in, "it was delivered by special messenger. This dirty big black car came and a man, must have been a flunkey, knocked on the door and—" Then Coral saw Tuta and, "Oh Tuta," she cried, opening her arms to him as if she hadn't seen him for days.

After that, of course, there was no turning back. The boss   6
from the factory called to put the hard word on Tuta. Mrs. Simmons RSVPed by telephone and—"Just in case, Tuta dear"—by letter and, once that was done, he had to go. The

rest of his mates at the factory got into the act, also, can-
celling the airline booking he made to get out of town and,
from thereon in, followed him everywhere. "Giz a break,
fellas," Tuta pleaded as he tried to get out, cajole or bribe
himself out of the predicament. But Crazy-Joe only said,
"Lissen, if you don't get there then I'm—" and he drew a finger across his throat, and Blackjack said, "Hey, man, I know
a man who knows a man who can get us a Rolls for the
night—" and Bigfoot just handed him the tiara. And boy, did
Coral ever turn out to be the walking compendium of What
To Do And How To Do It At A Ball. "Gloria says that we
have to take you to a tailor so you can hire a suit. Not just any
suit and none of your purple numbers either. A black *conservative* suit. And then we have to get you a bowtie and you have
to wear black shoes—so I reckon a paint job on your brown
ones will do. You've got a white shirt, thank goodness, but
we'll have to get some new socks—calf length so that when you
sit down people won't see your hairy legs. Now, what else? Oh
yes, I've already made an appointment for you to go to have
your hair cut, no buts, Tuta, and the boys are taking you there,
so don't think you're going to wriggle out of it. By the time
that dance comes around we'll have you decked out like the
Prince of Wales—" which was just what Tuta was afraid of.

But that was only the beginning. Not only did his appear-   7
ance have to be radically altered, but his manners had to be
brushed up also—and Mrs. Simmons was the first to have a
go. "Tuta dear," she said when he knocked on her door. "Do
come in. Yes, take your boots off but on THE NIGHT, the
shoes stay *on*. Please, come this way. No, Tuta, *after* me, just
a few steps behind. Never barge, Tuta and don't shamble
along. Be PROUD, Tuta, be HAUGHTY"—and she showed
him how to put his nose in the air. Tuta followed her, his
nose so high that he almost tripped, into the dining-room.
"Voila!" she said. "Ay?" Tuta answered. Mrs. Simmons then
realised that this was going to be very difficult. "I said, 'Ta
ra!'" She had set the table with a beautiful cloth—and it appeared to be laid with thousands of knives, forks and spoons.
"This is what it will be like at the ball," she explained. "Oh

boy," Tuta said. "Now, because I'm a lady you must escort me to my seat," Mrs. Simmons said. "Huh? Can't you walk there yourself?" Tuta asked. "Just *do* it," Mrs. Simmons responded dangerously, "and *don't* push me all the way under the table, Tuta, just to the edge will do—" and then, under her breath "—Patience, Gloria dear, *patienza*." Once seated, she motioned Tuta to a chair opposite her. "Gee, thanks," he said. Mrs. Simmons paused, thoughtfully, and said, "Tuta dear, when in doubt don't say *anything*. Just shut your mouth." She shivered, but really, the boy would only understand common language, "—and keep it shut." Then she smiled. "Now follow every action that I make." Exaggerating the movements for Tuta's benefit, Mrs. Simmons said, "First, take up the spoon. No, not that one, *that* one. That's for your soup, that's for the second course, that's for the third course, that's for the fourth—" Tuta looked helplessly at her. "Can't I use the same knives and things all the time?" he asked. "*Never,*" Mrs. Simmons shivered. "Well, what's all these courses for?" Tuta objected. "Why don't they just stick all the kai on the table at once?" Mrs. Simmons deigned not to answer. Instead she motioned to the glasses, saying, "Now *this* is for white wine, this for red wine, this for champagne and this for cognac." Tuta sighed, saying "No beer? Thought as much." Refusing to hear him, Mrs. Simmons proceeded, "You sip your wine just like you sip the soup. Like *so*," and she showed him. "No, Tuta, not too fast. And leave the bowl *on* the table, *don't* put it to your lips. No, *don't* slurp. Oh my goodness. Very GOOD, Tuta! Now wipe your lips with the napkin." Tuta looked puzzled. "Ay?" he asked. "The paper napkin on your lap," Mrs. Simmons said. "This hanky thing?" Tuta responded. "Why, Tuta!" Mrs. Simmons's teeth said, "How clever of you to work that out. Shall we proceed to the second course? Good!" Mrs. Simmons felt quite sure that Professor Higgins didn't have it *this* bad.

Then, of course, there was the matter of learning how to dance—not hot rock but slow *slow* dancing, holding a girl, "You know," Mrs. Simmons said, "*together,*" adding, "and young ladies at the ball are never allowed to decline." So

Tuta made a date with Desirée Dawn after hours at the club. Desirée was just overwhelmed to be asked for advice and told her friends Alexis Dynamite and Chantelle Derrier to help her. "Lissun, honey," Desirée said as she cracked her gum. "No matter what the dance is, there's always a basic rhythm." Chantelle giggled and said, "Yeah, very basic." Ignoring her, Desirée hauled Tuta on to the floor, did a few jeté's and, once she had limbered up, said, "Now *you* lead," and "Oo, honey, I didn't know you were so masterful." Alexis fluttered her false eyelashes and, "You two don't need music at *all*," she whispered. Nevertheless, Alexis ran the tape and the music boomed across the club floor. "This isn't ball music," Tuta said as he heard the raunch scream out of the saxes. "How do *you* know?" Chantelle responded. And Tuta had the feeling that he wasn't going to learn how to dance in any way except improperly. "Lissun," Desirée said, "Alexis and I will show you. Move your butt over here, Lexie. Now, Tuta honey, just watch. Can ya hear the rhythum? Well you go *boom* and a *boom* and a *boom boom boom*." And Alexis screamed and yelled, "Desirée, he wants to dance with the girl, not *make* her in the middle of the floor." And Chantelle only made matters worse by laughing, "Yeah, you stupid slut, you want him to end up in prison like you?" At which Desirée gasped, walked over to Chantelle, peeled off both Chantelle's false eyelashes, said, "Can you see better? Good," and lammed her one in the mouth. As he exited, Tuta knew he would have better luck with Sheree at the pinball parlour—she used to be good at roller skating and could even do the splits in mid-air.

So it went on. The fitting at the tailor's was duly accomplished ("Hmmmmnnnn," the tailor said as he measured Tuta up. "Your shoulders are too wide, your hips too large, you have shorter legs than you should have but—Hmmmmnnnn"), his hair was trimmed to within an inch of propriety, and he painted his brown shoes black. His lessons continued with Mrs. Simmons, Tuta's mother, the workers from the factory— even the boss—all pitching in to assist Tuta in the etiquette required. For instance: "If you're talking you ask about the weather. This is called polite conversation. You say "Isn't it lovely?" to everything, even if it isn't. You always say "Yes" if you're offered something, even if you don't want it. The man with the medals is *not* the waiter. He is His Excellency. The lady who looks like a horse is not in drag and you should *not* ask if her tiara fell off the same truck as Bigfoot's."

Then, suddenly it was time for Tuta to go to the ball. "Yes,   10 Mum," he said to Coral as she fussed around him with a clothes brush, "I've got a hanky, I've brushed my teeth three times already, the invite is in my pocket—" And when Tuta stepped out the door the whole world was there—the boss, Mrs. Simmons, Crazy-Joe, Blackjack, Bigfoot and others from the factory, Desirée Dawn and the neighbours. "Don't let us down," the boss said. "Not too much food on the fork," Mrs. Simmons instructed. "The third boom is the one that does it," Desirée Dawn called. "Don't forget the Diplo plates," Blackjack whispered. "And don't drink too much of the beer," Coral said. Then, there was the car, a Jaguar festooned with white ribbons and two small dolls on the bonnet. "It's a ball I'm off to," Tuta said sarcastically, "not a wedding." Blackjack shrugged his shoulders. "Best I could do, mate, and this beauty was just sitting there outside the church and—" He got in and started the motor. Tuta sat in the back and, suddenly, Bigfoot and Crazy-Joe were in either side. "The boss's orders," they said. "We deliver you to the door or else—" Outside, Tuta saw the boss draw a line across their necks. The car drew away and as it did so, Mrs. Simmons gave a small scream. "Oh my goodness, I forgot to tell Tuta that if Nature calls he should not use the bushes," she said.

Looking back, Tuta never quite understood how he ever   11 survived that journey. At one point a police car drew level on the motorway, but when they looked over at the Jaguar and saw Tuta he could just imagine their disbelief, Nah. Couldn't possibly . . . Nah. His head was whirling with all the etiquette he had learnt and all the instructions he had to remember. He trembled, squirmed, palpitated and sweated all over the seat. Then he was there, and Blackjack was showing the invitation, and the officer at the gate was looking doubtfully at the wedding decorations, and then

"Proceed ahead, sir," the officer said. *What a long drive,* Tuta thought. *What a big palace. And look at all those flash people. And they're all going in.* "Well, mate," Blackjack said, "Good luck. Look for us in the car park." And Crazy-Joe said, "Hey, give the missus a whirl for me, ay?" and with that, and a squeal of tires (Blackjack was always such a show-off), they were gone.

He was alone. Him. Tuta Wharepapa. Standing there. At 12 the entrance way. Inside he heard music and the laughter of the guests. Then someone grabbed his arm and said, "Come along!" and before he knew it he was inside and being propelled along a long hallway. And the young woman who had grabbed him was suddenly pulled away by her companion, and Tuta was alone again. *Oh boy,* he thought. *Look at this red carpet.* He felt quite sure that the paint was running off his shoes and that there were great big black footmarks all the way to where he was now standing. Then a voice BOOMED ahead, and Tuta saw that there was a line of people in front and they were handing their invitations in to the bouncer. Tuta joined them. The bouncer was very old and very dignified—he looked, though, as if he should have been retired from the job years ago. *Nah,* Tuta thought. *He couldn't be a bouncer. Must be a toff.* The toff looked Tuta up and down and thrust out his white-gloved hand. "I got an invitation," Tuta said. "True. I got one." The toff read the card and his eyebrows arched. "Your name?" he BOOMED. "Tuta." Couldn't he read? Then the toff turned away in the direction of a huge ballroom that stretched right to the end of the world. The room seemed to be hung with hundreds of chandeliers and *thousands* of people were either dancing or standing around the perimeter. There were steps leading down to the ballroom and, at the bottom, was a man wearing medals and a woman whose tiara wasn't as sparkly as Bigfoot's—*them.* And Tuta felt *sure,* when the Major-Domo—for that was who the toff was—stepped forward and opened his mouth to announce him, that *everybody* must have heard him BOOM—

"Your Excellencies, Mr. Tutae Tockypocka."   13

Tuta looked for a hole to disappear into. He tried to   14
backpedal down the hallway but there were people behind
him. "No, you got it wrong," he said between clenched teeth
to the Major-Domo. "Tutae's a rude word." But the Major-
Domo simply sniffed, handed back the invitation, and motioned Tuta down the stairs. Had *they* heard? In trembling
anticipation Tuta approached the Governor-General. "Mr.
Horrynotta?" the Governor-General smiled. "Splendid that
you were able to come along. Dear? Here's Mr. Tutae." And
in front of him was Mrs. Governor-General. "Mr. Forrimoppa,
how kind of you to come. May I call you Tutae? Please let me
introduce you to Lord Wells." And Lord Wells, too. "Mr.
Mopperuppa, quite a mouthful, what. Not so with Tutae,
what?" *You don't know the half of it,* Tuta thought gloomily.
And then Mrs. Governor-General just *had* to, didn't she, giggle and pronounce to all and sundry, "Everybody, you must
meet Mr. Tutae." And that's who Tuta became all that
evening. "Have you met Mr. Tutae yet? No? Mr. Tutae, this
is Mr.—" And Tuta would either shake hands or do a stiff little bow and look around for that hole in the floor. He once
made an attempt to explain what "tutae" was but heard Mrs.
Simmons's voice: "If in doubt, Tuta, *don't.*" So instead he
would draw attention away from that word by asking about
the weather. "Do you think it will rain?" he would ask. "Oh,
not inside, Mr. Tutae!"—and the word got around that Mr.
Tutae was such a wit, so funny, so quaint, that he soon found
himself exactly where he didn't want to be—at the centre of
attention. In desperation, he asked every woman to dance.
"Why, certainly, Mr. Tutae!" they said, because ladies never
said no. So he danced with them all—a fat lady, a slim lady, a
lady whose bones cracked all the time—and, because he was
nervous, he went *boom* at every third step, and *that* word got
around too. And as the Governor-General waltzed past he
shouted, "Well done, Tutae, jolly good show."

No matter what he tried to do Tuta could never get away   15
from being at the centre of the crowd or at the centre of attention. Instead of being gratified, however, Tuta became
more embarrassed. Everybody seemed to laugh at his every

word, even when it wasn't funny, or to accept his way of dancing because it was so *daring*. It seemed as if he could get away with anything. At the same time, Tuta suddenly realised that he was the only Maori there and that perhaps people were mocking him. He wasn't a real person to them, but rather an Entertainment. Even when buffet dinner was served, the crowd still seemed to mock him, pressing in upon him with "Have some hors d'oeuvres, Mr. Tutae. Some *escalope* of veal, perhaps? You must try the pâté de foie gras! A slice of *jambon*? What about some langouste? Oh, the raspberry gâteau is just divine!" It was as if the crowd knew very well his ignorance of such delicacies and, by referring to them, was putting him down. In desperation Tuta tried some caviar. "Oh, Mr. Tutae, we can see that you just love caviar!" Tuta gave a quiet, almost dangerous, smile. "Yes," he said. "I think it's just divine."

So it went on. But then, just after the buffet, a Very Important Person arrived and, relieved, Tuta found himself deserted. Interested, he watched as the one who had just arrived became the centre of attention. "It always happens this way," a voice said behind Tuta. "I wouldn't worry about it." Startled, Tuta turned around and saw a huge fern. "Before you," the fern continued, "it was me." Then Tuta saw that a young woman was sitting behind the fern. "I'm not worried," he said to her, "I'm glad." The woman sniffed and said, "You certainly looked as if you were enjoying it." Tuta parted the frons to get a good look at the woman's face—it was a pleasant face, one which could be pretty if it didn't frown so much. "Shift over," Tuta said. "I'm coming to join you." He sidled around the plant and sat beside her. "My name is—" he began. "Yes, I know," the woman said quickly, "Mr. Tutae." Tuta shook his head vigorously, "*No,* not Tutae. Tuta." The woman looked at him curiously and, "Is there a difference?" she asked. "You better believe it," Tuta said. "Oh—" the woman sniffed. "I'm Joyce." 16

The music started to play again. Joyce squinted her eyes and Tuta sighed, "Why don't you put on your glasses?" Joyce squealed, "How did you know?" before popping them on 17 and parting the fronds. "I'm a sociology student," Joyce muttered. "Don't you think people's behaviour is just amazing? I mean ay-*may*zing?" Tuta shrugged his shoulders and wondered if Joyce was looking at something he couldn't see. "I mean," Joyce continued, "look at them out there, just *look* at them. This could be India under the Raj. All this British Imperial graciousness and yet the carpet is being pulled from right beneath their feet." Puzzled, Tuta tried to see the ball through Joyce's eyes, but failed. "Ah well," Joyce sighed. Then she put her hand out to Tuta so that he could shake it, saying "Goodbye, Mr. Tuta." Tuta looked at her and, "Are you going?" he asked. "Oh no," Joyce said, "I'm staying here until everybody leaves. But *you* must go out and reclaim attention." Tuta laughed. "That new guy's welcome," he said. "But don't you want to fulfil their expectations?" Joyce asked. Tuta paused, and "If that means what I think it means, no," he said. "Good," Joyce responded, "You are perfectly capable of beating them at their own game. Good luck."

Then, curious, Tuta asked, "What did you mean when you said that before me it had been *you?*" Joyce shifted uneasily, took off her glasses and said, "Well, I'm not a Maori, but I thought it would have been obvious—" *Oh,* Tuta thought, *she's a plain Jane and people have been making fun of her.* "But that doesn't matter to me," Tuta said gallantly. "Really?" Joyce asked. "I'll prove it," Tuta said. "How about having the next dance." Joyce gasped, "Are you *sure?*" Taken aback, Tuta said, "Of course, I'm sure." And Joyce said, "But are you *sure* you're sure!" To show her, Tuta stood up and took her hand. Joyce sighed and shook her head. "Well, don't say I didn't warn you." Then she stood up . . . and up . . . and UP. 18

"Oh," Tuta said as he parted the fronds to look up at Joyce's face. She must have been six feet six at least. He and Joyce regarded each other miserably. Joyce bit her lip. *Well you asked for it,* Tuta thought. "Come on," he said, "let's have a good time." He reached up, grabbed her waist, put his face against her chest, and they waltzed into the middle of 19 the floor. There, Tuta stood as high on his toes as possible. *Oh, why did I come?* he thought. Then the music ended and he took Joyce back to the fern. "I'm sorry I'm such a bad dancer," she apologised. "I always took the man's part at school." Tuta smiled at her. "That's no sweat. Well—" And he was just about to leave her when he suddenly realised that after all he and Joyce were both outsiders really. And it came to him that, bloody hell, if you could not join them—as if he would really want to do *that*—then, yes, he could beat them if he wanted to. Not by giving in to them, but by being strong enough to stand up to them. Dance, perhaps, but using his own steps. Listen, also, not to the music of the band but to the music in his head. He owed it, after all, to generous but silly wonderful mixed-up Mum, Mrs. Simmons, Desirée Dawn, and the boys—Crazy-Joe, Blackjack and Bigfoot—who were out *there* but wanting to know enough to get *in*. But they needed to come in on their own terms—that's what they would have to learn—as the real people they were and not as carbon copies of the people already on the inside. Once they learnt that, *oh, world, watch out, for your walls will come down in a flash, like Jericho.*

"Look," Tuta said, "how about another dance!" Joyce   20
looked at him in disbelief. "You're a sucker for punishment, aren't you!" she muttered. "Why?" Tuta bowed, mockingly. "Well, for one thing, it would be just divine." At that, Joyce let out a peal of laughter. She stood up again. "Thank you," Joyce whispered. Then, "You know, this is my first ball." And Tuta smiled and "It's *my* first ball too," he said. "From now on, balls like these will never be the same again." He took her hand and the band began to wail a sweet but *oh-so-mean* saxophone solo as he led her on to the floor.

COMMENT ON "HIS FIRST BALL"

"His First Ball" is a vivid and humorous comparison of cross-cultural misunderstanding. Tuta Wharepapa, a Maori factory worker, is invited to a formal ball thrown by the British government of New Zealand. With coaching from his friends, Tuta polishes his manners and dancing, trying to transform himself into something he is not—a British gentleman. When he arrives at the ball, the British treat him as entertainment rather than as a guest. At the end of this colonial *Pygmalion,* Tuta realizes that he must be his own person—not the creation of the dominant culture.

Comparison and Contrast as a Writing Strategy

1. Select a place in your childhood neighborhood—perhaps a garden, a playground, or a movie theater. Then, in an essay addressed to your writing class, write a short comparison of the way the place used to be and the way it is now. Consider the example of Mark Twain's "Two Views of the River" as you compare your childhood and adult visions. Consider also what you have learned about the place or about yourself by making the comparison. That lesson should help control your decisions about purpose and audience.

2. Select two contrasting concepts that are paired together, such as introvert and extrovert, passive and aggressive, and yin and yang. Then, like Sobel, explain each concept and how they come to be paired.

3. Conduct some research on the conversational patterns in your home (or dormitory) and in your classroom. Keep track of who talks, what they talk about, and how they use conversation—for example, to make friends, to report information, to win approval. Keep track of who doesn't talk and in what situations they are likely to stay silent. Then write an essay in which you compare the patterns of home and school conversation.

4. In "A Tale of Two Divorces," Anne Roiphe contrasts two women's reactions to the same situation. Select a subject you know well—a family celebration—and then compare your version with the way it is represented on television.

5. Write an essay comparing the way two magazines or newspapers cover the same story. Or, like Laura Bohannan, compare the way a story might be told in one culture with the way it might be told in another. For example, how would you compare the way the American media and the African media might tell the story of America's last presidential election?

6. Compare and contrast arguments on both sides of a controversial issue, such as welfare reform or gun control. Such issues produce controversy because there are legitimate arguments on each side. They also produce controversy because people can simplify them in slogans (Reading is good; Television is bad). Select two slogans that present the opposing sides of the controversy you are writing about. Compare and contrast the assumptions, evidence, and logic of both slogans. Like Sarah Vowell, use your research to advance a larger argument about cultural differences.

DIVISION
AND
CLASSIFICATION

Division and **classification** are mental processes that often work together. When you *divide,* you separate something (a college, a city) into sections (departments, neighborhoods). When you *classify,* you place examples of something (restaurants, jobs) into categories or classes (restaurants: moderately expensive, very expensive; jobs: unskilled, semiskilled, and skilled).

When you divide, you move downward from a concept to the subunits of that concept. When you classify, you move upward from specific examples to classes or categories that share a common characteristic. For example, you could *divide* a television news program into subunits such as news, features, editorials, sports, and weather. And you could *classify* some element of that program—such as the editorial commentator on the six o'clock news—according to his or her style, knowledge, and trustworthiness. You can use either division or classification singly, depending on your purpose, but most of the time you will probably use them together when you are writing a classification essay. First you might identify the subunits in a college sports program—football, basketball, hockey, volleyball, tennis; then you could classify them according to their budgets—most money budgeted for football, the least budgeted for volleyball.

PURPOSE

When you write a classification essay, your chief purpose is to *explain*. You might want to explain an established method for organizing information, such as the Library of Congress system, or a new plan for arranging data, such as the Internal Revenue Service's latest schedule for itemizing tax deductions. On one level, your purpose in such an essay is simply to show how the system works. At a deeper level, your purpose is to define, analyze, and justify the organizing principle that underlies the system.

You can also write a classification essay to *entertain* or to *persuade*. If you classify to entertain, you have an opportunity to be clever and witty. If you classify to persuade, you have a chance to be cogent and forceful. If you want to entertain, you might concoct an elaborate scheme for classifying fools, pointing out the distinguishing features of each category and giving particularly striking examples of each type. But if you want to persuade, you could explain how some new or controversial plan, such as the metric system or congressional redistricting, is organized, pointing out how the schemes use new principles to identify and organize information. Again, although you may give your readers a great deal of information in such an essay, your main purpose is to persuade them that the new plan is better than the old one.

AUDIENCE

As with any writing assignment, when you write a classification essay, you need to think carefully about what your readers already know and what they need to get from your writing. If you're writing on a new topic (social patterns in a primitive society) or if you're explaining a specialized system of classification (the botanist's procedure for identifying plants), your readers need precise definitions and plenty of illustrations for each subcategory. If your readers already know about your subject and the system it uses for classification (the movies' G, PG, PG-13, R, and NC-17 rating codes), then you don't need to give them an extensive demonstration. In that kind of writing situation, you might want to sketch the system briefly to refresh your readers' memories but then move on, using examples of specific movies to analyze whether the system really works.

You also need to think about how your readers might use the classification system that you explain in your essay. If you're classifying rock musicians, your readers are probably going to regard the system you create as something self-enclosed—interesting and amusing, perhaps something to quibble about, but not something they're likely to use in their everyday lives. On the other hand, if you write an essay classifying stereo equipment, your readers may want to use your system when they shop. For the first audience, you can use an informal approach to classification, dividing your subject into interesting subcategories and illustrating them with vivid examples. For the other audience, you need to be careful and strict in your approach, making sure you divide your topic into all its possible classes and illustrating each class with concrete examples.

STRATEGIES

When you write a classification essay, your basic strategy for organization should be to *divide your subject* into major categories that exhibit a common trait, then subdivide those categories into smaller units. Next, *arrange your categories* into a sequence that shows a logical or a dramatic progression. Finally, *define each of your categories*. First, show how each category is different from the others; then discuss its most vivid examples.

To make this strategy succeed, you must be sure that your classification system is *consistent, complete, emphatic,* and *significant*. Here is a method for achieving this goal. First, when you divide your subject into categories, *apply the same principle of selection to each class*. You may find this hard to do if you're trying to explain a system that someone else has already established but that is actually inconsistent. You have undoubtedly discovered that record stores use overlapping and inconsistent categories. CDs by Shania Twain, for example, may be found in sections labeled *country, pop,* and *female vocal*. You can avoid such tangles if you create and control your own classification system.

For instance, James H. Austin classifies "four kinds of chance," and Judith Viorst classifies four types of lies. By contrast, the other three writers in this section explain existing systems of classification. In "Shades of Black," Mary Mebane classifies the arbitrary and unfair assessment of students by color and class. In "Modern Friendships," Phillip Lopate classifies friendships according to age. And in "The Dramaturgy of Death," Garry Wills classifies the fourteen motives for capital punishment.

After you have divided your subject into separate and consistent categories, *make sure your division is complete*. The simplest kind of division separates a subject into two categories: A and Not-A (for example, conformists and nonconformists). This kind of division, however, is rarely encouraged. It allows you to tell your readers about category A (conformists), but you won't tell them much about Not-A (nonconformists). For this reason, you should try to exhaust your subject by finding at least three separate categories and by acknowledging any examples that don't fit into the system. When an author writes a formal classification essay, like Phillip Lopate in this section, he or she tries to be definitive—to include everything significant. Or if an author realizes that his or her divisions do not exhaust the subject, he or she may, like Garry Wills, admit that the categories may conflict with each other on one level and reinforce each other on another level.

Once you have completed your process of division, *arrange your categories and examples in an emphatic order.* Lopate arranges his categories of friendship from childhood to adulthood. Austin arranges his classification of chance from blind luck to personal sensibility. Viorst arranges her categories by the degree of social and moral harm they may cause. Mebane arranges her categories into increasingly subtle codes of class and color. The authors of these essays reveal the principal purpose underlying their classification schemes: to show variety in similarity, to challenge the arbitrariness of an established system, and to point out how concepts change.

Finally, *you need to show the significance of your system of classification.* The strength of the classification process is that you can use it to analyze a subject in any number of ways. Its weakness is that you can use it to subdivide a subject into all kinds of trivial or pointless categories. You can classify people by their educational backgrounds, their work experience, or their significant achievements. You can also classify them by their shoe size, the kind of socks they wear, or their tastes in ice cream. Notice that, when Mary Mebane explains her classification system, she questions the social and psychological impact it has on self-esteem, and that Garry Wills classifies the historical reasons for capital punishment in order to demonstrate its ineffectiveness.

USING DIVISION AND CLASSIFICATION IN PARAGRAPHS

Here are two division-and-classification paragraphs. The first is written by a professional writer and is followed by an analysis. The second is written by a student writer and is followed by questions.

WENDELL BERRY
Conservation Is Good Work

Divides conservation into three categories:
1. preservation of wild or "scenic" places
2. conservation of natural resources
3. limit, stop, or remedy abuses

There are, as nearly as I can make out, three kinds of conservation currently operating. The first is the preservation of places that are grandly wild or "scenic" or in some other way spectacular. The second is what is called "conservation of natural resources"—That is, of the things of nature that we intend to use: soil, water, timber, and minerals. The third is what you might call industrial troubleshooting: the attempt to limit or stop or remedy the most flagrant abuses of the industrial system. All three kinds of conservation are inadequate, both separately and together.

Concludes that all three are inadequate.

Comment In this paragraph, Wendell Berry points out the "three kinds of conservation currently operating" in our culture. As his last sentence suggests, Berry's purpose for establishing these categories is to demonstrate—in subsequent paragraphs—why they are "inadequate, both separately and together."

GARETH TUCKER
Gentlemen! Start Your Engines

On a typical weekend, most couch potatoes can channel-surf past about a dozen car races. As they watch brightly colored machines circling the track again and again, like images on some manic video game, they may conclude that a race is a race is a race. Actually automobile racing is divided into many subtle subcategories. For example, the three most popular forms can be identified by the image of the car and driver. Stock cars are perceived as souped-up versions of "stock" cars driven by "good ole boys" who talk as if they have just outrun the local police. Indy cars are perceived as masterpieces of engineering driven by "test pilots" who speak the technobabble of rocket scientists. Formula One cars are almost as technologically advanced as Indy cars, but they still retain the image of the European "Grand Prix" car—the sports car driven by some count who talks as if he's just finished a jolly little tour through the countryside.

1. What principle does Tucker use to establish his three categories?
2. How does his characterization of the race car driver help clarify each category?

DIVISION AND CLASSIFICATION

Points to Remember

1. Determine whether you want to (a) explain an existing system of classification or (b) create your own system.
2. Divide your subject into smaller categories by applying the same principle of selection to each category.
3. Make sure that your division is complete by establishing separate and consistent types of categories.
4. Arrange your categories (and the examples you use to illustrate each category) in a logical and emphatic sequence.
5. Demonstrate the significance of your system by calling your readers' attention to its significance.

CLOUD CHART

LONERS

Single clouds that like to hang out in an otherwise cloudless sky.

SHEEP

Little clouds that always appear in bunches.

SPEEDY GONZALI

Clouds in a huge hurry to get to the next sky.

BLOCKERS

Mischievous clouds with a fondness for popping up just as one decides to go in the ocean.

GRAY BLANKET

One vast gray cloud that usually covers several states at once.

INDUSTRIOS

Beautiful clouds that are most often seen over large manufacturing plants.

SIGMUNDS

Clouds with an uncanny ability to make you feel anxious or depressed.

DUHS

No-name, generic clouds having no meteorological significance whatsoever.

R. Chst

In this quirky cartoon, Roz Chast classifies the different kinds of clouds one can see in the sky. Examine the various categories in her "Cloud Chart." Reflect on your own experience watching clouds. What categories has she omitted or mislabeled? Write an essay that explains how meteorologists classify clouds or, alternatively, how clouds figure metaphorically in expressions ("his face clouded over"), literature (including song lyrics), or art.

JAMES H. AUSTIN

James H. Austin was born in 1925 in Cleveland, Ohio, and educated at Brown University and Harvard University Medical School. After an internship at Boston City Hospital and a residency at the Neurological Institute of New York, Austin established a private practice in neurology, first in Portland, Oregon, and then in Denver, Colorado. He currently serves as professor and head of the department of neurology at the University of Colorado Medical School. His major publication, *Chase, Chance, and Creativity: The Lucky Art of Novelty* (1978), addresses the issue of how "chance and creativity interact in biomedical research." His most recent book is *Zen and the Brain: Toward an Understanding of Meditation and Consciousness* (1999). In this essay, published originally in *Saturday Review,* Austin distinguishes four kinds of chance by the way humans react to their environment.

Four Kinds of Chance

W HAT IS CHANCE? Dictionaries define it as something 1
fortuitous that happens unpredictably without dis-
cernible human intention. Chance is unintentional and capricious, but we needn't conclude that chance is immune from
human intervention. Indeed, chance plays several distinct
roles when humans react creatively with one another and
with their environment.

We can readily distinguish four varieties of chance if we 2
consider that they each involve a different kind of motor activity and a special kind of sensory receptivity. The varieties of

chance also involve distinctive personality traits and differ in the way one particular individual influences them.

Chance I is the pure blind luck that comes with no effort   3
on your part. If, for example, you are sitting at a bridge table of four, it's "in the cards" for you to receive a hand of all 13 spades, but it will come up only once in every 6.3 trillion deals. You will ultimately draw this lucky hand—with no intervention on your part—but it does involve a longer wait than most of us have time for.

Chance II evokes the kind of luck Charles Kettering had in   4
mind when he said: "Keep on going and the chances are you

The term serendipity *describes the facility for encountering unexpected good luck, as the result of accident, general exploratory behavior, or sagacity.*

---

will stumble on something, perhaps when you are least expecting it. I have never heard of anyone stumbling on something sitting down."

In the sense referred to here, Chance II is not passive, but   5
springs from an energetic, generalized motor activity. A certain basal level of action "stirs up the pot," brings in random ideas that will collide and stick together in fresh combinations, lets chance operate. When someone, *anyone,* does swing into motion and keeps on going, he will increase the number of collisions between events. When a few events are linked together, they can then be exploited to have a fortuitous outcome, but many others, of course, cannot. Kettering was right. Press on. Something will turn up. We may term this the Kettering Principle.

In the two previous examples, a unique role of the individ-   6
ual person was either lacking or minimal. Accordingly, as we move on to Chance III, we see blind luck, but in camouflage.

Chance presents the clue, the opportunity exists, but it would be missed except by that one person uniquely equipped to observe it, visualize it conceptually, and fully grasp its significance. Chance III involves a special receptivity and discernment unique to the recipient. Louis Pasteur characterized it for all time when he said: "Chance favors only the prepared mind."

Pasteur himself had it in full measure. But the classic example of his principle occurred in 1928, when Alexander Fleming's mind instantly fused at least five elements into a conceptually unified nexus. His mental sequences went something like this: (1) I see that a mold has fallen by accident into my culture dish; (2) the staphylococcal colonies residing near it failed to grow; (3) the mold must have secreted something that killed the bacteria; (4) I recall a similar experience once before; (5) if I could separate this new "something" from the mold, it could be used to kill staphylococci that cause human infections.

Actually, Fleming's mind was exceptionally well prepared for the penicillin mold. Six years earlier, while he was suffering from a cold, his own nasal drippings had found their way into a culture dish, for reasons not made entirely clear. He noted that nearby bacteria were killed, and astutely followed up the lead. His observations led him to discover a bactericidal enzyme present in nasal mucus and tears, called lysozyme. Lysozyme proved too weak to be of medical use, but imagine how receptive Fleming's mind was to the penicillin mold when it later happened on the scene!

One word evokes the quality of the operations involved in the first three kinds of chance. It is *serendipity.* The term describes the facility for encountering unexpected good luck, as the result of: accident (Chance I), general exploratory behavior (Chance II), or sagacity (Chance III). The word itself was coined by the Englishman-of-letters Horace Walpole, in 1754. He used it with reference to the legendary tales of the Three Princes of Serendip (Ceylon), who quite unexpectedly encountered many instances of good fortune on their travels. In today's parlance, we have usually watered down *serendipity* to mean the good luck that comes solely by accident. We think of it as a result, not an ability. We have tended to lose sight of the element of sagacity, by which term Walpole wished to emphasize that some distinctive personal receptivity is involved.

There remains a fourth element in good luck, an uninten- 10 tional but subtle personal prompting of it. The English Prime Minister Benjamin Disraeli summed up the principle underlying Chance IV when he noted that "we make our fortunes and we call them fate." Disraeli, a politician of considerable practical experience, appreciated that we each shape our own destiny, at least to some degree. One might restate the principle as follows: *Chance favors the individualized action.*

In Chance IV the kind of luck is peculiar to one person, 11 and like a personal hobby, it takes on a distinctive individual flavor. This form of chance is one-man-made, and it is as personal as a signature. . . . Chance IV has an elusive, almost miragelike, quality. Like a mirage, it is difficult to get a firm grip on, for it tends to recede as we pursue it and advance as we step back. But we still accept a mirage when we see it, because we vaguely understand the basis for the phenomenon. A strongly heated layer of air, less dense than usual, lies next to the earth, and it bends the light rays as they pass through. The resulting image may be magnified as if by a telescopic lens in the atmosphere, and real objects, ordinarily hidden far out of sight over the horizon, are brought forward and revealed to the eye. What happens in a mirage then, and in this form of chance, not only appears farfetched but indeed is farfetched.

About a century ago, a striking example of Chance IV 12 took place in the Spanish cave of Altamira.* There, one day in 1879, Don Marcelino de Sautuola was engaged in his hobby of archaeology, searching Altamira for bones and stones. With him was his daughter, Maria, who had asked him if she could come along to the cave that day. The

*The cave had first been discovered some years before by an enterprising hunting dog in search of game. Curiously, in 1932 the French cave of Lascaux was discovered by still another dog.

indulgent father had said she could. Naturally enough, he first looked where he had always found heavy objects before, on the *floor* of the cave. But Maria, unhampered by any such preconceptions, looked not only at the floor but also all around the cave with the open-eyed wonder of a child! She looked up, exclaimed, and then he looked up, to see incredible works of art on the cave ceiling! The magnificent colored bison and other animals they saw at Altamira, painted more than 15,000 years ago, might lead one to call it "the Sistine Chapel of Prehistory." Passionately pursuing his interest in archaeology, de Sautuola, to his surprise, discovered man's first paintings. In quest of science, he happened upon Art.

Yes, a dog did "discover" the cave, and the initial receptivity was his daughter's, but the pivotal reason for the cave paintings' discovery hinged on a long sequence of prior events originating in de Sautuola himself. For when we dig into the background of this amateur excavator, we find he was an exceptional person. Few Spaniards were out probing into caves 100 years ago. The fact that he—not someone else—decided to dig that day in the cave of Altamira was the culmination of his passionate interest in his hobby. Here was a rare man whose avocation had been to educate himself from scratch, as it were, in the science of archaeology and cave exploration. This was no simple passive recognizer of blind luck when it came his way, but a man whose unique interests served as an active creative thrust—someone whose own actions and personality would focus the events that led circuitously but inexorably to the discovery of man's first paintings. 13

Then, too, there is a more subtle matter. How do you give full weight to the personal interests that imbue your child with your own curiosity, that inspire her to ask to join you in your own musty hobby, and that then lead you to agree to her request at the critical moment? For many reasons, at Altamira, more than the special receptivity of Chance III was required—this was a different domain, that of the personality and its actions. 14

A century ago no one had the remotest idea our caveman   15
ancestors were highly creative artists. Weren't their talents
rather minor and limited to crude flint chippings? But the
paintings at Altamira, like a mirage, would quickly magnify
this diminutive view, bring up into full focus a distant, hidden
era of man's prehistory, reveal sentient minds and well-
developed aesthetic sensibilities to which men of any age
might aspire. And like a mirage, the events at Altamira grew
out of de Sautuola's heated personal quest and out of the invisible forces of chance we know exist yet cannot touch. Accordingly, one may introduce the term *altamirage* to identify
the quality underlying Chance IV. Let us define it as the facility for encountering unexpected good luck as the result of
highly individualized action. *Altamirage* goes well beyond
the boundaries of serendipity in its emphasis on the role of
personal action in chance.

Chance IV is favored by distinctive, if not eccentric, hob-   16
bies, personal life-styles, and modes of behavior peculiar to
one individual, usually invested with some passion. The farther apart these personal activities are from the area under
investigation, the more novel and unexpected will be the
creative product of the encounter.

For Study and Discussion

QUESTIONS FOR RESPONSE

1. Would you consider yourself a lucky or an unlucky person? What
   evidence would you use to support your case?
2. Do you agree with Austin's assessment of the dictionary's
   definitions of the word *chance*? How would you define the word?

QUESTIONS ABOUT PURPOSE

1. What elements of human behavior and attitude does Austin
   demonstrate by dividing chance into four varieties?
2. What relationship does Austin discover between the words *luck,*
   serendipity, sagacity, and *altamirage*?

QUESTIONS ABOUT AUDIENCE

1. What assumptions does Austin make about his readers when he offers them *the best example* rather than several examples to illustrate each category?
2. How does Austin's attitude toward his audience change during the essay? For example, why does he speak directly to his readers when he explains Chance I but address them more formally in his discussion of other categories?

QUESTIONS ABOUT STRATEGIES

1. How does Austin arrange his four categories? Why doesn't he give equal treatment to each category?
2. How does Austin use transitions and summaries to clarify the differences between the major categories? In particular, see paragraphs 6 and 9.

QUESTIONS FOR DISCUSSION

1. What incidents in your personal experience would support Austin's classification system? How many examples can you cite in each category?
2. What do you think is the relationship between *ability* and *result*? For example, what is your opinion of Disraeli's assertion that "we make our fortunes and we call them fate"?

JUDITH VIORST

Judith Viorst was born in 1931 in Newark, New Jersey, and educated at Rutgers University and Washington Psychoanalytic Institute. She began her career by writing a science book about NASA's space program, *Projects: Space* (1962). Viorst then turned to poetry, *The Village Square* (1965), and eventually children's literature, *Sunday Morning* (1968). In her distinguished career as a poet, fiction writer, and children's author, she has blended her wry humor with critical analysis. Her more recent books include *Super-Completely and Totally the Messiest* (2000) and *Suddenly Sixty and Other Shocks of Later Life* (2000). In "The Truth About Lying," reprinted from *Redbook,* Viorst classifies lying in terms of "a series of moral puzzles."

The Truth About Lying

I'VE BEEN WANTING to write on a subject that intrigues and challenges me: the subject of lying. I've found it very difficult to do. Everyone I've talked to has a quite intense and personal but often rather intolerant point of view about what we can—and can never *never*—tell lies about. I've finally reached the conclusion that I can't present any ultimate conclusions, for too many people would promptly disagree. Instead, I'd like to present a series of moral puzzles, all concerned with lying. I'll tell you what I think about them. Do you agree?

SOCIAL LIES

Most of the people I've talked with say that they find social lying acceptable and necessary. They think it's the civilized way for folks to behave. Without these little white lies, they say, our relationships would be short and brutish and nasty. It's arrogant, they say, to insist on being so incorruptible and so brave that you cause other people unnecessary embarrassment or pain by compulsively assailing them with your honesty. I basically agree. What about you?

Will you say to people, when it simply isn't true, "I like your new hairdo," "You're looking much better," "It's so nice to see you," "I had a wonderful time"? 3

Will you praise hideous presents and homely kids? 4

Will you decline invitations with "We're busy that night— so sorry we can't come," when the truth is you'd rather stay home than dine with the So-and-sos? 5

And even though, as I do, you may prefer the polite evasion of "You really cooked up a storm" instead of "The 6

Everyone I've talked to has a quite intense and personal but often rather intolerant view about what we can—and can never never—*tell lies about.*

---

soup"—which tastes like warmed-over coffee—"is wonderful," will you, if you must, proclaim it wonderful?

There's one man I know who absolutely refuses to tell social lies. "I can't play that game," he says; "I'm simply not made that way." And his answer to the argument that saying nice things to someone doesn't cost anything is, "Yes, it does—it destroys your credibility." Now, he won't, unsolicited, offer his views on the painting you just bought, but you don't ask his frank opinion unless you want *frank,* and his silence at those moments when the rest of us liars are muttering, "Isn't it lovely?" is, for the most part, eloquent enough. My friend does not indulge in what he calls "flattery, false praise and mellifluous comments." When others tell fibs he will not go along. He says that social lying is lying, that 7 little white lies are still lies. And he feels that telling lies is morally wrong. What about you?

PEACE-KEEPING LIES

Many people tell peace-keeping lies; lies designed to avoid irritation or argument; lies designed to shelter the liar from possible blame or pain; lies (or so it is rationalized) designed to keep trouble at bay without hurting anyone. 8

I tell these lies at times, and yet I always feel they're wrong. I understand why we tell them, but still they feel wrong. And whenever I lie so that someone won't disapprove of me or think less of me or holler at me, I feel I'm a bit of a coward, I feel I'm dodging responsibility, I feel . . . guilty. What about you? 9

Do you, when you're late for a date because you overslept, say that you're late because you got caught in a traffic jam? 10

Do you, when you forget to call a friend, say that you called several times but the line was busy? 11

Do you, when you didn't remember that it was your father's birthday, say that his present must be delayed in the mail? 12

And when you're planning a weekend in New York City and you're not in the mood to visit your mother, who lives there, do you conceal—with a lie, if you must—the fact that you'll be in New York? Or do you have the courage—or is it the cruelty?—to say, "I'll be in New York, but sorry—I don't plan on seeing you"? 13

(Dave and his wife Elaine have two quite different points of view on this very subject. He calls her a coward. She says she's being wise. He says she must assert her right to visit New York sometimes and not see her mother. To which she always patiently replies: "Why should we have useless fights? My mother's too old to change. We get along much better when I lie to her.") 14

Finally, do you keep the peace by telling your husband lies on the subject of money? Do you reduce what you really paid for your shoes? And in general do you find yourself ready, 15 willing and able to lie to him when you make absurd mistakes or lose or break things?

"I used to have a romantic idea that part of intimacy was   16
confessing every dumb thing that you did to your husband. But after a couple of years of that," says Laura, "have I changed my mind!"

And having changed her mind, she finds herself telling   17
peace-keeping lies. And yes, I tell them too. What about you?

PROTECTIVE LIES

Protective lies are lies folks tell—often quite serious lies—   18
because they're convinced that the truth would be too damaging. They lie because they feel there are certain human values that supersede the wrong of having lied. They lie, not for personal gain, but because they believe it's for the good of the person they're lying to. They lie to those they love, to those who trust them most of all, on the grounds that breaking this trust is justified.

They may lie to their children on money or marital   19
matters.

They may lie to the dying about the state of their health.   20

They may lie about adultery, and not—so they insist—to   21
save their own hide, but to save the heart and the pride of the men they are married to.

They may lie to their closest friend because the truth about   22
her talents or son or psyche would be—or so they insist—utterly devastating.

I sometimes tell such lies, but I'm aware that it's quite pre-   23
sumptuous to claim I know what's best for others to know. That's called playing God. That's called manipulation and control. And we never can be sure, once we start to juggle lies, just where they'll land, exactly where they'll roll.

And furthermore, we may find ourselves lying in order to   24
back up the lies that are backing up the lie we initially told.

And furthermore—let's be honest—if conditions were   25
reversed, we certainly wouldn't want anyone lying to us.

Yet, having said all that, I still believe that there are times   26
when protective lies must nonetheless be told. What about
you?

If your Dad had a very bad heart and you had to tell him   27
some bad family news, which would you choose: to tell him
the truth or lie?

If your former husband failed to send his monthly child-   28
support check and in other ways behaved like a total rat,
would you allow your children—who believed he was simply
wonderful—to continue to believe that he was wonderful?

If your dearly beloved brother selected a wife whom you   29
deeply disliked, would you reveal your feelings or would you
fake it?

And if you were asked, after making love, "And how was   30
that for you?" would you reply, if it wasn't too good, "Not
too good"?

Now, some would call a sex lie unimportant, little more   31
than social lying, a simple act of courtesy that makes all
human intercourse run smoothly. And some would say all sex
lies are bad news and unacceptably protective. Because, says
Ruth, "a man with an ego that fragile doesn't need your
lies—he needs a psychiatrist." Still others feel that sex lies are
indeed protective lies, more serious than simple social lying,
and yet at times they tell them on the grounds that when it
comes to matters sexual, everybody's ego is somewhat fragile.

"If most of the time things go well in sex," says Sue, "I   32
think you're allowed to dissemble when they don't. I can't
believe it's good to say, 'Last night was four stars, darling, but
tonight's performance rates only a half.'"

I'm inclined to agree with Sue. What about you?   33

TRUST-KEEPING LIES

Another group of lies are trust-keeping lies, lies that involve   34
triangulation, with *A* (that's you) telling lies to *B* on behalf of
C (whose trust you'd promised to keep). Most people
concede that once you've agreed not to betray a friend's confidence, you can't betray it, even if you must lie. But I've

talked with people who don't want you telling them anything that they might be called on to lie about.

"I don't tell lies for myself," says Fran, "and I don't want to have to tell them for other people." Which means, she agrees, that if her best friend is having an affair, she absolutely doesn't want to know about it. 35

"Are you saying," her best friend asks, "that if I went off with a lover and I asked you to tell my husband I'd been with you, that you wouldn't lie for me, that you'd betray me?" 36

Fran is very pained but very adamant. "I wouldn't want to betray you, so . . . don't ask me." 37

Fran's best friend is shocked. What about you? 38

Do you believe you can have close friends if you're not prepared to receive their deepest secrets? 39

Do you believe you must always lie for your friends? 40

Do you believe, if your friend tells a secret that turns out to be quite immoral or illegal, that once you've promised to keep it, you must keep it? 41

And what if your friend were your boss—if you were perhaps one of the President's men—would you betray or lie for him over, say, Watergate? 42

As you can see, these issues get terribly sticky. 43

It's my belief that once we've promised to keep a trust, we must tell lies to keep it. I also believe that we can't tell Watergate lies. And if these two statements strike you as quite contradictory, you're right—they're quite contradictory. But for now they're the best I can do. What about you? 44

Some say that truth will out and thus you might as well tell the truth. Some say you can't regain the trust that lies lose. Some say that even though the truth may never be revealed, our lies pervert and damage our relationships. Some say . . . well, here's what some of them have to say. 45

"I'm a coward," says Grace, "about telling close people important, difficult truths. I find that I'm unable to carry it off. And so if something is bothering me, it keeps building up inside till I end up just not seeing them any more." 46

"I lie to my husband on sexual things, but I'm furious," says Joyce, "that he's too insensitive to know I'm lying." 47

"I suffer most from the misconception that children can't   48
take the truth," says Emily. "But I'm starting to see that
what's harder and more damaging for them is being told lies,
is *not* being told the truth."

"I'm afraid," says Joan, "that we often wind up feeling a   49
bit of contempt for the people we lie to."

And then there are those who have no talent for lying.   50

"Over the years, I tried to lie," a friend of mine explained,   51
"but I always got found out and I always got punished. I
guess I gave myself away because I feel guilty about any kind
of lying. It looks as if I'm stuck with telling the truth."

For those of us, however, who are good at telling lies, for   52
those of us who lie and don't get caught, the question of
whether or not to lie can be a hard and serious moral problem. I liked the remark of a friend of mine who said, "I'm willing to lie. But just as a last resort—the truth's always better."

"Because," he explained, "though others may completely   53
accept the lie I'm telling, I don't."

I tend to feel that way too.   54

What about you?   55

Questions for Study and Discussion

QUESTIONS FOR RESPONSE

1. When do you think it is acceptable and appropriate to lie?
2. How often have you had to tell one lie to cover another lie?

QUESTIONS ABOUT PURPOSE

1. How does Viorst's confession that she finds the subject of lying
   intriguing, challenging, and difficult establish the purpose of her
   essay?
2. How does her inability to "present any ultimate conclusions"
   explain the design of her essay?

QUESTIONS ABOUT AUDIENCE

1. What assumptions does Viorst make about her readers' interest in and familiarity with her subject?
2. How does she use the pronoun *you* to establish a connection with her readers?

QUESTIONS ABOUT STRATEGIES

1. Into what main categories does Viorst divide the subject of lying? Can you think of other categories she might have included?
2. What inconsistencies does she admit she has created in some of her categories?

QUESTIONS FOR DISCUSSION

1. What does Viorst suggest about the relationship between telling the truth and maintaining trust?
2. How does she characterize people who tell lies and the people who are lied to?

MARY MEBANE

Mary Mebane was born in 1933 in Durham,
North Carolina, and educated at North Carolina
Central University and the University of North
Carolina. She taught in the public schools of
North Carolina before moving on to teaching
writing at the University of South Carolina and
the University of Wisconsin. She has written essays
for the *New York Times;* a two-act play, *Take a Sad
Song* (1975); and two volumes of her autobiography, *Mary: An Autobiography* (1981) and *Mary,
Wayfarer* (1983). In "Shades of Black," excerpted
from the first autobiographical volume, Mebane
reveals how class and color have been used to classify members of the African-American community.

Shades of Black

D URING MY FIRST week of classes as a freshman, I was 1
stopped one day in the hall by the chairman's wife,
who was indistinguishable in color from a white woman. She
wanted to see me, she said.

This woman had no official position on the faculty, except 2
that she was an instructor in English; nevertheless, her summons had to be obeyed. In the segregated world there were
(and remain) gross abuses of authority because those at the
pinnacle, and even their spouses, felt that the people "under"
them had no recourse except to submit—and they were right
except that sometimes a black who got sick and tired of it
would go to the whites and complain. This course of action
was severely condemned by the blacks, but an interesting
thing happened—such action always got positive results.
Power was thought of in negative terms: I can deny someone
something, I can strike at someone who can't strike back, I

can ride someone down; that proves I am powerful. The concept of power as a force for good, for affirmative response to people or situations, was not in evidence.

When I went to her office, she greeted me with a big   3
smile. "You know," she said, "you made the highest mark on the verbal part of the examination." She was referring to the examination that the entire freshman class took upon entering the college. I looked at her but I didn't feel warmth, for in spite of her smile her eyes and tone of voice were saying, "How could this black-skinned girl score higher on the verbal than some of the students who've had more advantages than she? It must be some sort of fluke. Let me talk to her." I felt it, but I managed to smile my thanks and back off. For here at North Carolina College at Durham, as it had been since the beginning, social class and color were the primary criteria used in determining status on the campus.

First came the children of doctors, lawyers, and college   4
teachers. Next came the children of public-school teachers, businessmen, and anybody else who had access to more money than the poor black working class. After that came the

---

*At my college . . . social class and color were
the primary criteria used in determining
status on the campus.*

---

bulk of the student population, the children of the working class, most of whom were the first in their families to go beyond high school. The attitude toward them was: You're here because we need the numbers, but in all other things defer to your betters.

The faculty assumed that light-skinned students were   5
more intelligent, and they were always a bit nonplussed when a dark-skinned student did well, especially if she was a girl. They had reason to be appalled when they discovered that I

planned to do not only well but better than my light-skinned peers.

I don't know whether African men recently transported to   6
the New World considered themselves handsome or, more important, whether they considered African women beautiful in comparison with Native American Indian women or immigrant European women. It is a question that I have never heard raised or seen research on. If African men considered African women beautiful, just when their shift in interest away from black black women occurred might prove to be an interesting topic for researchers. But one thing I know for sure: by the twentieth century, really black skin on a woman was considered ugly in this country. This was particularly true among those who were exposed to college.

Hazel, who was light brown, used to say to me, "You are   7
dark, but not *too* dark." The saved commiserating with the damned. I had the feeling that if nature had painted one more brushstroke on me, I'd have had to kill myself.

Black skin was to be disguised at all costs. Since a black   8
face is rather hard to disguise, many women took refuge in ludicrous makeup. Mrs. Burry, one of my teachers in elementary school, used white face powder. But she neglected to powder her neck and arms, and even the black on her face gleamed through the white, giving her an eerie appearance. But she did the best she could.

I observed all through elementary and high school that for   9
various entertainments the girls were placed on the stage in order of color. And very black ones didn't get into the front row. If they were past caramel-brown, to the back row they would go. And nobody questioned the justice of these decisions—neither the students nor the teachers.

One of the teachers at Wildwood School, who was from the   10
Deep South and was just as black as she could be, had been a strict enforcer of these standards. That was another irony—that someone who had been judged outside the realm of beauty herself because of her skin tones should have adopted them so wholeheartedly and applied them herself without question.

One girl stymied that teacher, though. Ruby, a black 11
cherry of a girl, not only got off the back row but off the
front row as well, to stand alone at stage center. She could
outsing, outdance, and outdeclaim everyone else, and talent
proved triumphant over pigmentation. But the May Queen
and her Court (and in high school, Miss Wildwood) were
always chosen from among the lighter ones.

When I was a freshman in high school, it became clear that 12
a light-skinned sophomore girl named Rose was going to get
the "best girl scholar" prize for the next three years, and
there was nothing I could do about it, even though I knew I
was the better. Rose was caramel-colored and had shoulder-
length hair. She was highly favored by the science and math
teacher, who figured the averages. I wasn't. There was only
one prize. Therefore, Rose would get it until she graduated.
I was one year behind her, and I would not get it until after
she graduated.

To be held in such low esteem was painful. It was diffi- 13
cult not to feel that I had been cheated out of the medal,
which I felt that, in a fair competition, I perhaps would
have won. Being unable to protest or do anything about it
was a traumatic experience for me. From then on I instinctively tended to avoid the college-exposed, dark-skinned
male, knowing that when he looked at me he saw himself
and, most of the time, his mother and sister as well, and
since he had rejected his blackness, he had rejected theirs
and mine.

Oddly enough, the lighter-skinned black male did not 14
seem to feel so much prejudice toward the black black
woman. It was no accident, I felt, that Mr. Harrison, the
eighth-grade teacher, who was reddish-yellow himself, once
protested to the science and math teacher about the fact that
he always assigned sweeping duties to Doris and Ruby Lee,
two black black girls. Mr. Harrison said to them one day,
right in the other teacher's presence, "You must be some bad
girls. Every day I come down here ya'll are sweeping." The
science and math teacher got the point and didn't ask them
to sweep anymore.

Uneducated black males, too, sometimes related very well   15
to the black black woman. They had been less firmly indoc-
trinated by the white society around them and were more
securely rooted in their own culture.

Because of the stigma attached to having dark skin, a black   16
black woman had to do many things to find a place for herself. One possibility was to attach herself to a light-skinned
woman, hoping that some of the magic would rub off on her.
A second was to make herself sexually available, hoping to attract a mate. Third, she could resign herself to a more chaste
life-style—either (for the professional woman) teaching and
work in established churches or (for the uneducated woman)
domestic work and zealous service in the Holy and Sanctified
churches.

Even as a young girl, Lucy had chosen the first route. Lucy   17
was short, skinny, short-haired, and black black, and thus un-
acceptable. So she made her choice. She selected Patricia, the
lightest-skinned girl in the school, as her friend, and followed
her around. Patricia and her friends barely tolerated Lucy,
but Lucy smiled and doggedly hung on, hoping that some
who noticed Patricia might notice her, too. Though I felt
shame for her behavior, even then I understood.

As is often the case of the victim agreeing with and adopt-   18
ing the attitudes of oppressor, so I have seen it with black
black women. I have seen them adopt the oppressor's attitude that they are nothing but "sex machines," and their supposedly superior sexual performance becomes their sole
reason for being and for esteeming themselves. Such women
learn early that in order to make themselves attractive to men
they have somehow to shift the emphasis from physical
beauty to some other area—usually sexual performance.
Their constant talk is of their desirability and their ability to
gratify a man sexually.

I knew two such women well—both of them black black.   19
To hear their endless talk of sexual conquests was very sad. I
have never seen the category that these women fall into described anywhere. It is not that of promiscuity or nympho-
mania. It is the category of total self-rejection: "Since I am

black, I am ugly, I am nobody. I will perform on the level that they have assigned to me." Such women are the pitiful results of what not only white America but also, and more important, black America has done to them.

Some, not taking the sexuality route but still accepting black society's view of their worthlessness, swing all the way across to intense religiosity. Some are staunch, fervent workers in the more traditional Southern churches—Baptist and Methodist—and others are leaders and ministers in the lower status, more evangelical Holiness sects.

Another avenue open to the black black woman is excellence in a career. Since in the South the field most accessible to such women is education, a great many of them prepared to become teachers. But here, too, the black black woman had problems. Grades weren't given to her lightly in school, nor were promotions on the job. Consequently, she had to prepare especially well. She had to pass examinations with flying colors or be left behind; she knew that she would receive no special consideration. She had to be overqualified for a job because otherwise she didn't stand a chance of getting it— and she was competing only with other blacks. She had to have something to back her up: not charm, not personality— but training.

The black black woman's training would pay off in the 1970s. With the arrival of integration the black black woman would find, paradoxically enough, that her skin color in an integrated situation was not the handicap it had been in an all-black situation. But it wasn't until the middle and late 1960s, when the post-1945 generation of black males arrived on college campuses, that I noticed any change in the situation at all. *He* wore an afro and *she* wore an afro, and sometimes the only way you could tell them apart was when his afro was taller than hers. Black had become beautiful, and the really black girl was often selected as queen of various campus activities. It was then that the dread I felt at dealing with the college-educated black male began to ease. Even now, though, when I have occasion to engage in any type of transaction with a college-educated black man, I gauge his age. If

I guess he was born after 1945, I feel confident that the transaction will turn out all right. If he probably was born before 1945, my stomach tightens, I find myself taking shallow breaths, and I try to state my business and escape as soon as possible.

For Study and Discussion

QUESTIONS FOR RESPONSE

1. How do you respond when you or your friends are judged by some physical feature—weight, height, hair?
2. How do you and your friends identify various social classes? What assumptions do you make about people in each class?

QUESTIONS ABOUT PURPOSE

1. Why does Mebane use the concept of power to introduce her classification?
2. How does Mebane use her essay to explain the impulse of the victim to adopt the attitudes of the oppressor?

QUESTIONS ABOUT AUDIENCE

1. Does Mebane envision her readers as primarily black or primarily white, primarily men or primarily women? Explain your answer.
2. In what way do you think Mebane's system may apply to the attitudes of today's African-American students? Explain your answer.

QUESTIONS ABOUT STRATEGIES

1. How does Mebane classify her college classmates by color and class? What assumptions do her teachers make about black black working-class women?

2. What options does Mebane suggest are available to black black women? How are these options enforced?

QUESTIONS FOR DISCUSSION

1. How did the civil rights movement of the 1950s and the black consciousness movement of the 1960s change the African-American community's definition of beauty?
2. Do subtle judgments about class and color still control the power structure of the African-American community? In what way?

Phillip Lopate was born in Jamaica Heights, New York, in 1943 and educated at Columbia University. He taught creative writing with the Teachers and Writers Collaborative in the New York Public Schools before devoting his full attention to his own writing. He has contributed fiction to *Paris Review*, poetry to *Yale Literary Review*, and film criticism to the *Cinemabook*. His essays have appeared in collections such as *Against Joie de Vivre* (1989); he has also edited numerous writing collections such as *The Anchor Essay Annual* (1997) and *Writing New York: A Literary Anthology* (2000). In "Modern Friendships," reprinted from *Against Joie de Vivre*, Lopate classifies his changing attitude toward various kinds of "friends."

Modern Friendships

I S THERE ANYTHING left to say about friendship after so 1
many great essayists have picked over the bones of the
subject? Probably not. Aristotle and Cicero, Seneca and
Montaigne, Bacon and Samuel Johnson, Hazlitt, Emerson,
and Lamb have all taken their cracks at it; since the ancients,
friendship has been a sort of examination subject for the personal essayist. It is partly the very existence of such wonderful prior models that lures the newcomer to follow in the
others' footsteps, and partly a self-referential aspect of the
genre, since the personal essay is itself an attempt to establish
a friendship on the page between writer and reader.

Friendship has been called "love without wings," implying 2
a want of lyrical afflatus. On the other hand, the Stoic definition of love ("Love is the attempt to form a friendship
inspired by beauty") seems to suggest that friendship came

first. Certainly a case can be made that the buildup of affection and the yearning for more intimacy, without the release
of sexual activity, keeps friends in a state of sweet-sorrowful
itchiness that has as much romantic quality as a love affair. We
know that a falling-out between two old friends can leave a
deeper and more perplexing hurt than the ending of a love
affair, perhaps because we are more pessimistic about the latter's endurance from the start.

Our first attempted friendships are within the family. It is   3
here we practice the techniques of listening sympathetically

---

*Friendship is a school for character,
allowing us the chance to study in great
detail and over time temperaments
very different from our own.*

---

and proving that we can be trusted, and learn the sort of
kindness we can expect in return. I have a sister, one year
younger than I, who often took care of me when I was growing up. Once, when I was about fifteen, unable to sleep and
shivering uncontrollably with the start of a fever, I decided in
the middle of the night to go into her room and wake her.
She held me, performing the basic service of a friend—
presence—and the chills went away.

There is something tainted about these family friendships,   4
however. This same sister, in her insecure adolescent phase,
told me: "You love me because I'm related to you, but if you
were to meet me for the first time at a party, you'd think I was
a jerk and not worth being your friend." She had me in a
bind: I had no way of testing her hypothesis. I should have
argued that even if our bond was not freely chosen, our decision to work on it had been. Still, we are quick to dismiss the
partiality of our family members when they tell us we are

talented, cute, or lovable; we must go out into the world and seduce others.

It is just a few short years from the promiscuity of the sandbox to the tormented, possessive feelings of a fifth grader who has just learned that his best and only friend is playing at another classmate's house after school. There may be worse betrayals in store, but probably none is more influential than the sudden fickleness of an elementary school friend who has dropped us for someone more popular after all our careful, patient wooing. Often we lose no time inflicting the same betrayal on someone else, just to ensure that we have got the victimization dynamic right.

What makes friendships in childhood and adolescence so poignant is that we need the chosen comrade to be everything in order to rescue us from the gothic inwardness of family life. Even if we are lucky enough to have several companions, there must be a Best Friend, knightly dubbed as though victor of an Arthurian tournament.

I clung to the romance of the Best Friend all through high school, college, and beyond, until my university circle began to disperse. At that point, in my mid-twenties, I also "acted out" the dark competitive side of friendship that can exist between two young men fighting for a place in life and love, by doing the one unforgivable thing: sleeping with my best friend's girl. I was baffled at first that there was no way to repair the damage. I lost this friendship forever, and came away from that debacle much more aware of the amount of injury that friendship can and cannot sustain. Perhaps I needed to prove to myself that friendship was not an all-permissive, resilient bond, like a mother's love, but something quite fragile. Precisely because Best Friendship promotes such a merging of identities, such seeming boundarylessness, the first major transgression of trust can cause the injured party to feel he is fighting for his violated soul against his darkest enemy. There is not much room to maneuver in a best friendship between unlimited intimacy and unlimited mistrust.

Still, it was not until the age of thirty that I reluctantly abandoned the Best Friend expectation and took up a more pluralistic model. At present, I cherish a dozen friends for their unique personalities, without asking that any one be my soul-twin. Whether this alteration constitutes a movement toward maturity or toward cowardly pragmatism is not for me to say. It may be that, in refusing to depend so much on any one friend, I am opting for self-protection over intimacy. Or it may be that, as we advance into middle age, the life problem becomes less that of establishing a tight dyadic bond and more one of making our way in a broader world, "society." Indeed, since Americans have so indistinct a notion of society, we often try to put friendship networks in its place. If a certain intensity is lost in the pluralistic model of friendship, there is also the gain of being able to experience all of one's potential, half-buried selves, through witnessing the spectacle of the multiple fates of our friends. Since we cannot be polygamists in our conjugal life, at least we can do so with friendship. As it happens, the harem of friends, so tantalizing a notion, often translates into feeling pulled in a dozen different directions, with the guilty sense of having disappointed everyone a little. It is also a risky, contrived enterprise to try to make one's friends behave in a friendly manner toward each other: if the effort fails one feels obliged to mediate; if it succeeds too well, one is jealous.

Whether friendship is intrinsically singular and exclusive, or plural and democratic, is a question that has vexed many commentators. Aristotle distinguished three types of friendship in *The Nicomachean Ethics:* "friendship based on utility," such as businessmen cultivating each other for benefit; "friendship based on pleasure," like young people interested in partying; and "perfect friendship." The first two categories Aristotle calls "qualified and superficial friendships," because they are founded on circumstances that could easily change; the last, which is based on admiration for another's good character, is more permanent, but also rarer, because good men "are few." Cicero, who wrote perhaps the best treatise on friendship, also insisted that what brings true friends together is "a mutual belief in each other's goodness." This insistence on virtue as a precondition for true friendship may strike us as impossibly demanding: who, after all, feels himself good nowadays? And yet, if I am honest, I must admit that the friendships of mine which have lasted longest have been with those whose integrity, or humanity, or strength to bear their troubles I continue to admire. Conversely, when I lost respect for someone, however winning he otherwise remained, the friendship petered away almost immediately. "Remove respect from friendship," said Cicero, "and you have taken away the most splendid ornament it possesses."

Montaigne distinguished between friendship, which he saw as a once-in-a-lifetime experience, and the calculating worldly alliances around him, which he thought unworthy of the name. In paying tribute to his late friend Etienne de la Boetie, Montaigne wrote: "Having so little time to last, and having begun so late, for we were both grown men, and he a few years older than I, it could not lose time and conform to the pattern of mild and regular friendships, which need so many precautions in the form of long preliminary association. Our friendship has no other model than itself, and can be compared only with itself. It is not one special consideration, nor two, nor three, nor four, nor a thousand: it is I know not what quintessence of all this mixture, which, having seized my whole will, led it to plunge and lose itself in his; which, having seized his whole will, led it to plunge and lose itself in mine, with equal hunger, equal rivalry. . . . So many coincidences are needed to build up such a friendship that it is a lot if fortune can do it once in three centuries." This seems a bit high hat: since the sixteenth century, our expectations of friendship may have grown more plebeian. Even Emerson, in his grand romantic essay on the subject, allowed as how he was not up to the Castor-and-Pollux standard: "I am not quite so strict in my terms, perhaps because I have never known so high a fellowship as others." Emerson contents himself with a circle of intelligent men and women, but warns us not to throw them together: "You shall have very useful and cheering discourse at several times with two several men, but let all three of you come together, and you shall not have one new and hearty word. Two may talk and one may hear, but three cannot take part in a conversation of the most sincere and searching sort."

Friendship is a long conversation. I suppose I could imagine a nonverbal friendship revolving around shared physical work or sport, but for me, good talk is the point of the thing. Indeed, the ability to generate conversation by the hour is the most promising indication, during its uncertain early stages, that a possible friendship will take hold. In the first few conversations there may be an exaggeration of agreement, as both parties angle for adhesive surfaces. But later on, trust builds through the courage to assert disagreement, through the tactful acceptance that differences of opinion will have to remain. 11

Some view like-mindedness as both the precondition and product of friendship. Myself, I distrust it. I have one friend who keeps assuming that we see the world eye-to-eye. She is intent on enrolling us in a flattering aristocracy of taste, on the short "we" list against the ignorant "they"; sometimes I do not have the strength to fight her need for consensus with my own stubborn disbelief in the existence of any such inner circle of privileged, cultivated sensibility. Perhaps I have too much invested in a view of myself as idiosyncratic to be eager to join any coterie, even a coterie of two. What attracts me to friends' conversation is the give-and-take, not necessarily that we come out at the same point. 12

"Our tastes and aims and views were identical—and that is where the essence of a friendship must always lie," wrote Cicero. To some extent, perhaps, but then the convergence must be natural, not, as Emerson put it, "a mush of concession. Better be a nettle in the side of your friend than his echo." And Francis Bacon observed that "the best preservative to keep the mind in health is the faithful admonition of a friend." 13

Friendship is a school for character, allowing us the chance to study in great detail and over time temperaments very different from our own. These charming quirks, these contradictions, these nobilities, these blind spots of our friends we track not out of disinterested curiosity: we must have this information before knowing how far we may relax our guard, 14 how much we may rely on them in crises. The learning curve of friendship involves, to no small extent, filling out this picture of the other's limitations and making peace with the results. (With one's own limitations there may never be peace.) Each time I hit up against a friend's inflexibility I am relieved as well as disappointed: I can begin to predict, and arm myself in advance against repeated bruises. I have one friend who is always late, so I bring a book along when I am to meet her. If I give her a manuscript to read and she promises to look at it over the weekend, I start preparing myself for a month-long wait.

Not that one ever gives up trying to educate the friend to one's needs. I approach such matters experimentally: sometimes I will pride myself in tactfully circumventing the friend's predicted limitation, even if it means relinquishing all hope of getting the response I want; at other times I will confront a problem with intentional tactlessness, just to see if any change is still possible.   15

I have a dear old friend, Richard, who shies away from personal confidences. Years go by without my learning anything about his love life, and he does not encourage the baring of my soul either, much as I like that sort of thing. But we share so many other interests and values that that limitation seems easily borne, most of the time. Once, however, I found myself in a state of emotional despair; I told him I had exhausted my hopes of finding love or success, that I felt suicidal, and he changed the topic, patently embarrassed. I was annoyed both at his emotional rigidity and at my own stupidity—after all, I'd enough friends who ate up this kind of confessional talk, why foist on Richard what I might have predicted he couldn't, or wouldn't, handle? For a while I sulked, annoyed at him for having failed me, but I also began to see my despair through his eyes as melodramatic, childish petulance, and I began to let it go. As it happened, he found other ways during our visit to be so considerate that I ended up feeling better, even without our having had a heart-to-heart talk. I suppose the moral is that a friend can serve as a corrective to our insular miseries simply by offering up his essential otherness.   16

Though it is often said that with a true friend there is no   17
need to hold anything back ("A friend is a person with whom
I may be sincere. Before him I may think aloud," wrote
Emerson), I have never found this to be entirely the case.
Certain words may be too cruel if spoken at the wrong
moment—or may fall on deaf ears, for any number of reasons. I also find with each friend, as they must with me, that
some initial resistance, restlessness, psychic weather must be
overcome before that tender ideal attentiveness may be called
forth.

I have a good friend, Charlie, who is often very distracted   18
whenever we first get together. If we are sitting in a cafe he
will look around constantly for the waiter, or be distracted by
a pretty woman or the restaurant's cat. It would be foolish for
me to broach an important subject at such moments, so I resign myself to waiting the half hour or however long it takes
until his jumpiness subsides. Or else I draw this pattern
grumpily to his attention. Once he has settled down, however, I can tell Charlie virtually anything, and he me. But the
candor cannot be rushed. It must be built up to with the
verbal equivalent of limbering exercises.

The Friendship Scene—a flow of shared confidences,   19
recognitions, humor, advice, speculation, even wisdom—is
one of the key elements of modern friendships. Compared to
the rest of life, this ability to lavish one's best energies on an
activity utterly divorced from the profit motive and free from
the routines of domination and inequality that affect most relations (including, perhaps, the selfsame friendship at other
times) seems idyllic. The Friendship Scene is by its nature not
an everyday occurrence. It represents the pinnacle, the fruit
of the friendship, potentially ever-present but not always
arrived at. Both friends' dim yet self-conscious awareness that
they are wandering conversationally toward a goal that they
have previously accomplished but which may elude them this
time around creates a tension, an obligation to communicate
as sincerely as possible, like actors in an improvisation exercise
struggling to shape their baggy material into some climactic
form. This very pressure to achieve "quality" communication

may induce a sort of inauthentic epiphany, not unlike what happens sometimes in the last ten minutes of a psychotherapy session. But a truly achieved Friendship Scene can be among the best experiences life has to offer.

I remember one such afternoon when Michael, a close writer-friend, and I met at a cafeteria on a balmy Saturday in early spring and talked for three and a half hours. There were no outside time pressures that particular afternoon, a rare occurrence for either of us. At first we caught up with our latest business, the sort of items that might have gone into a biweekly bulletin sent to any number of acquaintances. Then gradually we settled into an area of perplexing unresolved impressions. I would tell Michael about A's chance, seemingly hostile remark toward me at a gathering, and he would report that the normally ebullient B looked secretly depressed. These were the memory equivalents of food grains stuck in our teeth, which we were now trying to free with our tongues: anecdotal fragments I was not even sure had any point, until I started fashioning them aloud for Michael's interest. Together we diagnosed our mutual acquaintances, each other's character, and, from there, the way of the world. In the course of our free associations we eventually descended into what was really bothering us. I learned he was preoccupied with the fate of an old college friend who was dying of AIDS; he, that my father was in poor health and needed two operations. We had touched bottom—mortality— and it was reassuring to settle there awhile. Gradually we rose again, drawn back to the questions of ego and career, craft and romance. It was, as I've said, a pretty day, and we ended up walking through a new mall in Houston, gawking at the window displays of that bland emporium with a reawakened curiosity about the consumer treats of America, our attentions turned happily outward now that we had dwelt long enough in the shared privacies of our psyches.

Contemporary urban life, with its tight schedules and crowded appointment books, has helped to shape modern friendship into something requiring a good deal of intentionality and pursuit. You phone a friend and make a date a week or more in advance; then you set aside an evening, like a tryst, during which to squeeze in all your news and advice, confession and opinion. Such intimate compression may add a romantic note to modern friendships, but it also places a strain on the meeting to yield a high quality of meaning and satisfaction, closer to art than life, thereby increasing the chance for disappointment. If I see certain busy or out-of-town friends only once every six months, we must not only catch up on our lives but convince ourselves within the allotted two hours together that we still share a special affinity, an inner track to each other's psyches, or the next meeting may be put off for years. Surely there must be another, saner rhythm to friendship in rural areas—or maybe not? I think about "the gold old days" when friends would go on walking tours through England together, when Edith Wharton would bundle poor Henry James into her motorcar and they'd drive to the South of France for a month. I'm not sure my friendships could sustain the strain of travel for weeks at a time, and the truth of the matter is that I've gotten used to this urban arrangement of serial friendship "dates," where the pleasure of the rendezvous is enhanced by the knowledge that it will only last, at most, six hours. If the two of us don't happen to mesh that day (always a possibility)—well, it's only a few hours; and if it should go beautifully, one needs an escape hatch from exaltation as well as disenchantment. I am capable of only so much intense, exciting communication before I start to fade; I come to these encounters equipped with a six-hour oxygen tank. Is this an evolutionary pattern of modern friendship, or only a personal limitation?

Perhaps because I conceive of the modern Friendship Scene   22
as a somewhat theatrical enterprise, a one-act play, I tend to be very affected by the "set," so to speak. A restaurant, a museum, a walk in the park through the zoo, even accompanying a friend on shopping errands—I prefer public turf where the stimulation of the city can play a backdrop to our dialogue, feeding it with details when inspiration flags. True, some of the most cherished friendship scenes have occurred

around a friend's kitchen table. The problem with restricting
the date to one another's houses is that the entertaining
friend may be unable to stop playing the host, or may sink too
passively into his or her surroundings. Subtle struggles may
also develop over which domicile should serve as the venue.

I have a number of *chez moi* friends, friends who always in-   23
vite me to come to their homes while evading offers to visit
mine. What they view as hospitality I see as a need to control
the *mise-en-scène* of friendship. I am expected to fit in where
they are most comfortable, while they play lord of the manor,
distracted by the props of decor, the pool, the unexpected
phone call, the swirl of children, animals, and neighbors. Indeed, *chez moi* friends often tend to keep a sort of open
house, so that in going over to see them—for a *tête-à-tête*, I
had assumed—I will suddenly find their other friends and
neighbors, whom they have also invited, dropping in all afternoon. There are only so many Sundays I care to spend hanging out with a friend's entourage before becoming impatient
for a private audience.

Married friends who own their own homes are much more   24
apt to try to draw me into their domestic fold, whereas single
people are often more sensitive about establishing a discreet
space for the friendship to occur. Perhaps the married assume
that a bachelor like myself is desperate for home cooking and
a little family life. I have noticed that it is not an easy matter
to pry a married friend away from mate and milieu. For married people, especially those with children, the home often
becomes the wellspring of all their nurturing feelings, and the
single friend is invited to partake in the general flow. Maybe
there is also a certain tendency on their parts to kill two birds
with one stone: they don't see enough of their spouse and
kids, and figure they can visit with you all at the same time.
And maybe they need one-on-one friendship less, hampered
as they are by responsibilities that no amount of camaraderie
or discussion can change. Often friendship in these circumstances is not even a pairing, but a mixing together of two
sets of parents and children willy-nilly. What would the ancients say about this? In Rome, according to Bacon, "the

whole senate dedicated an altar to Friendship, as to a goddess. . . ." From my standpoint, friendship is a jealous
goddess. Whenever a friend of mine marries, I have to fight
to overcome the feeling that I am being "replaced" by the
spouse. I don't mind sharing a friend with his family milieu—
in fact I like it, up to a point—but eventually I must get the
friend alone, or else, as a bachelor at a distinct power disad-
vantage, I risk becoming a mere spectator of familial rituals
instead of a key player in the drama of friendship.

A person living alone usually has more control over his or   25
her schedule, hence more energy to give to friendship. If anything, the danger is of investing too much emotional energy in
one's friends. When a single person is going through a romantic dry spell he or she often tries to extract the missing passion
from a circle of friends. This works only up to a point: the
frayed nerves of protracted celibacy can lead to hypersensitive
imaginings of slights and rejections, during which times one's
platonic friends seem to come particularly into the line of fire.

Today, with the partial decline of the nuclear family and   26
the search for alternatives to it, we also see attempts to substitute the friendship web for intergenerational family life.
Since psychoanalysis has alerted us to regard the family as a
minefield of unrequited love, manipulation, and ambivalence, it is only natural that people may look to friendship as a
more supportive ground for relation. But in our longing for an
unequivocally positive bond, we should beware of sentimental-
izing friendship, as saccharine "buddy" movies or certain
feminist novels do, of neutering its problematic, destructive
aspects. Besides, friendship can never substitute for the true
meaning of family: if nothing else, it will never be able to
duplicate the family's wild capacity for concentrating neurosis.

In short, friends can't be your family, they can't be your   27
lovers, they can't be your psychiatrists. But they can be your
friends, which is plenty. For, as Cicero tells us, "friendship is
the noblest and most delightful of all the gifts the gods have
given to mankind." And Bacon adds: "It is a mere and miserable solitude to want true friends, without which the world is
but a wilderness. . . ."

When I think about the qualities that characterize the best   28
friendships I've known, I can identify five: rapport, affection,
need, habit, and forgiveness. Rapport and affection can only
take you so far; they may leave you at the formal, outer gate
of goodwill, which is still not friendship. A persistent need for
the other's company, for their interest, approval, opinion,
will get you inside the gates, especially when it is recipro-
cated. In the end, however, there are no substitutes for habit
and forgiveness. A friendship may travel for years on cozy
habit. But it is a melancholy fact that unless you are a saint
you are bound to offend every friend deeply at least once in
the course of time. The friends I have kept the longest are
those who forgave me for wronging them, unintentionally,
intentionally, or by the plain catastrophe of my personality,
time and again. There can be no friendship without
forgiveness.

For Study and Discussion

QUESTIONS FOR RESPONSE

1. In your life as a student, how many times have you had to write
   or read an essay on *friendship*? Which ones made the biggest impression on you?
2. How often do you enact the Friendship Scene (page 267)? What
   is your favorite setting for this scene?

QUESTIONS ABOUT PURPOSE

1. In what way does Lopate distinguish between the classical definition of friendship and friendships shaped by "contemporary
   urban life"?
2. What evidence does he supply for his argument that "friends
   can't be your family"?

QUESTIONS ABOUT AUDIENCE

1. Lopate acknowledges that many classical essayists have written about friendship. How does he help his readers understand what these essayists said? Does he agree or disagree with them?
2. He suggests, "The personal essay is an attempt to establish a friendship on the page between writer and reader." In what passages in the essay do you sense that Lopate is trying to establish such a friendship with his readers?

QUESTIONS ABOUT STRATEGIES

1. How does Lopate use maturity as a principle for classifying friendships? What kind of problems occur among "pluralistic" friends?
2. How does he use the scenes with Richard, Charlie, and Michael to demonstrate the difficulties of sustaining a friendship?

QUESTIONS FOR DISCUSSION

1. Only one of the friends Lopate mentions in this essay is a woman. How do you respond to the famous line in the movie *When Harry Met Sally* that "men and women can't be friends"?
2. What do you think about the five qualities Lopate identifies as characterizing the best friendships? Has he left out an important quality? Explain your answer.

GARRY WILLS

Garry Wills was born in 1934 in Atlanta, Georgia, and was educated at St. Louis University, Xavier University, and Yale University. He has taught humanities at Johns Hopkins University and American culture and public policy at Northwestern University. His many books on American politics and history include *Nixon Agonistes: The Crisis of the Self-Made Man* (1970), *Inventing America: Jefferson's Declaration of Independence* (1978), *Reagan's America: The Innocents at Home* (1987), *Lincoln at Gettysburg: The Words That Remade America* (1992), and *James Madison* (2002). In "The Dramaturgy of Death," reprinted from *The New York Review of Books*, Wills classifies fourteen reasons for killing someone to demonstrate that capital punishment is an ineffective ritual.

The Dramaturgy of Death

1. CAPITAL PUNISHMENT: THE RATIONALES

A slight perusal of the laws by which the measures of vindictive and coercive justice are established will discover so many disproportions between crimes and punishments, such capricious distinctions of guilt, and such confusion of remissness and severity as can scarcely be believed to have been produced by public wisdom, sincerely and calmly studious of public happiness.
—SAMUEL JOHNSON, *Rambler* 114

NIETZSCHE DENIED THAT capital punishment ever arose   1
from a single or consistent theory of its intent or effect. It erupted from a tangle of overlapping yet conflicting urges, which would be fitted out with later rationalizations.

274

The only common denominator he found in the original urges was some form of grievance (he used the French term *ressentiment*). One can expand his own list of such urges:

Killing as Exclusion. This occurs when society does not   2 want to admit any responsibility for persons considered outsiders. Abandonment of wounded or captured people one does not want to feed or support is an example, or exposure of unwanted children, or exiling the defenseless (as the blind

---

The bad faith of the [death penalty] process shows in the insistence on using the deterrence argument when it has been discredited by all the most reputable studies.

---

and old Oedipus was extruded from Thebes), or "outlawing" —leaving people without protection to any predators on them. Outlawing was an English practice continued in our colonies. In fact, Thomas Jefferson, when he revised the laws of Virginia for the new republic, left certain categories of offenders "out of the protection of the laws"—freed slaves who either enter the state or refuse to leave it, a white woman bearing a black child who does not leave the state within a year. These could be killed or mistreated in any way without remedy at law. The ancient Greeks denied offenders recourse to law by the penalty of *atimia* (loss of rights). There were lesser degrees of this, but the full degree of "atimia . . . and condemnation to death are interchangeable." Nietzsche calls this "Punishment as the expulsion of a degenerate element . . . as a means of preserving the purity of a race or maintaining a social type."

Killing as Cleansing. Outlawing abandons people to possible or probable death but does not directly bring it about.   3 Other forms of extrusion require society's purification by *destruction* of a polluted person. Unless society or its agents effect this purification, the pollution continues to taint them. Lesser pollutions can be robbed of their effect by simply driving away the affected person. But deeper taints are removed only by accompanying the expulsion with something like stoning the polluter to death or throwing him off a cliff. Plato said that the murderer of anyone in his own immediate family was to be killed by judicial officers and magistrate, then "thrown down naked on a designated crossroads outside the city; whereupon every official present must throw his own stone at the head of the corpse, to cleanse the whole city, and finally must take him beyond the land's outer boundaries and cast him out, all rites of burial denied" (*Laws* 873b–c).

Killing as Execration. Sometimes the community must   4
thrust away contamination by ritual curses *(arai)*, joining the punitive cry of the Furies, who are also called Arai (Aeschylus, *Eumenides* 417). When Prometheus is punished by exposure as the penalty of theft, Brute Force (Bia) tells the technician clamping him to the rock (Hephaistos) that he should curse as well as immobilize him (Aeschylus, *Prometheus* 38, 67–68). Southern lynch mobs stayed to curse with fury their hanged victim from a similar impulse.

Killing to Maintain Social Order. Superiors dramatize   5
their dominance by showing that it is easy for those higher in the social scale to kill those lower, but harder for the lower to kill the higher. Plato's legal code devised a penalty for a slave who kills a free man—public scourging to death before the free man's tomb and family—that had no symmetrical penalty for a free man who kills a slave (*Laws* 872b–c). In Jefferson's legal code, slaves could not testify against whites, but whites could testify against slaves. In parts of this country still, a black killing a white is far more likely to receive a death sentence than a white killing a black. Nietzsche calls this "Punishment as a means of inspiring fear of those who determine and execute the punishment."

Killing to Delegitimize a Former Social Order. Revolution-   6
ary tribunals execute officials of an overthrown regime. Even without a coup, critics of Athenian democracy claimed that mass juries were too ready to condemn their leaders. When

the Turkish general Lala Mustafa Pasha captured Cyprus from the Venetians in 1570, the podestà who had held out against him, Marcantonio Bragadin, was mutilated (nose and ears cut off), dragged around the city walls, dangled from a ship's mast, tied naked to a post, skinned alive, beheaded, and "quartered" (his four limbs cut off). Then his skin, stuffed with straw, was tied to a cow and led through the streets of the Famagusta, before being returned as a victory prize to Constantinople. Venetian rule was pulverized in its representative. Nietzsche calls this "Punishment as a festival, namely as the rape and mockery of a finally defeated enemy."

Killing as Posthumous Delegitimation. Some inquisitors 7 tried dead men and symbolically executed them. The leaders of the Gowrie Plot that tried to supplant King James VI of Scotland in 1600 were tried posthumously and their corpses were hanged, drawn (eviscerated), and quartered. In 897, Stephen VI had the corpse of his predecessor, Pope Formosus, exhumed, propped up in his papal garb, tried and condemned for usurpation, stripped of his vestments, his head (that had borne the tiara) cut off, along with the three fingers of his right hand used in benediction, and head, fingers, and body then thrown in the Tiber—all to declare Formosus's consecration of bishops and ordination of priests invalid.

Killing as Total Degradation. The previous three forms of 8 execution punished an offender as a member of a class (lower or higher); but other humiliating deaths are contrived to deprive a person of humanity as such. Public torture before death was one means for this—scourging that makes the offender scream and writhe, losing dignity along with his composure. The Greek punishment for theft was *apotympanismos,* the beating of a naked man clamped down in a crouched position before he was left to die of exposure (it is the punishment given to Prometheus in his play, though he cannot die). The death for traitors in Elizabethan England was an elaborate piece of theater. First the offender was dragged backward on a hurdle to the place of execution—signifying, said the attorney general Sir Edward Coke, that the man was "not worthy any more to tread upon the face of the earth where of he was made; also for that he hath been retrograde to nature, therefore is he drawn backward at a horse-tail." Then the man (it was a male punishment) was stripped, hanged, cut down living, castrated, disemboweled, his heart and viscera thrown in boiling water, decapitated, quartered, and his head exposed on Tower Bridge. When Jesuit priests were hanged, drawn, and quartered, their head, members, torso, and clothes were hidden away to prevent the taking of relics.

Killing and Posthumous Degradation. Refusal of burial led   9
the ancient Greeks to let bodies be exposed for ravaging by dogs and kites (Creon's treatment of Polyneices in Sophocles' *Antigone*). Romans let crucified bodies hang to be pecked at and decompose. Florentines in the Renaissance dangled the corpses of criminals from the high windows of the Bargello till they rotted, and commissioned artists like Andrea del Sarto to depict them there, prolonging the shame after they were gone. Joan of Arc was killed by a slow fire that consumed her clothes and skin, then the flames were raked away, to expose her body as a woman's and to show that no demon had spirited her away. Then intense fire was mounted to burn her down to ashes for scattering in the Seine, to prevent any collection of relics.

Killing by Ordeal. In this punishment, the innocent were   10
supposed to be protected if subjected to ordeal by combat, ordeal by fire (walking through it, as Saint Francis is supposed to have done in Egypt), or ordeal by water. The latter was especially reserved for suspected witches, who would sink only if innocent. A less lethal form of this punishment survived in the "ducking stool" for immersing witches. Jefferson's revised code says this: "All attempts to delude the people, or to abuse their understanding by exercise of the pretended [claimed] arts of witchcraft, conjuration, enchantment, or sorcery or by pretended prophecies, shall be punished by ducking and whipping at the discretion of a jury, not exceeding 15 stripes."

Threatened Killing as Inducement to Remorse. Refusal to   11
undergo trial by ordeal could be taken as a confession, leading to a lesser penalty than death. Recanting could have the

same effect. Joan of Arc, when first brought out to the stake with its kindling, renounced her voices as "idolatry" (devil worship), and was given life imprisonment. Only when she abjured her recantation was she actually put to the stake. Scaffold repentance could reduce the sentence to less than death—or, at the least, make officials perform a "merciful" (a swifter, not a lingering) execution—e.g., letting a man die in the noose before being cut down for disemboweling. Nietzsche calls this punishment for the "improvement" of the criminal.

Killing as Repayment. The *lex talionis,* as it exacts "an eye for an eye," must exact a life for a life. We say, "You're going to *pay* for this." Jefferson followed the logic of his state's *lex talionis:*

> *Whosoever shall be guilty of Rape, Polygamy, or Sodomy with man or woman shall be punished, if a man, by castration, if a woman, by cutting thro' the cartilage of her nose a hole of one half inch diameter at the least . . . Whosoever on purpose and of malice forethought shall maim another, or shall disfigure him, by cutting out or disabling the tongue, slitting or cutting off a nose, lip or ear, branding, or otherwise, shall be maimed or disfigured in like sort: or if that cannot be for want of the same part, then as nearly as may be in some other part of at least equal value and estimation in the opinion of a jury, and moreover shall forfeit one half of his lands and goods to the sufferer.*

Taking a life for a life on this principle is called by Nietzsche "Punishment as recompense to the injured party for the harm done."

Killing as Repayment-Plus. In Athenian law, repayment was of equal value if the crime was unintentional, but of double if it was intentional. On that principle, death has not been reserved only for taking a life, but can be considered an added penalty for crimes like major theft, rape, treasonous speech, and the like.

Killing as Victim Therapy. The Attic orator Antiphon has the father of a son killed by accident plead that the unintentional killer must be punished; the death leaves the father aggrieved (*epithymion*—much like Nietzsche's *ressentiment*). The grievance, of course, would be even greater if the killing were intentional. Soothing this sense of grievance is now called "giving closure" to the ordeal of victims.   14

Killing as a Form of Pedagogy. We say that punishing a man will "teach him a lesson." More important, it may teach others the consequence of crime, deterring anyone who contemplates a similar offense. Kant said that the person should be treated as his own end, not as a means for others' advantage. But the person executed is, by this theory, turned into a teaching instrument for the benefit of others.   15

2. PUBLIC EXECUTION

Experience of past times gives us little reason to hope that any reformation will be effected by a periodical havoc of our fellow beings.
—SAMUEL JOHNSON, *Rambler* 114

The fourteen types of capital punishment listed above do not exhaust all the possible urges expressed in our havocking of others. And as Nietzsche said, they are not neat little separate rationales. They conflict with each other at an intellectual level, but they reinforce each other at the emotional level. They are more powerful for certain people in certain combinations. But they have one thing in common: *they all demand, in logic, maximum display and publicity.* The outlaw's status must be proclaimed for people to act on it. The other effects sought—whether cleansing, order enforcement, delegitimation, humiliation, repayment, therapy, deterrence—can only be achieved if an audience sees what is being done to satisfy, intimidate, soothe, or instruct it.   16

In fact, various means to dramatize the process, to make its meaning clear, to show the right way to "read" it, were   17 invented. Those going to the scaffold often had their crimes blazoned on their backs. Joan of Arc wore a fool's cap with her four crimes printed on it. A crucified man had his crime posted on the cross. Lesser criminals were branded to sustain the memory of their crime. Ingenious means of execution were invented to express society's horror, anger, power, and the like. Any punishment that fits the crime should be *seen* to fit the crime. Indeed, the only urges that people now commonly admit to—the last four in the above list (repayment of two kinds, "closure," and deterrence)—are closely linked with publicity. The repayment is to us, to society as well as to the victims, the therapy is for the victims' contemplation, and an act meant to deter should vividly catch the attention of those who might benefit from it. How can they "learn their lesson" if it is not spelled out for them?

Our unconfessed difficulty is that we have given up what- 18 ever logic there was to the death penalty, since we have become unable to embrace most of the practices of the past. We no longer believe in a divine miasma to be purged, or divine guidance to be revealed in survival by ordeal. We have given up the desecration of corpses, killing as a reinforcement of class distinctions, torture, maiming, evisceration, and all the multiple methods used to reduce the criminal to a *corpus vile*. Even Jefferson wavered on the *lex talionis* when it came to blinding an offender (he could go as far as a nose for a nose, but not as far as an eye for an eye). Our Constitution forbids cruel and unusual punishment, and we take that to mean that there will be no gratuitous humiliation of the convict—we do not even put people in the stocks anymore, much less invite the public to see a condemned man being strapped onto a gurney. We want painless executions, so we have recurred to one of the few humane-looking methods of the Greeks— lethal injection (hemlock), though among the many deterrents to becoming a philosopher, Socrates' quiet (and self-chosen) death in his seventies has never ranked very high.

So far from stigmatizing or humiliating the inmate of death 19 row, we now provide him with a long and costly process meant to ascertain guilt, with free legal aid if he cannot afford his own, with counseling and family visits, with reading of his choice and TV, a last meal to his specifications, a last request, religious attendance, guaranteed burial, a swift and nearly painless death. We shut up his last hours from the general public, and act as if this secret rite will deter by some magic of mere occurrence. We treat the killing as a dirty little secret, as if we are ashamed of it. Well, we should be ashamed. Having given up on most of the previous justifications for the death penalty, we cling to a mere vestige of the practice, relying most urgently on one of the least defensible defenses of it.

3 . DETERRENCE

The gibbet, indeed, certainly disables those who die upon it from infesting the community; but their death seems not to contribute more to the reformation of their associates than any other method of separation.
—SAMUEL JOHNSON, *Rambler* 114

The bad faith of the process shows in the insistence on   20
using the deterrence argument when it has been discredited by all the most reputable studies. This is an old story. In the eighteenth century, Samuel Johnson, who liked to defend any tradition he could, discovered no deterrent effect following on traditional executions, though they were far more numerous and far more public than they are now (factors, some people think, that add to deterrent effect). In the middle of the twentieth century, Arthur Koestler could refer to a strong scholarly record on the matter:

> *This belief in the irreplaceable deterrent value of the death-penalty has been proved to be a superstition by the long and patient inquiries of the Parliamentary Select Committee of 1930 and the Royal Commission on Capital Punishment of 1948; yet it pops up again and again. Like all superstitions, it has the nature of a Jack-in-the-box; however often you hit it over the head with facts and statistics, it will solemnly pop up again, because the hidden spring*

> *inside it is the unconscious and irrational power of traditional beliefs.*

Present and former presidents of the most prestigious criminological societies, polled in 1995, overwhelmingly said they did not think the death penalty significantly reduces the homicide rate (94 percent), and they knew of no empirical evidence that would support such a claim (94.1 percent). They held (79.2 percent) that execution causes no reduction in crime—a finding confirmed by the fact that states with the death penalty have higher murder rates than those without (the region with the highest number of homicides, the South, accounts for over 80 percent of the nation's executions). Furthermore, countries in Europe that have given up the death penalty have far lower murder rates than does the United States (since those countries *do* have gun control laws). Disbelief in the deterring power of execution is also expressed, though not so overwhelmingly, by police chiefs and sheriffs—not a far-left part of the community—surveyed by Peter D. Hart Research Associates in 1995. They did not think (67 percent) that executions significantly reduce homicides. In fact, New York's former police chief Patrick V. Murphy responded that "the flimsy notion that the death penalty is an effective law enforcement tool is being exposed as mere political puffery."

Expert criminologists said (100 percent, joined in this by 85 percent of the police chiefs) that politicians support the death penalty for symbolic reasons, to show they are tough on crime, though that distracts them (86.6 percent of the criminologists, 56 percent of the police chiefs) from addressing better methods of reducing the homicide rate. The police listed four things that would be more effective in fighting crime, including longer sentences, more police, and gun control. It takes little observation of actual politicians to confirm that politicians support the death penalty for electoral reasons. Now-Senator Dianne Feinstein, who had opposed capital punishment as a very active member of the California

parole board, embraced it in 1990 when she ran for governor. When I asked her during that campaign what had made
her change her position, she said that she had become convinced that executions do deter other criminals. I said that
most studies I had seen denied this, but she told me she had
read new and better research, though she could not name it
for me. "I'll send it to you," she promised—but she never
did. The only empirical evidence that mattered to her was her
knowledge of the way Rose Bird had been resoundingly defeated for reelection as the chief justice of the Supreme Court
of California because she opposed capital punishment.

When Andrew Young ran for governor of Georgia in   22
1990, he too abandoned his early opposition to the death
penalty (though his daughter remained an activist opponent
of it, because of its disproportionate rate among blacks—the
NAACP Legal Defense Fund discovered that a black's chance
of being executed in Georgia was eleven times that of a
white). I asked Young if he too had been convinced that executions deter. He said that he had not, but that as mayor of
Atlanta he had listened to police tell him that it discouraged
them to catch criminals and see them escape execution—"I
did it for their morale." (He did it, though, only when he was
leaving the mayor's office and addressing a much whiter con-
stituency in his race for governor.)

Other politicians obviously look to the polls, not to policy   23
studies, when taking their stand on executions. Campaigning
to become the senator from New York, Hillary Clinton knew
how much support the state's former governor Mario
Cuomo had lost because of his resolute stand against executions. William Weld, while he was still governor of Massachusetts, said that he relied not on studies but on "my gut":
"My gut is that . . . capital punishment is deterrent." The
deft use of the death penalty issue by Bob Graham as governor of Florida and in his 1986 race for the Senate is studied
in a book that Timothy McVeigh is known to have read in
prison. In 1984, Graham dismissed scholarly studies on the
death penalty by saying, "This is an issue that is inherently
beyond what empirical research can validate," making him

another gut-truster like Weld. But if we cannot know the deterrent effect, we are certainly killing one man for a hypothetical effect on others that is uncertain.

Actually, the deterrent theory of capital punishment, always weak, is especially flimsy now, when a rash of cases—some involving DNA evidence—has proved that some innocent men are on death row. The evidence of incompetent defenses, faked evidence, and negligent procedures has led to announced or informal moratoria on executions. In Oklahoma alone, where Timothy McVeigh's crime was committed, the evidence in approximately three thousand cases is now tainted by the defective lab work of one technician, Joyce Gilchrist. The execution of the innocent is not a new issue, but widespread public awareness of it is. The British study by the Select Committee on Capital Punishment, cited by Arthur Koestler, found cases of mistaken executions, including "many" reported by the governor of Sing Sing in America. 24

Some try to separate the problem of killing the *right* person from the question of whether we should execute *any* person at all. But since the principal prop of the death penalty is deterrence theory, that prop is knocked out when uncertainty of guilt enters the national consciousness. Even if we were to grant that executions deter, they may not deter people who think it is a random matter whether the right person is caught. If they might get off while guilty, or be killed while innocent, that fact is not a very stable basis for forswearing a particular homicide. And executing the mentally defective or marginally juvenile, like the disproportionate killing of blacks, cannot much intimidate a would-be murderer who is mentally sound, of mature age, or white. 25

These considerations join longer-term flaws in the deterrence argument. Juries are readiest to convict people for crimes of passion, sexually charged rape-murders, child-abuse murders, or serial killings. To see these offenders caught will not necessarily affect the person most likely to have the coolness and calculation that deterrence requires. And obviously 26 they do not affect other people in the grip of obsessions, mental instability, or drug- or alcohol-induced frenzy. Plato was against executing those guilty of a crime of passion (*Laws* 867c–d), but our juries reflect more the anger of society than the didactic strategies of deterrence. In doing this, the juries fail to make the calculations that we are told future murderers will make. The whole theory is senseless.

4. "CLOSURE"

[People come] in thousands to the legal massacre and look with carelessness, perhaps with triumph, on the utmost exacerbations of human misery.
—SAMUEL JOHNSON, *Rambler* 114

"Closure" has become a buzzword, not only for discussing   27 the death penalty but for addressing any kind of social discontent. When the unmarried mother of Jesse Jackson's child sued Reverend Jackson, it was not about anything so crass as money, it was to find "closure" for herself and her child. Who can deprive a grieving person of solace? This is the argument Antiphon's prosecutor made when he demanded emotional relief for the loss of his child to an accident. Attorney General John Ashcroft endorsed the argument by arranging for the families of Timothy McVeigh's victims to see him die. This conflicts with the logic of deterrence, since the families are not viewing the event to deter them from becoming mass murderers. If the real point of executions is to act *in terrorem* for other criminals, the Oklahoma families are the least appropriate audience.

Ashcroft's response to the hot pressures of the McVeigh   28 case is just that of Dianne Feinstein or Andrew Young to less emotionally charged instances of capital punishment, where no mass murder is involved. McVeigh, the cold killer revealed in *American Terrorist,* by Lou Michel and Dan Herbeck, triggers all the upsurges of emotion Nietzsche described. We feel that the very existence of a McVeigh is an affront to society, a pollutant of our life, a thing we cannot be clean of without execration. But the politician does not want to be seen ministering to atavistic reactions in their raw state. So he invokes deterrence where it does not apply, or says that humane consideration of the victims' sympathies trumps all other considerations. Seeing the murderer die, we are told, will just help the families to "close a chapter of their lives."

But is this really likely? The aim of emotional healing is to bring inflamed emotions of loss and *ressentiment* back into a manageable relationship with other parts of one's life. Does that happen when, for many years in most cases (six years so far in McVeigh's case), a victim's survivors focus on seeing that someone pays for his or her loss? This tends to reenact the outrage in a person's mind, rather than to transcend it. It prolongs the trauma, delaying and impeding the healing process. When I asked Sister Helen Prejean, the author of *Dead Man Walking,* what she has observed, she said that families are asked by prosecutors to attend the trial of a relative's murderer, but to show no emotion lest they cause a mistrial. "They learn new details of the crime, and with each new turn of the trial and its aftermath the media call them to get a reaction." This is less like healing than like tearing scabs open again and again. Some relatives who want to escape this process are accused by their own of not loving the victim, says Sister Helen: "I have seen families torn apart over the death penalty." 29

What's more, the sterile, anodyne, and bureaucratic procedures of a modern execution can baffle the desire for revenge encouraged before its performance. Sister Helen recalls a man who said he wished to see more suffering, and who comes with pro-death demonstrators to all later executions. This is hardly one who has found "closure." The eeriness of the closure language was revealed when McVeigh himself, through his lawyer, Rob Nigh, expressed sympathy for the relatives' "disappointment" after his execution was delayed. He is more the manipulator of these grieving people than an offering to them. 30

Emotional counselors work toward reconciliation with the facts, as religious leaders recommend forgiveness. Many church bodies oppose the death penalty, drawing on rich 31 traditions in the various faiths. Saint Augustine resisted the killing of murderers, even of two men who had murdered one of his own priests, arguing that the fate of souls is in God's hands (Letters 133, 134). It is true that Thomas Aquinas likened the killing of murderers to the amputation of a limb for the good of the whole body, but his fellow Dominican Niceto Blázquez points out how defective this argument is: Thomas was drawing an analogy with the excommunication of sinners from the Church, the body of Christ—but that is a move meant to promote reunion, to rescue a person from the death of his soul, not to impose a death on the body.

Conservative Catholics, who are aghast at fellow believers'   32
willingness to ignore the pope on matters like contraception, blithely ignore in their turn papal pleas to renounce the death penalty (addressed most recently to the McVeigh case). And I have not seen Bible-quoting fundamentalists refer to the one place in the Gospels where Jesus deals with capital punishment. At John 8:3–11, he interrupts a legal execution (for adultery) and tells the officers of the state that their own sinfulness deprives them of jurisdiction. Jesus himself gives up any jurisdiction for this kind of killing: "Neither do I condemn you." George W. Bush said during the campaign debates of [2002] that Jesus is his favorite philosopher—though he did not hesitate to endorse the execution of 152 human beings in Texas, where half of the public defenders of accused murderers were sanctioned by the Texas bar for legal misbehavior or incompetence. Mr. Bush clearly needs some deeper consultation with the philosopher of his choice.

For Study and Discussion

QUESTIONS FOR RESPONSE

1. In the court cases you know something about, has the punishment fit the crime?
2. In what ways do you think punishment teaches a lesson?

QUESTIONS ABOUT PURPOSE

1. How does Wills's detailed—and often gruesome—classification of the motives for killing someone support his argument against the death penalty?
2. How does Wills dispute the argument that capital punishment teaches would-be criminals not to commit a crime?

QUESTIONS ABOUT AUDIENCE

1. How does Wills use quotations from historical figures—such as Plato and Jefferson—to shock his readers?
2. How does he anticipate the reactions of those readers who believe that capital punishment provides healing and closure?

QUESTIONS ABOUT STRATEGIES

1. How does Wills explain why some of the motives he lists overlap one another?
2. How does Wills use statistical research to counteract the "gut" responses of politicians?

QUESTIONS FOR DISCUSSION

1. How do you account for our culture's preference for "secret ritual" over "public execution"?
2. How does Wills use Sister Helen Prejean's observations to explain why families have been "torn apart over the death penalty"?

Flannery O'Connor (1925–1964) was born in Savannah, Georgia, and was educated at the Women's College of Georgia and the University of Iowa. She returned to her mother's farm near Milledgeville, Georgia, when she discovered that she had contracted lupus erythematosus, the systemic disease that had killed her father and of which she herself was to die. For the last fourteen years of her life, she lived a quiet, productive life on the farm—raising peacocks, painting, and writing the extraordinary stories and novels that won her worldwide acclaim. Her novels, *Wise Blood* (1952), which was adapted for film in 1979, and *The Violent Bear It Away* (1960), deal with fanatical preachers. Her thirty-one carefully crafted stories, combining grotesque comedy and violent tragedy, appear in *A Good Man Is Hard to Find* (1955), *Everything That Rises Must Converge* (1965), and *The Complete Stories* (1971), which won the National Book Award. "Revelation" dramatizes the ironic discoveries a woman makes about how different classes of people fit into the order of things.

Revelation

T HE DOCTOR'S WAITING room, which was very small, was almost full when the Turpins entered and Mrs. Turpin, who was very large, made it look even smaller by her presence. She stood looming at the head of the magazine table set in the center of it, a living demonstration that the room was inadequate and ridiculous. Her little bright black eyes took in all the patients as she sized up the seating

1

situation. There was one vacant chair and a place on the sofa occupied by a blond child in a dirty blue romper who should have been told to move over and make room for the lady. He was five or six, but Mrs. Turpin saw at once that no one was going to tell him to move over. He was slumped down in the seat, his arms idle at his sides and his eyes idle in his head; his nose ran unchecked.

Mrs. Turpin put a firm hand on Claud's shoulder and said in a voice that included anyone who wanted to listen, "Claud, you sit in that chair there," and gave him a push down into the vacant one. Claud was florid and bald and sturdy, somewhat shorter than Mrs. Turpin, but he sat down as if he were accustomed to doing what she told him to. 2

Mrs. Turpin remained standing. The only man in the room besides Claud was a lean stringy old fellow with a rusty hand spread out on each knee, whose eyes were closed as if he were asleep or dead or pretending to be so as not to get up and offer her his seat. Her gaze settled agreeably on a well-dressed gray-haired lady whose eyes met hers and whose expression said: if that child belonged to me, he would have some manners and move over—there's plenty of room there for you and him too. 3

Claud looked up with a sigh and made as if to rise. 4

"Sit down," Mrs. Turpin said. "You know you're not supposed to stand on that leg. He has an ulcer on his leg," she explained. 5

Claud lifted his foot onto the magazine table and rolled his trouser leg up to reveal a purple swelling on a plump marble-white calf. 6

"My!" the pleasant lady said. "How did you do that?" 7

"A cow kicked him," Mrs. Turpin said. 8

"Goodness!" said the lady. 9

Claud rolled his trouser leg down. 10

"Maybe the little boy would move over," the lady suggested, but the child did not stir. 11

"Somebody will be leaving in a minute," Mrs. Turpin said. She could not understand why a doctor—with as much money as they made charging five dollars a day to just stick 12 their head in the hospital door and look at you—couldn't afford a decent-sized waiting room. This one was hardly bigger than a garage. The table was cluttered with limp-looking magazines and at one end of it there was a big green glass ash tray full of cigarette butts and cotton wads with little blood spots on them. If she had had anything to do with the running of the place, that would have been emptied every so often. There were no chairs against the wall at the head of the room. It had a rectangular-shaped panel in it that permitted a view of the office where the nurse came and went and the secretary listened to the radio. A plastic fern in a gold pot sat in the opening and trailed its fronds down almost to the floor. The radio was softly playing gospel music.

Just then the inner door opened and a nurse with the highest stack of yellow hair Mrs. Turpin had ever seen put her face in the crack and called for the next patient. The woman sitting beside Claud grasped the two arms of her chair and hoisted herself up; she pulled her dress free from her legs and lumbered through the door where the nurse had disappeared.   13

Mrs. Turpin eased into the vacant chair, which held her tight as a corset. "I wish I could reduce," she said, and rolled her eyes and gave a comic sigh.   14

"Oh, *you* aren't fat," the stylish lady said.   15

"Ooooo I am too," Mrs. Turpin said. "Claud he eats all he wants to and never weighs over one hundred and seventy-five pounds, but me I just look at something good to eat and I gain some weight," and her stomach and shoulders shook with laughter. "You can eat all you want to, can't you, Claud?" she asked, turning to him.   16

Claud only grinned.   17

"Well, as long as you have such a good disposition," the stylish lady said, "I don't think it makes a bit of difference what size you are. You just can't beat a good disposition."   18

Next to her was a fat girl of eighteen or nineteen, scowling into a thick blue book which Mrs. Turpin saw was entitled *Human Development*. The girl raised her head and directed her scowl at Mrs. Turpin as if she did not like her looks. She appeared annoyed that anyone should speak while she tried   19 to read. The poor girl's face was blue with acne and Mrs. Turpin thought how pitiful it was to have a face like that at that age. She gave the girl a friendly smile but the girl only scowled the harder. Mrs. Turpin herself was fat but she had always had good skin, and, though she was forty-seven years old, there was not a wrinkle in her face except around her eyes from laughing too much.

Next to the ugly girl was the child, still in exactly the same position, and next to him was a thin leathery old woman in a cotton print dress. She and Claud had three sacks of chicken feed in their pump house that was in the same print. She had seen from the first that the child belonged with the old woman. She could tell by the way they sat—kind of vacant and white-trashy, as if they would sit there until Doomsday if nobody called and told them to get up. And at right angles but next to the well-dressed pleasant lady was a lank-faced woman who was certainly the child's mother. She had on a yellow sweat shirt and wine-colored slacks, both gritty-looking, and the rims of her lips were stained with snuff. Her dirty yellow hair was tied behind with a little piece of red paper ribbon. Worse than niggers any day, Mrs. Turpin thought. 20

The gospel hymn playing was, "When I looked up and He looked down," and Mrs. Turpin, who knew it, supplied the last line mentally, "And wona these days I know I'll weear a crown." 21

Without appearing to, Mrs. Turpin always noticed people's feet. The well-dressed lady had on red and gray suede shoes to match her dress. Mrs. Turpin had on her good black patent leather pumps. The ugly girl had on Girl Scout shoes and heavy socks. The old woman had on tennis shoes and the white-trashy mother had on what appeared to be bedroom slippers, black straw with gold braid threaded through them—exactly what you would have expected her to have on. 22

Sometimes at night when she couldn't go to sleep, Mrs. Turpin would occupy herself with the question of who she would have chosen to be if she couldn't have been herself. If Jesus had said to her before he made her, "There's only two places available for you. You can either be a nigger or 23 white-trash," what would she have said? "Please, Jesus, please," she would have said, "just let me wait until there's another place available," and he would have said, "No, you have to go right now and I have only those two places so make up your mind." She would have wiggled and squirmed and begged and pleaded but it would have been no use and finally she would have said, "All right, make me a nigger then—but that don't mean a trashy one." And he would have made her a neat clean respectable Negro woman, herself but black.

Next to the child's mother was a red-headed youngish   24
woman, reading one of the magazines and working a piece of chewing gum, hell for leather, as Claud would say. Mrs. Turpin could not see the woman's feet. She was not white-trash, just common. Sometimes Mrs. Turpin occupied herself at night naming the classes of people. On the bottom of the heap were most colored people, not the kind she would have been if she had been one, but most of them; then next to them—not above, just away from—were the white-trash; then above them were the home-owners, and above them the home-and-land-owners, to which she and Claud belonged. Above she and Claud were people with a lot of money and much bigger houses and much more land. But here the complexity of it would begin to bear in on her, for some of the people with a lot of money were common and ought to be below she and Claud and some of the people who had good blood had lost their money and had to rent and then there were colored people who owned their homes and land as well. There was a colored dentist in town who had two red Lincolns and a swimming pool and a farm with registered white-face cattle on it. Usually by the time she had fallen asleep all the classes of people were moiling and roiling around in her head, and she would dream they were all crammed in together in a box car, being ridden off to be put in a gas oven.

"That's a beautiful clock," she said and nodded to her   25
right. It was a big wall clock, the face encased in a brass sunburst.

"Yes, it's very pretty," the stylish lady said agreeably. "And right on the dot too," she added, glancing at her watch.   26

The ugly girl beside her cast an eye upward at the clock, smirked, then looked directly at Mrs. Turpin and smirked again. Then she returned her eyes to her book. She was obviously the lady's daughter because, although they didn't look anything alike as to disposition, they both had the same shape of face and the same blue eyes. On the lady they sparkled pleasantly but in the girl's seared face they appeared alternately to smolder and to blaze.   27

What if Jesus had said, "All right, you can be white-trash or a nigger or ugly"!   28

Mrs. Turpin felt an awful pity for the girl, though she thought it was one thing to be ugly and another to act ugly.   29

The woman with the snuff-stained lips turned around in her chair and looked up at the clock. Then she turned back and appeared to look a little to the side of Mrs. Turpin. There was a cast in one of her eyes. "You want to know wher you can get you one of themther clocks?" she asked in a loud voice.   30

"No, I already have a nice clock," Mrs. Turpin said. Once somebody like her got a leg in the conversation, she would be all over it.   31

"You can get you one with green stamps," the woman said. "That's most likely wher he got hisn. Save you up enough, you can get you most anythang. I got me some joo'ry."   32

Ought to have got you a wash rag and some soap, Mrs. Turpin thought.   33

"I get contour sheets with mine," the pleasant lady said.   34

The daughter slammed her book shut. She looked straight in front of her, directly through Mrs. Turpin and on through the yellow curtain and the plate glass window which made the wall behind her. The girl's eyes seemed lit all of a sudden with a peculiar light, an unnatural light like night road signs give. Mrs. Turpin turned her head to see if there was anything going on outside that she should see, but she could not see anything. Figures passing cast only a pale shadow   35 through the curtain. There was no reason the girl should single her out for her ugly looks.

"Miss Finley," the nurse said, cracking the door. The gum-chewing woman got up and passed in front of her and Claud and went into the office. She had on red high-heeled shoes.   36

Directly across the table, the ugly girl's eyes were fixed on Mrs. Turpin as if she had some very special reason for disliking her.   37

"This is wonderful weather, isn't it?" the girl's mother said.   38

"It's good weather for cotton if you can get the niggers to pick it," Mrs. Turpin said, "but niggers don't want to pick cotton any more. You can't get the white folks to pick it and now you can't get the niggers—because they got to be right up there with the white folks."   39

"They gonna *try* anyways," the white-trash woman said, leaning forward.   40

"Do you have one of the cotton-picking machines?" the pleasant lady asked.   41

"No," Mrs. Turpin said, "they leave half the cotton in the field. We don't have much cotton anyway. If you want to make it farming now, you have to have a little of everything. We got a couple of acres of cotton and a few hogs and chickens and just enough white-face that Claud can look after them himself."   42

"One thang I don't want," the white-trash woman said, wiping her mouth with the back of her hand. "Hogs. Nasty stinking things, a-gruntin and a-rootin all over the place."   43

Mrs. Turpin gave her the merest edge of her attention. "Our hogs are not dirty and they don't stink," she said. "They're cleaner than some children I've seen. Their feet never touch the ground. We have a pig-parlor—that's where you raise them on concrete," she explained to the pleasant lady, "and Claud scoots them down with the hose every afternoon and washes off the floor." Cleaner by far than that child right there, she thought. Poor nasty little thing. He had not moved except to put the thumb of his dirty hand into his mouth.   44

The woman turned her face away from Mrs. Turpin. "I   45
know I wouldn't scoot down no hog with no hose," she said
to the wall.

You wouldn't have no hog to scoot down, Mrs. Turpin   46
said to herself.

"A-gruntin and a-rootin and a-groanin," the woman   47
muttered.

"We got a little of everything," Mrs. Turpin said to the   48
pleasant lady. "It's no use in having more than you can handle yourself with help like it is. We found enough niggers to
pick our cotton this year but Claud he has to go after them
and take them home again in the evening. They can't walk
that half a mile. No they can't. I tell you," she said and
laughed merrily, "I sure am tired of buttering up niggers, but
you got to love em if you want em to work for you. When
they come in the morning, I run out and I say, 'Hi yawl this
morning?' and when Claud drives them off to the field I just
wave to beat the band and they just wave back." And she
waved her hand rapidly to illustrate.

"Like you read out of the same book," the lady said, show-   49
ing she understood perfectly.

"Child, yes," Mrs. Turpin said. "And when they come in   50
from the field, I run out with a bucket of icewater. That's the
way it's going to be from now on," she said. "You may as well
face it."

"One thang I know," the white-trash woman said. "Two   51
thangs I ain't going to do: love no niggers or scoot down no
hog with no hose." And she let out a bark of contempt.

The look that Mrs. Turpin and the pleasant lady ex-   52
changed indicated they both understood that you had to
have certain things before you could *know* certain things. But
every time Mrs. Turpin exchanged a look with the lady, she
was aware that the ugly girl's peculiar eyes were still on her,
and she had trouble bringing her attention back to the
conversation.

"When you got something," she said, "you got to look   53
after it." And when you ain't got a thing but breath and
britches, she added to herself, you can afford to come to

town every morning and just sit on the Court House coping and spit.

A grotesque revolving shadow passed across the curtain behind her and was thrown palely on the opposite wall. Then a bicycle clattered down against the outside of the building. The door opened and a colored boy glided in with a tray from the drugstore. It had two large red and white paper cups on it with tops on them. He was a tall, very black boy in discolored white pants and a green nylon shirt. He was chewing gum slowly, as if to music. He set the tray down in the office opening next to the fern and stuck his head through to look for the secretary. She was not in there. He rested his arms on the ledge and waited, his narrow bottom stuck out, swaying to the left and right. He raised a hand over his head and scratched the base of his skull.   54

"You see that button there, boy?" Mrs. Turpin said. "You can punch that and she'll come. She's probably in the back somewhere."   55

"Is thas right?" the boy said agreeably, as if he had never seen the button before. He leaned to the right and put his finger on it. "She sometime out," he said and twisted around to face his audience, his elbows behind him on the counter. The nurse appeared and he twisted back again. She handed him a dollar and he rooted in his pocket and made the change and counted it out to her. She gave him fifteen cents for a tip and he went out with the empty tray. The heavy door swung too slowly and closed at length with the sound of suction. For a moment no one spoke.   56

"They ought to send all them niggers back to Africa," the white-trash woman said. "That's wher they come from in the first place."   57

"Oh, I couldn't do without my good colored friends," the pleasant lady said.   58

"There's a heap of things worse than a nigger," Mrs. Turpin agreed. "It's all kinds of them just like it's all kinds of us."   59

"Yes, and it takes all kinds to make the world go round," the lady said in her musical voice.   60

As she said it, the raw-complexioned girl snapped her teeth 61
together. Her lower lip turned downwards and inside out, revealing the pale pink inside of her mouth. After a second it
rolled back up. It was the ugliest face Mrs. Turpin had ever
seen anyone make and for a moment she was certain that the
girl had made it at her. She was looking at her as if she had
known and disliked her all her life—all of Mrs. Turpin's life,
it seemed too, not just all the girl's life. Why, girl, I don't
even know you, Mrs. Turpin said silently.

She forced her attention back to the discussion. "It would- 62
n't be practical to send them back to Africa," she said. "They
wouldn't want to go. They got it too good here."

"Wouldn't be what they wanted—if I had anythang to do 63
with it," the woman said.

"It wouldn't be a way in the world you could get all the 64
niggers back over there," Mrs. Turpin said. "They'd be hid-
ing out and lying down and turning sick on you and wailing
and hollering and raring and pitching. It wouldn't be a way
in the world to get them over there."

"They got over here," the trashy woman said. "Get back 65
like they got over."

"It wasn't so many of them then," Mrs. Turpin explained. 66

The woman looked at Mrs. Turpin as if here was an idiot 67
indeed but Mrs. Turpin was not bothered by the look, considering where it came from.

"Nooo," she said, "they're going to stay here where they 68
can go to New York and marry white folks and improve their
color. That's what they all want to do, every one of them, improve their color."

"You know what comes of that, don't you?" Claud asked. 69

"No, Claud, what?" Mrs. Turpin said. 70

Claud's eyes twinkled. "White-faced niggers," he said with 71
never a smile.

Everybody in the office laughed except the white-trash 72
and the ugly girl. The girl gripped the book in her lap with
white fingers. The trashy woman looked around her from face
to face as if she thought they were all idiots. The old woman
in the feed sack dress continued to gaze expressionless across

the floor at the high-top shoes of the man opposite her, the one who had been pretending to be asleep when the Turpins came in. He was laughing heartily, his hands still spread out on his knees. The child had fallen to the side and was lying now almost face down in the old woman's lap.

While they recovered from their laughter, the nasal chorus on the radio kept the room from silence.   73

> *You go to blank blank*
> *And I'll go to mine*
> *But we'll all blank along*
> *To-geth-ther,*
> *And all along the blank*
> *We'll hep eachother out*
> *Smile-ling in any kind of*
> *Weath-ther!*

Mrs. Turpin didn't catch every word but she caught   74
enough to agree with the spirit of the song and it turned her thoughts sober. To help anybody out that needed it was her philosophy of life. She never spared herself when she found somebody in need, whether they were white or black, trash or decent. And of all she had to be thankful for, she was most thankful that this was so. If Jesus had said, "You can be high society and have all the money you want and be thin and svelte-like, but you can't be a good woman with it," she would have had to say, "Well don't make me that then. Make me a good woman and it don't matter what else, how fat or how ugly or how poor!" Her heart rose. He had not made her a nigger or white-trash or ugly! He had made her herself and given her a little of everything. Jesus, thank you! she said. Thank you thank you thank you! Whenever she counted her blessings she felt as buoyant as if she weighed one hundred and twenty-five pounds instead of one hundred and eighty.

"What's wrong with your little boy?" the pleasant lady   75
asked the white-trashy woman.

"He has a ulcer," the woman said proudly. "He ain't give   76
me a minute's peace since he was born. Him and her are just

alike," she said, nodding at the old woman, who was running her leathery fingers through the child's pale hair. "Look like I can't get nothing down them two but Co' Cola and candy."

That's all you try to get down em, Mrs. Turpin said to herself. Too lazy to light the fire. There was nothing you could tell her about people like them that she didn't know already. And it was not just that they didn't have anything. Because if you gave them everything, in two weeks it would all be broken or filthy or they would have chopped it up for lightwood. She knew all this from her own experience. Help them you must, but help them you couldn't. 77

All at once the ugly girl turned her lips inside out again. Her eyes fixed like two drills on Mrs. Turpin. This time there was no mistaking that there was something urgent behind them. 78

Girl, Mrs. Turpin exclaimed silently, I haven't done a thing to you! The girl might be confusing her with somebody else. There was no need to sit by and let herself be intimidated. "You must be in college," she said boldly, looking directly at the girl. "I see you reading a book there." 79

The girl continued to stare and pointedly did not answer. 80

Her mother blushed at this rudeness. "The lady asked you a question, Mary Grace," she said under her breath. 81

"I have ears," Mary Grace said. 82

The poor mother blushed again. "Mary Grace goes to Wellesley College," she explained. She twisted one of the buttons on her dress. "In Massachusetts," she added with a grimace. "And in the summer she just keeps right on studying. Just reads all the time, a real book worm. She's done real well at Wellesley; she's taking English and Math and History and Psychology and Social Studies," she rattled on, "and I think it's too much. I think she ought to get out and have fun." 83

The girl looked as if she would like to hurl them all through the plate glass window. 84

"Way up north," Mrs. Turpin murmured and thought, well, it hasn't done much for her manners. 85

"I'd almost rather to have him sick," the white-trash woman said, wrenching the attention back to herself. "He's so mean when he ain't. Look like some children just take 86 natural to meanness. It's some gets bad when they get sick but he was the opposite. Took sick and turned good. He don't give me no trouble now. It's me waitin to see the doctor," she said.

If I was going to send anybody back to Africa, Mrs. Turpin   87
thought, it would be your kind, woman. "Yes, indeed," she said aloud, but looking up at the ceiling, "it's a heap of things worse than a nigger." And dirtier than a hog, she added to herself.

"I think people with bad dispositions are more to be pitied   88
than anyone on earth," the pleasant lady said in a voice that was decidedly thin.

"I thank the Lord he has blessed me with a good one,"   89
Mrs. Turpin said. "The day has never dawned that I couldn't find something to laugh at."

"Not since she married me anyways," Claud said with a   90
comical straight face.

Everybody laughed except the girl and the white-trash.   91

Mrs. Turpin's stomach shook. "He's such a caution," she   92
said, "that I can't help but laugh at him."

The girl made a loud ugly noise through her teeth.   93

Her mother's mouth grew thin and tight. "I think the   94
worst thing in the world," she said, "is an ungrateful person. To have everything and not appreciate it. I know a girl," she said, "who has parents who would give her anything, a little brother who loves her dearly, who is getting a good education, who wears the best clothes, but who can never say a kind word to anyone, who never smiles, who just criticizes and complains all day long."

"Is she too old to paddle?" Claud asked.   95

The girl's face was almost purple.   96

"Yes," the lady said, "I'm afraid there's nothing to do but   97
leave her to her folly. Some day she'll wake up and it'll be too late."

"It never hurt anyone to smile," Mrs. Turpin said. "It just   98
makes you feel better all over."

"Of course," the lady said sadly, "but there are just some   99
people you can't tell anything to. They can't take criticism."

"If it's one thing I am," Mrs. Turpin said with feeling, "it's 100
grateful. When I think who all I could have been besides
myself and what all I got, a little of everything, and a good
disposition besides, I just feel like shouting, 'Thank you,
Jesus, for making everything the way it is!' It could have been
different!" For one thing, somebody else could have got
Claud. At the thought of this, she was flooded with gratitude
and a terrible pang of joy ran through her. "Oh thank you,
Jesus, Jesus, thank you!" she cried aloud.

The book struck her directly over her left eye. It struck al- 101
most at the same instant that she realized the girl was about
to hurl it. Before she could utter a sound, the raw face came
crashing across the table toward her, howling. The girl's fingers sank like clamps into the soft flesh of her neck. She heard
the mother cry out and Claud shout, "Whoa!" There was an
instant when she was certain that she was about to be in an
earthquake.

All at once her vision narrowed and she saw everything as 102
if it were happening in a small room far away, or as if she
were looking at it through the wrong end of a telescope.
Claud's face crumpled and fell out of sight. The nurse ran
in, then out, then in again. Then the gangling figure of the
doctor rushed out of the inner door. Magazines flew this
way and that as the table turned over. The girl fell with a
thud and Mrs. Turpin's vision suddenly reversed itself and
she saw everything large instead of small. The eyes of the
white-trashy woman were staring hugely at the floor. There
the girl, held down on one side by the nurse and on the
other by her mother, was wrenching and turning in their
grasp. The doctor was kneeling astride her, trying to hold
her arm down. He managed after a second to sink a long
needle into it.

Mrs. Turpin felt entirely hollow except for her heart which 103
swung from side to side as if it were agitated in a great empty
drum of flesh.

"Somebody that's not busy call for the ambulance," the 104
doctor said in the off-hand voice young doctors adopt for
terrible occasions.

Mrs. Turpin could not have moved a finger. The old man   105
who had been sitting next to her skipped nimbly into the office
and made the call, for the secretary still seemed to be gone.

"Claud!" Mrs. Turpin called.   106

He was not in his chair. She knew she must jump up and   107
find him but she felt like some one trying to catch a train in a
dream, when everything moves in slow motion and the faster
you try to run the slower you go.

"Here I am," a suffocated voice, very unlike Claud's, said. 108

He was doubled up in the corner on the floor, pale as   109
paper, holding his leg. She wanted to get up and go to him
but she could not move. Instead, her gaze was drawn slowly
downward to the churning face on the floor, which she could
see over the doctor's shoulder.

The girl's eyes stopped rolling and focused on her. They   110
seemed a much lighter blue than before, as if a door that had
been tightly closed behind them was now open to admit light
and air.

Mrs. Turpin's head cleared and her power of motion re-   111
turned. She leaned forward until she was looking directly
into the fierce brilliant eyes. There was no doubt in her mind
that the girl did know her, knew her in some intense and personal way, beyond time and place and condition. "What you
got to say to me?" she asked hoarsely and held her breath,
waiting, as for a revelation.

The girl raised her head. Her gaze locked with Mrs.   112
Turpin's. "Go back to hell where you came from, you old
wart hog," she whispered. Her voice was low but clear. Her
eyes burned for a moment as if she saw with pleasure that her
message had struck its target.

Mrs. Turpin sank back in her chair.   113

After a moment the girl's eyes closed and she turned her   114
head wearily to the side.

The doctor rose and handed the nurse the empty syringe.   115
He leaned over and put both hands for a moment on the
mother's shoulders, which were shaking. She was sitting on
the floor, her lips pressed together, holding Mary Grace's
hand in her lap. The girl's fingers were gripped like a baby's

around her thumb. "Go on to the hospital," he said. "I'll call and make the arrangements."

"Now let's see that neck," he said in a jovial voice to Mrs. Turpin. He began to inspect her neck with his first two fingers. Two little moon-shaped lines like pink fish bones were indented over her windpipe. There was the beginning of an angry red swelling above her eye. His fingers passed over this also. [116]

"Lea' me be," she said thickly and shook him off. "See about Claud. She kicked him." [117]

"I'll see about him in a minute," he said and felt her pulse. He was a thin gray-haired man, given to pleasantries. "Go home and have yourself a vacation the rest of the day," he said and patted her on the shoulder. [118]

Quit your pattin me, Mrs. Turpin growled to herself. [119]

"And put an ice pack over that eye," he said. Then he went and squatted down beside Claud and looked at his leg. After a moment he pulled him up and Claud limped after him into the office. [120]

Until the ambulance came, the only sounds in the room were the tremulous moans of the girl's mother, who continued to sit on the floor. The white-trash woman did not take her eyes off the girl. Mrs. Turpin looked straight ahead at nothing. Presently the ambulance drew up, a long dark shadow, behind the curtain. The attendants came in and set the stretcher down beside the girl and lifted her expertly onto it and carried her out. The nurse helped the mother gather up her things. The shadow of the ambulance moved silently away and the nurse came back in the office. [121]

"That ther girl is going to be a lunatic, ain't she?" the white-trash woman asked the nurse, but the nurse kept on to the back and never answered her. [122]

"Yes, she's going to be a lunatic," the white-trash woman said to the rest of them. [123]

"Po' critter," the old woman murmured. The child's face was still in her lap. His eyes looked idly out over her knees. He had not moved during the disturbance except to draw one leg up under him. [124]

"I thank Gawd," the white-trash woman said fervently, "I   125
ain't a lunatic."

Claud came limping out and the Turpins went home.   126

As their pick-up truck turned into their own dirt road and   127
made the crest of the hill, Mrs. Turpin gripped the window
ledge and looked out suspiciously. The land sloped gracefully
down through a field dotted with lavender weeds and at the
start of the rise their small yellow frame house, with its little
flower beds spread out around it like a fancy apron, sat primly
in its accustomed place between two giant hickory trees. She
would not have been startled to see a burnt wound between
two blackened chimneys.

Neither of them felt like eating so they put on their house   128
clothes and lowered the shade in the bedroom and lay down,
Claud with his leg on a pillow and herself with a damp washcloth over her eye. The instant she was flat on her back, the
image of a razor-backed hog with warts on its face and horns
coming out behind its ears snorted into her head. She
moaned, a low quiet moan.

"I am not," she said tearfully, "a wart hog. From hell."   129
But the denial had no force. The girl's eyes and her words,
even the tone of her voice, low but clear, directed only to her,
brooked no repudiation. She had been singled out for the
message, though there was trash in the room to whom it
might justly have been applied. The full force of this fact
struck her only now. There was a woman there who was ne-
glecting her own child but she had been overlooked. The
message had been given to Ruby Turpin, a respectable, hardworking, church-going woman. The tears dried. Her eyes
began to burn instead with wrath.

She rose on her elbow and the washcloth fell into her hand.   130
Claud was lying on his back, snoring. She wanted to tell him
what the girl had said. At the same time, she did not wish to
put the image of herself as a wart hog from hell into his mind.

"Hey, Claud," she muttered and pushed his shoulder.   131

Claud opened one pale baby blue eye.   132

She looked into it warily. He did not think about any   133
thing. He just went his way.

"Wha, whasit?" he said and closed the eye again.   134

"Nothing," she said. "Does your leg pain you?"   135

"Hurts like hell," Claud said.   136

"It'll quit terreckly," she said and lay back down. In a mo-   137
ment Claud was snoring again. For the rest of the afternoon
they lay there. Claud slept. She scowled at the ceiling. Occasionally she raised her fist and made a small stabbing motion
over her chest as if she was defending her innocence to invisible guests who were like the comforters of Job, reasonable-
seeming but wrong.

About five-thirty Claud stirred. "Got to go after those nig-   138
gers," he sighed, not moving.

She was looking straight up as if there were unintelligible   139
handwriting on the ceiling. The protuberance over her eye
had turned a greenish-blue. "Listen here," she said.

"What?"   140

"Kiss me."   141

Claud leaned over and kissed her loudly on the mouth. He   142
pinched her side and their hands interlocked. Her expression
of ferocious concentration did not change. Claud got up,
groaning and growling, and limped off. She continued to
study the ceiling.

She did not get up until she heard the pick-up truck com-   143
ing back with the Negroes. Then she rose and thrust her feet
in her brown oxfords, which she did not bother to lace, and
stumped out onto the back porch and got her red plastic
bucket. She emptied a tray of ice cubes into it and filled it half
full of water and went out into the back yard. Every afternoon after Claud brought the hands in, one of the boys
helped him put out hay and the rest waited in the back of the
truck until he was ready to take them home. The truck was
parked in the shade under one of the hickory trees.

"Hi yawl this evening?" Mrs. Turpin asked grimly, appear-   144
ing with the bucket and the dipper. There were three women
and a boy in the truck.

"Us doin nicely," the oldest woman said. "Hi you doin?"   145
and her gaze stuck immediately on the dark lump on Mrs.
Turpin's forehead. "You done fell down, ain't you?" she

asked in a solicitous voice. The old woman was dark and almost toothless. She had on an old felt hat of Claud's set back on her head. The other two women were younger and lighter and they both had new bright green sunhats. One of them had hers on her head; the other had taken hers off and the boy was grinning beneath it.

Mrs. Turpin set the bucket down on the floor of the truck. 146 "Yawl hep yourselves," she said. She looked around to make sure Claud had gone. "No, I didn't fall down," she said, folding her arms. "It was something worse than that."

"Ain't nothing bad happen to you!" the old woman said. 147 She said it as if they all knew that Mrs. Turpin was protected in some special way by Divine Providence. "You just had you a little fall."

"We were in town at the doctor's office for where the cow 148 kicked Mr. Turpin," Mrs. Turpin said in a flat tone that indicated they could leave off their foolishness. "And there was this girl there. A big fat girl with her face all broke out. I could look at that girl and tell she was peculiar but I couldn't tell how. And me and her mama was just talking and going along and all of a sudden WHAM! She throws this big book she was reading at me and . . ."

"Naw!" the old woman cried out. 149

"And then she jumps over the table and commences to 150 choke me."

"Naw!" they all exclaimed, "naw!" 151

"Hi come she do that?" the old woman asked. "What ail 152 her?"

Mrs. Turpin only glared in front of her. 153

"Somethin ail her," the old woman said. 154

"They carried her off in an ambulance," Mrs. Turpin con- 155 tinued, "but before she went she was rolling on the floor and they were trying to hold her down to give her a shot and she said something to me." She paused. "You know what she said to me?"

"What she say?" they asked. 156

"She said," Mrs. Turpin began, and stopped, her face very 157 dark and heavy. The sun was getting whiter and whiter, blanching the sky overhead so that the leaves of the hickory tree were black in the face of it. She could not bring forth the words. "Something real ugly," she muttered.

"She sho shouldn't said nothin ugly to you," the old woman said. "You so sweet. You the sweetest lady I know." 158

"She pretty too," the one with the hat on said. 159

"And stout," the other one said. "I never knowed no sweeter white lady." 160

"That's the truth befo' Jesus," the old woman said. "Amen! You des as sweet and pretty as you can be." 161

Mrs. Turpin knew exactly how much Negro flattery was worth and it added to her rage. "She said," she began again and finished this time with a fierce rush of breath, "that I was an old wart hog from hell." 162

There was an astounded silence. 163

"Where she at?" the youngest woman cried in a piercing voice. 164

"Lemme see her. I'll kill her!" 165

"I'll kill her with you!" the other one cried. 166

"She b'long in the sylum," the old woman said emphatically. "You the sweetest white lady I know." 167

"She pretty too," the other two said. "Stout as she can be and sweet. Jesus satisfied with her!" 168

"Deed he is," the old woman declared. 169

Idiots! Mrs. Turpin growled to herself. You could never say anything intelligent to a nigger. You could talk at them but not with them. "Yawl ain't drunk your water," she said shortly. "Leave the bucket in the truck when you're finished with it. I got more to do than just stand around and pass the time of day," and she moved off and into the house. 170

She stood for a moment in the middle of the kitchen. The dark protuberance over her eye looked like a miniature tornado cloud which might any moment sweep across the horizon of her brow. Her lower lip protruded dangerously. She squared her massive shoulders. Then she marched into the front of the house and out the side door and started down the road to the pig parlor. She had the look of a woman going single-handed, weaponless, into battle. 171

The sun was a deep yellow now like a harvest moon and   172
was riding westward very fast over the far tree line as if it
meant to reach the hogs before she did. The road was rutted
and she kicked several good-sized stones out of her path as
she strode along. The pig parlor was on a little knoll at the
end of a lane that ran off from the side of the barn. It was a
square of concrete as large as a small room, with a board
fence about four feet high around it. The concrete floor
sloped slightly so that the hog wash could drain off into a
trench where it was carried to the field for fertilizer. Claud
was standing on the outside, on the edge of the concrete,
hanging onto the top board, hosing down the floor inside.
The hose was connected to the faucet of a water trough
nearby.

Mrs. Turpin climbed up beside him and glowered down at   173
the hogs inside. There were seven long-snouted bristly shoats
in it—tan with liver-colored spots—and an old sow a few
weeks off from farrowing. She was lying on her side grunting.
The shoats were running about shaking themselves like idiot
children, their little slit pig eyes searching the floor for anything left. She had read that pigs were the most intelligent
animal. She doubted it. They were supposed to be smarter
than dogs. There had even been a pig astronaut. He had performed his assignment perfectly but died of a heart attack
afterwards because they left him in his electric suit, sitting
upright throughout his examination when naturally a hog
should be on all fours.

A-gruntin and a-rootin and a-groanin.   174

"Gimme that hose," she said, yanking it away from Claud.   175
"Go on and carry them niggers home and then get off that
leg."

"You look like you might have swallowed a mad dog,"   176
Claud observed, but he got down and limped off. He paid no
attention to her humors.

Until he was out of earshot, Mrs. Turpin stood on the side   177
of the pen, holding the hose and pointing the stream of water
at the hind quarters of any shoat that looked as if it might try
to lie down. When he had had time to get over the hill, she

turned her head slightly and her wrathful eyes scanned the path. He was nowhere in sight. She turned back again and seemed to gather herself up. Her shoulders rose and she drew in her breath.

"What do you send me a message like that for?" she said in a low fierce voice, barely above a whisper but with the force of a shout in its concentrated fury. "How am I a hog and me both? How am I saved and from hell too?" Her free fist was knotted and with the other she gripped the hose, blindly pointing the stream of water in and out of the eye of the old sow whose outraged squeal she did not hear. 178

The pig parlor commanded a view of the back pasture where their twenty beef cows were gathered around the hay-bales Claud and the boy had put out. The freshly cut pasture sloped down to the highway. Across it was their cotton field and beyond that a dark green dusty wood which they owned as well. The sun was behind the wood, very red, looking over the paling of trees like a farmer inspecting his own hogs. 179

"Why me?" she rumbled. "It's no trash around here, black or white, that I haven't given to. And break my back to the bone every day working. And do for the church." 180

She appeared to be the right size woman to command the arena before her. "How am I a hog?" she demanded. "Exactly how am I like them?" and she jabbed the stream of water at the shoats. "There was plenty of trash there. It didn't have to be me. 181

"If you like trash better, go get yourself some trash then," she railed. "You could have made me trash. Or a nigger. If trash is what you wanted why didn't you make me trash?" She shook her fist with the hose in it and a watery snake appeared momentarily in the air. "I could quit working and take it easy and be filthy," she growled. "Lounge about the sidewalks all day drinking root beer. Dip snuff and spit in every puddle and have it all over my face. I could be nasty. 182

"Or you could have made me a nigger. It's too late for me to be a nigger," she said with deep sarcasm, "but I could act like one. Lay down in the middle of the road and stop traffic. Roll on the ground." 183

In the deepening light everything was taking on a mysteri-   184
ous hue. The pasture was growing a peculiar glassy green and
the streak of highway had turned lavender. She braced herself
for a final assault and this time her voice rolled out over the
pasture. "Go on," she yelled, "call me a hog! Call me a hog
again. From hell. Call me a wart hog from hell. Put that
bottom rail on top. There'll still be a top and bottom!"

A garbled echo returned to her.   185

A final surge of fury shook her and she roared, "Who do   186
you think you are?"

The color of everything, field and crimson sky, burned for   187
a moment with a transparent intensity. The question carried
over the pasture and across the highway and the cotton field
and returned to her clearly like an answer from beyond the
wood.

She opened her mouth but no sound came out of it.   188

A tiny truck, Claud's, appeared on the highway, heading   189
rapidly out of sight. Its gears scraped thinly. It looked like a
child's toy. At any moment a bigger truck might smash into
it and scatter Claud's and the niggers' brains all over the
road.

Mrs. Turpin stood there, her gaze fixed on the highway, all   190
her muscles rigid, until in five or six minutes the truck reappeared, returning. She waited until it had had time to turn
into their own road. Then like a monumental statue coming
to life, she bent her head slowly and gazed, as if through the
very heart of mystery, down into the pig parlor at the hogs.
They had settled all in one corner around the old sow who
was grunting softly. A red glow suffused them. They appeared to pant with a secret life.

Until the sun slipped finally behind the tree line, Mrs.   191
Turpin remained there with her gaze bent to them as if she
were absorbing some abysmal life-giving knowledge. At last
she lifted her head. There was only a purple streak in the sky,
cutting through a field of crimson and leading, like an extension of the highway, into the descending dusk. She raised her
hands from the side of the pen in a gesture hieratic and profound. A visionary light settled in her eyes. She saw the streak

as a vast swinging bridge extending upward from the earth through a field of living fire. Upon it a vast horde of souls were rumbling toward heaven. There were whole companies of white-trash, clean for the first time in their lives, and bands of black niggers in white robes, and battalions of freaks and lunatics shouting and clapping and leaping like frogs. And bringing up the end of the procession was a tribe of people whom she recognized at once as those who, like herself and Claud, had always had a little of everything and the God-given wit to use it right. She leaned forward to observe them closer. They were marching behind the others with great dignity, accountable as they had always been for good order and common sense and respectable behavior. They alone were on key. Yet she could see by their shocked and altered faces that even their virtues were being burned away. She lowered her hands and gripped the rail of the hog pen, her eyes small but fixed unblinkingly on what lay ahead. In a moment the vision faded but she remained where she was, immobile.

At length she got down and turned off the faucet and 192 made her slow way on the darkening path to the house. In the woods around her the invisible cricket choruses had struck up, but what she heard were the voices of the souls climbing upward into the starry field and shouting hallelujah.

COMMENT ON "REVELATION"

Ruby Turpin, the central character in Flannery O'Connor's "Revelation," is obsessed with the classification process. At night she occupies herself "naming the classes of people": most "colored people" are on the bottom; "next to them— not above, just away from—are the white trash"; and so on. Mrs. Turpin puzzles about the exceptions to her system—the black dentist who owns property and the decent white folks who have lost their money—but for the most part she is certain about her system and her place in it. In the doctor's waiting room, she sizes up the other patients, placing them in their appropriate classes. But her internal and external dialogue reveals the ironies and inconsistencies in her rigid system. Self-satisfied, pleased that Jesus is on her side, she is not prepared for the book on *Human Development* that is thrown at her or the events that follow—the transparent flattery of the black workers, her cleaning of the pig parlor, and finally her vision of the highway to heaven that reveals her real place in God's hierarchy.

Division and Classification as a Writing Strategy

1. Write a column for your local newspaper in which you develop a system for classifying a concept such as *trash*. You may decide to interpret this word literally, developing a scheme to categorize the type of objects people throw away. Or you may decide to interpret the word figuratively, focusing on things that some people consider worthless—gossip columns, romance magazines, game shows. Here are a few possibilities: although people throw trash away, it won't go away; people's distaste for trash is the cause of its creation; people are so saturated by trash that they accept it as part of their culture with its own subtle subcategories.

2. In an essay addressed to a class in criminal justice, research the various punishments for murder. Then explain the different punishments for intentional and unintentional murder.

3. Mary Mebane argues that the system of class and color is used to impose power in a negative way. Consider some other system that uses power in a positive way. For example, you may want to classify people by the various ways they empower others.

4. Write an essay that classifies various kinds of bad luck. You may want to follow Austin's pattern by arranging the types of bad luck in an ascending order of complexity.

5. Focus on Phillip Lopate's pluralistic category in "Modern Friendships," and classify it into smaller subcategories. For example, you may wish to draft a feature in which you identify various kinds of "work friends" or you may wish to take on the *When Harry Met Sally* line—explaining why men and women can or cannot be friends.

6. Judith Viorst presents many examples that reveal the relationship between telling the truth and maintaining trust. Instead of classifying types of lies, consider some other complicated moral issues, such as trust, loyalty, or courage. Divide the issue into categories, and then write an essay classifying and illustrating those categories.

DEFINITION

As a writer, both in and out of college, you're likely to spend a good deal of time writing definitions. In an astronomy class, you may be asked to explain what the Doppler effect is or what a white dwarf star is. In a literature class, you may be asked to define a sonnet and identify its different forms. If you become an engineer, you may write to define problems your company proposes to solve or to define a new product your company has developed. If you become a business executive, you may have to write a brochure to describe a new service your company offers or draft a letter that defines the company's policy on credit applications.

Writers use definitions to establish boundaries, to show the essential nature of something, and to explain the special qualities that identify a purpose, place, object, or concept and distinguish it from others similar to it. Writers often write extended definitions—definitions that go beyond the one-sentence or one-paragraph explanations that you find in a dictionary or encyclopedia to expand on and examine the essential qualities of a policy, an event, a group, or a trend. Sometimes an extended definition becomes an entire book. Some books are written to define the good life; others are written to define the ideal university or the best kind of government. In fact, many of the books on any current nonfiction best-seller list are primarily definitions. The essays in this section of *The Riverside Reader* are all extended definitions.

PURPOSE

When you write, you can use definitions in several ways. For instance, you can define to *point out the special nature* of something. You may want to show the special flavor of San Francisco that makes it different from other major cities in the world, or you may want to describe the unique features that make the Macintosh computer different from other personal computers.

You can also define to *explain*. In an essay about cross-country skiing, you might want to show your readers what the sport is like and point out why it's less hazardous and less expensive than downhill skiing but better exercise. You might also define to *entertain*—to describe the essence of what it means to be a "good old boy," for instance. Often you define to *inform;* that is what you are doing in college papers when you write about West Virginia folk art or postmodern architecture. Often you write to *establish a standard,* perhaps for a good exercise program, a workable environmental policy, or even the ideal pair of running shoes. Notice that when you define to set a standard, you may also be defining to *persuade,* to convince your reader to accept the ideal you describe. Many definitions are essentially arguments.

Sometimes you may even write to *define yourself.* That is what you are doing when you write an autobiographical statement for a college admissions officer or a scholarship committee, or when you write a job application letter. You hope to give your readers the special information that will distinguish you from all other candidates. When that is your task, you'll profit by knowing the common strategies for defining and by recognizing how other writers have used them.

AUDIENCE

When you're going to use definition in your writing, you can benefit by thinking ahead of time about what your readers expect from you. Why are they reading, and what questions will they want you to answer? You can't anticipate all their questions, but you should plan on responding to at least two kinds of queries.

First, your readers are likely to ask, "What distinguishes what you're writing about? What's typical or different about it? How do I know when I see one?" For example, if you were writing about the Olympic games, your readers would perhaps want to know the difference between today's Olympic games and the original games in ancient Greece. With a little research, you could tell them about several major differences.

Second, for more complex topics you should expect that your readers will also ask, "What is the basic character or the essential nature of what you're writing about? What do you mean when you say 'alternative medicine,' 'Marxist theory,' or 'white-collar crime'?" Answering questions such as these is more difficult, but if you're going to use terms like these in an essay, you have an obligation to define them, using as many strategies as you need to clarify your terms. To define white-collar crime, for instance, you could specify that it is nonviolent, likely to happen within businesses, and involves illegal manipulation of funds or privileged information. You should also strengthen your definition by giving examples that your readers might be familiar with.

STRATEGIES

You can choose from several strategies for defining, using them singly or in combination. A favorite strategy we all use is *giving examples,* something we do naturally when we point to a special automobile we like or show a child a picture of a raccoon in a picture book. Writers use the same method when they describe a scene, create a visual image, or cite a specific instance of something.

Every author in this section uses an abundance of examples. Diane Ackerman introduces a wealth of examples from across several societies to make her point that to some extent the way people experience pain is cultural. Anthony Giddens also provides a wide range of cross-cultural examples to illustrate the extensive and complex process of "globalization."

You can define by *analyzing qualities* to emphasize what specific traits distinguish the person or thing you're defining. When you use this strategy for people, you focus on certain qualities or behaviors that reveal that individual's personality and character. James Gleick uses this strategy to illustrate how people try to complete multiple tasks in smaller and smaller periods of time. In the opening paragraph of "Pain," Diane Ackerman shows what she calls T. E. Lawrence's "quintessential machismo" by describing him holding his hand in a candle flame.

A similar strategy is *attributing characteristics*. This is Stephen Harrigan's chief tactic in "The Tiger Is God." He begins by describing tigers' characteristic method of attack, points out that zookeepers know that tigers are dangerous, and then identifies tigers as predators whose mission is to kill.

Another strategy is *defining negatively;* one of John Berendt's chief strategies in "The Hoax" is showing what something is not. Simple deception or trickery may be a prank, but it is not a hoax. In order to qualify as a hoax, a trick must have something witty and original about it.

Another way to define is by *using analogies.* In "Pain" Ackerman draws an analogy between the painful rituals that young people go through in tribal initiation rites in some parts of the world and some of the procedures that women endure in beauty parlors to enhance their appearance. Harrigan uses analogy when he compares the window in the tiger's cage to "a portal through which mankind's most primeval terrors were allowed to pass unobstructed."

You can also define by *showing function.* Often the most important feature about an object, agency, or institution is what it does. The element of function figures centrally in

Toni Cade Bambara's story as Miss Moore tries to teach her students the meaning of the word *cost*. Harrigan also focuses on function in "The Tiger Is God," stressing that the primary function of a tiger is to kill for food; it's a predator.

COMBINING STRATEGIES

Even when you're writing an essay that is primarily an exercise in definition, you may want to do as professional writers often do and bring in other strategies, perhaps narration or argument or process analysis. For instance, in "A Chinaman's Chance" (pages 465–476), Eric Liu gives his own definition of the American Dream and then argues that young people who feel they have no chance to achieve that dream are mistaken.

Some writers also combine definition with narration and description. In "Beauty: When the Other Dancer Is the Self" (pages 39–48), Alice Walker defines beauty by describing how her child responds to her eye. Diane Ackerman uses several mini-narratives to illustrate that people in different cultures have different outlooks about the experience of pain. In "Stone Soup" (pages 485–494), Barbara Kingsolver uses stories about children as a way of defining a strong family. So you can mix and mingle strategies even though one may dominate. As you read essays in this section, and especially as you reread them, try to be conscious of the strategies authors are using. You may find that you can incorporate some of them into your own writing.

USING DEFINITION IN PARAGRAPHS

Here are two definition paragraphs. The first is written by a professional writer and is followed by an analysis. The second is written by a student writer and is followed by questions.

JOYCE CAROL OATES
When Tristram Met Isolde

Romantic love isn't so much a love that defies conventions, for romantic love is of all love types the most conventional, as a love that arises with

Romantic love is spontaneous

seeming spontaneity: unwilled, undirected by others' suggestions or admonitions, raw and un-premeditated and of the heart; not cerebral and not genital. Romantic love is forever in opposi-tion to formal, cultural, and tribal prescriptions of behavior: arranged marriages, for instance, in which brides and their dowries are possessions to be handed over to a bridegroom and his family, or in which titled names are wed in business-like arrangements that have little to do with the feelings of the individuals. Diana, Princess of Wales, would seem to have been a martyr to such an arrangement: her political marriage to Prince Charles ending in dissolution and divorce, and her "quest for personal happiness" (i.e., roman-tic love) ending in a grotesquely public death on a Parisian boulevard.

Opposed to rules and restrictions

Princess Diana as perfect example

Comment In this paragraph taken from a short essay whose title, "When Tristram Met Isolde," invokes the tragic legend of two fatally smitten lovers, the novelist Joyce Carol Oates defines romantic love as an irrational, compulsive emotion that overwhelms all caution and good sense. Those who em-brace it are rebelling against the practical economic and social concerns that families in non-Western cultures often value more than spontaneous feelings and individual desires. In both real life and in fiction, the surrender to romantic love often has disastrous consequences. To illustrate her point, Oates calls up what must be the most publicized example of a romantic disaster in the last decade: the death of Princess Diana and her lover in a high-speed automobile crash in that most romantic of cities, Paris.

JASON UTESCH
Personality

"She has a great personality." Translation: she goes to bed early to watch the shopping channel. "He has a great personality." Translation: he tells dirty jokes at funerals. The "p" word is trouble-some not only because all the great personalities we've been told about have proved disappoint-ing, but also because all the great personalities we know don't seem to measure up to other peo-ple's expectations. Even the old song suggests that <u>personality</u> is a complicated quality to define because to have it a person has to have a special <u>walk,</u> <u>talk,</u> <u>smile,</u> <u>charm,</u> <u>love,</u> and PLUS she (or he) has to have a great big <u>heart.</u>

1. What do you see as Utesch's purpose in listing so many contradictions in the way people define *personality*?
2. What does the writer imply by using the phrase "the 'p' word"?

DEFINITION

Points to Remember

1. Remember that you are obligated to define key terms that you use in your writing—such as *Marx-ism, alternative medicine,* or *nontraditional student.*
2. Understand your purpose in defining: to explain, to entertain, to persuade, to set boundaries, or to es-tablish a standard.
3. Understand how writers construct an argument from a definition. For example, by defining the good life or good government, they argue for that kind of life or government.
4. Know the several ways of defining: giving examples, analyzing qualities, attributing characteristics, defining negatively, using analogies, and showing function.
5. Learn to use definition in combination with other strategies, as a basis on which to build an argument, or as supporting evidence.

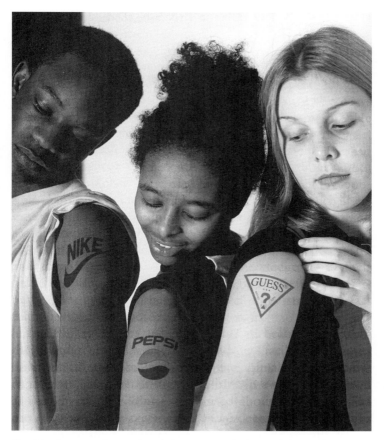

In this photograph, reprinted from an early issue of the anticommercial, anticonsumption magazine Adbusters, *Shannon Mendes captures three high school students showing off their tattoos. In what ways do these tattoos define these students? In what ways are some of these tattoos dated? Write an essay in which you explain how your choice of some product—beverage, clothes, car—defines you.*

JOHN BERENDT

John Berendt was born in Syracuse, New York, in 1939 and was educated at Harvard University. He began his writing career as an associate editor at *Esquire,* before editing *Holiday Magazine* and writing and producing television programs such as *The David Frost Show* and *The Dick Cavett Show.* In 1979, he returned to *Esquire* as a columnist after serving as editor of *New York Magazine* from 1977 to 1979. In 1994, he published his first book, *Midnight in the Garden of Good and Evil,* a "nonfiction novel" about a controversial murder in Savannah, Georgia. The book has since been transformed into a major film by director Clint Eastwood. In "The Hoax," reprinted from *Esquire,* Berendt defines the magical ingredients of a hoax.

The Hoax

W HEN THE HUMORIST Robert Benchley was an under-   1
graduate at Harvard eighty years ago, he and a couple of friends showed up one morning at the door of an elegant Beacon Hill mansion, dressed as furniture repairmen. They told the housekeeper they had come to pick up the sofa. Five minutes later they carried the sofa out the door, put it on a truck, and drove it three blocks away to another house, where, posing as deliverymen, they plunked it down in the parlor. That evening, as Benchley well knew, the couple living in house A were due to attend a party in house B. Whatever the outcome—and I'll get to that shortly—it was guaranteed to be a defining example of how proper Bostonians handle social crises. The wit inherent in Benchley's practical joke elevated it from the level of prank to the more respectable realm of hoax.

To qualify as a hoax, a prank must have magic in it—the   2
word is derived from *hocus-pocus,* after all. Daring and irony
are useful ingredients, too. A good example of a hoax is the
ruse perpetrated by David Hampton, the young black man
whose pretense of being Sidney Poitier's son inspired John
Guare's *Six Degrees of Separation.* Hampton managed to in-
sinuate himself into two of New York's most sophisticated
households—one headed by the president of the public-
television station WNET, the other by the dean of the
Columbia School of Journalism. Hampton's hoax touched a
number of sensitive themes: snobbery, class, race, and sex, all
of which playwright Guare deftly exploited.

Hampton is a member of an elite band of famous impos-   3
tors that includes a half-mad woman who for fifty years

To qualify as a hoax, a prank must have
magic in it. . . .

---

claimed to be Anastasia, the lost daughter of the assassinated
czar Nicholas II; and a man named Harry Gerguson, who became a Hollywood restaurateur and darling of society in the
1930s and 1940s as the ersatz Russian prince Mike
Romanoff.

Forgeries have been among the better hoaxes. Fake   4
Vermeers painted by an obscure Dutch artist, Hans van
Meegeren, were so convincing that they fooled art dealers,
collectors, and museums. The hoax came to light when Van
Meegeren was arrested as a Nazi collaborator after the war.
To prove he was not a Nazi, he admitted he had sold a fake
Vermeer to Hermann Göring for $256,000. Then he owned
up to having created other "Vermeers," and to prove he
could do it, he painted *Jesus in the Temple* in the style of
Vermeer while under guard in jail.

In a bizarre twist, a story much like Van Meegeren's be-   5
came the subject of the book *Fake!,* by Clifford Irving, who

in 1972 attempted to pull off a spectacular hoax of his own: a wholly fraudulent "authorized" biography of Howard Hughes. Irving claimed to have conducted secret interviews with the reclusive Hughes, and McGraw-Hill gave him a big advance. Shortly before publication, Hughes surfaced by telephone and denied that he had ever spoken with Irving. Irving had already spent $100,000 of the advance; he was convicted of fraud and sent to jail.

As it happens, we are used to hoaxes where I come from. I 6 grew up just a few miles down the road from Cardiff, New York—a town made famous by the Cardiff Giant. As we learned in school, a farmer named Newell complained, back in 1889, that his well was running dry, and while he and his neighbors were digging a new one, they came upon what appeared to be the fossilized remains of a man twelve feet tall. Before the day was out, Newell had erected a tent and posted a sign charging a dollar for a glimpse of the "giant"—three dollars for a longer look. Throngs descended on Cardiff. It wasn't long before scientists determined that the giant had been carved from a block of gypsum. The hoax came undone fairly quickly after that, but even so—as often happens with hoaxes—the giant became an even bigger attraction *because* it was a hoax. P. T. Barnum offered Newell a fortune for the giant, but Newell refused, and it was then that he got his comeuppance. Barnum simply made a replica and put it on display as the genuine Cardiff Giant. Newell's gig was ruined.

The consequences of hoaxes are what give them spice. 7 Orson Welles's lifelike 1938 radio broadcast of H. G. Wells's *War of the Worlds* panicked millions of Americans, who were convinced that martians had landed in New Jersey. The forged diary of Adolf Hitler embarrassed historian Hugh Trevor-Roper, who had vouched for its authenticity, and *Newsweek* and *The Sunday Times* of London, both of which published excerpts in 1983 shortly before forensic tests proved that there were nylon fibers in the paper it was written on, which wouldn't have been possible had it originated before 1950. The five-hundred-thousand-year-old remains of Piltdown man, found in 1912, had anthropologists confused about human evolution until 1953, when fluoride tests exposed the bones as an elaborate modern hoax. And as for Robert Benchley's game on Beacon Hill, no one said a word about the sofa all evening, although there it sat in plain sight. One week later, however, couple A sent an anonymous package to couple B. It contained the sofa's slipcovers.

For Study and Discussion

QUESTIONS FOR RESPONSE

1. What hoaxes do you know about or have you been involved in? Which of them had elements that might be described as daring or witty?
2. What's your reaction to those incidents in Berendt's account that involve criminal fraud? How do you explain that reaction?

QUESTIONS ABOUT PURPOSE

1. How do you think Berendt wants you to respond to the tricksters he describes in his essay? To what extent did you respond that way?
2. Berendt's examples of people duped by hoaxes include scientists, a historian, a college president, an eminent publisher, and curators of several museums. What does he accomplish by telling stories about such a wide range of dupes?

QUESTIONS ABOUT AUDIENCE

1. This essay originally appeared in *Esquire* magazine. What traits and attitudes do you think a writer for *Esquire* assumes characterize its readers? (If necessary, browse through an issue of *Esquire* in the library to get a feel for its audience.)
2. Berendt seems to assume that everyone enjoys stories about tricksters' getting the best of their victims. In your case, is the assumption justified? Why or why not?

QUESTIONS ABOUT STRATEGIES

1. What does the writer achieve by opening and closing the essay with the anecdote about the sofa?

2. How would you characterize the tone of this essay? What attitude of the writer toward his subject do you think the tone reflects? Do you find that attitude engaging or off-putting?

QUESTIONS FOR DISCUSSION

1. Which of Berendt's anecdotes do you find the most entertaining? Why?
2. When would you say a deception ceases to be a hoax and turns into something else? What examples can you think of?

Diane Ackerman was born in 1948 in Waukegan, Illinois, and was educated at Boston University, Pennsylvania State University, and Cornell University. After jobs as a researcher and editorial assistant, Ackerman began teaching writing at such schools as Pittsburgh University; Washington University, St. Louis; and Cornell University. Her own writing includes several collections of poems (*The Planets: A Cosmic Pastoral,* 1976; and *The Senses of Animals,* 2000), a play (*Reverse Thunder: A Dramatic Poem,* 1988), two television documentaries (*Ideas,* 1990; and *The Senses,* 1995), and numerous works of nonfiction (*The Natural History of the Senses,* 1990; *A Natural History of Love,* 1994; and *A Natural History of My Garden,* 2001). In "Pain," reprinted from *A Natural History of the Senses,* Ackerman examines the difficulty of defining *pain.*

Pain

IN THE SAND-SWEPT sprawl of the panoramic film   1
Lawrence of Arabia a scene of quintessential machismo
stands out: T. E. Lawrence holding his hand over a candle
flame until the flesh starts to sizzle. When his companion
tries the same thing, he recoils in pain, crying "Doesn't that
hurt you?" as he nurses his burned hand. "Yes," Lawrence
replies coolly. "Then what is the trick?" the companion asks.
"The trick," Lawrence answers, "is not to mind."

One of the great riddles of biology is why the experience   2
of pain is so subjective. Being able to withstand pain depends
to a considerable extent on culture and tradition. Many soldiers have denied pain despite appalling wounds, not even

requesting morphine, although in peacetime they would
have demanded it. Most people going into the hospital for an
operation focus completely on their pain and suffering,
whereas soldiers or saints and other martyrs can think about
something nobler and more important to them, and this
clouds their sense of pain. Religions have always encouraged
their martyrs to experience pain in order to purify the spirit.
We come into this world with only the slender word "I," and
giving it up in a sacred delirium is the painful ecstasy religions

*Being able to withstand pain depends to a
considerable extent on culture and tradition.*

demand. When a fakir runs across hot coals, his skin does
begin to singe—you can smell burning flesh; he just doesn't
feel it. In Bali a few years ago, my mother saw men go into
trances and pick up red-hot cannonballs from an open fire,
then carry them down the road. As meditation techniques
and biofeedback have shown, the mind can learn to conquer
pain. This is particularly true in moments of crisis or exaltation, when concentrating on something outside oneself
seems to distract the mind from the body, and the body from
suffering and time. Of course, there are those who welcome
pain in order to surmount it. In 1989, I read about a new
craze in California: well-to-do business people taking weekend classes in hot-coal-walking. Pushing the body to or beyond its limits has always appealed to human beings. There is
a part of our psyche that is pure timekeeper and weather
watcher. Not only do we long to know how fast we can run,
how high we can jump, how long we can hold our breath
under water—we also like to keep checking these limits regularly to see if they've changed. Why? What difference does it
make? The human body is miraculous and beautiful, whether
it can "clean and jerk" three hundred pounds, swim the

English Channel, or survive a year riding the subway. In anthropological terms, we've come to be who we are by evolving sharper ways to adapt to the environment, and, from the outset, what has guided us has been an elaborate system of rewards. Small wonder we're addicted to quiz shows and lotteries, paychecks and bonuses. We've always explored our mental limits, too, and pushed them without letup. In the early eighties, I spent a year as a soccer journalist, following the dazzling legwork of Pelé, Franz Beckenbauer, and virtually every other legendary international star the New York Cosmos had signed up for equally legendary sums of American cash. Choose your favorite sport; now imagine seeing all the world's best players on one team. I was interested in the ceremonial violence of sports, the psychology of games, the charmed circle of the field, the breezy rhetoric of the legs, the anthropological spectacle of watching twenty-two barely clad men run on grass in the sunlight, hazing the quarry of a ball toward the net. The fluency and grace of soccer appealed for a number of reasons, and I wanted to absorb some of its atmosphere for a novel I was writing. I was amazed to discover that the players frequently realized only at halftime or after a match that they'd hurt themselves badly and were indeed in wicked pain. During the match, there hadn't been the rumor of pain, but once the match was over and they could afford the luxury of suffering, pain screamed like a noon factory whistle.

Often our fear of pain contributes to it. Our culture expects childbirth to be a deeply painful event, and so, for us, it is. Women from other cultures stop their work in the fields to give birth, returning to the fields immediately afterward. Initiation and adolescence rites around the world often involve penetrating pain, which initiates must endure to prove themselves worthy. In the sun dance of the Sioux, for instance, a young warrior would allow the skin of his chest to be pierced by iron rods; then he was hung from a stanchion. When I was in Istanbul in the 1970s, I saw teenage boys dressed in shiny silk fezzes and silk suits decorated with glitter. They were preparing for circumcision, a festive event in the life of a

Turk, which occurs at around the age of fifteen. No anesthetic is used; instead, a boy is given a jelly candy to chew. Sir
Richard Burton's writings abound with descriptions of tribal
mutilation and torture rituals, including one in which a
shaman removes an apron of flesh from the front of a boy,
cutting all the way from the stomach to the thighs, producing a huge white scar.

Women in some cultures go through many painful initia-   4
tion rites, often including circumcision, which removes or
destroys the clitoris. Being able to endure the pain of childbirth is expected of women, but there are also disguised rites
of pain, pain that is endured for the sake of health or beauty.
Women have their legs waxed as a matter of fashion, and have
done so throughout the ages. When mine were waxed at a
Manhattan beauty salon recently, the pain, which began like
10,000 bees stinging me simultaneously, was excruciating.
Change the woman from a Rumanian cosmetician to a
German Gestapo agent. Change the room from a cubicle in a
beauty emporium to a prison cell. Keep the level of pain exactly the same, and it easily qualifies as torture. We tend to
think of torture in the name of beauty as an aberration of the
ancients, but there are modern scourging parlors. People
have always mutilated their skins, often enduring pain to be
beautiful, as if the pain chastened the beauty, gave it the special veneer of sacrifice. Many women experience extreme pain
during their periods each month, but they accept the pain because they understand that it's not caused by someone else,
it's not malicious, and it doesn't surprise them; and this
makes all the difference.

There are also illusions of pain as vivid as optical illusions,   5
times when the sufferer imagines he or she feels pain that
cannot possibly exist. In some cultures, the father experiences
a false pregnancy—*couvade* as it's called—and takes to bed
with childbirth pains, going through his own arduous experience of having a baby. The internal organs don't have many
pain receptors (the skin is supposed to be the guard post), so
people often feel "referred pain" when one of their organs is
in trouble. Heart attacks frequently produce a pain in the

stomach, the left arm, or the shoulder. When this happens, the brain can't figure out exactly where the message is coming from. In the classic phenomenon of phantom-limb pain, the brain gets faulty signals and continues to feel pain in a limb that has been amputated; such pain can be torturous, perverse, and maddening, since there is nothing physically present to hurt.

Pain has plagued us throughout the history of our species. 6 We spend our lives trying to avoid it, and, from one point of view, what we call "happiness" may be just the absence of pain. Yet it is difficult to define pain, which may be sharp, dull, shooting, throbbing, imaginary, or referred. We have many pains that surge from within as cramps and aches. And we also talk about emotional distress as pain. Pains are often combined, the emotional with the physical, and the physical with the physical. When you burn yourself, the skin swells and blisters, and when the blister breaks, the skin hurts in yet another way. A wound may become infected. Then histamine and serotonin are released, which dilate the blood vessels and trigger a pain response. Not all internal injuries can be felt (it's possible to do brain surgery under a local anesthetic), but illnesses that constrict blood flow often are: Angina pectoris, for example, which occurs when the coronary arteries shrink too tight for blood to comfortably pass. Even intense pain often eludes accurate description, as Virginia Woolf reminds us in her essay "On Being Ill": "English, which can express the thoughts of Hamlet and the tragedy of Lear, has no words for the shiver and the headache . . . let a sufferer try to describe a pain in his head to a doctor and language at once runs dry."

For Study and Discussion

QUESTIONS FOR RESPONSE

1. If you come from our traditional Western culture, how do you react to Ackerman's reports about the extreme pain that some members of other cultures seem to be able to endure?

2. Ackerman says that T. E. Lawrence displays the "quintessential machismo." How do you interpret that comment?

QUESTIONS ABOUT PURPOSE

1. What assumptions about pain do you think Ackerman is challenging in this essay?
2. How might her discussion of the many ways different people deal with pain cause some people to rethink their conventional wisdom about the sensation?

QUESTIONS ABOUT AUDIENCE

1. What message about dealing with pain do you think our culture gives the average person? How is that message communicated?
2. How would you describe your most painful physical experience? What resources helped you get through it?

QUESTIONS ABOUT STRATEGIES

1. How does Ackerman's opening paragraph introduce the reader to a central concept in her essay?
2. What does Ackerman achieve by packing her essay with such a broad range of examples from diverse cultures?

QUESTIONS FOR DISCUSSION

1. What incentives can people have to endure pain? What incentive might work for you?
2. In what ways is pain management big business in this country? How might that reality affect people's attitudes about pain?

JAMES GLEICK

James Gleick was born in 1954 in New York City and began his career as a copyeditor for the *New York Times.* He began writing articles on science for the *Times,* eventually publishing a series of widely acclaimed books, such as *Chaos: Making a New Science* (1987), *Genius: The Life and Science of Richard Feynman* (1993), and *Faster: The Acceleration of Just About Everything* (1999). In his more recent books, *What Just Happened: A Chronicle of the Information Frontier* (2002) and *Isaac Newton* (2003), he continues to explore the impact of technology and science on social and cultural issues. In "Attention! Multitaskers," reprinted from *Faster: The Acceleration of Just About Everything,* Gleick defines the origin and significance of the word that describes the "simultaneous fragmentation and overloading of human attention."

Attention! Multitaskers

T HE FINAL, FATAL flaw in the time-use pie chart is that we 1 are multitasking creatures. It is possible, after all, to tie shoes and watch television, to eat and read, to shave and talk with the children. These days it is possible to drive, eat, listen to a book, and talk on the phone, all at once, if you dare. No segment of time—not a day, not a second—can really be a zero-sum game.

"Attention! Multitaskers," says an advertisement for an 2 AT&T wireless telephone service. "Demo all these exciting features"—namely E-mail, voice telephone, and pocket organizer. Pay attention if you can. We have always multitasked—inability to walk and chew gum is a time-honored cause for

derision—but never so intensely or so self-consciously as
now. If haste is the gas pedal, multitasking is overdrive. We
are multitasking connoisseurs—experts in crowding, pressing, packing, and overlapping distinct activities in our all-too-
finite moments. Some reports from the front lines:

David Feldman, in New York, schedules his tooth-flossing   3
to coincide with his regular browsing of on-line discussion
groups (the latest in food, the latest in Brian Wilson). He has
learned to hit Page Down with his pinky. Mark Maxham of
California admits to even more embarrassing arrangements
of tasks. "I find myself doing strange little optimizations,"
he says, "like life is a set of computer code and I'm a com-
piler." Similarly, by the time Michael Hartl heads for the

---

*If haste is the gas pedal, multitasking
is overdrive.*

---

bathroom in his California Institute of Technology digs
each morning, he has already got his computer starting its
progress through the Windows boot sequence, and then, as
he runs to breakfast, he hits Control-Shift-D to dial into
the campus computer network, and then he gets his Web
browser started, downloading graphics, so he can check the
news while he eats. "I figure I save at least two or three minutes a day this way," he says. "Don't laugh." Then there's
the subroutine he thinks of as "the mouthwash gambit,"
where he swigs a mouthful on one pass by the sink, swishes
it around in his mouth as he gets his bicycle, and spits out as
he heads back in the other direction, toward a class in general relativity.

The word *multitasking* came from computer scientists of   4
the 1960s. They arranged to let a single computer serve multiple users on a network. When a computer multitasks, it usually just alternates tasks, but on the finest of time scales. It

slices time and interleaves its tasks. Unless, that is, it has more than one processor running, in which case multitasking can be truly parallel processing. Either way, society grabbed the term as fast as it did *Type A*. We apply it to our own flesh-and-blood CPUs. Not only do we multitask, but, with computers as our guides, we multitask self-consciously.

Multitasking begins in the service of efficiency. Working at a computer terminal in the London newsroom of Bloomberg News, Douglas McGill carried on a long telephone conversation with a colleague in New York. His moment of realization came when, still talking on the phone, he sent off an E-mail message to another colleague in Connecticut and immediately received her reply. "It squeezes more information than was previously squeezable into a given amount of time," he says. "I wonder if this contributes to that speeding-up sensation we all feel?" Clearly it does.   5

Is there any limit? A few people claim to be able to listen to two different pieces of music at once. Many more learn to take advantage of the brain's apparent ability to process spoken and written text in separate channels. Mike Holderness, in London, watches television with closed captioning so that he can keep the sound off and listen to the unrelated music of his choice. Or he writes several letters at once—"in the sense that I have processes open and waiting." None of this is enough for a cerebral cortex conditioned to the pace of life on-line, he realizes: 6

> *Ten years ago, I was delighted and enthralled that I could get a telegram-like E-mail from Philadelphia to London in only fifteen minutes. Three years ago, I was delighted and enthralled that I could fetch an entire thesis from Texas to London in only five minutes. Now, I drum my fingers on the desk when a hundred-kilobyte file takes more than twenty seconds to arrive . . . damn, it's coming from New Zealand . . .*

It seems natural to recoil from this simultaneous fragmentation and overloading of human attention. How well can   7 people really accomplish their multitasks? "It's hard to get around the forebrain bottleneck," said Earl Hunt, a professor of psychology and computer science at the University of Washington. "Our brains function the same way the Cro-Magnon brains did, so technology isn't going to change that." But for many—humans, not computers—a sense of satisfaction and well-being comes with this saturation of parallel pathways in the brain. We divide ourselves into parts, perhaps, each receiving sensations, sending messages, or manipulating the environment in some way. We train ourselves as Samuel Renshaw would have trained us. Or, then again, we slice time just as a computer does, feeding each task a bit of our attention in turn. Perhaps the young have an advantage because of the cultural conditioning they received from early exposure to computers and fast entertainment media. Corporate managers think so. Marc Prensky, a Bankers Trust vice president, had to learn to overcome instinctive annoyance when a young subordinate began reading E-mail during a face-to-face conversation; the subordinate explained: "I'm still listening; I'm parallel processing." This whole generation of workers, Prensky decided, weaned on video games, operates at *twitch speed*—"your thumbs going a million miles a minute," and a good thing, if managers can take advantage of it.

At least one computer manufacturer, Gateway, applies 8 multitasking to technical support. Customers call in for help, wait on hold, and then hear voices. "Hello," they are told. "You are on a conference call." William Slaughter, a lawyer calling from Philadelphia, slowly realizes that he has joined a tech-support group therapy session. He listens to Brian helping Vince. Next, Vince listens to Brian helping William. It's like a chess master playing a simultaneous exhibition, William thinks, though Brian seems a bit frazzled. Somehow the callers cope with their resentment at not being deemed worthy of Brian's undivided attention. Why should he sit daydreaming while they scurry to reboot? "Hello, Vicky," they hear him say. "You are on a conference call."

There is ample evidence that many of us choose this style   9
of living. We're willing to pay for the privilege. An entire class
of technologies is dedicated to the furthering of multitasking.
Waterproof shower radios and, now, telephones. Car phones,
of course. Objects as innocent-seeming as trays for magazines
on exercise machines are tools for multitasking (and surely
television sets are playing in the foreground, too). Picture-in-
picture display on your television set. (Gregory Stevens, in
Massachusetts: "PIP allows me to watch PBS/C-Span or the
like, and keep the ball game on or an old movie. Of course, it
is impossible for anyone else to enjoy this, with me changing
the pictures and audio feed every few seconds. When the
computer and the phone are available in a multiwindow form
on the television, things are going to be very different.")
Even without picture-in-picture, the remote control enables
a time-slicing variation on the same theme. Marc Weiden-
baum, in San Francisco, has a shorthand for describing an
evening's activities to his girlfriend: "Got home. Ate some
soup. Watched twenty or thirty shows." He means this more
or less literally:

> *I'll watch two sitcoms and a* Star Trek: Voyager
> *episode and routinely check MTV (didn't they used
> to run music videos?) and CNN (didn't they used to
> run news?) in a single hour.*
>
>   *And really not feel like I'm missing out on
> anything.*

Nothing could be more revealing of the transformation of   10
human sensibility over the past century than this widespread
unwillingness to settle for soaking up, in single-task fashion,
the dynamic flow of sound and picture coming from a television screen. Is any one channel, in itself, monotonous?
Marshall McLuhan failed to predict this: the medium of television seemed *cool* and all-absorbing to him, so different from
the experience available to us a generation later. For the
McLuhan who announced that the medium was the message,
television was a black-and-white, unitary stream. McLuhan

did not surf with remote control. Sets were tiny and the resolution poor—"visually low in data," he wrote in 1964, "a
ceaselessly forming contour of things limned by the scanning
finger." People were seen mostly in close-up, perforce. Thus
he asserted: "TV will not work as background. It engages
you. You have to be *with* it."

No longer paradoxically, perhaps, as television has gained   11
in vividness and clarity, it has lost its command of our foreground. For some people television has been bumped off its
pedestal by the cool, fast, fluid, indigenously multitasking activity of browsing the Internet. Thus anyone—say, Steven
Leibel of California—can counter McLuhan definitively (typing in one window while reading a World Wide Web page in
another): "The Web and TV complement each other perfectly. TV doesn't require much attention from the viewer. It
fits perfectly into the spaces created by downloading Web
pages." If he really needs to concentrate, he turns down the
sound momentarily. Not everyone bothers concentrating.
Eight million American households report television sets and
personal computers running, together in the same room,
"often" or "always."

Not long ago, listening to the simpler audio stream of   12
broadcast radio was a single-task activity for most people.
The radio reached into homes and grabbed listeners by the
lapel. It could dominate their time and attention—for a few
decades. "A child might sit," Robinson and Godbey recall
sentimentally, "staring through the window at the darkening
trees, hearing only the Lone Ranger's voice and the hooves
of horses in the canyon." Now it is rare for a person to listen
to the radio *and do nothing else*. Programmers structure
radio's content with the knowledge that they can count on
only a portion of the listener's attention, and only for intermittent intervals. And rarely with full attention. Much of the
radio audience at any given moment has its senses locked up
in a more demanding activity—probably driving. Or shower-
ing, or cooking, or jogging. Radio has become a secondary
task in a multitasking world.

For Study and Discussion

QUESTIONS FOR RESPONSE

1. How often do you find yourself multitasking?
2. When you are multitasking, how efficiently do you perform each task?

QUESTIONS ABOUT PURPOSE

1. How does the title of Gleick's book, *Faster: The Acceleration of Just About Everything,* help explain the purpose of this essay?
2. What is he attempting to prove about the relationship between time and productivity?

QUESTIONS ABOUT AUDIENCE

1. What assumptions does Gleick make about his readers' attitude toward the effective use of time?
2. How does he identify generational differences in his readers' attitude toward multitasking?

QUESTIONS ABOUT STRATEGIES

1. How does Gleick explain the origin of the word *multitasking?*
2. How does he use the routines of people like David Feldman, Mark Maxham, and Michael Hart to illustrate the word?

QUESTIONS FOR DISCUSSION

1. How has multitasking created the demand for an entire class of technologies?
2. In what ways does Marshall McLuhan's failure to explain multitasking reveal how this new behavior has changed our lives?

ANTHONY GIDDENS

Anthony Giddens was born in 1938 in London, England, and educated at the University of Hull, London School of Economics, and Cambridge University. Considered by many as England's most prominent sociologist, Giddens is the co-founder of Polity Press and director of the London School of Economics. His many books include *Capitalism and Modern Social Theory: An Analysis of the Writings of Marx, Durkheim and Max Weber* (1971); *The Class Structure of Advanced Societies* (1981); and *The Third Way: The Renewal of Social Democracy* (1999). Prime Minister Anthony Blair borrowed the phrase "the third way" to define the new platform of the British Labour Party. One of Giddens's recent books is *Runaway World: How Globalization Is Reshaping Our World* (2000). In "Globalisation," Giddens uses the British spelling of the word in his BBC Reith Lectures (1999) to define a word that is a "complex set of processes."

Globalisation

A FRIEND OF mine studies village life in central Africa. A few years ago, she paid her first visit to a remote area where she was to carry out her fieldwork. The evening she got there, she was invited to a local home for an evening's entertainment. She expected to find out about the traditional pastimes of this isolated community. Instead, the evening turned out to be a viewing of *Basic Instinct* on video. The film at that point hadn't even reached the cinemas in London.

Such vignettes reveal something about our world. And what they reveal isn't trivial. It isn't just a matter of people

1

2

adding modern paraphernalia—videos, TVs, personal computers and so forth—to their traditional ways of life. We live in a world of transformations, affecting almost every aspect of what we do. For better or worse, we are being propelled into a global order that no one fully understands, but which is making its effects felt upon all of us.

Globalisation is the main theme of my lecture tonight, and 3 of the lectures as a whole. The term may not be—it isn't—a particularly attractive or elegant one. But absolutely no-one who wants to understand our prospects and possibilities at century's end can ignore it. I travel a lot to speak abroad. I haven't been to a single country recently where globalisation isn't being intensively discussed. In France, the word is *mondialisation*. In Spain and Latin America, it is *globalización*. The Germans say *Globalisierung*.

The global spread of the term is evidence of the very developments to which it refers. Every business guru talks about it. No political speech is complete without reference to it. Yet as little as 10 years ago the term was hardly used, either in the academic literature or in everyday language. It has

---

Globalisation . . . isn't developing in an even-handed way, and is by no means wholly benign in its consequences.

---

come from nowhere to be almost everywhere. Given its sudden popularity, we shouldn't be surprised that the meaning of the notion isn't always clear, or that an intellectual reaction has set in against it. Globalisation has something to do with the thesis that we now all live in one world—but in what ways exactly, and is the idea really valid?

Different thinkers have taken almost completely opposite 5 views about globalisation in debates that have sprung up over the past few years. Some dispute the whole thing. I'll call them the sceptics. According to the sceptics, all the talk about globalisation is only that—just talk. Whatever its benefits, its trials and tribulations, the global economy isn't especially different from that which existed at previous periods. The world carries on much the same as it has done for many years.

Most countries, the sceptics argue, only gain a small   6
amount of their income from external trade. Moreover, a good deal of economic exchange is between regions, rather than being truly world-wide. The countries of the European Union, for example, mostly trade among themselves. The same is true of the other main trading blocs, such as those of the Asia Pacific or North America.

Others, however, take a very different position. I'll label   7
them the radicals. The radicals argue that not only is globalisation very real, but that its consequences can be felt everywhere. The global marketplace, they say, is much more developed than even two or three decades ago, and is indifferent to national borders. Nations have lost most of the sovereignty they once had, and politicians have lost most of their capability to influence events. It isn't surprising that no one respects political leaders any more, or has much interest in what they have to say. The era of the nation state is over. Nations, as the Japanese business writer Keniche Ohmae puts it, have become mere "fictions." Authors like Ohmae see the economic difficulties of last year and this as demonstrating the reality of globalisation, albeit seen from its disruptive side.

The sceptics tend to be on the political left, especially the   8
old left. For if all of this is essentially a myth, governments can still intervene in economic life and the welfare state remain intact. The notion of globalisation, according to the sceptics, is an ideology put about by free-marketeers who wish to dismantle welfare systems and cut back on state expenditures. What has happened is at most a reversion to how the world was a century ago. In the late 19th Century there was already an open global economy, with a great deal of trade, including trade in currencies.

Well, who is right in this debate? I think it is the radicals.   9
The level of world trade today is much higher than it ever was

before, and involves a much wider range of goods and services. But the biggest difference is in the level of finance and
capital flows. Geared as it is to electronic money—money that
exists only as digits in computers—the current world economy has no parallels in earlier times. In the new global electronic economy, fund managers, banks, corporations, as well
as millions of individual investors, can transfer vast amounts of
capital from one side of the world to another at the click of a
mouse. As they do so, they can destabilise what might have
seemed rock-solid economies—as happened in East Asia.

The volume of world financial transactions is usually   10
measured in US dollars. A million dollars is a lot of money
for most people. Measured as a stack of thousand dollar
notes, it would be eight inches high. A billion dollars—in
other words, a million million—would be over 120 miles
high, 20 times higher than Mount Everest.

Yet far more than a trillion dollars is now turned over each   11
day on global currency markets, a massive increase from only
10 years ago, let alone the more distant past. The value of
whatever money we may have in our pockets, or our bank accounts, shifts from moment to moment according to fluctuations in such markets. I would have no hesitation, therefore,
in saying that globalisation, as we are experiencing it, is in
many respects not only new, but revolutionary.

However, I don't believe either the sceptics or the radicals   12
have properly understood either what it is or its implications
for us. Both groups see the phenomenon almost solely in
economic terms. This is a mistake. Globalisation is political,
technological and cultural, as well as economic. It has been
influenced above all by developments in systems of communication, dating back only to the late 1960's.

In the mid-19th Century, a Massachusetts portrait painter,   13
Samuel Morse, transmitted the first message, "What hath
god wrought?", by electric telegraph. In so doing, he initiated a new phase in world history. Never before could a message be sent without someone going somewhere to carry it.
Yet the advent of satellite communications marks every bit as
dramatic a break with the past. The first communications

satellite was launched only just over 30 years ago. Now there are more than 200 such satellites above the earth, each carrying a vast range of information. For the first time ever, instantaneous communication is possible from one side of the world to the other. Other types of electronic communication, more and more integrated with satellite transmission, have also accelerated over the past few years. No dedicated transatlantic or transpacific cables existed at all until the late 1950's. The first held less than 100 voice paths. Those of today carry more than a million.

On the first of February 1999, about 150 years after Morse invented his system of dots and dashes, Morse code finally disappeared from the world stage, discontinued as a means of communication for the sea. In its place has come a system using satellite technology, whereby any ship in distress can be pinpointed immediately. Most countries prepared for the transition some while before. The French, for example, stopped using Morse as a distress code in their local waters two years ago, signing off with a Gallic flourish: "Calling all. This is our last cry before our eternal silence."

Instantaneous electronic communication isn't just a way in which news is or information is conveyed more quickly. Its existence alters the very texture of our lives, rich and poor alike. When the image of Nelson Mandela maybe is more familiar to us than the face of our next door neighbour, something has changed in the nature of our everyday experience.

Nelson Mandela is a global celebrity, and celebrity itself is largely a product of new communications technology. The reach of media technologies is growing with each wave of innovation. It took 40 years for radio in the United States to gain an audience of 50 million. The same number were using personal computers only 15 years after the PC was introduced. It needed a mere four years, after it was made available for 50 million Americans to be regularly using the Internet.

It is wrong to think of globalisation as just concerning the big systems, like the world financial order. Globalisation isn't only about what is "out there" remote and far away from the individual. It is an "in here" phenomenon too, influencing intimate and personal aspects of our lives. The debate about family values, for example, that is going on in many countries, might seem far removed from globalising influences. It isn't. Traditional family systems are becoming transformed, or are under strain, in many parts of the world, particularly as women stake claim to greater equality. There has never before been a society, so far as we know from the historical record, in which women have been even approximately equal to men. This is a truly global revolution in everyday life, whose consequences are being felt around the world in spheres from work to politics.

Globalisation thus is a complex set of processes, not a single one. And these operate in a contradictory or oppositional fashion. Most people think of it as simply "pulling away" power or influence from local communities and nations into the global arena. And indeed this is one of its consequences. Nations do lose some of the economic power they once had. However, it also has an opposite effect. Globalisation not only pulls upwards, it pushes downwards, creating new pressures for local autonomy. The American sociologist Daniel Bell expresses this very well when he says that the nation becomes too small to solve the big problems, but also too large to solve the small ones. 18

Globalisation is the reason for the revival of local cultural identities in different parts of the world. If one asks, for example, why the Scots want more independence in the UK, or why there is a strong separatist movement in Quebec, the answer is not to be found only in their cultural history. Local nationalisms spring up as a response to globalising tendencies, as the hold of older nation-states weakens. 19

Globalisation also squeezes sideways. It creates new economic and cultural zones within and across nations. Examples are the Hong Kong region, northern Italy, or Silicon Valley in California. The area around Barcelona in northern Spain extends over into France. Catalonia, where Barcelona is located, is closely integrated into the European Union. It is part of Spain, yet also looks outwards. 20

The changes are being propelled by a range of factors, 21
some structural, others more specific and historical. Economic influences are certainly among the driving forces, especially the global financial system. Yet they aren't like forces
of nature. They have been shaped by technology, and cultural
diffusion, as well as by the decisions of governments to liber-
alise and deregulate their national economies.

The collapse of Soviet communism has added further 22
weight to such developments, since no significant group of
countries any longer stands outside. That collapse wasn't just
something that happened to occur. Globalisation explains
both why and how Soviet communism met its end. The
Soviet Union and the East European countries were comparable to the West in terms of growth rates until somewhere
around the early 1970s. After that point, they fell rapidly behind. Soviet communism, with its emphasis upon state-run
enterprise and heavy industry, could not compete in the
global electronic economy. The ideological and cultural control upon which communist political authority was based
similarly could not survive in an era of global media.

The Soviet and the East European regimes were unable to 23
prevent the reception of western radio and TV broadcasts.
Television played a direct role in the 1989 revolutions, which
have rightly been called the first "television revolutions."
Street protests taking place in one country were watched by
the audiences in others, large numbers of whom then took to
the streets themselves.

Globalisation, of course, isn't developing in an even- 24
handed way, and is by no means wholly benign in its consequences. To many living outside Europe and North
America, it looks uncomfortably like Westernisation—or,
perhaps, Americanisation, since the US is now the sole superpower, with a dominant economic, cultural and military
position in the global order. Many of the most visible cultural expressions of globalisation are American—Coca-
Cola, McDonald's.

Most of giant multinational companies are based in the US 25
too. Those that aren't all come from the rich countries, not the

poorer areas of the world. A pessimistic view of globalisation would consider it largely an affair of the industrial North, in which the developing societies of the South play little or no active part. It would see it as destroying local cultures, widening world inequalities and worsening the lot of the impoverished. Globalisation, some argue, creates a world of winners and losers, a few on the fast track to prosperity, the majority condemned to a life of misery and despair.

And indeed the statistics are daunting. The share of the poorest fifth of the world's population in global income has dropped from 2.3% to 1.4% over the past 10 years. The proportion taken by the richest fifth, on the other hand, has risen from 70% to 85%. In Sub-Saharan Africa, 20 countries have lower incomes per head in real terms than they did two decades ago. In many less developed countries, safety and environmental regulations are low or virtually non-existent. Some trans-national companies sell goods there that are controlled or banned in the industrial countries—poor quality medical drugs, destructive pesticides or high tar and nicotine content cigarettes. As one writer put it recently, rather than a global village, this is more like global pillage. 26

Along with ecological risk, to which it is related, expanding inequality is the most serious problem facing world society. It will not do, however, merely to blame it on the wealthy. It is fundamental to my argument that globalisation today is only partly Westernisation. Of course the western nations, and more generally the industrial countries, still have far more influence over world affairs than do the poorer states. But globalisation is becoming increasingly de-centred—not under the control of any group of nations, and still less of the large corporations. Its effects are felt just as much in the western countries as elsewhere. 27

This is true of the global financial system, communications and media, and of changes affecting the nature of government itself. Examples of "reverse colonisation" are becoming more and more common. Reverse colonisation means that non-western countries influence developments in the west. Examples abound—such as the Latinising of Los Angeles, the 28 emergence of a globally-oriented high-tech sector in India, or the selling of Brazilian TV programmes to Portugal.

Is globalisation a force promoting the general good? The   29
question can't be answered in a simple way, given the complexity of the phenomenon. People who ask it, and who
blame globalisation for deepening world inequalities, usually
have in mind economic globalisation, and within that, free
trade. Now it is surely obvious that free trade is not an unal-
loyed benefit. This is especially so as concerns the less developed countries. Opening up a country, or regions within it,
to free trade can undermine a local subsistence economy. An
area that becomes dependent upon a few products sold on
world markets is very vulnerable to shifts in prices as well as
to technological change.

Trade always needs a framework of institutions, as do   30
other forms of economic development. Markets cannot be
created by purely economic means, and how far a given economy should be exposed to the world marketplace must
depend upon a range of criteria. Yet to oppose economic
globalisation, and to opt for economic protectionism, would
be a misplaced tactic for rich and poor nations alike. Protectionism may be a necessary strategy at some times and in
some countries. In my view, for example, Malaysia was correct
to introduce controls in 1998, to stem the flood of capital
from the country. But more permanent forms of protectionism will not help the development of the poor countries, and
among the rich would lead to warring trade blocs.

The debates about globalisation I mentioned at the begin-   31
ning have concentrated mainly upon its implications for the
nation-state. Are nation-states, and hence national political
leaders, still powerful, or are they becoming largely irrelevant
to the forces shaping the world? Nation-states are indeed still
powerful and political leaders have a large role to play in the
world. Yet at the same time the nation-state is being reshaped
before our eyes. National economic policy can't be as effective as it once was. More importantly, nations have to rethink
their identities now the older forms of geopolitics are becoming obsolete. Although this is a contentious point, I would

say that, following the dissolving of the cold war, nations no longer have enemies. Who are the enemies of Britain, or France, or Japan? Nations today face risks and dangers rather than enemies, a massive shift in their very nature.

It isn't only of the nation that such comments could be   32
made. Everywhere we look, we see institutions that appear the same as they used to be from the outside, and carry the same names, but inside have become quite different. We continue to talk of the nation, the family, work, tradition, nature, as if they were all the same as in the past. They are not. The outer shell remains, but inside all is different—and this is happening not only in the US, Britain, or France, but almost everywhere. They are what I call shell institutions, and I shall talk about them quite a bit in the lectures to come. They are institutions that have become inadequate to the tasks they are called upon to perform.

As the changes I have described in this lecture gather   33
weight, they are creating something that has never existed before, a global cosmopolitan society. We are the first generation to live in this society, whose contours we can as yet only dimly see. It is shaking up our existing ways of life, no matter where we happen to be. This is not—at least at the moment—a global order driven by collective human will. Instead, it is emerging in an anarchic, haphazard, fashion, carried along by a mixture of economic, technological and cultural imperatives.

It is not settled or secure, but fraught with anxieties, as   34
well as scarred by deep divisions. Many of us feel in the grip of forces over which we have no control. Can we re-impose our will upon them? I believe we can. The powerlessness we experience is not a sign of personal failings, but reflects the incapacities of our institutions. We need to reconstruct those we have, or create new ones, in ways appropriate to the global age.

We should and we can look to achieve greater control over   35
our runaway world. We shan't be able to do so if we shirk the challenges, or pretend that all can go on as before. For globalisation is not incidental to our lives today. It is a shift in our very life circumstances. It is the way we now live.

For Study and Discussion

QUESTIONS FOR RESPONSE

1. Where do you hear the word *globalization* used?
2. Do the people you know who use the word think of it as a force for good or for evil?

QUESTIONS ABOUT PURPOSE

1. How does Giddens use the *skeptics* and the *radicals* to establish a context for his definition?
2. Why does he think the economic definition of *globalization* is too limited?

QUESTIONS ABOUT AUDIENCE

1. This essay was given as a lecture on the BBC. What assumptions does Giddens make about the knowledge of his listeners?
2. How does he use the comparison between "out there" and "in here" to identify with his audience?

QUESTIONS ABOUT STRATEGIES

1. How does Giddens use the examples of Samuel Morse and satellites to illustrate globalization?
2. How does he use *Westernization* and *Americanization* as synonyms for *globalization*?

QUESTIONS FOR DISCUSSION

1. In what ways has 9/11 and the events that have followed altered Giddens's assertions about "enemies"?
2. How has reverse globalization increased or changed since he delivered this lecture?

STEPHEN HARRIGAN

Stephen Harrigan was born in Oklahoma City in 1948 and educated at the University of Texas. After working as a journalist, including a term as senior editor at *Texas Monthly,* Harrigan turned his attention to fiction and screenplays. His novels include *Aransas* (1980) and *Jacob's Well* (1984), and his screenplays include *The Last of His Tribe* (1992) and *The O. J. Simpson Story* (1995). Harrigan has also published two collections of essays, *A Natural State* (1988) and *Comanche Midnight* (1995). In "The Tiger Is God," reprinted from the former collection, Harrigan provides dramatic examples that help define a tiger "just being a tiger."

The Tiger Is God

W HEN TIGERS ATTACK men, they do so in a character- 1 istic way. They come from behind, from the right side, and when they lunge it is with the intent of snapping the neck of the prey in their jaws. Most tiger victims die swiftly, their necks broken, their spinal cords compressed or severed high up on the vertebral column.

Ricardo Tovar, a fifty-nine-year-old keeper at the Houston 2 Zoo, was killed by a tiger on May 12, 1988. The primary cause of death was a broken neck, although most of the ribs on the left side of his chest were fractured as well, and there were multiple lacerations on his face and right arm. No one witnessed the attack, and no one would ever know exactly how and why it took place, but the central nightmarish event was clear. Tovar had been standing at a steel door separating the zookeepers' area from the naturalistic tiger display outside. Set into the door was a small viewing window—only

slightly larger than an average television screen—made of
wire-reinforced glass. Somehow the tiger had broken the
glass, grabbed the keeper, and pulled him through the window to his death.

Fatal zoo accidents occur more frequently than most peo-   3
ple realize. The year before Tovar died, a keeper in the Fort
Worth Zoo was crushed by an elephant, and in 1985, an em-
ployee of the Bronx Zoo was killed by two Siberian tigers—
the same subspecies as the one that attacked Tovar—when
she mistakenly entered the tiger display while the animals

---

*One point is beyond dispute: A tiger is a
predator, its mission on the earth is to kill,
and in doing so it often displays awesome
strength and dexterity.*

---

were still there. But there was something especially haunting
about the Houston incident, something that people could
not get out of their minds. It had to do with the realization
of a fear built deep into our genetic code: the fear that a beast
could appear out of nowhere—through a window!—and
snatch us away.

The tiger's name was Miguel. He was eleven years old—   4
middle-aged for a tiger—and had been born at the Houston
Zoo to a mother who was a wild-caught Siberian. Siberians
are larger in size than any of the other subspecies, and their
coats are heavier. Fewer than three hundred of them are now
left in the frozen river valleys and hardwood forests of the
Soviet Far East, though they were once so plentiful in that
region that Cossack troops were sent in during the construction of the Trans-Baikal railway specifically to protect the
workers from tiger attacks. Miguel was of mixed blood—his
father was a zoo-reared Bengal—but his Siberian lineage was
dominant. He was a massive 450-pound creature whose

disposition had been snarly ever since he was a cub. Some of the other tigers at the zoo were as placid and affectionate as house cats, but Miguel filled his keepers with caution. Oscar Mendietta, a keeper who retired a few weeks before Tovar's death, remembers the way Miguel would sometimes lunge at zoo personnel as they walked by his holding cage, his claws unsheathed and protruding through the steel mesh. "He had," Mendietta says, "an intent to kill."

Tovar was well aware of Miguel's temperament. He had been working with big cats in the Houston Zoo since 1982, and his fellow keepers regarded him as a cautious and responsible man. Like many old-time zookeepers, he was a civil servant with no formal training in zoology, but he had worked around captive animals most of his life (before coming to Houston, he had been a keeper at the San Antonio Zoo) and had gained a good deal of practical knowledge about their behavior. No one regarded Miguel's aggressiveness as aberrant. Tovar and the other keepers well understood the fact that tigers were supposed to be dangerous.

In 1987 the tigers and other cats had been moved from their outdated display cages to brand-new facilities with outdoor exhibit areas built to mimic the animals' natural environments. The Siberian tiger exhibit—in a structure known as the Phase II building—comprised about a quarter of an acre. It was a wide rectangular space decorated with shrubs and trees, a few fake boulders, and a water-filled moat. The exhibit's backdrop was a depiction, in plaster and cement, of a high rock wall seamed with stress fractures.

Built into the wall, out of public view, was a long corridor lined with the cats' holding cages, where the tigers were fed and confined while the keepers went out into the display to shovel excrement and hose down the area. Miguel and the other male Siberian, Rambo, each had a holding cage, and they alternated in the use of the outdoor habitat, since two male tigers occupying the same space guaranteed monumental discord. Next to Rambo's cage was a narrow alcove through which the keepers went back and forth from the corridor into the display. The alcove was guarded by two doors.

The one with the viewing window led outside. Another door, made of steel mesh, closed off the interior corridor.

May 12 was a Thursday. Tovar came to work at about six-thirty in the morning, and at that hour he was alone. Rambo was secure in his holding cage and Miguel was outside—it had been his turn that night to have the run of the display. [8]

Thursdays and Sundays were "fast" days. Normally the tigers were fed a daily ration of ten to fifteen pounds of ground fetal calf, but twice a week their food was withheld in order to keep them from growing obese in confinement. The animals knew which days were fast days, and on those mornings they were sometimes balky about coming inside, since no food was being offered. Nevertheless, the tigers had to be secured in their holding cages while the keepers went outside to clean the display. On this morning, Tovar had apparently gone to the viewing window to check the whereabouts of Miguel when the tiger did not come inside, even though the keepers usually made a point of not entering the alcove until they were certain that both animals were locked up in their holding cages. The viewing window was so small and the habitat itself so panoramic that the chances of spotting the tiger from the window were slim. Several of the keepers had wondered why there was a window there at all, since it was almost useless as an observation post and since one would never go through the door in the first place without being certain that the tigers were in their cages. [9]

But that was where Tovar had been, standing at a steel door with a panel of reinforced glass, when the tiger attacked. John Gilbert, the senior zookeeper who supervised the cat section, stopped in at the Phase II building a little after seven-thirty, planning to discuss with Tovar the scheduled sedation of a lion. He had just entered the corridor when he saw broken glass on the floor outside the steel mesh door that led to the alcove. The door was unlocked—it had been opened by Tovar when he entered the alcove to look out the window. Looking through the mesh, Gilbert saw the shards of glass hanging from the window frame and Tovar's cap, watch, and a single rubber boot lying on the floor. Knowing [10] something dreadful had happened, he called Tovar's name, then pushed on the door and cautiously started to enter the alcove. He was only a few paces away from the broken window when the tiger's head suddenly appeared there, filling its jagged frame. His heart pounding, Gilbert backed off, slammed and locked the mesh door behind him and radioed for help.

Tom Dieckow, a wiry, white-bearded Marine veteran of the Korean War, was the zoo's exhibits curator. He was also in charge of its shooting team, a seldom-convened body whose task was to kill, if necessary, any escaped zoo animal that posed an immediate threat to the public. Dieckow was in his office in the service complex building when he heard Gilbert's emergency call. He grabbed a twelve-gauge shotgun, commandeered an electrician's pickup truck, and arrived at the tiger exhibit two minutes later. He went around to the front of the habitat and saw Miguel standing there, calm and unconcerned, with Tovar's motionless body lying face down fifteen feet away. Dieckow did not shoot. It was his clear impression that the keeper was dead, that the harm was already done. By that time the zoo's response team had gathered outside the exhibit. Miguel stared at the onlookers and then picked up Tovar's head in his jaws and started to drag him off.

"I think probably what crossed that cat's mind at that point," Dieckow speculated later, "is 'look at all those scavengers across there that are after my prey. I'm gonna move it.' He was just being a tiger."

Dieckow raised his shotgun again, this time with the intention of shooting Miguel, but because of all the brush and ersatz boulders in the habitat, he could not get a clear shot. He fired into the water instead, causing the startled tiger to drop the keeper, and then fired twice more as another zoo worker discharged a fire extinguisher from the top of the rock wall. The commotion worked, and Miguel retreated into his holding cage.

The Houston Zoo opened a half-hour late that day. Miguel and all the other big cats were kept inside until zoo

officials could determine if it was safe—both for the cats and
for the public—to exhibit them again. For a few days the
zoo switchboard was jammed with calls from people wanting to express their opinion on whether the tiger should live
or die. But for the people at the zoo that issue had never
been in doubt.

"It's automatic with us," John Werler, the zoo director,   15
told me when I visited his office a week after the incident.
"To what end would we destroy the tiger? If we followed this
argument to its logical conclusion, we'd have to destroy
every dangerous animal in the zoo collection."

Werler was a reflective, kindly looking man who was obvi-   16
ously weighed down by a load of unpleasant concerns. There
was the overall question of zoo safety, the specter of lawsuits,
and most recently the public anger of a number of zoo
staffers who blamed Tovar's death on the budget cuts,
staffing shortages, and bureaucratic indifference that forced
keepers to work alone in potentially dangerous environments. But the dominant mood of the zoo, the day I was
there, appeared to be one of simple sadness and shock.

"What a terrible loss," read a sympathy card from the staff   17
of the Fort Worth Zoo that was displayed on a coffee table.
"May you gain strength and support to get you through this
awful time."

The details of the attack were still hazy, and still eerie to   18
think about. Unquestionably, the glass door panel had not
been strong enough, but exactly how Miguel had broken it,
how he had killed Tovar—and why—remained the subjects
of numb speculation. One point was beyond dispute: A tiger
is a predator, its mission on the earth is to kill, and in doing
so it often displays awesome strength and dexterity.

An Indian researcher, using live deer and buffalo calves as   19
bait, found that the elapsed time between a tiger's secure grip
on the animal's neck and the prey's subsequent death was
anywhere from thirty-five to ninety seconds. In other circumstances the cat will not choose to be so swift. Sometimes a
tiger will kill an elephant calf by snapping its trunk and waiting for it to bleed to death, and it is capable of dragging the

carcass in its jaws for miles. (A full-grown tiger possesses the traction power of thirty men.) When a mother tiger is teaching her cubs to hunt, she might move in on a calf, cripple it with a powerful bite to its rear leg, and stand back and let the cubs practice on the helpless animal.

Tigers have four long canine teeth—fangs. The two in the upper jaw are tapered along the sides to a shearing edge. Fourteen of the teeth are molars, for chewing meat and grinding bone. Like other members of the cat family, tigers have keen, night-seeing eyes, and their hearing is so acute that Indonesian hunters—convinced that a tiger could hear the wind whistling through a man's nose hairs—always kept their nostrils carefully barbered. The pads on the bottom of a tiger's paws are surprisingly sensitive, easily blistered or cut on hot, prickly terrain. But the claws within, five on each front paw and four in the hind paws, are protected like knives in an upholstered box.

They are not idle predators; when they kill, they kill to eat. Even a well-fed tiger in a zoo keeps his vestigial repertoire of hunting behaviors intact. (Captive breeding programs, in fact, make a point of selecting in favor of aggressive predatory behavior, since the ultimate hope of these programs is to bolster the dangerously low stock of free-living tigers.) In the zoo, tigers will stalk birds that land in their habitats, and they grow more alert than most people would care to realize when children pass before their gaze. Though stories of man-eating tigers have been extravagantly embellished over the centuries, the existence of such creatures is not legendary. In the Sunderbans, the vast delta region that spans the border of India and Bangladesh, more than four hundred people have been killed by tigers in the last decade. So many fishermen and honey collectors have been carried off that a few years ago officials at the Sunderbans tiger preserve began stationing electrified dummies around the park to encourage the tigers to seek other prey. One percent of all tigers, according to a German biologist who studied them in the Sunderbans, are "dedicated" man-eaters: when they go out hunting, they're after people. Up to a third of all tigers will kill and eat

20

21

a human if they come across one, though they don't make a special effort to do so.

It is not likely that Miguel attacked Ricardo Tovar out of hunger. Except for the killing wounds inflicted by the tiger, the keeper's body was undisturbed. Perhaps something about Tovar's movements on the other side of the window intrigued the cat enough to make him spring, a powerful lunge that sent him crashing through the glass. Most likely the tiger was surprised, and frightened, and reacted instinctively. There is no evidence that he came all the way through the window. Probably he just grabbed Tovar by the chest with one paw, crushed him against the steel door, and with unthinkable strength pulled him through the window and killed him outside. 22

John Gilbert, the senior keeper who had been the first on the scene that morning, took me inside the Phase II building to show me where the attack had taken place. Gilbert was a sandy-haired man in his thirties, still shaken and subdued by what he had seen. His recitation of the events was as formal and precise as that of a witness at an inquest. 23

"When I got to this point," Gilbert said as we passed through the security doors that led to the keepers' corridor, "I saw the broken glass on the floor. I immediately yelled Mr. Tovar's name . . ." 24

The alcove in which Tovar had been standing was much smaller than I had pictured it, and seeing it firsthand made one thing readily apparent: it was a trap. Its yellow cinderblock walls were no more than four feet apart. The ceiling was made of steel mesh and a door of the same material guarded the exit to the corridor. The space was so confined it was not difficult to imagine—it was impossible *not* to imagine—how the tiger had been able to catch Tovar by surprise with a deadly swipe from his paw. 25

And there was the window. Covered with a steel plate now, its meager dimensions were still visible. The idea of being hauled through that tiny space by a tiger had an almost supernatural resonance—as if the window were a portal through which mankind's most primeval terrors were allowed to pass unobstructed. 26

Gilbert led me down the corridor. We passed the holding   27
cage of Rambo, who hung his head low and let out a grum-
bling basso roar so deep it sounded like a tremor in the earth.
Then we were standing in front of Miguel.

"Here he is," Gilbert said, looking at the animal with an   28
expression on his face that betrayed a sad welter of emotions.
"He's quite passive right now."

The tiger was reclining on the floor, looking at us without   29
concern. I noticed his head, which seemed to me wider than
the window he had broken out. His eyes were yellow, and
when the great head pivoted in my direction and Miguel's
eyes met mine I looked away reflexively, afraid of their hyp-
notic gravity. The tiger stood up and began to pace, his
gigantic pads treading noiselessly on the concrete. The
bramble of black stripes that decorated his head was as neatly
symmetrical as a Rorschach inkblot, and his orange fur—
conceived by evolution as camouflage—was a florid, provoca-
tive presence in the featureless confines of the cage.

Miguel idly pawed the steel guillotine door that covered   30
the entrance to his cage, and then all of a sudden he reared
on his hind legs. I jumped back a little, startled and dwarfed.
The top of Miguel's head nestled against the ceiling mesh of
his cage, his paws were spread to either side. In one silent
moment, his size and scale seemed to have increased expo-
nentially. He looked down at Gilbert and me. In Miguel's
mind, I suspected, his keeper's death was merely a vignette,
a mostly forgotten moment of fright and commotion that
had intruded one day upon the tiger's torpid existence in the
zoo. But it was hard not to look up at that immense animal
and read his posture as a deliberate demonstration of the
power he possessed.

I thought of Tipu Sultan, the eighteenth-century Indian   31
mogul who was obsessed with the tiger and used its likeness
as his constant emblem. Tipu Sultan's imperial banner had
borne the words "The Tiger Is God." Looking up into
Miguel's yellow eyes I felt the strange appropriateness of
those words. The tiger was majestic and unknowable, a beast
of such seeming invulnerability that it was possible to believe

that he alone had called the world into being, and that a given life could end at his whim. The truth, of course, was far more literal. Miguel was a remnant member of a species never far from the brink of extinction, and his motivation for killing Ricardo Tovar probably did not extend beyond a behavioral quirk. He had a predator's indifference to tragedy; he had killed without culpability. It was a gruesome and unhappy incident, but as far as Miguel was concerned most of the people at the zoo had reached the same conclusion: he was just being a tiger.

For Study and Discussion

QUESTIONS FOR RESPONSE

1. In your visits to zoos, how have you responded to tigers you've seen? With admiration? with awe? with fear? How do you think reading Harrigan's essay might affect your feelings on any future visit?
2. How do you respond to the zoo professionals' feeling that Miguel was "just being a tiger"? Does that reflect a callous or careless attitude?

QUESTIONS ABOUT PURPOSE

1. What attitude about the tiger do you think Harrigan wants to bring about in his readers?
2. Why does Harrigan go into minute detail about the physical arrangements of the zoo and about the schedules? Why would readers want to know these details?

QUESTIONS ABOUT AUDIENCE

1. On what basis do you think that Harrigan can assume that a general audience would want to read about tigers and about the fatal incident at the Houston Zoo?
2. What questions does Harrigan anticipate that his readers will have? How does he attempt to answer those questions?

QUESTIONS ABOUT STRATEGIES

1. What is the impact on the reader of Harrigan's first paragraph? What tone does it set for the essay?
2. What details does the author give that are most important in defining the nature of the tiger? Pick out three or four specific paragraphs that are most important.

QUESTIONS FOR DISCUSSION

1. In what ways are zoos important institutions in this country? Does their value to the public warrant their cost in money, in risk, and in the treatment of animals?
2. What do you think is the appeal of an article like this? What special significance does it have that the animal was a tiger rather than another animal that can be just as dangerous, for instance, an elephant or rhinoceros?

TONI CADE BAMBARA

Toni Cade Bambara (1939–1995) was born in New York City and educated at Queens College, the University of Florence, the Ecole de Mme. Etienne Decroux in Paris, and the City College of the City University of New York. Her work experience was extremely varied: a social investigator for the New York State Department of Welfare, a director of recreation in the psychiatry department of New York's Metropolitan Hospital, a visiting professor of Afro-American studies (Stephens College in Columbia, Missouri), a consultant on women's studies (Emory University in Atlanta), and a writer-in-residence at Spelman College in Atlanta. She contributed stories and essays to magazines as diverse as *Negro Digest*, *Prairie Schooner*, and *Redbook*. Her two collections of short stories, *Gorilla, My Love* (1971) and *The Sea Birds Are Still Alive: Collected Stories* (1977), deal with the emerging sense of self of black women. "The Lesson," reprinted from *Gorilla, My Love*, focuses on the experiences of several black children who learn how much things "cost."

The Lesson

BACK IN THE days when everyone was old and stupid or   1
young and foolish and me and Sugar were the only ones just right, this lady moved on our block with nappy hair and proper speech and no makeup. And quite naturally we laughed at her, laughed the way we did at the junk man who went about his business like he was some big-time president and his sorry-ass horse his secretary. And we kinda hated her too, hated the way we did the winos who cluttered up our

parks and pissed on our handball walls and stank up our hallways and stairs so you couldn't halfway play hide-and-seek
without a goddamn gas mask. Miss Moore was her name.
The only woman on the block with no first name. And she
was black as hell, cept for her feet, which were fish-white and
spooky. And she was always planning these boring-ass things
for us to do, us being my cousin, mostly, who lived on the
block cause we all moved North the same time and to the
same apartment then spread out gradual to breathe. And our
parents would yank our heads into some kinda shape and
crisp up our clothes so we'd be presentable for travel with
Miss Moore, who always looked like she was going to
church, though she never did. Which is just one of the things
the grownups talked about when they talked behind her back
like a dog. But when she came calling with some sachet she'd
sewed up or some gingerbread she'd made or some book,
why then they'd all be too embarrassed to turn her down and
we'd get handed over all spruced up. She'd been to college
and said it was only right that she should take responsibility
for the young ones' education, and she not even related by
marriage or blood. So they'd go for it. Specially Aunt
Gretchen. She was the main gofer in the family. You got some
ole dumb shit foolishness you want somebody to go for, you
send for Aunt Gretchen. She been screwed into the go-along
for so long, it's a blood-deep natural thing with her. Which is
how she got saddled with me and Sugar and Junior in the
first place while our mothers were in a la-de-da apartment up
the block having a good ole time.

So this one day Miss Moore rounds us all up at the mail- 2
box and it's puredee hot and she's knockin herself out about
arithmetic. And school suppose to let up in summer I heard,
but she don't never let up. And the starch in my pinafore
scratching the shit outta me and I'm really hating this
nappy-head bitch and her goddamn college degree. I'd
much rather go to the pool or to the show where it's cool.
So me and Sugar leaning on the mailbox being surly, which
is a Miss Moore word. And Flyboy checking out what everybody brought for lunch. And Fat Butt already wasting his

peanut-butter-and-jelly sandwich like the pig he is. And Junebug punchin on Q. T.'s arm for potato chips. And Rosie Giraffe shifting from one hip to the other waiting for somebody to step on her foot or ask her if she from Georgia so she can kick ass, preferably Mercedes'. And Miss Moore asking us do we know what money is, like we a bunch of retards. I mean real money, she say, like it's only poker chips or monopoly papers we lay on the grocer. So right away I'm tired of this and say so. And would much rather snatch Sugar and go to the Sunset and terrorize the West Indian kids and take their hair ribbons and their money too. And Miss Moore files that remark away for next week's lesson on brotherhood, I can tell. And finally I say we oughta get to the subway cause it's cooler and besides we might meet some cute boys. Sugar done swiped her mama's lipstick, so we ready.

So we heading down the street and she's boring us silly 3 about what things cost and what our parents make and how much goes for rent and how money ain't divided up right in this country. And then she gets to the part about we all poor and live in the slums, which I don't feature. And I'm ready to speak on that, but she steps out in the street and hails two cabs just like that. Then she hustles half the crew in with her and hands me a five-dollar bill and tells me to calculate 10 percent tip for the driver. And we're off. Me and Sugar and Junebug and Flyboy hangin out the window and hollering to everybody, putting lipstick on each other cause Flyboy a faggot anyway, and making farts with our sweaty armpits. But I'm mostly trying to figure how to spend this money. But they all fascinated with the meter ticking and Junebug starts laying bets as to how much it'll read when Flyboy can't hold his breath no more. Then Sugar lays bets as to how much it'll be when we get there. So I'm stuck. Don't nobody want to go for my plan, which is to jump out at the next light and run off to the first bar-b-que we can find. Then the driver tells us to get the hell out cause we there already. And the meter reads eighty-five cents. And I'm stalling to figure out the tip and Sugar say give him a dime. And I decide he don't need it bad as I do, so later for him. But then he tries to take off with

Junebug foot still in the door so we talk about his mama something ferocious. Then we check out that we on Fifth Avenue and everybody dressed up in stockings. One lady in a fur coat, hot as it is. White folks crazy.

"This is the place," Miss Moore say, presenting it to us in the voice she uses at the museum. "Let's look in the windows before we go in."   4

"Can we steal?" Sugar asks very serious like she's getting the ground rules squared away before she plays. "I beg your pardon," say Miss Moore, and we fall out. So she leads us around the windows of the toy store and me and Sugar screamin, "This is mine, that's mine, I gotta have that, that was made for me, I was born for that," till Big Butt drowns us out.   5

"Hey, I'm goin to buy that there."   6

"That there? You don't even know what it is, stupid."   7

"I do so," he say punchin on Rosie Giraffe. "It's a microscope."   8

"Whatcha gonna do with a microscope, fool?"   9

"Look at things."   10

"Like what, Ronald?" ask Miss Moore. And Big Butt ain't got the first notion. So here go Miss Moore gabbing about the thousands of bacteria in a drop of water and the somethi-norother in a speck of blood and the million and one living things in the air around us is invisible to the naked eye. And what she say that for? Junebug go to town on that "naked" and we rolling. Then Miss Moore ask what it cost. So we all jam into the window smudgin it up and the price tag say $300. So then she ask how long'd take for Big Butt and Junebug to save up their allowances. "Too long," I say. "Yeh," adds Sugar, "outgrown it by that time." And Miss Moore say no, you never outgrow learning instruments. "Why, even medical students and interns and," blah, blah, blah. And we ready to choke Big Butt for bringing it up in the first damn place.   11

"This here costs four hundred eighty dollars," say Rosie Giraffe. So we pile up all over her to see what she pointin out. My eyes tell me it's a chunk of glass cracked with something   12 heavy, and different-color inks dripped into the splits, then the whole thing put into a oven or something. But for $480 it don't make sense.

"That's a paperweight made of semi-precious stones fused   13
together under tremendous pressure," she explains slowly, with her hands doing the mining and all the factory work.

"So what's a paperweight?" asks Rosie Giraffe.   14

"To weigh paper with, dumbbell," say Flyboy, the wise   15
man from the East.

"Not exactly," say Miss Moore, which is what she say   16
when you warm or way off too. "It's to weigh paper down so it won't scatter and make your desk untidy." So right away me and Sugar curtsy to each other and then to Mercedes who is more the tidy type.

"We don't keep paper on top of the desk in my class," say 17
Junebug, figuring Miss Moore crazy or lyin one.

"At home, then," she say. "Don't you have a calendar and   18
a pencil case and a blotter and a letter-opener on your desk at home where you do your homework?" And she know damn well what our homes look like cause she nosys around in them every chance she gets.

"I don't even have a desk," say Junebug. "Do we?"   19

"No. And I don't get no homework neither," says Big   20
Butt.

"And I don't even have a home," say Flyboy like he do at   21
school to keep the white folks off his back and sorry for him. Send this poor kid to camp posters, is his specialty.

"I do," says Mercedes. "I have a box of stationery on my   22
desk and a picture of my cat. My godmother bought the stationery and the desk. There's a big rose on each sheet and the envelopes smell like roses."

"Who wants to know about your smelly-ass stationery,"   23
say Rosie Giraffe fore I can get my two cents in.

"It's important to have a work area all your own so that . . ."   24

"Will you look at this sailboat, please," say Flyboy, cuttin 25
her off and pointin to the thing like it was his. So once again we tumble all over each other to gaze at this magnificent thing in the toy store which is just big enough to maybe sail

two kittens across the pond if you strap them to the posts tight. We all start reciting the price tag like we in assembly. "Handcrafted sailboat of fiberglass at one thousand one hundred ninety-five dollars."

"Unbelievable," I hear myself say and am really stunned. I read it again for myself just in case the group recitation put me in a trance. Same thing. For some reason this pisses me off. We look at Miss Moore and she lookin at us, waiting for I dunno what. 26

"Who'd pay all that when you can buy a sailboat set for a quarter at Pop's, a tube of glue for a dime, and a ball of string for eight cents? It must have a motor and a whole lot else besides," I say. "My sailboat cost me about fifty cents." 27

"But will it take water?" say Mercedes with her smart ass. 28

"Took mine to Alley Pond Park once," say Flyboy. "String broke. Lost it. Pity." 29

"Sailed mine in Central Park and it keeled over and sank. Had to ask my father for another dollar." 30

"And you got the strap," laugh Big Butt. "The jerk didn't even have a string on it. My old man wailed on his behind." 31

Little Q. T. was staring hard at the sailboat and you could see he wanted it bad. But he too little and somebody'd just take it from him. So what the hell. "This boat for kids, Miss Moore?" 32

"Parents silly to buy something like that just to get all broke up," say Rosie Giraffe. 33

"That much money it should last forever," I figure. 34

"My father'd buy it for me if I wanted it." 35

"Your father, my ass," say Rosie Giraffe getting a chance to finally push Mercedes. 36

"Must be rich people shop here," say Q. T. 37

"You are a very bright boy," say Flyboy. "What was your first clue?" And he rap him on the head with the back of his knuckles, since Q. T. the only one he could get away with. Though Q. T. liable to come up behind you years later and get his licks in when you half expect it. 38

"What I want to know is," I says to Miss Moore though I never talk to her, I wouldn't give the bitch that satisfaction, 39 "is how much a real boat costs? I figure a thousand'd get you a yacht any day."

"Why don't you check that out," she says, "and report   40
back to the group?" Which really pains my ass. If you gonna mess up a perfectly good swim day least you could do is have some answers. "Let's go in," she say like she got something up her sleeve. Only she don't lead the way. So me and Sugar turn the corner to where the entrance is, but when we get there I kinda hang back. Not that I'm scared, what's there to be afraid of, just a toy store. But I feel funny, shame. But what I got to be shamed about? Got as much right to go in as anybody. But somehow I can't seem to get hold of the door, so I step away from Sugar to lead. But she hangs back too. And I look at her and she looks at me and this is ridiculous. I mean, damn, I have never ever been shy about doing nothing or going nowhere. But then Mercedes steps up and then Rosie Giraffe and Big Butt crowd in behind and shove, and next thing we all stuffed into the doorway with only Mercedes squeezing past us, smoothing out her jumper and walking right down the aisle. Then the rest of us tumble in like a glued-together jigsaw done all wrong. And people lookin at us. And it's like the time me and Sugar crashed into the Catholic church on a dare. But once we got in there and everything so hushed and holy and the candles and the bowin and the handkerchiefs on all the drooping heads, I just couldn't go through with the plan. Which was for me to run up to the altar and do a tap dance while Sugar played the nose flute and messed around in the holy water. And Sugar kept givin me the elbow. Then later teased me so bad I tied her up in the shower and turned it on and locked her in. And she'd be there till this day if Aunt Gretchen hadn't finally figured I was lyin about the boarder takin a shower.

Same thing in the store. We all walkin on tiptoe and hardly   41
touchin the games and puzzles and things. And I watched Miss Moore who is steady watchin us like she waitin for a sign. Like Mama Drewery watches the sky and sniffs the air and takes note of just how much slant is in the bird formation. Then me and Sugar bump smack into each other, so

busy gazing at the toys, 'specially the sailboat. But we don't laugh and go into our fat-lady bump-stomach routine. We just stare at that price tag. Then Sugar run a finger over the whole boat. And I'm jealous and want to hit her. Maybe not her, but I sure want to punch somebody in the mouth.

"Watcha bring us here for, Miss Moore?"   42

"You sound angry, Sylvia. Are you mad about some-   43
thing?" Givin me one of them grins like she tellin a grown-up joke that never turns out to be funny. And she's lookin very closely at me like maybe she plannin to do my portrait from memory. I'm mad, but I won't give her that satisfaction. So I slouch around the store bein very bored and say, "Let's go."

Me and Sugar at the back of the train watchin the tracks   44
whizzin by large then small then gettin gobbled up in the dark. I'm thinking about this tricky toy I saw in the store. A clown that somersaults on a bar then does chin-ups just cause you yank lightly at his leg. Cost $35. I could see me askin my mother for a $35 birthday clown. "You wanna who that costs what?" she'd say, cocking her head to the side to get a better view of the hole in my head. Thirty-five dollars could buy new bunk beds for Junior and Gretchen's boy. Thirty five dollars and the whole household could go visit Grand-daddy Nelson in the country. Thirty-five dollars would pay for the rent and the piano bill too. Who are these people that spend that much for performing clowns and $1000 for toy sailboats? What kinda work they do and how they live and how come we ain't in on it? Where we are is who we are, Miss Moore always pointin out. But it don't necessarily have to be that way, she always adds then waits for somebody to say that poor people have to wake up and demand their share of the pie and don't none of us know what kind of pie she talking about in the first damn place. But she ain't so smart cause I still got her four dollars from the taxi and she sure ain't gettin it. Messin up my day with this shit. Sugar nudges me in my pocket and winks.

Miss Moore lines us up in front of the mailbox where we   45
started from, seem like years ago, and I got a headache for thinkin so hard. And we lean all over each other so we can

hold up under the draggy-ass lecture she always finishes us off with at the end before we thank her for borin us to tears. But she just looks at us like she readin tea leaves. Finally she say, "Well, what did you think of F.A.O. Schwarz?"

Rosie Giraffe mumbles, "White folks crazy." 46

"I'd like to go there again when I get my birthday money," 47 says Mercedes, and we shove her out the pack so she has to lean on the mailbox by herself.

"I'd like a shower. Tiring day," say Flyboy. 48

Then Sugar surprises me by sayin, "You know, Miss 49 Moore, I don't think all of us here put together eat in a year what that sailboat costs." And Miss Moore lights up like somebody goosed her. "And?" she say, urging Sugar on. Only I'm standin on her foot so she don't continue.

"Imagine for a minute what kind of society it is in which 50 some people can spend on a toy what it would cost to feed a family of six or seven. What do you think?"

"I think," say Sugar pushing me off her feet like she never 51 done before, cause I whip her ass in a minute, "that this is not much of a democracy if you ask me. Equal chance to pursue happiness means an equal crack at the dough, don't it?" Miss Moore is besides herself and I am disgusted with Sugar's treachery. So I stand on her foot one more time to see if she'll shove me. She shuts up, and Miss Moore looks at me, sorrowfully I'm thinkin. And somethin weird is goin on, I can feel it in my chest.

"Anybody else learn anything today?" lookin dead at me. 52 I walk away and Sugar has to run to catch up and don't even seem to notice when I shrug her arm off my shoulder.

"Well, we got four dollars anyway," she says. 53

"Uh hunh." 54

"We could go to Hascombs and get half a chocolate layer 55 and then go to the Sunset and still have plenty money for potato chips and ice cream sodas."

"Uh hunh." 56

"Race you to Hascombs," she say. 57

We start down the block and she gets ahead which is O.K. 58 by me cause I'm going to the West End and then over to the

Drive to think this day through. She can run if she want to
and even run faster. But ain't nobody gonna beat me at
nuthin.

COMMENT ON "THE LESSON"

"The Lesson" is an excellent illustration of how narration
and description are used in short fiction. Although the plot
seems arranged in a simple chronology, the narrator, Sylvia,
suggests that the events took place "Back in the days when
everyone was old and stupid or young and foolish and me
and Sugar were the only ones just right." Sylvia's tough talk
is directed at an audience she presumes will understand why
she sees Miss Moore and her activities as "boring-ass." But as
Sylvia describes the various toys at F.A.O. Schwarz, she reveals that her point of view is defensive. She is stunned by
what things cost, embarrassed by her ignorance, and confused by her anger and Sugar's treachery. She will not acknowledge publicly that she has learned Miss Moore's lesson
about the inequities in society, but privately she concludes
that "ain't nobody gonna beat me at nuthin."

Definition as a Writing Strategy

1. Select a category of objects in which you have a special interest and that you could illustrate with pictures or your own sketches, and put together an illustrated, annotated essay that defines the object. Several possibilities suggest themselves:

   - Bridges
   - Sports cars
   - SUVs
   - Kayaks or canoes
   - Tree houses
   - Stereo, video, and television complexes
   - Stairways

   You may think of other possibilities from your own interests or hobbies. In your comments on different examples, mention special features and the advantages or disadvantages of each one.

2. For a challenging assignment focusing on a person, pick someone you find especially interesting—an athlete like Tiger Woods, a businessperson like Bill Gates or Michael Dell, an entertainment personality like Oprah Winfrey or Barbra Streisand, a public figure like Jesse Jackson or Justice Ruth Ginsberg. Through a computer search, locate several magazine articles on that person, and read them. Be sure to use substantial articles, not just items from gossip columns. Write a definition essay in which you describe the person—his or her professional activities and personal interests—trying to bring out the unique traits that have made the person successful. Remember that anecdotes are useful in this kind of essay. Your hypothetical audience could be readers of a magazine like *Parade* or *Esquire*.

3. If you are a person with special knowledge about a particular kind of animal, reread Harrigan's essay "The Tiger Is God," paying special attention to his strategies for

defining the nature of the tiger. Then write an essay in which you describe and define a breed or type of animal that you know well. Some possibilities are the cutting horse; the dressage horse; hunting dogs or sheep dogs; a particular breed of dog, such as golden retriever or Weimaraner; or a particular breed of cat, such as Burmese or Russian blue. Certainly there are many other possibilities. Use concrete details and examples of particular actions that illustrate the animal's distinctive temperament and behavior.

4. James Gleick and Anthony Giddens define words that are relatively new additions to popular vocabulary. Select a word that is relatively new or has been given new meaning, such as *bling* or *spam,* and then write an extended definition—explaining the word's origins and cultural significance.

5. In "The Hoax," John Berendt defines a hoax as a special kind of practical joke that involves wit as well as a physical element, and he gives several examples. In a special feature for your college newspaper or humor magazine, explain the defining characteristics of something you have fun with. Some possibilities might be a great Halloween costume, a grade B horror movie, an April Fool's gag, or a cartoon or picture that satirizes some work of art that is so well known it's become a cliché. Have fun with this one.

6. Writers and speakers often argue from definition, trying to get their audiences to agree with or approve of something by defining it positively (for example, a good education) or to criticize something by defining it negatively (for example, a bad grading policy). Drawing on material and information you are getting in one of your courses, write a paper suitable for that course defining a concept, policy, theory, or event either negatively or positively. For a course in early childhood development, you could define a good day-care center. For a chemistry course, you could do a process paper on how to set up a good laboratory experiment. For a government course, you could define a well-run local campaign. For a speech course, you could define an effective speaking style.

CAUSE
AND
EFFECT

If you are like most people, you're just naturally curious: you look at the world around you and wonder why things happen. But you're also curious because you want some control over your life and over your environment, and you can't have that control unless you can understand **causes.** That's why so much writing is cause-and-effect writing, writing that seeks to explain the causes for change and new developments. In almost every profession you will be asked to do writing that analyzes causes; that's why such writing has an important place in college composition courses.

You also want to understand **effects.** If A happens, will B be the effect? You want to try to predict the consequences of putting some plan into effect or look at some effect and explain what brought it about. Or you want to set a goal (the effect) and plan a strategy for reaching it. This kind of writing also prepares you for writing you're likely to do later in your career.

PURPOSE

When you write cause-and-effect essays, you're likely to have one of three purposes. Sometimes you want to *explain* why something happened or what might be likely to happen under certain circumstances. Daniel Goleman is writing that kind of essay in "Peak Performance: Why Records Fall" when he explains how new knowledge about training practices and about human mental capacities have led to athletic feats that seemed impossible only a few decades ago. At other times, you might write a cause-and-effect paper to *speculate* about an interesting topic—for instance, to speculate why a new computer game has become so popular or what the effects of a new kind of body suit will be for competitive swimmers.

Writers often use a cause-and-effect essay to *argue,* or prove a point. In "Examined Life," Malcolm Gladwell argues that Stanley Kaplan proved that students could get a desired effect—a high grade on the SAT—by understanding how the test worked and preparing for it. In "Why McDonald's Fries Taste So Good," Eric Schlosser argues that the fast-food industry achieves its goal of making customers happy by hiring chemists to create tasty artificial flavors. In "Why Boys Don't Play with Dolls," Katha Pollitt argues that parental—and cultural—messages shape our attitudes toward sex roles.

AUDIENCE

When you begin to analyze your audience for a cause-and-effect argument, it helps to think of them as jurors to whom you are going to present a case. You can make up a list of questions just as a lawyer would to help him or her formulate an argument. For example:

- How should I prepare my readers for my argument? What background information do they need?
- What kind of evidence are they likely to want? Factual, statistical, anecdotal?
- How much do I have to explain? Will they have enough context to understand my points and make connections without my spelling them out?

Like a trial lawyer, you're trying to establish a chain of cause and effect. Perhaps you can't establish absolute proof, but you can show probability. The format for such arguments can be

- State your claim early, usually in the first paragraph.
- Show the connection you want to establish.
- Present your supporting evidence.
- Repeat your claim in your conclusion.

STRATEGIES

One good strategy for cause-and-effect arguments is *drawing analogies*. Daniel Goleman draws analogies between winning performers in sports, music, chess, and feats of memory in "Peak Performance: Why Records Fall." You could use a similar strategy in drawing an analogy between a culture that glorifies male sports stars, particularly in bruising sports like professional football, and a social environment that erupts into street violence among gangs of young men. You could seek support for your thesis by doing keyword searches with entries like Violence + Sports + Gangs.

You could also use cause and effect in writing an essay about how your encounter with an unfamiliar situation changed your attitude toward major social issues. Jonathan Kozol uses this strategy to catalogue the social (and moral) effects of illiteracy. Your version might recount how a brief trip to another country prompted you to learn its language, read about its history, and eventually arrange to travel there again for a "study abroad" semester.

USING CAUSE AND EFFECT IN PARAGRAPHS

Here are two cause-and-effect paragraphs. The first is written by a professional writer and is followed by an analysis. The second is written by a student writer and is followed by questions.

JONATHAN WEINER
Elephant Evolution

For poachers, elephants with big tusks were prime targets. Elephants with small tusks were more likely to be passed over, and those with no tusks at all were not shot. In effect, though no one realized it at the time, African elephants in places where poaching was rife were under enormous selection pressure for tusklessness. And in fact, elephant watchers in the most heavily poached areas began noticing more and more tuskless elephants in the wild. Andrew Dobson, an ecologist at Princeton, has compiled graphs of this trend, tracing the evolution of tusklessness in five African wildlife preserves, Ambroseli, Mikumi, Tsavo East, Tsavo West, and Queen Elizabeth. In Ambroseli, where the elephants are relatively safe, the proportion of tuskless female elephants is small, just under a few percent. But in Mikumi, a park where the elephants are heavily poached, tusklessness is rising. The longer each generation lives the fewer tusks the elephants carry. Among females aged five through ten about 10 percent are tuskless; among females aged thirty to thirty-five, about 50 percent are tuskless.

Sets up evidence

Shows effect

Statistics that support his point

Comment In this paragraph taken from his book *The Beak of the Finch,* which documents the evolutionary patterns two scientists have traced by measuring the beaks of finches on an isolated island in the Galápagos, the science writer Jonathan Weiner shows how poaching on elephant preserves in Africa has directly affected the physical characteristics of the elephants on those preserves. He sets up a direct "if-then" cause-and-effect equation. When poachers killed the elephants with the largest tusks because those tusks were in the greatest demand, fewer elephants who carried the genes for that characteristic were left to breed. Therefore fewer elephants with large tusks appeared in subsequent generations. By citing the graphs that an identified academic ecologist compiled from observations in five specific wildlife preserves, Weiner shores up his cause-and-effect argument; he's not relying only on hearsay evidence or casual observation.

EMILY LINDERMAN
Barrier-Free Design

Many merchants view the Americans with Disabilities Act as expensive social engineering. They have established an attractive and affordable space for their businesses. Their customers seem satisfied. Then the federal government requires them to provide accessible ramps and elevators, wider doorways and halls, larger bathrooms, and lower drinking fountains. Seen from another perspective, however, making these changes may pay off in the long run. How many times have you tried to move furniture into a building or up to the third floor? How many times have you tried to find a place for your packages in a cramped bathroom stall? And how many times have you had to lift your little brother up to the fountain to get a drink? All customers, not simply disabled customers, will benefit from and reward merchants who invest in these barrier-free buildings.

1. Whom do you think Linderman is addressing with her argument for the benefits of barrier-free buildings?
2. How does the significance of the extra benefits that Linderman mentions compare with the significance of the benefits that the Disabilities Act was designed to provide?

CAUSE AND EFFECT

Points to Remember

1. Remember that, in human events, you can almost never prove direct, simple, cause-and-effect relationships. Qualify your claims.
2. Be careful not to oversimplify your cause-and-effect statements; be cautious about saying that a cause always produces a certain effect or that a remedy never succeeds.
3. Avoid confusing coincidence or simple sequence with cause and effect; because B follows A doesn't mean that A caused B.
4. Build your cause-and-effect argument as a trial lawyer would. Present as much evidence as you can, and argue for your hypothesis.

In this documentary photograph, Frank Hurley chronicles a dramatic moment during Sir Ernest Shackleton's journey across the Antarctic (1914–1916). Research the Shackleton expedition. What prompted them to go? What caused their ship, Endurance, *to be trapped in the ice? What happened to the expedition? Write an essay analyzing the causes and effects of this legendary voyage.*

KATHA POLLITT

Katha Pollitt was born in 1949 in New York City and educated at Radcliffe College. She has worked as a writer, literary editor, and contributing editor for *Nation,* and has made numerous television appearances on news and opinion programs. Her first book, a collection of poems, *Antarctic Traveller* (1982), enjoyed immense critical success. But she is perhaps best known for her political and cultural commentary on television and in the essays she has written for the *New Yorker, Atlantic Monthly,* and *Harper's.* Her written commentary has been collected in two volumes, *Reasonable Creatures: Essays on Women and Feminism* (1994) and *Subject to Debate: Sense and Dissents on Women, Politics, and Culture* (2001). In "Why Boys Don't Play with Dolls," reprinted from the *New York Times Magazine,* Pollitt speculates on why the old rules still seem to apply to sex roles.

Why Boys Don't Play with Dolls

I T'S 28 YEARS since the founding of NOW, and boys still like trucks and girls still like dolls. Increasingly, we are told that the source of these robust preferences must lie outside society—in prenatal hormonal influences, brain chemistry, genes—and that feminism has reached its natural limits. What else could possibly explain the love of preschool girls for party dresses or the desire of toddler boys to own more guns than Mark from Michigan.

True, recent studies claim to show small cognitive differences between the sexes: he gets around by orienting himself in space, she does it by remembering landmarks. Time will tell if any deserve the hoopla with which each is invariably greeted, over the

protests of the researchers themselves. But even if the results
hold up (and the history of such research is not encouraging),
we don't need studies of sex-differentiated brain activity in reading, say, to understand why boys and girls still seem so unalike.

The feminist movement has done much for some women,   3
and something for every woman, but it has hardly turned
America into a playground free of sex roles. It hasn't even got
women to stop dieting or men to stop interrupting them.

Instead of looking at kids to "prove" that differences in   4
behavior by sex are innate, we can look at the ways we raise
kids as an index to how unfinished the feminist revolution
really is, and how tentatively it is embraced even by adults
who fully expect their daughters to enter previously male-
dominated professions and their sons to change diapers.

I'm at a children's birthday party. "I'm sorry," one mom   5
silently mouths to the mother of the birthday girl, who has
just torn open her present—Tropical Splash Barbie. Now,

---

*With sex roles, as in every area of life, people
aspire to what is possible and conform to
what is necessary.*

---

you can love Barbie or you can hate Barbie, and there are
feminists in both camps. But *apologize* for Barbie? Inflict
Barbie, against your own convictions, on the child of a friend
you know will be none too pleased?

Every mother in that room had spent years becoming a   6
person who had to be taken seriously, not least by herself.
Even the most attractive, I'm willing to bet, had suffered
over her body's failure to fit the impossible American ideal.
Given all that, it seems crazy to transmit Barbie to the
next generation. Yet to reject her is to say that what Barbie
represents—being sexy, thin, stylish—is unimportant, which
is obviously not true, and children know it's not true.

Women's looks matter terribly in this society, and so Barbie, 7
however ambivalently, must be passed along. After all, there
are worse toys. The Cut and Style Barbie styling head, for example, a grotesque object intended to encourage "hair play."
The grown-ups who give that probably apologize, too.

How happy would most parents be to have a child who 8
flouted sex conventions? I know a lot of women, feminists,
who complain in a comical, eyeball-rolling way about their
sons' passion for sports: the ruined weekends, obnoxious
coaches, macho values. But they would not think of discour-
aging their sons from participating in this activity they find so
foolish. Or do they? Their husbands are sports fans, too, and
they like their husbands a lot.

Could it be that even sports-resistant moms see athletics as 9
part of manliness? That if their sons wanted to spend the
weekend writing up their diaries, or reading, or baking, they'd
find it disturbing? Too antisocial? Too lonely? Too gay?

Theories of innate differences in behavior are appealing. 10
They let parents off the hook—no small recommendation in
a culture that holds moms, and sometimes even dads, responsible for their children's every misstep on the road to bliss
and success.

They allow grown-ups to take the path of least resistance 11
to the dominant culture, which always requires less psychic
effort, even if it means more actual work: just ask the working mother who comes home exhausted and nonetheless
finds it easier to pick up her son's socks than make him do it
himself. They let families buy for their children, without too
much guilt, the unbelievably sexist junk that the kids, who
have been watching commercials since birth, understandably
crave.

But the thing the theories do most of all is tell adults that 12
the *adult* world—in which moms and dads still play by many
of the old rules even as they question and fidget and chafe
against them—is the way it's supposed to be. A girl with a
doll and a boy with a truck "explain" why men are from Mars
and women are from Venus, why wives do housework and
husbands just don't understand.

The paradox is that the world of rigid and hierarchal sex   13
roles evoked by determinist theories is already passing
away. Three-year-olds may indeed insist that doctors are
male and nurses female, even if their own mother is a
physician. Six-year-olds know better. These days, something like half of all medical students are female, and male
applications to nursing school are inching upward. When
tomorrow's 3-year-olds play doctor, who's to say how
they'll assign the roles?

With sex roles, as in every area of life, people aspire to   14
what is possible and conform to what is necessary. But
these are not fixed, especially today. Biological determinism
may reassure some adults about their present, but it is feminism, the ideology of flexible and converging sex roles,
that fits our children's future. And the kids, somehow,
know this.

That's why, if you look carefully, you'll find that for every   15
kid who fits a stereotype, there's another who's breaking one
down. Sometimes it's the same kid—the boy who skate-
boards *and* takes cooking in his after-school program; the girl
who collects stuffed animals *and* A-pluses in science.

Feminists are often accused of imposing their "agenda"   16
on children. Isn't that what adults always do, consciously
and unconsciously? Kids aren't born religious, or polite, or
kind, or able to remember where they put their sneakers.
Inculcating these behaviors, and the values behind them, is
a tremendous amount of work, involving many adults.
We don't have a choice, really, about *whether* we should give
our children messages about what it means to be male
and female—they're bombarded with them from morning
till night.

The question, as always, is what do we want those   17
messages to be?

For Study and Discussion

QUESTIONS FOR RESPONSE

1. How do you feel about boys who play with dolls and girls who play with trucks?
2. How do your parents respond to such boys and girls?

QUESTIONS ABOUT PURPOSE

1. What major point is Pollitt making about the difference between *nature* and *nurture*?
2. Why does she believe adults are responsible for the "old rules"?

QUESTIONS ABOUT AUDIENCE

1. How does Pollitt use the example of the birthday party to identify her readers?
2. Why does she think her readers might be attracted to "theories of innate differences"?

QUESTIONS ABOUT STRATEGIES

1. How does Pollitt's commentary on parental attitudes help establish her argument about the cause of gender stereotyping?
2. How does she illustrate the contradictions of sexual stereotyping?

QUESTIONS FOR DISCUSSION

1. What is Pollitt's attitude toward research on the differences between men and women?
2. Why does she feel that feminism is the ideology "that fits our children's future"?

DANIEL GOLEMAN

Daniel Goleman was born in 1946 in Stockton, California, and was educated at Amherst College and Harvard University. After working for several years as a professor of psychology, he began his career as an editor for *Psychology Today*. He has contributed more than fifty articles to psychology journals and has written a dozen books, including *The Meditative Mind* (1988); *The Creative Spirit* (1992); *Mind, Body Medicine: How to Use Your Mind for Better Health* (1993); *Emotional Intelligence* (1995); and *Working with Emotional Intelligence* (1998). In "Peak Performance: Why Records Fall," reprinted from a 1994 *New York Times* article, Goleman analyzes how dedication to practice contributes to peak performances.

Peak Performance: Why Records Fall

T HE OLD JOKE—How do you get to Carnegie Hall? Practice, practice, practice—is getting a scientific spin. Researchers are finding an unexpected potency from deliberate practice in world-class competitions of all kinds, including chess matches, musical recitals and sporting events.

Studies of chess masters, virtuoso musicians and star athletes show that the relentless training routines of those at the top allow them to break through ordinary limits in memory and physiology, and so perform at levels that had been thought impossible.

World records have been falling inexorably over the last century. For example, the marathon gold medalist's time in the 1896 Olympics Games was, by 1990, only about as good as the qualifying time for the Boston Marathon.

"Over the last century Olympics have become more and more competitive, and so athletes steadily have had to put in more total lifetime hours of practice," said Dr. Michael Mahoney, a psychologist at the University of North Texas in Denton, who helps train the United States Olympic weightlifting team. "These days you have to live your sport."

That total dedication is in contrast to the relatively leisurely attitude taken at the turn of the century, when even world-class athletes would train arduously for only a few months before their competition.

"As competition got greater, training extended to a whole season," said Dr. Anders Ericsson, a psychologist at Florida State University in Tallahassee who wrote an article on the role of deliberate practice for star performance recently in the journal *American Psychologist*. "Then it extended through

---

Through their hours of practice, elite performers of all kinds master shortcuts that give them an edge.

---

the year, and then for several years. Now the elite performers start their training in childhood. There is a historical trend toward younger starting ages, which makes possible a greater and greater total number of hours of practice time."

To be sure, there are other factors at work: coaching methods have become more sophisticated, equipment has improved and the pool of people competing has grown. But new studies are beginning to reveal the sheer power of training itself.

Perhaps the most surprising data show that extensive practice can break through barriers in mental capacities, particularly short-term memory. In short-term memory, information is stored for the few seconds that it is used and then fades, as in hearing a phone number which one forgets as soon as it is dialed.

The standard view, repeated in almost every psychology   9
textbook, is that the ordinary limit on short-term memory is
for seven or so bits of information—the length of a phone
number. More than that typically cannot be retained in
short-term memory with reliability unless the separate units
are "chunked," as when the numbers in a telephone prefix
are remembered as a single unit.

But, in a stunning demonstration of the power of sheer   10
practice to break barriers in the mind's ability to handle information, Dr. Ericsson and associates at Carnegie-Mellon University have taught college students to listen to a list of as
many as 102 random digits and then recite it correctly. After
50 hours of practice with differing sets of random digits, four
students were able to remember up to 20 digits after a single
hearing. One student, a business major not especially talented in mathematics, was able to remember 102 digits. The
feat took him more than 400 hours of practice.

The ability to increase memory in a particular domain is at   11
the heart of a wide range high-level performance, said Dr.
Herbert Simon, professor of computer science and psychol-
ogy at Carnegie-Mellon University and a Nobel laureate.
Dr. Ericsson was part of a team studying expertise led by
Dr. Simon.

"Every expert has acquired something like this memory   12
ability" in his or her area of expertise, said Dr. Simon. "Memory is like an index; experts have approximately 50,000
chunks of familiar units of information they recognize. For a
physician, many of those chunks are symptoms."

A similar memory training effect, Dr. Simon said, seems to   13
occur with many chess masters. The key skill chess players re-
hearse in practicing is, of course, selecting the best move.
They do so by studying games between two chess masters
and guessing the next move from their own study of the
board as the game progresses.

Repeated practice results in a prodigious memory for chess   14
positions. The ability of some chess masters to play blind-
folded, while simply told what moves their opponents make,
has long been known; in the 1940s Adrian DeGroot, himself

a Dutch grandmaster, showed that many chess masters are able to look at a chess board in midgame for as little as five seconds and then repeat the position of every piece on the board.

Later systematic studies by Dr. Simon's group showed that the chess masters' memory feat was limited to boards used in actual games; they had no such memory for randomly placed pieces. "They would see a board and think, that reminds me of Spassky versus Lasker," said Dr. Simon.　　15

This feat of memory was duplicated by a college student who knew little about chess, but was given 50 hours of training in remembering chess positions by Dr. Ericsson in a 1990 study.　　16

Through their hours of practice, elite performers of all kinds master shortcuts that give them an edge. Dr. Bruce Abernathy, a researcher at the University of Queensland in Australia, has found that the most experienced players in racquet sports like squash and tennis are able to predict where a serve will land by cues in the server's posture before the ball is hit.　　17

A 1992 study of baseball greats like Hank Aaron and Rod Carew by Thomas Hanson, then a graduate student at the University of Virginia in Charlottesville, found that the all-time best hitters typically started preparing for games by studying films of the pitchers they would face, to spot cues that would tip off what pitch was about to be thrown. Using such fleeting cues demands rehearsing so well that the response to them is automatic, cognitive scientists have found.　　18

The maxim that practice makes perfect has been borne out through research on the training of star athletes and artists. Dr. Anthony Kalinowski, a researcher at the University of Chicago, found that swimmers who achieved the level of national champion started their training at an average age of 10, while those who were good enough to make the United States Olympic teams started on average at 7. This is the same age difference found for national and international chess champions in a 1987 study.　　19

Similarly, the best violinists of the 20th century, all with international careers as soloists for more than 30 years, were found to have begun practicing their instrument at an　　20 average age of 5, while violinists of only national prominence, those affiliated with the top music academy in Berlin, started at 8, Dr. Ericsson found in research reported last year in *The Psychological Review.*

Because of limits on physical endurance and mental alert-   21
ness, world-class competitors—whether violinists or weight lifters—typically seem to practice arduously no more than four hours a day, Dr. Ericsson has found from studying a wide variety of training regimens.

"When we train Olympic weight lifters, we find we often   22
have to throttle back the total time they work out," said Dr. Mahoney. "Otherwise you find a tremendous drop in mood, and a jump in irritability, fatigue and apathy."

Because their intense practice regimen puts them at risk for   23
burnout or strain injuries, most elite competitors also make rest part of their training routine, sleeping a full eight hours and often napping a half-hour a day, Dr. Ericsson found.

Effective practice focuses not just on the key skills in-   24
volved, but also systematically stretches the person's limits. "You have to tweak the system by pushing, allowing for more errors at first as you increase your limits," said Dr. Ericsson. "You don't get benefits from mechanical repetition, but by adjusting your execution over and over to get closer to your goal."

Violin virtuosos illustrate the importance of starting early   25
in life. In his 1993 study Dr. Ericsson found that by age 20 top-level violinists in music academies had practiced a life-time total of about 10,000 hours, while those who were slightly less accomplished had practiced an average of about 7,500 hours.

A study of Chinese Olympic divers, done by Dr. John Shea   26
of Florida State University, found that some 11-year-old divers had spent as many hours in training as had 21-year-old American divers. The Chinese divers started training at age 4.

"It can take 10 years of extensive practice to excel in   27
anything," said Dr. Simon. "Mozart was 4 when he started composing, but his world-class music started when he was about 17."

Total hours of practice may be more important than time   28
spent in competition, according to findings not yet published
by Dr. Neil Charness, a colleague of Dr. Ericsson at Florida
State University. Dr. Charness, comparing the rankings of
107 competitors in the 1993 Berlin City Tournament, found
that the more time they spent practicing alone, the higher
their ranking as chess players. But there was no relationship
between the chess players' rankings and the time they spent
playing others.

As has long been known, the extensive training of an elite   29
athlete molds the body to fit the demands of a given sport.
What has been less obvious is the extent of these changes.

"The sizes of hearts and lungs, joint flexibility and bone   30
strength all increase directly with hours of training," said Dr.
Ericsson. "The number of capillaries that supply blood to
trained muscles increases."

And the muscles themselves change, Dr. Ericsson said.   31
Until very recently, researchers believed that the percentage
of muscle fiber types was more than 90 percent determined
by heredity. Fast-twitch muscles, which allow short bursts of
intense effort, are crucial in sports like weight lifting and
sprinting, while slow-twitch muscles, richer in red blood
cells, are essential for endurance sports like marathons.
"Muscle fibers in those muscles can change from fast twitch
to slow twitch, as the sport demands," said Dr. Ericsson.

Longitudinal studies show that years of endurance training   32
at champion levels leads athletes' hearts to increase in size
well beyond the normal range for people their age.

Such physiological changes are magnified when training oc-   33
curs during childhood, puberty and adolescence. Dr. Ericsson
thinks this may be one reason virtually all top athletes today
began serious practice as children or young adolescents,
though some events, like weight training, may be exceptions
because muscles need to fully form before intense lifting
begins.

The most contentious claim made by Dr. Ericsson is that   34
practice alone, not natural talent, makes for a record-breaking
performance. "Innate capacities have very little to do with

becoming a champion," said his colleague, Dr. Charness. "What's key is motivation and temperament, not a skill specific to performance. It's unlikely you can get just any child to apply themselves this rigorously for so long."

But many psychologists argue that the emphasis on practice alone ignores the place of talent in superb performance. "You can't assume that random people who practice a lot will rise to the top," said Dr. Howard Gardner, a psychologist at Harvard University. Dr. Ericsson's theories "leave out the question of who selects themselves—or are selected—for intensive training," adding, "It also leaves out what we most value in star performance, like innovative genius in a chess player or emotional expressiveness in a concert musician."   35

Dr. Gardner said: "I taught piano for many years, and there's an enormous difference between those who practice dutifully and get a little better every week, and those students who break away from the pack. There's plenty of room for innate talent to make a difference over and above practice time. Mozart was not like you and me."   36

For Study and Discussion

QUESTIONS FOR RESPONSE

1. Think of some top performers who started very young—for instance, violinist Midori, chess prodigy Bobby Fischer, or tennis player Jennifer Capriati. What do you know about their subsequent lives? To what extent can you generalize about such individuals?
2. If you hope to be a top performer in your chosen field, does this essay encourage you or discourage you? Explain why.

QUESTIONS ABOUT PURPOSE

1. What message do you think the experts quoted in this essay are giving to young people who want to excel in something? What do you see as the impact of that message?
2. What role do you think science plays in sports these days? What is your feeling about that role?

QUESTIONS ABOUT AUDIENCE

1. What groups of readers do you see as people who would particularly benefit from learning about the research reported here? In what way would they benefit?
2. How would the value system of a reader—that is, the complex of things that the reader thinks is important—affect the way he or she responds to this essay?

QUESTIONS ABOUT STRATEGIES

1. What is the impact of Goleman's pointing out that the marathon runner who won an Olympic gold medal a hundred years ago could barely qualify for the Boston Marathon today?
2. How does Goleman's use of diverse authorities strengthen his essay?

QUESTIONS FOR DISCUSSION

1. What impact do you think the new realities about becoming a winner will have on the families of young artists and athletes? How might it differ among families?
2. What factors in a competitor's performance that are not discussed here might affect his or her achievement? How important are those elements?

JONATHAN KOZOL

Jonathan Kozol was born in 1936 in Boston, Massachusetts, and educated at Harvard University and, as a Rhodes Scholar, at Oxford University. He began his career as an elementary, secondary, and college teacher. But his interest in illiteracy and the educational and economic problems that caused it prompted him to write books such as *Death at an Early Age: The Destruction of the Hearts and Minds of Negro Children in the Boston Schools* (1967)— winner of the National Book Award—*Illiterate America* (1985), *Savage Inequalities: Children in American Schools* (1991), and *Ordinary Resurrections: Children in the Years of Hope* (2000). In "The Human Cost of an Illiterate Society," reprinted from *Illiterate America,* Kozol catalogs the effects of illiteracy on a democratic culture.

The Human Cost of an Illiterate Society

PRECAUTIONS. READ BEFORE USING.
Poison: Contains sodium hydroxide (caustic soda-lye).
Corrosive: Causes severe eye and skin damage, may cause blindness.
Harmful or fatal if swallowed.
If swallowed, give large quantities of milk or water.
Do not induce vomiting.
Important: Keep water out of can at all times to prevent contents
from violently erupting. . . .
—Warning on a Can of Drano

W E ARE SPEAKING here no longer of the dangers faced by passengers on Eastern Airlines or the dollar costs incurred by U.S. corporations and taxpayers. We are speaking now of human suffering and of the ethical dilemmas that are

1

faced by a society that looks upon such suffering with qualified concern but does not take those actions which its wealth
and ingenuity would seemingly demand.

Questions of literacy, in Socrates' belief, must at length be
judged as matters of morality. Socrates could not have had in
mind the moral compromise peculiar to a nation like our
own. Some of our Founding Fathers did, however, have this
question in their minds. One of the wisest of those Founding
Fathers (one who may not have been most compassionate
but surely was more prescient than some of his peers) recognized the special dangers that illiteracy would pose to basic
equity in the political construction that he helped to shape.

"A people who mean to be their own governors," James
Madison wrote, "must arm themselves with the power
knowledge gives. A popular government without popular

---

*Questions of literacy . . . must at length be
judged as matters of morality.*

---

information or the means of acquiring it, is but a prologue to
a farce or a tragedy, or perhaps both."

Tragedy looms larger than farce in the United States
today. Illiterate citizens seldom vote. Those who do are
forced to cast a vote of questionable worth. They cannot
make informed decisions based on serious print information.
Sometimes they can be alerted to their interests by aggressive
voter education. More frequently, they vote for a face, a smile,
or a style, not for a mind or character or body of beliefs.

The number of illiterate adults exceeds by 16 million the
entire vote cast for the winner in the 1980 presidential contest. If even one third of all illiterates could vote, and read
enough and do sufficient math to vote in their self-interest,
Ronald Reagan would not likely have been chosen president.
There is, of course, no way to know for sure. We do know
this: Democracy is a mendacious term when used by those

who are prepared to countenance the forced exclusion of one third of our electorate. So long as 60 million people are denied significant participation, the government is neither of, nor for, nor by, the people. It is a government, at best, of those two thirds whose wealth, skin color, or parental privilege allows them opportunity to profit from the provocation and instruction of the written word.

The undermining of democracy in the United States is one   6
"expense" that sensitive Americans can easily deplore because it represents a contradiction that endangers citizens of all political positions. The human price is not so obvious at first.

Since I first immersed myself within this work I have often   7
had the following dream: I find that I am in a railroad station or a large department store within a city that is utterly unknown to me and where I cannot understand the printed words. None of the signs or symbols are familiar. Everything looks strange: like mirror writing of some kind. Gradually I understand that I am in the Soviet Union. All the letters on the walls around me are Cyrillic. I look for my pocket dictionary but I find that it has been mislaid. Where have I left it? Then I recall that I forgot to bring it with me when I packed my bags in Boston. I struggle to remember the name of my hotel. I try to ask somebody for directions. One person stops and looks at me in a peculiar way. I lose the nerve to ask. At last I reach into my wallet for an ID card. The card is missing. Have I lost it? Then I remember that my card was confiscated for some reason, many years before. Around this point, I wake up in a panic.

This panic is not so different from the misery that millions   8
of adult illiterates experience each day within the course of their routine existence in the U.S.A.

Illiterates cannot read the menu in a restaurant.   9

They cannot read the cost of items on the menu in the   10
window of the restaurant before they enter.

Illiterates cannot read the letters that their children bring   11
home from their teachers. They cannot study school department circulars that tell them of the courses that their children must be taking if they hope to pass the SAT exams. They

cannot help with homework. They cannot write a letter to the teacher. They are afraid to visit in the classroom. They do not want to humiliate their child or themselves.

Illiterates cannot read instructions on a bottle of prescrip-   12
tion medicine. They cannot find out when a medicine is past the year of safe consumption; nor can they read of allergenic risks, warnings to diabetics, or the potential sedative effect of certain kinds of nonprescription pills. They cannot observe preventive health care admonitions. They cannot read about "the seven warning signs of cancer" or the indications of blood-sugar fluctuations or the risks of eating certain foods that aggravate the likelihood of cardiac arrest.

Illiterates live, in more than literal ways, an uninsured exis-   13
tence. They cannot understand the written details on a health insurance form. They cannot read the waivers that they sign preceding surgical procedures. Several women I have known in Boston have entered a slum hospital with the intention of ob-taining a tubal ligation and have emerged a few days later after having been subjected to a hysterectomy. Unaware of their rights, incognizant of jargon, intimidated by the unfamiliar air of fear and atmosphere of ether that so many of us find oppres-sive in the confines even of the most attractive and expensive medical facilities, they have signed their names to documents they could not read and which nobody, in the hectic situation that prevails so often in those overcrowded hospitals that serve the urban poor, had even bothered to explain.

Childbirth might seem to be the last inalienable right of   14
any female citizen within a civilized society. Illiterate moth-ers, as we shall see, already have been cheated of the power to protect their progeny against the likelihood of demolition in deficient public schools and, as a result, against the verbal servitude within which they themselves exist. Surgical denial of the right to bear that child in the first place represents an ultimate denial, an unspeakable metaphor, a final darkness that denies even the twilight gleamings of our own humanity. What greater violation of our biological, our biblical, our spir-itual humanity could possibly exist than that which takes place nightly, perhaps hourly these days, within such overburdened

and benighted institutions as the Boston City Hospital? Illiteracy has many costs; few are so irreversible as this.

Even the roof above one's head, the gas or other fuel for   15
heating that protects the residents of northern city slums
against the threat of illness in the winter months become uncertain guarantees. Illiterates cannot read the lease that they
must sign to live in an apartment which, too often, they cannot afford. They cannot manage check accounts and therefore seldom pay for anything by mail. Hours and entire days
of difficult travel (and the cost of bus or other public transit)
must be added to the real cost of whatever they consume.
Loss of interest on the check accounts they do not have, and
could not manage if they did, must be regarded as another of
the excess costs paid by the citizen who is excluded from the
common instruments of commerce in a numerate society.

"I couldn't understand the bills," a woman in Washington,   16
D.C., reports, "and then I couldn't write the checks to pay
them. We signed things we didn't know what they were."

Illiterates cannot read the notices that they receive from   17
welfare offices or from the IRS. They must depend on word-
of-mouth instruction from the welfare worker—or from other
persons whom they have good reason to mistrust. They do not
know what rights they have, what deadlines and requirements
they face, what options they might choose to exercise. They
are half-citizens. Their rights exist in print but not in fact.

Illiterates cannot look up numbers in a telephone direc-   18
tory. Even if they can find the names of friends, few possess
the sorting skills to make use of the yellow pages; categories
are bewildering and trade names are beyond decoding capabilities for millions of nonreaders. Even the emergency numbers
listed on the first page of the phone book—"Ambulance,"
"Police," and "Fire"—are too frequently beyond the recognition of nonreaders.

Many illiterates cannot read the admonition on a pack of   19
cigarettes. Neither the Surgeon General's warning nor its reproduction on the package can alert them to the risks. Although most people learn by word of mouth that smoking is
related to a number of grave physical disorders, they do not

get the chance to read the detailed stories which can document this danger with the vividness that turns concern into determination to resist. They can see the handsome cowboy or the slim Virginia lady lighting up a filter cigarette; they cannot heed the words that tell them that this product is (not "may be") dangerous to their health. Sixty million men and women are condemned to be the unalerted, high-risk candidates for cancer.

Illiterates do not buy "no-name" products in the super- 20
markets. They must depend on photographs or the familiar logos that are printed on the packages of brand-name groceries. The poorest people, therefore, are denied the benefits of the least costly products.

Illiterates depend almost entirely upon label recognition. 21
Many labels, however, are not easy to distinguish. Dozens of different kinds of Campbell's soup appear identical to the nonreader. The purchaser who cannot read and does not dare to ask for help, out of the fear of being stigmatized (a fear which is unfortunately realistic), frequently comes home with something which she never wanted and her family never tasted.

Illiterates cannot read instructions on a pack of frozen 22
food. Packages sometimes provide an illustration to explain the cooking preparations; but illustrations are of little help to someone who must "boil water, drop the food—*within* its plastic wrapper—in the boiling water, wait for it to simmer, instantly remove."

Even when labels are seemingly clear, they may be easily 23
mistaken. A woman in Detroit brought home a gallon of Crisco for her children's dinner. She thought that she had bought the chicken that was pictured on the label. She had enough Crisco now to last a year—but no more money to go back and buy the food for dinner.

Recipes provided on the packages of certain staples some- 24
times tempt a semiliterate person to prepare a meal her children have not tasted. The longing to vary the uniform and often starchy content of low-budget meals provided to the family that relies on food stamps commonly leads to ruinous results. Scarce funds have been wasted and the food must be

thrown out. The same applies to distribution of food-surplus produce in emergency conditions. Government inducements to poor people to "explore the ways" by which to make a tasty meal from tasteless noodles, surplus cheese, and powdered milk are useless to nonreaders. Intended as benevolent advice, such recommendations mock reality and foster deeper feelings of resentment and of inability to cope. (Those, on the other hand, who cautiously refrain from "innovative" recipes in preparation of their children's meals must suffer the opprobrium of "laziness," "lack of imagination. . . .")

Illiterates cannot travel freely. When they attempt to do so,   25 they encounter risks that few of us can dream of. They cannot read traffic signs and, while they often learn to recognize and to decipher symbols, they cannot manage street names which they haven't seen before. The same is true for bus and subway stops. While ingenuity can sometimes help a man or woman to discern directions from familiar landmarks, buildings, cemeteries, churches, and the like, most illiterates are virtually immobilized. They seldom wander past the streets and neighborhoods they know. Geographical paralysis becomes a bitter metaphor for their entire existence. They are immobilized in almost every sense we can imagine. They can't move up. They can't move out. They cannot see beyond. Illiterates may take an oral test for drivers' permits in most sections of America. It is a questionable concession. Where will they go? How will they get there? How will they get home? Could it be that some of us might like it better if they stayed where they belong?

Travel is only one of many instances of circumscribed exis-   26 tence. Choice, in almost all of its facets, is diminished in the life of an illiterate adult. Even the printed TV schedule, which provides most people with the luxury of preselection, does not belong within the arsenal of options in illiterate existence. One consequence is that the viewer watches only what appears at moments when he happens to have time to turn the switch. Another consequence, a lot more common, is that the TV set remains in operation night and day. Whatever the program offered at the hour when he walks into the room will be the nutriment that he accepts and swallows. Thus, to passivity, is added frequency—indeed, almost uninterrupted continuity. Freedom to select is no more possible here than in the choice of home or surgery or food.

"You don't choose," said one illiterate woman. "You take   27
your wishes from somebody else." Whether in perusal of a menu, selection of highways, purchase of groceries, or determination of affordable enjoyment, illiterate Americans must trust somebody else: a friend, a relative, a stranger on the street, a grocery clerk, a TV copywriter.

"All of our mail we get, it's hard for her to read. Settin' down   28
and writing a letter, she can't do it. Like if we get a bill . . . we take it over to my sister-in-law . . . My sister-in-law reads it."

Billing agencies harass poor people for the payment of the   29
bills for purchases that might have taken place six months before. Utility companies offer an agreement for a staggered payment schedule on a bill past due. "You have to trust them," one man said. Precisely for this reason, you end up by trusting no one and suspecting everyone of possible deceit. A submerged sense of distrust becomes the corollary to a constant need to trust. "They are cheating me . . . I have been tricked . . . I do not know . . ."

Not knowing: This is a familiar theme. Not knowing the   30
right word for the right thing at the right time is one form of subjugation. Not knowing the world that lies concealed behind those words is a more terrifying feeling. The longitude and latitude of one's existence are beyond all easy apprehension. Even the hard, cold stars within the firmament above one's head begin to mock the possibilities for self-location. Where am I? Where did I come from? Where will I go?

"I've lost a lot of jobs," one man explains. "Today, even if   31
you're a janitor, there's still reading and writing . . . They leave a note saying, 'Go to room so-and-so . . .' You can't do it. You can't read it. You don't know."

"The hardest thing about it is that I've been places where   32
I didn't know where I was. You don't know where you are . . . You're lost."

"Like I said: I have two kids. What do I do if one of my   33
kids starts choking? I go running to the phone . . . I can't

look up the hospital phone number. That's if we're at home. Out on the street, I can't read the sign. I get to a pay phone. 'Okay, tell us where you are. We'll send an ambulance.' I look at the street sign. Right there, I can't tell you what it says. I'd have to spell it out, letter for letter. By that time, one of my kids would be dead . . . These are the kinds of fears you go with, every single day . . ."

"Reading directions, I suffer with. I work with chemicals   34 . . . That's scary to begin with . . ."

"You sit down. They throw the menu in front of you.   35 Where do you go from there? Nine times out of ten you say, 'Go ahead. Pick out something for the both of us.' I've eaten some weird things, let me tell you!"

Menus. Chemicals. A child choking while his mother   36 searches for a word she does not know to find assistance that will come too late. Another mother speaks about the inability to help her kids to read: "I can't read to them. Of course that's leaving them out of something they should have. Oh, it matters. You *believe* it matters! I ordered all these books. The kids belong to a book club. Donny wanted me to read a book to him. I told Donny: 'I can't read.' He said: 'Mommy, you sit down. I'll read it to you.' I tried it one day, reading from the pictures. Donny looked at me. He said, 'Mommy, that's not right.' He's only five. He knew I couldn't read . . ."

A landlord tells a woman that her lease allows him to evict   37 her if her baby cries and causes inconvenience to her neighbors. The consequence of challenging his words conveys a danger which appears, unlikely as it seems, even more alarming than the danger of eviction. Once she admits that she can't read, in the desire to maneuver for the time in which to call a friend, she will have defined herself in terms of an explicit impotence that she cannot endure. Capitulation in this case is preferable to self-humiliation. Resisting the definition of oneself in terms of what one cannot do, what others take for granted, represents a need so great that other imperatives (even one so urgent as the need to keep one's home in winter's cold) evaporate and fall away in face of fear. Even the loss of home and shelter, in this case, is not so terrifying as the loss of self.

"I come out of school. I was sixteen. They had their meet-   38
ings. The directors meet. They said that I was wasting their
school paper. I was wasting pencils . . ."

Another illiterate, looking back, believes she was not wor-   39
thy of her teacher's time. She believes that it was wrong of
her to take up space within her school. She believes that it
was right to leave in order that somebody more deserving
could receive her place.

Children choke. Their mother chokes another way: on   40
more than chicken bones.

People eat what others order, know what others tell them,   41
struggle not to see themselves as they believe the world per-
ceives them. A man in California speaks about his own loss of
identity, of self-location, definition:

"I stood at the bottom of the ramp. My car had broke down   42
on the freeway. There was a phone. I asked for the police. They
was nice. They said to tell them where I was. I looked up at the
signs. There was one that I had seen before. I read it to them:
ONE WAY STREET. They thought it was a joke. I told them I
couldn't read. There was other signs above the ramp. They
told me to try. I looked around for somebody to help. All the
cars was going by real fast. I couldn't make them understand
that I was lost. The cop was nice. He told me: 'Try once
more.' I did my best. I couldn't read. I only knew the sign
above my head. The cop was trying to be nice. He knew that I
was trapped. 'I can't send out a car to you if you can't tell me
where you are.' I felt afraid. I nearly cried. I'm forty-eight years
old. I only said: 'I'm on a one-way street . . .' "

Perhaps we might slow down a moment here and look at   43
the realities described above. This is the nation that we live
in. This is a society that most of us did not create but which
our President and other leaders have been willing to sustain
by virtue of malign neglect. Do we possess the character and
courage to address a problem which so many nations, poorer
than our own, have found it natural to correct?

The answers to these questions represent a reasonable test   44
of our belief in the democracy to which we have been asked
in public school to swear allegiance.

For Study and Discussion

QUESTIONS FOR RESPONSE

1. How have you felt when you discovered you were lost?
2. How have you responded when you tried to read written instructions—for fixing your computer or filing your taxes—that you could not understand?

QUESTIONS ABOUT PURPOSE

1. How does Kozol use the quotation from James Madison to establish a historical and political context for his analysis?
2. How does he use his concluding questions to summarize the purpose of his essay?

QUESTIONS ABOUT AUDIENCE

1. How does Kozol use voting statistics to capture the attention of his audience?
2. How does he use his dream to help his readers understand illiteracy?

QUESTIONS ABOUT STRATEGIES

1. How does Kozol use cataloging to illustrate the social effects of illiteracy?
2. How does he use quotations to dramatize the cost of illiteracy?

QUESTIONS FOR DISCUSSION

1. How does Kozol demonstrate that "capitulation is preferable to self-humiliation"?
2. In what ways does Kozol's analysis relate to the national debate about "English only" and immigration?

MALCOLM GLADWELL

Malcolm Gladwell was born in 1963 in England, grew up in Canada, and graduated with a degree in history from the University of Toronto. He has worked at the *Washington Post*, first as a science writer and then as New York City bureau chief. He is currently a staff writer for the *New Yorker*, where he has written on a range of issues concerning media, education, and business. His international best-seller, *The Tipping Point: How Little Things Can Make a Big Difference* (2000), describes how ideas and trends start and spread. In "Examined Life," reprinted from the *New Yorker*, Gladwell discusses a range of problems caused by the Kaplan program that helps students improve their scores on the SAT.

Examined Life

O NCE, IN FOURTH grade, Stanley Kaplan got a B-plus on his report card and was so stunned that he wandered aimlessly around the neighborhood, ashamed to show his mother. This was in Brooklyn, on Avenue K in Flatbush, between the wars. Kaplan's father, Julius, was from Slutsk, in Belorussia, and ran a plumbing and heating business. His mother, Ericka, ninety pounds and four feet eight, was the granddaughter of the chief rabbi of the synagogue of Prague, and Stanley loved to sit next to her on the front porch, immersed in his schoolbooks while his friends were off playing stickball. Stanley Kaplan had Mrs. Holman for fifth grade, and when she quizzed the class on math equations, he would shout out the answers. If other students were having problems, Stanley would take out pencil and paper and pull them aside. He would offer them a dime sometimes if they would

1

just sit and listen. In high school, he would take over algebra class, and the other kids, passing him in the hall, would call him Teach. One classmate, Aimee Rubin, was having so much trouble with math that she was in danger of being dropped from the National Honor Society. Kaplan offered to help her, and she scored a ninety-five on her next exam. He tutored a troubled eleven-year-old named Bob Linker, and Bob Linker ended up a successful businessman. In Kaplan's sophomore year at City College, he got a C in biology and

---

The SAT . . . had an ideology, and Kaplan realized that anyone who understood that ideology would have a tremendous advantage.

---

was so certain that there had been a mistake that he marched in to see the professor and proved that his true grade, an A, had accidentally been switched with that of another, not quite so studious Stanley Kaplan. Thereafter, he became Stanley H. Kaplan, and when people asked him what the "H" stood for, he would say "Higher scores!" or, with a sly wink, "Preparation!" He graduated Phi Beta Kappa and hung a shingle outside his parent's house on Avenue K—"Stanley H. Kaplan Educational Center"—and started tutoring kids in the basement. In 1946, a high school junior named Elizabeth, from Coney Island, came to him for help on an exam he was unfamiliar with. It was called the Scholastic Aptitude Test, and from that moment forward the business of getting into college in America was never quite the same.

The SAT, at that point, was just beginning to go into ² widespread use. Unlike existing academic exams, it was intended to measure innate ability—not what a student had learned but what a student was capable of learning—and it stated clearly in the instructions that "cramming or last-minute reviewing" was pointless. Kaplan was puzzled. In Flatbush you always studied for tests. He gave Elizabeth pages of math problems and reading-comprehension drills. He grilled her over and over, doing what the SAT said should not be done. And what happened? On test day, she found the SAT "a piece of cake," and promptly told all her friends, and her friends told their friends, and soon word of Stanley H. Kaplan had spread throughout Brooklyn.

A few years later, Kaplan married Rita Gwirtzman, who   3
had grown up a mile away, and in 1951 they moved to a two-story brick-and-stucco house on Bedford Avenue, a block from his alma mater, James Madison High School. He renovated his basement, dividing it into classrooms. When the basement got too crowded, he rented a podiatrist's office near King's Highway, at the Brighton Beach subway stop. In the 1970s, he went national, setting up educational programs throughout the country, creating an SAT-preparation industry that soon became crowded with tutoring companies and study manuals. Kaplan has now written a memoir, *Test Pilot,* which has as its subtitle *How I Broke Testing Barriers for Millions of Students and Caused a Sonic Boom in the Business of Education.* That actually understates his importance. Stanley Kaplan changed the rules of the game.

The SAT is now seventy-five years old, and it is in trouble.   4
Earlier this year, the University of California—the nation's largest public university system—stunned the educational world by proposing a move toward a "holistic" admissions system, which would mean abandoning its heavy reliance on standardized-test scores. The school backed up its proposal with a devastating statistical analysis, arguing that the SAT is virtually useless as a tool for making admissions decisions.

The report focused on what is called predictive validity, a   5
statistical measure of how well a high school student's performance in any given test or program predicts his or her performance as a college freshman. If you wanted to, for instance, you could calculate the predictive validity of prowess at Scrabble, or the number of books a student reads in his senior year, or, more obviously, high school grades.

What the Educational Testing Service (which creates the SAT) and the College Board (which oversees it) have always argued is that most performance measures are so subjective and unreliable that only by adding aptitude-test scores into the admissions equation can a college be sure it is picking the right students.

This is what the UC study disputed. It compared the pre-   6
dictive validity of three numbers: a student's high school GPA, his or her score on the SAT (or, as it is formally known, the SAT I), and his or her score on what is known as the SAT II, which is a so-called achievement test, aimed at gauging mastery of specific areas of the high school curriculum. Drawing on the transcripts of 78,000 University of California freshmen from 1996 through 1999, the report found that overall, the most useful statistic in predicting freshman grades was the SAT II, which explained 16 percent of the "variance" (which is another measure of predictive validity). The second most useful was high school GPA, at 15.4 percent. The SAT was the least useful, at 13.3 percent. Combining high school GPA and the SAT II explained 22.2 percent of the variance in freshman grades. Adding in SAT I scores increased that number by only 0.1 percent. Nor was the SAT better at what one would have thought was its strong suit: identifying high-potential students from bad schools. In fact, the study found that achievement tests were ten times more useful than the SAT in predicting the success of students from similar backgrounds. "Achievement tests are fairer to students because they measure accomplishment rather than promise," Richard Atkinson, the president of the University of California, told a conference on college admissions last month. "They can be used to improve performance; they are less vulnerable to charges of cultural or socioeconomic bias; and they are more appropriate for schools because they set clear curricular guidelines and clarify what is important for students to learn. Most important, they tell students that a college education is within the reach of anyone with the talent and determination to succeed."

This argument has been made before, of course. The SAT   7
has been under attack, for one reason or another, since its

inception. But what is happening now is different. The University of California is one of the largest single customers of the SAT. It was the UC system's decision, in 1968, to adopt the SAT that affirmed the test's national prominence in the first place. If UC defects from the SAT, it is not hard to imagine it being followed by a stampede of other colleges. Seventy-five years ago, the SAT was instituted because we were more interested, as a society, in what a student was capable of learning than in what he had already learned. Now, apparently, we have changed our minds, and few people bear more responsibility for that shift than Stanley H. Kaplan.

From the moment he set up shop on Avenue K, Stanley   8
Kaplan was a pariah in the educational world. Once, in 1956, he went to a meeting for parents and teachers at a local high school to discuss the upcoming SAT, and one of the teachers leading the meeting pointed his finger at Kaplan and shouted, "I refuse to continue until *that man* leaves the room." When Kaplan claimed that his students routinely improved their scores by a hundred points or more, he was denounced by the testing establishment as a "quack" and "the cram king" and a "snake oil salesman." At the Educational Testing Service, "it was a cherished assumption that the SAT was uncoachable," Nicholas Lemann writes in his history of the SAT, *The Big Test*:

> *The whole idea of psychometrics was that mental tests are a measurement of a psychical property of the brain, analogous to taking a blood sample. By definition, the test-taker could not affect the result. More particularly, ETS's main point of pride about the SAT was its extremely high test-retest reliability, one of the best that any standardized test had ever achieved. . . . So confident of the SAT's reliability was ETS that the basic technique it developed for catching cheaters was simply to compare first and second scores, and to mount an investigation in the case of any very large increase. ETS was sure that substantially increasing one's score could be accomplished only by nefarious means.*

But Kaplan wasn't cheating. His great contribution was to   9
prove that the SAT was eminently coachable—that whatever
it was that the test was measuring was less like a blood sample than like a heart rate, a vital sign that could be altered
through the right exercises. In those days, for instance, the
test was a secret. Students walking in to take the SAT were
often in a state of terrified ignorance about what to expect.
(It wasn't until the early eighties that the ETS was forced to
release copies of old test questions to the public.) So Kaplan
would have "Thank Goodness It's Over" pizza parties after
each SAT. As his students talked about the questions they
had faced, he and his staff would listen and take notes, trying
to get a sense of how better to structure their coaching.
"Every night I stayed up past midnight writing new questions and study materials," he writes. "I spent hours trying to
understand the design of the test, trying to think like the test
makers, anticipating the types of questions my students
would face." His notes were typed up the next day, cranked
out on a Gestetner machine, hung to dry in the office, then
snatched off the line and given to waiting students. If students knew what the SAT was like, he reasoned, they would
be more confident. They could skip the instructions and save
time. They could learn how to pace themselves. They would
guess more intelligently. (For a question with five choices, a
right answer is worth one point but a wrong answer results in
minus one-quarter of a point—which is why students were always warned that guessing was penalized. In reality, of
course, if a student can eliminate even one obviously wrong
possibility from the list of choices, guessing becomes an intelligent strategy.) The SAT was a test devised by a particular
institution, by a particular kind of person, operating from a
particular mindset. It had an ideology, and Kaplan realized
that anyone who understood that ideology would have a
tremendous advantage.

Critics of the SAT have long made a kind of parlor game of   10
seeing how many questions on the reading-comprehension
section (where a passage is followed by a series of multiple-
choice questions about its meaning) can be answered without

reading the passage. David Owen, in the anti-SAT account "None of the Above," gives the following example, adapted from an actual SAT exam:

1. The main idea of the passage is that:
   A) a constricted view of [this novel] is natural and acceptable
   B) a novel should not depict a vanished society
   C) a good novel is an intellectual rather than an emotional experience
   D) many readers have seen only the comedy [in this novel]
   E) [this novel] should be read with sensitivity and an open mind

If you've never seen an SAT before, it might be difficult to guess the right answer. But if, through practice and exposure, you have managed to assimilate the ideology of the SAT—the kind of decent, middlebrow earnestness that permeates the test—it's possible to develop a kind of gut feeling for the right answer, the confidence to predict, in the pressure and rush of examination time, what the SAT is looking for. A is suspiciously postmodern. B is far too dogmatic. C is something that you would never say to an eager, college-bound student. Is it D? Perhaps, but D seems too small a point. It's probably E—and sure enough, it is.

With that in mind, try this question:

2. The author of [this passage] implies that a work of art is properly judged on the basis of its:
   A) universality of human experience truthfully recorded
   B) popularity and critical acclaim in its own age
   C) openness to varied interpretations, including seemingly contradictory ones
   D) avoidance of political and social issues of minor importance
   E) continued popularity through different eras and with different societies

Is it any surprise that the answer is A? Bob Schaeffer, the public education director of the anti-test group FairTest, says that when he got a copy of the latest version of the SAT, the first thing he did was try the reading comprehension section blind. He got twelve out of thirteen questions right.

The math portion of the SAT is perhaps a better example ₁₃ of how coachable the test can be. Here is another question, cited by Owen, from an old SAT:

> *In how many different color combinations can 3 balls be painted if each ball is painted one color and there are 3 colors available? (Order is not considered; e.g. red, blue, red is considered the same combination as red, red, blue.)*
>   A) 4   B) 6   C) 9   D) 10   E) 27

This was, Owen points out, the twenty-fifth question in a ₁₄ twenty-five-question math section. SATs—like virtually all standardized tests—rank their math questions from easiest to hardest. If the hardest questions came first, the theory goes, weaker students would be so intimidated as they began the test that they might throw up their hands in despair. So this is a "hard" question. The second thing to understand about the SAT is that it only really works if good students get the hard questions right and poor students get the hard questions wrong. If anyone can guess or blunder his way into the right answer to a hard question, then the test isn't doing its job. So this is the second clue: the answer to this question must not be something that an average student might blunder into answering correctly. With these two facts in mind, Owen says, don't focus on the question. Just look at the numbers: there are three balls and three colors. The average student is most likely to guess by doing one of three things—adding three and three, multiplying three times three, or, if he is feeling more adventurous, multiplying three by three by three. So six, nine, and twenty-seven are out. That leaves four and ten. Now, he says, read the problem. It can't be four, since anyone can think of more than four combinations. The correct answer must be D, ten.

Does being able to answer that question mean that a stu-   15
dent has a greater "aptitude" for math? Of course not. It just
means that he had a clever teacher. Kaplan once determined
that the testmakers were fond of geometric problems involving the Pythagorean theorem. So an entire generation of
Kaplan students were taught "boo, boo, boo, square root of
two," to help them remember how the Pythagorean formula
applies to an isosceles right triangle. "It was usually not lack of
ability," Kaplan writes, "but poor study habits, inadequate instruction, or a combination of the two that jeopardized students' performance." The SAT was not an aptitude test at all.

In proving that the SAT was coachable, Stanley Kaplan did   16
something else, which was of even greater importance. He
undermined the use of aptitude tests as a means of social engineering. In the years immediately before and after World
War I, for instance, the country's elite colleges faced what became known as "the Jewish problem." They were being
inundated with the children of Eastern European Jewish
immigrants. These students came from the lower middle class
and they disrupted the genteel WASP sensibility that had
been so much a part of the Ivy League tradition. They were
guilty of "underliving and overworking." In the words of
one writer, they "worked far into each night [and] their lessons next morning were letter perfect." They were "socially
untrained," one Harvard professor wrote, "and their bodily
habits are not good." But how could a college keep Jews out?
Columbia University had a policy that the New York State
Regents Examinations—the statewide curriculum-based high
school graduation examination—could be used as the basis
for admission, and the plain truth was that Jews did extraordinarily well on the Regents Exams. One solution was simply
to put a quota on the number of Jews, which is what Harvard
explored. The other idea, which Columbia followed, was to
require applicants to take an aptitude test. According to
Herbert Hawkes, the dean of Columbia College during this period, because the typical Jewish student was simply a "grind,"
who excelled on the Regents Exams because he worked so

hard, a test of innate intelligence would put him back in his place. "We have not eliminated boys because they were Jews and do not propose to do so," Hawkes wrote in 1918.

> *We have honestly attempted to eliminate the lowest grade of applicant and it turns out that a good many of the low grade men are New York City Jews. It is a fact that boys of foreign parentage who have no back ground in many cases attempt to educate themselves beyond their intelligence. Their accomplishment is over 100 percent of their ability on account of their tremendous energy and ambition. I do not believe however that a College would do well to admit too many men of low mentality who have ambition but not brains.*

Today Hawkes's anti-Semitism seems absurd, but he was by no means the last person to look to aptitude tests as a means of separating ambition from brains. The great selling point of the SAT has always been that it promises to reveal whether the high school senior with a 3.0 GPA is someone who could have done much better if he had been properly educated or someone who is already at the limit of his abilities. We want to know that information because, like Hawkes, we prefer naturals to grinds: we think that people who achieve based on vast reserves of innate ability are somehow more promising and more worthy than those who simply work hard. 17

But is this distinction real? Some years ago, a group headed by the British psychologist John Sloboda conducted a study of musical talent. The group looked at 256 young musicians, between the ages of ten and sixteen, drawn from elite music academies and public school music programs alike. They interviewed all the students and their parents and recorded how each student did in England's national music-examination system, which, the researchers felt, gave them a relatively objective measure of musical ability. "What we found was that the best predictor of where you were on that 18 scale was the number of hours practiced," Sloboda says. This is, if you think about it, a little hard to believe. We conceive musical ability to be a "talent"—people have an aptitude for music—and so it would make sense that some number of students could excel at the music exam without practicing very much. Yet Sloboda couldn't find any. The kids who scored the best on the test were, on average, practicing *800 percent more* than the kids at the bottom. "People have this idea that there are those who learn better than others, can get further on less effort," Sloboda says. "On average, our data refuted that. Whether you're a dropout or at the best school, where you end up can be predicted by how much you practice."

Sloboda found another striking similarity among the "musical" children. They all had parents who were unusually invested in their musical education. It wasn't necessarily the case that the parents were themselves musicians or musically inclined. It was simply that they wanted their children to be that way. "The parents of the high achievers did things that most parents just don't do," he said. "They didn't simply drop their child at the door of the teacher. They went into the practice room. They took notes on what the teacher said, and when they got home they would say, Remember when your teacher said do this and that. There was a huge amount of time and motivational investment by the parents."   19

Does this mean that there is no such thing as musical talent? Of course not. Most of those hardworking children with pushy parents aren't going to turn out to be Itzhak Perlmans; some will be second violinists in their community orchestra. The point is that when it comes to a relatively well defined and structured task—like playing an instrument or taking an exam—how hard you work and how supportive your parents are have a lot more to do with success than we ordinarily imagine. Ability cannot be separated from effort. The test-makers never understood that, which is why they thought they could weed out the grinds. But educators increasingly do, and that is why college admissions are now in such upheaval. The Texas state university system, for example, has, since 1997, automatically admitted any student who places in   20 the top 10 percent of his or her high school class—regardless of SAT score. Critics of the policy said that it would open the door to students from marginal schools whose SAT scores would normally have been too low for admission to the University of Texas—and that is exactly what happened. But so what? The "top 10 percenters," as they are known, may have lower SAT scores, but they get excellent grades. In fact, their college GPAs are the equal of students who scored two hundred to three hundred points higher on the SAT. In other words, the determination and hard work that propel someone to the top of his high school class—even in cases where that high school is impoverished—are more important to succeeding in college (and, for that matter, in life) than whatever abstract quality the SAT purports to measure. The importance of the Texas experience cannot be overstated. Here, at last, is an intelligent alternative to affirmative action, a way to find successful minority students without sacrificing academic performance. But we would never have got this far without Stanley Kaplan—without someone first coming along and puncturing the mystique of the SAT. "Acquiring test-taking skills is the same as learning to play the piano or ride a bicycle," Kaplan writes. "It requires practice, practice, practice. Repetition breeds familiarity. Familiarity breeds confidence." In this, as in so many things, the grind *was* the natural.

To read Kaplan's memoir is to be struck by what a representative figure he was in the postwar sociological miracle that was Jewish Brooklyn. This is the lower-middle-class, second- and third-generation immigrant world, stretching from Prospect Park to Sheepshead Bay, that ended up peopling the upper reaches of American professional life. Thousands of students from those neighborhoods made their way through Kaplan's classroom in the fifties and sixties, many along what Kaplan calls the "heavily traveled path" from Brooklyn to Cornell, Yale, and the University of Michigan. Kaplan writes of one student who increased his score by 340 points and ended up with a Ph.D. and a position as a scientist at Xerox. "Debbie" improved her SAT by 500 points, got into the University of Chicago, and earned a Ph.D. in clinical psychology. Arthur Levine, the president of Teachers College at Columbia University, raised his SATs by 282 points, "making it possible," he writes on the book's jacket, "for me to attend a better university than I ever would have imagined." Charles Schumer, the senior senator from New York, studied while he worked the mimeograph machine in Kaplan's office, and ended up with close to a perfect 1600.

These students faced a system designed to thwart the hard 22
worker, and what did they do? They got together with their pushy parents and outworked it. Kaplan says that he knew a "strapping athlete who became physically ill before taking the SAT because his mother was so demanding." There was the mother who called him to say, "Mr. Kaplan, I think I'm going to commit suicide. My son made only one thousand on the SAT." "One mother wanted her straight-A son to have an extra edge, so she brought him to my basement for years for private tutoring in basic subjects," Kaplan recalls. "He was extremely bright and today is one of the country's most successful ophthalmologists." Another student was "so nervous that his mother accompanied him to class armed with a supply of terry-cloth towels. She stood outside the classroom, and when he emerged from our class sessions dripping in sweat, she wiped him dry and then nudged him back into the classroom." Then, of course, there was the formidable four-foot-eight figure of Ericka Kaplan, granddaughter of the chief rabbi of the synagogue of Prague. "My mother was a perfectionist whether she was keeping the company books or setting the dinner table," Kaplan writes, still in her thrall today. "She was my best cheerleader, the reason I performed so well, and I constantly strove to please her." What chance did even the most artfully constructed SAT have against the mothers of Brooklyn?

Stanley Kaplan graduated number two in his class at City 23
College and won the school's Award for Excellence in Natural Sciences. He wanted to be a doctor, and he applied to five medical schools, confident that he would be accepted. To his shock, he was rejected by every single one. Medical schools did not take public colleges like City College seriously. More

important, in the forties there was a limit to how many Jews they were willing to accept. "The term *meritocracy*—or success based on merit rather than heritage, wealth, or social status—wasn't even coined yet," Kaplan writes, "and the methods of selecting students based on talent, not privilege, were still evolving."

That's why Stanley Kaplan was always pained by those who   24
thought that what went on in his basement was somehow subversive. He loved the SAT. He thought that the test gave people like him the best chance of overcoming discrimination. As he saw it, he was simply giving the middle-class students of Brooklyn the same shot at a bright future that their counterparts in the private schools of Manhattan had. In 1983, after years of hostility, the College Board invited him to speak at its annual convention. It was one of the highlights of Kaplan's life. "Never, in my wildest dreams," he began, "did I ever think I'd be speaking to you here today."

The truth is, however, that Stanley Kaplan was wrong.   25
What he did in his basement *was* subversive. The SAT was designed as an abstract intellectual tool. It never occurred to its makers that aptitude was a social matter: that what people were capable of was affected by what they knew, and what they knew was affected by what they were taught, and what they were taught was affected by the industry of their teachers and parents. And if what the SAT was measuring, in no small part, was the industry of teachers and parents, then what did it mean? Stanley Kaplan may have loved the SAT. But when he stood up and recited "boo, boo, boo, square root of two," he killed it.

For Study and Discussion

QUESTIONS FOR RESPONSE

1. If you took the SAT tests to be admitted to college, how does your experience mesh with Gladwell's claim that one can often choose the right answer on the test without really understanding the problem?

2. Thinking about the high achievers you know in college and other enterprises, to what extent do you believe that hard work and application had more to do with their success than a natural intelligence?

QUESTIONS ABOUT PURPOSE

1. When Gladwell explains the methods Kaplan devised for coaching students for the SAT test, what kind of commonsense wisdom emerges about test taking?
2. What weaknesses about the admissions processes of many colleges does Gladwell bring out?

QUESTIONS ABOUT AUDIENCE

1. Most high school students who plan to go to college hear about the importance of the SAT tests by the time they're in the seventh or eighth grade. How does your experience with that knowledge affect your reading of this essay?
2. If you took a Kaplan course to raise your SAT scores to increase your competitive advantage for college admission, how do you think the coaching helped (or didn't help) you?

QUESTIONS ABOUT STRATEGIES

1. How does the list of very specific examples that Gladwell gives in the opening paragraph engage your interest and preview the thesis of the essay?
2. What is the intellectual and philosophical conflict that Gladwell establishes between Kaplan and the administrators of the Educational Testing Service?

QUESTIONS FOR DISCUSSION

1. Some critics say that Kaplan's coaching courses create their own kind of elite applicants: those whose parents can afford to pay for such courses. What kinds of issues does that possibility raise?
2. In the United States, tests created and administered by the Educational Testing Service—the GRE, MCAT, LSAT, and so on—act as major hurdles that any student must overcome to enter almost any professional school. Are such barriers useful or detrimental to students and to the graduate schools?

ERIC SCHLOSSER

Eric Schlosser is a correspondent for the *Atlantic* and author of the best-selling book *Fast Food Nation: The Dark Side of the All-American Meal* (2001). Schlosser lives in New York City and is currently at work on a book about the American prison system. After he published his essay "Why McDonald's Fries Taste So Good," Schlosser became a media celebrity—being interviewed on *60 Minutes,* NPR, and CNN. His disclosure that McDonald's fries tasted so good because they were fried in "beef tallow" caused Hindus to destroy McDonald's restaurants in India and vegetarians to file class action suits against McDonald's in America.

Why McDonald's Fries Taste So Good

T HE FRENCH FRY was "almost sacrosanct for me," Ray   1
Kroc, one of the founders of McDonald's, wrote in his autobiography, "its preparation a ritual to be followed religiously." During the chain's early years french fries were made from scratch every day. Russet Burbank potatoes were peeled, cut into shoestrings, and fried in McDonald's kitchens. As the chain expanded nationwide, in the mid-1960s, it sought to cut labor costs, reduce the number of suppliers, and ensure that its fries tasted the same at every restaurant. McDonald's began switching to frozen french fries in 1966—and few customers noticed the difference. Nevertheless, the change had a profound effect on the nation's agriculture and diet. A familiar food had been transformed into a highly processed industrial commodity. McDonald's fries now come from huge manufacturing plants

that can peel, slice, cook, and freeze 2 million pounds of potatoes a day. The rapid expansion of McDonald's and the popularity of its low-cost, mass-produced fries changed the way Americans eat. In 1960 Americans consumed an average of about eighty-one pounds of fresh potatoes and four pounds of frozen french fries. In 2000 they consumed an average of about fifty pounds of fresh potatoes and thirty

---

The rise and fall of corporate empires—of soft-drink companies, snack-food companies, and fast-food chains—is often determined by how their products taste.

---

pounds of frozen fries. Today McDonald's is the largest buyer of potatoes in the United States.

The taste of McDonald's french fries played a crucial role   2
in the chain's success—fries are much more profitable than hamburgers—and was long praised by customers, competitors, and even food critics. James Beard loved McDonald's fries. Their distinctive taste does not stem from the kind of potatoes that McDonald's buys, the technology that processes them, or the restaurant equipment that fries them: other chains use Russet Burbanks, buy their french fries from the same large processing companies, and have similar fryers in their restaurant kitchens. The taste of a french fry is largely determined by the cooking oil. For decades McDonald's cooked its french fries in a mixture of about 7 percent cottonseed oil and 93 percent beef tallow. The mixture gave the fries their unique flavor—and more saturated beef fat per ounce than a McDonald's hamburger.

In 1990, amid a barrage of criticism over the amount of   3
cholesterol in its fries, McDonald's switched to pure vegetable oil. This presented the company with a challenge: how to make fries that subtly taste like beef without cooking them

in beef tallow. A look at the ingredients in McDonald's french fries suggests how the problem was solved. Toward the end of the list is a seemingly innocuous yet oddly mysterious phrase: "natural flavor." That ingredient helps to explain not only why the fries taste so good but also why most fast food—indeed, most of the food Americans eat today—tastes the way it does.

Open your refrigerator, your freezer, your kitchen cupboards, and look at the labels on your food. You'll find "natural flavor" or "artificial flavor" in just about every list of ingredients. The similarities between these two broad categories are far more significant than the differences. Both are man-made additives that give most processed food most of its taste. People usually buy a food item the first time because of its packaging or appearance. Taste usually determines whether they buy it again. About 90 percent of the money that Americans now spend on food goes to buy processed food. The canning, freezing, and dehydrating techniques used in processing destroy most of food's flavor—and so a vast industry has arisen in the United States to make processed food palatable. Without this flavor industry today's fast food would not exist. The names of the leading American fast-food chains and their best-selling menu items have become embedded in our popular culture and famous worldwide. But few people can name the companies that manufacture fast food's taste.

The flavor industry is highly secretive. Its leading companies will not divulge the precise formulas of flavor compounds or the identities of clients. The secrecy is deemed essential for protecting the reputations of beloved brands. The fast-food chains, understandably, would like the public to believe that the flavors of the food they sell somehow originate in their restaurant kitchens, not in distant factories run by other firms. A McDonald's french fry is one of countless foods whose flavor is just a component in a complex manufacturing process. The look and the taste of what we eat now are frequently deceiving—by design.

The New Jersey Turnpike runs through the heart of the flavor industry, an industrial corridor dotted with refineries and chemical plants. International Flavors & Fragrances (IFF), the world's largest flavor company, has a manufacturing facility off Exit 8A in Dayton, New Jersey; Givaudan, the world's second-largest flavor company, has a plant in East Hanover. Haarmann & Reimer, the largest German flavor company, has a plant in Teterboro, as does Takasago, the largest Japanese flavor company. Flavor Dynamics has a plant in South Plainfield; Frutarom is in North Bergen; Elan Chemical is in Newark. Dozens of companies manufacture flavors in the corridor between Teaneck and South Brunswick. Altogether the area produces about two-thirds of the flavor additives sold in the United States.

The IFF plant in Dayton is a huge pale-blue building with a modern office complex attached to the front. It sits in an industrial park, not far from a BASF plastics factory, a Jolly French Toast factory, and a plant that manufactures Liz Claiborne cosmetics. Dozens of tractor-trailers were parked at the IFF loading dock the afternoon I visited, and a thin cloud of steam floated from a roof vent. Before entering the plant, I signed a nondisclosure form, promising not to reveal the brand names of foods that contain IFF flavors. The place reminded me of Willy Wonka's chocolate factory. Wonderful smells drifted through the hallways, men and women in neat white lab coats cheerfully went about their work, and hundreds of little glass bottles sat on laboratory tables and shelves. The bottles contained powerful but fragile flavor chemicals, shielded from light by brown glass and round white caps shut tight. The long chemical names on the little white labels were as mystifying to me as medieval Latin. These odd-sounding things would be mixed and poured and turned into new substances, like magic potions.

I was not invited into the manufacturing areas of the IFF plant, where, it was thought, I might discover trade secrets. Instead I toured various laboratories and pilot kitchens, where the flavors of well-established brands are tested or adjusted, and where whole new flavors are created. IFF's snack-and-savory lab is responsible for the flavors of potato chips, corn chips, breads, crackers, breakfast cereals, and pet food.

The confectionery lab devises flavors for ice cream, cookies, candies, toothpastes, mouthwashes, and antacids. Everywhere I looked, I saw famous, widely advertised products sitting on laboratory desks and tables. The beverage lab was full of brightly colored liquids in clear bottles. It comes up with flavors for popular soft drinks, sports drinks, bottled teas, and wine coolers, for all-natural juice drinks, organic soy drinks, beers, and malt liquors. In one pilot kitchen I saw a dapper food technologist, a middle-aged man with an elegant tie beneath his crisp lab coat, carefully preparing a batch of cookies with white frosting and pink-and-white sprinkles. In another pilot kitchen I saw a pizza oven, a grill, a milk-shake machine, and a french fryer identical to those I'd seen at innumerable fast-food restaurants.

In addition to being the world's largest flavor company, IFF   9 manufactures the smells of six of the ten best-selling fine perfumes in the United States, including Estée Lauder's Beautiful, Clinique's Happy, Lancôme's Trésor, and Calvin Klein's Eternity. It also makes the smells of household products such as deodorant, dishwashing detergent, bath soap, shampoo, furniture polish, and floor wax. All these aromas are made through essentially the same process: the manipulation of volatile chemicals. The basic science behind the scent of your shaving cream is the same as that governing the flavor of your TV dinner.

Scientists now believe that human beings acquired the sense   10 of taste as a way to avoid being poisoned. Edible plants generally taste sweet, harmful ones bitter. The taste buds on our tongues can detect the presence of half a dozen or so basic tastes, including sweet, sour, bitter, salty, astringent, and umami, a taste discovered by Japanese researchers—a rich and full sense of deliciousness triggered by amino acids in foods such as meat, shellfish, mushrooms, potatoes, and seaweed. Taste buds offer a limited means of detection, however, compared with the human olfactory system, which can perceive thousands of different chemical aromas. Indeed, "flavor" is primarily the smell of gases being released by the chemicals you've just put in your mouth. The aroma of a food can be responsible for as much as 90 percent of its taste.

The act of drinking, sucking, or chewing a substance re- 11
leases its volatile gases. They flow out of your mouth and up
your nostrils, or up the passageway in the back of your
mouth, to a thin layer of nerve cells called the olfactory epithelium, located at the base of your nose, right between your
eyes. Your brain combines the complex smell signals from
your olfactory epithelium with the simple taste signals from
your tongue, assigns a flavor to what's in your mouth, and
decides if it's something you want to eat.

A person's food preferences, like his or her personality, are 12
formed during the first few years of life, through a process of
socialization. Babies innately prefer sweet tastes and reject
bitter ones; toddlers can learn to enjoy hot and spicy food,
bland health food, or fast food, depending on what the people around them eat. The human sense of smell is still not
fully understood. It is greatly affected by psychological factors and expectations. The mind focuses intently on some of
the aromas that surround us and filters out the overwhelming
majority. People can grow accustomed to bad smells or good
smells; they stop noticing what once seemed overpowering.
Aroma and memory are somehow inextricably linked. A
smell can suddenly evoke a long-forgotten moment. The flavors of childhood foods seem to leave an indelible mark, and
adults often return to them, without always knowing why.
These "comfort foods" become a source of pleasure and
reassurance—a fact that fast-food chains use to their advantage. Childhood memories of Happy Meals, which come
with french fries, can translate into frequent adult visits to
McDonald's. On average, Americans now eat about four
servings of french fries every week.

The human craving for flavor has been a largely unac- 13
knowledged and unexamined force in history. For millennia
royal empires have been built, unexplored lands traversed,
and great religions and philosophies forever changed by
the spice trade. In 1492 Christopher Columbus set sail to
find seasoning. Today the influence of flavor in the world
marketplace is no less decisive. The rise and fall of corporate
empires—of soft-drink companies, snack-food companies,

and fast-food chains—is often determined by how their products taste.

The flavor industry emerged in the mid-nineteenth cen-   14
tury, as processed foods began to be manufactured on a large scale. Recognizing the need for flavor additives, early food processors turned to perfume companies that had long experience working with essential oils and volatile aromas. The great perfume houses of England, France, and the Netherlands produced many of the first flavor compounds. In the early part of the twentieth century Germany took the technological lead in flavor production, owing to its powerful chemical industry. Legend has it that a German scientist discovered methyl anthranilate, one of the first artificial flavors, by accident while mixing chemicals in his laboratory. Suddenly the lab was filled with the sweet smell of grapes. Methyl anthranilate later became the chief flavor compound in grape Kool-Aid. After World War II much of the perfume industry shifted from Europe to the United States, settling in New York City near the garment district and the fashion houses. The flavor industry came with it, later moving to New Jersey for greater plant capacity. Man-made flavor additives were used mostly in baked goods, candies, and sodas until the 1950s, when sales of processed food began to soar. The invention of gas chromatographs and mass spectrometers— machines capable of detecting volatile gases at low levels— vastly increased the number of flavors that could be synthesized. By the mid-1960s flavor companies were churning out compounds to supply the taste of Pop Tarts, Bac-Os, Tab, Tang, Filet-O-Fish sandwiches, and literally thousands of other new foods.

The American flavor industry now has annual revenues of   15
about $1.4 billion. Approximately ten thousand new processed-food products are introduced every year in the United States. Almost all of them require flavor additives. And about nine out of ten of these products fail. The latest flavor innovations and corporate realignments are heralded in publications such as *Chemical Market Reporter, Food Chemical News, Food Engineering,* and *Food Product Design.* The

progress of IFF has mirrored that of the flavor industry as a whole. IFF was formed in 1958, through the merger of two small companies. Its annual revenues have grown almost fifteenfold since the early 1970s, and it currently has manufacturing facilities in twenty countries.

Today's sophisticated spectrometers, gas chromatographs, and headspace-vapor analyzers provide a detailed map of a food's flavor components, detecting chemical aromas present in amounts as low as one part per billion. The human nose, however, is even more sensitive. A nose can detect aromas present in quantities of a few parts per trillion—an amount equivalent to about 0.000000000003 percent. Complex aromas, such as those of coffee and roasted meat, are composed of volatile gases from nearly a thousand different chemicals. The smell of a strawberry arises from the interaction of about 350 chemicals that are present in minute amounts. The quality that people seek most of all in a food—flavor—is usually present in a quantity too infinitesimal to be measured in traditional culinary terms such as ounces or teaspoons. The chemical that provides the dominant flavor of bell pepper can be tasted in amounts as low as 0.02 parts per billion; one drop is sufficient to add flavor to five average-size swimming pools. The flavor additive usually comes next to last in a processed food's list of ingredients and often costs less than its packaging. Soft drinks contain a larger proportion of flavor additives than most products. The flavor in a twelve-ounce can of Coke costs about half a cent. 16

The color additives in processed foods are usually present in even smaller amounts than the flavor compounds. Many of New Jersey's flavor companies also manufacture these color additives, which are used to make processed foods look fresh and appealing. Food coloring serves many of the same decorative purposes as lipstick, eye shadow, mascara—and is often made from the same pigments. Titanium dioxide, for example, has proved to be an especially versatile mineral. It gives many processed candies, frostings, and icings their bright white color; it is a common ingredient in women's cosmetics; and it 17 is the pigment used in many white oil paints and house paints. At Burger King, Wendy's, and McDonald's coloring agents have been added to many of the soft drinks, salad dressings, cookies, condiments, chicken dishes, and sandwich buns.

Studies have found that the color of a food can greatly af-   18
fect how its taste is perceived. Brightly colored foods frequently seem to taste better than bland-looking foods, even when the flavor compounds are identical. Foods that somehow look off-color often seem to have off tastes. For thousands of years human beings have relied on visual cues to help determine what is edible. The color of fruit suggests whether it is ripe, the color of meat whether it is rancid. Flavor researchers sometimes use colored lights to modify the influence of visual cues during taste tests. During one experiment in the early 1970s people were served an oddly tinted meal of steak and french fries that appeared normal beneath colored lights. Everyone thought the meal tasted fine until the lighting was changed. Once it became apparent that the steak was actually blue and the fries were green, some people became ill.

The federal Food and Drug Administration does not re-   19
quire companies to disclose the ingredients of their color or flavor additives so long as all the chemicals in them are considered by the agency to be GRAS ("generally recognized as safe"). This enables companies to maintain the secrecy of their formulas. It also hides the fact that flavor compounds often contain more ingredients than the foods to which they give taste. The phrase "artificial strawberry flavor" gives little hint of the chemical wizardry and manufacturing skill that can make a highly processed food taste like strawberries.

A typical artificial strawberry flavor, like the kind found in   20
a Burger King strawberry milk shake, contains the following ingredients: amyl acetate, amyl butyrate, amyl valerate, anethol, anisyl formate, benzyl acetate, benzyl isobutyrate, butyric acid, cinnamyl isobutyrate, cinnamyl valerate, cognac essential oil, diacetyl, dipropyl ketone, ethyl acetate, ethyl amyl ketone, ethyl butyrate, ethyl cinnamate, ethyl heptanoate, ethyl heptylate, ethyl lactate, ethyl methylphenylglycidate, ethyl nitrate, ethyl propionate, ethyl valerate,

heliotropin, hydroxyphenyl-2-butanone (10 percent solution in alcohol), α-ionone, isobutyl anthranilate, isobutyl butyrate, lemon essential oil, maltol, 4-methylacetophenone, methyl anthranilate, methyl benzoate, methyl cinnamate, methyl heptine carbonate, methyl naphthyl ketone, methyl salicylate, mint essential oil, neroli essential oil, nerolin, neryl isobutyrate, orris butter, phenethyl alcohol, rose, rum ether, γ-undecalactone, vanillin, and solvent.

Although flavors usually arise from a mixture of many different volatile chemicals, often a single compound supplies the dominant aroma. Smelled alone, that chemical provides an unmistakable sense of the food. Ethyl-2-methyl butyrate, for example, smells just like an apple. Many of today's highly processed foods offer a blank palette: whatever chemicals are added to them will give them specific tastes. Adding methyl-2-pyridyl ketone makes something taste like popcorn. Adding ethyl-3-hydroxy butanoate makes it taste like marshmallow. The possibilities are now almost limitless. Without affecting appearance or nutritional value, processed foods could be made with aroma chemicals such as hexanal (the smell of freshly cut grass) or 3-methyl butanoic acid (the smell of body odor). 21

The 1960s were the heyday of artificial flavors in the United States. The synthetic versions of flavor compounds were not subtle, but they did not have to be, given the nature of most processed food. For the past twenty years food processors have tried hard to use only "natural flavors" in their products. According to the FDA, these must be derived entirely from natural sources—from herbs, spices, fruits, vegetables, beef, chicken, yeast, bark, roots, and so forth. Consumers prefer to see natural flavors on a label, out of a belief that they are more healthful. Distinctions between artificial and natural flavors can be arbitrary and somewhat absurd, based more on how the flavor has been made than on what it actually contains. 22

"A natural flavor," says Terry Acree, a professor of food science at Cornell University, "is a flavor that's been derived with an out-of-date technology." Natural flavors and artificial 23 flavors sometimes contain exactly the same chemicals, produced through different methods. Amyl acetate, for example, provides the dominant note of banana flavor. When it is distilled from bananas with a solvent, amyl acetate is a natural flavor. When it is produced by mixing vinegar with amyl alcohol and adding sulfuric acid as a catalyst, amyl acetate is an artificial flavor. Either way it smells and tastes the same. "Natural flavor" is now listed among the ingredients of everything from Health Valley Blueberry Granola Bars to Taco Bell Hot Taco Sauce.

A natural flavor is not necessarily more healthful or purer   24
than an artificial one. When almond flavor—benzaldehyde—is derived from natural sources, such as peach and apricot pits, it contains traces of hydrogen cyanide, a deadly poison. Benzaldehyde derived by mixing oil of clove and amyl acetate does not contain any cyanide. Nevertheless, it is legally considered an artificial flavor and sells at a much lower price. Natural and artificial flavors are now manufactured at the same chemical plants, places that few people would associate with Mother Nature.

The small and elite group of scientists who create most of the   25
flavor in most of the food now consumed in the United States are called "flavorists." They draw on a number of disciplines in their work: biology, psychology, physiology, and organic chemistry. A flavorist is a chemist with a trained nose and a poetic sensibility. Flavors are created by blending scores of different chemicals in tiny amounts—a process governed by scientific principles but demanding a fair amount of art. In an age when delicate aromas and microwave ovens do not easily coexist, the job of the flavorist is to conjure illusions about processed food and, in the words of one flavor company's literature, to ensure "consumer likeability." The flavorists with whom I spoke were discreet, in keeping with the dictates of their trade. They were also charming, cosmopolitan, and ironic. They not only enjoyed fine wine but could identify the chemicals that give each grape its unique aroma. One flavorist compared his work to composing music. A well-made flavor compound will have a "top note" that is often followed by a "dry-down" and a "leveling-off," with

different chemicals responsible for each stage. The taste of a food can be radically altered by minute changes in the flavoring combination. "A little odor goes a long way," one flavorist told me.

In order to give a processed food a taste that consumers will find appealing, a flavorist must always consider the food's "mouthfeel"—the unique combination of textures and chemical interactions that affect how the flavor is perceived. Mouthfeel can be adjusted through the use of various fats, gums, starches, emulsifiers, and stabilizers. The aroma chemicals in a food can be precisely analyzed, but the elements that make up mouthfeel are much harder to measure. How does one quantify a pretzel's hardness, a french fry's crispness? Food technologists are now conducting basic research in rheology, the branch of physics that examines the flow and deformation of materials. A number of companies sell sophisticated devices that attempt to measure mouthfeel. The TA.XT2i Texture Analyzer, produced by the Texture Technologies Corporation, of Scarsdale, New York, performs calculations based on data derived from as many as 250 separate probes. It is essentially a mechanical mouth. It gauges the most important rheological properties of a food—bounce, creep, breaking point, density, crunchiness, chewiness, gumminess, lumpiness, rubberiness, springiness, slipperiness, smoothness, softness, wetness, juiciness, spreadability, springback, and tackiness. 26

Some of the most important advances in flavor manufacturing are now occurring in the field of biotechnology. Complex flavors are being made using enzyme reactions, fermentation, and fungal and tissue cultures. All the flavors created by these methods—including the ones being synthesized by fungi—are considered natural flavors by the FDA. The new enzyme-based processes are responsible for extremely true-to-life dairy flavors. One company now offers not just butter flavor but also fresh creamy butter, cheesy butter, milky butter, savory melted butter, and super-concentrated butter flavor, in liquid or powder form. The development of new fermentation techniques, along with new techniques for 27 heating mixtures of sugar and amino acids, have led to the creation of much more realistic meat flavors.

The McDonald's Corporation most likely drew on these   28
advances when it eliminated beef tallow from its french fries. The company will not reveal the exact origin of the natural flavor added to its fries. In response to inquiries from *Vegetarian Journal*, however, McDonald's did acknowledge that its fries derive some of their characteristic flavor from "an animal source." Beef is the probable source, although other meats cannot be ruled out. In France, for example, fries are sometimes cooked in duck fat or horse tallow.

Other popular fast foods derive their flavor from unex-   29
pected ingredients. McDonald's Chicken McNuggets contain beef extracts, as does Wendy's Grilled Chicken Sandwich. Burger King's BK Broiler Chicken Breast Patty contains "natural smoke flavor." A firm called Red Arrow Products specializes in smoke flavor, which is added to barbecue sauces, snack foods, and processed meats. Red Arrow manufactures natural smoke flavor by charring sawdust and capturing the aroma chemicals released into the air. The smoke is captured in water and then bottled, so that other companies can sell food that seems to have been cooked over a fire.

The Vegetarian Legal Action Network recently petitioned   30
the FDA to issue new labeling requirements for foods that contain natural flavors. The group wants food processors to list the basic origins of their flavors on their labels. At the moment vegetarians often have no way of knowing whether a flavor additive contains beef, pork, poultry, or shellfish. One of the most widely used color additives—whose presence is often hidden by the phrase "color added"—violates a number of religious dietary restrictions, may cause allergic reactions in susceptible people, and comes from an unusual source. Cochineal extract (also known as carmine or carminic acid) is made from the desiccated bodies of female *Dactylopius coccus Costa,* a small insect harvested mainly in Peru and the Canary Islands. The bug feeds on red cactus berries, and color from the berries accumulates in the females and their unhatched larvae. The insects are collected, dried, and ground into a pigment. It takes about seventy thousand of them to produce a pound of

carmine, which is used to make processed foods look pink, red, or purple. Dannon strawberry yogurt gets its color from carmine, and so do many frozen fruit bars, candies, and fruit fillings, and Ocean Spray pink-grapefruit juice drink.

In a meeting room at IFF, Brian Grainger let me sample some of the company's flavors. It was an unusual taste test—there was no food to taste. Grainger is a senior flavorist at IFF, a soft-spoken chemist with graying hair, an English accent, and a fondness for understatement. He could easily be mistaken for a British diplomat or the owner of a West End brasserie with two Michelin stars. Like many in the flavor industry, he has an Old World, old-fashioned sensibility. When I suggested that IFF's policy of secrecy and discretion was out of step with our mass-marketing, brand-conscious, self-promoting age, and that the company should put its own logo on the countless products that bear its flavors, instead of allowing other companies to enjoy the consumer loyalty and affection inspired by those flavors, Granger politely disagreed, assuring me that such a thing would never be done. In the absence of public credit or acclaim, the small and secretive fraternity of flavor chemists praise one another's work. By analyzing the flavor formula of a product, Grainger can often tell which of his counterparts at a rival firm devised it. Whenever he walks down a supermarket aisle, he takes a quiet pleasure in seeing the well-known foods that contain his flavors.

Grainger had brought a dozen small glass bottles from the lab. After he opened each bottle, I dipped a fragrance-testing filter into it—a long white strip of paper designed to absorb aroma chemicals without producing off notes. Before placing each strip of paper in front of my nose, I closed my eyes. Then I inhaled deeply, and one food after another was conjured from the glass bottles. I smelled fresh cherries, black olives, sautéed onions, and shrimp. Grainger's most remarkable creation took me by surprise. After closing my eyes, I suddenly smelled a grilled hamburger. The aroma was uncanny, almost miraculous—as if someone in the room were flipping burgers on a hot grill. But when I opened my eyes, I saw just a narrow strip of white paper and a flavorist with a grin.

For Study and Discussion

QUESTIONS FOR RESPONSE

1. What are some of the implications of the changes in American eating habits that Schlosser describes in his opening paragraph?
2. What is your personal reaction to learning so much about the way our food in the United States is processed and flavored?

QUESTIONS ABOUT PURPOSE

1. This essay is a chapter from Schlosser's book *Fast Food Nation*. What purpose do you think he might have had in writing a book with that title?
2. Why does he want his readers to know more about the way large food corporations flavor processed food?

QUESTIONS ABOUT AUDIENCE

1. What experience with fast food does Schlosser assume most Americans have? How justified are his assumptions?
2. This essay first appeared in the *Atlantic,* a magazine with a relatively small circulation drawn from well-educated readers, and then appeared in book form. Why could readers like that be important for Schlosser to reach?

QUESTIONS ABOUT STRATEGIES

1. What do you think Schlosser accomplishes by using statistics (paragraphs 1 and 16) and lists (paragraphs 8, 17, and 20) to develop his explanations about how food flavors are created?
2. What does Schlosser tell you about his research and his methods in order to establish his credibility?

QUESTIONS FOR DISCUSSION

1. What do you think might be some of the consequences of ingesting the multiple chemicals that food companies use to make their products appeal to customers?
2. How could the practices Schlosser described be controlled? Should they be? Why or why not?

ARTHUR C. CLARKE

Arthur C. Clarke was born in 1917 in Somerset, England. Although he was interested in science at an early age, building his first telescope at the age of thirteen, he could not afford a formal university education. He went to work for the British Civil Service as an auditor and became treasurer for the British Interplanetary Society. During World War II, he was a radar specialist with the Royal Air Force. After the war he received educational assistance and entered King's College, University of London, where in two years he graduated with honorary degrees in math and physics. He worked briefly as an editor for *Science Abstracts* but soon devoted his full attention to his lifetime vocation, writing about science. His nonfiction publications, such as *Interplanetary Flight* (1950), *The Exploration of Space* (1951), and *The Making of a Moon* (1957), explain space travel, but his science fiction is concerned with the complex effect of such travel on human emotions and values. His novels include *The Sounds of Mars* (1951) and *Rendezvous with Rama* (1974); and his screenplay for Stanley Kubrick's *2001: A Space Odyssey* is considered a classic. In "The Star," reprinted from *The Nine Billion Names of God* (1955), a Jesuit astronomer tells of a space journey that challenges his faith in God.

The Star

I T IS THREE thousand light-years to the Vatican. Once, I   1
believed that space could have no power over faith, just as I believed that the heavens declared the glory of God's

handiwork. Now I have seen that handiwork, and my faith is sorely troubled. I stare at the crucifix that hangs on the cabin wall above the Mark VI Computer, and for the first time in my life I wonder if it is no more than an empty symbol.

I have told no one yet, but the truth cannot be concealed. The facts are there for all to read, recorded on the countless miles of magnetic tape and the thousands of photographs we are carrying back to Earth. Other scientists can interpret them as easily as I can, and I am not one who would condone that tampering with the truth which often gave my order a bad name in the olden days.

The crew were already sufficiently depressed: I wonder how they will take this ultimate irony. Few of them have any religious faith, yet they will not relish using this final weapon in their campaign against me—that private, good-natured, but fundamentally serious war which lasted all the way from Earth. It amused them to have a Jesuit as chief astrophysicist: Dr. Chandler, for instance, could never get over it. (Why are medical men such notorious atheists?) Sometimes he would meet me on the observation deck, where the lights are always low so that the stars shine with undiminished glory. He would come up to me in the gloom and stand staring out of the great oval port, while the heavens crawled slowly around us as the ship turned end over end with the residual spin we had never bothered to correct.

"Well, Father," he would say at last, "it goes on forever and forever, and perhaps *Something* made it. But how you can believe that Something has a special interest in us and our miserable little world—that just beats me." Then the argument would start, while the stars and nebulae would swing around us in silent, endless arcs beyond the flawlessly clear plastic of the observation port.

It was, I think, the apparent incongruity of my position that caused most amusement to the crew. In vain I would point to my three papers in the *Astrophysical Journal,* my five in the *Monthly Notices of the Royal Astronomical Society.* I would remind them that my order has long been famous for its scientific works. We may be few now, but ever since the eighteenth century we have made contributions to astronomy and geophysics out of all proportion to our numbers. Will my report on the Phoenix Nebula end our thousand years of history? It will end, I fear, much more than that.

I do not know who gave the nebula its name, which seems   6
to me a very bad one. If it contains a prophecy, it is one that cannot be verified for several billion years. Even the word "nebula" is misleading: this is a far smaller object than those stupendous clouds of mist—the stuff of unborn stars—that are scattered throughout the length of the Milky Way. On the cosmic scale, indeed, the Phoenix Nebula is a tiny thing—a tenuous shell of gas surrounding a single star.

Or what is left of a star . . .   7

The Rubens engraving of Loyola seems to mock me as it   8
hangs there above the spectrophotometer tracings. What would *you*, Father, have made of this knowledge that has come into my keeping, so far from the little world that was all the Universe you knew? Would your faith have risen to the challenge, as mine has failed to do?

You gaze into the distance, Father, but I have traveled a   9
distance beyond any that you could have imagined when you founded our order a thousand years ago. No other survey ship has been so far from Earth: we are at the very frontiers of the explored Universe. We set out to reach the Phoenix Nebula, we succeeded, and we are homeward bound with our burden of knowledge. I wish I could lift that burden from my shoulders, but I call to you in vain across the centuries and the light-years that lie between us.

On the book you are holding the words are plain to read.   10
AD MAIOREM DEI GLORIAM, the message runs, but it is a message I can no longer believe. Would you still believe it, if you could see what we have found?

We knew, of course, what the Phoenix Nebula was. Every   11
year, in our Galaxy alone, more than a hundred stars explode, blazing for a few hours or days with thousands of times their normal brilliance before they sink back into death and obscurity. Such are the ordinary novae—the commonplace disasters of the Universe. I have recorded the spectrograms and

light curves of dozens since I started working at the Lunar Observatory.

But three or four times in every thousand years occurs   12
something beside which even a nova pales into total insignificance.

When a star becomes a *supernova,* it may for a little while   13
outshine all the massed suns of the Galaxy. The Chinese astronomers watched this happen in A.D. 1054, not knowing what it was they saw. Five centuries later, in 1572, a supernova blazed in Cassiopeia so brilliantly that it was visible in the daylight sky. There have been three more in the thousand years that have passed since then.

Our mission was to visit the remnants of such a catastrophe,   14
to reconstruct the events that led up to it, and, if possible, to learn its cause. We came slowly in through the concentric shells of gas that had been blasted out six thousand years before, yet were expanding still. They were immensely hot, radiating even now with a fierce violet light, but were far too tenuous to do us any damage. When the star had exploded, its outer layers had been driven upward with such speed that they had escaped completely from its gravitational field. Now they formed a hollow shell large enough to engulf a thousand solar systems, and at its center burned the tiny, fantastic object which the star had now become—a White Dwarf, smaller than the Earth, yet weighing a million times as much.

The glowing gas shells were all around us, banishing the   15
normal night of interstellar space. We were flying into the center of the cosmic bomb that had detonated millennia ago and whose incandescent fragments were still hurtling apart. The immense scale of the explosion, and the fact that the debris already covered a volume of space many billions of miles across, robbed the scene of any visible movement. It would take decades before the unaided eye could detect any motion in these tortured wisps and eddies of gas, yet the sense of turbulent expansion was overwhelming.

We had checked our primary drive hours before, and were   16
drifting slowly toward the fierce little star ahead. Once it had been a sun like our own, but it had squandered in a few hours

the energy that should have kept it shining for a million years. Now it was a shrunken miser, hoarding its resources as if trying to make amends for its prodigal youth.

No one seriously expected to find planets. If there had been any before the explosion, they would have been boiled into puffs of vapor, and their substance lost in the greater wreckage of the star itself. But we made the automatic search, as we always do when approaching an unknown sun, and presently we found a single small world circling the star at an immense distance. It must have been the Pluto of this vanished Solar System, orbiting on the frontiers of the night. Too far from the central sun ever to have known life, its remoteness had saved it from the fate of all its lost companions.

The passing fires had seared its rocks and burned away the mantle of frozen gas that must have covered it in the days before the disaster. We landed, and we found the Vault.

Its builders had made sure that we should. The monolithic marker that stood above the entrance was now a fused stump, but even the first long-range photographs told us that here was the work of intelligence. A little later we detected the continent-wide pattern of radioactivity that had been buried in the rock. Even if the pylon above the vault had been destroyed, this would have remained, an immovable and all but eternal beacon calling to the stars. Our ship fell toward this gigantic bull's-eye like an arrow into its target.

The pylon must have been a mile high when it was built, but now it looked like a candle that had melted down into a puddle of wax. It took us a week to drill through the fused rock, since we did not have the proper tools for a task like this. We were astronomers, not archaeologists, but we could improvise. Our original purpose was forgotten: this lonely monument, reared with such labor at the greatest possible distance from the doomed sun, could have only one meaning. A civilization that knew it was about to die had made its last bid for immortality.

It will take us generations to examine all the treasures that were placed in the Vault. They had plenty of time to prepare, for their sun must have given its first warnings many years before the final detonation. Everything that they wished to preserve, all the fruit of their genius, they brought here to this distant world in the days before the end, hoping that some other race would find it and that they would not be utterly forgotten. Would we have done as well, or would we have been too lost in our own misery to give thought to a future we could never see or share?

If only they had had a little more time! They could travel freely enough between the planets of their own sun, but they had not yet learned to cross the interstellar gulfs, and the nearest Solar System was a hundred light-years away. Yet even had they possessed the secret of the Transfinite Drive, no more than a few millions could have been saved. Perhaps it was better thus.   22

Even if they had not been so disturbingly human as their sculpture shows, we could not have helped admiring them and grieving for their fate. They left thousands of visual records and the machines for projecting them, together with elaborate pictorial instructions from which it will not be difficult to learn their written language. We have examined many of these records, and brought to life for the first time in six thousand years the warmth and beauty of a civilization that in many ways must have been superior to our own. Perhaps they only showed us the best, and one can hardly blame them. But their worlds were very lovely, and their cities were built with a grace that matches anything of man's. We have watched them at work and play, and listened to their musical speech sounding across the centuries. One scene is still before my eyes—a group of children on a beach of strange blue sand, playing in the waves as children play on Earth. Curious whiplike trees line the shore, and some very large animal is wading in the shallows yet attracting no attention at all.   23

And sinking into the sea, still warm and friendly and life-giving, is the sun that will soon turn traitor and obliterate all this innocent happiness.   24

Perhaps if we had not been so far from home and so vulnerable to loneliness, we should not have been so deeply moved. Many of us had seen the ruins of ancient civilizations on other worlds, but they had never affected us so   25 profoundly. This tragedy was unique. It is one thing for a race to fail and die, as nations and cultures have done on Earth. But to be destroyed so completely in the full flower of its achievement, leaving no survivors—how could that be reconciled with the mercy of God?

My colleagues have asked me that, and I have given what answers I can. Perhaps you could have done better, Father Loyola, but I have found nothing in the *Exercitia Spiritualia* that helps me here. They were not an evil people: I do not know what gods they worshiped, if indeed they worshiped any. But I have looked back at them across the centuries, and have watched while the loveliness they used their last strength to preserve was brought forth again into the light of their shrunken sun. They could have taught us much: why were they destroyed? 26

I know the answers that my colleagues will give when they get back to Earth. They will say that the Universe has no purpose and no plan, that since a hundred suns explode every year in our Galaxy, at this very moment some race is dying in the depths of space. Whether that race has done good or evil during its lifetime will make no difference in the end: there is no divine justice, for there is no God. 27

Yet, of course, what we have seen proves nothing of the sort. Anyone who argues thus is being swayed by emotion, not logic. God has no need to justify His actions to man. He who built the Universe can destroy it when He chooses. It is arrogance—it is perilously near blasphemy—for us to say what He may or may not do. 28

This I could have accepted, hard though it is to look upon whole worlds and peoples thrown into the furnace. But there comes a point when even the deepest faith must falter, and now, as I look at the calculations lying before me, I know I have reached that point at last. 29

We could not tell, before we reached the nebula, how long ago the explosion took place. Now, from the astronomical evidence and the record in the rocks of that one surviving planet, I have been able to date it very exactly. I know in what year the light of this colossal conflagration reached our Earth. 30

I know how brilliantly the supernova whose corpse now dwindles behind our speeding ship once shone in terrestrial skies. I know how it must have blazed low in the east before sunrise, like a beacon in that oriental dawn.

There can be no reasonable doubt: the ancient mystery is solved at last. Yet, oh God, there were so many stars you could have used. What was the need to give these people to the fire, that the symbol of their passing might shine above Bethlehem? 31

COMMENT ON "THE STAR"

The distressed narrator of this story is a Jesuit scientist who, on the basis of evidence that he cannot refute professionally or ethically, finds himself forced to acknowledge a scientific discovery that he fears may destroy his religious faith, the rock of his very existence. Two arguments are going on in the story. The first is a vocal one between the Jesuit and the crew, particularly a medical doctor who represents the traditional scientific view that, although there may be order in the universe, there is no God who takes a special interest in the affairs of humans. The Jesuit represents the argument for faith in God and His concern for humankind. The second argument is the silent one that the Jesuit astrophysicist has seen building as his spaceship penetrated the outer reaches of space to investigate the origins of the Phoenix Nebula. He collects evidence from three sources: from the interstellar space debris that testifies to the explosion of a supernova; from irrefutable evidence left purposefully by a superior, cultured civilization that flourished on a lost planet several thousand years before; and finally, from the evidence that allows him to calculate the date of the explosion that destroyed that planet. When he puts all the pieces together, the Jesuit sees the conclusion of the second argument. Ironically, it destroys the first argument but almost destroys the Jesuit also. God does indeed take special interest in the affairs of humans; the proof is that the date of the supernova that destroyed the beautiful lost civilization coincides precisely with the Star of Bethlehem announcing the birth of Jesus.

Cause and Effect as a Writing Strategy

1. Jonathan Kozol has a sweeping topic in his essay "The Human Cost of Illiteracy," but you could write on a similar topic that illustrates how literacy changed your life. For example, if you're a returning student who has come late to computers, you could write about how computers have changed your life. If LASIK surgery freed you from having to wear glasses, you could write about how that operation changed your life. If you have moved to the United States from another, very different culture, you could write about a specific way in which that move has changed your life. You could also pick out some significant way in which your life has changed in recent years and, with the help of your instructor and your fellow students, work out a closely focused topic of this kind. Your audience could be your classmates, a chat room, or the newsletter of an organization you belong to.

2. In the last year or two, many newspaper and magazine articles, two or three books (such as Schlosser's *Fast Food Nation*), and a film (*Super Size Me*) about the food industry have appeared. In them the authors have cited the rising rates of obesity in the United States, pointing out the health risks the trend poses and the likely consequences for future generations. Write an essay about the menus and ambience of some of the restaurants you and your friends frequent near your campus or in your hometown that feature high-calorie food and drinks, many of which contain the flavor-enhancing chemicals Schlosser describes in "Why McDonald's Fries Taste So Good." Do these restaurants *cause* obesity? What do you think the effect would be if they were required to list the number of calories in each item on their menus? Would such a requirement be justified? You could write this essay for the college newspaper or post it on a blog to which you contribute. Give it some flavor-enhancing details.

3. Pick out some fairly recent innovation that you've incorporated into your life, and write about the effects it has had on your day-to-day routine. Some examples might be a global positioning system either for your car or as a locating device in some outdoor activity, a DVD player (portable or at home), a wireless laptop computer, a cell phone with a visual screen, or a top-of-the-line digital camera. What have been the effects for you? Have there been drawbacks, such as difficult instructions or trouble keeping the batteries charged? What would you say is your net satisfaction from having purchased this device? Write for an audience of other owners of the device, either among your classmates or for a chat room.

4. Write an essay for your classmates telling why you have chosen the profession you currently plan to go into. What are your reasons? Why do you think it will be rewarding? What caused you to choose this profession? Whom do you know in the profession, and how have their experiences affected your choice? What kind of training and education will be necessary, and what sacrifices, both financial and personal, might be involved? What kind of conflicts, if any, do you think you might experience between your personal and professional lives? What effects do you think those conflicts might have on you?

5. Movies, on and off television, play a major role in modern culture, yet no one seems to have a clear idea of how much influence they have on young people. Write a short essay, perhaps for the movie section of your local newspaper, in which you speculate about the influence a very popular movie or kind of movie has on how under-twenty-one-year-old viewers view sexual identity.

As an alternative topic, consider this: American movies, particularly action movies with stars like Bruce Willis and Tom Cruise, are extremely popular in other countries. What effect do you think such movies—name some you've seen recently—may have on the image of the United States abroad? If you're a student from another country, draw on your own experience in seeing American movies, and discuss how they colored your opinions.

6. For an editorial or feature article in your local or campus newspaper, write an account of an environmental problem you have heard about in your community or your state. Such a problem might be a toxic waste dump close to a neighborhood, a leaky natural gas or oil pipeline that caused hazards, or the accumulation in the walls of a school of a substance that made students and teachers ill. Do some research in the files of your local paper or on the Web to find out the causes of the problem and how long it existed before someone noticed. Conclude by speculating what might be done to prevent such problems from developing in the future.

PERSUASION
AND
ARGUMENT

Intuitively, you already know a good deal about **argument.**
For one thing, you use it all the time as you go through the
day talking or writing and making claims and giving reasons.
But you also live surrounded by arguments. They come not
only from people you talk to and deal with in everyday personal or business situations, but also from television, radio,
newspapers, subway posters, billboards, and signs and
brochures of all kinds. Any time someone is trying to persuade you to buy something, contribute money, take action,
make a judgment, or change your mind about anything, that
person is arguing with you.

This introduction offers an overview of some important argument theory, tips about the kinds of arguments that you can make, points to keep in mind as you write arguments, and some tips about pitfalls you should avoid. Remember that what we offer here barely scrapes the surface of the complex topic of argument and persuasion. If you want to learn more about argument theory and about writing good arguments, you can find several useful books in your college bookstore or through an on-line book seller.

KINDS OF ARGUMENTS

Traditionally, arguments fall into three categories: logical, emotional, and ethical. *Logical arguments* appeal to the reason; they depend primarily on evidence and logic. *Emotional arguments* appeal to the feelings; they depend heavily on images and connotative language. *Ethical arguments* appeal on the basis of the writer or speaker's character. In practice, of course, most writers and speakers combine all of these appeals when they try to persuade or convince their audiences. All the writers in this section combine reason and emotion, but some appeal more strongly to the feelings, depending heavily on imagery and figurative language, whereas others try to make a strong rational appeal, citing historical evidence and giving examples. And all of them use various strategies to give readers the impression that they're ethical; that is, that they have integrity and character.

It's important to remember that rational arguments aren't necessarily better than emotional arguments. Some occasions call for appeals to pride, loyalty, and compassion; for using vivid metaphors and images; and for strong language that touches the passions. When someone is speaking at a political rally or at a graduation or award ceremony, the audience is probably more interested in stories and images than in logical analysis and data. The kind of writing done for such occasions is called *ceremonial discourse,* and often it's successful precisely because it is emotional. The speech by Martin Luther King, Jr., "I Have a Dream," fits into this category.

When you write arguments for your college courses or in your work, however, you should plan on appealing primarily to reason and on providing strong evidence and clear examples. Your writing situation is *not* ceremonial; you're now writing to convince a thoughtful and skeptical audience, one that expects you to make a good case for your position. Again, take your cue from courtroom lawyers: state your case and prove it.

Notice that the eight essays in this section are arranged in pairs. Each pair treats a single topic, but the two writers take a different point of view on that topic. The topic of the essays by Martin Luther King, Jr., and Eric Liu is racial discrimination. The paired essays by Richard Doerflinger and Peggy Prichard Ross deal with ethical and scientific debate about stem cell research. The essays by Barbara Kingsolver and Barbara Dafoe Whitehead focus on child rearing and family values. The topic of the essays by Joan Acocella and Harold Bloom is the popular Harry Potter series of children's books.

PURPOSE

When you hear the term *argument,* you may automatically connect it with controversy and conflict. That's not necessarily the case, however, particularly in academic writing. There—and at other times too—you may have many purposes other than winning a dispute.

Sometimes you may argue *to support a cause.* For instance, you might write an editorial in favor of subsidized child care on your campus. You may also argue *to urge people to action* or *to promote change*—for instance, when you write a campaign brochure or a petition to reduce student fees. Sometimes you may argue *to refute a theory*—perhaps a history paper claiming that antislavery sentiment was not the chief cause of the Civil War. You can also write arguments *to arouse sympathy*—for better laws against child abuse, for example; *to stimulate interest*— for more participation in student government; *to win agreement*—to get condominium residents to agree to abolish regulations against pets; and *to provoke anger*—to arouse outrage against a proposed tax. And, of course, you might incorporate several of these purposes into one piece of writing.

AUDIENCE

When you write arguments, you must think about your readers. Who are they, what do they know, what do they believe, and what do they expect? Unless you can answer these questions at least partially, you cannot expect to write an effective argument. There simply is no such thing as a good argument in the abstract, separated from its purpose and its audience. Any argument you write is a good one only if it does what you want it to do with the particular readers who are going to read it. So, by no later than the second draft of any argument you write, you need to know why you are writing and for whom you are writing.

If you are trying to choose an audience for your paper, ask yourself the following questions:

1. Who is likely to be interested in what I am writing about?
2. What groups could make the changes I'm arguing for?

When you know the answers to these questions, you can direct your writing to readers to whom you have something to say—otherwise, there's little point in writing.

Once you have settled on your audience, ask yourself these questions:

1. What do my readers already know about my topic?
   a. What experience and knowledge do they have that I can use?
   b. Can I use specialized language? Should I?
   c. How can I teach them something they want to know?
2. How do my readers feel about my topic?
   a. What shared values can I appeal to?
   b. What prejudices or preconceptions must I pay attention to?
   c. What kind of approach will work best with them—casual or formal, objective or personal, factual or anecdotal?
3. What questions will my readers want me to answer?

You may find it especially useful to write out the answers to that last question.

When you have worked your way through all of these questions, either as a brainstorming exercise or in a prewriting group discussion, you'll have a stronger sense of who your readers are and how you can appeal to them.

STRATEGIES

When you are writing arguments, you can use a wide range of strategies, but most of them will fall into one of these three categories: *emotional appeal, logical appeal, or ethical appeal.*

Emotional Appeal

You argue by emotional or nonlogical appeal when you appeal to the emotions, to the senses, and to personal biases or prejudices. You incorporate such appeals into your writing when you use *connotative language* that elicits feelings or reactions—words like *melancholy, crimson, slovenly,* or *villainous.* Usually you're also using nonlogical appeal when you use *figurative language*—metaphors, allusions, or colorful phrases that make the reader draw comparisons or make associations. Phrases like "environmental cancer" or "industrial Goliath" evoke images and comparisons and play on the emotions.

Creating a tone is also a nonlogical strategy and an important one. The tone you choose can exert a powerful force on your readers, catching their attention, ingratiating you into their favor, conveying an air of authority and confidence. You can establish a friendly, close-to-your-reader tone by using contractions and the pronouns *I, we,* and *you.* You can create a relaxed tone by bringing in humor or personal anecdote, or you can give your writing an air of authority and detachment by avoiding personal pronouns and writing as objectively as possible.

All writers in this group of arguments use emotional appeal, but those who rely on it most heavily are Martin Luther King, Jr., Richard Doerflinger, and Peggy Prichard Ross. All of them are writing on strongly emotional topics, King on racism and Doerflinger and Ross on stem cell research.

Logical Appeal

You employ logical or rational strategies when you appeal mainly to your readers' intelligence, reason, and common sense. Your chief strategies are

> Making claims and supporting them
> Giving testimony
> Citing authorities
> Arguing from precedent
> Drawing comparisons and analogies
> Arguing from cause and effect

Eric Liu argues logically when he cites the past experience of minorities in the United States to support his claim that minorities can succeed in this country. Barbara Dafoe Whitehead makes a rational case that fathers are important to stable families, but there are also strong emotional undertones to her argument.

Ethical Appeal

Ethical appeal is the most subtle and often the most powerful because it comes from the character and evident expertise of the author, not directly from reason or emotion. All the writers in this section rely on their ethical appeal, but it works most effectively for Martin Luther King, Jr., because it rests on his record as a fighter for civil rights and on his having won the Nobel Peace Prize for his work. Joan Acocella's essay on the Harry Potter books has strong ethical appeal because it's evident that she understands and appreciates the generations of myths and legends that underlie the appeal of the books.

Eric Liu's ethical appeal comes from his own experience and that of his family, and Barbara Dafoe Whitehead's comes from her calm tone and obvious concern for children. As a novice writer, you're not yet in a position to convince through your reputation, but if can you show your readers that you're knowledgeable, thoughtful, and have done your homework, you're likely to succeed with your arguments.

USING PERSUASION AND
ARGUMENT IN PARAGRAPHS

Here are two persuasive paragraphs. The first is written by a
professional writer and is followed by an analysis. The second
is written by a student and is followed by questions.

NICHOLAS LEMANN
The Promised Land

Until 1950 one   During the first half of the twentieth century, it
could think only   was at least possible to think of race as a Southern
the South had
race problems   issue. The South, and only the South, had to con-
tend with the contradiction between the national
creed of democracy and the local reality of a caste
system; consequently the South lacked the optimism and confidence that characterized the
After 1950   country as a whole. The great black migration
black migration   made race a national issue in the second half of
to North
the century—an integral part of the politics, the
social thought, and the organization of everyday
life in the United States. Not coincidentally, by
the time the migration was over, the country had
acquired a good measure of the tragic sense that
Had to realize   had previously been confined to the South. Race
racism a   relations stood out nearly everywhere as the one
national
problem   thing most plainly wrong in America, the flawed
portion of the great tableau, the chief generator
of doubt about how essentially noble the whole
national enterprise really was.

Comment In this paragraph from the first chapter of
Nicholas Lemann's book *The Promised Land,* the author lays
out one of the central arguments of the book: the migration
of blacks from the South to the North after World War II
forced Americans to realize that racial discrimination and its
consequences constituted a national problem and were not
simply remnants of the South's defeat in the Civil War. They
could no longer claim that America was a great democracy

with liberty and justice for all. Once hundreds of thousands of blacks were living in the North, the struggle for equal rights and fair treatment began to permeate the political, economic, and social life of the whole nation. Lemann is particularly eloquent in the last sentence when he says, "Race relations stood out . . . as . . . the flawed portion of the great tableau, the chief generator of doubt about how essentially noble the whole national enterprise really was."

JIM F. SALOMAN
Genetic Engineering

We need to regulate experiments in genetic engineering. Scientists can reconfigure the genetic makeup of an organism. They can literally change life. But without appropriate controls, such tampering can lead to unpredictable and violent results. What would happen if scientists were able to resurrect an extinct species that would reverse the order of natural selection? And what would happen if they produced a superior organism that destroyed the balance of our present ecosystem? And what would happen if they started "creating" people for particular tasks? They could design aggressive men to fight wars and passive women to breed children. Whole new social classes could be created, some genetically advanced, some genetically restricted. If we are to protect the rights of individuals and prevent evolutionary chaos, we must create a thoughtful public policy that protects us from our own scientific experiments.

1. How might Saloman go on to develop this paragraph into a full-length persuasive essay?
2. Saloman gives several examples of what he calls "unpredictable and violent results." How would you evaluate the persuasive value of the several generalizations that he gives as examples of such results?

PERSUASION AND ARGUMENT

Points to Remember

1. To argue well, you have to know your audience and your purpose. Do you understand your audience's interests, their backgrounds, and what questions they might have? Do you know what you want to accomplish with this particular group of readers? It's useful to write out the answers to both of these questions before you start.

2. Understand the three principal kinds of persuasive appeals.
   - *Appeal to reason.* Emphasizes logic, evidence, authority, cause and effect, precedent, and comparison and analogy.
   - *Appeal to emotion.* Emphasizes feelings, the senses, personal biases, connotative language, and images and metaphor.
   - *Appeal from integrity and character.* Emphasizes the writer's competence, experience, and reputation.

   The most persuasive writers usually combine elements from all three kinds of appeals.

3. Construct your arguments as a lawyer would construct a case to present to a jury: state your claim and back it up with evidence and reason, but, when appropriate, also use metaphor and connotation.

4. Always assume your audience is intelligent, if perhaps uninformed about some particulars. Be respectful; avoid a superior tone.

5. Argue responsibly.
   - Don't overstate your claim.
   - Don't oversimplify complex issues.
   - Support your claims with specific details and evidence.

In this public service advertisement created by the Leo Burnett advertising company, PALM, or Physicians Against Land Mines, presents its argument about the death, dismemberment, and disability caused by land mines. The text below Emina Uzicanin's missing leg describes how, as a child playing on the outskirts of Sarajevo, she stepped on a land mine. In addition to this emotional story, the text offers other compelling evidence: "every 22 minutes another civilian is killed or maimed by a land mine"; "there are over 60 million unexploded land mines in nearly 70 countries." Select another public service advertising campaign—such as those sponsored by MADD (Mothers Against Drunk Driving) or ADL (Anti-Defamation League)—and analyze the visual and textual features that make it a persuasive argument.

A Debate About Racism

MARTIN LUTHER KING, JR.

Martin Luther King, Jr. (1929–1968), was born in Atlanta, Georgia, and was educated at Morehouse College, Crozer Theological Seminary, and Boston University. Ordained a Baptist minister in his father's church in 1947, King soon became involved in civil rights activities in the South. In 1957 he founded the Southern Christian Leadership Conference and established himself as America's most prominent spokesman for nonviolent racial integration. In 1963 he was named *Time* magazine's Man of the Year; in 1964 he was given the Nobel Peace Prize. In 1968 he was assassinated in Memphis, Tennessee. His writing includes *Letter from Birmingham Jail* (1963), *Why We Can't Wait* (1964), and *Where Do We Go from Here: Chaos or Community?* (1967). "I Have a Dream" is the famous speech King delivered at the Lincoln Memorial at the end of the March on Washington in 1963 to commemorate the one hundredth anniversary of the Emancipation Proclamation. King argues that realization of the dream of freedom for all American citizens is long overdue.

I Have a Dream

FIVE SCORE YEARS ago, a great American, in whose symbolic shadow we stand, signed the Emancipation Proclamation. This momentous decree came as a great beacon light of hope to millions of Negro slaves who had been seared in the flames of withering injustice. It came as a joyous daybreak to end the long night of captivity.

But one hundred years later, we must face the tragic fact   2
that the Negro is still not free. One hundred years later, the
life of the Negro is still sadly crippled by the manacles of segregation and the chains of discrimination. One hundred years
later, the Negro lives on a lonely island of poverty in the
midst of a vast ocean of material prosperity. One hundred
years later, the Negro is still languishing in the corners of
American society and finds himself an exile in his own land.
So we have come here today to dramatize an appalling
condition.

In a sense we have come to our nation's Capitol to cash a   3
check. When the architects of our republic wrote the magnificent words of the Constitution and the Declaration of

---

*There will be neither rest nor tranquility in
America until the Negro is granted his
citizenship rights.*

Independence, they were signing a promissory note to which
every American was to fall heir. This note was a promise that
all men would be guaranteed the unalienable rights of life,
liberty, and the pursuit of happiness.

It is obvious today that America has defaulted on this   4
promissory note insofar as her citizens of color are concerned. Instead of honoring this sacred obligation, America
has given the Negro people a bad check; a check which has
come back marked "insufficient funds." But we refuse to believe that the bank of justice is bankrupt. We refuse to believe
that there are insufficient funds in the great vaults of opportunity of this nation. So we have come to cash this check—a
check that will give us upon demand the riches of freedom
and the security of justice. We have also come to this hal-
lowed spot to remind America of the fierce urgency of *now*.
This is no time to engage in the luxury of cooling off or to

take the tranquilizing drug of gradualism. *Now* is the time to make real the promises of Democracy. *Now* is the time to rise from the dark and desolate valley of segregation to the sunlit path of racial justice. *Now* is the time to open the doors of opportunity to all of God's children. *Now* is the time to lift our nation from the quicksands of racial injustice to the solid rock of brotherhood.

It would be fatal for the nation to overlook the urgency of the moment and to underestimate the determination of the Negro. This sweltering summer of the Negro's legitimate discontent will not pass until there is an invigorating autumn of freedom and equality. 1963 is not an end, but a beginning. Those who hope that the Negro needed to blow off steam and will now be content will have a rude awakening if the nation returns to business as usual. There will be neither rest nor tranquility in America until the Negro is granted his citizenship rights. The whirlwinds of revolt will continue to shake the foundations of our nation until the bright day of justice emerges. 5

But there is something I must say to my people who stand on the warm threshold which leads into the palace of justice. In the process of gaining our rightful place we must not be guilty of wrongful deeds. Let us not seek to satisfy our thirst for freedom by drinking from the cup of bitterness and hatred. We must forever conduct our struggle on the high plane of dignity and discipline. We must not allow our creative protest to degenerate into physical violence. Again and again we must rise to the majestic heights of meeting physical force with soul force. The marvelous new militancy which has engulfed the Negro community must not lead us to a distrust of all white people, for many of our white brothers, as evidenced by their presence here today, have come to realize that their destiny is tied up with our destiny and their freedom is inextricably bound to our freedom. We cannot walk alone. 6

And as we walk, we must make the pledge that we shall march ahead. We cannot turn back. There are those who are asking the devotees of civil rights, "When will you be satisfied?" We can never be satisfied as long as the Negro is the 7 victim of the unspeakable horrors of police brutality. We can never be satisfied as long as our bodies, heavy with the fatigue of travel, cannot gain lodging in the motels of the highways and the hotels of the cities. We cannot be satisfied as long as the Negro's basic mobility is from a smaller ghetto to a larger one. We can never be satisfied as long as a Negro in Mississippi cannot vote and a Negro in New York believes he has nothing for which to vote. No, no, we are not satisfied, and we will not be satisfied until justice rolls down like waters and righteousness like a mighty stream.

I am not unmindful that some of you have come here out of great trials and tribulations. Some of you have come fresh from narrow jail cells. Some of you have come from areas where your quest for freedom left you battered by the storms of persecution and staggered by the winds of police brutality. You have been the veterans of creative suffering. Continue to work with the faith that unearned suffering is redemptive. 8

Go back to Mississippi, go back to Alabama, go back to South Carolina, go back to Georgia, go back to Louisiana, go back to the slums and ghettoes of our northern cities, knowing that somehow this situation can and will be changed. Let us not wallow in the valley of despair. 9

I say to you today, my friends, that in spite of the difficulties and frustrations of the moment I still have a dream. It is a dream deeply rooted in the American dream. 10

I have a dream that one day this nation will rise up and live out the true meaning of its creed: "We hold these truths to be self-evident; that all men are created equal." 11

I have a dream that one day on the red hills of Georgia the sons of former slaves and the sons of former slaveowners will be able to sit down together at the table of brotherhood. 12

I have a dream that the state of Mississippi, a desert state sweltering with the heat of injustice and oppression, will be transformed into an oasis of freedom and justice. 13

I have a dream that my four little children will one day live in a nation where they will not be judged by the color of their skin but by the content of their character. 14

I have a dream today. 15

I have a dream that the state of Alabama, whose gover-   16
nor's lips are presently dripping with the words of interposi-
tion and nullification, will be transformed into a situation
where little black boys and black girls will be able to join
hands with little white boys and white girls and walk together
as sisters and brothers.

I have a dream today.   17

I have a dream that one day every valley shall be exalted,   18
every hill and mountain shall be made low, the rough places
will be made plain, and the crooked places will be made
straight, and the glory of the Lord shall be revealed, and all
flesh shall see it together.

This is our hope. This is the faith with which I return to   19
the South. With this faith we will be able to hew out of the
mountain of despair a stone of hope. With this faith we will
be able to transform the jangling discords of our nation into
a beautiful symphony of brotherhood. With this faith we will
be able to work together, to pray together, to struggle together, to go to jail together, to stand up for freedom together, knowing that we will be free one day.

This will be the day when all of God's children will be able   20
to sing with new meaning.

> *My country, 'tis of thee*
> *Sweet land of liberty,*
> *   Of thee I sing:*
> *Land where my fathers died,*
> *Land of the pilgrims' pride,*
> *From every mountainside*
> *   Let freedom ring.*

And if America is to be a great nation this must become   21
true. So let freedom ring from the prodigious hilltops of New
Hampshire. Let freedom ring from the mighty mountains of
New York. Let freedom ring from the heightening Alleghenies
of Pennsylvania!

Let freedom ring from the snowcapped Rockies of   22
Colorado!

Let freedom ring from the curvaceous peaks of California!   23

But not only that; let freedom ring from Stone Mountain   24
of Georgia!

Let freedom ring from Lookout Mountain of Tennessee!   25

Let freedom ring from every hill and molehill of Missis-   26
sippi. From every mountainside, let freedom ring.

When we let freedom ring, when we let it ring from every   27
village and every hamlet, from every state and every city, we
will be able to speed up that day when all of God's children,
black men and white men, Jews and Gentiles, Protestants and
Catholics, will be able to join hands and sing in the words of
the old Negro spiritual, "Free at last! free at last! thank God
almighty, we are free at last!"

For Study and Discussion

QUESTIONS FOR RESPONSE

1. What experiences of injustice have you had (or perhaps witnessed, read about, or seen in a movie) that help you to identify
   with King's dreams and feel the force of his speech?
2. What did you already know about the life of King and of his
   place in modern U.S. history that prepared you for reading "I
   Have a Dream"? How well did the speech live up to what you
   expected of it?

QUESTIONS ABOUT PURPOSE

1. King has at least two strong messages. One message is local and
   immediate; the other one is national and long range. How
   would you summarize those two messages?
2. How does King use his speech to reinforce his belief in nonvio-
   lence as the appropriate tool in the struggle for civil rights?

QUESTIONS ABOUT AUDIENCE

1. King gave this speech to a huge live audience that had come to
   Washington for a march for freedom and civil rights. How much
   larger is the national audience he is addressing, and why is that
   audience also important?

2. This speech is one of the most widely anthologized of modern speeches. What audiences does it continue to appeal to and why?

QUESTIONS ABOUT STRATEGIES

1. How does King draw on metaphor to engage his listeners' feelings of injustice and give them hope for a new day? What are some of the most powerful metaphors?
2. In what way do King's talents as a minister serve his purposes in the speech? What African-American leader today do you think most resembles King in style and in mission?

QUESTIONS FOR DISCUSSION

1. If King were alive today, more than forty years after this speech, how much of his dream do you think he would feel has come true? Look particularly at the visions he speaks of in paragraph 7 and paragraphs 11 through 16.
2. What elements in the speech reveal those qualities that contributed to King's power as a major civil rights leader, effective with whites as well as with blacks?

ERIC LIU

Eric Liu was born in Poughkeepsie, New York, in 1968 and was educated at Yale University. He worked as a legislative aide for Senator David Boren of Oklahoma and then as a speechwriter for Secretary of State Warren Christopher and President Bill Clinton. He is currently the publisher and editor of *The Next Progressive,* a journal of opinion; the editor of *NEXT: Young American Writers on the New Generation* (1994); and the author of *The Accidental Asian: Notes of a Native Speaker* (1998). In "A Chinaman's Chance: Reflections on the American Dream," reprinted from *NEXT,* Liu argues that the American Dream is more about seizing opportunity than about claiming prosperity.

A Chinaman's Chance: Reflections on the American Dream

A LOT OF people my age seem to think that the American Dream is dead. I think they're dead wrong. 1

Or at least only partly right. It is true that for those of us in our twenties and early thirties, job opportunities are scarce. There looms a real threat that we will be the first American generation to have a lower standard of living than our parents. 2

But what is it that we mean when we invoke the American Dream? 3

In the past, the American Dream was something that held people of all races, religions, and identities together. As James Comer has written, it represented a shared aspiration among all Americans—black, white, or any other color—"to provide 4 well for themselves and their families as valued members of a democratic society." Now, all too often, it seems the American Dream means merely some guarantee of affluence, a birthright of wealth.

At a basic level, of course, the American Dream is about 5 prosperity and the pursuit of material happiness. But to me, its meaning extends beyond such concerns. To me, the dream is not just about buying a bigger house than the one I grew up in or having shinier stuff now than I had as a kid. It also represents a sense of opportunity that binds generations

---

*I want to prove . . . that a Chinaman's
chance is as good as anyone else's.*

---

together in commitment, so that the young inherit not only property but also perseverance, not only money but also a mission to make good on the strivings of their parents and grandparents.

The poet Robert Browning once wrote that "a man's 6 reach must exceed his grasp—else what's a heaven for?" So it is in America. Every generation will strive, and often fail. Every generation will reach for success, and often miss the mark. But Americans rely as much on the next generation as on the next life to prove that such struggles and frustrations are not in vain. There may be temporary setbacks, cutbacks, recessions, depressions. But this is a nation of second chances. So long as there are young Americans who do not take what they have—or what they can do—for granted, progress is always possible.

My conception of the American Dream does not take 7 progress for granted. But it does demand the *opportunity* to achieve progress—and values the opportunity as much as the achievement. I come at this question as the son of immigrants. I see just as clearly as anyone else the cracks in the idealist vision of fulfillment for all. But because my parents came here with virtually nothing, because they did build something, I see the enormous potential inherent in the ideal.

I happen still to believe in our national creed: freedom and opportunity, and our common responsibility to uphold them. This creed is what makes America unique. More than any demographic statistic or economic indicator, it animates the American Dream. It infuses our mundane struggles—to plan a career, do good work, get ahead—with purpose and possibility. It makes America the only country that could produce heroes like Colin Powell—heroes who rise from nothing, who overcome the odds. 8

I think of the sacrifices made by my own parents. I appreciate the hardship of the long road traveled by my father—one of whose first jobs in America was painting the yellow line down a South Dakota interstate—and by my mother—whose first job here was filing pay stubs for a New York restaurant. From such beginnings, they were able to build a comfortable life and provide me with a breadth of resources—through arts, travel, and an Ivy League education. It was an unspoken obligation for them to do so. 9

I think of my boss in my first job after college, on Capitol Hill. George is a smart, feisty, cigar-chomping, take-no-shit Greek-American. He is about fifteen years older than I, has different interests, a very different personality. But like me, he is the son of immigrants, and he would joke with me that the Greek-Chinese mafia was going to take over one day. He was only half joking. We'd worked harder, our parents doubly harder, than almost anyone else we knew. To people like George, talk of the withering of the American Dream seems foreign. 10

It's undeniable that principles like freedom and opportunity, no matter how dearly held, are not enough. They can inspire a multiracial March on Washington, but they can not bring black salaries in alignment with white salaries. They can draw wave after wave of immigrants here, but they can not provide them the means to get out of our ghettos and barrios 11 and Chinatowns. They are not sufficient for fulfillment of the American Dream.

But they are necessary. They are vital. And not just to the   12
children of immigrants. These ideals form the durable thread that weaves us all in union. Put another way, they are one of the few things that keep America from disintegrating into a loose confederation of zip codes and walled-in communities.

What alarms me is how many people my age look at our   13
nation's ideals with a rising sense of irony. What good is such a creed if you are working for hourly wages in a dead-end job? What value do such platitudes have if you live in an urban war zone? When the only apparent link between homeboys and housepainters and bike messengers and in-vestment bankers is pop culture—MTV, the NBA, movies, dance music—then the social fabric is flimsy indeed.

My generation has come of age at a time when the country   14
is fighting off bouts of defeatism and self-doubt, at a time when racism and social inequities seem not only persistent but intractable. At a time like this, the retreat to one's own kind is seen by more and more of my peers as an advance. And that retreat has given rise again to the notion that there are essen-tial and irreconcilable differences among the races—a notion that was supposed to have disappeared from American dis-course by the time my peers and I were born in the sixties.

Not long ago, for instance, my sister called me a "banana."   15

I was needling her about her passion for rap and hip-hop   16
music. Every time I saw her, it seemed, she was jumping and twisting to Arrested Development or Chubb Rock or some other funky group. She joked that despite being the daugh-ter of Chinese immigrants, she was indeed "black at heart." And then she added, lightheartedly, "You, on the other hand—well, you're basically a banana." Yellow on the out-side, but white inside.

I protested, denied her charge vehemently. But it was too   17
late. She was back to dancing. And I stood accused.

Ever since then, I have wondered what it means to be   18
black, or white, or Asian "at heart"—particularly for my gen-eration. Growing up, when other kids would ask whether I

was Chinese or Korean or Japanese, I would reply, a little petulantly, "American." Assimilation can still be a sensitive subject. I recall reading about a Korean-born Congressman who had gone out of his way to say that Asian-Americans should expect nothing special from him. He added that he was taking speech lessons "to get rid of this accent." I winced at his palpable self-hate. But then it hit me: Is this how my sister sees me?

There is no doubt that minorities like me can draw strength from our communities. But in today's environment, anything other than ostentatious tribal fealty is taken in some communities as a sign of moral weakness, a disappointing dilution of character. In times that demand ever-clearer thinking, it has become too easy for people to shut off their brains: "It's a black/Asian/Latino/white thing," says the variable T-shirt. "You wouldn't understand." Increasingly, we don't. 19

The civil-rights triumphs of the sixties and the cultural revolutions that followed made it possible for minorities to celebrate our diverse heritages. I can appreciate that. But I know, too, that the sixties—or at least, my generation's grainy, hazy vision of the decade—also bequeathed to young Americans a legacy of near-pathological race consciousness. 20

Today's culture of entitlement—and of race entitlement in particular—tells us plenty about what we get if we are black or white or female or male or old or young. 21

It is silent, though, on some other important issues. For instance: What do we "get" for being American? And just as importantly, What do we owe? These are questions around which young people like myself must tread carefully, since talk of common interests, civic culture, responsibility, and integration sounds a little too "white" for some people. To the new segregationists, the "American Dream" is like the old myth of the "Melting Pot": an oppressive fiction, an opiate for the unhappy colored masses. 22

How have we allowed our thinking about race to become so twisted? The formal obstacles and the hateful opposition to civil rights have long faded into memory. By most external measures, life for minorities is better than it was a quarter 23

century ago. It would seem that the opportunities for tolerance and cooperation are commonplace. Why, then, are so
many of my peers so cynical about our ability to get along
with one another?

The reasons are frustratingly ambiguous. I got a glimpse   24
of this when I was in college. It was late in my junior year,
and as the editor of a campus magazine, I was sitting on a
panel to discuss "The White Press at Yale: What Is to Be
Done?" The assembly hall was packed, a diverse and noisy
crowd. The air was heavy, nervously electric.

Why weren't there more stories about "minority issues" in   25
the Yale *Daily News?* Why weren't there more stories on
Africa in my magazine, the foreign affairs journal? How many
"editors of color" served on the boards of each of the major
publications? The questions were volleyed like artillery, one
round after another, punctuated only by the applause of an
audience spoiling for a fight. The questions were not at all
unfair. But it seemed that no one—not even those of us on
the panel who *were* people of color—could provide, in this
context, satisfactory answers.

Toward the end of the discussion, I made a brief appeal for   26
reason and moderation. And afterward, as students milled
around restlessly, I was attacked: for my narrowmindedness—
How dare you suggest that Yale is not a fundamentally preju-
diced place!—for my simplemindedness—Have you, too,
been co-opted?

And for my betrayal—Are you just white inside?   27

My eyes were opened that uncomfortably warm early sum-   28
mer evening. Not only to the cynical posturing and the combustible opportunism of campus racial politics. But more
importantly, to the larger question of identity—my identity—
in America. Never mind that the aim of many of the loudest
critics was to generate headlines in the very publications they
denounced. In spite of themselves—against, it would seem,
their true intentions—they got me to think about who I am.

In our society today, and especially among people of my gen-   29
eration, we are congealing into clots of narrow commonality.
We stick with racial and religious comrades. This tribal

consciousness-raising can be empowering for some. But while America was conceived in liberty—the liberty, for instance, to associate with whomever we like—it was never designed to be a mere collection of subcultures. We forget that there is in fact such a thing as a unique American identity that transcends our sundry tribes, sets, gangs, and cliques.

I have grappled, wittingly or not, with these questions of identity and allegiance all my life. When I was in my early teens, I would invite my buddies overnight to watch movies, play video games, and beat one another up. Before too long, my dad would come downstairs and start hamming it up— telling stories, asking gently nosy questions, making corny jokes, all with his distinct Chinese accent. I would stand back, quietly gauging everyone's reaction. Of course, the guys loved it. But I would feel uneasy. 30

What was then cause for discomfort is now a source of strength. Looking back on such episodes, I take pride in my father's accented English; I feel awe at his courage to laugh loudly in a language not really his own. 31

It was around the same time that I decided that continued attendance at the community Chinese school on Sundays was uncool. There was no fanfare; I simply stopped going. As a child, I'd been too blissfully unaware to think of Chinese school as anything more than a weekly chore, with an annual festival (dumplings and spring rolls, games and prizes). But by the time I was a peer-pressured adolescent, Chinese school seemed like a badge of the woefully unassimilated. I turned my back on it. 32

Even as I write these words now, it feels as though I am revealing a long-held secret. I am proud that my ancestors— scholars, soldiers, farmers—came from one of the world's great civilizations. I am proud that my grandfather served in the Chinese Air Force. I am proud to speak even my clumsy brand of Mandarin, and I feel blessed to be able to think idiomatically in Chinese, a language so much richer in nuance and subtle poetry than English. 33

Belatedly, I appreciate the good fortune I've had to be the son of immigrants. As a kid, I could play Thomas Jefferson in 34

the bicentennial school play one week and the next week play
the poet Li Bai at the Chinese school festival. I could come
home from an afternoon of teen slang at the mall and sit
down to dinner for a rollicking conversation in our family's
hybrid of Chinese and English. I understood, when I went
over to visit friends, that my life was different. At the time, I
just never fully appreciated how rich it was.

Yet I know that this pride in my heritage does not cross into   35
prejudice against others. What it reflects is pride in what my
country represents. That became clear to me when I went
through Marine Corps Officer Candidates' School. During
the summers after my sophomore and junior years of college,
I volunteered for OCS, a grueling boot camp for potential officers in the swamps and foothills of Quantico, Virginia.

And once I arrived—standing 5′4″, 135 pounds, bespecta-   36
cled, a Chinese Ivy League Democrat—I was a target straight
out of central casting. The wiry, raspy-voiced drill sergeant,
though he was perhaps only an inch or two taller than I,
called me "Little One" with as much venom as can be
squeezed into such a moniker. He heaped verbal abuse on
me, he laughed when I stumbled, he screamed when I hesitated. But he also never failed to remind me that just because
I was a little shit didn't mean I shouldn't run farther, climb
higher, think faster, hit harder than anyone else.

That was the funny thing about the Marine Corps. It is,   37
ostensibly, one of the most conservative institutions in the
United States. And yet, for those twelve weeks, it represented
the kind of color-blind equality of opportunity that the rest
of society struggles to match. I did not feel uncomfortable at
OCS to be of Chinese descent. Indeed, I drew strength from
it. My platoon was a veritable cross section of America: forty
young men of all backgrounds, all regions, all races, all levels
of intelligence and ability, displaced from our lives (if only for
a few weeks) with nowhere else to go.

Going down the list of names—Courtemanche, Dough-   38
erty, Grella, Hunt, Liu, Reeves, Schwarzman, and so on—
brought to mind a line from a World War II documentary I
once saw, which went something like this: The reason why it

seemed during the war that America was as good as the rest of the world put together was that America *was* the rest of the world put together.

Ultimately, I decided that the Marines was not what I wanted to do for four years and I did not accept the second lieutenant's commission. But I will never forget the day of the graduation parade: bright sunshine, brisk winds, the band playing Sousa as my company passed in review. As my mom and dad watched and photographed the parade from the rafters, I thought to myself: this is the American Dream in all its cheesy earnestness. I felt the thrill of truly being part of something larger and greater than myself.

I do know that American life is not all Sousa marches and flag-waving. I know that those with reactionary agendas often find it convenient to cloak their motives in the language of Americanism. The "American Party" was the name of a major nativist organization in the nineteenth century. "America First" is the siren song of the isolationists who would withdraw this country from the world and expel the world from this country. I know that our national immigration laws were once designed explicitly to cut off the influx from Asia.

I also know that discrimination is real. I am reminded of a gentle old man who, after Pearl Harbor, was stripped of his possessions without warning, taken from his home, and thrown into a Japanese internment camp. He survived, and by many measures has thrived, serving as a community leader and political activist. But I am reluctant to share with him my wide-eyed patriotism.

I know the bittersweet irony that my own father—a strong and optimistic man—would sometimes feel when he was alive. When he came across a comically lost cause—if the Yankees were behind 14–0 in the ninth, or if Dukakis was down ten points in the polls with a week left—he would often joke that the doomed party had "a Chinaman's chance" of success. It was one of those insensitive idioms of a generation ago, and it must have lodged in his impressionable young mind when he first came to America. It spoke of a perceived stacked deck.

I know, too, that for many other immigrants, the dream   43
simply does not work out. Fae Myenne Ng, the author of
Bone, writes about how her father ventured here from China
under a false identity and arrived at Angel Island, the deten-
tion center outside the "Gold Mountain" of San Francisco.
He got out, he labored, he struggled, and he suffered "a bitter no-luck life" in America. There was no glory. For him, Ng
suggests, the journey was not worth it.

But it is precisely because I know these things that I want   44
to prove that in the long run, over generations and across
ethnicities, it *is* worth it. For the second-generation American, opportunity is obligation. I have seen and faced racism.
I understand the dull pain of dreams deferred or unmet. But
I believe still that there is so little stopping me from building
the life that I want. I was given, through my parents' labors,
the chance to bridge that gap between ideals and reality. Who
am I to throw away that chance?

Plainly, I am subject to the criticism that I speak too much   45
from my own experience. Not everyone can relate to the
second-generation American story. When I have spoken like
this with some friends, the issue has been my perspective.
*What you say is fine for you. But unless you grew up where I did,
unless you've had people avoid you because of the color of your
skin, don't talk to me about common dreams.*

But are we then to be paralyzed? Is respect for different ex-   46
periences supposed to obviate the possibility of shared aspira-
tions? Does the diversity of life in America doom us to a
fractured understanding of one another? The question is
basic: Should the failure of this nation thus far to fulfill its
stated ideals incapacitate its young people, or motivate us?

Our country was built on, and remains glued by, the idea   47
that everybody deserves a fair shot and that we must work together to guarantee that opportunity—the original American
Dream. It was this idea, in some inchoate form, that drew
every immigrant here. It was this idea, however sullied by
slavery and racism, that motivated the civil-rights movement.
To write this idea off—even when its execution is spotty—to
let American life descend into squabbles among separatist

tribes would not just be sad. It would be a total mishandling of a legacy, the squandering of a great historical inheritance.

Mine must not be the first generation of Americans to lose America. Just as so many of our parents journeyed here to find their version of the American Dream, so must young Americans today journey across boundaries of race and class to rediscover one another. We are the first American generation to be born into an integrated society, and we are accustomed to more race mixing than any generation before us. We started open-minded, and it's not too late for us to stay that way.   48

Time is of the essence. For in our national political culture today, the watchwords seem to be *decline* and *end*. Apocalyptic visions and dark millennial predictions abound. The end of history. The end of progress. The end of equality. Even something as ostensibly positive as the end of the Cold War has a bittersweet tinge, because for the life of us, no one in America can get a handle on the big question, "What Next?"   49

For my generation, this fixation on endings is particularly enervating. One's twenties are supposed to be a time of widening horizons, of bright possibilities. Instead, America seems to have entered an era of limits. Whether it is the difficulty of finding jobs from some place other than a temp agency, or the mountains of debt that darken our future, the message to my peers is often that this nation's time has come and gone; let's bow out with grace and dignity.   50

A friend once observed that while the Chinese seek to adapt to nature and yield to circumstance, Americans seek to conquer both. She meant that as a criticism of America. But I interpreted her remark differently. I *do* believe that America is exceptional. And I believe it is up to my generation to revive that spirit, that sense that we do in fact have control over our own destiny—as individuals and as a nation.   51

If we are to reclaim a common destiny, we must also reach out to other generations for help. It was Franklin Roosevelt who said that while America can't always build the future for its youth, it can—and must—build its youth for the future.   52

That commitment across generations is as central to the American Dream as any I have enunciated. We are linked, black and white, old and young, one and inseparable.

I know how my words sound. I am old enough to perceive   53
my own naïveté but young enough still to cherish it. I realize that I am coming of age just as the American Dream is showing its age. Yet I still have faith in this country's unique destiny—to create generation after generation of hyphenates like me, to channel this new blood, this resilience and energy into an ever more vibrant future for *all* Americans.

And I want to prove—for my sake, for my father's sake,   54
and for my country's sake—that a Chinaman's chance is as good as anyone else's.

For Study and Discussion

QUESTIONS FOR RESPONSE

1. Do you endorse or discount Liu's argument? How do you think your family background and history affect your response?
2. How would you define the American Dream? To what extent do you think it has been or will be fulfilled for you?

QUESTIONS ABOUT PURPOSE

1. To what criticisms *about* his generation is Liu responding? To what criticisms *from* his generation is he responding?
2. What specific attitudes among young people does Liu challenge?

QUESTIONS ABOUT AUDIENCE

1. Liu wrote this essay for a 1994 book titled *NEXT: Young American Writers on the New Generation,* a book he conceived of and also edited. What kind of readers do you think he envisioned for the book? How do you think you fit into that group?
2. What do you think Liu's appeal might be to generations older than his? Why?

QUESTIONS ABOUT STRATEGIES

1. What is the impact of Liu's writing about his parents' experience?
2. Liu was once one of President Clinton's speechwriters. What strategies does he use that he might have learned through that experience?

QUESTIONS FOR DISCUSSION

1. What evidence, if any, do you see that students are splitting into separate groups on your campus? What is your view of such splits? Why?
2. What factors in Liu's life and experiences do you think played a significant part in his success in college and beyond? How would those factors affect his outlook on life?

A Debate About Stem Cell Research

RICHARD DOERFLINGER

Richard Doerflinger is deputy director of the Secretariat for Pro-Life Activities at the United States Conference of Catholic Bishops in Washington, D.C. A Maryland resident, Doerflinger also serves as an adjunct fellow in bioethics and public policy at the National Catholic Bioethics Center in Boston. In "First Principles and the 'Frist Principles,'" Doerflinger presents arguments for why scientists should not conduct stem cell research.

First Principles and the "Frist Principles"

A COUPLE OF interesting things happened at a recent Senate hearing on stem cell research. News media covered one of those things, and not very well. The full picture has horrifying implications for our future.

The media reported that Senator Bill Frist of Tennessee, known as a pro-life Republican and the Senate's only physician member, testified in favor of funding stem cell research that requires destroying human embryos. Senator Frist claimed that while such research is "untried and untested" it also has "huge potential," and so should be funded even as we show "the highest moral regard" for the embryos we kill in the process.

So far this is the tale of another Senator who threw away his pro-life convictions citing a hope of medical benefits. Sadly, Frist's reference to "moral regard" sounded like the hypocrisy of President Clinton's National Bioethics Advisory Commission, which concluded that embryos deserve "respect" as human lives but should be killed for their stem cells. What is the "respectful" way to suck out a living being's innards and throw away the shell?

Receiving less media attention was Frist's announcement 4 that federal funding of this research "should be contingent on the implementation of strict new safeguards," to prevent abuse of his newfound loophole in respect for life. Without a trace of irony he presented these as "Frist Principles on Human Stem Cell Research."

Some of these "principles" are just silly. For example, one 5 calls for "independent scientific and ethical review" of the research by the Institute of Medicine and the Secretary of

---

There's no negotiating with the ideologues who want a Brave New World.

Health and Human Services. This is like calling for independent review of the henhouse by the foxes, since IOM and Secretary Thompson both favor destructive embryo research. Another principle would make standards for fetal tissue research "consistent" with the rules for embryo research. This seems to mean that researchers could perform abortions *solely to obtain fetal tissue for government research,* just as they may kill live embryos solely to obtain stem cells.

There were also "principles" that pro-life Americans can 6 and do support: Ban human cloning; continue the ban on directly funding destruction of human embryos; ban the creation of embryos solely for research. These should be pursued in their own right, not as "trade-offs" for government-sanctioned experimentation on some humans.

In this context, nonetheless, Frist proposed that it could 7 be "pro-life" for the government, for the first time in U.S. history, to fund research on stem cells obtained by killing human embryos. Only embryos "that would otherwise be discarded" will be used—which is like saying that the government will fund abortions only for unborn children not wanted by their parents.

Not covered at all by most media is what happened to the   8
"Frist Principles" when they were presented to Senators Arlen Specter (R-PA) and Tom Harkin (D-IA), the Senate's chief promoters of embryo research and the conveners of this hearing. The principles got massacred.

Frist's effort to limit the number of embryos killed was de-   9
nounced by Senator Specter and several like-minded scientists, who said hundreds of cell lines may be needed for valid scientific results. One researcher said that ten thousand may be needed, to obtain a close genetic "match" to most patients needing tissue. (Keep in mind that each cell line requires destroying many embryos. Recently a fertility clinic in Virginia created and destroyed over a hundred embryos to get three cell lines.) Human cloning—creating and killing embryonic "copies" of each patient to obtain genetically tailored stem cells—was called the best way to provide tissue that will not be rejected by patients' bodies, and Harkin and Specter raised no objection.

Senator Specter also asked a representative of the National   10
Institutes of Health whether the NIH needs to be able to destroy its own stock of human embryos to do high-quality research. When the official hesitated at taking this step, Specter angrily threatened to make massive cuts in total NIH spending unless she expressed support for federal embryo farms.

In other words, proponents of this grotesque research   11
have no need for Senator Frist's compromises. They think they have support for their real agenda: Government embryo farming, creating human life in the lab solely to destroy it, cloning to make multiple human guinea pigs. The whole frightening Brave New World is before our eyes—which should help us concentrate on what the real issue is.

Senator Frist said his support for funding embryonic stem   12
cell research is "contingent" on these principles, and the principles were ridiculed and rejected by his newfound pro-abortion friends. He now may realize they are no friends.

And President Bush might learn from the fate of the hapless Bill Frist: There's no negotiating with the ideologues who want a Brave New World. The only reasonable approach to embryonic stem cell research is not to do it at all.

For Study and Discussion

QUESTIONS FOR RESPONSE

1. How do you respond to arguments about controversial subjects?
2. What are the major arguments you have heard against stem cell research?

QUESTIONS ABOUT PURPOSE

1. Why does Doerflinger contest the political position of Senator Bill Frist?
2. How does he distort his argument by suggesting that stem cell research is similar to funding abortions?

QUESTIONS ABOUT AUDIENCE

1. What assumptions does Doerflinger make about his readers' attitude toward stem cell research?
2. How does he use the word *us* to identify with his readers?

QUESTIONS ABOUT STRATEGIES

1. What emotional appeals does Doerflinger use to support his argument?
2. What sort of ethical appeal does he have as deputy director of the Secretariat for Pro-Life Activities at the United States Conference of Catholic Bishops?

QUESTIONS FOR DISCUSSION

1. How has science fiction—in novels and films—portrayed the "Brave New World" where cloning and robotics have become commonplace?
2. What does this essay suggest about the relationship of politics, religion, and science?

PEGGY PRICHARD ROSS

Peggy Prichard Ross grew up in Pittsburgh, Pennsylvania, and was educated at the University of Florida, where she earned a master's degree in communications. She has worked as the director of communications for AvMed Health Plan in Gainesville, Florida. In "Stem Cell Research: It's About Life and Death, Not Politics," reprinted from the *Tallahassee Democrat*, Ross provides powerful reasons why scientists should be allowed to pursue stem cell research.

Stem Cell Research: It's About Life and Death, Not Politics

IN SIX MONTHS there is a good chance I'll be dead. This 1
doesn't bother me nearly as much as having a president
who wants to jail scientists and doctors who are trying to find
cures for people with my disease and other illnesses such as
diabetes, Alzheimer's, Parkinson's, and so many others.

In October 2001, I was diagnosed with a grade-three as- 2
trocytoma, which is a brain cancer with no known cause and
no known cure. I tried to learn all I could about the disease
and medical research in the field. I learned that brain cancer
is technically not really cancer. It is, in fact, a disease of stem
cells.

And just like that, the political debate on stem cell research 3
became more than a political argument to me. It became a
debate of hope versus despair.

I watched President Bush's 2003 State of the Union address 4
from my hospital bed in Shands Hospital in Gainesville. During the speech he urged Congress to ban "all human cloning."
Unfortunately, "all human cloning" includes therapeutic
cloning, which is one and the same with stem cell research.

The president likes to call it cloning because he knows it ⁵
creates images of mutant or butchered babies, when stem cell
research (also known as somatic cell nuclear transfer, or
SCNT) has nothing to do with babies or fetuses. In fact, the

---

*The arguments against stem cell research are
scientifically unfounded and at best, are
based on personal religious beliefs.*

---

egg cells used in therapeutic cloning have no chance of being
fertilized or transplanted into a woman's womb.

The arguments against stem cell research are scientifically ⁶
unfounded and at best, are based on personal religious beliefs. I take exception to the president using his religion to
dictate public health policy. Policy should be based on science, not sectarian beliefs.

The president describes himself as a compassionate conser- ⁷
vative. But what is compassionate about outlawing vital
research? What is conservative about using the federal government to dictate religion?

I fully realize that my time is limited, and any cures discov- ⁸
ered from stem cell research will be several years away. My
concern is with the future generations. Almost 20,000 Americans per year will get the same type of brain cancer I did.
They will be children and adults, men and women, black and
white, Christian and Muslim.

The disease is not hereditary, yet has no known environ- ⁹
mental cause either. There is no rhyme or reason to who gets
it and why. What we don't understand about the disease far
outweighs what we do understand about it. How can any of
this change if studying the very root cause of the disease is
made illegal?

There are bipartisan bills in Congress that recognize ¹⁰
the importance of stem cell research and I hope that our

representatives, senators, and president will give the millions of Americans who fight for their lives every day against life threatening illnesses the hope they need and deserve.

For Study and Discussion

QUESTIONS FOR RESPONSE

1. How have you responded to the diagnosis that someone you know has a serious disease?
2. How do you respond to the charge that "the arguments against stem cell research are scientifically unfounded"?

QUESTIONS ABOUT PURPOSE

1. Why does Ross contest the position of President Bush on stem cell research?
2. How does she distort her argument by suggesting that the president is using the federal government to dictate religion?

QUESTIONS ABOUT AUDIENCE

1. How does the title of Ross's essay reveal her assumptions about her audience?
2. How does her concern for future generations suggest that she is trying to expand her audience?

QUESTIONS ABOUT STRATEGIES

1. How does Ross's opening sentence make an emotional appeal to her readers?
2. What sort of ethical appeal does she have as director of communications for AvMed Health Plan?

QUESTIONS FOR DISCUSSION

1. How would you characterize the difference between a political and a personal argument?
2. What is the difference between a stem cell and a fetus?

A Debate About Family

BARBARA KINGSOLVER

Barbara Kingsolver was born in Annapolis, Maryland, in 1955 and educated at DePauw University and the University of Arizona. She began her writing career as a technical writer in the office of arid studies, then began working as a freelance journalist before publishing her first novel, *The Bean Trees* (1988). Her other novels include *Animal Dreams* (1990), *The Poisonwood Bible* (1998), and *Prodigal Summer* (2000). She has published short stories in *Homeland and Other Stories* (1989) and essays in *High Tide in Tucson: Essays from Now or Never* (1995) and *Small Wonder* (2002). In "Stone Soup," Kingsolver argues that there is not necessarily one best model for a successful family.

Stone Soup

IN THE CATALOG of family values, where do we rank an occasion like this? A curly-haired boy who wanted to run before he walked, age seven now, a soccer player scoring a winning goal. He turns to the bleachers with his fists in the air and a smile wide as a gap-toothed galaxy. His own cheering section of grown-ups and kids all leap to their feet and hug each other, delirious with love for this boy. He's Andy, my best friend's son. The cheering section includes his mother and her friends, his brother, his father and stepmother, a stepbrother and stepsister, and a grandparent. Lucky is the child with this many relatives on hand to hail a proud accomplishment. I'm there too, witnessing a family

1

fortune. But in spite of myself, defensive words take shape in my head. I am thinking: I dare *anybody* to call this a broken home.

Families change, and remain the same. Why are our names for home so slow to catch up to the truth of where we live? ₂

When I was a child, I had two parents who loved me without cease. One of them attended every excuse for attention I ever contrived, and the other made it to the ones with higher ₃

Arguing about whether nontraditional families deserve pity or tolerance is a little like the medieval debate about left-handedness as a mark of the devil.

---

production values, like piano recitals and appendicitis. So I was a lucky child too. I played with a set of paper dolls called "The Family of Dolls," four in number, who came with the factory-assigned names of Dad, Mom, Sis, and Junior. I think you know what they looked like, at least before I loved them to death and their heads fell off.

Now I've replaced the dolls with a life. I knit my days ₄ around my daughter's survival and happiness, and am proud to say her head is still on. But we aren't the Family of Dolls. Maybe you're not, either. And if not, even though you are statistically no oddity, it's probably been suggested to you in a hundred ways that yours isn't exactly a real family, but an impostor family, a harbinger of cultural ruin, a slapdash substitute—something like counterfeit money. Here at the tail end of our century, most of us are up to our ears in the noisy business of trying to support and love a thing called family. But there's a current in the air with ferocious moral force that finds its way even into political campaigns, claiming there is only one right way to do it, the Way It Has Always Been.

In the face of a thriving, particolored world, this narrow   5
view is so pickled and absurd I'm astonished that it gets air-
play. And I'm astonished that it still stings.

Every parent has endured the arrogance of a child-   6
unfriendly grump sitting in judgment, explaining what those
kids of ours really need (for example, "a good licking"). If
we're polite, we move our crew to another bench in the park.
If we're forthright (as I am in my mind, only, for the rest of
the day), we fix them with a sweet imperious stare and say,
"Come back and let's talk about it after you've changed a
thousand diapers."

But it's harder somehow to shrug off the Family-of-Dolls   7
Family Values crew when they judge (from their safe distance) that divorced people, blended families, gay families,
and single parents are failures. That our children are at risk,
and the whole arrangement is messy and embarrassing. A
marriage that ends is not called "finished," it's called *failed*.
The children of this family may have been born to a happy
union, but now they are called *the children of divorce*.

I had no idea how thoroughly these assumptions overlaid   8
my culture until I went through divorce myself. I wrote to
a friend: "This might be worse than being widowed.
Overnight I've suffered the same losses—companionship,
financial and practical support, my identity as a wife and partner, the future I'd taken for granted. I am lonely, grieving,
and hard-pressed to take care of my household alone. But instead of bringing casseroles, people are acting like I had a fit
and broke up the family china."

Once upon a time I held these beliefs about divorce: that   9
everyone who does it could have chosen not to do it. That
it's a lazy way out of marital problems. That it selfishly puts
personal happiness ahead of family integrity. Now I tremble
for my ignorance. It's easy, in fortunate times, to forget
about the ambush that could leave your head reeling: serious
mental or physical illness, death in the family, abandonment,
financial calamity, humiliation, violence, despair.

I started out like any child, intent on being the Family of   10
Dolls. I set upon young womanhood believing in most of the

doctrines of my generation: I wore my skirts four inches above the knee. I had the Barbie with her zebra-striped swimsuit and a figure unlike anything found in nature. And I understood the Prince Charming Theory of Marriage, a quest for Mr. Right that ends smack dab where you find him. I did not completely understand that another whole story *begins* there, and no fairy tale prepared me for the combination of bad luck and persistent hope that would interrupt my dream and lead me to other arrangements. Like a cancer diagnosis, a dying marriage is a thing to fight, to deny, and finally, when there's no choice left, to dig in and survive. Casseroles would help. Likewise, I imagine it must be a painful reckoning in adolescence (or later on) to realize one's own true love will never look like the soft-focus fragrance ads because Prince Charming (surprise!) is a princess. Or vice versa. Or has skin the color your parents didn't want you messing with, except in the Crayola box.

It's awfully easy to hold in contempt the straw broken   11
home, and that mythical category of persons who toss away nuclear family for the sheer fun of it. Even the legal terms we use have a suggestion of caprice. I resent the phrase "irreconcilable differences," which suggests a stubborn refusal to accept a spouse's little quirks. This is specious. Every happily married couple I know has loads of irreconcilable differences. Negotiating where to set the thermostat is not the point. A nonfunctioning marriage is a slow asphyxiation. It is waking up despised each morning, listening to the pulse of your own loneliness before the radio begins to blare its raucous gospel that you're nothing if you aren't loved. It is sharing your airless house with the threat of suicide or other kinds of violence, while the ghost that whispers, "Leave here and destroy your children," has passed over every door and nailed it shut. Disassembling a marriage in these circumstances is as much *fun* as amputating your own gangrenous leg. You do it, if you can, to save a life—or two, or more.

I know of no one who really went looking to hoe the   12
harder row, especially the daunting one of single parenthood. Yet it seems to be the most American of customs to blame the

burdened for their destiny. We'd like so desperately to believe in freedom and justice for all, we can hardly name that rogue bad luck, even when he's a close enough snake to bite us. In the wake of my divorce, some friends (even a few close ones) chose to vanish, rather than linger within striking distance of misfortune.

But most stuck around, bless their hearts, and if I'm any   13
the wiser for my trials, it's from having learned the worth of steadfast friendship. And also, what not to say. The least helpful question is: "Did you want the divorce, or didn't you?" Did I want to keep that gangrenous leg, or not? How to explain, in a culture that venerates choice: two terrifying options are much worse than none at all. Give me any day the quick hand of cruel fate that will leave me scarred but blameless. As it was, I kept thinking of that wicked third-grade joke in which some boy comes up behind you and grabs your ear, starts in with a prolonged tug, and asks, "Do you want this ear any longer?"

Still, the friend who holds your hand and says the wrong   14
thing is made of dearer stuff than the one who stays away. And generally, through all of it, you live. My favorite fictional character, Kate Vaiden (in the novel by Reynolds Price), advises: "Strength just comes in one brand—you stand up at sunrise and meet what they send you and keep your hair combed."

Once you've weathered the straits, you get to cross the   15
tricky juncture from casualty to survivor. If you're on your feet at the end of a year or two, and have begun putting together a happy new existence, those friends who were kind enough to feel sorry for you when you needed it must now accept you back to the ranks of the living. If you're truly blessed, they will dance at your second wedding. Everybody else, for heaven's sake, should stop throwing stones.

Arguing about whether nontraditional families deserve pity   16
or tolerance is a little like the medieval debate about lefthandedness as a mark of the devil. Divorce, remarriage, single parenthood, gay parents, and blended families simply are.

They're facts of our time. Some of the reasons listed by soci-
ologists for these family reconstructions are: the idea of marriage as a romantic partnership rather than a pragmatic one; a
shift in women's expectations, from servility to self-respect
and independence; and longevity (prior to antibiotics no
marriage was expected to last many decades—in Colonial
days the average couple lived to be married less than twelve
years). Add to all this, our growing sense of entitlement to
happiness and safety from abuse. Most would agree these are
all good things. Yet their result—a culture in which serial
monogamy and the consequent reshaping of families are the
norm—gets diagnosed as "failing."

For many of us, once we have put ourselves Humpty-   17
Dumpty-wise back together again, the main problem with our
reorganized family is that other people think we have a problem. My daughter tells me the only time she's uncomfortable
about being the child of divorced parents is when her friends
say they feel sorry for her. It's a bizarre sympathy, given that
half the kids in her school and nation are in the same boat, pursuing childish happiness with the same energy as their married-
parent peers. When anyone asks how *she* feels about it, she
spontaneously lists the benefits: our house is in the country
and we have a dog, but she can go to her dad's neighborhood
for the urban thrills of a pool and sidewalks for roller-skating.
What's more, she has three sets of grandparents!

Why is it surprising that a child would revel in a widened   18
family and the right to feel at home in more than one house?
Isn't it the opposite that should worry us—a child with no
home at all, or too few resources to feel safe? The child at risk
is the one whose parents are too immature themselves to
guide wisely; too diminished by poverty to nurture; too far
from opportunity to offer hope. The number of children in
the U.S. living in poverty at this moment is almost unfath-
omably large: twenty percent. There are families among us
that need help all right, and by no means are they new on the
landscape. The rate at which teenage girls had babies in 1957
(ninety-six per thousand) was twice what it is now. That remarkable statistic is ignored by the religious right—probably

because the teen birth rate was cut in half mainly by legalized abortion. In fact, the policy gatekeepers who coined the phrase "family values" have steadfastly ignored the desperation of too-small families, and since 1979 have steadily reduced the amount of financial support available to a single parent. But, this camp's most outspoken attacks seem aimed at the notion of families getting too complex, with add-ons and extras such as a gay parent's partner, or a remarried mother's new husband and his children.

To judge a family's value by its tidy symmetry is to purchase a book for its cover. There's no moral authority there. The famous family comprised of Dad, Mom, Sis, and Junior living as an isolated economic unit is not built on historical bedrock. In *The Way We Never Were*, Stephanie Coontz writes, "Whenever people propose that we go back to the traditional family, I always suggest that they pick a ballpark date for the family they have in mind." Colonial families were tidily disciplined, but their members (meaning everyone but infants) labored incessantly and died young. Then the Victorian family adopted a new division of labor, in which women's role was domestic and children were allowed time for study and play, but this was an upper-class construct supported by myriad slaves. Coontz writes, "For every nineteenth-century middle-class family that protected its wife and child within the family circle, there was an Irish or German girl scrubbing floors . . . a Welsh boy mining coal to keep the home-baked goodies warm, a black girl doing the family laundry, a black mother and child picking cotton to be made into clothes for the family, and a Jewish or an Italian daughter in a sweatshop making 'ladies' dresses or artificial flowers for the family to purchase." 19

The abolition of slavery brought slightly more democratic arrangements, in which extended families were harnessed together in cottage industries; at the turn of the century came a steep rise in child labor in mines and sweatshops. Twenty percent of American children lived in orphanages at the time; their parents were not necessarily dead, but couldn't afford to keep them. 20

During the Depression and up to the end of World War II,   21
many millions of U.S. households were more multigenerational than nuclear. Women my grandmother's age were
likely to live with a fluid assortment of elderly relatives, in-
laws, siblings, and children. In many cases they spent virtually every waking hour working in the company of other
women—a companionable scenario in which it would be easier, I imagine, to tolerate an estranged or difficult spouse.
I'm reluctant to idealize a life of so much hard work and so
little spousal intimacy, but its advantage may have been resilience. A family so large and varied would not easily be
brought down by a single blow: it could absorb a death, long
illness, an abandonment here or there, and any number of
irreconcilable differences.

The Family of Dolls came along midcentury as a great   22
American experiment. A booming economy required a mobile labor force and demanded that women surrender jobs to
returning soldiers. Families came to be defined by a single
breadwinner. They struck out for single-family homes at an
earlier age than ever before, and in unprecedented numbers
they raised children in suburban isolation. The nuclear family
was launched to sink or swim.

More than a few sank. Social historians corroborate that   23
the suburban family of the postwar economic boom, which
we have recently selected as our definition of "traditional,"
was no panacea. Twenty-five percent of Americans were poor
in the mid-1950s, and as yet there were no food stamps. Sixty
percent of the elderly lived on less than $1,000 a year, and
most had no medical insurance. In the sequestered suburbs,
alcoholism and sexual abuse of children were far more widespread than anyone imagined.

Expectations soared, and the economy sagged. It's hard to   24
depend on one other adult for everything, come what may.
In the last three decades, that amorphous, adaptable structure we call "family" has been reshaped once more by economic tides. Compared with fifties families, mothers are far
more likely now to be employed. We are statistically more
likely to divorce, and to live in blended families or other

extranuclear arrangements. We are also more likely to plan and space our children, and to rate our marriages as "happy." We are less likely to suffer abuse without recourse, or to stare out at our lives through a glaze of prescription tranquilizers. Our aged parents are less likely to be destitute, and we're half as likely to have a teenage daughter turn up a mother herself. All in all, I would say that if "intact" in modern family-values jargon means living quietly desperate in the bell jar, then hip-hip-hooray for "broken." A neat family model constructed to service the Baby Boom economy seems to be returning gradually to a grand, lumpy shape that human families apparently have tended toward since they first took root in the Olduvai Gorge. We're social animals, deeply fond of companionship, and children love best to run in packs. If there is a *normal* for humans, at all, I expect it looks like two or three Families of Dolls, connected variously by kinship and passion, shuffled like cards and strewn over several shoeboxes.

The sooner we can let go of the fairy tale of families functioning perfectly in isolation, the better we might embrace the relief of community. Even the admirable parents who've stayed married through thick and thin are very likely, at present, to incorporate other adults into their families— household help and baby-sitters if they can afford them, or neighbors and grandparents if they can't. For single parents, this support is the rock-bottom definition of family. And most parents who have split apart, however painfully, still manage to maintain family continuity for their children, creating in many cases a boisterous phenomenon that Constance Ahrons in her book *The Good Divorce* calls the "binuclear family." Call it what you will—when ex-spouses beat swords into plowshares and jump up and down at a soccer game together, it makes for happy kids.   25

Cinderella, look, who needs her? All those evil stepsisters? That story always seemed like too much cotton-picking fuss over clothes. A childhood tale that fascinated me more was the one called "Stone Soup," and the gist of it is this: Once upon a time, a pair of beleaguered soldiers straggled home to   26 a village empty-handed, in a land ruined by war. They were famished, but the villagers had so little they shouted evil words and slammed their doors. So the soldiers dragged out a big kettle, filled it with water, and put it on a fire to boil. They rolled a clean round stone into the pot, while the villagers peered through their curtains in amazement.

"What kind of soup is that?" they hooted.   27

"Stone soup," the soldiers replied. "Everybody can have   28
some when it's done."

"Well, thanks," one matron grumbled, coming out with a   29
shriveled carrot. "But it'd be better if you threw this in."

And so on, of course, a vegetable at a time, until the whole   30
suspicious village managed to feed itself grandly.

Any family is a big empty pot, save for what gets thrown   31
in. Each stew turns out different. Generosity, a resolve to turn bad luck into good, and respect for variety—these things will nourish a nation of children. Name-calling and suspicion will not. My soup contains a rock or two of hard times, and maybe yours does too. I expect it's a heck of a bouillabaise.

For Study and Discussion

QUESTIONS FOR RESPONSE

1. To what extent does the makeup of your family or the families of some of your close friends fit what Kingsolver calls the "traditional family"; that is, a father, stay-at-home mother, and two or three children? How do your experiences with different kinds of families affect your response to Kingsolver's essay?
2. The phrase "family values" is an ambiguous term, used by various factions for their own political purposes. How would you define the term in what seems to you an honest and legitimate way? What do you think Kingsolver's definition of family values might be?

QUESTIONS ABOUT PURPOSE

1. In paragraphs 19 through 23, Kingsolver gives several snapshots of what so-called traditional families have actually looked like for

the past several decades. What do you think she hopes to accomplish with these accounts?

2. What new insights do you think Kingsolver wants her readers to have about the divorce process?

QUESTIONS ABOUT AUDIENCE

1. What experience with divorce, single parenthood, and the step-families created by second marriages do you think today's readers under forty are likely to have? How do those experiences affect the way they are likely to respond to an essay like this?

2. What details in the essay suggest that Kingsolver feels she is writing more for women than for men?

QUESTIONS ABOUT STRATEGIES

1. Kingsolver has published several successful novels, two of which—*The Bean Trees* and *Pigs in Heaven*—tell the story of a single mother who adopts and raises a child. What strategies do you see in this essay that you think might have come from her talent for writing fiction?

2. Kingsolver draws examples from two sources: her own experience and observations, and historical examples from previous eras. What are the strengths of examples from each of these sources?

QUESTIONS FOR DISCUSSION

1. The variety of households in most communities suggests that there are several models for effective families. Drawing on your own experiences, describe one or two models that you have seen work well.

2. Kingsolver suggests that she's been severely criticized at times for being a divorced woman who is raising a child without a husband. Do you think such criticisms are common, and, if so, how justified do you believe them to be?

Barbara Dafoe Whitehead was born in Rochester, Minnesota, in 1944 and educated at the University of Wisconsin and the University of Chicago. She has contributed articles to *Commonweal*, the *New York Times,* and the *Wall Street Journal.* Her most controversial article, "Dan Quayle Was Right," published in the *Atlantic,* refers to former Vice President Dan Quayle's criticism of the television show *Murphy Brown* because its title character chose to have a baby without being married. She has also written another controversial article for the *Atlantic,* "The Failure of Sex Education." These articles have led to books such as *The Divorce Culture* (1997) and *Goodbye to Girlhood: What's Troubling Girls and What We Can Do About It* (1999). In "Women and the Future of Fatherhood," excerpted from *The Divorce Culture,* Whitehead argues that even the best mothers cannot be good fathers.

Women and the Future of Fatherhood

MUCH OF OUR contemporary debate over fatherhood is governed by the assumption that men can solve the fatherhood problem on their own. The organizers of last year's Million Man March asked women to stay home, and the leaders of Promise Keepers and other grass-roots fatherhood movements whose members gather with considerably less fanfare simply do not admit women.

There is a cultural rationale for the exclusion of women. The fatherhood movement sees the task of reinstating responsible fatherhood as an effort to alter today's norms of masculinity and correctly believes that such an effort cannot succeed unless it is voluntarily undertaken and supported by men. There is also a political rationale in defining fatherlessness as a men's issue. In the debate about marriage and parenthood, which women have dominated for at least 30 years, the fatherhood movement gives men a powerful collective voice and presence.

Yet however effective the grass-roots movement is at stirring men's consciences and raising their consciousness, the fatherhood problem will not be solved by men alone. To be sure, by signaling their commitment to accepting responsibility

---

[This] notion of marriage as a union of two sovereign selves may be inadequate to define a relationship that carries with it the obligations, duties and sacrifices of parenthood.

---

for the rearing of their children, men have taken the essential first step. But what has not yet been acknowledged is that the success of any effort to renew fatherhood as a social fact and a cultural norm also hinges on the attitudes and behavior of women. Men can't be fathers unless the mothers of their children allow it.

Merely to say this is to point to how thoroughly marital disruption has weakened the bond between fathers and children. More than half of all American children are likely to spend at least part of their lives in one-parent homes. Since the vast majority of children in disrupted families live with their mothers, fathers do not share a home or a daily life with their children. It is much more difficult for men to make the kinds of small, routine, instrumental investments in their children that help forge a good relationship. It is hard to fix a flat bike tire or run a bath when you live in

another neighborhood or another town. Many a father's instrumental contribution is reduced to the postal or electronic
transmission of money, or, all too commonly, to nothing at
all. Without regular contact with their children, men often
make reduced emotional contributions as well. Fathers must
struggle to sustain close emotional ties across time and space,
to "be there" emotionally without being there physically.
Some may pick up the phone, send a birthday card, or buy a
present, but for many fathers, physical absence also becomes
emotional absence.

Without marriage, men also lose access to the social and   5
emotional intelligence of women in building relationships.
Wives teach men how to care for young children, and they
also encourage children to love their fathers. Mothers who
do not live with the father of their children are not as likely as
married mothers to represent him in positive ways to the children; nor are the relatives who are most likely to have greatest
contact with the children—the mother's parents, brothers,
and sisters—likely to have a high opinion of the children's
father. Many men are able to overcome such obstacles, but
only with difficulty. In general, men need marriage in order
to be good fathers.

If the future of fatherhood depends on marriage, however, its   6
future is uncertain. Marriage depends on women as well as
men, and women are less committed to marriage than ever
before in the nation's history. In the past, women were economically dependent on marriage and assumed a dispropor-
tionately heavy responsibility for maintaining the bond, even
if the underlying relationship was seriously or irretrievably
damaged. In the last third of the 20th century, however, as
women have gained more opportunities for paid work and
the availability of child care has increased, they have become
less dependent on marriage as an economic arrangement.
Though it is not easy, it is possible for women to raise children on their own. This has made divorce far more attractive
as a remedy for an unsatisfying marriage, and a growing number of women have availed themselves of the option.

Today, marriage and motherhood are coming apart.   7
Remarriage and marriage rates are declining even as the rates
of divorce remain stuck at historic highs and childbearing
outside marriage becomes more common. Many women see
single motherhood as a choice and a right to be exercised if a
suitable husband does not come along in time.

The vision of the "first stage" feminism of the 1960s and   8
'70s, which held out the model of the career woman unfet-
tered by husband or children, has been accepted by women
only in part. Women want to be fettered by children, even to
the point of going through grueling infertility treatments or
artificial insemination to achieve motherhood. But they are
increasingly ambivalent about the ties that bind them to a
husband and about the necessity of marriage as a condition of
parenthood. In 1994, a National Opinion Research survey
asked a group of Americans. "Do you agree or disagree: one
parent can bring up a child as well as two parents together."
Women split 50/50 on the question; men disagreed by more
than two to one.

And indeed, women enjoy certain advantages over men in   9
a society marked by high and sustained levels of family
breakup. Women do not need marriage to maintain a close
bond to their children, and thus to experience the larger
sense of social and moral purpose that comes with raising
children. As the bearers and nurturers of children and
(increasingly) as the sole breadwinners for families, women
continue to be engaged in personally rewarding and socially
valuable pursuits. They are able to demonstrate their feminine virtues outside marriage.

Men, by contrast, have no positive identity as fathers outside   10
marriage. Indeed, the emblematic absent father today is the
infamous "deadbeat dad." In part, this is the result of efforts
to stigmatize irresponsible fathers who fail to pay alimony
and child support. But this image also reflects the fact that
men are heavily dependent on the marriage partnership to
fulfill their role as fathers. Even those who keep up their child
support payments are deprived of the social importance and

sense of larger purpose that comes from providing for children and raising a family. And it is the rare father who can develop the qualities needed to meet the new cultural ideal of the involved and "nurturing" father without the help of a spouse.

These differences are reflected in a growing virtue gap. American popular culture today routinely recognizes and praises the achievements of single motherhood, while the widespread failure of men as fathers has resulted in a growing sense of cynicism and despair about men's capacity for virtuous conduct in family life. The enormously popular movie *Waiting to Exhale* captures the essence of this virtue gap with its portrait of steadfast mothers and deadbeat fathers, morally sleazy men and morally unassailable women. And women feel free to vent their anger and frustration with men in ways that would seem outrageous to women if the shoe were on the other foot. In *Operating Instructions* (1993), her memoir of single motherhood, Anne Lamott mordantly observes, "On bad days, I think straight white men are so poorly wired, so emotionally unenlightened and unconscious that you must approach each one as if he were some weird cross between a white supremacist and an incredibly depressing T. S. Eliot poem."

Women's weakening attachment to marriage should not be taken as a lack of interest in marriage or in a husband-wife partnership in child rearing. Rather, it is a sign of women's more exacting emotional standards for husbands and their growing insistence that men play a bigger part in caring for children and the household. Given their double responsibilities as breadwinners and mothers, many working wives find men's need for ego reinforcement and other forms of emotional and physical upkeep irksome and their failure to share housework and child care absolutely infuriating. (Surveys show that husbands perform only one-third of all household tasks even if their wives are working full-time.) Why should men be treated like babies? women complain. If men fail to meet their standards, many women are willing to do without them. Poet and polemicist Katha Pollitt captures the prevailing sentiment: "If single women can have sex, their own homes, the respect of friends and interesting work, they don't need to tell themselves that any marriage is better than none. Why not have a child on one's own? Children are a joy. Many men are not."

For all these reasons, it is important to see the fatherhood problem as part of the larger cultural problem of the decline of marriage as a lasting relationship between men and women. The traditional bargain between men and women has broken down, and a new bargain has not yet been struck. It is impossible to predict what that bargain will look like—or whether there will even be one. However, it is possible to speculate about the talking points that might bring women to the bargaining table. First, a crucial proviso: there must be recognition of the changed social and economic status of women. Rightly or wrongly, many women fear that the fatherhood movement represents an effort to reinstate the status quo ante, to repeal the gains and achievements women have made over the past 30 years and return to the "separate spheres" domestic ideology that put men in the workplace and women in the home. Any effort to rethink marriage must accept the fact that women will continue to work outside the home. 13

Therefore, a new bargain must be struck over the division of paid work and family work. This does not necessarily mean a 50/50 split in the work load every single day, but it does mean that men must make a more determined and conscientious effort to do more than one-third of the household chores. How each couple arrives at a sense of what is fair will vary, of course, but the goal is to establish some mutual understanding and commitment to an equitable division of tasks. 14

Another talking point may focus on the differences in the expectations men and women have for marriage and intimacy. Americans have a "best friends" ideal for marriage that 15 includes some desires that might in fact be more easily met by a best friend—someone who doesn't come with all the complicated entanglements of sharing a bed, a bank account, and a bathroom. Nonetheless, high expectations for emotional intimacy in marriage often are confounded by the very different understandings men and women have of intimacy. Much more than men, women seek intimacy and affection through talking and emotional disclosure. Men often prefer sex to talking, and physical disrobing to emotional disclosing. They tend to be less than fully committed to (their own) sexual fidelity, while women view fidelity as a crucial sign of commitment. These are differences that the sexes need to engage with mutual recognition and tolerance.

In renegotiating the marital bargain, it may also be useful   16 to acknowledge the biosocial differences between mothers and fathers rather than to assume an androgynous model for the parental partnership. There can be a high degree of flexibility in parental roles, but men and women are not interchangeable "parental units," particularly in their children's early years. Rather than struggle to establish identical tracks in career and family lives, it may be more realistic to consider how children's needs and well-being might require patterns of paid work and child rearing that are different for mothers and fathers but are nevertheless equitable over the course of a lifetime.

Finally, it may be important to think and talk about marriage   17 in another kind of language than the one that suffuses our current discourse on relationships. The secular language of "intimate relationships" is the language of politics and psychotherapy, and it focuses on individual rights and individual needs. It can be heard most clearly in the personal-ad columns, a kind of masked ball where optimists go in search of partners who respect their rights and meet their emotional needs. These are not unimportant in the achievement of the contemporary ideal of marriage, which emphasizes egalitarianism and emotional fulfillment. But this notion of marriage as a union of two sovereign selves may be inadequate to define a relationship that carries with it the obligations, duties, and sacrifices of parenthood. There has always been a tension between marriage as an intimate relationship between a man and a woman and marriage as an institutional arrangement for raising children, and though the language of individual rights plays a part in defining the former, it cannot fully describe the latter. The parental partnership requires some language that acknowledges differences, mutuality, complementarity, and, more than anything else, altruism.

There is a potentially powerful incentive for women to respond to an effort to renegotiate the marriage bargain, and that has to do with their children. Women can be good mothers without being married. But especially with weakened communities that provide little support, children need levels of parental investment that cannot be supplied solely by a good mother, even if she has the best resources at her disposal. These needs are more likely to be met if the child has a father as well as a mother under the same roof. Simply put, even the best mothers cannot be good fathers.   18

For Study and Discussion

QUESTIONS FOR RESPONSE

1. In paragraph 9, Whitehead says that "women enjoy certain advantages over men in a society marked by high and sustained levels of family breakup." Considering your own experience and that of people you know well, how do you respond to this claim?
2. In her first paragraph, Whitehead talks about "the fatherhood problem." How would you describe that problem in our society? Or do you think it even exists? Why do you say so?

QUESTIONS ABOUT PURPOSE

1. What changes in women's behaviors and attitudes would Whitehead like to bring about?
2. What changes in men's behaviors and attitudes would Whitehead like to bring about?

QUESTIONS ABOUT AUDIENCE

1. Whom do you see as the principal audience that Whitehead hopes to reach with this essay—men or women? On what do you base your answer?
2. What differences in responses to this article would you expect from readers over forty and those under forty?

QUESTIONS ABOUT STRATEGIES

1. Whitehead's argument is built on strong statements like this: "Today, marriage and motherhood are coming apart" and "Men have no positive identity as fathers outside marriage." In light of your own observations about today's families, how credible do you find these statements? Why?
2. Although Whitehead is writing about a topic that often generates a great deal of emotion, she is careful not to sound angry or to blame anyone. How does her argument benefit from her maintaining this moderate tone?

QUESTIONS FOR DISCUSSION

1. In paragraph 15, Whitehead says that men and women have crucial differences in their expectations about marriage and family. Judging by the people you know who have married recently or who plan to marry soon, what do you think women expect? What do men expect?
2. What important contributions (other than money) do you think a father makes to a child's upbringing that can't be adequately taken care of by a mother? Are there other individuals who can make those contributions?

A Debate About Harry Potter

JOAN ACOCELLA

Joan Acocella was born in 1945 in San Francisco and was educated at the University of California at Berkeley and Rutgers University. She began her writing career as a dance critic for *Dance Magazine,* the *New York Daily News,* and the *Wall Street Journal* before joining the staff of the *New Yorker.* Her books include *Mark Morris* (1993), *Creating Hysteria: Women and Multiple Personality Disorder* (1999), and *Willa Cather and the Politics of Criticism* (2000). In "Under the Spell," reprinted from the *New Yorker,* Acocella argues that the appeal of the Harry Potter books lies in their willingness to raise complicated moral questions.

Under the Spell

N OT SINCE Y2K have we seen a fuss like the one over   1
"Harry Potter and the Goblet of Fire," the fourth volume in J. K. Rowling's series about a junior wizard. Biggest advance order ever (including Amazon.com's three hundred and fifty thousand), biggest first printing ever (three million eight hundred thousand copies in this country alone), biggest takeover, ever, of the *Times* best-seller list by a single writer, let alone a children's writer. As "The Goblet of Fire" was being printed, the three preceding volumes were all still in the ranking—a circumstance that resulted, last Sunday, in the creation of a separate, children's best-seller list, just what we didn't need. Prior to publication, the book was shrouded in ultra-tight, press-inflaming secrecy. There

were no copies for reviewers, or for anyone, before publication day, July 8th. Many stores stayed open late on July 7th—
indeed, threw Harry Potter parties—and started ringing up
the sales at a minute after midnight. I myself went to Books of
Wonder, on West Eighteenth Street, and stood in line for two
hours with a lot of excited children and bleary-eyed parents as
a Harry Potter lookalike, presumably associated with the
store, cruised the sidewalk, distributing press-on lightning-
bolt tattoos and fake cheer. Around 1:45 A.M., I made it to

---

*The subject of the Harry Potter series is
power, an important matter for children,
since they have so little of it.*

---

the front of the line and was allowed to buy "The Goblet of
Fire." After all that, I would love to tell you that the book is a
big nothing. In fact, it's wonderful, just like its predecessors.

   Part of the secret of Rowling's success is her utter   2
traditionalism. The Potter story is a fairy tale, plus a
bildungsroman, plus a murder mystery, plus a cosmic war of
good and evil, and there's almost no classic in any of those
genres that doesn't reverberate between the lines of Harry's
saga. The Arthurian legend, the Superman comics, "Star
Wars," "Cinderella," "The Lord of the Rings," the "Chronicles of Narnia," "The Adventures of Sherlock Holmes,"
Genesis, Exodus, the Divine Comedy, "Paradise Lost"—
they're all there. The Gothic paraphernalia, too: turreted cas-
tles, purloined letters, surprise visitors arriving in the dark of
night, backed by forked lightning. If you take a look at
Vladimir Propp's 1928 book "Morphology of the Folk
Tale," which lists just about every convention ever used in
fairy tales, you can check off, one by one, the devices that
Rowling has unabashedly picked up. At the beginning of the
story, Propp says, the villain harms someone in the hero's

family. (The evil wizard Voldemort murdered Harry's good-wizard parents when the boy was a year old, and tried to kill him, too.) The hero is branded. (Voldemort's attack left Harry with a scar in the shape of a lightning bolt on his forehead.) The hero is banished. (Harry is forced to go live with his loathsome aunt and uncle, the Dursleys.) The hero is released. (Harry is finally informed that he is a wizard, and goes off to live at Hogwarts School of Witchcraft and Wizardry.) The hero must survive ordeals, seek things, acquire a wise helper, all of which Harry does. The villain must change form and leave bloody trails; Voldemort obliges. According to Propp, a fairy tale is supposed to end with the hero's marriage, but Rowling may break ranks here. She has said that the series will be seven novels long, one for each of Harry's years at Hogwarts. He started there at age eleven, so he will be seventeen when we say goodbye to him. In the line in front of Books of Wonder, there was heated speculation as to who is going to end up as Harry's girl. (I say Ginny Weasley.) I doubt we'll have a wedding, though. Seventeen's a little young.

So Rowling's books are chock-a-block with archetypes, [3] and she doesn't just use them; she glories in them, plays with them, postmodernly. At the Dursleys' house, Harry lives in a cupboard under the stairs, with spiders. Rowling is also a great showoff when it comes to surprise endings, and this, I think, is actually a fault of the books, or of the last two. The dénouements last for pages and pages, as red herrings are eliminated, false identities cleared up, friends unmasked as foes, and vice versa. Not only is this too complicated, the surprises are too surprising. How can Sirius Black, who has been stalking Harry throughout "The Prisoner of Azkaban," turn out to be a good guy—indeed, the boy's godfather? How can Scabbers, whom we have known and loved for three volumes as a dusty, useless little rat, snoozing in the sun, emerge at the end of that book as a deep-dyed villain in disguise? It seems to invalidate all our prior experience of the series. Not to speak of the sheer confusion. Faced with the equally counter-intuitive revelations at the end of "The Goblet of Fire,"

Harry thinks, "It made no sense . . . no sense at all." I agree with him, but apparently we're in a minority.

Rowling has said that she has no trouble at all thinking her-   4
self back to age eleven, and the novels show it. There are toilet jokes, booger jokes. There is a ball game, Quidditch—with four kinds of players (all flying on brooms) and three kinds of balls—that sounds as though it were made up by a clever eleven-year-old. And the books are filled with children's problems. Do you have bad dreams? Did you find your Christmas presents rather a letdown? Do you hate the new baby in your house? Do you wish you had different parents? Is there something weird that lives under your bed and makes noises at night? If so, Joanne Rowling is thinking about you. Best of all is her treatment of the social nightmares of the schoolyard: cliques, bullying, ostracism, kids who like to remind you that your family doesn't have much money. Such problems are perhaps more pressing in the English boarding school, on which Hogwarts is modelled. (Last year, in the *Times Book Review*, Pico Iyer claimed that Hogwarts was a near-exact replica of Eton, where he did his time.) But the situation clearly rings a bell with Rowling's American readers, too.

More, even, than the Potter books' sensitivity to preteen   5
terrors, it is their wised-upness, their lack of sentimentality, that must appeal to Rowling's audience. However much they have to do with goodness, these are not prissy books. Harry lies to adults again and again. He also hates certain people, and Rowling hates them, too. Uncle Vernon Dursley is not only cruel; he spits when he talks. Harry says the Dursleys wish him dead, and he's right. As for the forces of good, they are often well out of reach. In "The Sorcerer's Stone" there is a heart-stopping scene in which Harry comes upon a mirror, the so-called Mirror of Erised, and sees his dead parents in it. His father waves at him; his mother weeps and smiles. Reading this, you think, Oh, good, thank God—Harry's not really alone, not really an orphan. Yes, he's being hunted down by a remorseless villain—in each of

the books, Voldemort pursues him—but his parents' spirits are there to protect him. Then Dumbledore, Hogwarts's wise headmaster, appears and tells Harry that the Mirror of Erised shows us not what is but what we desire. (Read "Erised" backward.) Harry is alone.

The great beauty of the Potter books is their wealth of 6 imagination, their sheer, shining fullness. Rowling has said that the idea for the series came to her on a train trip from Manchester to London in 1990, and that, even before she started writing the first volume, she spent years just working out the details of Harry's world. We reap the harvest: the inventory of magical treats (Ice Mice, Jelly Slugs, Fizzing Whizbees—levitating sherbet balls) in the wizard candy store; the wide range of offerings (Dungbombs, Hiccup Sweets, Nose-Biting Teacups) in the wizard joke store. Hogwarts is a grand, creepy castle, a thousand years old, with more dungeons and secret passages than you can shake a stick at. There are a hundred and forty-two staircases, some of which go to different places on different days of the week. There are suits of armor that sing carols at Christmastime, and get the words wrong. There are poltergeists—Peeves, for example, who busies himself jamming gum into keyholes. We also get ghosts, notably Nearly Headless Nick, whose executioner didn't quite finish the job, so that Nick's head hangs by an "inch or so of ghostly skin and muscle"—it keeps flopping over his ruff—thus, to his grief, excluding him from participating in the Headless Hunt, which is confined to the thoroughly decapitated.

The Hogwarts staff is a display case all its own: Mad-Eye 7 Moody, the professor of Defense Against the Dark Arts, who, apart from his ocular problems, has a chunk of his nose missing and a wooden leg ending in a clawed foot; Rubeus Hagrid, the gentle-giant gamekeeper, with his pet, Norbert, a baby dragon, whom he feeds a bucket of brandy mixed with chicken blood every half hour. Norbert isn't the only monster. There are also centaurs, basilisks, and hippogriffs, together with hinkypunks, boggarts, and, my favorites, the grindylows. Harry encounters his first grindylow in a tank in a professor's office: "A sickly green creature with sharp little horns had its face pressed against the glass, . . . flexing its long spindly fingers." (Later, the grindylow shakes its fist at him.) To deal with such encounters, and other life events, the students must learn many spells: "Expelliarmus," to get rid of something; "Waddiwasi," to extract gum from keyholes; "Peskipiksi Pesternomi," to make pixies leave you alone. Hogwarts is a whole, bursting world.

Most of Rowling's characters are types, and excellent as such, but some rise to a richness beyond the reach of British central casting. Voldemort, for example. When he failed to kill the infant Harry, Voldemort was disempowered, and it is in this weakened state that we first encounter him in "The Goblet of Fire." But he isn't just weak. He is—grotesquely, disgustingly, terrifyingly—a *baby:* "hairless and scaly-looking, a dark, raw, reddish black. Its arms and legs were thin and feeble, and its face—no child alive ever had a face like that—flat and snakelike, with gleaming red eyes." Soon—as soon as he is immersed in a potion made from Harry's blood and someone else's hacked-off hand and various other ingredients—he becomes his adult self again, which is not so handsome either, but that first sight of him, that little red thing, swaddled in blankets, is a triumph of horror fiction.

It's horror with a difference, though. Rowling's favorite writer, she has told interviewers, is Jane Austen. She also loves Dickens. And it is in their bailiwick—English morals-and-manners realism, the world of Pip and Miss Bates, of money and position and trying to keep your head up if you have neither—that she scores her greatest victories. A nice example is the scene, in "The Sorcerer's Stone," where Harry and Ron meet for the first time, on the train that is taking them, as entering students, to Hogwarts. Each is handicapped. Harry, though he is famous throughout the wizard world (because, as an infant, he repelled Voldemort's attack), and though he has a pile of gold left to him by his parents, is without family and utterly ignorant of wizardry. Ron comes from a long line of wizards, and he has family galore, but that is his problem: five older brothers, no position. He is always

ACOCELLA ☞ *Under the Spell*   **511**

dressed in hand-me-downs; his mother always forgets what kind of sandwich he likes; he has no spending money. Together, in the train compartment, the two boys comfort and help each other. Harry shares the wizard candies he buys from the vender (he can afford them); Ron explains the wizard trading cards that come with the candies (he understands them). Harry gives Ron prestige; Ron gives Harry a sense of belonging. All this is done very Englishly, very subtly, in small gestures, but in the end each boy, because of the other, arrives at Hogwarts slightly better armed against the harshness of the world.

The subject of the Harry Potter series is power, an important   10 matter for children, since they have so little of it. How does one acquire power? How can it be used well, and ill? Does ultimate power lie with the good? (In other words, is there a God?) If so, why is there so much cruelty around? These are questions that Milton, among others, addressed before Rowling, and she is not ashamed to follow in their wake. Voldemort is an avatar of Milton's Lucifer; Dumbledore of Milton's God, who so mysteriously permits evil in the world.

   Each of the novels approaches the problem from a differ-   11 ent angle. The first, "Harry Potter and the Sorcerer's Stone," is heroic. We meet our champion; he is a child; we watch him grow into competence and faith. The second volume, "Harry Potter and the Chamber of Secrets," is quite different: secular, topical, political. Sexism is not a major problem at Hogwarts. The school is coed. Several of the Quidditch champions are girls. Harry's friend Hermione, the know-it-all girl, the hand-up-in-class girl—Rowling has said she based the character on herself as a child—is not forced to go through the Katharine Hepburn treatment (take off her glasses, unpin her hair) before she becomes likable. But racism *is* a problem at Hogwarts. Yes, the student body includes Cho Chang and Parvati Patil and Dean Thomas, who has dreadlocks. (Rowling forgot about a few other groups, though. I would not have minded if the evil Professor Snape had not had a hook nose, greasy black hair, and sallow skin—standard features of the rapacious Jew—or if the chief villain of "The Sorcerer's Stone" had not worn a purple turban, been prone to faint and weep, and had the name Quirrell, which is rather close to "queer.") But the wizard world is in the grip of an overarching race war, a campaign to rid wizardry of those with Muggle, or non-wizard, blood. This ethnic-cleansing campaign, led by Voldemort, is the subject of "The Chamber of Secrets." It fails, but only for the time being. We will hear about it again.

The strangest volume is the third, "Harry Potter and the Prisoner of Azkaban," the psychological installment, featuring a pack of demons—operating at Voldemort's bidding—who are the most frightening monsters in the series so far. These are the Dementors: huge, cloaked, faceless creatures, with rotting hands, who, if they get you, clamp their jaws on your mouth and suck out of you every thought of happiness. The Dementors represent depression. Actually, if I'm not mistaken, they represent a specific, British theory of depression—John Bowlby's theory that loss of a parent in early childhood is a major risk factor for that disorder. At age one, Harry lost both his parents. (I don't know much about Rowling's childhood, but she has told interviewers that she suffered a period of depression as an adult, and had to get professional help.) In any case, the Dementors are after Harry, and he escapes them only with the help of a teacher named Lupin. To Lupin alone can he fully confide his fears, and Lupin's teachings are the closest thing, in the Potter series, to overt psychological counselling of child readers. At the end of "The Prisoner of Azkaban," this nice man turns out to be a werewolf (Rowling's antisentimentality again), but he's a good werewolf. 12

The new book, "Harry Potter and the Goblet of Fire," is the central pillar of the projected series of seven and is thus a transitional volume. It introduces many new subjects, notably sex. (Harry is fourteen now, and mightily taken with Cho Chang.) Also, the politics become more ambitious. Rowling now asks her readers to consider the cynicism of government officials, the injustice of the law courts, the vagaries of international relations, the mendacity of the press, 13 even the psychology of slavery. ("They're *happy*," Ron's brother says of the house-elves. Hermione does not agree.) This is a great, toppling heap of subjects, and Rowling takes seven hundred and thirty-four pages to deal with them. (Has there ever before been a children's story seven hundred and thirty-four pages long? What confidence!) Where the prior volumes moved like lightning, here the pace is slower, the energy more dispersed. At the same time, the tone becomes more grim. Voldemort has been restored to power. Things will now become harder for Harry, and for all the wizard world. Dumbledore says so.

There is much for Rowling to resolve in the remaining volumes, above all the question about power—is it reconcilable with goodness?—that she poses in the first four books. Already in "The Sorcerer's Stone," Quirrell says, "There is no good and evil, there is only power, and those too weak to seek it." As Harry has grown, he has become more powerful and ambitious and, at the same time, more virtuous. In "The Goblet of Fire," as in all the books, there is a big contest, which Harry longs to win. The contest is in three parts, and in each part, lest we miss the point, Rowling shows Harry handicapping himself, hurting his chances of victory, out of concern for others. He wins, but how will he do, thus compromised by altruism, in future contests? Remember: Voldemort is back.   14

Even more interesting, however, is a strange matter— something about the *kinship* of good and evil—that Rowling has been hinting at since the beginning of the series. Harry and Voldemort have a lot in common. Both have Muggle blood; both are orphans. Their wands contain feathers from the same phoenix. When they met in armed combat in "The Goblet of Fire," their wands, as they touch, produce a single stream of light, which binds them together. There is some connection between these two. (Shades of "Star Wars.") I don't know what Rowling has in mind here. Maybe it's the Miltonic idea of evil as merely good perverted. Or maybe not.   15

But that is the main virtue of these books, their philosophical seriousness. Rowling is a good psychotherapist, and she teaches excellent morals. (Those parents who have objected   16 to the Potter series on the ground that it promotes unchristian values should give it another read.) She also spins a good yarn. Undoubtedly, it is Voldemort and the Dementors and the grindylows that have gotten these books translated into forty languages and won them sales, *before* "The Goblet of Fire," of more than thirty million copies. But her great glory, and the thing that may place her in the pantheon, is that she asks her preteen readers to face the hardest questions of life, and does not shy away from the possibility that the answers may be sad: that loss may be permanent, evil ever-present, good exhaustible. In an odd, quiet moment in "The Goblet of Fire," Harry stands alone in Hogwarts's Owlery, gazing out into the twilight. He sees his friend Hagrid digging in the earth. Is Hagrid burying something? Or looking for something? Harry doesn't know, and for once he doesn't investigate. He seems tired. He just stays there, watching Hagrid, until he can see him no more, whereupon the owls in the Owlery awaken and swoosh past him, "into the night." In this volume, some darkness has fallen. With the light—the next three books—new griefs will surely come.

For Study and Discussion

QUESTIONS FOR RESPONSE

1. If you've enjoyed the Harry Potter books, where do you think their appeal lies for you? If you haven't read them, what do you think accounts for your lack of interest?
2. As Acocella points out, the Harry Potter books have been cleverly marketed to build up suspense among potential buyers. To what extent do you think the marketing strategies have influenced your reaction to them?

QUESTIONS ABOUT PURPOSE

1. Although the Harry Potter books are written for children, this serious review of them was written for the *New Yorker*, a magazine for sophisticated, well-educated readers. Why do you think Acocella chose them for her audience?

2. Why does Acocella trace the traditions, from the King Arthur legends to *Star Wars,* that underlie the books, giving references that range from the Bible and literary classics to comic books?

QUESTIONS ABOUT AUDIENCE

1. Educators know that young boys are a notoriously difficult audience for writers to reach, but both boys and girls are reading Harry Potter in record numbers. How does Acocella explain this wide appeal?

2. Who besides the readers of the Potter books themselves might be interested in learning more about this publishing phenomenon?

QUESTIONS ABOUT STRATEGIES

1. Acocella goes into great detail to show the lurid and gory details of the Potter stories. How does she engage her readers with these descriptions?

2. How does Acocella present herself in this essay? How does she establish her credentials to analyze the traditions and legends that are so important to the Potter series?

QUESTIONS FOR DISCUSSION

1. Acocella says that the main virtue of the Potter books is their philosophical seriousness and the fact that Rowling, the author, is a good psychotherapist. How does she support that claim?

2. Why do you think the books have drawn so much response? How is that response different from the attention paid to movies and sports?

Harold Bloom was born in 1930 in New York and was educated at Cornell University and Yale University. In his distinguished teaching career, he has taught literature at Yale, Cornell, Harvard, and New York University. A staunch defender of the Western literary tradition, his numerous critical books include *The Anxiety of Influence: A Theory of Poetry* (1973), *A Map of Misreading* (1975), *The Breaking of Vessels* (1982), *The Western Canon: The Books and School of the Ages* (1994), and most recently *Hamlet: Poem Unlimited* (2003). In "Can 35 Million Book Buyers Be Wrong? Yes," reprinted from the *Wall Street Journal*, Bloom argues that the Harry Potter books are inferior to classic children's books.

Can 35 Million Book Buyers Be Wrong? Yes.

T AKING ARMS AGAINST Harry Potter, at this moment, is 1
to emulate Hamlet taking arms against a sea of troubles. By opposing the sea, you won't end it. The Harry Potter epiphenomenon will go on, doubtless for some time, as J. R. R. Tolkien did, and then wane.

The official newspaper of our dominant counter-culture, 2
the *New York Times,* has been startled by the Potter books into establishing a new policy for its not very literate book review. Rather than crowd out the Grishams, Clancys, Crichtons, Kings and other vastly popular prose fictions on its fiction bestseller list, the Potter volumes will now lead a separate children's list. J. K. Rowling, the chronicler of Harry Potter, thus has an unusual distinction: She has changed the policy of the policy-maker.

IMAGINATIVE VISION

I read new children's literature, when I can find some of any   3
value, but had not tried Rowling until now. I have just concluded the 300 pages of the first book in the series, "Harry
Potter and the Sorcerer's Stone," purportedly the best of the
lot. Though the book is not well written, that is not in itself
a crucial liability. It is much better to see the movie, "The
Wizard of Oz," than to read the book upon which it was
based, but even the book possessed an authentic imaginative

---

*Hogwarts enchants many of Harry's fans,
perhaps because it is much livelier than the
schools they attend, but it seems to me an
academy more tiresome than grotesque.*

---

vision. "Harry Potter and the Sorcerer's Stone" does not, so
that one needs to look elsewhere for the book's (and its se-
quels') remarkable success. Such speculation should follow
an account of how and why Harry Potter asks to be read.

The ultimate model for Harry Potter is "Tom Brown's   4
School Days" by Thomas Hughes, published in 1857. The
book depicts the Rugby School presided over by the formidable Thomas Arnold, remembered now primarily as the father of Matthew Arnold, the Victorian critic-poet. But
Hughes's book, still quite readable, was realism, not fantasy.
Rowling has taken "Tom Brown's School Days" and re-seen
it in the magical mirror of Tolkien. The resultant blend of a
schoolboy ethos with a liberation from the constraints of re-
ality-testing may read oddly to me, but is exactly what millions of children and their parents desire and welcome at this
time.

In what follows, I may at times indicate some of the inad-   5
equacies of "Harry Potter." But I will keep in mind that a
host are reading it who simply will not read superior fare,

such as Kenneth Grahame's "The Wind in the Willows" or the "Alice" books of Lewis Carroll. Is it better that they read Rowling than not read at all? Will they advance from Rowling to more difficult pleasures?

Rowling presents two Englands, mundane and magical, divided not by social classes, but by the distinction between the "perfectly normal" (mean and selfish) and the adherents of sorcery. The sorcerers indeed seem as middle-class as the Muggles, the name the witches and wizards give to the common sort, since those addicted to magic send their sons and daughters off to Hogwarts, a Rugby School where only witchcraft and wizardry are taught. Hogwarts is presided over by Albus Dumbledore as Headmaster, he being Rowling's version of Tolkien's Gandalf. The young future sorcerers are just like any other budding Britons, only more so, sports and food being primary preoccupations. (Sex barely enters into Rowling's cosmos, at least in the first volume.) 6

Harry Potter, now the hero of so many millions of children and adults, is raised by dreadful Muggle relatives after his sorcerer parents are murdered by the wicked Voldemort, a wizard gone trollish and, finally, post-human. Precisely why poor Harry is handed over by the sorcerer elders to his piggish aunt and uncle is never clarified by Rowling, but it is a nice touch, suggesting again how conventional the alternative Britain truly is. They consign their potential hero-wizard to his nasty blood-kin, rather than let him be reared by amiable warlocks and witches, who would know him for one of their own. 7

The child Harry thus suffers the hateful ill treatment of the Dursleys, Muggles of the most Muggleworthy sort, and of their sadistic son, his cousin Dudley. For some early pages we might be in Ken Russell's film of "Tommy," the rock-opera by The Who, except that the prematurely wise Harry is much healthier than Tommy. A born survivor, Harry holds on until the sorcerers rescue him and send him off to Hogwarts, to enter upon the glory of his schooldays. 8

Hogwarts enchants many of Harry's fans, perhaps because it is much livelier than the schools they attend, but it seems 9 to me an academy more tiresome than grotesque. When the future witches and wizards of Great Britain are not studying how to cast a spell, they preoccupy themselves with bizarre intramural sports. It is rather a relief when Harry heroically suffers the ordeal of a confrontation with Voldemort, which the youth handles admirably.

One can reasonably doubt that "Harry Potter and the Sorcerer's Stone" is going to prove a classic of children's literature, but Rowling, whatever the aesthetic weakness of her work, is at least a millennial index to our popular culture. So huge an audience gives her importance akin to rock stars, movie idols, TV anchors, and successful politicians. Her prose style, heavy on cliché, makes no demands upon her readers. In an arbitrarily chosen single page—page 4—of the first Harry Potter book, I count seven clichés, all of the "stretch his legs" variety. 10

How to read "Harry Potter and the Sorcerer's Stone"? Why, very quickly, to begin with, perhaps also to make an end. Why read it? Presumably, if you cannot be persuaded to read anything better, Rowling will have to do. Is there any redeeming educational use to Rowling? Is there any to Stephen King? Why read, if what you read will not enrich mind or spirit or personality? For all I know, the actual wizards and witches of Britain, or of America, may provide an alternative culture for more people than is commonly realized. 11

Perhaps Rowling appeals to millions of reader non-readers because they sense her wistful sincerity, and want to join her world, imaginary or not. She feeds a vast hunger for unreality: can that be bad? At least her fans are momentarily emancipated from their screens, and so may not forget wholly the sensation of turning the pages of a book, any book. 12

INTELLIGENT CHILDREN

And yet I feel a discomfort with the Harry Potter mania, and I hope that my discontent is not merely a highbrow snobbery, or a nostalgia for a more literate fantasy to beguile (shall we say) intelligent children of all ages. Can more than 35 million 13 book buyers, and their offspring, be wrong? Yes, they have been, and will continue to be so for as long as they persevere with Potter.

A vast concourse of inadequate works, for adults and for children, crams the dustbins of the ages. At a time when public judgment is no better and no worse than what is proclaimed by the ideological cheerleaders who have so destroyed humanistic study, anything goes. The cultural critics will, soon enough, introduce Harry Potter into their college curriculum, and the *New York Times* will go on celebrating another confirmation of the dumbing-down it leads and exemplifies.   14

For Study and Discussion

QUESTIONS FOR RESPONSE

1. What impression do you get of the author, Harold Bloom, from the reasons he gives for disliking the Harry Potter books?
2. Either from your own reading of the Potter books or from reviewing the essay "Under the Spell," what is your response to Bloom's claim that J. K. Rowling lacks imagination?

QUESTIONS ABOUT PURPOSE

1. What do you think an eminent professor of Bloom's standing hopes to accomplish by taking time to read a popular children's book and then give it—and the *New York Times*—such a scathing review?
2. What kind of reading do you think Bloom would recommend as literature that would, as he says, "enrich the mind or spirit or personality"?

QUESTIONS ABOUT AUDIENCE

1. Bloom published this essay in the *Wall Street Journal*. How does he anticipate the knowledge and interests of his readers, who are predominantly business executives and people involved in the world of finance?

2. On the other hand, why might the readers of the *Wall Street Journal* be intrigued by the Harry Potter books?

QUESTIONS ABOUT STRATEGIES

1. What persona do you think Bloom wants to present to his readers? How does his first sentence contribute to that persona?
2. Why does he liken Harry's creator, J. K. Rowling, to the "rock stars, movie idols, TV anchors, and successful politicians" of the millennium? What's his point?

QUESTIONS FOR DISCUSSION

1. In his last paragraph, when Bloom condemns "the ideological cheerleaders who have so destroyed humanistic study," he refers to faculty across the country who have, in recent years, promoted a more culturally diverse curriculum in the humanities, one that includes more women writers and more writers from minority groups. He accuses such individuals of "dumbing down" literature courses. How does his criticism of the Harry Potter books fit into this complaint?
2. To what extent do you see Bloom's criticism as valid? To what extent do you see it as nostalgia for a "golden age of children's literature"?

KURT VONNEGUT, JR.

Kurt Vonnegut, Jr., was born in 1922 in Indianapolis, Indiana, and attended Cornell University before being drafted into the infantry in World War II. Vonnegut was captured by the Germans at the Battle of the Bulge and sent to Dresden, where he worked in the underground meat locker of a slaughterhouse. He survived the Allied firebombing of Dresden and, following the war, returned to the United States, where he studied anthropology, then worked for a news bureau, and later wrote publicity for the General Electric Research Laboratory in Schenectady, New York. In 1950 he began to devote all his time to his own writing. His first three novels, *Player Piano* (1952), *The Sirens of Titan* (1959), and *Cat's Cradle* (1963), established Vonnegut's reputation as a writer who could blend humor with serious insights into the human experience. His most successful novel, *Slaughterhouse-Five, or the Children's Crusade* (1969), is based on his wartime experiences in Dresden. Among his numerous other works are *God Bless You, Mr. Rosewater* (1966), *Galápagos* (1985), *Hocus Pocus* (1990), and *Timequake* (1997). His best-known short stories are collected in *Canary in the Cat House* (1961) and *Welcome to the Monkey House* (1968). "Harrison Bergeron," reprinted from the latter collection, is the story of the apparatus that a future society must create to make everyone equal.

Harrison Bergeron

T HE YEAR WAS 2081, and everybody was finally equal.   1
They weren't only equal before God and the law. They

were equal every which way. Nobody was smarter than anybody else. Nobody was better looking than anybody else.
Nobody was stronger or quicker than anybody else. All this
equality was due to the 211th, 212th, and 213th Amend-
ments to the Constitution, and to the unceasing vigilance of
agents of the United States Handicapper General.

Some things about living still weren't quite right, though.   2
April, for instance, still drove people crazy by not being
springtime. And it was in that clammy month that the H-G
men took George and Hazel Bergeron's fourteen-year-old
son, Harrison, away.

It was tragic, all right, but George and Hazel couldn't   3
think about it very hard. Hazel had a perfectly average intelligence, which meant she couldn't think about anything except in short bursts. And George, while his intelligence was
way above normal, had a little mental handicap radio in his
ear. He was required by law to wear it at all times. It was
tuned to a government transmitter. Every twenty seconds or
so, the transmitter would send out some sharp noise to keep
people like George from taking unfair advantage of their
brains.

George and Hazel were watching television. There were   4
tears on Hazel's cheeks, but she'd forgotten for the moment
what they were about.

On the television screen were ballerinas.   5

A buzzer sounded in George's head. His thoughts fled in   6
panic, like bandits from a burglar alarm.

"That was a real pretty dance, that dance they just did,"   7
said Hazel.

"Huh?" said George.   8

"That dance—it was nice," said Hazel.   9

"Yup," said George. He tried to think a little about the   10
ballerinas. They weren't really very good—no better than
anybody else would have been, anyway. They were burdened with sashweights and bags of birdshot, and their
faces were masked, so that no one, seeing a free and graceful gesture or a pretty face, would feel like something the
cat drug in. George was toying with the vague notion that

maybe dancers shouldn't be handicapped. But he didn't get very far with it before another noise in his ear radio scattered his thoughts.

George winced. So did two of the eight ballerinas.   11

Hazel saw him wince. Having no mental handicap herself,   12
she had to ask George what the latest sound had been.

"Sounded like somebody hitting a milk bottle with a ball   13
peen hammer," said George.

"I'd think it would be real interesting, hearing all the dif-   14
ferent sounds," said Hazel, a little envious. "All the things
they think up."

"Um," said George.   15

"Only, if I was Handicapper General, you know what I   16
would do?" said Hazel. Hazel, as a matter of fact, bore a
strong resemblance to the Handicapper General, a woman
named Diana Moon Glampers. "If I was Diana Moon
Glampers," said Hazel, "I'd have chimes on Sunday—just
chimes. Kind of in honor of religion."

"I could think, if it was just chimes," said George.   17

"Well—maybe make 'em real loud," said Hazel. "I think   18
I'd make a good Handicapper General."

"Good as anybody else," said George.   19

"Who knows better'n I do what normal is?" said Hazel.   20

"Right," said George. He began to think glimmeringly   21
about his abnormal son who was now in jail, about Harrison,
but a twenty-one-gun salute in his head stopped that.

"Boy!" said Hazel, "that was a doozy, wasn't it?"   22

It was such a doozy that George was white and trembling,   23
and tears stood on the rims of his red eyes. Two of the eight
ballerinas had collapsed on the studio floor, were holding
their temples.

"All of a sudden you look so tired," said Hazel. "Why   24
don't you stretch out on the sofa, so's you can rest your
handicap bag on the pillows, honeybunch." She was referring
to the forty-seven pounds of birdshot in a canvas bag, which
was padlocked around George's neck. "Go on and rest the
bag for a little while," she said. "I don't care if you're not
equal to me for a while."

George weighed the bag with his hands. "I don't mind it," 25
he said. "I don't notice it any more. It's just a part of me."

"You been so tired lately—kind of wore out," said Hazel. 26
"If there was just some way we could make a little hole in the
bottom of the bag, and just take out a few of them lead balls.
Just a few."

"Two years in prison and two thousand dollars fine for every 27
ball I took out," said George. "I don't call that a bargain."

"If you could just take a few out when you came home 28
from work," said Hazel. "I mean—you don't compete with
anybody around here. You just set around."

"If I tried to get away with it," said George, "then other 29
people'd get away with it—and pretty soon we'd be right
back to the dark ages again, with everybody competing
against everybody else. You wouldn't like that, would you?"

"I'd hate it," said Hazel. 30

"There you are," said George. "The minute people start 31
cheating on laws, what do you think happens to society?"

If Hazel hadn't been able to come up with an answer to 32
this question, George couldn't have supplied one. A siren
was going off in his head.

"Reckon it'd fall all apart," said Hazel. 33

"What would?" said George blankly. 34

"Society," said Hazel uncertainly. "Wasn't that what you 35
just said?"

"Who knows?" said George. 36

The television program was suddenly interrupted for a 37
news bulletin. It wasn't clear at first as to what the bulletin
was about, since the announcer, like all announcers, had a serious speech impediment. For about half a minute, and in a
state of high excitement, the announcer tried to say, "Ladies
and gentlemen—"

He finally gave up, handed the bulletin to a ballerina to 38
read.

"That's all right—" Hazel said to the announcer, "he 39
tried. That's the big thing. He tried to do the best he could
with what God gave him. He should get a nice raise for trying so hard."

"Ladies and gentlemen—" said the ballerina, reading the   40
bulletin. She must have been extraordinarily beautiful, because the mask she wore was hideous. And it was easy to see
that she was the strongest and most graceful of all the
dancers, for her handicap bags were as big as those worn by
two-hundred-pound men.

And she had to apologize at once for her voice, which was   41
a very unfair voice for a woman to use. Her voice was a warm,
luminous, timeless melody. "Excuse me—" she said, and she
began again, making her voice absolutely uncompetitive.

"Harrison Bergeron, age fourteen," she said in a grackle   42
squawk, "has just escaped from jail, where he was held on
suspicion of plotting to overthrow the government. He is a
genius and an athlete, is under-handicapped, and should be
regarded as extremely dangerous."

A police photograph of Harrison Bergeron was flashed on   43
the screen upside down, then sideways, upside down again,
then right side up. The picture showed the full length of
Harrison against a background calibrated in feet and inches.
He was exactly seven feet tall.

The rest of Harrison's appearance was Halloween and hard-   44
ware. Nobody had ever borne heavier handicaps. He had out-
grown hindrances faster than the H-G men could think them
up. Instead of a little ear radio for a mental handicap, he wore
a tremendous pair of earphones, and spectacles with thick wavy
lenses. The spectacles were intended to make him not only half
blind, but to give him whanging headaches besides.

Scrap metal was hung all over him. Ordinarily, there was a   45
certain symmetry, a military neatness to the handicaps issued
to strong people, but Harrison looked like a walking junk-
yard. In the race of life, Harrison carried three hundred
pounds.

And to offset his good looks, the H-G men required that   46
he wear at all times a red rubber ball for a nose, keep his eyebrows shaved off, and cover his even white teeth with black
caps at snaggle-tooth random.

"If you see this boy," said the ballerina, "do not—I repeat,   47
do not—try to reason with him."

There was the shriek of a door being torn from its hinges. 48

Screams and barking cries of consternation came from the 49
television set. The photograph of Harrison Bergeron on
the screen jumped again and again, as though dancing to the
tune of an earthquake.

George Bergeron correctly identified the earthquake, and 50
well he might have—for many was the time his own home
had danced to the same crashing tune. "My God—" said
George, "that must be Harrison!"

The realization was blasted from his mind instantly by the 51
sound of an automobile collision in his head.

When George could open his eyes again, the photograph 52
of Harrison was gone. A living, breathing Harrison filled the
screen.

Clanking, clownish, and huge, Harrison stood in the cen- 53
ter of the studio. The knob of the uprooted studio door was
still in his hand. Ballerinas, technicians, musicians, and
announcers cowered on their knees before him, expecting
to die.

"I am the Emperor!" cried Harrison. "Do you hear? I am 54
the Emperor! Everybody must do what I say at once!" He
stamped his foot and the studio shook.

"Even as I stand here—" he bellowed, "crippled, hobbled, 55
sickened—I am a greater ruler than any man who ever lived!
Now watch me become what I *can* become!"

Harrison tore the straps of his handicap harness like wet 56
tissue paper, tore straps guaranteed to support five thousand
pounds.

Harrison's scrap-iron handicaps crashed to the floor. 57

Harrison thrust his thumbs under the bars of the padlock 58
that secured his head harness. The bar snapped like celery.
Harrison smashed his headphones and spectacles against the
wall.

He flung away his rubber-ball nose, revealed a man that 59
would have awed Thor, the god of thunder.

"I shall now select my Empress!" he said, looking down 60
on the cowering people. "Let the first woman who dares rise
to her feet claim her mate and her throne!"

A moment passed, and then a ballerina arose, swaying like   61
a willow.

Harrison plucked the mental handicap from her ear,   62
snapped off her physical handicaps with marvelous delicacy.
Last of all, he removed her mask.

She was blindingly beautiful.   63

"Now—" said Harrison, taking her hand, "shall we show   64
the people the meaning of the word dance? Music!" he
commanded.

The musicians scrambled back into their chairs, and   65
Harrison stripped them of their handicaps, too. "Play your
best," he told them, "and I'll make you barons and dukes
and earls."

The music began. It was normal at first—cheap, silly, false.   66
But Harrison snatched two musicians from their chairs,
waved them like batons as he sang the music as he wanted it
played. He slammed them back into their chairs.

The music began again and was much improved.   67

Harrison and his Empress merely listened to the music for   68
a while—listened gravely, as though synchronizing their
heartbeats with it.

They shifted their weights to their toes.   69

Harrison placed his big hands on the girl's tiny waist, let-   70
ting her sense the weightlessness that would soon be hers.

And then, in an explosion of joy and grace, into the air   71
they sprang!

Not only were the laws of the land abandoned, but the law   72
of gravity and the laws of motion as well.

They reeled, whirled, swiveled, flounced, capered, gam-   73
boled, and spun.

They leaped like deer on the moon.   74

The studio ceiling was thirty feet high, but each leap   75
brought the dancers nearer to it.

It became their obvious intention to kiss the ceiling.   76

They kissed it.   77

And then, neutralizing gravity with love and pure will,   78
they remained suspended in air inches below the ceiling, and
they kissed each other for a long, long time.

It was then that Diana Moon Glampers, the Handicapper   79
General, came into the studio with a double-barreled ten-
gauge shotgun. She fired twice, and the Emperor and the
Empress were dead before they hit the floor.

Diana Moon Glampers loaded the gun again. She aimed it   80
at the musicians and told them they had ten seconds to get
their handicaps back on.

It was then that the Bergerons' television tube burned out.   81

Hazel turned to comment about the blackout to George.   82
But George had gone out into the kitchen for a can of beer.

George came back in with the beer, paused while a handi-   83
cap signal shook him up. And then he sat down again. "You
been crying?" he said to Hazel.

"Yup," she said.   84

"What about?" he said.   85

"I forgot," she said. "Something real sad on television."   86

"What was it?" he said.   87

"It's all kind of mixed up in my mind," said Hazel.   88

"Forget sad things," said George.   89

"I always do," said Hazel.   90

"That's my girl," said George. He winced. There was the   91
sound of a rivetting gun in his head.

"Gee—I could tell that one was a doozy," said Hazel.   92

"You can say that again," said George.   93

"Gee—" said Hazel, "I could tell that one was a doozy."   94

COMMENT ON "HARRISON BERGERON"

Known for his offbeat and sometimes bizarre vision of reality,
Kurt Vonnegut, Jr., has created in "Harrison Bergeron" a science fiction story full of black humor and grotesque details.
The society he creates in the story is reminiscent of the society pictured in Orwell's *1984,* totally controlled by a government that invades and interferes in every facet of its citizens'
lives. In a travesty of the famous declaration that "All men
are created equal," the government has set out to legislate
equality. Vonnegut portrays the results of such legislation in

macabre images of people forced to carry weighted bags to reduce their strength, wear grotesque masks to conceal their beauty, and wear headphones that emitted disruptive sounds to prevent them from thinking clearly. When a fourteen-year-old boy, Harrison Bergeron, shows signs of excellence, he is first arrested, then ruthlessly destroyed when he throws off his restraints and literally rises to the top.

Underneath the farce, Vonnegut has created a tragic picture of a culture so obsessed with equality that people must be leveled by decree. Mediocrity reigns; any sign of excellence or superiority threatens law and order and must be suppressed immediately. Ultimately, of course, such a society will perish because it will kill its talent and stagnate.

Vonnegut wrote this story in 1961, after the repressive Stalinist regime that wiped out thousands of leaders and intellectuals in Russia; it precedes by a few years the disastrous era of Mao's Red Guards in China, when hundreds of thousands of intellectuals and artists were killed or imprisoned in the name of equality. Is Vonnegut commenting on the leveling tendencies of these totalitarian societies? Or does he see such excesses reflected in our own society? No one knows, but it's the genius of artists to prod us to think about such concerns.

Persuasion and Argument as a Writing Strategy

1. In their essays, both Martin Luther King, Jr. and Eric Liu show how strong they still find the concept of the American Dream, the idea that in the United States a person can break away from the constraints of race and poverty and work to fulfill his or her ambition. For a short essay to post on your class website, argue either for or against this concept. If you're skeptical about it, show what limitations you think a person faces because of race, class, or economic circumstances. If you agree that many disadvantaged people in the United States still have a good chance to achieve the American Dream, give examples to support your view.

2. If you're a Harry Potter fan, reread Harold Bloom's essay "Can 35 Million Book Buyers Be Wrong? Yes." and critique his argument. What are his main arguments against the books? What problems do you find with those arguments? To what extent do you think his position as an eminent professor of literature and a famous Shakespeare scholar might influence his opinions about the Potter books? You could post your essay on the website that your hometown library maintains and to which it invites readers to contribute.

3. Reread Kingsolver's essay "Stone Soup" and Whitehead's essay "Women and the Future of Fatherhood," and compare the kinds of arguments the two authors are making. How would you describe the dominant appeal of each essay? How do the two authors use evidence to support their claims, and what kinds of evidence do they choose? Then decide which essay you find more effective and argue for your preference. Conclude your essay by briefly sketching what your experiences with family life have been, either your own or that of people close to you; then consider how those experiences have probably affected your response to these essays. You could write for the

audience of a chat room that's run for children of divorce, write for a discussion group in your writing class, or post your argument on the class website.

4. Many liberal arts colleges require that their students do considerable volunteer work in their community as one of the requirements for completing their degree. Such work might include tutoring in a structured program run by the local schools, being a counselor for four weeks in a summer camp for disadvantaged children, doing physical work one day a month on a Habitat for Humanity project, or serving meals at the Salvation Army charity kitchen twice a month. A student is not permitted to substitute service at his or her own church. In an editorial for your college newspaper, argue for or against this requirement. If you argue for it, give well-supported reasons about the benefits students gain; if you argue against it, do not simply claim that a college has no authority to make such a requirement—point out what you believe are real disadvantages to the students.

5. Argue that the role of the scientist has been distorted by movies featuring mad scientists toying with life and creating monsters.

6. Argue that the role of doctors has been distorted by television shows featuring godlike doctors curing all sorts of obscure diseases for distraught patients.

RESOURCES
FOR
WRITING

ENERGY:
A CASEBOOK

As you worked your way through this book, you discovered
that you already possess many resources for reading and writing. You read essays on a wide variety of themes. You encountered new and complicated information shaped by unusual

and unsettling assertions. But you discovered experiences and feelings that you recognize—the challenge of learning, the ordeal of disappointment, and the cost of achievement. As you examined these essays, you realized that you had something to say about your reading, something to contribute to the themes explored by the writers.

Your work with this book has also enabled you to identify and practice strategies that at each stage of the writing process helped you transform your ideas about a theme into writing. In the beginning, these strategies give rise to questions that you might ask to explore any topic.

Suppose you want to write an essay on the theme of women and science. You might begin by asking why so few women are ranked among the world's great scientists. You might continue asking questions: What historical forces have discouraged women from becoming scientists (cause and effect)? How do women scientists define problems, analyze evidence, and formulate conclusions (process analysis), and do they go about these processes differently than men (comparison and contrast)? If women scientists look at the world differently than men do, does this difference have an effect on the established notions of inquiry (persuasion and argument)? Such questions work like the different lenses you attach to a camera: each lens gives you a different perspective on a subject, a variation on a theme.

If your initial questions enable you to envision your theme from different perspectives, then answering one of these questions encourages you to develop your theme according to a purpose associated with one of the common patterns of organization. For instance, if you decide to write about the underwater discoveries you made on your first scuba dive, your choice of purpose seems obvious: to answer the question, "What happened?" You would then write a narrative essay. In drafting this essay, however, you may discover questions you had not anticipated: What caused explorers to develop scuba diving equipment? What kinds of discoveries have been made using scuba diving equipment? What are the limitations of scuba diving equipment for underwater exploration? How is scuba diving similar to or different from swimming?

Responding to these new questions forces you to decide whether your new information develops or distorts your draft. The history of underwater discovery—from diving bells to diving suits to small submarines—may help your readers see a context for your narrative. On the other hand, such information may confuse them, distracting them from your original purpose—to tell about the discoveries you made scuba diving.

As you struggle with your new themes, you may decide that your original purpose no longer drives your writing. You may decide to change your purpose and write a cause-and-effect essay. Instead of telling what happened to you on your first scuba dive, you might decide to use your personal experience, together with some reading, to write a more scientific essay analyzing the effects of underwater exploration on your senses of sight and hearing.

This book has helped you make such decisions by showing you how the common patterns of organization evoke different purposes, audiences, and strategies. In this thematic unit, you will have the opportunity to make decisions about a little anthology of writing on the theme of *energy*.

Before you begin reading these selections, take an initial inventory:

- *What kind of direct experience have you had with the energy problem?*
  How much attention do you pay to the cost of gasoline?
  How much of your income do you spend on utilities?
  How have you reacted when a storm knocked out your electrical power?

- *What kind of indirect experience have you had with the energy problem?*
  How often do your family members or friends discuss the gas consumption of their cars?
  What have you read about the "energy crisis" in your local newspaper or in your academic classes?
  What have you learned from the media about energy alternatives?

- *What do you know about the history and significance of energy to our culture?*
  How have different sources of energy—water, wind, coal, steam, oil—defined our history?
  Who have been the great energy inventors and innovators?
  How have the revolutions in technology enabled us to find new sources of energy?
  Why do the political debates about energy and the environment create so much controversy?

Thinking about such questions will remind you of the extensive resources you bring to the theme of *energy*. It is a subject that touches all of our lives in some way. And it affects our behavior in countless other ways—what we do with our time, with whom we associate, how we spend our money, what we think of ourselves and our culture.

After you have made a preliminary inventory of your knowledge of and attitudes toward energy, read the writings in this chapter. You will notice that each selection asks you to think about energy from a different perspective.

1. *What happened? (Narration and Description).* Stephen Doheny-Farina recounts the impact an ice storm—and the loss of electrical power—had on his family and community.
2. *How do you do it? How is it done? (Process Analysis).* Tom and Ray Magliozzi analyze different procedures for achieving better "miles per gallon."
3. *How is it similar to or different from something else? (Comparison and Contrast).* Greenpeace International presents a sardonic comparison between an accident at a nuclear power plant in England and the attitudes of Homer Simpson and his fellow workers at a nuclear plant in "Springfield."
4. *What kinds of subdivisions does it contain? (Division and Classification).* Susan Neville reflects on her experience with different types of "utilities."
5. *How would you characterize it? (Definition).* Joseph J. Romm defines *fuel cells* and explains why they have become the Holy Grails of energy technology.

6. *How did it happen? (Cause and Effect)*. Edward Cody analyzes the "high human cost" of China's decision to build the Three Gorges Dam.

7. *How do you prove it? (Persuasion and Argument)*. Francis Broadhurst and Robert F. Kennedy, Jr., present opposing arguments about the value of building a "wind farm" in the middle of Nantucket Sound.

This collection also includes a *photo essay* that present various "visual texts"—pictures, paintings, and images—that evoke questions about the way we *see* energy. Each page of images also contains a writing assignment that asks you to interpret the significance of what you are looking at.

The collection ends with Thomas Pynchon's story "Entropy," an experimental story that explores how *entropy* applies to social and cultural systems as well as to the matter in the universe.

As you examine these selections, keep track of how your reading and seeing expands the theme of energy—provoking memories, adding information, and suggesting questions you had not considered when you made your initial inventory about *energy*. Because this information will give you new ways to think about your original questions, you will want to explore your thinking in writing.

For that reason, this chapter concludes with a series of writing assignments asking you to draw on your own experience or to conduct some additional research so that you can contribute your own resources to the subject of *energy*.

STEPHEN DOHENY-FARINA

Stephen Doheny-Farina was born in 1954 in Harrisburg, Pennsylvania, and educated at the University of Maine and Rensselaer Polytechnic Institute. He is a professor of communication and media at Clarkson University, where he teaches courses in rhetoric, media studies, and digital video production. Most recently he is the recipient of a National Endowment for the Arts grant dedicated to digitizing, archiving, and making accessible via the Internet hundreds of unpublished audio recordings, photographs, and films from the 1970s black avant garde jazz era in New York City. He is the author of *The Wired Neighborhood* (1996) and *The Grid and the Village* (2001). In "The Grid and the Village," excerpted from his book of the same title, Doheny-Farina describes how an ice storm destroyed the power grid, but created a vibrant grid of social ties, in his community.

The Grid and the Village

EARLY MORNING, JANUARY 1998. In Potsdam, New 1
York, the power was out and the freezing rain was intensifying. Our roof, like all our neighbors' roofs, lay insulated beneath a creamy gray-white icing, rounding off the edges and dripping down every wall. Power and phone lines sagged deeply. Bushes and shrubs bowed gracefully down, embedded in glass. A gently undulating, pebbly white sheet stretched across yards and fields from the western horizon down to the frozen flat expanse of the Raquette River to the east. The only sound I could hear was the constant chattering of ice pellets punctuated by the intermittent gunshots of breaking branches. Tree limbs were snapping all around me.

One of our dogs was sniffing around my feet when I saw   2
an orange flash on the horizon, a fiery flare somewhere in the
village. A moment later a brilliant blue explosion lit up the
entire dome of the sky: one of the major power circuits sup-
plying energy to our entire town had just blown. Startled, I
ducked involuntarily and the dog skittered away from me. A
mile away, on the other side of the river, my neighbor's son,
Mike Warden, had just opened his eyes when the world outside his bedroom window was suddenly revealed in that silent
flash of light. For a moment he could see as clearly as if it
were midday, but under a sickly green sun. His wife, Marge,
slept on, the baby due in little more than a week.

For the first two days of the ice storm, my family and   3
neighbors were so cut off from the world that we had no

---

*The impact of the ice storm was less a sudden
catastrophe than an unforeseen change in
the way we had to live.*

---

concept of the severity of the problem. The storm had arrived
with little warning; we didn't know that it had knocked out
power grids from the Great Lakes to the North Atlantic, or
that thousands of people were already fleeing to makeshift
shelters. We didn't know that national emergencies were
being declared on both sides of the U.S.-Canada border and
utility crews from across both countries were steadily parad-
ing into this vast zone of darkness. We simply expected the
lights to come back on at any moment.

It was chillingly cold, and so dark at night that the ice   4
seemed to glow. By the third day without power my wife,
Kath, and I had begun working with our neighbors, the
Centofantis and the Wardens. We needed warmth, in at least
one of our houses, and we needed water from at least one of
our wells. The only way we could succeed in either of these

was to run a generator—and to do that we needed gasoline. As an essential ingredient for all those who had not taken refuge in one of the emergency shelters, finding gas was nearly impossible.

A plan to get some gasoline to us was on the mind of my $\quad$ 5 brother-in-law, Steve, who called us several days into the disaster from one of his service stations downstate. He knew far more about the scale of the storm than we did. He said that he'd be willing to sell a fifty-five gallon drum with gasoline and drive it and a generator to our house. Kath and I were somewhat taken aback by this proposal. It couldn't be that bad, I thought. You can't just wake up one morning and have to live off of a generator for the foreseeable future. That doesn't happen.

But within a day we realized that not only could it happen, $\quad$ 6 it had. We decided to take Steve up on his offer. And when he and Kath's father, Bob, arrived, they told us of a sharp line they had crossed as they descended out of the Adirondack mountains and into the St. Lawrence River valley. After that point, Bob said, the utter destruction of the trees reminded him of photos of European forests that had been shelled in World War II—for as far as he could see there were just tall sticks with craggy, broken branches drooping down. Kath and her father wired the generator into our furnace and water pump, and then set it up so that it could be disengaged and carried over to our neighbor's house intermittently to keep their pipes from freezing, too.

With this it had become clear that the power wasn't just $\quad$ 7 about to come back. We were in the middle of a major storm and we were all starting to realize that we'd better be prepared to take care of ourselves. We emptied the refrigerator and set up a makeshift one on our back deck, which had the effect of putting all our perishables in a freezer. Then we decided to join our neighbors in cooking supper each night at the Wardens' house. The families would pool some key resources.

With a baby due any day, Marge and Mike moved in with $\quad$ 8 their parents. The houses had all become public places; no one needed to knock, and we all moved freely in and out of each other's homes. I heard myself saying things like, "Let's see, with that fifty-five gallons of gas, the twenty-five you have in those cans, the other fifty or sixty gallons we have left in the tanks of all our vehicles, we'll be alright." Twenty-four hours earlier the storm was merely an annoyance that was keeping me from finishing my course syllabi for the coming semester. Suddenly I'm talking about siphoning off gas tanks so we don't freeze; suddenly we're making decisions like having the kids stay in the Wardens' rec room because that's the warmest spot of all our houses.

This was an ironic and deserved fate for me. A couple of   9
years before I had written a book that touted local life while warning people of the potential dangers of global networks. Yet all the while I was continually connected to these networks, participating in global discussions about the importance of protecting local communities. Now my network extended across one yard to the Wardens' house and across one road to the Centofantis' house. No matter how often I had preached about the importance of geophysical place before, I had never in my adult life been so totally consumed for so long by such a limited here and now. It was a moment-by-moment existence devoted to the people and property around me.

Life was focused on keeping generators running, and mov-   10
ing them between our houses. One day when several of us drove a generator over to Mike and Marge's now-abandoned house so that we could pump out its flooded basement, a woman appeared suddenly in the middle of the street and asked me if I knew of anyone who could spare a generator. She was nearly in tears. I hesitated. She said that there was a farm outside of town where the cows were threatened because they couldn't be milked. I didn't know what to say. Our little generator certainly couldn't handle that job. We suggested she contact the police or fire departments. Good Lord, I thought, are we going to find ourselves choosing between keeping our kids warm and fed or helping our neighbors save their livelihoods?

But events quickly pulled us back to our own situation. In   11
the middle of our fourth night without power, Marge went into labor and had to be rushed to the hospital, which itself

was operating in emergency mode under generator power. Then, as the temperatures dropped into the single digits, our generators started to falter. Mine had begun to run ragged and stall out under the strain of cold and overuse.

On the morning of the fifth day I awoke to discover that   12
Mike and Marge had a new baby boy and the Wardens' generator was silent and sitting in a pool of oil. Our genuine happiness was tinged with concern. Without some source of heat and water, we, too, might end up at the shelter. So the day was spent working on generators and with the expert help of a friend of the Wardens, we were able to get both of them back online for the moment.

After nearly a week without power, with Mike, Marge, and   13
baby safely ensconced in the hospital, and with two generators barely limping along, we all decided that we should treat ourselves by going to the shelter for supper. We had heard that they offered free food to anyone who could make it there, and although we hesitated to join what we considered a "refugee camp," we realized that we needed help, too.

The building that night had evolved into a kind of place   14
that has largely disappeared, even in small towns and villages; it became a public commons, a place where people met by chance and talked about whatever was on their minds. On this night, of course, conversations were focused. As we pushed our trays along the buffet line, the common question was "how are you doing?"—not the polite and empty how-are-you-doing but one that meant, What kind of heat do you have? How are you holding up? Who are you with? What have you seen? What do you know? The stories spilled out. Some people had generators; some had fireplaces or wood-stoves. Those who had were sharing with those who didn't. Multigenerational families far flung across the region were coalescing at one location. Others, like us, found themselves throwing in with small neighborhood groups. Whole households were living in one room, the rest of the house closed off and abandoned to the cold. Some were enjoying the company, others were suffocating. For young kids it was fun while teenagers were getting bored and difficult.

There were stories about unexpected predicaments and 15
amazing sights. There was grapevine information about the
state of the power grid and who was going to get power
first. People stood between tables holding trays of hot food
getting cold and just kept talking. Or they were leaning
back in their chairs and talking over their shoulders to someone behind them. Attitudes ranged from a resigned relax-
ation to a kind of subdued, exhausted agitation. All were
shocked by the state of the trees. At one point I realized that
each of the adults around our table was turned away talking
to a different person whom we may or may not have known
before. Talk was easy when everyone was bound by the same
necessities. For me it was a simple but powerful night.

On the night of our sixth day without power, a light over 16
the stove in our kitchen suddenly came on. It stayed on.
Later I would learn that we were among the first thirty percent to get power back in St. Lawrence County. After that,
every day brought more people back online. It would take
two more weeks to restore power to everyone in New York.
It took until February 8, nearly five weeks after the storm hit,
for the complete restoration of power in Quebec's "triangle
of darkness" south of Montreal.

A few days after power had been restored to our road, I 17
was home trying to bring myself to begin preparing again for
the upcoming semester. At that time there were still large
chunks of the north country without electricity, and the word
at Clarkson was that the semester's start would be pushed
back by a week or more. Even so I had little else to do but to
get back at it. The trouble was, I had zero interest in doing
so. The job seemed so distant to me. It was almost as if I had
changed careers over the course of two weeks from teacher to
home handyman—klutzy, semi-clueless, but coachable, very
willing to learn new skills like how to run and maintain a two-
cycle generator engine.

Suddenly the power went out again. I got up quickly and 18
looked out the window to see if there was evidence of power
anywhere in sight. I got on the phone and started calling
people. Power seemed to be out across the village. I was

alive—it was as if the power left the grid and poured into me. I started to check for essential materials throughout the house: candles, flashlights, et cetera. I turned on the radio. Was it a story yet? I was smiling and excited. But I knew there was something perverse about that. "This is nuts," I told myself. "Calm down. It can't last."

It didn't, of course. About an hour later power was re- 19
stored and the reality of pre-storm living continued to loom over me. A week or so later I heard a weather forecaster predict that we might be getting hit by another ice storm. That same day I heard the panicky voice of a local caller to North Country Public Radio who was clearly unnerved by the forecast. She said her husband was immobilized by fear of another ice storm. "We have to do something," she said, "to help each other handle all this." A wave of guilt washed over me. No one who lived through it—including myself—wants to live under those conditions. But why was I, like many others I knew, so unsettled by the prospect of returning to the energized grid?

Late that afternoon, outside the door to the Wardens' 20
house, I stood holding one of their gas cans that had found its way to my garage. I didn't just open the door and walk in. I knocked instead.

In the end, as in all major disasters, the ice storm numbers 21
were big. In the U.S. alone, the storm damaged about eighteen million acres of rural and urban forests. In New York over one thousand power transmission towers were damaged; power companies replaced over eight thousand poles, 1,800 transformers, and five hundred miles of wires. In Canada over 1,300 steel towers were damaged; power companies replaced over 35,000 poles and five thousand transformers. Dairy farmers in both countries lost millions of dollars in livestock and income. At least thirty-five people were killed by storm-related house fires, falling ice, carbon monoxide poisoning, or hypothermia. The Worldwatch Institute reported that the cost of the damage on both sides of the border totaled 2.5 billion dollars, about half of the cost inflicted by Hurricane Mitch ten months later.

But the impact of this experience goes beyond these quan- 22
tifiable items. Consider for a moment one more statistic—
one small, local, seemingly insignificant item: during the
week in which the village of Potsdam was without any type of
traffic signals or traffic control, only one minor fender-
bender was reported. Only one. Under normal circumstances
accidents happen every day around here. Yes, Potsdam is a
small town, but as in any active community, urban, suburban,
or rural, there is just the right combination of traffic and
tricky intersections to bring about a number of serious and
sometimes fatal accidents. There were fewer cars on the road,
thereby reducing the chance of an accident, but I drove
through a few of the most dangerous intersections enough
times in the early days of the storm to know that there were
plenty of chances for serious accidents to happen.

There was more going on than just fewer drivers on the 23
road. I think drivers were more mindful of the act of driving
during that experience. And it was this exercise of storm-
induced mindfulness that may have the most lasting impact
of the entire event. Like most people before the storm I
lived as if electricity came from light switches and power out-
lets. The storm changed that. It's as if I've started to trace
electricity back along the lines from my house to the pole on
the road to the local substation to the transmission lines to
one of the sources of that bulk power: the massive hy-
dropower dam twenty-five miles away on the St. Lawrence
Seaway.

From there I can go a number of places. I can examine the 24
environmental impact of the Seaway to illustrate the price we
pay for power. I can explore in depth that growing worldwide
movement to oppose the building of large dams, most notably
the gargantuan Three Gorges project in China, as a way to
gauge power's costs. I can follow the changes in the power
industry nationwide as state after state is moving to deregulate
its utilities. Or I can delve into the newly resurgent world of
alternate energy sources, especially the recent advances in home
power stations that promise to further atomize the home by
removing it from the power grid without sacrificing any

electronic convenience. But, ultimately, what I find particularly compelling is the way that community came to the fore in the absence of the grid that under normal conditions enables us to live and work quite independently from one another.

Although all disasters have their unique dangers, in many ways the impact of the ice storm was less a sudden catastrophe than an unforeseen change in the way we had to live. Many other types of disasters leave relatively clear boundaries between destruction and normality. For those who are fortunate enough to emerge safely from the mayhem of, say, an earthquake or tornado, escape is possible. The path of destruction is narrow and capricious. One person's world may be destroyed while a neighbor's goes untouched. Or in the case of all but the largest of hurricanes, a section of a town may be obliterated while others survive largely intact. There is some level of destruction and some level of normal living, and the distinction is clear. In contrast, the ice storm was far less violent, far less lethal, but far more democratic; it afflicted everyone within its vast boundaries. For most of the five million of us who lived through it, there was no escape. The only options were to adapt and endure.

And during that process a fascinating phenomenon evolved: as the power grid failed, in its place arose a vibrant grid of social ties—formal and informal, organized and serendipitous, public and private, official and ad hoc. While national news media reported on the standard three Ds of disaster news—deaths, destruction, and disorder—a spontaneous, ever-shifting group of citizen volunteers, public officials, corporate decision-makers, and neighbors helping neighbors pulled together to weather the storm.

By the time we all returned to the safety of the electrified grid, we had come to realize that there existed in this place at this time a web of support that many people thought had long since withered away from disuse. While the fruits of the power grid may make it seem as though each of us can live an autonomous life, we learned that that is an illusion. It is family and community, not global networks, that truly sustain us.

For Study and Response

QUESTIONS FOR RESPONSE

1. How have you reacted when you had to live without electrical power for an extended period?
2. What stories have you told or heard about the event after power was restored?

QUESTIONS ABOUT PURPOSE

1. What does Doheny-Farina want to demonstrate about our dependence on electrical energy?
2. What effect did the ice storm have on his community?

QUESTIONS ABOUT AUDIENCE

1. What assumptions does Doheny-Farina make about his readers' experience with natural disasters?
2. How does his reaction to the weather forecaster's predictions help him establish a connection with his audience?

QUESTIONS ABOUT STRATEGIES

1. How does Doheny-Farina's detailed narrative personalize the facts of the ice storm?
2. How does his obsession with the generator suggest how the ice storm affected his life?

QUESTIONS FOR DISCUSSION

1. What distinctions does Doheny-Farina make between a "refugee camp" and a "public commons"?
2. In what ways does this ice storm differ from other natural disasters—such as Hurricane Katrina?

TOM AND RAY MAGLIOZZI

Tom (b. 1939) and Ray (b. 1949) Magliozzi—
better known as Click and Clack, the Tappet
Brothers—were born in East Cambridge, Massachusetts; both were educated at Massachusetts
Institute of Technology. Tom earned additional
degrees from Northeastern University and
Boston University before working in marketing.
Ray was a VISTA volunteer, taught junior high
school, and worked in the Massachusetts State
Consumer Affairs Department. In 1973, the
brothers opened a "do-it-yourself" garage in
Cambridge called Good News Garage. In 1976,
they started a local radio show in which they answered questions about auto repair. This hilarious
and informative show, *Car Talk,* was syndicated
on National Public Radio in 1987. A sampling of
their most amusing conversations appears in their
book *Car Talk* (1991). In "Guide to Better Fuel
Economy," reprinted from the Car Talk website,
Tom and Ray provide advice about how to save
money on gasoline.

Guide to Better Fuel Economy

W E'RE USED TO taking the car everywhere we go.   1
Three blocks to the store? We just hop in the car
and go. However, if you stop and consider it for a moment,
you'll realize you there are lots of good alternatives.

You can walk, bike, or crawl! And there are other benefits,   2
besides saving money on gas. When you walk, you'll get exercise and live longer. When you bike, you can stop and meet
that new, single neighbor down the street. When you crawl,
you could pick up loose change!

THE
SOURCES
OF
ENERGY
A VISUAL ESSAY

PHOTO 1 *Thomas Hart Benton,* Boomtown,
*1928, 46 1/8 × 54 1/4 inches, oil on
canvas, collection of the Memorial Art
Gallery of the University of Rochester,
Marion Stratton Gould Fund. Photo
by James Via. Art © T. H. Benton
and R. P. Benton Testamentary
Trusts/UMB Bank Trustee/Licensed
by VAGA, New York, NY.*

Thomas Hart Benton's *Boomtown* (1928) evokes a major
era in the history of energy—the discovery of oil. Research
a major energy event in your lifetime and explain both its
personal and national significance.

PHOTO 2 *Michael Townsend,* Chinese Waterwheel, *copyright © Michael Townsend/Stone/Getty Images.*

PHOTO 3 *Viktor Korotayev,* Ukraine Coal Furnace, *copyright © Viktor Korotayev/Reuters/Corbis.*

Michael Townsend's *Chinese Waterwheel* and Viktor Korotayev's *Ukraine Coal Furnace* document two early sources of energy. Research and then describe the limitations of one of these energy sources.

PHOTO 4   *John McGrail,* Nuclear Plant Cooling Towers at Night, *copyright © John McGrail/Taxi/Getty Images.*

PHOTO 5   *Chinch Gryniewicz,* Solar Panels on Roof, *ca. 1970–1994, copyright © Chinch Gryniewicz; Ecoscene/Corbis.*

John McGrail's *Nuclear Plant Cooling Towers at Night* and Chinch Gryniewicz's *Solar Panels* suggest two new sources of energy. Research and then describe the possibilities of one of these energy sources.

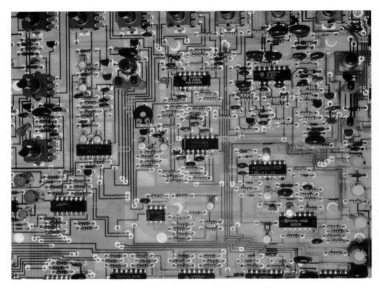

P H O T O 6   *Dia Max,* Computer Chip, *copyright © Dia Max/Taxi/Getty Images.*

Dia Max's *Computer Chip* reveals the miniature connections within a computer chip. Research and then describe how the computer chip has changed the design and use of an everyday electrical appliance.

P H O T O 7 *David McNew,* California Power Grid, *August 9, 2004, copyright © David McNew/Getty Images.*

David McNew's *California Power Grid* (2004) reveals the extensive connections necessary to deliver electricity to homes and businesses in California. Research and then explain the causes of California's frequent power outages.

P H O T O   8   *Galen Rowell,* Alaska Pipeline with Brooks
Range, *ca. 1993, copyright © Galen
Rowell/Corbis.*

Galen Rowell's *Alaska Pipeline with Brooks Range* (ca. 1993) suggests a benign relationship between energy technology and nature.
Research and then describe the benefits and dangers of this pipeline
to our economy and environment

P H O T O 9   *Juan Castromil,* Oil Covered Seagull,
*November 22, 2002, copyright © Juan
Castromil/Corbis.*

Juan Castromil's *Oil Covered Seagull* (2002) suggests a disastrous
relationship between energy technology and nature. Research and
then analyze the causes and costs of oil spills to our economy and
environment.

PHOTO 10   *David Cooper,* Smart Car Parked Behind
Hummer, *April 7, 2005,* © *David
Cooper/Toronto Star/ZUMA/Corbis*

David Cooper's *Smart Car Parked Behind Hummer* (2005) reveals
the dramatic differences between a ponderous machine and an
efficient vehicle. Research the advantages and disadvantages of each
car—cost, safety, fuel consumption, maneuverability—and then
present an argument for the car you would buy.

If you live in a town or city with decent public transportation, leave your car home and use the bus or train. Even if you use public transit just once or twice a week, you'll save wear and tear on your car, you won't be shelling out for all that gas, and you won't have to dodge cell-phone-addicted rush-hour commuters. Plus you get to people watch—an underappreciated activity.   3

Still not enough reasons for you? Consider this fact: Actress Debra Winger met her husband on the subway. We rest our case.   4

For more information on public transportation in your 'hood, check out the directory at the American Public Transportation Association website.   5

Time to buy a new car? Do the math and see what it'll cost you if gas costs, say, $5 a gallon in six years. If you're like   6

So slow down. You'll be a safer, more relaxed driver, and you'll increase your fuel efficiency.

---

most Americans, and drive about 20,000 miles a year, increasing your car's fuel efficiency by 10 MPG can save you over a thousand bucks a year—not to mention countless stops at the gas station where you breathe fumes and stand in the rain.

Our advice? Get the smallest, most efficient vehicle that makes sense for your daily driving. There are more hybrids on the market every year. And, when you really do need that Gigantisaurus SUV for loading up the family and hauling the 24-foot cabin cruiser to the beach, rent it for two weeks.   7

For more information, go to fueleconomy.gov.   8

Okay, so carpooling or using public transportation is not exactly a revolutionary idea. But the fact is we don't do enough of either one of these things. Admittedly, driving to work with Ned Flanders next door could be a colossal pain in   9 the butt. But then again, if you're lucky, you just might car-pool with an investment banker and get in on some valuable insider trading tips.

A new idea to the U.S., formal car co-ops have been around 10 for years in Europe. How do they work? Members share a fleet of vehicles and pay a monthly fee. And, since the organization takes care of all of the maintenance and repairs on the fleet, you'll never have to worry about making a boat payment to your mechanic . . . or even pumping gas in some cases. A vari-ety of programs exist around the country. In Our Fair City, there's a service called Zipcar. You become a member, log on to the website, and sign up for a car during the hours you want it. Then you take it from the designated parking spot, use it, and put it back. And you pay a reasonable hourly fee. That's it.

Is a car co-op right for you? If you drive 10,000 miles per 11 year or less, a car co-op may make sense. If you drive 5,000 miles a year you'll save at least $1,300 annually by joining a car co-op.

Car co-ops have been shown to reduce individual mem- 12 bers' driving by more than 50 percent. A study by the Swiss Office for Energy Affairs indicated that car co-op members reduced their driving by more than 70 percent, without feeling particularly bothered by not having immediate access to a car. For more information and for specifics about pro-grams in your area, check out the car sharing website for Zipcar, or Flexcar.

Tell your boss that you're going to be working at home 13 one day a week.

Then, get another job for that one day a week you're at 14 home. Think of all the gas you'll be able to afford! Seriously, by working from home just one day a week you'll avoid put-ting wear and tear on your car, using gas, getting stuck in traffic—and, quite possibly, you might even discover that you get more work done at home than in the office.

Use the grade of gas you need and nothing higher. 15

Does your owner's manual say "Premium Unleaded 16 Only"? No? Then don't ever use premium fuel. There. We just saved you 40 cents a gallon . . . or $8 on a 20-gallon fill up. If your engine is designed to run on regular gas, there's absolutely no benefit to putting in "high test." It pollutes more, it costs more, and doesn't give you any benefit in performance or fuel system cleanliness.

Now, what if your car DOES call for minimum 91 octane? Well, next time you buy a car, dumkoff, check what kind of fuel it requires first. We've always said that once you buy the car, you're stuck. You've got to use 91, because your high compression engine will ping if you don't. But now, most cars have "knock sensors," that retard the timing via the engine management computer (effectively lowering the compression) to protect the engine, in the event that you happen to get some bad gas, or have an emergency and can only get regular grade fuel. So we got to thinking, what would be wrong with using the knock sensor all the time? What if you put regular gas in the car all the time and let the knock sensor do its job and retard the timing? You'd have a little less power, but that extra 8 bucks a fill up might be more important to you than power right now. It would be to us. ⟨17⟩

It's a controversial theory, we admit it. But that's never bothered us before. And we can't think of any long-term effects of driving with the knock sensor retarding the timing. So our position (for the time being) is . . . use regular. Who cares? Now, if there are any actual automotive engineers in the audience who have worked on knock sensors, who want to tell us why we have our heads up our keisters, feel free to write to us. And if we're convinced that we're wrong, we'll happily change our recommendation. ⟨18⟩

Because wind resistance increases dramatically with speed, every mile that you drive at a speed over 55 MPH, your fuel economy actually goes down by two percent. In other words, you'll get about half the mileage driving at 70 MPH compared to 50 MPH! That's why aerodynamics has become so important in the last 15 years, and why all of our cars now look like jelly beans. ⟨19⟩

Here's another rule of thumb, from the EPA: Every 5 MPH you drive over 60 MPH you're paying an additional $0.21 per gallon for gas. ⟨20⟩

So slow down. You'll be a safer, more relaxed driver, and   21
you'll increase your fuel efficiency. And, believe it or not, due
to an unexplained Einsteinian time warp, you'll also get to
your destination in about the same time.

Getting into the highest gear you can, at the lowest possi-   22
ble speed, will save you plenty of gas.

Why? Because you use less gas when the engine is turning   23
slowly. The slower the engine turns, the fewer the number of
explosions in the cylinders. And fewer explosions means less
gas consumed.

So, if you drive a manual transmission car, shift sooner. As   24
long as the engine doesn't buck, shutter, or ping, you're fine.
You'll sacrifice the ability to accelerate quickly—but you can
always downshift if you need to accelerate.

Why is it that everyone feels they have to accelerate going   25
up a hill?

It turns out that accelerating uphill is a fabulous way to   26
burn up enormous amounts of gas. Don't believe us? If your
car has a display that shows your instantaneous gas mileage,
try it out. You'll see your mileage plummet—from 25 or
30 MPG . . . down to 6 MPG—or sometimes even as low as
2 or 3 MPG.

So, don't try to increase your speed when you're climbing   27
a hill—just maintain the same speed, or even allow the car to
go a little slower. Heck, it's a hill! Your wallet will thank you.

Every time you step on your car's brakes, you're wasting   28
gas.

Why is that? Simple. Every time you use the brakes, you're   29
wasting the "acceleration" you've already used. Instead of
moving your car, that energy is being transformed into
steaming hot brake pads.

How do you use the brakes less? Anticipate. If you're at a   30
stoplight, don't speed away when there's a good chance
you'll have to stop again soon. Accelerate slowly, and then
coast to the next light. If you see a need to stop up ahead,
coast. Don't continue to accelerate and then brake at the last
minute. If you anticipate your stops, you'll cut down on your
wasteful acceleration, and save lots of fuel.

You know that Thule roof rack you keep on your car to ³¹ convince people that you're really outdoorsy? (Even though you drive a Volvo.) It's costing up to 5 percent in MPG. So unless you need the rack to boost your flagging self-esteem, we suggest you pull off the entire rack. That also goes for standard luggage racks, kayak holders, ski racks, Labrador retriever holders and all the cross bars that go with them. Put it in the garage, and toss the rack back on the roof when you really need it. You'll reduce your aerodynamic drag significantly.

What's your MPG when you're idling? It's negative! ³² You're actually burning gas . . . and going nowhere.

If you're sitting outside a tattoo parlor waiting for your ³³ grandmother, and you know it's going to take her a good 15 minutes to get that new Komodo dragon tattooed on her left butt cheek, turn off your engine. You're just burning money. Some people have heard a myth that it takes more gas to start a car than to run it. So they use that as an excuse to leave a car idling. It's complete B.S. If you're stationary for more than a couple of minutes, shut it off, and save gas.

This tip also applies to warming up the car. Unless it's ³⁴ below freezing, cars don't need to be warmed up at all. Driving them gently is the best warm up there is. If it's 25 degrees out, you might want to let it warm up for 30 seconds. If it's 10 degrees out, warm it up for a minute. If it's −10 degrees out, move somewhere warmer.

Some members of our extended family seem to enjoy driving around with, say, 200 pounds of "dead" weight in the back of their cars. And, as it turns out, each 100 pounds in the truck will reduce your fuel economy by 1 to 2 percent.

So, take a moment, rifle through your trunk, and dispose ³⁶ of any extra bowling balls that are rolling around back there.

If you don't need to run your air conditioner, don't. Your ³⁷ car's air conditioner forces the engine to work harder—and that's energy that could instead be used to move your car forward. So if it's 74° Fahrenheit outside, open the windows instead of wasting fuel running the AC at 72° Fahrenheit.

Here's a tip e mailed to us from our pal Bernie Gwalthney: 38

> *I saw the following letter to the editor in the St.*
> *Petersburg (Florida) Times on October 9, 2005: In*
> *an effort to cut down on unnecessary driving, I've*
> *decided to stop and ask for directions when I'm lost.*
> *Richard Parvin, Clearwater*

Now, just imagine if every guy stopped and asked for   39
directions when he got lost. The US would never import
another barrel of oil! (Okay, we're kidding. But, you have to
admit it: the guy's got a good point.)

The softer your tires are, the greater the friction between   40
the road and the rubber, and the harder your engine will
have to work to move the car. When we check tire pressure
on our customers' cars, we notice that they are often nowhere near the recommended pressure. Here's why it matters:
Under-inflated tires lower gas mileage by 0.4 percent for
every one pound of drop in pressure of all four tires. So, if
you're down by 10 pounds . . . you're losing 4 percent in
fuel economy.

Don't get us wrong: This doesn't mean you should over-   41
inflate your tires (you don't want to be riding on stale
bagels), because that's not safe, either. Too much air in your
tires can seriously jeopardize your car's handling. But you
DO want to keep your tires right at the recommended pressure, which represents a good balance between ride, handling, and fuel efficiency.

If you're not sure what the correct tire pressure is for your   42
vehicle, you can find it on the door to the glove compartment or on the driver's-side door pillar.

When the seasons are changing, keep an even closer eye on   43
your tire pressure. For every drop of 10° Fahrenheit in air
temperature, your tires will lose one pound of pressure.

Getting your car serviced regularly is one of the most   44
important things you can do to maximize fuel efficiency.

Regular service can spot lots of problems that reduce gas   45
mileage and increase pollution, such as a broken thermostat,

low transmission fluid, sticky brake calipers—or even something as simple as a dirty air filter.

If you can't remember the last time you had your car serviced, take it in. In extreme situations, you might increase your mileage by up to 10 percent. So what? Well, if you drove 20,000 miles a year, you would save $250—enough to cover the cost of the service, buy yourself a super-size falafel sandwich and still have a few bucks left over to start tipping your mechanic. (You did know you're supposed to tip your mechanic, right?)   46

Modern engines have such precise engine tolerances that very lightweight oil is often required, such as 0-W20 or 0-W30.   47

Thicker oil, such as 10W30 or 10W40, may not lubricate as well, because it won't flow as quickly into key nooks and crevices.   48

Thicker than required oil will also reduce your gas mileage, because it takes more energy to push through thick oil than it does through thinner oil. Check your owner's manual for the recommended viscosity, and ask for it specifically when you get your oil changed. You don't just want whatever they have on special this week.   49

For Study and Discussion

QUESTIONS FOR RESPONSE

1. How often do you think about the cost of the gasoline your car consumes?
2. What alternatives have you considered to your current transportation routines?

QUESTIONS ABOUT PURPOSE

1. What do Tom and Ray Magliozzi hope to accomplish by writing this "guide"?
2. What benefits—other than saving money—do they see in following their advice?

QUESTIONS ABOUT AUDIENCE

1. How do Tom and Ray Magliozzi use the pronouns *we* and *you* to connect with their readers?
2. How do they use questions to engage their readers in their analysis?

QUESTIONS ABOUT STRATEGIES

1. How do Tom and Ray Magliozzi use web links to give authority to their recommendations?
2. How do they use humor to enhance the effectiveness of their advice?

QUESTIONS FOR DISCUSSION

1. Of the various recommendations provided in this essay, which one seems the most difficult to follow?
2. Which myth about how cars work does this essay correct?

Greenpeace International has been campaigning against environmental degradation since 1971, when a small boat of volunteers and journalists sailed into Amchitka, an area north of Alaska where the U.S. government was conducting underground nuclear tests. In pursuing its mission, the organization claims to have no permanent allies or enemies. Its primary purpose is to promote open, informed debate about society's environmental choices. "Sellafield = Springfield? Homer Simpson's Nuclear Swimming Pool," reprinted from the Greenpeace International website, creates a sardonic comparison between a real nuclear accident in England (Sellafield) and the blasé attitude toward the potential for nuclear accidents in Homer Simpson's fictional hometown, Springfield.

Sellafield = Springfield?
Homer Simpson's Nuclear Swimming Pool

HOMER SIMPSON DISCUSSING with Tony Blair what a great idea nuclear power is. Perfectly safe, clean and inexpensive. Maybe Homer is pasing on some advice: "Honest it will never be a problem, and if it does just try and keep it quiet." 1

Sellafield, United Kingdom—A massive leak in a nuclear facility lies unnoticed for 9 months until someone goes looking for an awful lot of missing radioactive material. Excellent! It must be the latest adventure of Homer Simpson, comically bumbling around in the incompetently run Springfield nuclear power plant, right? 2

Doh! Afraid not, cartoon fans. It's a real event at a real   3
nuclear reprocessing plant called THORP at the Sellafield
nuclear complex in the UK.

One closed chamber in the plant now has a highly   4
radioactive mixture containing 20 tonnes of uranium and
plutonium fuel dissolved in nitric acid spread across the
floor. It's enough liquid to fill half an Olympic swimming
pool. Unlike your average swimming pool this one is not for
swimming or even looking at. It's so radioactive that the

---

*"Honest it will never be a problem, and if it
does just try and keep it quiet."*

---

chamber can only be entered by robots. They will need to be
designed and built, before a clean up can even be attempted.

"I suppose that's normal background radiation, the kind   5
you'd find in any nuclear facility, or for that matter, play-
grounds and hospitals?"—Mr. Burns, owner of Sellafield, no,
Springfield, nuclear power plant.

D O H !

The leak was caused by ruptured pipe connected to a tank. The   6
tank moved when it was filled and emptied which eventually
ruptured the connecting pipe. Engineers had not considered
movement of the tank during construction. You can almost see
Homer during the construction—"if that suspended tank is
being constantly filled and emptied with thousands of litres of
radioactive liquid maybe we should consider it might move?"
Perhaps a Mr. Burns thought this was a minor quibble.

The leak probably started in August 2004 but significant   7
leakage started in January 2005. It went unnoticed until
operators couldn't find all the fuel the plant was supposed to
be reprocessing.

In April 2005, remote camera's revealed 83,000 litres of 8
spent nuclear fuel spread across the floor, containing enough
plutonium to make 20 nuclear bombs.

Perhaps, like Homer, the operators taped a picture of 9
themselves over Monty Burns' surveillance camera (upside
down of course) while they snuck off to watch the Springfield
Isotopes play the pesky Shelbyville Shelby-Villians.

"SERIOUS INCIDENT"

While no one was injured in the leak it has closed the plant 10
indefinitely, costing taxpayers millions of Euros for each week
of closure. On the nuclear accident scale of 1 to 7 it was rated
3—a "serious incident." If the plant remains closed for a long
period it could be the final nail in the coffin for the troubled
THORP plant. While workers at the plant are being blamed
for their negligence, it is the management of Sellafield, and
the UK government who support its continued operation
who are the guilty parties. Even though Homer isn't really in
charge, the accident shows once again that there is no such
thing as safe nuclear power.

Homers are expendable. Mr. Burns is always with us. 11

Mr. Burns: *"Ironic, isn't it Smithers? This anonymous clan* 12
of slack-jawed troglodytes may cost me the election, and yet if I
were to have them killed, I would be the one to go to jail. That's
democracy for you."

We, and many others, campaigned against the construc- 13
tion of the plant in the early 90's on the grounds that it was
too expensive, too dangerous, and too unnecessary. To the
pro-nuclear lobby it was (yet another) bright new hope in the
nuclear age and was supposed to usher in age of limitless
nuclear power.

Mr. Burns: *"Imagine, Smithers: energy too cheap to meter!* 14
And if they don't have meters, we can get away with charging
them a bundle!"

This optimistic vision quickly evaporated like so many 15
nuclear pipe dreams. Construction costs overran to a stagger-
ing US$4 billion. The plant has never operated at full

capacity due to accidents and failures. Expected orders never materialised because the new nuclear plants expected to place orders turned out to be too expensive to build. Customers are suing THORP because reprocessing is so behind schedule. If the customers suing THORP are successful it will be taxpayers again footing the expensive bill.

Marge: *"I'm not sure about the people Bart's working for. I think they're criminals."*   16

Homer: *"A job's a job. I mean, take me. If my plant pollutes the water and poisons the town, by your logic, that would make me a criminal."*   17

Even though the plant has been an expensive failure the Japanese government is busy wasting **US$21 billion** on a similar reprocessing plant.   18

Mr. Burns: *"What good is money if it can't inspire terror in your fellow man?"*   19

Far from solving some of the many problems of nuclear power the reprocessing of nuclear fuel just creates more weapons grade plutonium, swallows billions of tax payers money and pours more radioactivity in the environment.   20

If nuclear reprocessing were any other industry it would have been shut down long ago.   21

But as the Potbellied Yellow Sage has said, *"weaselling out of things is what separates us from the animals . . . except of course the weasel."*   22

For Study and Discussion

QUESTIONS FOR RESPONSE

1. How do you react to descriptions of nuclear disasters, such as Three Mile Island and Chernobyl?
2. How do you react to Homer Simpson's attitude toward his work at the Springfield power plant?

QUESTIONS ABOUT PURPOSE

1. What do the writers of this essay accomplish by comparing a real tragedy with a cartoon comedy?
2. What is the writers' position on "safe" nuclear power?

QUESTIONS ABOUT AUDIENCE

1. What assumptions do the writers of this essay make about its readers' knowledge of the television series *The Simpsons?*
2. How do they think their readers will react to their use of humor to explain a "serious incident"?

QUESTIONS ABOUT STRATEGIES

1. How do the writers of this essay use "counterpointing" to establish their comparison?
2. How do they use the exchanges between Mr. Burns and Smithers, and Marge and Homer, to make their case about the cost and ultimate responsibility for nuclear accidents?

QUESTIONS FOR DISCUSSION

1. How are nuclear accidents usually depicted in films and television programs?
2. How does the phrase "weaselling out of things" characterize the way many people avoid responsibility for "serious incidents"?

SUSAN NEVILLE

Susan Neville was born in 1951 in Indianapolis, Indiana, and was educated at DePauw University and Bowling Green State University. She has taught writing at St. Petersburg Junior College, Ball State University, and Butler University. Her own writing includes fiction—*The Invention of Flight* (1974), which won the Pushcart Prize, and *Indiana Winter* (1994)—and nonfiction—*Fabrication: Essays on Making Things and Making Meaning* (2001). In "Utilities," reprinted from *Fabrication,* Neville reflects on the history and significance of different kinds of *utilities.*

Utilities

A tool, device, or other implement used as an adjunct to a more important machine. Exists in reference to a machine as a dictionary exists in reference to a poem. Designed for usefulness often at the expense of beauty.

A ND SO, WHAT is that hulking monstrous postapocalyptic building? Towering, black, with squidlike chutes that spread around the perimeter. It's a building out of scale with everything around it; it's out of tone. And when you're walking from Nordstrom's to Planet Hollywood or you're watching a small white baseball float into the evening ether, you wonder what the building is, and you ask someone and no one has an answer to your question, no one knows what it's there for, no one can tell you why it hasn't been destroyed.

When you really stop to look at it, it's larger than the mall, it's larger than the new hotels. It's ugly and enormous and weirdly invisible. A remnant of something, its days are no doubt numbered. It can't be necessary. It should be someplace else, where we can't see it.

No one makes things anymore. It's a well-known fact. We 3
all know things like this fact, and that brings us money, which
is infinite and surreal and as green as a pop bottle. We use the
money to buy the things that no one makes, and we don't
wonder where they came from or how they're made. The
things we buy are easily expendable. We live in a perpetual
twilight.

So burn it down or blot it out, that dinosaur, blast it off 4
the earth, whatever it is, we just don't need it.

I have to go just once inside another aging building. 5
Because it's both enormous and invisible. Because all my life

---

*All my life I've looked for something that
could shake the foundations, something that
could shake the stem and roots of my hair.*

I've looked for something that could shake the foundations,
something that could shake the stem and roots of my hair.

COKE

The solid product resulting from the destructive distillation of
coal in an oven or closed chamber or by imperfect combustion,
consisting primarily of carbon.
—Webster's New International Dictionary

The coke plant covers several city blocks. You can see the city 6
from the coke plant because the city travels skyward, but you
can't see the coke plant from the city because, for the most
part, the coke plant travels closer to the ground. It's more
likely to make you feel the rush of awe than any skyscraper.
Skyscrapers are clean and sharp and rational. A skyscraper
feels like order. The coke plant is dirtier; it spreads over
blocks and spews hot steam. There are unexpected, mammoth shapes—triangular smoking towers and enormous silos.
The purpose of the coke plant is the creation of impossible

heat and the attempt to cool it down. Wherever you look, there are signs reminding you of dangers.

A section of Pleasant Creek runs through the plant. It's 7 lined with discarded chunks of coal. The houses right outside the plant are dusty colored, shotgun, porches filled with discarded upholstered furniture. There are hookers a block away, and clots of people who are out of work. The coke plant spews its steam behind tall chain-link fences. It fills the horizon. You can't see it unless you drive here among the dispossessed. The coke plant feels like suppressed rage.

Inside, they superheat the coal to make the blocks of 8 coke. They push the blocks into a quenching tower. Ten thousand gallons of water fall onto the hot, now steaming, coke. The flushing liquor cools the coke, and tar condenses out of it.

Out of tar, you make pitch and one hundred thousand 9 other things including dye, vitamins, saccharine, explosives, and chartreuse sulphur.

Coke-oven gas is hydrogen and is just as flammable. At 10 one time it was used to lift zeppelins. Coke is mostly carbon, and carbon is necessary in the production of cast iron. When you burn the coke to make iron, you gain both heat and carbon. The coke plant is powerful and efficient, as efficient as poetry.

To wit: the iron is used in automobiles that spin around on 11 concrete ribbons and isolate the coke plant from the neighborhoods and businesses surrounding it. The coke is shipped to Honda and to Saturn and to General Motors. The coke-oven gas is pumped to the Power and Light to help produce the steam that heats the pharmaceutical company that makes your Prozac and heats the hospital where you go to repair your broken bones or, in rare cases, to replace your failing eye or heart or kidney with that of the car crash victim's. In all this process, they say that nothing much is lost.

You wear protective glasses and metal-toed shoes when 12 you enter the plant. You pass by several guards. It covers several city blocks. It looms. When it was built a hundred years ago, it was out in the country. It's not intended to be pretty. When coke is exposed to air, it begins to consume itself.

ELECTRICITY

One of the basic properties of the elementary particles of matter
giving rise to all electric and magnetic forces and interactions.
—Webster's New International Dictionary

My home is home to two adults, two children, a guinea pig, a dog, and uncountable fish in glass aquariums lined with blue glass stones.   13

My home is also home to five televisions and many other corded objects made of black or grayish plastic: microwaves and clocks and stoves and VCRs and answering machines and modems and computers, many of them with digital red numbers, which usually track the time but which are, this morning, beating 12:00 exactly like a pulse because the electricity stopped, briefly, overnight.   14

Every single time I open the cabinet over my telephone, complicated manuals explaining how they can be reset tumble out at me, and I feel helpless.   15

When something electronic shuts down, I ask my son or daughter to fix it, and if that doesn't work, I dive into the sea of cars, and I take the object to the store where they will often say it's more expensive to fix it than to throw it out and buy a new one. So I throw it out. Last week it was a microwave, a month ago a printer. If the object is small enough, I put it in a trash bag and wait for it to disappear. If it's large enough, like an automobile, they'll let you trade it in and someone else will buy it and someone else and someone else, but eventually it too will disappear to the places these things go. Sometimes I'll put a larger object in a closet where it will sit, quite lifeless, with cords that tangle in coat hangers and get caught in boxes, and within a year or two the thing that looked so sleek at first will turn unaccountably and oddly quaint and heavy, but never charming enough to take out and put in the middle of a table with cut flowers and a bowl of fruit.   16

POWER

Work done or energy transferred per unit of time. See also, angels.

They suck it in through pipes and wires. They suck and suck   17
and suck at it. The television sucks at it, and the computer.
And the CD player and the clicking lamps and the miraculous
dishwasher, and the coughing disposal and the trash com-
pactor. While we sleep, the clocks and alarms and furnace
slurp the wires like drinking straws, and when we're away
from home they slurp at it, and when we wake up in
the morning they take a big long gulp and turn it into hot
brewed coffee, they turn it into air that warms the walls and
rocks the curtains, they turn it into steaming water for our
showers. They drink in power and light and do our bidding.

INDIANA GAS

*A subject possessing perfect molecular mobility and the
property of indefinite expansion.*

The industries that located here included but were not lim-   18
ited to those that require extraordinary heat: iron, steel, and
particularly glass. The county was known for glass: art glass,
window glass, glass ball paperweights, glass lamps, and circular Ball dome jars and sealing lids for preserving summer
where you could see and touch it on a shelf in your grandmother's basement.

   It was the supply of natural gas that was, we believed, lim-   19
itless, which is to say eternal. Gas burned in blue flambeaux
on street corners; there were fountains of the flaming stuff.
People kept the doors of their homes open wide all winter to
let the heat escape. The gas was as vast as the distance to the
stars, as blue in its burning as the atmosphere, the perpetual
turning of a wheel on a perpetual decline. The gas burned,
yet kept on rising. Miraculous. Circular. Four dollars a month
for all the gas you could consume. It would be the source of
power for the entire next century. We owned it all.

   In 1902 the needles dropped on the gas gauges. In an-   20
other year or two the gas was gone.

STEAM

The mist formed when the gas or vapor from boiling water
condenses in the air.
—Webster's New International Dictionary

This is the building that produces the steam made from the   21
coke oven gas. It produces heat. It produces warmth in winter:
for the pharmaceutical company and the hospital, for National
Starch and General Motors, for the university and the Hebrew
National Kosher Food Processing; for homes and gas stations.

The landfill where my old microwave is sitting, where my   22
old receipts and coffee grounds are mixed together, both
buys and helps create the steam. Everyone buys it; it runs underneath the city in large pipes. The pipes are cleaned out
regularly because this is not New York, and we mind the
plumes; we don't want those things that remind us of the underground, the pipes and sewers.

To get inside, you climb a fire escape. You climb three   23
stories.

Inside, the entire building shakes. The walls, the tables   24
where you put your hands, the floor, it shakes and rumbles.
Everything is covered with ash, and dark, and you're standing inside a large engine, a machine, inside the turn of the
nineteenth century.

In the winter they can make a million pounds of steam an   25
hour.

There are rooms filled with mills grinding the coal to the   26
consistency of face powder. The pulverized coal mixed with
air produces something like a gas that burns immediately, like
dryer lint. The flash, the heat, the constant explosions. This is
the second largest steam-producing plant in the country, second to New York City.

Outside the building: the baseballs, the families with their   27
shopping bags, the stock markets, the virtual reality palaces,
the computer screens in microbreweries. The football fans
paint their faces blue.

Inside here where the heat is made, it's dark and loud and   28
trembling, filled with pipes and boilers and things you're

afraid to brush past because they might burn you. One hundred years ago men crawled into holes in the boilers. They would put in wood, light it, crawl back out, and throw in coal.

When the lights go out in here, they say, it's terrifying. No 29 windows, all the noise and explosive heat and catwalks with drops of a hundred feet. Like Mammoth Cave without flares. You sit down where you are and wait for light to reappear.

SANITATION

*The application of measures to make environmental conditions
favorable to health.*
—*Webster's New International Dictionary*

Ash ponds, ash handlers, precipitators. The side of the build- 30 ing that faces the capital is kept cleaner than the back. The ash is removed dry, stored in silos, and dumped in an ash pond. A train hauls the ash away, five thousand tons of it, six or seven times a day.

Once there was a wedding at the Ramada Inn on the west. 31 The bride, the groom, the wedding cake, all covered with ash.

MONEY

Any circulating medium of exchange.
—*Webster's New International Dictionary*

What is it? Cotton and linen, it takes some craftsman seven 32 years to learn to engrave it, longer than medical school. The production goes on all day long, all night. Intaglio. Seventy-three hundred sheets of bills per hour; printers hover over the machines, inspecting sheets of freshly minted bills. Bins of dark green ink like wet grass clipping. Ink spots, smears, discolorations, mutilated shredded bills sold in the gift shop, in the barrels of pens, wrapped around golf balls and jewelry, in plastic bags to take back home to your family—$100 from the U.S. mint. Take your picture by a stack of it; see what you're worth. The windows so old they're purple, the glassed-in printing presses. It's all here, on the other side of the window, so much money, stacks and stacks and stacks of it.

The new bills, why don't they look as green? Beige and   33
simple, not as Victorian. I watch the money being made in
July, and by October I hold the first new ones in my hand.
Remember this? I ask my daughter. We took the bus to
Washington, D.C., and watched it being made. The bus
driver wore a tie printed with vintage buses. We saw the Capitol building and the monuments and all the busy, self-
important people. They filled the subways, they ran from one
station to the next in suits, and everyone looked busy and
nervous, like people wearing uncomfortable, ill-fitting shoes.

For some reason, no one trusts these bills. At McDonald's,   34
the drive-through woman holds it to the light to see some hidden blur. At Arby's, they mark it with a special pen. Decep-
tively simple to counterfeit, the man says, you can try to print
your own at Kinko's. Bleach a dollar bill and print this new one
on a color printer. But use this pen or hold it to the light, and
you can see the holographic images float inside of it, this
strange technology. Who needs the engraver, the strictly orna-
mental, the hidden messages in the elaborately coded text?

NUCLEAR POWER

Energy that can be liberated by changes in the nucleus of an atom.
—Webster's New International Dictionary

In 1955, Union Carbide built a 350,000-gallon swimming   35
pool reactor to take to the Geneva Conference on Peaceful
Uses of Atomic Energy. Lying safely, we thought, beneath
sixteen feet of water, the plates of uranium began slowly to
disintegrate inside their aluminum boxes, making the surrounding water glow blue from the radiation. They switched
the reactor off and let it cool a few weeks before lifting the
reactor out and heading for Geneva.

There was a column in the Hagerstown, Indiana, paper   36
about the laying of the cornerstone for the new nineteen-
story building adjoining Radio City in New York to house
the Crowell-Collier Publishing Company.

> *That cornerstone was put into place by atomic energy
> rather than by human hands. . . . The two-ton*

cornerstone was lowered into position at the end of a chain attached to a motor atop a hoist, which was powered by energy produced by splitting ten U-235 atoms. A miniature reactor, an amplifier, and two relays were used. One relay was attached to the hoist motor and the other to a magnesium flare imbedded in a ceremonial ribbon stretched between the motor and the suspended cornerstone. A half gram of radium-beryllium was used as the neutronic source for bombarding the uranium-235. Each time a neutron struck one of the atoms, the latter was split, releasing 200,000,000 volts of energy. We heard a pronounced click as this energy, picked up by the amplifier, caused a gong to ring and a 100-watt fluorescent lamp to flash.

This happened each time one of the ten atoms was split. After this the accumulated electrical impulse was transmitted to the motor and the magnesium flare. The ribbon broke with a loud report and bright flash. The activated motor lowered the cornerstone into position.

COAL

A black or brownish black solid combustible mineral substance formed by the partial decomposition of vegetable matter without free access of air and under the influence of moisture and in many cases increased pressure and temperature, the substance being widely used as a natural fuel and containing carbon, hydrogen, oxygen, nitrogen, and sulfur as well as inorganic constituents that are left behind as ash after burning.
—Webster's New International Dictionary

When the trains bring in the coal, there's a machine that lifts the car from off its bed. The car hovers over a large hole in the ground and then metal circles at each end turn it upside down. You can stand on the track and watch the coal fall into the pit: the roaring and clattering like a waterfall or, rather, like jars of pennies being dumped into a sorter or like sacks of marbles or gravel from a dump truck. Whatever you can bring to this image from your own experience, magnify it— the sound, the pit, the tons of coal.

37

The coal superheats the steam. The coke gas superheats   38
the steam. The water for the steam is piped in from the river.
And one thing more: 39
When things fall apart in this place, they fall apart quickly.   40
Some of the mechanical boilers need adjustments every
twenty minutes, and if the boilers fail, the buildings relying on
the steam need to have it up and running within ten minutes.
There are temperature and pressure gauges. There's fire.

And the thing you notice in this building is all the emptiness.   41
The vast space, and the abandoned desks, some of them close
to one hundred years old. In every room there's a dusty desk or
two where someone used to sit, watching. Room after room, it
goes on like this until you get to a single glassed-in room with
one man sitting, peering out. In some rooms there's the green
rectangle of a computer screen, a pair of aqua plastic gloves on
a table, a calamine-colored, coal-dusted untouched desk.

At the very top of the building there's a room where three   42
men sit on rotating chairs, surrounded by gauges and television
screens. They sit high above the city, at the same level, say, as
the governor who sits behind his own desk one street away. The
men wear black baseball caps. One cap says *Protect Freedom.*
On another there's a cross. Objects sit on top of their computer
screens: a Mickey Mouse hat with a feather, a toy airplane, a
walnut, a Santa Claus head, a boat, a plastic toilet, a radio station football by a snake. When things fall apart, these are the
men who fix it. They punch at buttons. There are no women.
On Christmas Day, there are sometimes only five men in the
entire building. Where are the sons and daughters of the men
who used to work here? What are they doing?

The three men type on keyboards. They make corrections.   43
They sit back in their chairs. For much of the day, they stare
at a television screen with what seems to be an unmoving
image. You look at it yourself, and you see the slightest
movement. It's a picture of the three smokestacks on the
outside of the building, centered in the screen in black and
white, a faint ribbon of the white exhaling from each one,
just the faintest breath of smoke. Three smokestacks, the
highest in the middle, the cross on the fireman's baseball cap.
It's eerie because it's all in tones of gray and because it doesn't

move and because it looks like Calvary. Why is the camera focused here? What or who is being sacrificed? Why is there such stillness? We watch, the fireman says. There are so many ways things go wrong in this life. And the statehouse is right across the street from us, and the stadiums, and the park. The senators get worried when the smoke gets thick. We make adjustments. This steam runs in pipes all through this city.

For Study and Discussion

QUESTIONS FOR RESPONSE

1. How do you respond to the large, anonymous buildings that produce power in your community?
2. Do you know anyone who works at such a power plant? How do they explain their jobs?

QUESTIONS ABOUT PURPOSE

1. What does Neville demonstrate by defining and classifying various utilities?
2. Why is she attracted to buildings that produce power?

QUESTIONS ABOUT AUDIENCE

1. Why does Neville create a sense of mystery about the buildings that produce power?
2. How do her confessions about how she deals with broken electrical appliances establish a connection with her readers?

QUESTIONS ABOUT STRATEGIES

1. How does Neville use dictionary definitions to establish the subcategories of her classification?
2. How does she justify the inclusion of some of her categories—such as sanitation and money?

QUESTIONS FOR DISCUSSION

1. How does the example of Indiana Natural Gas comment on the current energy crisis?
2. How does the following sentence comment on the function of utilities: "There are so many ways things go wrong in this life"?

JOSEPH J. ROMM

Joseph J. Romm was educated at the Massachusetts Institute of Technology and has had a long career as an energy consultant. He has held various positions at the U.S. Department of Energy, conducted research for the National Science Foundation, and founded the Center for Energy and Climate Solutions. He has contributed essays to magazine such as *Forbes, Science,* and *Industry Standard.* His books include *The Once and Future Superpower: How to Restore America's Economic, Energy, and Environmental Security* (1992); *Clean Management: How to Boost Profits and Productivity by Reducing Pollution* (1994); and *The Hype About Hydrogen: Fact and Fiction in the Race to Save the Climate* (2004). In "The Holy Grails of Energy Technology," excerpted from *The Hype About Hydrogen,* Romm defines fuel cells and explains their connection to the "hydrogen economy."

The Holy Grails of Energy Technology

FUEL CELLS ARE one of the Holy Grails of energy technology. They are pollution-free electric "engines" that run on hydrogen. Unlike virtually all other engines, fuel cells do not rely on the burning of fossil fuels. Hence, they produce no combustion by-products, such as oxides of nitrogen, sulfur dioxide, or particulates—the air pollutants that cause smog and acid rain and that have been most clearly documented as harmful to human health. [1]

Fuel cells have been reliably providing electricity to spacecraft since the 1960s, including the Gemini and Apollo [2] missions as well as the space shuttle. The leading manufacturer of fuel cells for the National Aeronautics and Space Administration (NASA), United Technologies Corporation, has sold commercial units for stationary power since the early 1990s, with more than 200 units in service.

But finding a fuel cell with the right combination of fea-   3
tures for powering a car or truck has proved much more difficult. Why is that hard? To begin with, you need a fuel cell that is lightweight and compact enough to fit under the hood of a car but that can still deliver the power and acceleration drivers have come to expect. You also need a fuel cell that can

---

Since fuel cells are more efficient than gasoline internal combustion engines, hydrogen fuel cell vehicles are, potentially, a double winner in the race to replace oil.

---

reach full power in a matter of seconds after start-up, which rules out a variety of fuel cells that operate at very high temperatures and thus take a long time to warm up. You also need cost and reliability comparable to that of the gasoline-powered internal combustion engine, which is an exceedingly mature technology, the product of more than a hundred years of development and real-world testing in hundreds of millions of vehicles.

Further, these hardware hurdles are all quite separate from   4
the way in which the fuel for fuel cells—hydrogen—would be produced and delivered to the vehicle. Hydrogen, first and foremost, is not a primary fuel, like natural gas or coal or wood, which we can drill or dig for or chop down and then use at once. Hydrogen is the most abundant element in the universe, true enough. But on Earth, it is bound up tightly in molecules of water, coal, natural gas, and so on. To unbind it, a great deal of energy must be used.

For all these reasons—plus the sharp drop in both the 5
price of oil and government funding for alternative energy—
hydrogen fuel cell vehicles received little attention through
most of the 1980s. Still, a few government and industry laboratories (together with a small and ardent group of hydrogen
advocates and state energy experts) kept plugging away, particularly on proton exchange membrane (PEM) fuel cells.

PEM fuel cells were developed in the early 1960s by the 6
General Electric Company for the Gemini space program.
Fuel cells require catalysts to speed up the electrochemical
reaction, and PEM fuel cells use platinum, a very expensive
metal. An early 1981 analysis for the DOE had presciently argued that PEM fuel cells would be ideal for transportation if
the catalyst loading could be significantly reduced. By the
early 1990s, Los Alamos National Laboratory (and others)
did succeed in cutting the amount of platinum by almost a
factor of ten, a remarkable improvement. This still did not
make PEM fuel cells cost-competitive with gasoline engines—
we are a long way away from that—but it did dramatically
reinvigorate interest in hydrogen-powered vehicles because
PEMS were exactly the kind of low-temperature fuel cell that
could be used in a car. . . .

Many other trends have driven the renewed interest in hy- 7
drogen. At the top of the list are worries about oil consumption and air pollution, including global warming. America's
dependence on imported oil has accelerated since the mid-
1990s, as many people predicted—including Charles Curtis,
then deputy secretary of the DOE, and me in a 1996 *Atlantic
Monthly* piece titled "Mideast Oil Forever?" By 2002, we
were importing more than half our oil, an outflow of $100
billion per year to foreign governments, including those in
the politically unstable Persian Gulf region.

The terrible September 11, 2001, terrorist attacks height- 8
ened this concern. Less than two weeks later, the DOE was
commenting publicly. "It is clear that our reliance on
imported oil—56% of the oil we use—has complicated our
response to the terrorist attack," noted David Garman, the
Bush administration's assistant secretary for energy efficiency

and renewable energy, on September 24, 2001. "There is also little doubt that some of the dollars we have exported in exchange for foreign oil have found their way into the hands of terrorists and would-be terrorists."

These seismic problems, together with worldwide population growth, economic growth, and urbanization, will dramatically increase global oil consumption in the coming decades, especially in the developing world. If by 2050 the per capita energy consumption of China and India were to approach that of South Korea, and if the Chinese and Indian populations increase at currently projected rates, those two supergiant countries *by themselves* would consume more oil than the entire world did in 2003.

Since oil is a finite, nonrenewable resource, analysts have attempted to predict when production will peak and start declining. Some believe this will occur by 2010. The Royal Dutch/Shell Group, probably the most successful predictor in the global oil business, adds fifteen to thirty years to that gloomy forecast. Worry about oil supplies is one of the factors behind Shell's growing research into hydrogen. This debate will not be resolved here, but it does appear credible that oil production will peak in the first half of this century and will possibly decline at a relatively rapid rate thereafter, even as demand increases. Thus, delaying action until we are past the peak may put us at significant risk.

A whopping two-thirds of U.S. oil consumption is in the transportation sector, the only sector of the U.S. economy wholly reliant on oil. The energy price shocks of the 1970s helped spur growth in use of natural gas for home heating and drove the electric utility sector and the industrial sector to reduce their dependence on petroleum. But roughly 97 percent of all energy consumed by our cars, sport utility vehicles, vans, trucks, and airplanes is still petroleum-based.

Not surprisingly, a high priority of R&D funding by the United States—and by any country, state, or company that takes the long view—is to develop both more fuel-efficient vehicles and alternative fuels. Only a limited number of fuels are plausible alternatives for gasoline, and one enormous

9

10

11

12

benefit of hydrogen over others is that it can be generated by a variety of different sources, thus potentially minimizing dependence on any one. Most important, hydrogen can be generated from renewable sources of energy such as wind power, raising the ultimate prospect of an inexhaustible, clean, domestic source of transportation fuel. Also, since fuel cells are more efficient than gasoline internal combustion engines, hydrogen fuel cell vehicles are, potentially, a double winner in the race to replace oil.

Hydrogen fuel cell vehicles would seem to be the perfect answer to our burgeoning and alarming dependence on imported oil. For some, like Peter Schwartz, chair of the Global Business Network, they are almost the deus ex machina—the quick, pure technological fix—that will avoid the need for difficult policy choices, such as federal mandates for increased vehicle efficiency. That is overoptimistic hype, as we will see.   13

The pollution generated by internal combustion engine automobiles is another key reason why so many people are drawn to hydrogen fuel cell vehicles. The transportation sector remains one of the largest sources of urban air pollution, especially the oxides of nitrogen that are a precursor to ozone smog and the particulates that do so much damage to our hearts and lungs. Vehicle emissions of such pollutants, however, have been declining steadily, and, by 2010, federal and state standards will have made new U.S. cars exceedingly clean.   14

Yet, even as new internal combustion engine vehicles dramatically cut the emissions of noxious urban air pollutants by automobiles, their contribution to global warming has begun to rise. In the 1990s, the transportation sector saw the fastest growth in carbon dioxide (CO_2) emissions of any major sector of the U.S. economy. And *the transportation sector is projected to generate nearly half of the 40 percent rise in U.S. CO_2 emissions forecast for 2025.*   15

When the United States takes serious action on global warming, the transportation sector will need to be a top priority. The two most straightforward ways to reduce vehicle CO_2 emissions are, first, by increasing the fuel efficiency of the vehicles themselves and, second, by using a fuel that has   16 lower net emissions than gasoline. Again, the attractiveness of hydrogen fuel cell vehicles is that they afford the possibility of pursuing both strategies at the same time: Fuel cells are more efficient than traditional internal combustion engines, and hydrogen, when produced from renewable energy sources, would create no net greenhouse gas emissions.

The possibility that hydrogen and fuel cells could play a   17 key role in combating pollution, particularly global warming, is, I believe, the strongest argument for expanded efforts in research and development. John Heywood, director of the Sloan Automotive Laboratory at the Massachusetts Institute of Technology, argues, "If the hydrogen does not come from renewable sources, then it is simply not worth doing, environmentally or economically."

The idea that hydrogen could be generated without releas-   18 ing any pollution is not a new one. In 1923, John Haldane, who later became one of the century's most famous geneticists, gave a lecture predicting that Britain would ultimately derive its energy from "rows of metallic windmills" generating electricity for the country and, when there was excess wind, producing hydrogen. "Among its more obvious advantages will be the fact that . . . no smoke or ash will be produced."

The problem with the vision of a pure hydrogen economy   19 has been that, until recently, most greenhouse-gas-free sources for hydrogen have been far too expensive to be practical. Haldane himself was imagining a future "four hundred years hence." Even today, nuclear, wind, and solar electric power would produce hydrogen that is far more expensive than hydrogen from fossil fuels. But for more than two decades, renewable energy, especially wind and solar energy, has been declining in price sharply. That has created a renewed interest in renewable hydrogen, although it will still be two or more decades before this is a competitive way to generate hydrogen.

There is another, more unexpected possible source of   20 greenhouse-gas-free hydrogen: fossil fuels. In the mid-1990s, Princeton University professor Bob Williams (and others) produced detailed reports arguing that fossil fuels could be both a cost-effective and an environmentally benign source of hydrogen *if* the CO_2 released during the production process could be captured and stored in underground geologic formations so that it would not be released into the atmosphere and thereby accelerate global warming. His briefings to DOE officials and others in government were a major reason why the department launched a major effort to explore this possibility. Today, carbon capture and storage is the subject of considerable research as well as demonstration projects around the globe and is widely seen as a potentially critical strategy for addressing global warming in the longer term.

21 With ongoing advances in transportation fuel cells and pollution-free hydrogen production, hydrogen vehicles would seem to be the perfect answer to global warming. Yet one of the conclusions of this book—the one that surprised me the most, as it was not my view before starting the current research—is that *hydrogen vehicles are unlikely to make a significant dent in U.S. greenhouse gas emissions in the first half of this century,* especially if U.S. energy policy is not significantly changed. Still, hydrogen-fueled *stationary* power plants could be critical in reducing greenhouse gas emissions much sooner. Further, hydrogen may well be the essential vehicle fuel in the second half of this century if we are to achieve the very deep reductions in CO_2 emissions that will almost certainly be needed then or if we are past the peak of oil production.

22 We are not used to thinking or planning in such giant, multi-decade time steps. But then again, we have never faced such a giant problem as global warming.

23 The term "hydrogen economy" describes a time when a substantial fraction of our energy is delivered by hydrogen made from sources of energy that have no net emissions of greenhouse gases. These would include renewable sources of energy, such as wind power and biomass (e.g., plant matter), but it could also include the scenario of converting fossil fuels into hydrogen and CO_2 and then permanently storing the carbon. It could also include generating hydrogen from nuclear power, should that prove practical.

We are unlikely to know whether a hydrogen economy is   24
practical and economically feasible for at least one decade and
possibly two or even more. A hydrogen economy would require dramatic changes in our transportation system because,
at room temperature and pressure, hydrogen takes up three
thousand times more space than gasoline containing an
equivalent amount of energy. We will need tens of thousands
of hydrogen fueling stations, and, unless hydrogen is generated on-site at those stations, we will also need a massive infrastructure for delivering that hydrogen from wherever it is
generated.

Substantial technological and cost breakthroughs will be   25
needed in many areas, not the least of which is fuel cells for
vehicles. In 2003, fuel cell vehicles cost $1 million each or
more. Were we to build a hydrogen infrastructure for fueling
vehicles, the total delivered cost of hydrogen generated from
fossil fuel sources would likely be at least triple the cost of
gasoline for the foreseeable future. Hydrogen generated
from renewable energy sources would be considerably more
expensive. Hydrogen storage is currently expensive, ineffi-
cient, and subject to onerous codes and standards. The DOE
does not foresee making a decision about commercializing
fuel cell vehicles until 2015. One detailed 2003 analysis of a
hydrogen economy by two leading European fuel cell experts
concluded, "The 'pure-hydrogen-only-solution' may never
become reality."

And if the imposing technical and cost problems can be   26
substantially solved, we will still have an imposing chicken-
and-egg problem: Who will spend hundreds of billions of
dollars on a wholly new nationwide infrastructure to provide
ready access to hydrogen for consumers with fuel cell vehicles
until millions of hydrogen vehicles are on the road? Yet who
will manufacture and market such vehicles—and who will
buy them—until the infrastructure is in place to fuel those vehicles? A 2002 analysis by Argonne National Laboratory
found that "with current technologies, the hydrogen delivery
infrastructure to serve 40% of the light duty fleet is likely to cost
over $500 billion." I fervently hope to see an economically,

environmentally, and politically plausible scenario for bridging this classic catch-22 chasm; it does not yet exist.

For Study and Discussion

QUESTIONS FOR RESPONSE

1. What have you heard about fuel cells from the media reporting on various NASA missions?
2. What other sorts of "gadgets" have you read about as possible replacements for the gasoline internal combustion engine?

QUESTIONS ABOUT PURPOSE

1. Why does Romm refer to hydrogen fuel cells as the "Holy Grails" of energy technology?
2. Why does he refer to the speculation about such technology as "hype"?

QUESTIONS ABOUT AUDIENCE

1. What assumptions does Romm make about his readers' scientific knowledge?
2. How does he make the possibility of a "hydrogen economy" appealing to his readers?

QUESTIONS ABOUT STRATEGIES

1. How does Romm combine other strategies—cause and effect, persuasion and argument—with his definition?
2. How does he connect hydrogen fuel cells to the problems of imported oil and global warming?

QUESTIONS FOR DISCUSSION

1. What is Romm's attitude toward long-term planning?
2. How does he use the "chicken and egg" metaphor to explain the problem with hydrogen fuel cells?

EDWARD CODY

Edward Cody was born in 1943 in Portland, Oregon, and educated at Gonzaga University, the University of Paris Law School, and Columbia University Graduate School of Journalism. He worked at the *Charlotte Observer* and the Associated Press before joining the *Washington Post,* where he writes for the foreign desk. He lives in Beijing, China. In "China's Symbol, and Source, of Power," reprinted from the *Washington Post,* Cody analyzes the reasons why China built the Three Gorges Dam and speculates on its effect on people and the environment.

China's Symbol, and Source, of Power
Three Gorges Dam Nears Completion, at High Human Cost

A FTER 13 YEARS of breakneck construction that displaced more than a million villagers, China is about to pour the final concrete on an enormous dam across the mighty Yangtze River, seeking to tame the flood-prone waterway that has nurtured and tormented the Chinese people for 5,000 years.

Engineers, many of whom have spent their entire careers on the site, will gather on Saturday for a ceremony to mark their achievement: The dun-colored barrier at last has reached its full height of 606 feet and stretches 7,575 feet across the Yangtze's murky green waters in the Three Gorges area of central China's Hubei province, 600 miles southwest of Beijing.

The Three Gorges Project, with 25,000 workers and a budget of $24 billion, is China's most ambitious engineering

582

undertaking since the Great Wall. It has replaced Brazil's Itaipu Dam as the world's largest hydroelectric and flood-control installation, Chinese officials said, with the strength to hold back more water than Lake Superior and power 26 generators to churn out 85 billion kilowatt-hours of electricity a year when the final touches are completed in 2008. Hoover Dam on the Nevada-Arizona border, by comparison, generates more than 4 billion kilowatt-hours a year.

"This is the grandest project the Chinese people have undertaken in thousands of years," said Li Yong'an, general manager 4

In its scope and ambition—as well as its human costs—the Three Gorges Project has become a symbol of China's relentless energy and determination to take its place among the world's great economic powers.

---

of the government's Three Gorges corporation, which runs the project under the direct leadership of Premier Wen Jiabao.

In its scope and ambition—as well as its human costs—the 5 Three Gorges Project has become a symbol of China's relentless energy and determination to take its place among the world's great economic powers. At the same time, the project has demonstrated the Communist Party's willingness to sacrifice individual rights for the country's general welfare and to take high-stake risks in the name of progress.

The Chinese have long dreamed of a dam across the 6 Yangtze to alleviate flooding and facilitate navigation. Sun Yat-sen, revered as the founder of the Chinese republic, urged construction of a dam as early as 1918. U.S. engineers suggested one right after World War II. Mao Zedong, whose Communist Party took over in 1949, wrote seven years later that "walls of stone" should rise from the river.

It was left to the present-day Communist leadership, dom- 7 inated by engineers and driven to build, to put the project into motion. Li Peng, a former waterworks official, got the project off the ground in the late 1980s when he was premier. The first earth was turned in 1993 under the president at the time, Jiang Zemin, a Soviet-educated engineer. The dam's completion is now being celebrated under President Hu Jintao, who was trained as a hydraulic engineer and has adopted "scientific development" as a mantra.

But critics of the project—they are many, in China and abroad—have questioned whether building a giant dam is really scientific in the 21st century, when the United States and other nations are weighing the wisdom of damming their rivers. Despite the $24 billion price tag, they note, the Three Gorges Dam will produce only 2 percent of China's electricity by 2010. Moreover, environmentalists have warned that the backup of water behind the dam could end up as a giant waste-collection pool for Chongqing, China's largest urban conglomeration about 250 miles upstream. 8

"There are two sides to everything, and the Three Gorges Project is no exception," said Cao Guangjing, the building company's deputy manager. "But many studies, undertaken since the beginning, have shown that the advantages outweigh the disadvantages." 9

The government has set aside $5 billion to build sewage treatment plants around Chongqing and other upstream cities to prevent the river from turning into a cesspool, officials pointed out. Tests so far show that the water quality has not suffered, even though water has been backing up for several years, they said. 10

"Look at that," Feng Zhengpeng, head of hydroelectrics, told reporters walking atop the dam Wednesday as he gestured toward the river far below. "Do you think my water looks dirty?" 11

Li Yong'an, the dam-building company's manager, said that despite its difficulties, the project is running ahead of schedule and will solve "one of the Chinese people's most important afflictions," the flooding that has ravaged the Yangtze basin for centuries. Floods killed more than 145,000 in 1931, according to Chinese records, and another 142,000 four 12 years later. As late as 1998, with the dam under construction, more than 2,000 were reported killed by river waters that spilled over the banks.

Now, said deputy director Cao, engineers will be able to   13
control the flow of water during the peak flooding months of summer, letting it back up in a huge basin that will reach as far as 385 miles upstream.

To make way for the impounded water, which has risen to   14
more than 400 feet above its natural level, at least 1,200 villages and two towns had to be moved. Displaced residents already total about 1.1 million, according to a government count. Wen, who heads the government's Committee for Construction of the Three Gorges Project, last week authorized a further rise to 470 feet next fall, which will displace another 80,000.

Zigui, a community of 60,000 people, baked under a   15
warm sun Wednesday several thousand feet away from its for-mer location—now underwater. The village of Zhongbao, whose inhabitants once prospered growing oranges by the riverside, also was submerged, reduced to a reflection on the river's surface just under the dam. One city farther upstream, Fengjie, was rebuilt about 10 miles inland from its traditional riverside location, only to be moved again nearby when engi-neers discovered the new site was unstable.

"The displaced people problem is a big one," acknowl-   16
edged Li, the manager, "and ultimately our ability to deal with it will determine whether the Three Gorges Project is successful or not."

Li said Wen's government had guaranteed that all those   17
displaced would be compensated and provided new houses and livelihoods. But many displaced families have com-plained from the beginning that their compensation was si-phoned off by corrupt local officials and that they cannot make a living in their new locations.

The state audit office reported as early as 1999 that mil-   18
lions of dollars in compensation funds were being embezzled. Scores of officials were investigated and many prosecuted, according to the official New China News Agency. But the complaints have not stopped.

Chen Qun, a disgruntled Zhongbao villager, said Wednes-   19
day that his community's 2,000 residents were promised
$450 each when they had to pack and leave in 1993. So far,
he said, they have received only a third of that amount and
corrupt local officials have pocketed the rest.

When they heard that foreign reporters were about to visit   20
the dam, Chen said, several villagers put up banners urging
Beijing to "Punish the corrupt officials" and "Give us back
our space for survival." But police jailed the activists for several hours Monday and tore down the banners, he said.

For Study and Discussion

QUESTIONS FOR RESPONSE

1. What experience have you had with major construction projects'
   solving or creating problems in your community?
2. What do you know about the causes and effects of China's decision to build the Great Wall?

QUESTIONS ABOUT PURPOSE

1. How does Cody's title preview the purpose of his essay?
2. How does his presentation of the critics of the project clarify his
   purpose?

QUESTIONS ABOUT AUDIENCE

1. What assumptions does Cody make about his readers' knowledge of other hydroelectric projects?
2. How does he help his readers understand the history of the project?

QUESTIONS ABOUT STRATEGIES

1. How does Cody explain the reasons for building the dam?
2. How does he analyze the possible effects—good and bad—of
   building the dam?

QUESTIONS FOR DISCUSSION

1. What issues should be considered when a government sacrifices
   individual rights for general welfare?
2. Why does China's commitment to scientific development represent a new "mantra"?

A Debate About Windmills

ROBERT F. KENNEDY, JR.

Robert F. Kennedy, Jr., was born in 1954 and educated at Harvard University, London School of
Economics, and the University of Virginia Law
School. In 1978 he published his first book, based
on his Harvard senior thesis—a biography of
Alabama federal judge Frank M. Johnson, Jr., who
opposed the segregation policies of Governor
George Wallace. In recent years, Kennedy has become a strong advocate for environmental issues,
cohosting *Ring of Fire* on Air American Radio,
contributing articles to magazines such as *Sierra
Magazine* and *Rolling Stone,* and teaching environmental law at Pace University. In 1997, together
with John Cronin, he co-authored *The Riverkeep-
ers: Two Activists Fight to Reclaim Our Environment as a Basic Human Right.* In "An Ill Wind Off
Cape Cod," an op-ed column reprinted from the
New York Times, Kennedy argues against Energy
Management's proposal to build giant windmills in
Nantucket Sound.

An Ill Wind Off Cape Cod

A S AN ENVIRONMENTALIST, I support wind power, includ-   1
ing wind power on the high seas. I am also involved in
siting wind farms in appropriate landscapes, of which there are
many. But I do believe that some places should be off limits to
any sort of industrial development. I wouldn't build a wind
farm in Yosemite National Park. Nor would I build one on
Nantucket Sound, which is exactly what the company Energy
Management is trying to do with its Cape Wind project.

Environmental groups have been enticed by Cape Wind,   2
but they should be wary of lending support to energy
companies that are trying to privatize the commons—in this
case 24 square miles of a heavily used waterway. And because
offshore wind costs twice as much as gas-fired electricity and
significantly more than onshore wind, the project is finan-
cially feasible only because the federal and state governments
have promised $241 million in subsidies.

Cape Wind's proposal involves construction of 130 giant   3
turbines whose windmill arms will reach 417 feet above the
water and be visible for up to 26 miles. These turbines are less
than six miles from shore and would be seen from Cape Cod,

---

*Environmental groups have been enticed by
Cape Wind, but they should be wary of
lending support to energy companies that are
trying to privatize the commons.*

Martha's Vineyard and Nantucket. Hundreds of flashing
lights to warn airplanes away from the turbines will steal the
stars and nighttime views. The noise of the turbines will be
audible onshore. A transformer substation rising 100 feet
above the sound would house giant helicopter pads and
40,000 gallons of potentially hazardous oil.

According to the Massachusetts Historical Commission,   4
the project will damage the views from 16 historic sites and
lighthouses on the cape and nearby islands. The Humane Society estimates the whirling turbines could every year kill
thousands of migrating songbirds and sea ducks.

Nantucket Sound is among the most densely traveled boat-   5
ing corridors in the Atlantic. The turbines will be perilously
close to the main navigation channels for cargo ships, ferries
and fishing boats. The risk of collisions with the towers would
increase during the fogs and storms for which the area is
famous. That is why the Steamship Authority and HyLine

Cruises, which transport millions of passengers to and from the cape and islands every year, oppose the project. Thousands of small businesses, including marina owners, hotels, motels, whale watching tours and charter fishing operations will also be hurt. The Beacon Hill Institute at Suffolk University in Boston estimates a loss of up to 2,533 jobs because of the loss of tourism—and over a billion dollars to the local economy.

Nantucket Sound is a critical fishing ground for the commercial fishing families of Martha's Vineyard and Cape Cod. Hundreds of fishermen work Horseshoe Shoal, where the Cape Wind project would be built, and make half their annual income from the catch. The risks that their gear will become fouled in the spider web of cables between the 130 towers will largely preclude fishing in the area, destroying family-owned businesses that enrich the palate, economy and culture of Cape Cod.

Many environmental groups support the Cape Wind project, and that's unfortunate because making enemies of fishermen and marina owners is bad environmental strategy in the long run. Cape Cod's traditional-gear commercial fishing families and its recreational anglers and marina owners have all been important allies for environmentalists in our battles for clean water.

There are those who argue that unlike our great Western national parks, Cape Cod is far from pristine, and that Cape Wind's turbines won't be a significant blot. I invite these critics to see the pods of humpback, minke, pilot, finback and right whales off Nantucket, to marvel at the thousands of harbor and gray seals lolling on the bars off Monomoy and Horseshoe Shoal, to chase the dark clouds of terns and shorebirds descending over the thick menhaden schools exploding over acre-sized feeding frenzies of striped bass, bluefish and bonita.

I urge them to come diving on some of the hundreds of historic wrecks in this "graveyard of the Atlantic," and to visit the endless dune-covered beaches of Cape Cod, our fishing villages immersed in history and beauty, or to spend an afternoon netting blue crabs or mucking clams, quahogs and scallops by the bushel on tidal mud flats—some of the reasons my uncle, John F. Kennedy, authorized the creation of the Cape Cod National Seashore in 1961, and why Nantucket Sound is under consideration as a national marine sanctuary, a designation that would prohibit commercial electrical generation.

All of us need periodically to experience wilderness to 10 renew our spirits and reconnect ourselves to the common history of our nation, humanity and to God. The worst trap that environmentalists can fall into is the conviction that the only wilderness worth preserving is in the Rocky Mountains or Alaska. To the contrary, our most important wildernesses are those that are closest to our densest population centers, like Nantucket Sound.

There are many alternatives that would achieve the same 11 benefits as Cape Wind without destroying this national treasure. Deep water technology is rapidly evolving, promising huge bounties of wind energy with fewer environmental and economic consequences. Scotland is preparing to build wind turbines in the Moray Firth more than 12 miles offshore. Germany is considering placing turbines as far as 27 miles off its northern shores.

If Cape Wind were to place its project further offshore, it 12 could build not just 130, but thousands of windmills—where they can make a real difference in the battle against global warming without endangering the birds or impoverishing the experience of millions of tourists and residents and fishing families who rely on the sound's unspoiled bounties.

For Study and Discussion

QUESTIONS FOR RESPONSE

1. How have you responded to projects that endanger the environment in your community?
2. How have you and your family members responded to unsightly or noisy intrusions into your neighborhood?

QUESTIONS ABOUT PURPOSE

1. What is Kennedy's main argument against the building of the Cape Wind project?
2. What suggestions does he make that would allow the project to be built?

QUESTIONS ABOUT AUDIENCE

1. Why does Kennedy begin by telling his readers that he is an environmentalist who supports wind power?
2. How does his assertion that "all of us" need to experience wilderness establish a connection with his readers?

QUESTIONS ABOUT STRATEGIES

1. How does Kennedy use expert testimony from organizations such as the Massachusetts Historical Commission, the Humane Society, and the Beacon Hill Institute to support his argument?
2. How does he use his "invitations" to his critics to help explain what would be lost if the project were built?

QUESTIONS FOR DISCUSSION

1. Why does Kennedy claim that support for Cape Wind is "bad environmental strategy"?
2. How does his reference to his uncle, John F. Kennedy, and the Cape Cod National Seashore establish his ethical appeal?

FRANCIS BROADHURST

Francis Broadhurst was born in 1935 in Becket, Massachusetts, and educated at the University of Massachusetts at Amherst. He has written for numerous newspapers in New England, such as the *Boston Herald* and the *Cape Cod Times*. He has also worked as the news editor for several New England radio stations, including WQRC radio where he produced the *Broadhurst Report,* a daily commentary and news analysis program. In "Cape Wind Is Sound for the Sound," which appeared as an op-ed column in the *Cape Cod Times* and also broadcast on Cape Cod's National Public Radio station, Broadhurst argues that the Cape Wind project presents no environmental dangers and promises valuable economic benefits.

Cape Wind Is Sound for the Sound

C APE WIND IS the foundation for our renewable energy   1
future—an opportunity to put Massachusetts on the map as a clean energy leader while paving the way for other renewable energy projects. Cape Wind will provide the Cape and Islands with 75% of our energy needs. In conjunction with the future of offshore wind, it will reduce our dependence on foreign oil and slow global warming. Wind Power is a clean, renewable energy resource that does not pollute our air with dirty fossil fuel emissions that cause global warming. By reducing greenhouse gas emissions, properly sited wind farms will also help prevent bird populations from becoming extinct.

A recent study published in the journal *Nature* indicates   2
that 15–37 percent of all bird species could face extinction

due to global warming by the year 2050. Radar studies conducted by Denmark's National Environmental Research Institute indicate that wind farms have no adverse impact on bird populations, concluding that most bird species exhibit an avoidance reaction to wind turbines, thereby reducing the probability of a collision. Jack Clarke, director of public policy and government relations at the Massachusetts Audubon Society states that the Demark studies are quite credible. Moreover, Mass. Audubon conducted their own study, concluding that roseate terns avoid Horseshoe Shoals completely. "If it looked like these birds were going to be further

---

*Cape Wind is the gateway to our
renewable energy future.*

---

jeopardized in the northeast as a result of this project then we would have some very, very serious concerns and strong doubts about whether it's a viable project, but we don't see that," Jack Clarke said in an interview with the PBS News Hour this fall.

Cape Wind will also bring significant economic benefits to 3 the local region by creating jobs, stimulating the local economy, and diversifying the region's energy sources. Renewable energy in Nantucket Sound will displace energy we currently generate using fossil fuels without any additional back-up power being required. Forty-five percent of Southeastern Massachusetts' generating capacity is oil-fired, which means Cape Wind will reduce our dependence on foreign oil. Further, in contrast to the skyrocketing energy prices we are currently experiencing, the cost of wind energy remains constant and brings a stabilizing influence to energy prices.

In light of the increasing costs of heating our homes this 4 winter, local residents would stand to benefit greatly from the Cape Wind Project through a fixed-price deal where electricity rates would remain the same. The Cape Light Compact could negotiate long-term contracts on behalf of the 197,000 Cape and Martha's Vineyard residents they supply. This would benefit local residents by providing a fixed-price electricity supply well into the future.

Cape Wind is a stepping-stone for deep-water technology 5 and this near-shore experience is essential to deep-water success. Currently, there are no deep-water wind turbines anywhere in the world. The purpose of the first proposed deep-water site, the Beatrice "demonstrator" project in Scotland, is to test new technology. Unlike the Cape Wind project, the Beatrice demonstrator is heavily subsidized, receiving almost $16 million for two turbines. Furthermore, the developer acknowledges that deep-water technology is not currently viable. The future of deep-water offshore wind energy is promising. The present viability of near-shore wind energy is real. The near-shore Cape Wind project can supply our short-term needs and lay the foundation for the coming of deep-water wind.

Cape Wind is the gateway to our renewable energy future. 6 The project has been undergoing an environmental review for four years, and no major flaws have been found. It is the right project, for the right place, at the right time.

For Study and Discussion

QUESTIONS FOR RESPONSE

1. How do you respond to a controversial issue when both sides seem to have reasonable arguments?
2. How do you react to "bandwagon" appeals, such as "Everyone agrees with us; you should too"?

QUESTIONS ABOUT PURPOSE

1. How does Broadhurst's title suggest his position in the Cape Wind controversy?
2. What is the primary reason he supports the Cape Wind project?

QUESTIONS ABOUT AUDIENCE

1. How does Broadhurst use the pronoun *our* to establish a relationship with his readers?
2. How does he use the promise of "fixed-price electricity" to appeal to his readers?

QUESTIONS ABOUT STRATEGIES

1. How does Broadhurst use expert testimony from organizations such as the Audubon Society to support his argument?
2. How does he use the difference between deep-water and near-shore technology to advance his argument?

QUESTIONS FOR DISCUSSION

1. How do you determine the reliability of expert witnesses when they disagree?
2. A controversy occurs when both sides can present reasonable arguments. How do you resolve the aesthetic, environmental, and economic issues in the Cape Wind controversy?

THOMAS PYNCHON

Thomas Pynchon was born in 1937 in Glen Cove, Long Island, New York, and was educated at Cornell University. After working briefly at Boeing Aircraft, Seattle, as a technical writer, Pynchon traveled to Mexico to finish his first novel, *V* (1963). Since that time, the most noteworthy biographical fact about Pynchon has been his anonymity. He never claimed the William Faulkner First Novel Award for *V* and refused the National Book Award for *Gravity's Rainbow* (1973), preferring to avoid publicity and to live in seclusion. Pynchon's other work includes two novels, *The Crying of Lot 49* (1966) and *Vineland* (1990), and a collection of short stories, *Slow Learner* (1984). "Entropy," reprinted from *Slow Learner,* explores the changes in an "open" and a "closed" information system.

Entropy

Boris has just given me a summary of his views.
He is a weather prophet. The weather will continue bad, he says.
There will be more calamities, more death, more despair.
Not the slightest indication of a change anywhere. . . . We must get
into step, a lockstep toward the prison of death. There is no escape.
The weather will not change.
—Tropic of Cancer

Downstairs, Meatball Mulligan's lease-breaking party was moving into its 40th hour. On the kitchen floor, amid a litter of empty champagne fifths, were Sandor Rojas and three friends, playing spit in the ocean and staying awake on Heidseck and benzedrine pills. In the living room Duke, Vincent, Krinkles and Paco sat crouched over a 15-inch speaker which had been bolted into the top of a wastepaper basket, listening to 27 watts' worth of *The Heroes' Gate at Kiev.* They all wore hornrimmed sunglasses and rapt expressions, and smoked funny-looking cigarettes which contained not, as you might expect, tobacco, but an adulterated form of *cannabis sativa.* This group was the Duke di Angelis quartet. They recorded for a local label called Tambú and had to their credit one 10″ LP entitled *Songs of Outer Space.* From time to time one of them would flick the ashes from his cigarette into the speaker cone to watch them dance around. Meatball himself was sleeping over by the window, holding an empty magnum to his chest as if it were a teddy bear. Several government girls, who worked for people like the State Department and NSA, had passed out on couches, chairs and in one case the bathroom sink.

This was in early February of '57 and back then there were ₂ a lot of American expatriates around Washington, D.C., who would talk, every time they met you, about how someday they were going to go over to Europe for real but right now it seemed they were working for the government. Everyone saw a fine irony in this. They would stage, for instance, polyglot parties where the newcomer was sort of ignored if he couldn't carry on simultaneous conversations in three or four languages. They would haunt Armenian delicatessens for weeks at a stretch and invite you over for bulghour and lamb in tiny kitchens whose walls were covered with bullfight posters. They would have affairs with sultry girls from Andalucía or the Midi who studied economics at Georgetown. Their Dôme was a collegiate Rathskeller out on Wisconsin Avenue called the Old Heidelberg and they had to settle for cherry blossoms instead of lime trees when spring came, but in its lethargic way their life provided, as they said, kicks.

At the moment, Meatball's party seemed to be gathering ₃ its second wind. Outside there was rain. Rain splatted against the tar paper on the roof and was fractured into a fine spray off the noses, eyebrows and lips of wooden gargoyles under the eaves, and ran like drool down the windowpanes. The day before, it had snowed and the day before that there had been winds of gale force and before that the sun had made the city glitter bright as April, though the calendar read early February. It is a curious season in Washington, this false spring. Somewhere in it are Lincoln's Birthday and the Chinese New Year, and a forlornness in the streets because cherry blossoms are weeks away still and, as Sarah Vaughan has put it, spring will be a little late this year. Generally crowds like the one which would gather in the Old Heidelberg on weekday afternoons to drink Würtzburger and to sing Lili Marlene (not to mention The Sweetheart of Sigma Chi) are inevitably and incorrigibly Romantic. And as every good Romantic knows, the soul (*spiritus, ruach, pneuma*) is nothing, substantially, but air; it is only natural that warpings in the atmosphere should be recapitulated in those who breathe it. So that over and above the public components—holidays, tourist attractions—there are private meanderings, linked to the climate as if this spell were a *stretto* passage in the year's fugue: haphazard weather, aimless loves, unpredicted commitments: months one can easily spend *in* fugue, because oddly enough, later on, winds, rains, passions of February and March are never remembered in that city, it is as if they had never been.

The last bass notes of *The Heroes' Gate* boomed up   4 through the floor and woke Callisto from an uneasy sleep. The first thing he became aware of was a small bird he had been holding gently between his hands, against his body. He turned his head sidewise on the pillow to smile down at it, at its blue hunched-down head and sick, lidded eyes, wondering how many more nights he would have to give it warmth before it was well again. He had been holding the bird like that for three days: it was the only way he knew to restore its health. Next to him the girl stirred and whimpered, her arm thrown across her face. Mingled with the sounds of the rain came the first tentative, querulous morning voices of the other birds, hidden in philodendrons and small fan palms: patches of scarlet, yellow and blue laced through this Rousseau-like fantasy, this hothouse jungle it had taken him seven years to weave together. Hermetically sealed, it was a tiny enclave of regularity in the city's chaos, alien to the vagaries of the weather, of national politics, of any civil disorder. Through trial-and-error Callisto had perfected its ecological balance, with the help of the girl its artistic harmony, so that the swayings of its plant life, the stirrings of its birds and human inhabitants were all as integral as the rhythms of a perfectly-executed mobile. He and the girl could no longer, of course, be omitted from that sanctuary; they had become necessary to its unity. What they needed from outside was delivered. They did not go out.

"Is he all right," she whispered. She lay like a tawny question mark facing him, her eyes suddenly huge and dark and blinking slowly. Callisto ran a finger beneath the feathers at the base of the bird's neck; caressed it gently. "He's going to be well, I think. See: he hears his friends beginning to wake up." The girl had heard the rain and the birds even before she was fully awake. Her name was Aubade: she was part French and part Annamese, and she lived on her own curious and lonely planet, where the clouds and the odor of poincianas, the bitterness of wine and the accidental fingers at the small of her back or feathery against her breasts came to her reduced inevitably to the terms of sound: of music which emerged at intervals from a howling darkness of discordancy. "Aubade," he said, "go see." Obedient, she arose; padded to the window, pulled aside the drapes and after a moment said: "It is 37. Still 37." Callisto frowned. "Since Tuesday, then," he said. "No change." Henry Adams, three generations before his own, had stared aghast at Power; Callisto found himself now in much the same state over Thermodynamics, the inner life of that power, realizing like his predecessor that the Virgin and the dynamo stand as much for love as for power; that the two are indeed identical; and that love therefore not only makes the world go round but also makes the boccie ball spin, the nebula precess. It was this latter or sidereal element which disturbed him. The cosmologists had predicted an eventual heat-death for the universe (something like Limbo: form and motion abolished, heat-energy identical at every point in it); the meteorologists, day-to-day, staved it off by contradicting with a reassuring array of varied temperatures.

But for three days now, despite the changeful weather, the   6
mercury had stayed at 37 degrees Fahrenheit. Leery at omens
of apocalypse, Callisto shifted beneath the covers. His fingers
pressed the bird more firmly, as if needing some pulsing or
suffering assurance of an early break in the temperature.

It was that last cymbal crash that did it. Meatball was   7
hurled wincing into consciousness as the synchronized wag-
ging of heads over the wastebasket stopped. The final hiss
remained for an instant in the room, then melted into the
whisper of rain outside. "Aarrgghh," announced Meatball in
the silence, looking at the empty magnum. Krinkles, in slow
motion, turned, smiled and held out a cigarette. "Tea time,
man," he said. "No, no," said Meatball. "How many times I
got to tell you guys. Not at my place. You ought to know,
Washington is lousy with Feds." Krinkles looked wistful.
"Jeez, Meatball," he said, "you don't want to do nothing no
more." "Hair of dog," said Meatball. "Only hope. Any juice
left?" He began to crawl toward the kitchen. "No champagne, I don't think," Duke said. "Case of tequila behind the
icebox." They put on an Earl Bostic side. Meatball paused at
the kitchen door, glowering at Sandor Rojas. "Lemons," he
said after some thought. He crawled to the refrigerator and
got out three lemons and some cubes, found the tequila and
set about restoring order to his nervous system. He drew
blood once cutting the lemons and had to use two hands
squeezing them and his foot to crack the ice tray but after
about ten minutes he found himself, through some miracle,
beaming down into a monster tequila sour. "That looks
yummy," Sandor Rojas said. "How about you make me
one." Meatball blinked at him. *"Kitchi lofass a shegitbe,"* he
replied automatically, and wandered away into the bathroom.
"I say," he called out a moment later to no one in particular.
"I say, there seems to be a girl or something sleeping in the
sink." He took her by the shoulders and shook. "Wha," she
said. "You don't look too comfortable," Meatball said.
"Well," she agreed. She stumbled to the shower, turned on
the cold water and sat down crosslegged in the spray. "That's
better," she smiled.

"Meatball," Sandor Rojas yelled from the kitchen. "Some-   8
body is trying to come in the window. A burglar, I think. A
second-story man." "What are you worrying about," Meatball said. "We're on the third floor." He loped back into the
kitchen. A shaggy woebegone figure stood out on the fire escape, raking his fingernails down the windowpane. Meatball
opened the window. "Saul," he said.

"Sort of wet out," Saul said. He climbed in, dripping.   9
"You heard, I guess."

"Miriam left you," Meatball said, "or something, is all I   10
heard."

There was a sudden flurry of knocking at the front door.   11
"Do come in," Sandor Rojas called. The door opened and
there were three coeds from George Washington, all of whom
were majoring in philosophy. They were each holding a gallon
of Chianti. Sandor leaped up and dashed into the living room.
"We heard there was a party," one blonde said. "Young
blood," Sandor shouted. He was an ex-Hungarian freedom
fighter who had easily the worst chronic case of what certain
critics of the middle class have called Don Giovannism in the
District of Columbia. *Purche porti la gonnella, voi sapete quel
che fa.* Like Pavlov's dog: a contralto voice or a whiff of Arpège
and Sandor would begin to salivate. Meatball regarded the trio
blearily as they filed into the kitchen; he shrugged. "Put the
wine in the icebox," he said "and good morning."

Aubade's neck made a golden bow as she bent over the   12
sheets of foolscap, scribbling away in the green murk of the
room. "As a young man at Princeton," Callisto was dictating,
nestling the bird against the gray hairs of his chest, "Callisto
had learned a mnemonic device for remembering the Laws of
Thermodynamics: you can't win, things are going to get
worse before they get better, who says they're going to get
better. At the age of 54, confronted with Gibbs' notion of the
universe, he suddenly realized that undergraduate cant had
been oracle, after all. That spindly maze of equations became,
for him, a vision of ultimate, cosmic heat-death. He had
known all along, of course, that nothing but a theoretical engine or system ever runs at 100% efficiency; and about the

theorem of Clausius, which states that the entropy of an
isolated system always continually increases. It was not,
however, until Gibbs and Boltzmann brought to this principle
the methods of statistical mechanics that the horrible significance of it all dawned on him: only then did he realize that
the isolated system—galaxy, engine, human being, culture,
whatever—must evolve spontaneously toward the Condition
of the More Probable. He was forced, therefore, in the sad
dying fall of middle age, to a radical reëvaluation of everything
he had learned up to then; all the cities and seasons and casual
passions of his days had now to be looked at in a new and elusive light. He did not know if he was equal to the task. He was
aware of the dangers of the reductive fallacy and, he hoped,
strong enough not to drift into the graceful decadence of an
enervated fatalism. His had always been a vigorous, Italian
sort of pessimism: like Machiavelli, he allowed the forces of
virtù and *fortuna* to be about 50/50; but the equations now
introduced a random factor which pushed the odds to some
unutterable and indeterminate ratio which he found himself
afraid to calculate." Around him loomed vague hothouse
shapes; the pitifully small heart fluttered against his own.
Counterpointed against his words the girl heard the chatter of
birds and fitful car honkings scattered along the wet morning
and Earl Bostic's alto rising in occasional wild peaks through
the floor. The architectonic purity of her world was constantly
threatened by such hints of anarchy: gaps and excrescences
and skew lines, and a shifting or tilting of planes to which she
had continually to readjust lest the whole structure shiver into
a disarray of discrete and meaningless signals. Callisto had described the process once as a kind of "feedback": she crawled
into dreams each night with a sense of exhaustion, and a desperate resolve never to relax that vigilance. Even in the brief
periods when Callisto made love to her, soaring above the
bowing of taut nerves in haphazard double-stops would be
the one singing string of her determination.

  "Nevertheless," continued Callisto, "he found in entropy   13
or the measure of disorganization for a closed system an ade-
quate metaphor to apply to certain phenomena in his own

world. He saw, for example, the younger generation responding to Madison Avenue with the same spleen his own had
once reserved for Wall Street: and in American 'consumerism'
discovered a similar tendency from the least to the most probable, from differentiation to sameness, from ordered individuality to a kind of chaos. He found himself, in short, restating
Gibbs' prediction in social terms, and envisioned a heat-death
for his culture in which ideas, like heat-energy, would no
longer be transferred, since each point in it would ultimately
have the same quantity of energy; and intellectual motion
would, accordingly, cease." He glanced up suddenly. "Check
it now," he said. Again she rose and peered out at the
thermometer. "37," she said. "The rain has stopped." He
bent his head quickly and held his lips against a quivering
wing. "Then it will change soon," he said, trying to keep his
voice firm.

Sitting on the stove Saul was like any big rag doll that a kid 14
has been taking out some incomprehensible rage on. "What
happened," Meatball said. "If you feel like talking, I mean."

"Of course I feel like talking," Saul said. "One thing I did, 15
I slugged her."

"Discipline must be maintained." 16

"Ha, ha. I wish you'd been there. Oh Meatball, it was a 17
lovely fight. She ended up throwing a *Handbook of Chemistry
and Physics* at me, only it missed and went through the window, and when the glass broke I reckon something in her
broke too. She stormed out of the house crying, out in the
rain. No raincoat or anything."

"She'll be back." 18

"No." 19

"Well." Soon Meatball said: "It was something earth- 20
shattering, no doubt. Like who is better, Sal Mineo or Ricky
Nelson."

"What it was about," Saul said, "was communication theory. 21
Which of course makes it very hilarious."

"I don't know anything about communication theory." 22

"Neither does my wife. Come right down to it, who does? 23
That's the joke."

When Meatball saw the kind of smile Saul had on his face   24
he said: "Maybe you would like tequila or something."

"No. I mean, I'm sorry. It's a field you can go off the deep   25
end in, is all. You get where you're watching all the time for
security cops: behind bushes, around corners. MUFFET is
top secret."

"Wha."   26

"Multi-unit factorial field electronic tabulator."   27

"You were fighting about that."   28

"Miriam has been reading science fiction again. That and   29
Scientific American. It seems she is, as we say, bugged at this
idea of computers acting like people. I made the mistake of
saying you can just as well turn that around, and talk about
human behavior like a program fed into an IBM machine."

"Why not," Meatball said.   30

"Indeed, why not. In fact it is sort of crucial to communi-   31
cation, not to mention information theory. Only when I said
that she hit the roof. Up went the balloon. And I can't figure
out *why*. If anybody should know why, I should. I refuse to
believe the government is wasting taxpayers' money on me,
when it has so many bigger and better things to waste it on."

Meatball made a moue. "Maybe she thought you were   32
acting like a cold, dehumanized amoral scientist type."

"My god," Saul flung up an arm. "Dehumanized. How   33
much more human can I get? I worry, Meatball, I do. There
are Europeans wandering around North Africa these days
with their tongues torn out of their heads because those
tongues have spoken the wrong words. Only the Europeans
thought they were the right words."

"Language barrier," Meatball suggested.   34

Saul jumped down off the stove. "That," he said, angry, "is   35
a good candidate for sick joke of the year. No, ace, it is *not* a
barrier. If it is anything it's a kind of leakage. Tell a girl: 'I love
you.' No trouble with two-thirds of that, it's a closed circuit.
Just you and she. But that nasty four-letter word in the middle,
that's the one you have to look out for. Ambiguity. Redun-
dance. Irrelevance, even. Leakage. All this is noise. Noise
screws up your signal, makes for disorganization in the circuit."

Meatball shuffled around. "Well, now, Saul," he muttered, 36 "you're sort of, I don't know, expecting a lot from people. I mean, you know. What it is is, most of the things we say, I guess, are mostly noise."

"Ha! Half of what you just said, for example." 37

"Well, you do it too." 38

"I know." Saul smiled grimly. "It's a bitch, ain't it." 39

I bet that's what keeps divorce lawyers in business. 40 Whoops."

"Oh I'm not sensitive. Besides," frowning, "you're right. 41 You find I think that most 'successful' marriages—Miriam and me, up to last night—are sort of founded on compromises. You never run at top efficiency, usually all you have is a minimum basis for a workable thing. I believe the phrase is Togetherness."

"Aarrgghh." 42

"Exactly. You find that one a bit noisy, don't you. But the 43 noise content is different for each of us because you're a bachelor and I'm not. Or wasn't. The hell with it."

"Well sure," Meatball said, trying to be helpful, "you were 44 using different words. By 'human being' you meant something that you can look at like it was a computer. It helps you think better on the job or something. But Miriam meant something entirely—"

"The hell with it." 45

Meatball fell silent. "I'll take that drink," Saul said after a 46 while.

The card game had been abandoned and Sandor's friends 47 were slowly getting wasted on tequila. On the living room couch, one of the coeds and Krinkles were engaged in amorous conversation. "No," Krinkles was saying, "no, I can't put Dave *down*. In fact I give Dave a lot of credit, man. Especially considering his accident and all." The girl's smile faded. "How terrible," she said. "What accident?" "Hadn't you heard?" Krinkles said. "When Dave was in the army, just a private E-2, they sent him down to Oak Ridge on special duty. Something to do with the Manhattan Project. He was handling hot stuff one day and got an overdose of radiation.

So now he's got to wear lead gloves all the time." She shook her head sympathetically. "What an awful break for a piano-player."

Meatball had abandoned Saul to a bottle of tequila and was about to go to sleep in a closet when the front door flew open and the place was invaded by five enlisted personnel of the U.S. Navy, all in varying stages of abomination. "This is the place," shouted a fat, pimply seaman apprentice who had lost his white hat. "This here is the hoorhouse that chief was telling us about." A stringy-looking 3rd class boatswain's mate pushed him aside and cased the living room. "You're right, Slab," he said. "But it don't look like much, even for Stateside. I seen better tail in Naples, Italy." "How much, hey," boomed a large seaman with adenoids, who was holding a Mason jar full of white lightning. "Oh, my god," said Meatball. 48

Outside the temperature remained constant at 37 degrees Fahrenheit. In the hot-house Aubade stood absently caressing the branches of a young mimosa, hearing a motif of sap-rising, the rough and unresolved anticipatory theme of those fragile pink blossoms which, it is said, insure fertility. That music rose in a tangled tracery: arabesques of order competing fugally with the improvised discords of the party downstairs, which peaked sometimes in cusps and ogees of noise. That precious signal-to-noise ratio, whose delicate balance required every calorie of her strength, seesawed inside the small tenuous skull as she watched Callisto, sheltering the bird. Callisto was trying to confront any idea of the heat-death now, as he nuzzled the feathery lump in his hands. He sought correspondences. Sade, of course. And Temple Drake, gaunt and hopeless in her little park in Paris, at the end of *Sanctuary*. Final equilibrium, *Nightwood*. And the tango. Any tango, but more than any perhaps the sad sick dance in Stravinsky's *L'Histoire du Soldat*. He thought back: what had tango music been for them after the war, what meanings had he missed in all the stately coupled automatons in the *cafés-dansants*, or in the metronomes which had ticked behind the eyes of his own partners? Not even the clean 49 constant winds of Switzerland could cure the *grippe espagnole:* Stravinsky had had it, they all had had it. And how many musicians were left after Passchendaele, after the Marne? It came down in this case to seven: violin, double-bass. Clarinet, bassoon. Cornet, trombone. Tympani. Almost as if any tiny troupe of saltimbanques had set about conveying the same information as a full pit-orchestra. There was hardly a full complement left in Europe. Yet with violin and tympani Stravinsky had managed to communicate in that tango the same exhaustion, the same airlessness one saw in the slicked-down youths who were trying to imitate Vernon Castle, and in their mistresses, who simply did not care. *Ma maîtresse.* Celeste. Returning to Nice after the second war he had found that café replaced by a perfume shop which catered to American tourists. And no secret vestige of her in the cobblestones or in the old pension next door; no perfume to match her breath heavy with the sweet Spanish wine she always drank. And so instead he had purchased a Henry Miller novel and left for Paris, and read the book on the train so that when he arrived he had been given at least a little forewarning. And saw that Celeste and the others and even Temple Drake were not all that had changed. "Aubade," he said, "my head aches." The sound of his voice generated in the girl an answering scrap of melody. Her movement toward the kitchen, the towel, the cold water, and his eyes following her formed a weird and intricate canon; as she placed the compress on his forehead his sigh of gratitude seemed to signal a new subject, another series of modulations.

"No," Meatball was still saying, "no, I'm afraid not. This is not a house of ill repute. I'm sorry, really I am." Slab was adamant. "But the chief said," he kept repeating. The seaman offered to swap the moonshine for a good piece. Meatball looked around frantically, as if seeking assistance. In the middle of the room, the Duke di Angelis quartet were engaged in a historic moment. Vincent was seated and the others standing: they were going through the motions of a group having a session, only without instruments. "I say," Meatball

50

said. Duke moved his head a few times, smiled faintly, lit a cigarette, and eventually caught sight of Meatball. "Quiet, man," he whispered. Vincent began to fling his arms around, his fists clenched; then, abruptly, was still, then repeated the performance. This went on for a few minutes while Meatball sipped his drink moodily. The navy had withdrawn to the kitchen. Finally at some invisible signal the group stopped tapping their feet and Duke grinned and said, "At least we ended together."

Meatball glared at him. "I say," he said. "I have this new conception, man," Duke said. "You remember your name-sake. You remember Gerry." 51

"No," said Meatball. "I'll remember April, if that's any help." 52

"As a matter of fact," Duke said, "it was Love for Sale. Which shows how much you know. The point is, it was Mulligan, Chet Baker and that crew, way back then, out yonder. You dig?" 53

"Baritone sax," Meatball said. "Something about a baritone sax." 54

"But no piano, man. No guitar. Or accordion. You know what that means." 55

"Not exactly," Meatball said. 56

"Well first let me just say, that I am no Mingus, no John Lewis. Theory was never my strong point. I mean things like reading were always difficult for me and all—" 57

"I know," Meatball said drily. "You got your card taken away because you changed key on Happy Birthday at a Kiwanis Club picnic." 58

"Rotarian. But it occurred to me, in one of these flashes of insight, that if that first quartet of Mulligan's had no piano, it could only mean one thing." 59

"No chords," said Paco, the baby-faced bass. 60

"What he is trying to say," Duke said, "is no root chords. Nothing to listen to while you blow a horizontal line. What one does in such a case is, one *thinks* the roots." 61

A horrified awareness was dawning on Meatball. "And the next logical extension," he said. 62

"Is to think everything," Duke announced with simple dignity. "Roots, line, everything." 63

Meatball looked at Duke, awed. "But," he said. 64

"Well," Duke said modestly, "there are a few bugs to work out." 65

"But," Meatball said. 66

"Just listen," Duke said. "You'll catch on." And off they went again into orbit, presumably somewhere around the asteroid belt. After a while Krinkles made an embouchure and started moving his fingers and Duke clapped his hand to his forehead. "Oaf!" he roared. "The new head we're using, you remember, I wrote last night?" "Sure," Krinkles said, "the new head. I come in on the bridge. All your heads I come in then." "Right," Duke said. "So why—" "Wha," said Krinkles, "16 bars, I wait, I come in—" "16?" Duke said. "No. No, Krinkles. Eight you waited. You want me to sing it? A cigarette that bears a lipstick's traces, an airline ticket to romantic places." Krinkles scratched his head. "These Foolish Things, you mean." "Yes," Duke said, "yes, Krinkles. Bravo." "Not I'll Remember April," Krinkles said. *"Minghe morte,"* said Duke. "I *figured* we were playing it a little slow," Krinkles said. Meatball chuckled. "Back to the old drawing board," he said. "No, man," Duke said, "back to the airless void." And they took off again, only it seemed Paco was playing in G sharp while the rest were in E flat, so they had to start all over. 67

In the kitchen two of the girls from George Washington and the sailors were singing Let's All Go Down and Piss on the Forrestal. There was a two-handed, bilingual *morra* game on over by the icebox. Saul had filled several paper bags with water and was sitting on the fire escape, dropping them on passersby in the street. A fat government girl in a Bennington sweatshirt, recently engaged to an ensign attached to the Forrestal, came charging into the kitchen, head lowered, and butted Slab in the stomach. Figuring this was as good an excuse for a fight as any, Slab's buddies piled in. The *morra* players were nose-to-nose, screaming *trois, sette* at the tops of their lungs. From the shower the girl Meatball had taken out 68 of the sink announced that she was drowning. She had apparently sat on the drain and the water was now up to her neck. The noise in Meatball's apartment had reached a sustained, ungodly crescendo.

Meatball stood and watched, scratching his stomach lazily.   69
The way he figured, there were only about two ways he could cope: (a) lock himself in the closet and maybe eventually they would all go away, or (b) try to calm everybody down, one by one. (a) was certainly the more attractive alternative. But then he started thinking about that closet. It was dark and stuffy and he would be alone. He did not feature being alone. And then this crew off the good ship Lollipop or whatever it was might take it upon themselves to kick down the closet door, for a lark. And if that happened he would be, at the very least, embarrassed. The other way was more a pain in the neck, but probably better in the long run.

So he decided to try and keep his lease-breaking party   70
from deteriorating into total chaos: he gave wine to the sailors and separated the *morra* players; he introduced the fat government girl to Sandor Rojas, who would keep her out of trouble; he helped the girl in the shower to dry off and get into bed; he had another talk with Saul; he called a repairman for the refrigerator, which someone had discovered was on the blink. This is what he did until nightfall, when most of the revellers had passed out and the party trembled on the threshold of its third day.

Upstairs Callisto, helpless in the past, did not feel the faint   71
rhythm inside the bird begin to slacken and fail. Aubade was by the window, wandering the ashes of her own lovely world; the temperature held steady, the sky had become a uniform darkening gray. Then something from downstairs—a girl's scream, an overturned chair, a glass dropped on the floor, he would never know what exactly—pierced that private time-warp and he became aware of the faltering, the constriction of muscles, the tiny tossings of the bird's head; and his own pulse began to pound more fiercely, as if trying to compensate. "Aubade," he called weakly, "he's dying." The girl, flowing and rapt, crossed the hothouse to gaze down at

Callisto's hands. The two remained like that, poised, for one minute, and two, while the heartbeat ticked a graceful diminuendo down at last into stillness. Callisto raised his head slowly. "I held him," he protested, impotent with the wonder of it, "to give him the warmth of my body. Almost as if I were communicating life to him, or a sense of life. What has happened? Has the transfer of heat ceased to work? Is there no more . . ." He did not finish.

"I was just at the window," she said. He sank back, terri-   72
fied. She stood a moment more, irresolute; she had sensed his obsession long ago, realized somehow that that constant 37 was now decisive. Suddenly then, as if seeing the single and unavoidable conclusion to all this she moved swiftly to the window before Callisto could speak; tore away the drapes and smashed out the glass with two exquisite hands which came away bleeding and glistening with splinters; and turned to face the man on the bed and wait with him until the moment of equilibrium was reached, when 37 degrees Fahrenheit should prevail both outside and inside, and forever, and the hovering, curious dominant of their separate lives should resolve into a tonic of darkness and the final absence of all motion.

COMMENT ON "ENTROPY"

Thomas Pynchon is obsessed with the word *entropy*—the measure of random motion in a system and therefore a measure of the limit of the amount of work that can be extracted from an energy system. The second law of thermodynamics states that entropy always increases, and therefore more and more energy becomes available for work. However, Pynchon is particularly interested in the way entropy is used to describe both energy and communication, because the word is also a measure of the energy and communication that is unable to work—waste, noise.

In "Entropy" Pynchon uses this slippery scientific concept as a metaphor, as he creates two plots. Meatball's lease-breaking party is an open, chaotic system. Callisto's sanctuary is a stable, closed system. Meatball's plot reaches its climax when he tries to contain the disorder in his party. Callisto's plot reaches its climax when Aubade smashes the window, rejecting the wisdom of the "hermetically sealed" environment and hoping for some sort of eventual equilibrium between the outside and the inside.

The two plots take place within a larger system—Washington, D.C.—and deal with the same theme: man's ability to influence and control the larger system. Meatball's efforts to stem chaos and Callisto's efforts to impose order both prove inadequate, suggesting that entropy applies to the social system as well as to the matter in the universe. In other words, our culture is moving from "differentiation to sameness, from ordered individuality to chaos."

Writing About Energy

1. *Narration and Description.* Write a narrative for your local newspaper's Sunday supplement about how the members of your community or neighborhood bonded over a common cause or responded to a major event. Stephen Doheny-Farina writes about how his community responded to an ice storm. Instead, you may want to write about an event that prompted your neighbors to circulate a petition or attend a town meeting.

2. *Process Analysis.* Analyze various methods you have developed for saving money on energy. Like Tom and Ray Magliozzi, you may want to write about how to save money on gasoline or get better miles per gallon, but you may also want to analyze the steps you have discovered or developed for saving money on keeping warm in the winter or cool in the summer.

3. *Comparison and Contrast.* Write a film review for your student newspaper comparing several disaster films. Greenpeace International compares a real nuclear accident with the fictional presentation of nuclear energy on *The Simpsons.* You may instead want to compare films that present such crises as global warming or environmental pollution. In particular, you may want to compare the "scientific solutions" the films create to avoid what appears to be an inevitable disaster.

4. *Division and Classification.* Sort through the utility bills you pay each month. Then call the customer service number on each bill and ask the person who answers to explain the various charges on your bill. Then write an essay classifying (and ranking) the various utilities by their ability to answer your questions effectively.

5. *Definition.* Select some device related to energy—a gasoline pump, an electricity transformer—and write an essay defining it for nonscientific readers, such as those who frequent a website such as "How Stuff Works." Or you may want to select a slippery scientific term such as *entropy* and define it for readers who are scientifically challenged.

6. *Cause and Effect.* Analyze the causes and possible effects of a construction project. Edward Cody analyzes the causes and possible effects of building Three Gorges Dam. Instead, you may wish to write about the causes and effects of building the new football stadium at your university or a new housing addition in your community.

7. *Persuasion and Argument.* Write an op-ed column for your local newspaper persuading people to invest in an energy alternative. Robert F. Kennedy, Jr., and Francis Broadhurst present arguments against and for the Cape Wind project in Nantucket Sound, Massachusetts. But, depending on where you live, people in your area may be considering other alternatives, such as using corn to make ethanol or coal to make a synthetic liquid fuel, or synfuel.

USING
AND
DOCUMENTING
SOURCES

The essays in *The Riverside Reader* are sources. Many of the writing assignments at the end of each essay ask you to *analyze* these sources or to use them to support your own ideas. Most academic writing asks you to use sources—from books, journals, magazines, newspapers, and the Internet—to augment and advance the ideas in your writing. Every time you cite a source, or use it in some way, you must *document*

it. For example, in the student research paper at the end of this chapter, Erin McMullen uses the Modern Language Association Style to cite print and electronic sources.

This chapter explains the style recommended by the Modern Language Association (MLA) for documenting sources in academic papers. It also analyzes some of the implications of MLA style for your research and composing. More detailed information is given in the *MLA Handbook* and the *MLA Style Manual.*

MLA documentation style has three major features:

- A brief **parenthetical reference** within the text is used to document material borrowed from another source and to direct readers to the full citation (which is provided at the end of the paper in the list of works cited).
- Numbered **footnotes** or **endnotes** are used to present two types of supplementary information—*commentary* or explanation that the text cannot accommodate and *bibliographical notes* that contain several source citations.
- A section entitled **Works Cited** is placed at the end of the paper and lists all sources cited in a paper.

Planning and Writing the Research Paper

MLA style emphasizes the importance of following the procedures for planning and writing the research paper outlined in any standard writing textbook. In particular, MLA style requires you to devote considerable attention to certain steps in your research and composing:

- Evaluating sources
- Compiling source information
- Taking notes (quoting, summarizing, and paraphrasing sources)
- Avoiding plagiarism

Evaluating Sources

As you begin collecting sources to advance your research, evaluate them according to the following criteria:

1. **A source should be relevant.** Ask yourself: Does the content of this source apply directly to the topic of the paper? Whether a particular source is relevant is not always apparent. When you begin your research, your lack of perspective on your subject may make every source seem potentially relevant. Titles of sources may be misleading or vague, prompting you to examine a source unrelated to your subject or to dismiss a source as too theoretical or general when it actually gives you vital perspective on your subject. The status of your sources may also change as you restrict and define your subject. A source that seemed irrelevant yesterday may appear more pertinent today.

2. **A source should be authoritative.** Ask yourself: Does the author of a particular source have the necessary expertise or experience to speak authoritatively about the subject of your paper? Most print sources enable you to judge the credentials and bias of the author. You can usually judge the authority of books and articles because the book has been reviewed by knowledgeable persons or the article has been evaluated by the journal's editorial board. But you have no way to evaluate the authority of many electronic sources. A source that you assume is authoritative may have been posted by a hacker or by someone who wishes to further his or her own agenda.

3. **A source must be current.** Ask yourself: Is this source current? You don't want to cite a twenty-year-old source if you are writing about the latest cures for cancer. However, you may want to use that same twenty-year-old source if you are writing about the history of cancer therapy. Writers often cite standard print sources to establish the reliability of their arguments. Then they will cite recent electronic sources to address issues that have arisen since the print source sources were originally published. Keep in

mind that electronic sources are not necessarily the most current since many print sources are now posted on the Internet. To make sure your sources are reliable and current, you may need to mix print and electronic sources.

4. **A source should be comprehensive.** Ask yourself: Does this source cover all the major issues I need to discuss in my paper? Some sources will focus on an extremely narrow aspect of your subject; others will cover every feature and many related, or unrelated, topics as well. Begin reading the most comprehensive first because it will cover the essential information in the more specialized sources and give you the related subtopics within your subject. Most books, for example, are comprehensive sources whereas most websites provide only "bits" of information.

5. **A source should be stable.** Ask yourself: If I use this source, will my readers be able to locate it if they want to read more about the topic of my paper? You want to cite sources that provide the best and most stable information on your topic. There is nothing more stable than a book. Even if a library does not own a book or a book goes out of print, librarians can find a copy for your readers through interlibrary loan. The same is true for most articles. But electronic sources are not stable. The source you stumble on today may not be there tomorrow. Your readers will not be able to find it because it may have been renamed, reclassified, or often simply deleted. If your readers want to check your sources, you should cite sources they can find.

6. **A source should provide links.** Ask yourself: Does this source help me locate other sources? The best sources lead to other sources, which can further your research. The subject headings on a source provide an excellent system for linking up with other sources. Annotated bibliographies not only link you to other sources but also provide you with an assessment of their value. Of course, the chief advantage of the Internet and its various search engines is that they allow you to link up with thousands of sources

by simply pointing and clicking. If your source provides such links, your readers can use them to trace the research that informs the source and the way you have used it to broaden and deepen the research in your paper.

Compiling Source Information

Once you have located sources that you suspect will prove useful, create a computer file for each item. List the source in the appropriate format. To guarantee that each file is complete and accurate, take your information directly from the source rather than from the card or on-line catalog or a bibliographical index. Your collection of files will help you keep track of your sources throughout your research. Alphabetizing the files will enable you to prepare a provisional list of works cited.

The provisional list must be in place *before* you begin writing your paper. You may expand or refine the list as you write, but to document each source in your text, you first need to know its correct citation. Thus, although Works Cited will be the last section of your paper, you must prepare it first.

Taking Notes

Note-taking demands that you read, select, interpret, and evaluate the information that will form the substance of your paper. After you return books and articles to the library, your notes will be the only record of your research. If you have taken notes carelessly, you will be in trouble when you try to use them in the body of your paper. Many students inadvertently plagiarize because they have incorrectly copied and pasted sources into their files. As you select information from a source, use one of three methods to record it: quoting, summarizing, or paraphrasing.

Quoting sources: Although quoting an author's text word for word is the easiest way to record information, use this method selectively and quote only the passages that deal directly with your subject in memorable language. When you copy a quotation into a file, place quotation marks at the beginning and the end of the passage. If you decide to omit part of the passage, use ellipsis points to indicate that you have omitted words from the original source. To indicate an omission from the middle of a sentence, use three periods (. . .), and leave a space before and after each period. For an omission at the end of a sentence, type three spaced periods following the sentence period.

To move a quotation from your notes to your paper, making it fit smoothly into the flow of your text, use one of the following methods.

1. Work the quoted passage into the syntax of your sentence.

Morrison points out that social context prevented the authors of slave narratives "from dwelling too long or too carefully on the more sordid details of their experience" (109).

2. Introduce the quoted passage with a sentence and a colon.

Commentators have tried to account for the decorum of most slave narratives by discussing social context: "popular taste discouraged the writers from dwelling too long or too carefully on the more sordid details of their experience" (Morrison 109).

3. Set off the quoted passage with an introductory sentence followed by a colon.

This method is reserved for long quotations (four or more lines of prose; three or more lines of poetry). Double-space the quotation, and indent it one inch (ten spaces) from the left margin. Because this special placement identifies the passage as a quotation, do not enclose it within quotation marks. Notice that the final period goes *before* rather than *after* the parenthetical reference. Leave one space after the final period. If the long quotation extends to two or more paragraphs, then indent the first line of these additional paragraphs one-quarter inch (three spaces).

Toni Morrison, in "The Site of Memory," explains how social context shaped slave narratives:

> No slave society in the history of the world wrote more—or more thoughtfully—about its own enslavement. The milieu, however, dictated the purpose and the style. The narratives are instructive, moral and obviously representative. Some of them are patterned after the sentimental novel that was in vogue at the time. But whatever the level of eloquence or the form, popular taste discouraged the writers from dwelling too long or too carefully on the more sordid details of their experience. (109)

Summarizing and paraphrasing sources: Summarizing and paraphrasing an author's text are the most efficient ways to record information. The terms *summary* and *paraphrase* are often used interchangeably to describe a brief restatement of the author's ideas in your own words, but they may be used more precisely to designate different procedures.

- A *summary* condenses the content of a lengthy passage. When you write a summary, you reformulate the main idea and outline the main points that support it.
- A *paraphrase* restates the content of a short passage. When you paraphrase, you reconstruct the passage phrase by phrase, recasting the author's words in your own.

A summary or a paraphrase is intended as a complete and objective presentation of an author's ideas, so be careful not to distort the original passage by omitting major points or by adding your own opinion. Because the words of a summary or a paraphrase are yours, they are not enclosed by quotation marks. But because the ideas you are restating came from someone else, you need to cite the source in your notes and in your text.

The following examples illustrate two common methods of introducing a summary or a paraphrase into your paper.

1. **Summary of a long quotation:** Often, the best way to proceed is to name the author of a source in the body of your sentence and place the page numbers in parentheses. This procedure informs your reader that you are about to quote or paraphrase. It also gives you an opportunity to state the credentials of the authority you are citing.

2. **Paraphrase of a short quotation:** You may decide to vary the pattern of documentation by presenting the information from a source and placing the author's name and page numbers in parentheses at the end of the sentence. This method is particularly useful if you have already established the identity of your source in a previous sentence and now want to develop the author's ideas in some detail without having to clutter your sentences with constant references to his or her name.

Slave narratives sometimes imitated the popular fiction of their era (Morrison 109).

Works Cited

Morrison, Toni. "The Site of Memory." Inventing the Truth: The Art and Craft of Memoir. Ed. William Zinsser. Boston: Houghton, 1987. 101–24.

Avoiding Plagiarism

Plagiarism is theft. It is using someone else's words or ideas without giving proper credit—or without giving any credit at all—to the writer of the original. Whether plagiarism is intentional or unintentional, it is a serious offense that your professor and school will deal with severely. You can avoid plagiarism by taking notes carefully, by formulating and developing your own ideas, and by using quotes responsibly to support, rather than to replace, your own work. Adhere to the advice for research and composing outlined above and demonstrated below.

The following excerpt is from Robert Hughes's *The Fatal Shore*, an account of the founding of Australia. The examples of how students tried to use this excerpt illustrate the problem of plagiarism.

1. Original version

Transportation did not stop crime in England or even slow it down. The "criminal class" was not eliminated by transportation, and could not be, because transportation did not deal with the causes of crime.

2. Version A

Transportation did not stop crime in England or even slow it down. Criminals were not eliminated by transportation because transportation did not deal with the causes of crime.

Version A is plagiarism. Because the writer of Version A does not indicate in the text or in a parenthetical reference that the words and ideas belong to Hughes, her readers will believe the words are hers. She has stolen the words and ideas and has attempted to cover the theft by changing or omitting an occasional word.

3. Version B

Robert Hughes points out that transportation did not stop crime in England or even slow it down. The criminal class was not eliminated by transportation, and could not be, because transportation did not deal with the causes of crime (168).

Version B is also plagiarism, even though the writer acknowledges his source and documents the passage with a parenthetical reference. He has worked from careless notes and has misunderstood the difference between quoting and paraphrasing. He has copied the original word for word yet has supplied no quotation marks to indicate the extent of the borrowing. As written and documented, the passage masquerades as a paraphrase when in fact it is a direct quotation.

4. Version C

Hughes argues that transporting criminals from England to Australia "did not stop crime. . . . The 'criminal class' was not eliminated by transportation, and could not be, because transportation did not deal with the causes of crime" (168).

Version C is one satisfactory way of handling this source material. The writer has identified her source at the beginning of the sentence, letting readers know who is being quoted. She then explains the concept of transportation in her own words, placing within quotation marks the parts of the original she wants to quote and using ellipsis points to delete the parts she wants to omit. She provides a parenthetical reference to the page number in the source listed in Works Cited.

Works Cited

Hughes, Robert. The Fatal Shore. New York: Knopf, 1987.

Preparing the List of Works Cited

In an academic paper that follows MLA style, the list of works cited is the *only* place where readers will find complete information about the sources you have cited. For that reason, your list must be thorough and accurate.

The list of works cited appears at the end of your paper and, as its title suggests, *lists only the works you have cited in your paper.* Occasionally, your instructor may ask you to prepare a list of works consulted. The Works Consulted list would include not only the sources you cite but also the sources you consulted as you conducted your research. In either case, MLA prefers Works Cited or Works Consulted to the more limited heading Bibliography (literally, "description of books") because those headings are more likely to accommodate the variety of sources—articles, films, Internet sources—that writers may cite in a research paper.

To prepare the list of works cited, follow these general guidelines:

1. Paginate the Works Cited section as a continuation of your text. If the conclusion of your paper appears on page 8, then begin your list on page 9 (unless there is an intervening page of endnotes).
2. Double-space between successive lines of an entry and between entries.
3. Begin the first line of an entry flush left, and indent successive lines five spaces or one-half inch.
4. List entries in alphabetical order according to the last name of the author.
5. If you are listing more than one work by the same author, alphabetize the works according to title (excluding the articles *a, an,* and *the*). Instead of repeating the author's name, type *three* hyphens and a period, and then give the title.
6. Underline the titles of works published independently: books, plays, long poems, pamphlets, periodicals, films.
7. Although you do not *need* to underline the spaces between words, a continuous line is easier to type and guarantees that all features of the title are underlined. Type a continuous line under titles unless you are instructed to do otherwise.
8. If you are citing a book whose title includes the title of another book, underline the main title, but do not

underline the other title (for example, A Casebook on Ralph Ellison's Invisible Man).

9. Use quotation marks to indicate titles of short works that appear in larger works (for example, "Minutes of Glory." African Short Stories). Also use quotation marks for song titles and for titles of unpublished works, including dissertations, lectures, and speeches.

10. Use arabic numerals except with names of monarchs (Elizabeth II) and except for the preliminary pages of a work (ii–xix), which are traditionally numbered with roman numerals.

11. Use lowercase abbreviations to identify the parts of a work (for example, *vol.* for *volume*), a named translator (*trans.*), and a named editor (*ed.*). However, when these designations follow a period, they should be capitalized (for example, Woolf, Virginia. A Writer's Diary. Ed. Leonard Woolf).

12. Whenever possible, use appropriate shortened forms for the publisher's name (*Random* instead of *Random House*).

13. Separate author, title, and publication information with a period followed by one space.

14. Use a colon and one space to separate the volume number and year of a periodical from the page numbers (for example, Trimmer, Joseph. "Memoryscape: Jean Shepherd's Midwest." Old Northwest 2 (1976): 357–69).

In addition to these guidelines, MLA recommends procedures for documenting an extensive variety of sources, including electronic sources and nonprint materials such as films and television programs. The following models illustrate sources most commonly cited.

Sample Entries: Books

When citing books, provide the following general categories of information:

Author's last name, first name. Book title. Additional information.

City of publication: Publishing company, publication date.

Entries illustrating variations on this basic format appear below.

A BOOK BY ONE AUTHOR

Light, Richard J. Making the Most of College: Students Speak

Their Minds. Cambridge: Harvard UP, 2001.

TWO OR MORE BOOKS BY THE SAME AUTHOR

Rose, Mike. Lives on the Boundary: The Struggles and

Achievements of America's Underprepared. New York:

Free Press, 1989.

— — —. The Mind at Work: Valuing the Intelligence of the American

Worker. New York: Viking, 2004.

A BOOK BY TWO OR THREE AUTHORS

Wynn, Charles M., and Arthur Wiggins. Quantum Leaps in the

Wrong Direction: Where Real Science Ends . . . and

Pseudoscience Begins. Washington: National Academy,

2001.

Peel, Robin, Annette Patterson, and Jeanne Gerlach. Questions of

English: Ethics, Aesthetics, Rhetoric and the Formation of the

Subject in England, Australia, and the United States. London:

Routledge, 2000.

A BOOK BY FOUR OR MORE AUTHORS

Lassiter, Luke Eric, et al. The Other Side of Middletown: Exploring

Muncie's African American Community. Walnut Creek, CA:

AltaMira, 2004.

A BOOK BY A CORPORATE AUTHOR

National Geographic Society. Cradle and Crucible: History and Faith
in the Middle East. Washington: National Geographic, 2002.

A BOOK BY AN ANONYMOUS AUTHOR

Literary Market Place 2001: The Dictionary of the American Book
Publishing Industry. New Providence, NJ: Bowker, 2000.

A BOOK WITH AN EDITOR

Jackson, Kenneth T., ed. The Encyclopedia of New York City. New
Haven: Yale UP, 1995.

A BOOK WITH AN AUTHOR AND AN EDITOR

Toomer, Jean. Cane. Ed. Darwin T. Turner. New York: Norton, 1988.

A BOOK WITH A PUBLISHER'S IMPRINT

Hillenbrand, Laura. Seabiscuit: An American Legend. New York:
Ballantine-Random, 2001.

AN ANTHOLOGY OR COMPILATION

Smith, Barbara Leigh, and John McCann, eds. Reinventing
Ourselves: Interdisciplinary Education, Collaborative
Learning, and Experimentation in Higher Education.
Bolton, MA: Anker, 2001.

A WORK IN AN ANTHOLOGY

Peterson, Rai. "My Tribe outside the Global Village." Visual Media
and the Humanities: A Pedagogy of Representation. Ed. Kecia
Driver McBride. Knoxville: U of Tennessee P, 2004.

AN INTRODUCTION, PREFACE, FOREWORD, OR AFTERWORD

Shulman, Lee S. Foreword. Disciplinary Styles in the Scholarship

of Teaching and Learning. Eds. Mary Taylor Huber and

Sherwyn P. Morreale. Washington: American Assn. of

Higher Educ., 2002.

A MULTIVOLUME WORK

Blotner, Joseph. Faulkner: A Biography. 2 vols. New York:

Random, 1974.

AN EDITION OTHER THAN THE FIRST

Chaucer, Geoffrey. The Riverside Chaucer. Ed. Larry D. Benson.

3rd ed. Boston: Houghton, 1987.

A BOOK IN A SERIES

Eggers, Dave, ed. The Best American Nonrequired Reading, 2004.

The Best American Series. Boston: Houghton, 2004.

A REPUBLISHED BOOK

Malamud, Bernard. The Natural. 1952. New York: Avon, 1980.

A SIGNED ARTICLE IN A REFERENCE BOOK

Tobias, Richard. "Thurber, James." Encyclopedia Americana.

2002 ed.

AN UNSIGNED ARTICLE IN A REFERENCE BOOK

"Tharp, Twyla." Who's Who of American Women. 17th ed. 1991–92.

A GOVERNMENT DOCUMENT

National Commission on Terrorist Attacks upon the United States.
The 9/11 Commission Report: Final Report of the National
Commission on Terrorists Attacks upon the United States.
Washington: GPO, 2004.

PUBLISHED PROCEEDINGS OF A CONFERENCE

Sass, Steven A., and Robert K. Triest. Social Security Reform:
Conference Proceedings: Links to Saving, Investment and
Growth. Boston: Federal Reserve Bank of Boston, 1997.

A TRANSLATION

Giroud, Françoise. Marie Curie: A Life. Trans. Lydia Davis. New
York: Holmes, 1986.

A BOOK WITH A TITLE IN ITS TITLE

Habich, Robert D. Transcendentalism and the Western Messenger:
A History of the Magazine and Its Contributors, 1835–1841.
Rutherford: Fairleigh Dickinson UP, 1985.

A BOOK PUBLISHED BEFORE 1900

Field, Kate. The History of Bell's Telephone. London, 1878.

AN UNPUBLISHED DISSERTATION

Geissinger, Shirley Burry. "Openness versus Secrecy in
Adoptive Parenthood." Diss. U of North Carolina at
Greensboro, 1984.

A PUBLISHED DISSERTATION

Schottler, Beverly A. <u>A Handbook for Dealing with Plagiarism in</u>

    <u>Public Schools</u>. Diss. Kansas State U, 2003. Ann Arbor: UMI,

    2004. AAT 3113929.

Sample Entries: Articles in Periodicals

When citing articles in periodicals, provide the following general categories of information:

Author's last name, first name. "Article title." <u>Periodical title</u> Date:

    inclusive pages.

Entries illustrating variations on this basic format appear below.

A SIGNED ARTICLE FROM A DAILY NEWSPAPER

Glanz, James. "Iraqi Insurgents Step Up Attacks after Elections."

    <u>New York Times</u> 13 Feb. 2005, late ed.: A1.

AN UNSIGNED ARTICLE FROM A DAILY NEWSPAPER

"Sunnis Worry of Future in New Shiite-run Iraq." <u>Chicago Tribune</u>

    13 Feb. 2005, sec. 1: 1: 16?.

AN ARTICLE FROM A MONTHLY OR BIMONTHLY MAGAZINE

Fallows, James. "Success without Victory." <u>Atlantic Monthly</u>

    Jan.–Feb. 2005: 80–90.

AN ARTICLE FROM A WEEKLY OR BIWEEKLY MAGAZINE

Mayer, Jane. "Outsourcing Torture." <u>New Yorker</u> 14–21 Feb. 2005:

    106–23.

AN ARTICLE IN A JOURNAL WITH CONTINUOUS PAGINATION

Flower, Linda. "Intercultural Inquiry and the Transformation of

Service." College English 65 (2002): 181–201.

AN ARTICLE IN A JOURNAL THAT NUMBERS PAGES IN EACH ISSUE SEPARATELY

Madden, Thomas F. "Revisiting the Crusades." Wilson Quarterly

26.4 (2002): 100–03.

AN EDITORIAL

"Poverty and Health." Editorial. Washington Post 31 Aug. 2004: A20.

A REVIEW

Nathan, Daniel A. "Of Grades and Glory: Rethinking Intercollegiate

Athletics." Rev. of The Game of Life: College Sports and

Educational Values by James L. Shulman and William G.

Bowen. American Quarterly 54.1 (2002): 139–47.

AN ARTICLE WHOSE TITLE CONTAINS A QUOTATION OR A TITLE WITHIN QUOTATION MARKS

DeCuir, Andre L. "Italy, England and the Female Artist in George

Eliot's 'Mr. Gilfil's Love-Story.'" Studies in Short Fiction 29

(1992): 67–75.

AN ABSTRACT FROM *DISSERTATION ABSTRACTS* OR *DISSERTATION ABSTRACTS INTERNATIONAL*

Creek, Mardena Bridges. "Myth, Wound, Accommodation:

American Literary Responses to the War in Vietnam."

DAI 43 (1982): 3539A. Ball State U.

Sample Entries: Miscellaneous Print and Nonprint Sources

FILMS; RADIO AND TELEVISION PROGRAMS

Chicago. Dir. Rob Marshall. With Renée Zellweger, Catherine
Zeta-Jones, Richard Gere. Miramax, 2002.

"New York, New York (1944–1951)." Leonard Bernstein: An
American Life. Prods. Steve Rowland and Larry Abrams.
NPR. WBST, Muncie. 18 Jan. 2005.

"Seeds of Destruction." Slavery and the Making of America. Prod.
Clara Gazit. PBS. WNET, New York. 16 Feb. 2005.

PERFORMANCES

The Producers. By Mel Brooks. Dir. Susan Stroman. With Nathan
Lane and Matthew Broderick. St. James Theater, 8 October
2002.

Spano, Robert, cond. Wagner, Mendelssohn, Wyner and Haydn.
Concert. Boston Symphony Orch. Symphony Hall, Boston.
17 Feb. 2005.

RECORDINGS

Mozart, Wolfgang A. Cosi Fan Tutte. Record. With Kiri Te Kanawa,
Frederica von Stade, David Rendall, and Philippe Hutten-
locher. Cond. Alain Lombard. Strasbourg Philharmonic Orch.
RCA, SRL3-2629, 1978.

Jones, Norah. Come Away with Me. Blue Note, 2002.

WORKS OF ART

Botticelli, Sandro. Giuliano de' Medici. Samuel H. Kress Collection.

  National Gallery of Art, Washington.

Rodin, Auguste. The Gates of Hell. Rodin Museum, Paris.

INTERVIEWS

Ellison, Ralph. "Indivisible Man." Interview. By James Alan

  McPherson. Atlantic Dec. 1970: 45–60.

Martone, Michael. Telephone interview. 6 Jan. 2005.

Patterson, Annette. E-mail interview. 16 Feb. 2005.

MAPS AND CHARTS

Wine Country Map. Map. Napa Valley: Wine Zone, 2004.

CARTOONS AND ADVERTISEMENTS

Lynch, Mike. Cartoon. *Chronicle Review* 18 Feb. 2005: B17.

Lufthansa. Advertisement. *New Yorker* 11 Oct. 2004: 27.

LECTURES, SPEECHES, AND ADDRESSES

Paglia, Camille. "Art and Poetry v. Hollywood and Media." 92nd

  Street YMCA. New York, 28 Mar. 2005.

Scholes, Robert. "The Presidential Address." MLA Convention.

  Philadelphia, 29 Dec. 2004.

PUBLISHED AND UNPUBLISHED LETTERS

Fitzgerald, F. Scott. "To Ernest Hemingway." 1 June 1934. The Let-

  ters of F. Scott Fitzgerald. Ed. Andrew Turnbull. New York:

  Scribner's, 1963. 308–10.

Stowe, Harriet Beecher. Letter to George Eliot. 25 May 1869. Berg

> Collection, New York: New York Public Library.

Sample Entries: Electronic Publications

MLA style for electronic sources resembles the MLA format for books and periodicals in most respects except for the inclusion of the user's date of access and the electronic address. Because many electronic documents are periodically updated, you need to supply the date of access—that is, the date you viewed the document. The date of access should be placed immediately *before* the electronic address. The electronic address, or URL (uniform resource locator), may have more information than you need—that is, the URL may be so long and complex that it invites transcription errors.

Enclose the URL in angle brackets. For lengthy or complex URLs, give enough information about the path so a reader can locate the exact page you are referring to from the search page of the site or database. If you need to break a URL at the end of a line, do so only after a slash and do not add punctuation or hyphens that are not in the original URL. *Note:* MLA suggests placing <> angle brackets at the beginning and at the end of the electronic address. However, many software systems read these signs as instructions to convert the address into color.

When citing information from an electronic source, provide the following general categories of information:

Author's last name, first name. "Article title" or Book title. Publica-

> tion information for any printed version. Or subject line of

> forum or discussion group. Indication of online posting or

> home page. Title of Electronic Journal. Date of electronic pub-

> lication. Page numbers of paragraphs or section. Name of

> institution or organization sponsoring website. Date of access

> to the source <URL>.

The best way to confirm the accuracy of your electronic citations is to click the "Frequently Asked Questions" link in the MLA Style section of the MLA website at <http://www.mla.org>.

A PROFESSIONAL SITE

"College Research paper." 2005. National Council of Teachers of

　　English. 24 Oct. 2005 <http://www.ncte.org/collections/

　　collegeresearch>.

A HOME PAGE FOR A COURSE

Papper, Carole Clark. Writing technologies. Course home page. Jan.

　　2005–May 2005. Dept. of English, Ball State U. 17 Feb 2005

　　<http://www.bsu.edu/web/cpapper/692>.

A PERSONAL SITE

Hawisher, Gail. Home page. University of Illinois Urbana-Champaign.

　　26 Mar. 2003 <<http://www.english.uiuc.edu/facpages/

　　Hawisher.htm>>.

AN ONLINE BOOK

Anderson, Sherwood. Winesburg, Ohio. 1919. Bartleby.com: Great

　　Books Online. 1999. 17 Feb. 2005 <http://www.bartelby.com/

　　156/index.html>.

AN ONLINE POEM

Roethke, Theodore. "My Papa's Waltz," Favorite Poem Project. 5

　　May 2003 <http://www.favoritepoem.org/roethke/waltz.html>.

AN ARTICLE IN A SCHOLARLY JOURNAL

Butler, Darrell L., and Martin Sellbom. "Barriers to Adopting
Technology for Teaching and Learning." Educause Quarterly
25.2 (2002); 22–28. Educause. 17 Feb. 2005
<http://www.educause.edu/ ir/library/pdf/eqm0223.pdf>.

AN ARTICLE IN A REFERENCE DATABASE

"Women in American History." Britannica Online. Vers. 98.1.1.
Nov. 1997. Encyclopaedia Britannica. 10 Mar. 1998
<http://eb.com>.

AN ARTICLE IN A MAGAZINE

Glasser, Ronald J. "We Are Not Immune." Harper's Oct. 2004.
12 Dec. 2004 <http://www.harpers.org/WeAreNotImune.
html>.

A REVIEW

Chabon, Michael. "Inventing Sherlock Holmes." Rev. of The New
Annotated Sherlock Holmes, Vols. 1 and 2, by Sir Arthur
Conan Doyle. Ed. Leslie S. Klinger. New York Review of Books
10 Feb. 2005. 17 Feb. 2005 <http://www.nybooks.com/articles/
17718>.

A POSTING TO A DISCUSSION GROUP

Inman, James. "Re: Technologist." Online posting. 24 Sept. 1997.
Alliance for Computers in Writing. 27 Feb. 2005 .
<acw1@unicorn.acs.ttu.edu>.

A PERSONAL E-MAIL MESSAGE

Johnson, Alfred B. "Audio Interactive Awards." E-mail to James W.

Miles. 14 Feb. 2005.

CD-ROM: PERIODICAL PUBLICATION WITH PRINTED SOURCE OR PRINTED ANALOGUE

West, Cornel. "The Dilemma of the Black Intellectual." Critical

Quarterly 29 (1987): 39–52. MLA International Bibliography.

CD-ROM. Silver Platter. Feb. 1995.

CD-ROM: NONPERIODICAL PUBLICATION

"Entropy." The Oxford English Dictionary. 2nd ed. CD-ROM.

Oxford: Oxford UP, 1992.

CD-ROM: A WORK IN MORE THAN ONE ELECTRONIC MEDIUM

Mozart. CD-ROM, laser disk. Union City, CA: Ebook, 1992.

Sample Outline and Research Paper

The author of the following research paper used many features of MLA style to document her paper. Adhering to MLA style, she did not include a title page with her outline or her paper. Instead, she typed her name, her instructor's name, the course title, and the date on separate lines (double-spacing between lines) at the upper left margin. Then, after double-spacing again, she typed the title of her paper, double-spaced, and started the first line of her text. On page 1 and successive pages, she typed her last name and the page number in the upper right-hand corner, as recommended by MLA.

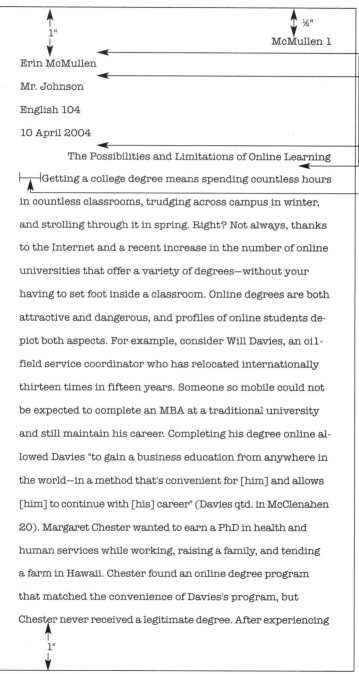

½"
McMullen 1

Erin McMullen

Mr. Johnson

English 104

10 April 2004

The Possibilities and Limitations of Online Learning

Getting a college degree means spending countless hours in countless classrooms, trudging across campus in winter, and strolling through it in spring. Right? Not always, thanks to the Internet and a recent increase in the number of online universities that offer a variety of degrees—without your having to set foot inside a classroom. Online degrees are both attractive and dangerous, and profiles of online students depict both aspects. For example, consider Will Davies, an oil-field service coordinator who has relocated internationally thirteen times in fifteen years. Someone so mobile could not be expected to complete an MBA at a traditional university and still maintain his career. Completing his degree online allowed Davies "to gain a business education from anywhere in the world—in a method that's convenient for [him] and allows [him] to continue with [his] career" (Davies qtd. in McClenahen 20). Margaret Chester wanted to earn a PhD in health and human services while working, raising a family, and tending a farm in Hawaii. Chester found an online degree program that matched the convenience of Davies's program, but Chester never received a legitimate degree. After experiencing

1"

Double-space

Indent
five spaces
or one-half
inch.

Short
quotation:
A quotation
embedded
in a quota-
tion

McMullen 2

Paraphrase:
Source is
paraphrased
and the
author and
page are
placed
within
parentheses.

communication problems with the university, Chester dis-

covered that it had been operating without state approval

while claiming to offer legitimate degrees (Mannix 68).

Online universities offer a convenient and career-specific

alternative to the traditional degrees granted by brick-and-

mortar institutions, and they usually attract professionals

and adult learners with families who desire advanced de-

grees in their fields. However, buyer beware: online degrees

are convenient for many professionals and adult learners,

but they cannot replicate the benefits of traditional universi-

ties such as student services, multidimensional instructor-

student communication, and a real, not a virtual, student

community.

From what kinds of institutions can a student pursue an

online degree? Virtual universities, hubs of learning that

exist completely on the Internet, provide online degrees to

students who never set foot on a campus or in a classroom.

In addition, traditional universities such as the University of

California at Berkeley, the University of Michigan, Ohio State

University, and Duke University have begun to create their

own online degrees. And finally, some universities have

teamed up with for-profit online organizations to create de-

gree programs culled from courses at a variety of universi-

ties and managed by the for-profit organization. For exam-

ple, Unext.com has created Cardean University by blending

McMullen 3

course material and syllabi from Columbia University, Stanford University, the University of Chicago, Carnegie-Mellon, and the London School of Economics (Clayton 15; Carr A50).

No matter what kind of institution a student selects to provide his or her online education, online courses on the whole are increasingly popular. In fact, International Data Corporation, a respected research firm in Framingham, Massachusetts, claimed that in 2002, 2.2 million students would be enrolled in online courses, a number significantly higher than the 710,000 online students enrolled in 1998 (Clayton 15). Students gravitate to online learning because of the convenience of asynchronous learning. This style of education assumes that the students and instructor will not participate in the class at the same time, but the variety of schedules is not seen as a hindrance. On the contrary, students working toward online degrees usually choose courses that allow them to work asynchronously so that they can go to class when it is convenient for them (Willis 119). Asynchronous learning also allows students to "go to class" from any location in the world- -as long as they can access the Internet.

Although online students benefit from asynchronous communication, they find that campus life and its accompanying student benefits are missing from online programs and universities. Online classes are oftentimes more expensive than traditional ones- -Duke University's online global

Documentation: Information from two sources is summarized with authors and pages placed within parentheses.

Paraphrase: Source is paraphrased and the author and page are placed within parentheses.

McMullen 4

Documen-
tation: A
page num-
ber that in-
cludes a
capital letter
to designate
a section of
the source

Documen-
tation: An
electronic
address for
a website
placed
within
parentheses

Executive MBA costs $85,000 (Mangan A27)--and less

financial aid is available to students. Also, taking online

courses through a brick-and-mortar university does not nec-

essarily qualify students for traditional forms of financial aid

(teaching assistantships and fellowships) for graduate work

(Hartigan 6). The nature of completely online universities,

such as Jones International University and the University of

Phoenix, has impeded their abilities to make government-

subsidized funding and grants available to their students

(<http://www.jonesinternational.edu>). Students in a tradi-

tional university also benefit from a physical space in which

they can solve problems that arise with funding, course

work, instructors, and billing procedures. Online universities

do not have corresponding student service components that

can compete with the efficiency and convenience of the on-

site help offered at a traditional university (Shea 55).

    In spite of online education's lack of student services and

financial aid, many adult learners who have completed on-

line degrees welcome the virtual environment. In a virtual

classroom, they do not have to worry about negotiating the

aspects of college for which they may care very little, such as

sporting events and social occasions that are geared toward

eighteen- to twenty-two-year-olds. In an online environment,

adult learners can focus completely on their course work,

and the chat-room environment is a more comfortable

McMullen 5

means of communication if they find face-to-face communica-

tion threatening. Additionally, students have found the online

discussions to be more fruitful than traditional classroom dis-

cussions in which "if you don't know the answer, you can hun-

ker down and hope the professor doesn't call on you" (Tapley

qtd. in Mangan A27). As this online student explained, in the

chat-room environment, where there will be a printed-out

record of who participated in discussion, students feel a

greater responsibility to participate consistently and thought-

fully than they might feel in a traditional classroom. Students

for whom English is a second language can also benefit from

the chat-room system. If those students are not confident

about their communication skills in English, sending written

communications in an asynchronous environment allows

them more time to prepare a remark than they would have if

they were participating in a classroom discussion. Online pro-

grams foster a more comfortable communication environ-

ment, but these programs can also demand a higher level of

accountability than courses taught in traditional classrooms.

Online universities and degree programs do offer the

ease of communicating in a virtual, equalizing environment,

but the nuances in communication that often drive a

course's direction and speed are missing from an online

class centered around e-mail and chat-room communication.

In his Distance Education: A Practical Guide, Barry Willis

Marginal notes:

Documentation: The parenthetical reference to a run-in quotation precedes the final mark of punctuation.

Long quotation: Author and title establish credibility of source.

McMullen 6

Long quo-
tation: A
quotation
of more
than four
lines is set
off from
text and is
not placed
in quota-
tion marks.
Indent ten
spaces or
one inch.

comments on the importance of face-to-face interaction:

> Effective classroom teachers rely on a number of
> visual and unobtrusive cues and clues from their
> students. A quick glance . . . reveals who is atten-
> tively taking notes, pondering a difficult concept, or
> enthusiastically preparing to make a comment. . . .
> [T]he delivery of information, and often the course
> content itself, is adapted to meet the unique charac-
> teristics and needs of the class. (6)

Documenta-
tion: The
parenthetical
reference to
a block
quotation
follows
the final
mark of
punctuation.

The communication techniques used in online courses do
not provide a rich array of visual cues from which instructors can effectively shape their course content and direction.
The amount of online communication, or lack of it, can also
be a problem. In fact, many students drop out of their online
courses because there is not enough communication, a situation that leaves them feeling disconnected and lost in work
that should be supported by group discussion. Programs
with courses that suffer from this communication problem
claim that 60 percent of their students drop out of the
courses before completion (Shea 46). Online courses can
reduce this dropout rate through improved communication,
but they cannot replicate the nuances and dimensions available in classroom communication.

Online courses offer more than convenience and comfort; they are often specifically designed on the basis of

McMullen 7

recommendations or requests from corporations. This
means that online students can take courses that can provide them with present, direct, and immediate professional
application. Most online students are twenty-five or older
with at least a few years of working experience in their professions, so the lure to earn a degree tailored to help them
pursue promotion in their field is very enticing. As Rachel
Hartigan writes, "Students are seeking master's degrees because they have become the passport to entry-level jobs in
many fields, or at least the key to moving up the ladder. . . .
With business and technology seeping into nursing, education, science, public policy, and diplomacy, employees must
learn new skills or risk being passed over" (6). Although
these programs are infinitely valuable for some students, it
is clear that many of them could not pursue an advanced
degree that was not taught through the lens of business,
technology, or education. Online degrees are a valuable and
important innovation, but they are not for everyone. Those
pursuing careers in business will benefit, but the liberal
arts and sciences are generally left out of online degree programs and universities.

Students in all disciplines benefit from clear instructor
and institution communication- -something that online
universities do not always offer. Students in traditional
universities benefit from on-campus learning by having

Short quo-
tation: Au-
thor is iden-
tified at the
beginning of
the sen-
tence, and
quotation is
worked into
sentence.

Use ellipsis
points to
show where
you have
omitted
words from
the original.

McMullen 8

instructor support throughout a course--through e-mail, office hours, and class time. Students in brick-and-mortar universities know who provides them with information, generates class discussion, and grades their work because they physically see their instructors and teaching assistants in class. Online universities are murkier in this area. Jones International University, the first online university to receive accreditation, claims an "all-star cast of professors from top universities." As the university's Web site explains, "Courses are designed by faculty and content experts from around the globe." The Web site goes on to claim that faculty come from twenty-five countries and from prestigious institutions such as the University of California at Berkeley, Columbia University, the London School of Economics, and Stanford University (<http://www.jonesinternational.edu>, emphasis added). Although this sounds promising, a look through the names of faculty listed on the Web site shows that these "all-stars" do not actually teach JIU's courses. Students taking these all-star-designed courses through JIU do not interact with the academic experts who have created them. More than likely, they communicate with adjunct instructors, almost half of whom also teach classes at brick-and-mortar universities. Unclear and implied associations between professors and courses can easily mislead students

Short quotation: Author is identified as an organization.

Documentation: A citation to an electronic address with an editorial comment on the source included within parentheses

aspiring to study with those intellectual "all-stars" lauded on online university Web sites. Traditional universities benefit from a clearer connection between course content and instructor.

The recent shift to online education, predominantly at the advanced degree level, has raised a plethora of new issues in higher education. Online degrees are more convenient for many students, with more direct relationships to their current professions or professions they are hoping to enter. Studies from the 1960s to the present, ending with one by University of North Carolina at Chapel Hill's Thomas Russell, have consistently concluded that students learn just as well in correspondence or online courses as they do in on-campus courses (Keegan 73; Willis 11; Shea 55). However, online universities have not taken the place of traditional brick-and-mortar institutions. Fortunately, those pursuing degrees online can take advantage of a hybrid mix of traditional and online education. For example, the online MBA program at Ohio University requires six weekend sessions and three one-week residencies, requirements that demand that online students come to campus and interact face to face with one another. The combination of on-campus and online education helps promote more effective team-building and a more developed relationship with one's classmates while also retaining the freedom and convenience that online courses offer. As Ohio University professor John Stinson reflects, "It would be hard

Documentation: Information from three sources is paraphrased with authors and pages placed within parentheses.

Short quotation: A quotation embedded within a quotation

to learn how to give an effective presentation and do it all over the Web" (qtd. in McClenahen 20).

The online degree program has firmly established a new model for universities--the students are demanding consumers, and they have the freedom to shop around to find the best program for them, one that meets more of their requirements than any other program. Viewing students as consumers and the university as a business implies that universities will tailor their online programs to student demands and to the demands of companies that want their employees to be better informed in any area or skill of the company's choosing. The student population and the business world, not the faculty and administration, shape the kinds of classes and degrees offered online. This shift in higher education is more career- and consumer-driven and less concerned about learning for the sake of learning. Nevertheless, students with specific requirements that brick-and-mortar institutions cannot meet may find a haven in learning online.

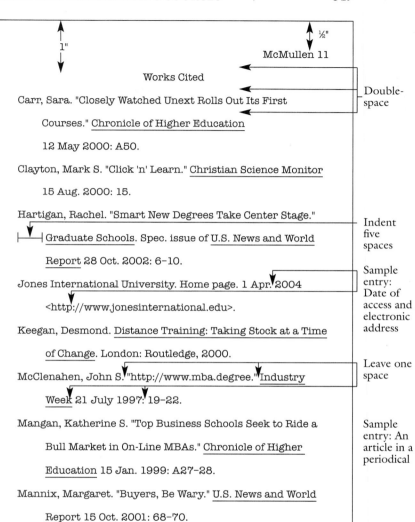

McMullen 11

Works Cited

Carr, Sara. "Closely Watched Unext Rolls Out Its First
    Courses." Chronicle of Higher Education
    12 May 2000: A50.

Clayton, Mark S. "Click 'n' Learn." Christian Science Monitor
    15 Aug. 2000: 15.

Hartigan, Rachel. "Smart New Degrees Take Center Stage."
    Graduate Schools. Spec. issue of U.S. News and World
    Report 28 Oct. 2002: 6–10.

Jones International University. Home page. 1 Apr. 2004
    <http://www.jonesinternational.edu>.

Keegan, Desmond. Distance Training: Taking Stock at a Time
    of Change. London: Routledge, 2000.

McClenahen, John S. "http://www.mba.degree." Industry
    Week 21 July 1997: 19–22.

Mangan, Katherine S. "Top Business Schools Seek to Ride a
    Bull Market in On-Line MBAs." Chronicle of Higher
    Education 15 Jan. 1999: A27–28.

Mannix, Margaret. "Buyers, Be Wary." U.S. News and World
    Report 15 Oct. 2001: 68–70.

Shea, Rachel Hartigan. "So Where's the Beef?" U.S. News and
    World Report 15 Oct. 2001: 44–50.

Willis, Barry. Distance Education: A Practical Guide.
    Englewood Cliffs, NJ: Educ. Technology Publ., 1993.

Double-
space

Indent
five
spaces

Sample
entry:
Date of
access and
electronic
address

Leave one
space

Sample
entry: An
article in a
periodical

Sample
entry: A
book by
one author

ACKNOWLEDGMENTS

DIANE ACKERMAN "Pain" from *A Natural History of the Senses* by Diane Ackerman, copyright © 1990 by Diane Ackerman. Used by permission of Random House, Inc.

JOAN ACOCELLA "Under the Spell," used by permission of the author. Copyright © 2000 by Joan Acocella. This article first appeared in *The New Yorker.*

ALICE ADAMS "Truth or Consequences," from *To See You Again* by Alice Adams, copyright © 1982 by Alice Adams. Used by permission of Alfred A. Knopf, a division of Random House.

JULIA ALVAREZ "Grounds for Fiction," copyright © 1998 by Julia Alvarez. Published in *Something to Declare,* Algonquin Books of Chapel Hill, 1998. Reprinted by permission of Susan Bergholz Literary Services, New York. All rights reserved.

JAMES H. AUSTIN "Four Kinds of Chance," by James H. Austin. Reprinted by author's permission from *Saturday Review/World,* November 2, 1974.

TONI CADE BAMBARA "The Lesson," copyright © 1972 by Toni Cade Bambara, from *Gorilla, My Love* by Toni Cade Bambara. Used by permission of Random House, Inc.

JOHN BERENDT "The Hoax," by John Berendt. Reprinted by permission from John Berendt.

HAROLD BLOOM "Can 35 Million Book Buyers Be Wrong? Yes." From the *Wall Street Journal,* July 11, 2000. Reprinted with the permission of Harold Bloom.

LAURA BOHANNAN "Shakespeare in the Bush," by Laura Bohannan, from *Ants, Indians, and Little Dinosaurs,* ed. by A. Ternes (Charles Scribner's Sons, 1975). Reprinted with the permission of Dennis Bohannan.

FRANCIS BROADHURST "Cape Wind Is Sound for the Sound," Broadcast February 17, 2006, WCAI. Reprinted by permission of Francis Broadhurst, Centerville, MA, freelance writer (email fibcape@comcast.net).

ARTHUR C. CLARKE "The Star," by Arthur C. Clarke, from *The Nine Billion Names of God* (Harcourt, 1955).

EDWARD CODY "China's Symbol, and Source, of Power: Three Gorges Dam Nears Completion, at High Human Cost," The *Washington Post,* Thursday, May 18, 2006, p. A01. Copyright © 2006 The *Washington Post,* reprinted with permission.

JUDITH ORTIZ COFER "The Myth of the Latin Woman: I Just Met a Girl Named María," from *The Latin Deli* (New York: Norton, 1993), pp. 148–154. Reprinted by permission of University of Georgia Press.

RICHARD DOERFLINGER "First Principles and the 'Frist Principles,'" from *Pro-Life Activities,* www.uscccb.org/profile. Reprinted with permission.

STEPHEN DOHENY-FARINA "The Grid and the Village." This article originally appeared in the Autumn 2001 issue of *Orion,* 187 Main Street, Great Barrington, MA 02130, 888/909-6568, www.orionmagazine.org.

ANDRE DUBUS "Digging," from *Meditations from a Movable Chair* by Andre Dubus, copyright © 1998 by Andre Dubus. Used by permission of Alfred A. Knopf, a division of Random House, Inc.

KRISTIE FERGUSON "The Scenic Route" (student essay).

ANTHONY GIDDENS "Globalisation," Reich Lecture 1999, BBC.

NIKKI GIOVANNI "Campus Racism 101," from *Racism 101* by Nikki Giovanni. Copyright © 1994 by Nikki Giovanni. Reprinted by permission of HarperCollins Publishers, Inc.

MALCOLM GLADWELL "Examined Life," *The New Yorker,* December 17, 2001. Reprinted by permission of the author.

JAMES GLEICK "Attention! Multitaskers," from *Faster: The Acceleration of Just About Everything* by James Gleick, copyright © 1999 by James Gleick. Used by permission of Pantheon Books, a division of Random House, Inc.

DANIEL GOLEMAN Excerpt from "Peak Performance: Why Records Fall," by Daniel Goleman. Copyright © 1994 by The New York Times Co. Reprinted with permission.

GREENPEACE "Sellafield = Springfield? Homer Simpson's Nuclear Swimming Pool" from http://www.greenpeace.org/international/news/sellafield-springfield. Copyright Stichting Greenpeace Council.

STEPHEN HARRIGAN "The Tiger Is God," by Stephen Harrigan. From *Comanche Midnight* (1995) by Stephen Harrigan. Reprinted by permission.

WITI IHIMAERA "His First Ball," by Witi Ihimaera. From *Dear Miss Mansfield* by Witi Ihimaera, published by Penguin Books New Zealand. Reprinted by permission.

ROBERT F. KENNEDY, JR. "An Ill Wind Off Cape Cod," *The New York Times,* September 16, 2005. Copyright © 2005 *The New York Times.* Reprinted by permission.

GEORGE ORWELL   "Shooting an Elephant" from *Shooting an Elephant and Other Essays,* by George Orwell, copyright © 1950 by Harcourt, Inc. and renewed 1979 by Sonia Brownell Orwell, reprinted by permission of Harcourt, Inc.

KATHA POLLITT   "Why Boys Don't Play with Dolls," from *The New York Times Magazine,* October 8, 1995. Reprinted by permission of the author.

SISTER HELEN PREJEAN   "Memories of a Dead Man Walking," from *Oxford American Magazine,* Spring 1996, pp. 19–22. Reprinted by permission of Helen Prejean and the Watkins/Loomis Agency.

THOMAS PYNCHON   "Entropy" from *Slow Learner: Early Stories.* Copyright © 1984 by Thomas Pynchon. By permission of Little, Brown and Co., Inc.

ANNA QUINDLEN   From "How Reading Changed My Life" by Anna Quindlen, copyright © 1998 by Anna Quindlen. Used by permission of Ballantine Books, a division of Random House, Inc.

ANNE ROIPHE   "A Tale of Two Divorces" from *Women on Divorce: A Bedside Companion* by Penny Kaganoff and Susan Spano, copyright © 1995 by Anne Roiphe, reprinted by permission of Harcourt, Inc.

JOSEPH J. ROMM   Excerpt adapted from "The Holy Grails of Energy Technology," from *The Hype about Hydrogen: Fact and Fiction in the Race to Save the Climate* (Washington, DC: Island Press, 2004).

PEGGY PRICHARD ROSS   "Stem Cell Research: It's About Life and Death, Not Politics," as it appeared in the *Tallahassee Democrat* and was reprinted in *The Stem Cell Research Foundation,* www.stemcellresearchfoundation.org. Copyright © 2003 by Knight-Ridder Newspapers.

SCOTT RUSSELL SANDERS   "Digging Limestone," copyright © 1982 by Scott Russell Sanders. First appeared in *The North American Review;* from *The Paradise of Bombs;* reprinted by permission of the author and the author's agents, the Virginia Kidd Agency, Inc.

ERIC SCHLOSSER   "Why McDonald's Fries Taste So Good," from *Fast Food Nation: The Dark Side of the All-American Meal* by Eric Schlosser. Excerpted and reprinted by permission of Houghton Mifflin Company. All rights reserved. First published in the *Atlantic Monthly,* January 2001.

DAVA SOBEL   "Imaginary Lines," from *Longitude,* pp. 1–10. Published by arrangement with Walker & Co.

KURT VONNEGUT, JR.   "Harrison Bergeron," from *Welcome to the Monkey House* by Kurt Vonnegut, Jr., copyright © 1961 by Kurt Vonnegut Jr. Used by permission of Dell Publishing, a division of Random House, Inc.

JUDITH VIORST   "The Truth About Lying," *Redbook,* March 1981, pp. 34–42. Reprinted by permission.

SARAH VOWELL   "Cowboys v. Mounties," reprinted with the permission of Simon & Schuster Adult Publishing Group from *The Partly Cloudy Patriot* by Sarah Vowell. Copyright © 2002 by Sarah Vowell.

ALICE WALKER "Beauty: When the Other Dancer Is the Self," from *In Search of Our Mothers' Gardens: Womanist Prose,* copyright © 1983 by Alice Walker, reprinted by permission of Harcourt, Inc.

BARBARA DAFOE WHITEHEAD "Women and the Future of Fatherhood," from *The Divorce Culture* by Barbara Dafoe Whitehead, copyright © 1996 by Barbara Dafoe Whitehead. Used by permission of Alfred A. Knopf, a division of Random House, Inc.

GARY WILLS "The Dramaturgy of Death," first published in *The New York Review of Books,* June 21, 2001. Copyright © 2001 by Gary Wills, permission of The Wylie Agency.

ELIZABETH WINTHROP "The Golden Darters," first published in *American Short Fiction.* Copyright © 1991 by Elizabeth Winthrop. Reprinted by permission of the author.

ANN ZWINGER "Drawing on Experience," from *Finding Home.* This article originally appeared in the Winter 1987 issue of *Orion Magazine,* 187 Main Street, Great Barrington, MA 01230.

INDEX

Ackerman, Diane, 319, 320, 329
 "Pain," 319, 329–334
Acocella, Joan, 450, 453, 505
 "Under the Spell," 505–515
Adams, Alice, 75
 "Truth or Consequences," 75–89
Addresses, in Works Cited, 634
Advertisements, in Works Cited, 634
Alternating strategy, for comparison
 and contrast, 163–164
Alvarez, Julia, 95, 96, 121
 "Grounds for Fiction," 121–135
Analogies
 in cause and effect, 378
 in definition, 319
 in persuasion and
  argument, 453
Analysis, 92–93. *See also* Process
 analysis.
Anecdotes
 in narration and description, 20
 in process analysis, 96
Annotated essays
 in cause and effect, 379–381
 in comparison and contrast,
  164–166
 in definition, 320–322
 in division and classification,
  233–235
 in narration and description,
  24–25

 in persuasion and argument,
  454–455
 in process analysis, 97–99
 in sample analysis, 8–11
 when reading, 2
Arguing a point
 cause and effect to, 377
 narration and description to, 20
Argument, 448–453. *See also*
 Persuasion and argument.
Arguments, types of, 449
"Arranging a Marriage in India"
 (Nanda), 136–148
Articles in periodicals, in Works
 Cited, 631–632
"Attention! Multitaskers" (Gleick),
 335–341
Attitude, relating to person and
 position of author, 23–24
Audience, 3, 6, 13
 of cause and effect, 377–378
 of comparison and contrast, 162
 of definition, 318
 of division and classification, 231
 of narration and description, 21
 of persuasion and argument,
  451–452
 of process analysis, 93–94
Austin, James H., 232, 233, 237
 "Four Kinds of Chance,"
  237–243

Balance, in comparison and
   contrast, 164
Bambara, Toni Cade, 320, 364
   "The Lesson," 364–373
"Barrier-Free Design" (Linderman),
   380–381
"Beauty: When the Other Dancer Is
   the Self" (Walker), 39–48, 320
Berendt, John, 319, 324
   "The Hoax," 319, 324–328
Berry, Wendell, "Conservation Is
   Good Work," 234
Bloom, Harold, 450, 516
   "Can 35 Million Book Buyers Be
   Wrong? Yes.," 516–521
Bohannan, Laura, 163, 164, 199
   "Shakespeare in the Bush: An
   American Anthropologist Set
   Out to Study the Tiv of West
   Africa and Was Taught the True
   Meaning of Hamlet," 163,
   199–212
Books, in Works Cited, 626–631
Brainstorming, 12, 452
Briner, Lauren, "Deloris," 25–26
Broadhurst, Francis, 537, 592
   "Cape Wind Is Sound for the
   Sound," 592–595

"Campus Racism 101" (Giovanni),
   115–120
"Can 35 Million Book Buyers Be
   Wrong? Yes." (Bloom), 516–521
"Cape Wind Is Sound for the
   Sound" (Broadhurst), 592–595
Cartoons, in Works Cited, 634
Cause and effect, 5, 534, 537
   annotated paragraphs of, 379–381
   to argue a point, 377
   audience of, 377–378
   definition of, 376–377
   drawing analogies in, 378
   examples of, 379–381, 383–444,
   582–586
   for explanation, 377
   points to remember for, 381
   purposes of, 377
   for speculation, 377
   strategies for, 378–379, 445–447

CD–ROM, in Works Cited, 638
Ceremonial discourse, 449
Characteristics, attributing in
   definition strategy, 319
"A Chinaman's Chance: Reflections
   on the American Dream" (Liu),
   320, 465–477
"China's Symbol, and Source, of
   Power: Three Gorges Dam
   Nears Completion, at High
   Human Cost" (Cody),
   582–586
Citations, *see* MLA style;
   Works Cited.
Clarke, Arthur C., "The Star,"
   437–444
Classification, 229–230. *See also*
   Division and classification.
Cody, Edward, 537, 582
   "China's Symbol, and Source, of
   Power: Three Gorges Dam
   Nears Completion, at High
   Human Cost," 582–586
Cofer, Judith Ortez, 22, 23, 24, 49
   "The Myth of the Latin Woman: I
   Just Met a Girl Named María,"
   49–57
Comparison and contrast, 4,
   534, 536
   alternating (point-by-point)
   strategy for, 163–164
   annotated paragraphs of, 164–166
   audience of, 162
   balance in, 164
   combining strategies for, 164
   definition of, 160–161
   divided (subject–by–subject)
   strategy for, 163–164
   examples of, 164–166, 168–226,
   557–561
   fanciful, 161–162
   points to remember for, 164, 166
   purpose of, 161–162
   reasons in, 164
   reminders in, 164
   strategies for, 163–164, 227–228
   strict, 161
Comparisons, in process analysis,
   96–97

Conflict, 22, 450
Connotative language, 452
"Conservation Is Good Work"
    (Berry), 234
Contrast, 160. *See also* Comparison
    and contrast.
"Cowboys v. Mounties" (Vowell),
    172–179

Definition, 4, 536
    analogies in, 319
    analyzing qualities in, 319
    annotated paragraphs of, 320–322
    attributing characteristics in, 319
    audience for, 318
    combining strategies with, 320
    defining key terms in, 318
    defining negatively, 319
    definition of, 316–317
    establishing standards in, 317
    examples of, 320–322, 324–373,
        573–581
    extended, 316–317
    giving examples in, 318–319
    for persuasion, 317
    point out special nature with, 317
    points to remember for, 322
    purposes of, 317–318
    reasons for using, 317–318
    for self–definition, 317–318
    showing function in, 319–320
    strategies for, 318–320, 374–375
"Deloris" (Briner), 25–26
Description. *See* Narration and
    description.
Details
    in division and classification, 231
    in narration and description, 23
"Digging" (Dubus), 22, 23, 28–38
"Digging Limestone" (Sanders),
    97–98
Directions, process analysis
    to give, 93
Divided strategy, in comparison and
    contrast, 163–164
Division and classification, 4, 536
    annotated paragraphs of, 233–235
    audience for, 231
    definition of, 229–230

details in, 231
examples of, 233–235, 237–314,
    562–572
for explanation, 230
organization in, 231–232
for persuasion, 230
points to remember for, 235
purposes of, 230
strategies for, 231–233, 315
Documentation, of sources,
    615–649. *See also* MLA style;
    Works Cited.
Doerflinger, Richard, 450, 452, 478
    "First Principles and the 'Frist
    Principles,'" 478–481
Doheny-Farina, Stephen, 536, 538
    "The Grid and the Village,"
    538–547
"The Dramaturgy of Death"
    (Wills), 232, 274–289
"Drawing on Experience"
    (Zwinger), 101–108
Dubus, Andre, 28
    "Digging," 22, 23, 24, 28–38

Effects, 377. *See also* Cause
    and effect.
Electronic publications, in Works
    Cited, 635–638
"Elephant Evolution" (Weiner),
    379–380
Emotional appeal, 452
Emotional arguments, 449
Endnotes, 616
Entertainment
    definition for, 317
    division and classification
    for, 230
"Entropy" (Pynchon), 537,
    596–612
Essay guidelines
    for reading, 6–7
    for writing, 12–13
Ethical appeal, 453
Ethical arguments, 449
Evidence, in persuasion and
    argument, 449–450
"Examined Life" (Gladwell), 4, 377,
    407–421

Examples, use of in writing, 96–97, 318–319
Explanation
    cause and effect for, 377
    definition for, 317
    division and classification for, 230
    narration and description for, 20
Extended definition, 316–317

Fanciful comparison, 161–162
"FDR and Truman" (McCullough), 164–165
Ferguson, Kristie, "The Scenic Route," 14–17
Figurative language, 452
Films, in Works Cited, 633
"First Principles and the 'Frist Principles'" (Doerflinger), 478–481
Footnotes, 616
"Four Kinds of Chance" (Austin), 237–243
Function, showing using definition, 319–320

"Genetic Engineering" (Saloman), 455
"Gentleman! Start Your Engines" (Tucker), 234–235
Giddens, Anthony, 319, 342
    "Globalisation," 342–352
Giovanni, Nikki, 95, 115
    "Campus Racism 101," 115–120
Gladwell, Malcolm, 4, 377, 407
    "Examined Life," 407–421
Gleick, James, 319, 335
    "Attention! Multitaskers," 335–341
"Globalisation" (Giddens), 342–352
"The Golden Darters" (Winthrop), 149–158
Goleman, Daniel, 377, 378, 388
    "Peak Performance: Why Records Fall," 377, 378, 388–395
Greenpeace International, 536, 557
    "Sellafield = Springfield? Homer Simpson's Nuclear Swimming Pool," 557–561

"The Grid and the Village" (Doheny–Farina), 538–547
"Grounds for Fiction" (Alvarez), 121–135
"Guide to Better Fuel Economy" (Magliozzi and Magliozzi), 548–556

Harms, Nathan M., "Howard and Rush," 165–166
Harrigan, Stephen, 319, 320, 353
    "The Tiger Is God," 319, 320, 353–363
"Harrison Bergeron" (Vonnegut), 522–530
"His First Ball" (Ihimaera), 213–226
"The Hoax" (Berendt), 319, 324–328
"The Holy Grails of Energy Technology" (Romm), 573–581
"How Reading Changed My Life" (Quindlen), 2, 8–10
"Howard and Rush" (Harms), 165–166
"The Human Cost of an Illiterate Society" (Kozol), 396–406

"I Have a Dream" (King), 449, 458–464
Ihimaera, Witi, 213
    "His First Ball," 213–226
"An Ill Wind Off Cape Cod" (Kennedy), 587–591
"Imaginary Lines" (Sobel), 164, 180–187
Information
    definition to provide, 317
    process analysis to provide, 93
Interviews, in Works Cited, 634

Kennedy, Robert F., Jr., 537, 587
    "An Ill Wind Off Cape Cod," 587–591
King, Martin Luther, Jr., 449, 450, 452, 453, 458
    "I Have a Dream," 449, 458–464
Kingsolver, Barbara, 320, 450, 485
    "Stone Soup," 320, 485–495

Kingston, Maxine Hong, "A Song for a Barbarian Reed Pipe," 24–25
Kozol, Jonathan, 378, 396
    "The Human Cost of an Illiterate Society," 396–406

Lectures, in Works Cited, 634
Lemann, Nicholas, "The Promised Land," 454
"The Lesson" (Bambara), 364–373
Letters (published and unpublished), in Works Cited, 634
Linderman, Emily, "Barrier–Free Design," 380–381
List of works cited. See Works Cited.
Liu, Eric, 320, 450, 453, 465
    "A Chinaman's Chance: Reflections on the American Dream," 320, 465–477
Logical appeal, 453
Logical arguments, 449
Lopate, Phillip, 232, 260
    "Modern Friendships," 232, 260–273

Magliozzi, Ray, 536, 548
    "Guide to Better Fuel Economy," 548–556
Magliozzi, Tom, 536, 548
    "Guide to Better Fuel Economy," 548–556
"Making Stained Glass" (Temple), 98–99
Maps, in Works Cited, 634
Margin notes, 2. See also Annotated essays.
McCullough, David, "FDR and Truman," 164–165
McMullen, Erin, 616
Mebane, Mary, 232, 233, 252
    "Shades of Black," 232, 252–259
"Memories of a Dead Man Walking" (Prejean), 22, 58–64
MLA style, 616–649
    endnotes and footnotes in, 616
    features of, 616
    guidelines for, 625–626
    implications on research and composition, 616–622

for paraphrase, 621–622
    parenthetical references and, 616
    for quotations, 619–621
    for sample research paper, 638–648
    for summary, 621–622
    See also Works Cited.
"Modern Friendships" (Lopate), 232, 260–273
Modern Language Association, see MLA style; Works Cited.
"The Myth of the Latin Woman: I Just Met a Girl Named María" (Cofer), 49–57

Nanda, Serena, 96, 136
    "Arranging a Marriage in India," 136–148
Narration and description, 4, 19–20, 536
    annotated paragraphs of, 24–25
    audience of, 21
    conflict in, 22
    definition of, 19–20
    details in, 23
    examples of, 24–25, 28–89, 538–547
    pace in, 22–23
    plot in, 22
    point of view in, 23–24
    points to remember for, 26
    position in, 23–24
    purpose of, 20–21
    strategies for, 21–24, 90–91
Negative definition, 319
Neville, Susan, 536, 562
    "Utilities," 562–572
Note-taking, from sources, 619–622

Oates, Joyce Carol, "When Tristram Met Isolde," 320–321
O'Connor, Flannery, 290
    "Revelation," 290–314
Organizational patterns. See Writing strategies.
O'Rourke, P. J., 96, 109
    "Third World Driving Hints and Tips," 109–114

Orwell, George, 22, 23, 24, 65
  "Shooting an Elephant," 65–74
Overview, in process analysis, 94–95

Pace, 22–23
"Pain" (Ackerman), 319, 329–334
Paraphrasing sources, 621–622
Parenthetical references, 616,
  619–621
"Peak Performance: Why Records
  Fall" (Goleman), 377, 378,
  388–395
Performances, in Works Cited, 633
Periodicals. *See* Articles in periodicals.
"Personality" (Utesch), 321–322
Persuasion
  in definition, 317
  in division and classification, 230
Persuasion and argument, 5,
  534, 537
  agreement won with, 450
  anger provoked with, 450
  annotated paragraphs of, 454–455
  arousing sympathy with, 450
  audience for, 451–452
  as call to action, 450
  ceremonial discourse and, 449
  changes promoted by, 450
  connotative language in, 452
  creating a tone in, 452
  definition for, 448–449
  emotional appeal in, 452
  ethical appeal in, 453
  examples of, 454–455, 458–530,
    587–595
  figurative language in, 452
  logical appeal in, 453
  points to remember for, 456
  purposes of, 450
  rational versus emotional, 449
  refuting theory through, 450
  stimulate interest with, 450
  strategies for, 452–453, 531–532
  for supporting a cause, 450
  types of, 449–450
  using cause and effect for, 377
  using definition for, 317
  using division and classification
    for, 230

Pictures, in process analysis, 96
Plagiarism, 622–624
Plot, 22
Point-by-point strategy, in
  comparison and contrast,
  163–164
Point of view
  in narration and description, 23
  in process analysis, 94
Pollitt, Katha, 377, 383
  "Why Boys Don't Play with
    Dolls," 377, 383–387
Position, 23–24
Prejean, Sisten Helen, 58
  "Memories of a Dead Man
    Walking," 22, 23, 24, 58–64
Process analysis, 5, 534, 536
  anecdotes in, 96
  annotated paragraphs of, 97–99
  audience of, 93–94
  comparisons in, 96–97
  definition of, 92–93
  examples of, 97–99, 101–158,
    548–556
  organization of, 94–95
  overview in, 94–95
  pictures in, 96
  points to remember for, 99
  purpose of, 93
  results in, 97
  sequence of steps in, 95–97
  special terms in, 95
  strategies for, 94–97, 159
  variants in, 96
"The Promised Land"
  (Lemann), 454
Purpose
  analyzing in reading process,
    2–3, 6
  analyzing in writing process, 12
  in cause and effect, 377
  in comparison and contrast,
    161–162
  in definition, 317–318
  in division and classification, 230
  in narration and description,
    20–21
  in process analysis, 93
  revising as you write, 535

Pynchon, Thomas, 537, 596
  "Entropy," 537, 596–612

Questions
  for reading, 2–3
  for writing, 534–535
Quindlen, Anna, "How Reading
  Changed My Life," 2, 8–10
Quotations, 619–621

Radio programs, in Works
  Cited, 633
Reading process, 1–5
  guidelines for, 6–7
  improving writing with, 2–3
  response to reading and, 2, 6
  sample analysis of an essay and,
    8–11
  steps of, 1–2
  writing strategies analyzed in,
    3–5, 7
Reasons, in comparison and
  contrast, 164
Recordings, in Works Cited, 633
Refuting a theory, in persuasion and
  argument, 450
Reminders, in comparison and
  contrast, 164
Research paper, sample of using
  MLA style, 638–648
Resources for writing, 533–537
  examples of, 538–612
  questions and, 534–537
  purpose and, 534–535
  strategies and, 534, 536–537
Response, to reading, 2, 6
Results, in process analysis, 95, 97
"Revelation" (O'Connor),
  290–314
Roiphe, Anne, 188
  "A Tale of Two Divorces,"
    188–198
Romm, Joseph J., 536, 573
  "The Holy Grails of Energy
    Technology," 573–581
Ross, Peggy Prichard, 450, 452, 482
  "Stem Cell Research: It's About
    Life and Death, Not Politics,"
    482–484

Saloman, Jim F., "Genetic
  Engineering," 455
Sanders, Scott Russell, "Digging
  Limestone," 97–98
"The Scenic Route" (Ferguson), 3,
  14–17
Schlosser, Eric, 377, 422
  "Why McDonald's Fries Taste So
    Good," 377, 422–436
"Sellafield = Springfield? Homer
  Simpson's Nuclear Swimming
  Pool" (Greenpeace
  International), 557–561
Sequence, in process analysis, 94,
  95–97
"Shades of Black" (Mebane), 232,
  252–259
"Shakespeare in the Bush: An
  American Anthropologist Set
  Out to Study the Tiv of West
  Africa and Was Taught the True
  Meaning of Hamlet"
  (Bohannan), 163, 199–212
"Shooting an Elephant" (Orwell),
  65–74
Sobel, Dava, 164, 180
  "Imaginary Lines," 164, 180–187
"A Song for a Barbarian Reed Pipe"
  (Kingston), 24–25
Source(s)
  compiling, 619
  documenting, 615–616, 626–638
  evaluating, 617–619
  plagiarism of, 622–624
  quoting, 619–622
  summarizing and paraphrasing,
    621–622
  taking notes from, 619–622
Special terms, in process analysis, 95
Speculation, cause and effect
  for, 377
Speeches, in Works Cited, 634
Standards, using definition to
  establish, 317
"The Star" (Clarke), 437–444
"Stem Cell Research: It's About Life
  and Death, Not Politics"
  (Ross), 482–484
Steps. *See* Sequence.

"Stone Soup" (Kingsolver), 320,
    485–495
Strategies. *See* Writing strategies.
Strict comparison, 161
Subject-by-subject strategy, in
    comparison and contrast,
    163–164
Summarizing sources, 621–622

"A Tale of Two Divorces" (Roiphe),
    188–198
Television programs, in Works
    Cited, 633
Temple, Sara, "Making Stained
    Glass," 98–99
Theory, persuasion and argument to
    refute, 450
"Third World Driving Hints and
    Tips" (O'Rourke), 109–114
"The Tiger Is God" (Harrigan),
    319, 320, 353–363
Tone, creating in persuasion and
    argument, 452
Topic, for your writing,
    12, 18
"The Truth About Lying" (Viorst),
    244–251
"Truth or Consequences" (Adams),
    75–89
Tucker, Gareth, "Gentleman! Start
    Your Engines," 234–235
Twain, Mark, 163, 168
    "Two Views of the River," 163,
        168–171
"Two Views of the River" (Twain),
    163, 168–171

"Under the Spell" (Acocella),
    505–515
URLs (uniform resource locator),
    documenting, 635–637
Utesch, Jason, "Personality,"
    321–322
"Utilities" (Neville), 562–572

Variants, in process analysis, 96
Viorst, Judith, 232, 233, 244
    "The Truth About Lying,"
        244–251

Vonnegut, Kurt, Jr., 522
    "Harrison Bergeron," 522–530
Vowell, Sarah, 164, 172
    "Cowboys v. Mounties,"
        172–179

Walker, Alice, 22, 24, 39, 320
    "Beauty: When the Other Dancer
        Is the Self," 39–48, 320
Web sources, in Works Cited,
    636–637
Weiner, Jonathan, "Elephant
    Evolution," 379–380
"When Tristram Met Isolde"
    (Oates), 320–321
Whitehead, Barbara Dafoe, 450,
    453, 496
    "Women and the Future of
        Fatherhood," 496–504
"Why Boys Don't Play with Dolls"
    (Pollitt), 377, 383–387
"Why McDonald's Fries Taste So
    Good" (Schlosser), 377,
    422–436
Wills, Garry, 232, 233, 274
    "The Dramaturgy of Death," 232,
        274–289
Winthrop, Elizabeth, 149
    "The Golden Darters," 149–158
"Women and the Future of
    Fatherhood" (Whitehead),
    496–504
Works Cited, 616, 619, 624–638
    articles in periodicals in, 631–632
    books in, 626–631
    cartoons and advertisements
        in, 634
    electronic publications, 635–638
    films, radio, and television
        programs in, 633
    guidelines for, 625–626
    interviews in, 634
    lectures, speeches, and addresses
        in, 634
    maps and charts in, 634
    performances in, 633
    preparing, 624–626
    published and unpublished letters
        in, 634

recordings in, 633
  sample of, 649
  works of art in, 633
Works Consulted, 625
Works of art, in Works
    Cited, 633
Writing
  audience and, 3, 6, 13
  organization of, 13
  purpose and, 2–3, 6, 12
Writing assignments, 18, 90–91,
    159, 227–228, 315, 374–375,
    445–447, 531–532, 613–614
Writing process, 2–3
  guidelines for, 12–13

Writing strategies
  analyzing through reading,
    3–5, 7
  combining, 4, 20, 164, 320
  examples when writing, 4–5
  See also Narration and description;
    Process analysis; Comparison
    and contrast; Division and
    classification; Definition; Cause
    and effect; Persuasion and
    argument.

Zwinger, Ann, 95, 96, 101
  "Drawing on Experience,"
    101–108